Inspectors General (Ireland)

Inspectors General : appendix to fifty-fourth report on general state of prisons of Ireland, Separate Reports on County and City Gaols and Bridewells

Inspectors General (Ireland)

Inspectors General : appendix to fifty-fourth report on general state of prisons of Ireland, Separate Reports on County and City Gaols and Bridewells

ISBN/EAN: 9783741104572

Manufactured in Europe, USA, Canada, Australia, Japa

Cover: Foto ©ninafisch / pixelio.de

Manufactured and distributed by brebook publishing software
(www.brebook.com)

Inspectors General (Ireland)

Inspectors General : appendix to fifty-fourth report on general state of prisons of Ireland, Separate Reports on County and City Gaols and Bridewells

APPENDIX

to the

FIFTY-FOURTH REPORT

of the

INSPECTORS-GENERAL

on

THE PRISONS OF IRELAND,

1875.

PART II.

SEPARATE REPORTS ON COUNTY AND CITY GAOLS AND BRIDEWELLS.

Presented to both Houses of Parliament by Command of Her Majesty.

DUBLIN:

PRINTED BY ALEXANDER THOM, 87 & 88, ABBEY-STREET,
PRINTER TO THE QUEEN'S MOST EXCELLENT MAJESTY.
FOR HER MAJESTY'S STATIONERY OFFICE.

1876.

[C.—1497. I.]   *Price 2s.*

CONTENTS.

APPENDIX—PART II.

SEPARATE REPORTS ON PRISONS BY INSPECTORS-GENERAL:

North District.

	Page
Antrim County Gaol, at Belfast; Antrim, Ballymena, and Ballymoney Bridewells,	5
Armagh County Gaol, at Armagh; Ballybot, Lurgan, Markethill, and Newtownhamilton Bridewells,	18
Cavan County Gaol, at Cavan; Bailieborough, Ballyconnell, and Cootehill Bridewells,	29
Donegal County Gaol, at Lifford; Buncrana, Donegal, Glenties, and Letterkenny Bridewells,	38
Down County Gaol, at Downpatrick; Newry and Newtownards Bridewells,	46
Dublin Gaol, City of, Richmond Bridewell,	57
Dublin Gaol, City of, Grangegorman Penitentiary,	69
Fermanagh County Gaol, at Enniskillen; Newtownbutler Bridewell,	81
Leitrim County Gaol, at Carrick-on-Shannon; Ballinamore and Manorhamilton Bridewells,	91
Londonderry County Gaol, at Londonderry; Coleraine, Magherafelt, and Limavady Bridewells,	101
Longford County Gaol, at Longford,	112
Louth County Gaol, at Dundalk; Ardee Bridewell,	123
Drogheda County of the Town Gaol,	134
Mayo County Gaol, at Castlebar; Ballina, Ballinrobe, Swineford, and Westport Bridewells,	142
Meath County Gaol, at Trim; Kells and Navan Bridewells,	152
Monaghan County Gaol, at Monaghan; Carrickmacross, Castleblayney, and Clones Bridewells,	163
Roscommon County Gaol, at Roscommon; Athlone, Boyle, Castlerea, and Strokestown Bridewells,	173
Sligo County Gaol, at Sligo; Ballymote Bridewell,	183
Tyrone County Gaol, at Omagh; Clogher and Dungannon Bridewells,	192
Westmeath County Gaol, at Mullingar; Moate Bridewell,	203

A 2

4   *Contents.*

SOUTH DISTRICT.

Page

Carlow County Gaol, at Carlow, ... 212

Clare County Gaol, at Ennis; Ennistimon, Killaloe, Kilrush, and Tulla
Bridewells, ... 219

Cork County Gaol, at Cork; Bandon, Bantry, Charleville, Clonakilty, Dunmanway, Fermoy, Kanturk, Kinsale, Macroom, Mallow, Midleton,
Mitchelstown, Queenstown, Skibbereen, and Youghal Bridewells, . . 229

Cork City Gaol, ... 242

Dublin County Gaol, at Kilmainham, ... 251

Galway County and Town Gaol, at Galway; Ballinasloe, Clifden, Eyrecourt,
Gort, Loughrea, Oughterard, Portumna, and Tuam Bridewells, . . 262

Kerry County Gaol, at Tralee; Cahersiveen, Castleisland, Dingle, Kenmare,
Killarney, Listowel, and Milltown Bridewells, ... 273

Kildare County Gaol, at Naas, ... 282

Kilkenny County and City Gaol, at Kilkenny; Callan, Thomastown, and
Urlingford Bridewells, ... 291

King's County Gaol, at Tullamore; Parsonstown Bridewell, . . . 299

Limerick County Gaol, at Limerick; Bruff and Rathkeale Bridewells, . 306

Limerick City Gaol, ... 315

Queen's County Gaol, at Maryborough, ... 322

Tipperary County (North Riding) Gaol, at Nenagh; Newport, Roscrea,
Templemore, and Thurles Bridewells, ... 329

Tipperary County (South Riding) Gaol, at Clonmel: Caher, Carrick-on-Suir,
Cashel, Clogheen, and Tipperary Bridewells, ... 338

Waterford County and City Gaol, at Waterford; Dungarvan and Lismore
Bridewells, ... 347

Wexford County Gaol, at Wexford; Enniscorthy, Gorey, and New Ross
Bridewells, ... 355

Wicklow County Gaol at Wicklow; Baltinglass and Tinahely Bridewells. . 364

INSPECTORS- ⎰SOUTH DISTRICT, . . JOHN LENTAIGNE.
GENERAL FOR ⎱NORTH DISTRICT, . . HON. CHARLES F. BOURKE.

APPENDIX—PART II.

SEPARATE REPORTS ON PRISONS.

NORTH DISTRICT.

ANTRIM COUNTY GAOL, AT BELFAST.—STATUTABLE INSPECTION,
4TH, 5TH, AND 7TH OCTOBER, 1875.

The following returns are made up to the second day of my inspection :—

Three hundred and fifty-five formed the total number of prisoners in custody at the above date, 203 being males and 152 females. Only forty-seven of these were cases serious enough to be tried by quarter sessions or assizes, and eleven were military offenders. Nineteen were untried, and one was a pauper debtor. The remainder were all disposed of summarily. Two juveniles were in charge at the time of my visit, and sixty-five had been in custody previously during the year. Twenty-five males and five females were sent to reformatories during the year 1875, and I observed during my inspection a boy in charge, and employed amongst the adults, said to be over seventeen years of age, but he certainly did not appear to be nearly so old. I would recommend that more care be taken before youths of this sort are committed to gaol, to ascertain their correct ages. Several juveniles have been committed here this year charged with stealing fruit, who, I fear, will have derived but little benefit from the short periods of imprisonment they have undergone. I would therefore submit that, if it were possible, such delinquents should receive a smart flogging, instead of sending them to prison, where little good is learned by prisoners of this class. I regret to state that as many as nineteen males and one female were committed here this year up to the time of my inspection who were known previously to have been in reformatories, twelve of whom were in custody at the time of my inspection. Three of them had been at Upton, three at Glencree, and fourteen at Malone; and during the year 1874 twenty-three males and one female had been in custody here who were known to have been previously in reformatories.

Numbers present.

Juveniles.

Number of Prisoners of all Classes in Gaol on the day of Inspection, and on the corresponding date in the three preceding years.

	M.	F.		M.	F.
1872,	275	123	1874,	260	154
1873,	251	140	1875 (day of Inspection),	203	152

Number of Returned Convicts in Gaol on the day of Inspection, and during each of the three preceding years, and the expired portion of 1875.

	M.	F.		M.	F.
1872,	11	6	1875 (up to and including day		
1873,	15	10	of Inspection).	8	4
1874,	14	5	Day of Inspection,	1	1

NORTH
DISTRICT.

———

Antrim
County
Gaol.

Commitments.

CLASSES.			From 1st January to 31st December, 1874.		From 1st January, 1875, to day of Inspection.	
			M.	F.	M.	F.
Debtors,	.	.	9	–	4	–
Criminals,	.	.	2,454	1,642	1,843	1,335
Vagrants,	.	.	16	17	33	43
Drunkards,	.	.	584	534	498	406
Total,	.	.	3,063	2,193	2,378	1,784

Commit-
ments.

It will be perceived by the foregoing table that during this year a good many returned convicts have found their way into this gaol, twelve having been committed here up to the time of my inspection. The quarters for debtors are now occupied by criminal prisoners, as very few of the former class are now committed here; and at the time of my inspection only one was in custody. He was sent here for contempt of court, and was, therefore, classed as a debtor, but expected to be released in a few days subsequent to my visit. The total number of commitments this year to this prison up to the time of my visit was 2,378 males and 1,784 females, against 3,063 of the former and 2,193 of the latter, during the whole of the previous year. Having regard to the time at which my inspection was made, it is to he hoped that the total number of commitments this year will be less than in 1874. It is satisfactory to perceive that there is a slight proportionate diminution in the number of commitments for drunkenness this year as compared with last, but the commitments of vagrants was, even at the time of my inspection, in excess this year as compared with 1874. The most serious criminals that were committed this year were three males for murder, and three males and a female for conspiring to take life, and two for manslaughter. Larceny, and assaults arising principally from drunkenness, formed the greater part of the commitments to this gaol.

Number of individual prisoners (exclusive of debtors) and number of times each had been committed during the following periods, distinguishing Adults from Juveniles.

NUMBER OF TIMES COMMITTED.			1874.				1875, to day of Inspection.			
			Juveniles.		Adults.		Juveniles.		Adults.	
			M.	F.	M.	F.	M.	F.	M.	F.
Once within the year,	.	.	59	8	1,437	465	49	10	1,155	416
Twice ,,	.	.	4	–	321	151	3	–	259	130
Thrice ,,	.	.	2	–	120	92	–	–	90	79
4 times ,,	.	.	–	–	64	35	–	–	44	61
5 ,, ,,	.	.	–	–	27	35	–	–	22	36
6 ,, ,,	.	.	–	–	13	29	–	–	11	42
7 ,, ,,	.	.	–	–	7	22	–	–	3	17
8 ,, ,,	.	.	–	1	3	17	–	–	–	6
9 ,, ,,	.	.	–	–	–	16	–	–	1	2
10 ,, ,,	.	.	–	–	–	4	–	–	–	–
11 ,, ,,	.	.	–	–	–	7	–	–	–	–
12 ,, ,,	.	.	–	–	–	4	–	–	–	–
13 ,, ,,	.	.	–	–	–	2	–	–	–	–
Total,	.	.	65	9	1,992	899	52	10	1,563	789
No. of above who had not been in Gaol previous to 1st January in .			56	8	1,065	315	47	9	784	254

Number of individual prisoners (exclusive of debtors) committed in the year 1874, and to the day of inspection in 1875, who had been once and oftener committed from their first commitment in any year, so far as can be ascertained, distinguishing Adults from Juveniles.

NORTH DISTRICT.

Antrim County Gaol.

NUMBER OF TIMES COMMITTED.	1874.				1875, to day of Inspection.			
	Juveniles.		Adults.		Juveniles.		Adults.	
	M.	F.	M.	F.	M.	F.	M.	F.
Once only,	55	8	913	259	46	9	694	199
Twice,	6	–	288	116	5	1	199	78
Thrice,	3	–	167	55	1	–	158	49
4 times,	2	–	126	45	–	–	89	38
5 ,,	–	–	91	27	–	–	80	30
6 ,,	–	–	59	32	–	–	52	30
7 to 11 ,,	–	1	172	106	–	–	133	107
12 to 16 ,,	–	–	76	69	–	–	86	63
17 to 20 ,,	–	.	35	42	–	–	28	32
21 to 30 ,,	–	–	35	46	–	–	35	47
31 to 40 ,,	–	–	14	31	–	–	15	31
41 to 50 ,,	–	–	9	20	–	–	7	31
51 to 60 ,,	–	–	4	10	–	–	7	16
61 to 70 ,,	–	–	1	9	–	–	–	9
71 to 80 ,,	–	–	1	5	–	–	1	6
81 to 90 ,,	–	–	–	5	–	–	–	4
91 to 100 ,,	–	–	–	4	–	–	–	4
101 to 120 ,,	–	–	–	7	–	–	–	4
121 to 140 ,,	–	–	1	3	–	–	1	7
141 to 160 ,,	–	–	–	1	–	–	–	2
161 to 180 ,,	–	–	–	1	–	–	–	1
181 to 200 ,,	–	–	–	3	–	–	–	–
201 to 250 ,,	–	–	–	1	–	–	–	3
Total No. of Individuals committed,	65	9	1,993	899	52	10	1,583	789
No. of Commitments represented in foregoing,	81	20	8,763	11639	62	11	7,704	12086

Re-commitments.

The two preceding tables will clearly show that this gaol is frequented by a certain class of individuals who almost spend their lives here, and upon whom imprisonment seems to have little effect for good. Up to the time of my visit this year one male and two females had been committed as often as nine times during the year, and twenty-two males and thirty-six females as often as six times during that period; while in 1874 two females were committed here thirteen times, and three males and seventeen females were committed nine times. The total number of adult individuals committed in 1874 was 1,992 males and 899 females whose known convictions since their first offence numbered 8,763 and 11,639 respectively. Previous to my inspection this year the total number of adult individuals committed was 1,583 males and 789 females. These individuals had respectively 7,704 and 12,086 commitments recorded against them since their first offence. Such figures, I submit, clearly show that some remedy should be applied to arrest this deplorable state of things; and every exertion should, therefore, be made in the prison to enforce discipline, and to carry out a more strict and rigid system of punishment amongst both sexes. The daily average number in

NORTH
DISTRICT.
___
*Antrim
County
Gaol.*

custody this year was somewhat higher than last, of both sexes, more especially of females ; and the numbers in charge at one period this year was higher than it had been for the last eight years.

Accommodation.

	M.	F.		M.	F.
Wards,	11	3	Store Rooms,	8	6
Yards,	23	20	Laundries,	–	2
Day Rooms,	4	–	Drying Rooms,	–	2
Solitary Cells,	16	–	Lavatories,	2	2
Single Cells, not less in size than 9 ft. long, 6 ft. wide, 8 ft. high, = 432 cubic feet,	382	153	Baths, with hot and cold water laid on,	6	2
			Privies,	8	–
Do., heated and furnished with bells,	382	153	Water-closets,	366	154
Hospital Rooms,	5	5	Fumigating Apparatus,	1	–
Chapel,	One.		Reception Rooms or Cells,	14	–
School-room,	One.		Pump,	1	–
Workshops,	2	–	Crank do.,	1	–
Worksheds,	107	–	Wells,	2	–
Kitchen,	1		Tell-tale Clocks,	2	–

New
Buildings.

Since my last inspection of this gaol a considerable addition has been made to its accommodation. The wings A and D have each had a story added to them, and altogether there has been added to the prison 129 cells fitted and suited for separate confinement. These were very badly wanted, for of late it had been found necessary to put two or three women in a cell, so that the separate system could not possibly be carried out. I trust now, therefore, that a more strict system of discipline and greater separation will be enforced, and that much benefit will, consequently, arise from the greater amount of system, regularity, and order in the whole establishment ; but I have no hesitation in saying that unless every exertion is made by the prison authorities here to enforce more dis-

Want of
discipline.

cipline and order than has existed for some time here, that crime will increase, and that another addition will have to be made to the gaol in a very few years. The same arrangements exist as at my last inspection as to the reception of prisoners. They are all bathed at once on admission, and the males who come in after look-up, or late in the evening, are sent to some reception cells, which are set apart for them in the basement of

Reception.

D wing. As a rule all prisoners are washed and cleansed immediately on admission, and as the Medical Officer attends here twice a day, they are

Baths.

at once passed by him into their proper ward. Two baths are provided in the female prison, and five in the male, with hot and cold water laid on. Men are said to be bathed once in three weeks, and women once a fortnight, but there is evidently no fixed rule as to bathing prisoners at certain periods ; and too much discretion in this matter is left to the subordinate officers. I submit that each class warder and matron should be responsible to the Governor and Head Matron for the bathing of all healthy prisoners at least once a week in their respective class, and at the end of each week certify to the Governor in writing that this rule has been carried out ; any exception to the rule should be noted in such report, for, with large numbers to deal with, as there are here, it is impossible to expect subordinate officers to be as precise in such matters as if they were constantly supervised by the Governor and Head Matron, as is the case in small gaols. All the cells, with the exception of those in the old

Lavatories,
&c.

debtors' quarters, are fitted with a lavatory and water-closet, which were generally in good order, with the exception of one on the basement floor of D wing, from which there was a most offensive smell, the same as at my last inspection, and to which I then called attention. . A door should be put up here, with a strong spring to it, in order to exclude the effluvia from the passage. The water is supplied by the same means as at my last inspection, namely, from the town main to a large cistern on the premises from which it is pumped by a donkey engine to a cistern above the gaol. The sewerage is reported to be excellent, and has lately been overhauled. All the cells are artificially heated, and the apparatus was in good working order at the time of my visit. The separate cellular accommodation for males is now 390, and for females 155, all provided with every means for carrying on the separate system in its integrity. There are also twenty small exercise yards for each sex, so that even at exercise separation can be maintained. One hundred and seven stonebreaking sheds are provided, in which men can be kept entirely apart one from the other. There are also workshops, such as carpenter's shop and smith's forge, in which men can work alone; but I regret to state that I found three carpenters working together in one room, and also four men in association in the blacksmith's shop, making a boiler for the Governor's house. I cannot help observing that I do not think the Governor pays sufficient attention to such matters, as there is no excuse for men being employed in association now in this gaol. The carpenters could easily have been put to work in separation in empty cells in the old debtors' quarters, and two men in the forge, under the supervision of an officer, would have been ample for the work in which they were engaged. Over 3,000 tons of broken stones were on hand at the time of my visit, as I was informed there had been some difficulty in getting the contractors to remove them. Only one fumigating apparatus is provided, in which all the clothing of males is purified before being put away, but only that of females which is considered dirty is subjected to this process. . I am clearly of opinion that all prisoners' clothing should be purified before being put away, and therefore submit that a fumigating apparatus should be provided for the female prison. No improvement has been made in the chapel since my last visit, except that all the painting has now been rubbed off in order to prevent scribbling. The improvements in the laundry were almost completed at the time of my visit. A new boiler has been put up there, which will supply water for the laundry, will heat the drying-rooms, and the water for the baths in the female prison. Twelve new ironing rooms have been made, and the drying-rooms have been enlarged. Altogether this department of the prison, which is a source of much profit to the gaol, has been very much improved, but I am bound to remark that there exists here a great deal too much association, the laundry being more like a free institution than a place for punishment. This is a matter to which I would draw the serious attention of the Board of Superintendence, for although it is of great importance to carry on as much profitable labour as possible in prisons, yet as punishment and reformation should be the principal objects of a gaol, I am strongly of opinion that those important results should not be sacrificed for the sake of obtaining large profits of labour. By a little more arrangement in the laundry women could be kept a great deal more apart than at present; and I am of opinion that fewer women should be employed there at the same time than are now. There are plenty of other means of employing prisoners, though perhaps not quite as profitable; but I submit that if these women were kept more in separation, and not allowed to communicate with one another as much as they do, that there would be a sensible diminution in the number of commitments in a very short time, for when one contemplates that some of the women have been in this gaol over 200 times, it cannot be considered that the results from the discipline and reformatory system maintained here is by any

(marginal notes:)
NORTH DISTRICT.
Antrim County Gaol.
Water.
Sewerage and heating.
Fumigator.
Chapel.
Laundry.

NORTH
DISTRICT.

*Antrim
County
Gaol.*

Gas.

Kitchen.

means satisfactory. Gas is provided throughout the prison, and the arrangements for lighting the new cells are upon an improved system, such as has been found to work well in the Cork county prison for some years; the bells also in these cells are upon the spiral system, which is an improvement on the old bells with the handles. I have again to remark upon the impropriety of employing a prisoner in the gas-house, which I submit is not within the prison boundary, and from which he could escape without any difficulty if he were so inclined. The arrangements in the kitchen are the same as at my last visit. A large steam boiler is provided, which serves for cooking the provisions and for heating the water for the baths of the male wing, and also provides steam for working the donkey engine. Five or six prisoners are employed here daily under the supervision of the cook warder, and are all in association, so that imprisonment to them can hardly be considered irksome or punitive. I have drawn attention to this subject in former reports on this prison, but am sorry to find that this abuse still exists, and the Governor is quite heedless of my recommendations on the subject. In Londonderry gaol the whole of the cooking, washing of the tins, &c., is performed by one female, and although the numbers here are certainly much larger than there, and doubtless there are many more utensils to wash and clean, yet it is clear that this number of prisoner-cooks employed here is in excess of the requirements of this gaol. They are also too much in association, for other arrangements could easily be made under good management, whereby the prisoners, though employed in the basement for culinary purposes, could be kept almost quite separate. The duty of photographing has not yet been allotted to one of the officers, as recommended in previous reports, and the artist from the town who performs the duty receives almost as much per year for photographing prisoners as is the salary of some of the subordinate officers. For this and other reasons already stated I would again urge upon the Board the necessity of requiring this duty to be performed by one of the officers. The Deputy Governor, I believe, understands the art, and if he were given a little assistance in the office by one of the turnkeys, he could very well manage to carry on the photographing of prisoners. Two tell-tale clocks are provided, which are marked alternately every quarter of an hour from 10 P.M. to 6 A.M. This duty is performed by the warders in rotation, two being on each night, the first from 6 P.M. to midnight, and the other from that time until 6 A.M. There is no patrol outside the gaol. The markings of the tell-tale clock are entered in the Lockings Book, and are entered by the Deputy Governor every morning; and all omissions of duty in this respect are noted in the Conduct Book; but I am glad to observe that the clocks are very regularly marked, and few omissions occur. Lock-up takes place at 5.45 P.M. all the year round, and unlock at 6 A.M. I am informed that the principal keys of the gaol are taken to the Governor at ten o'clock at night, and are kept by him in his bedroom. The others are locked up in a safe in the office during the night. As the Governor is solely responsible for the safe keeping of prisoners, I consider that he alone should have custody of all the keys of the prison during the night. This is a matter which I referred to in my last report of this gaol. The rules for visitors to prisoners are the same as at my last inspection. Visitors are chiefly admitted by order of the Local Inspector, but members of the Board occasionally exercise their privilege of giving orders to admit visitors. A suitable place has recently been fitted up for visitors to females, which is a great improvement. I published in full in my report for 1873 the regulations in force here respecting letter-writing and visiting of prisoners, to which, if necessary, reference can be made.

Photo-
graphy.

ight-
watch.

Visitors.

Stock at the time of Inspection.

	In Use.	In Store.	Male Clothing.	In Use.	In Store.	Female Clothing.	In Use.	In Store.
Blankets, pairs of,	475	229	Shirts, . .	550	31	Shifts, . .	330	94
Sheets, pairs of,	950	84	Jackets,	302	87	Jackets,Cloaks,	30	–
Rugs, .	460	176	Vests, . .	302	16	Gowns, . .	380	12
Hammocks or Cots, .	350	121	Trowsers, .	302	87	Petticoats, .	350	12
Bedticks, .	450	75	Caps, . .	302	14	Aprons, . .	350	10
Bedsteads, .	52	16	Socks or Stockings, pairs of,	504	506	Neckerchiefs,	150	50
			Shoes, Slippers, and Clogs, pairs of,	486	197	Caps, . .	350	–
						Stockings,pairs of, .	350	114
						Shoes,Slippers, and Clogs, pairs of, .	305	70

The general store of prison clothing is kept by the Deputy Governor,
who issues articles from it to the warders and to the Matron, by order
of the Governor, and these warders are required to have a suit of clothes
and bedding for each cell in their class, for which they are responsible
to the Deputy Governor. The supply of bedding and clothing at the time
of my visit was abundant; the sheets are said to he changed fortnightly,
but I cannot think that this rule is strictly adhered to, for it is, like the
bathing of prisoners, left too much to the discretion of the subordinate
officers. Some of the sheeting was by no means as clean as it should be,
which, however, is not surprising, inasmuch as the person of some of
the prisoners was certainly dirty. All the clothing is made up in the
prison, and also the uniform of the officers, under the superintendence
of the tailor and shoemaker warders, who appear to be efficient and
painstaking officers. I regret to find that prisoners on being admitted
to gaol are not all provided with clean pairs of sheets. This is a matter
that I referred to in my last report, and which, I submit, should be
attended to, as for obvious reasons it is highly objectionable that any
individual should be required to sleep in sheets that have been already
used by another.

Number of Punishments for Prison Offences.

	From 1st January to 31st December, 1874.		From 1st January, 1875, to day of Inspection.	
	M.	F.	M.	F.
By Magisterial authority, .	–	1	1	–.
By Governor—				
Dark or Refractory Cells, .	52	15	57	10
Stoppage of Diet, .	1,591	87	983	67
Other Punishments, .	18	4	40	7
Total, .	1,661	107	1,080	84

There are eight solitary cells for males, but only four of them are
boarded or made use of. Two of the ordinary cells in D wing have been
darkened and used as solitary cells for females, but properly arranged
punishment cells in the female prison are very much required, such as
exist in the male prison. I find the Matron has been in the habit of
putting noisy and obstreperous women into one of those darkened cells,
without the authority of the Governor, and also that females have been put
under restraint without his authority. This, I submit, is quite illegal,
and should not be permitted. All prisoners should be brought before the
Governor when punishment is required, or in his absence before the
Deputy Governor, as no other gaol officer is empowered by law to
administer punishment. At the time of my visit I saw two or three
very refractory female prisoners in custody, and I have no doubt
that their misconduct may be very much attributed to the want of
properly fitted solitary cells. I therefore trust that one or two of these

NORTH DISTRICT.

Antrim County Gaol.

requirements will be fitted up at once in the female section of the prison. I would also refer to the 15th rule of the 109th section of the Prisons Act, which alone regulates the power of the Governor as to the nature of the punishment he is to inflict, for I perceive he is in the habit of punishing prisoners by stopping their milk alone, and sometimes their diet, without sentencing them to refractory cells. This system is so irregular, and open to such gross abuse, that it should be discontinued, and in the event of a prisoner being punished by the Governor, he or she should be sent to the refractory cell, which sentence carries with it a diet of bread and water, for a term not exceeding three days.

Schools.

	From 1st Jan. to 31st Dec., 1874.		From 1st Jan., 1875, to day of Inspection	
	M.	F.	M.	F.
Number of individual prisoners who attended school,	397	153	278	92
Average daily number of pupils,	14	14	14	14
Number of days on which school was held,	186	141	95	58

School-hours.—Males—10 to 12 o'clock.   Females—12 to 1 o'clock.

School.

The male school is, I am informed, conducted from ten to twelve daily, and the female from twelve to one o'clock. They are both taught by the schoolmaster, the females in the presence of the Matron. I cannot think the system of conducting the school here is at all satisfactory. The different religions are still taught at different hours and on different days, and only those whose sentence exceeds two months and juveniles are allowed to go to school. The Governor does not appear to take any responsibility in the selection of people who are sent to school, and leaves this matter entirely to others. I consider that it is as much his duty to see that the proper people are sent to school as it is to regulate other matters in the gaol. At the time of my visit I found an old woman, who must have been to school for the purpose of idling her time, as her eyesight was defective, and she could not see letters without the aid of spectacles, which were not provided for her; the Master, too, did not appear aware of this, although the woman had been in the school for some time. This officer, in my opinion, is quite unsuited to manage a school, unless he were closely supervised by a competent person. The Episcopalian Chaplain, who has lately been appointed, accompanied me through the school, and I drew his attention to several matters, so that I trust that some steps will be taken for the more close inspection of the school by the Chaplains than has hitherto been the case. I find the Episcopalian Chaplain has visited the school twenty-eight times this year, the Presbyterian fifteen times, and the Roman Catholic Chaplain only four times. As the school is not in connexion with any board of education, I submit that these gentlemen should give it more of their time, and endeavour, as far as possible, to establish a more efficient system of teaching than is practised at present. The progress in the school registry is so small that I fear little good results from the secular instruction imparted in this prison, and if such be the case, it would be far better to close the school altogether; but I would strongly recommend it to be entirely remodelled, and to be placed in connexion with the National Board of Education. On a previous visit to this gaol one of the male prisoners (M'E.), complained to me about not being allowed to go to school, and on this occasion he repeated the same complaint, and stated that as he had only one arm, if he could obtain some instruction in reading and writing he would be able to earn his bread honestly when at large. I was informed that the reason this man was not allowed to go to school was that he had disturbed others while there, but this excuse was

not at all established to my satisfaction, and I certainly consider that the NORTH
man was fully entitled, under the 106th section of the Prisons Act, to be DISTRICT.
allowed to go to school. In the event of any prisoner misbehaving himself in school, he should certainly be punished for so doing, but that is *Antrim*
not a valid reason for expelling him altogether, and depriving him entirely *County*
of the advantages of instruction. *Gaol.*

Summary of Employment.

	M.	F.
Hard labour,	23	1
Industrial labour,	166	124
Sick,	1	3
Unemployed,	5	6
Discharged (before labour hours),	7	15
Debtors (unemployed),	1	–
Nursing,	–	3
Total in custody,	**203**	**152**

Amount received for produce of Prisoners' labour disposed of outside the Gaol for the last three years.

1872, . £854 10s. 0d. | 1873, . £1,196 8s. 9d. | 1874, . £1,102 11s. 4d.

Stone-breaking and oakum picking are the principal means of carrying Labour.
on hard labour here. The only difference made between prisoners sentenced and those not sentenced to hard labour is, that the former go out
for an hour's stone-breaking in the morning before breakfast, while the
latter are allowed to remain during that time in their cells unemployed.
I am of opinion that all prisoners should be required to work immediately
the gaol is open in the morning, but a sensible difference should be made
in the quantity and quality of the work exacted from those sentenced and
those not sentenced to hard labour. For example, hard labour prisoners
might be required to pick hard oakum, whereas the oakum given to
those not so sentenced might be somewhat opened. These, however,
are matters of detail, which should be arranged and carried out as a matter of course by the Governor of the gaol. No difference is made, as far as
I could ascertain, among the females sentenced and those not sentenced to
hard labour. Their chief employment is in the laundry, sewing, and
other prison duties. Although a vast amount of work is performed in this
gaol during the year, yet with the facilities that exist here for supervision
and for carrying on industries, I am of opinion that a greater amount
should be done, and that many of the prisoners are not sufficiently
employed. I find on the day of my inspection no fewer than ten male
prisoners were nominally employed as orderlies and six as cooks. All the
orderly duty of the gaol should be completed by breakfast time in the Orderlies.
morning, and I am of opinion that the system of orderlies, who are supposed to brush and clean about the gaol during the day, is most objectionable, and detrimental to discipline and order. I also observed that one of
the men on the basement floor is occupied during the day as a servant to
the warders. This is an abuse which should not be permitted, as such an
employment is an indulgence to the prisoner that is not contemplated in
the punishment imposed upon him by law. There is also a prisoner
orderly at the gate, attending on the gatekeeper. This also should
not be permitted, and I cannot too strongly protest against the habit
in this gaol of employing prisoners to assist officers, and to perform
their duties for them. The amount received for the produce of prisoners'
labour is, as I have said, very large as compared with other gaols in Ire- Profits.
land, reaching in 1874 the sum of £1,102 11s. 4d., by which means the
rates are relieved by so much, and the cost of the prison is proportionately
reduced.

Contracts.

Bread, white, 12s. per 112 lb. ; new milk, per gallon, 9½d. ; butter-milk, per gal.,
2½d. ; coal, per ton, for house, 13s. 9d. ; do. for gas, 15s. 9d. ; gas made in the gaol.

NORTH
DISTRICT.
―――
Antrim
County
Gaol.

Provisions.

The contracts are taken and sanctioned by the Board for bread, coals, and milk; meal and potatoes are bought as required, their price being always submitted to and sanctioned by that body. The provisions are kept by the cook warder, who receives about a ton of meal at a time; this officer weighs it out daily, and has sole charge of the meal stores. I am of opinion that the Deputy Governor should certainly issue the provisions daily, and serve them out to the cook warder as required, for obvious reasons. The materials for clothing are all obtained by contract, sanctioned by the Board of Superintendence. The samples of diet which I saw appeared to be excellent, and it is regularly inspected by the Chaplains, who, I find, have occasionally during this year taken exception to the quality of the bread, milk, and potatoes, but none of the prisoners preferred any complaint to me on this score.

Net average daily cost of Ordinary Diet for each Prisoner in the three preceding years.

1872,   .   4d. | 1873,   .   4½d. | 1874,   .   4½d.

Net cost of Gaol, including Diet and Salaries, for the three preceding years

1872, . £5,280 12s. 6d. | 1873, . £6,140 10s. 4d. | 1874, . £6,313 8s. 1d.

Total cost of Officers, including Clothing, Value of Rations, &c.

1872, . £2,054 12s. 1d. | 1873, . £2,294 8s. 1d. | 1874, . £2,302 14s. 1d.

Average cost of each Prisoner per annum in each of the last three years.

1872,   .   £17 5s. 4d. | 1873,   .   £16 2s. 1d. | 1874,   .   £16 4s. 7d.

Amounts repaid by the War Department for Military Prisoners in each of the last three years.

1872,   .   £78 14s. 0d. | 1873,   .   £72 10s. 0d. | 1874,   .   £65 19s. 8d.

Amounts repaid from the Consolidated Fund for the maintenance, &c., of Prisoners during the years—

1872,   .   £696 3s. 6d. | 1873,   .   £798 0s. 5d. | 1874,   .   £857 8s. 10d.

Expenditure.

The net cost of this gaol in 1874 amounted to £6,313 8s. 1d., and from that sum the cost of officers came to £2,302 14s. 1d., which latter sum is larger than in either of the two previous years, but this may be somewhat accounted for by the extra number of warders, namely, six, which were employed during the construction of the new building. These, however, should now be discontinued, as the ordinary staff of the gaol is quite sufficient for the maintenance of order and discipline. The average annual cost of a prisoner in this gaol amounted in 1874 to £16 4s. 7d., which is lower than in any other gaol in Ireland, and demonstrates clearly the absurdity of maintaining small and badly constructed gaols, where supervision is both expensive and difficult, and where discipline, punishment, and labour cannot be properly carried out.

Officers and Salaries.

Non-resident.	£	s.	d.	Resident.	£	s.	d.
Rev. Richard Oulton, Local Inspector, . . .	130	0	0	Captain T. M. Keogh, Governor, . . .	350	0	0
Rev. John Spence, Episcopal Chaplain, . . .	50	0	0	Robert Auld, Deputy Governor, . . .	107	10	0
Rev. Geo. Shaw, Presbyterian Chaplain, . . .	50	0	0	Robert Dick, Clerk, . .	65	0	0
Rev. Murty Hamill, Roman Catholic Chaplain, . .	50	0	0	James Shaw, Schoolmaster, .	55	0	0
Henry Murray, esq., Apothecary, . . .	15	0	0	James Gorman, Shoemaker, .	62	10	0
John Moore, esq., Surgeon, .	100	0	0	David Beattle, . .	62	10	0
				John Martin, . .	62	10	0
				George Handcock, Matmaker,	62	10	0
				William Gorman, Shoemaker, . . .	55	0	0

Inspectors-General of Prisons in Ireland.   **15**

Officers and Salaries—continued.

NORTH DISTRICT.

	£	s.	d.		£	s.	d.	
James Dawson, . . .	50	0	0	Annie Greer, Assist.-Matron,	38	10	0	*Antrim*
Archibald Thompson, *Tailor,*	50	0	0	Matilda Holmes, do. do.	38	0	0	*County*
William John M'Nair, .	42	10	0	Anne Shaw, *Laundress,* .	35	0	0	*Gaol.*
John Archibold, . . .	42	10	0	Margaret Cashe, Hospital				
Robert Hodgins, . . .	42	10	0	Nurse, ...	30	0	0	
John Davison, . .	42	10	0	Mary Cook, Servant, . .	20	0	0	
Stewart Taylor, *Plasterer,* .	42	10	0					
John Legg, ...	42	10	0	*Non-resident.*				
John Craig, ...	42	10	0	Alice Anderson, *Laundress,* .	42	10	0	
Sarah Bramble, Matron, - .	54	0	0	George Campbell, *Gas-man,* .	56	2	0	
Margt. Holmes, Assistant do.	38	10	0	James Anderson, Assist. do.,	52	0	0	

Officers on Gaol Allowance.

A Servant, half-pint new milk daily.

Visits paid by Officers.

	From 1st Jan. to 31st Dec., 1874.	From 1st Jan., 1875, to day of Inspection.
Number of times the Board of Super-intendence met and discharged business, ...	15	11
Local Inspector to Gaol, . . .	70	32
Do. do. to each Bridewell, .	3	.*|
Protestant Episcopal Chaplain, . .	159	121
Presbyterian Chaplain, . . .	139	107
Roman Catholic Chaplain, . .	167	119
Surgeon, ...	707	520
Apothecary, ...	310	243

* And twice by other parties for Inspector, by order of the Board.

All the subordinate officers of this prison have apartments within the gaol, but the married ones are permitted to sleep out in their turn every second night. They have a good mess-room, and are allowed half an hour for breakfast, and three-quarters of an hour for dinner. The mess-room is tidily fitted up, and each officer is provided with a press, in which his provisions are kept. No officer is permitted to leave the prison without the permission of the Governor, except those whose turn it is to go out when off duty. I regret that during my visit I had not the pleasure of seeing the Local Inspector, and more especially as the cause of his absence was through illness.

Books and Journals.

The registries and books of finance are chiefly kept by the clerk, assisted by the schoolmaster. The authorized Daily Employment Book and Work Ledger are not kept, but one which serves the same purpose is now in use. All these books appear to be well and regularly kept, and are duly checked and supervised by the Governor, who appears to devote much time and attention to this part of his duties. Owing to the illness of the Local Inspector his journal was necessarily not written up of late, but the journal of the Governor is full, and regularly kept; the Chaplains also write their journals regularly, but I was unable to ascertain from these books whether the prisoners are visited by them in accordance with the requirements of the 69th section of the Prisons Act. I was, however, informed that unless the prisoners ask to see the Chaplains in their cells they do not as a rule visit them. This system is, I submit, not in accordance with the provisions of the above-named section. I cannot but think that if these gentlemen were to comply with the Act in the performance of their duty that they would obtain some influence for good over some of the many unfortunate people who are so repeatedly confined here, and who would consequently come under their notice so frequently. I was accompanied through the gaol by the Medical Officer, who devotes much of his time and talents to this establishment. His books and journal fully testify how carefully he performs his prison duties.

NORTH DISTRICT.

Antrim County Gaol.

Hospitals.

	1872.		1873.		1874.		1875 (to day of Inspection).	
	M.	F.	M.	F.	M.	F.	M.	F.
No. of prisoners in hospital,	18	7	31	10	33	82	4	11
Average daily number in hospital,	·7	·6	1·	·3	1·2	1·2	·176	·526
No. of prisoners prescribed for and treated out of hospital,	1,146	732	1,246	940	693	469	560	854
No. of deaths in the gaol,	2	–	4	1	–	2	–	1
Cost of medicine,	£51 5s. 3d.		£24 11s. 5d.		£21 14s. 11d.		—	
Cost of extra diet for prisoners in hospital,	£12 8s. 2d.		£17 14s. 8½d.		£18 9s. 4½d.		—	
Cost of all extra diet ordered by Medical Officer for prisoners not in hospital,	£16 14s. 1d.		£22 15s. 3d.		£40 17s. 6d.		—	

Hospital.
The hospital arrangements in this gaol have undergone no alterations since my last inspection. This department has frequently been condemned by Inspectors-General, so that it is unnecessary for me to dwell further upon the subject than to suggest that until a proper hospital is built, a portion of the old debtors' day-room in D wing be fitted up as a male hospital, in which non-infectious cases and those for observation can be dealt with without being removed to the present hospital.

The Matron still sleeps in the middle wing of the hospital, and retains the keys of the cells, and also of the outer door of this building at night, and I find a prisoner orderly is also still permitted to spend her days here. These are abuses that I have already referred to in former reports. The medicines are procured from Dublin as required by the requisition of the Medical Officer, the cost of which amounted in 1874 to £21 14s. 11d. This sum though large is somewhat less than during the two previous years.

Miscellaneous.

Complaints.
Several complaints were made to me by the male prisoners during my inspection on different subjects, but on investigating them I was unable to come to any other conclusion than that they were frivolous, and not well founded. One man complained of his milk being stopped in the morning, but as I have already expressed my opinion upon the Governor's discretion in this matter, it is not necessary to further refer to it. I was glad to find that a number of books had been procured for the prisoners to read in their cells, and trust the Board will keep the selection of the secular library in their own hands, and make it common to prisoners of all religions, though each Chaplain should have the power of selecting a certain number of books of religious character for prisoners of their own persuasion. I make these suggestions as I have received complaints in other gaols from prisoners who, in my opinion, naturally object to the Chaplains being permitted to be the sole judges of the secular books which they are permitted to read. At the time of my visit certain commitments struck me as being irregular. I therefore submitted them to the Executive, who, I understand, has communicated with the committing justices on the subject with a view to putting at an end such commitments in future. I regret to find that the work of the Governor's garden is still performed by prison labour, an abuse to which I have already called attention in previous reports, and which I again submit should not be permitted, as being contrary to prison rule.

Board of Superintendence.

Geo. J. Clarke, esq., J.P., D.L.
Henry H. M'Neill, esq., J.P.
John Young, esq., J.P., D.L.
Sir Charles Lanyon, J.P.
David Taylor, esq., J.P.

W. T. B. Lyons, esq., J.P., D.L.
James Owens, esq., J.P.
Hon. E. O'Neill, J.P., D.L., M.P.

General Viscount Templetown, K.C.B., D.L.
Capt. R. C. Thomson, J.P.
Saml. Thompson, esq., J.P.
John Hind, esq., J.P.

The Board of Superintendence meets in this gaol on the first Friday of the month, and held eleven meetings during this year previous to my inspection. On these occasions the cheques are drawn for the payment of the monthly bills, and the subordinate officers receive their salaries. Those of the superior officers are paid half-yearly at assizes. I annex my reports upon the three bridewells of this county.

NORTH
DISTRICT.

*Antrim
County.*

STATE OF BRIDEWELLS.

Bridewells.

	Antrim.		Ballymena.		Ballymoney.	
	M.	F.	M.	F.	M.	F.
No. of Committals in past year, . .	64	30	181	40	65	43
Of whom were Drunkards, .	34	22	134	29	43	33
No. of Committals in the quarter preceding inspection, .	23	8	44	15	12	7
Of whom were Drunkards, .	7	5	26	12	4	7

	Antrim.	Ballymena.	Ballymoney.
Petty Sessions and Transmittals, how often?	Petty Sessions on last Tuesday in each month. Transmittals immediate. Criminal Quarter Sessions once a Quarter; but I am told that after this month the Criminal Quarter Sessions will be removed to Belfast.	Petty Sessions fortnightly; transmittals immediate. Criminal Quarter Sessions quarterly.	Petty Sessions first and third Monday of the month; Transmittals direct. Criminal Quarter Sessions four times a year.
Committals, . .	Regular.	Regular, but each remand should have a fresh stamp attached to it.	Regular; but one missing.
Registry, . . .	Regular.	Well kept.	Regular.
Repairs and Order, .	Good.	Good.	Good.
Security, . . .	Fair, with care.	Fair, except yards, which are very insecure.	Fair, with care.
Accommodation, .	Three cells for males, two for females; two day-rooms.	Three cells for each sex; 2 day-rooms.	Four cells for males, two for females; two day-rooms.
Furniture, Bedding, and Utensils.	Good, clean, and sufficient.	Good, clean, and sufficient.	Some blankets are light, and some sheets not as clean as they should be.
Water, how supplied?	By pumps in each yard, but still too close to the sewer.	By a good pump on premises.	By good pump in each yard.
Sewerage, . .	Effective.	Effective.	None; soil must be carried through the house.
Cleanliness, Dryness, and Ventilation.	Clean, and well ventilated.	Clean, and well ventilated.	Clean, and well ventilated.
Cost of Dietary, .	5d. per day.	5d. per head per day.	5d. per head per day.
Salary of Keeper, and whether he follows any other employment.	£25, and £10 to his mother. Is Court-keeper at £10; is also weighing-master at £50.	£27 10s.; wife £12 10s.; also fuel and light. Is Court-keeper at £10.	£23, and wife £12. Is Court-keeper, £10.
Date of Inspection, .	October 2nd, 1875.	October 2nd, 1875.	October 2nd, 1875.
Remarks, . . .	No prisoner in custody.	No prisoner in custody.	No prisoner in custody.

CHARLES F. BOURKE, *Inspector-General.*

B

NORTH
DISTRICT.

*Armagh
County
Gaol.*

Number in
custody.

Juveniles.

ARMAGH COUNTY GAOL, AT ARMAGH.—STATUTABLE INSPECTION,
29TH SEPTEMBER, 1875.

Fifty-two males and 24 females formed the total number of prisoners in custody at the above date. Fifty of these were disposed of summarily, 16 were cases tried at quarter sessions or assizes, 3 were untried, 6 were military offenders, and 1 was classed as a debtor—a female under an attachment from the Court of Chancery. No juveniles were in custody at the time of my visit, but 8 had been in charge previously during the year, 2 of whom were sent to reformatories. I am informed that care is taken to keep juveniles quite apart from the other prisoners, and I have no doubt that the Governor pays attention to this important matter. None of the above juveniles were known to have been previously in custody.

Number of Prisoners of all classes in Gaol on the day of Inspection, and on the corresponding date in the three preceding years.

		M.	F.		M.	F.
1872,		53	17	1874,	37	18
1873,		40	19	1875 (day of Inspection),	52	24

Number of Returned Convicts in Gaol on the day of Inspection, and during each of the three preceding years, and the expired portion of 1875.

		M.	F.		M.	F.
1872,		1	4	1875 (up to and including		
1873,		–	2	day of Inspection),	1	1
1874,		3	1	Day of Inspection,	1	–

Commitments.

CLASSES.					From 1st January to 31st Dec., 1874.		From 1st Jan., 1875, to day of Inspection.	
					M.	F.	M.	F.
Debtors,					7	1	4	2
Criminals,					272	86	201	58
Vagrants,					10	1	4	–
Drunkards,					157	78	130	72
Total,					446	166	339	132

Commit-
ments.

One prisoner was in custody at the time of my visit who was a returned convict, and was to be tried for the robbery from the person of £120. He had been committed here before, having been arrested with the man M'Dead, who was subsequently hung for an atrocious murder at Sligo. I have no doubt the Governor will trace this man's history, and lay it before the judge of assize on his trial—a course which should always be pursued where old offenders are concerned. The total number of commitments up to the time of my inspection, was 339 of males and 132 of females, against 446 of the former and 166 of the latter in the previous year. It will be observed by the previous table, that having regard to the time my inspection was made the offence of drunkenness this year is proportionably somewhat larger than last, especially amongst females; but I am in hopes that the criminal commitments at the close of the year will be somewhat smaller than in 1874, though I am afraid that the total number of commitments in 1875 will be in excess of those of the previous year. Four males and 2 females were committed here for debt during 1875; but I am in hopes that this class of prisoners will now cease to frequent our gaols, as the time is fast approaching when it will be no longer legal to imprison people for that offence.

Number of Individual Prisoners (exclusive of Debtors), and number of times each had been Committed during the following periods, distinguishing Adults from Juveniles.

NORTH DISTRICT. *Armagh County Gaol.*

NUMBER OF TIMES COMMITTED.	1874.				1875, to day of Inspection.			
	Juveniles.		Adults.		Juveniles.		Adults.	
	M.	F.	M.	F.	M.	F.	M.	F.
Once within the year,	20	-	325	102	7	1	268	82
Twice „	-	-	25	13	-	-	20	11
Thrice „	-	-	5	8	-	-	3	5
4 times „	-	-	3	2	-	-	1	1
5 „ „	-	-	2	1	-	-	-	-
6 „ „	-	-	1	-	-	-	-	1
7 „ „	-	-	-	-	-	-	1	-
Total,	20	-	361	126	7	1	293	100
No. of above who had not been in Gaol previous to 1st Jan. in	20	-	279	56	7	1	209	46

Number of Individual Prisoners (exclusive of Debtors) committed in the year 1874, and to the day of Inspection in 1875, who had been Once, Twice, Thrice, Four Times, Five Times, &c., &c., from their first Commitment in any year, so far as can be ascertained, distinguishing Adults from Juveniles.

NUMBER OF TIMES COMMITTED.	1874.				1875, to day of Inspection.			
	Juveniles.		Adults.		Juveniles.		Adults.	
	M.	F.	M.	F.	M.	F.	M.	F.
Once only,	20	-	265	51	7	1	204	46
Twice,	-	-	30	17	-	-	30	14
Thrice,	-	-	16	11	-	-	18	6
4 times,	-	-	9	11	-	-	8	4
5 „	-	-	10	6	-	-	4	3
6 „	-	-	5	3	-	-	4	2
7 to 11 „	-	-	17	8	-	-	16	10
12 to 16 „	-	-	7	2	-	-	6	3
17 to 20 „	-	-	-	-	-	-	-	4
21 to 30 „	-	-	-	9	-	-	2	4
31 to 40 „	-	-	-	3	-	-	-	2
41 to 50 „	-	-	1	2	-	-	-	-
51 to 60 „	-	-	-	2	-	-	-	1
91 to 100 „	-	-	-	1	-	-	-	-
181 to 200 „	-	-	-	-	-	-	-	1
201 to 250 „	-	-	1	-	-	-	1	-
Total No. of Individuals committed,	20	-	361	126	7	1	293	100
No. of Commitments represented in foregoing,	20	-	1,015	897	7	1	900	760

Up to the time of my visit this year, seven was the greatest number of times that any individual was committed to this gaol during the year ; but 20 males and 11 females had been committed twice during that period. At the same time it is evident from the last of the foregoing tables, that there are a certain number of individuals in this district who must spend a great portion of their lives in gaol, for it will be seen that in both years

Re-commitments.

B 2

NORTH
DISTRICT.

*Armagh
County
Gaol.*

one male was in custody who had been over 200 times in prison from his first offence, and one female, in 1875, who had been over 180 times in gaol. Those who have been committed ten and twelve times are very numerous; but serious offences are, I am happy to state, rare in this county, there having been only one prisoner in custody during this year who was charged with conspiring to take life. The offences for which the greatest number are committed are common assaults and drunkenness, and as the assaults are generally committed under the influence of drink, it may be fairly concluded, that the inordinate love of drink is the principal cause of crime in this county.

Averages, and Highest and Lowest Numbers (exclusive of Debtors).

—	From 1st January to 31st December, 1874.			From 1st January, 1875, to day of Inspection.		
	M.	F.	Date.	M.	F.	Date.
Average daily number of prisoners in custody,	50	18	—	54	20	—
Highest number of prisoners at any one time,	87		8th March.	103		22nd Aug.
Lowest ditto,	53		24th Sept.	58		26th Jan.
Highest number of males at any one time,	70		8th March.	77		22nd Aug.
Do. of females,		25	14th March.		27	24th Aug.
Lowest number of males at any one time,	35		14th Sept.	38		26th Jan.
Do. of females,		12	1st Sept.		14	12th Jan.

Highest Number of Prisoners (exclusive of Debtors) in Gaol during each of the previous seven years, and up to day of Inspection in 1875.

6th February, 1868,	. . . 76		15th September, 1872,	. . . 72
21st July, 1869,	. . . 142		3rd December, 1873,	. . . 80
5th August, 1870,	. . . 101		8th March, 1874,	. . . 87
1st January, 1871,	. . . 76		22nd August, 1875,	. . . 103

I regret to remark that the preceding tables show an increase this year up to the time of my inspection, in the daily average number of prisoners in custody, and also that a larger number were in charge at one time during this year than at any period since July, 1869.

Accommodation.

	M.	F.		M.	F.
Wards, . . .	3	2	Worksheds, . .	20	–
Yards, . . .	9	1	Kitchen, . .	1	–
Day Rooms, . .	2	–	Store Rooms, . .	4	–
Solitary Cells, .	3	–	Laundry, . .	–	1
Single Cells, 9 feet long, 6 feet wide, 8 feet high=432 cubic feet,	–	–	Drying Room, . .	–	1
			Lavatory, . .	–	1
Do., heated & furnished with bells,	61	38	Baths, with Hot and Cold Water		
Cells to contain three persons,	11	–	laid on, . .	1	1
Sleeping Rooms, .	5	–	Privies, . .	4	–
No. of Beds in such Rooms,	10	–	Water-closets, . .	66	5
Hospital Rooms, .	1	1	Fumigating Bath used.		
Chapel, . .	1	–	Reception Rooms or Cells,	3	–
School-room, . .	1	–	Pumps, . .	2	–
Workshop, . .	1	–	Tell-tale Clock, .	1	–

Cells.

Since my last inspection of this gaol some of the suggestions of my colleague and myself have been adopted. Tables are now provided in the cells for females. Altogether this prison is now very suitably arranged for carrying out the separate system in its integrity, being provided with sixty-one cells for males and thirty-eight for females of the required size, both heated and furnished with bells. Both the male and female prisons are amply supplied with water-closets and lavatories, and gas is furnished to all the cells except in the upper ward of the female prison. Good arrangements now exist for the bathing of prisoners as they come in, and subsequently during imprisonment, consequently the cells and bedding presented a very creditable cleanly appearance. The water supply is abundant, and is obtained from the town main at the rate of £10 a year. The sewerage is reported as effective, and is emptied into the river Callan. The laundry arrangements are very good, except that the washing stalls are not enclosed. I would therefore recommend that a latticed door be put to each compartment so as to prevent prisoners communicating one with another, as separation is considered now the most effective deterrent to ordinary offenders, and having regard to the large numbers recommitted it here behoves the authorities to use every means in their power to deter habitual offenders from frequenting the neighbourhood. The only washing done is that for the gaol ; but as the daily average number of females here is large, I would again recommend that the laundry be turned to more profitable account, for in this large town I cannot but think, that washing contracts could be procured, and as this labour is very well suited to the class of females who are continually coming to this prison, I think every effort should be made to obtain such suitable employment for them. The drying-room has a separate heating apparatus. This fire I submit, might be saved by connecting the heating of this department with the steam boiler. The chapel has lately been altered, and is now very suitably arranged, and all three services are performed here. That is one of the improvements that has been effected since my last visit. Photography is still done by an artist in the town—a system which both my colleague and I object to for obvious reasons. I therefore again submit, that this duty should be performed by an officer of the prison. The kitchen arrangements are the same as at my last visit, an excellent steam boiler is provided which cooks the food, heats the water for the laundry, and for the baths, and provides steam for the purification of the clothing. I am glad also to find, that the cook, in compliance with my recommendation, is now locked up in his cell at night. The vigilance of the night-watch is tested by means of one tell-tale clock, which is marked hourly from 10 P.M. to 6 A.M. Up to 10 o'clock P.M. there is an evening guard in the inside of the prison. The markings of the clock are taken by the head warder, and are entered by him in the Lockings Book, and all omissions of duty on the part of the night watchman are marked against him in the Officers Conduct Book. As both my colleague and I do not consider one tell-tale clock sufficient for this large gaol, I must recommend that another be procured and placed at a distance from the present one, so as to ensure a more perfect patrol of the prison during the night. I regret to observe several omissions in the markings of the tell-tale clock, and as this is a serious dereliction of duty, I would recommend that a scale of fines be established, which I have no doubt would have the effect, as it has in other gaols, of having this duty performed with greater care and attention. At 10 o'clock at night the Governor takes charge of all the keys of the prison, and brings them to his bed-room, so that after that time no person except the officers who are sleeping in the different wards can have access to the prison. I would again call attention to the very unsuitable arrangements existing here for visitors to prisoners, and submit that a proper visiting place, as suggested in my last report should be put up. Convicted prisoners are permitted to receive a visit once a month, and the untried once a week by order of the Local Inspector or the Board of Superintendence. This is an indulgence which should, I submit, be permitted as rarely as possible as it is one that is open to a great deal of

Side notes: NORTH DISTRICT. Armagh County Gaol. Lavatories, &c. Baths. Water. Sewerage. Laundry. Chapel. Photography. Kitchen. Night-watch. Visitors.

abuse, and it is found that when prisoners are not permitted to see their friends except upon rare occasions, that it adds considerably to their punishment while in gaol, and tends to their future good conduct. I am informed, that visitors to prisoners are all searched when they are suspected of being inclined to convey any prohibited article into the prison; but I submit that this rule should be invariably carried out, considering that the prison visiting place is so badly arranged.

Stock at the time of Inspection.

	In Use.	In Store.	Male Clothing.	In Use.	In Store.	Female Clothing.	In Use.	In Store.
Blankets, pairs of,	122	18	Shirts, . .	108	45	Shifts, . .	34	21
Sheets, pairs of, .	196	30	Jackets, . .	70	14	Gowns, . .	30	49
Rugs, . .	123	69	Vests, . .	70	14	Petticoats, .	66	46
Hammocks or Cots,	99	–	Trowsers, . .	64	15	Aprons, . .	36	41
Bed-ticks, .	122	11	Caps, . .	66	–	Caps, . .	30	37
Bedsteads, . .	–	33	Stockings or Socks, pairs of,	34	44	Stockings, pairs of,	14	25
			Shoes, Slippers, & Clogs, pairs of,	74	–	Shoes, Slippers, & Clogs, pairs of, .	20	–

At the time of my inspection there was an abundant supply of clothing and bedding throughout the prison, which was all in good repair and well stored. The storekeeper keeps the store of new clothing; but does not issue anything from it without the Governor's order, either to the matron or to the reception warder, which latter officer has the responsibilty of dressing all male prisoners as they come in. The private clothing of the males was properly labelled and stored away, but the system of labelling the female clothing was not as well observed as it should be; however, I drew the attention of the Governor and the matron to this defect, and I trust it will be in future corrected. All clothing is made up in the prison, and is immediately entered in the general store kept by the storekeeper. Stock is taken by the Governor of all prison clothing once a quarter.

Number of Punishments for Prison Offences.

	From 1st January to 31st Dec., 1874. M.	F.	From 1st Jan., 1875, to day of Inspection. M.	F.
By Magisterial authority, . .	2	–	–	–
By Governor—				
Dark or Refractory Cells, . .	35	4	23	–
Total, . .	37	4	23	–

The want of proper solitary cells is now one of the principal defects of this gaol. Some of the cells at the gateway are at present used as male solitary cells; but they are not heated or provided with bells, and are very unsuited to that purpose, and owing to the want of solitary cells for females, I have no doubt it is found very difficult at times to deal with obstreperous prisoners of this sex. Twenty-three males and no females were I perceive sentenced to the refractory cells previous to my visit this year. The 106th sec. of the "Prisons Act" require that a competent number of punishment cells should be provided in all gaols. I therefore submit, that this defect here should be remedied as soon as possible.

Schools.

	From 1st Jan. to 31st Dec., 1874. M.	F.	From 1st Jan., 1875, to day of Inspection. M.	F.
Number of individual prisoners who attended school, ...	149	47	106	40
Average daily number of pupils, .	.13	5	13·4	6
Number of days on which school was held, .	261	249	211	207

School hours.—Males—4 to 5·30, P.M.   Females—Noon to 2, P.M.

Since my last visit the school has been stalled and much improved; but I would suggest that it be further altered, as under the present arrangement prisoners face one another which is always objectionable. I would recommend that the stalls be placed on a raised tier, one row on a higher level than the other, and that all face in the same direction in order to prevent any communication between prisoners. The school is not in connexion with any educational body, but is occasionally inspected by the Chaplains. The schoolmaster has, I am informed, been taught under the Church Education Society, and the deputy-matron, who instructs the females, is a certified trained teacher. The progress noted in the school registry is on the whole satisfactory. I would recommend that the school be connected with the Board of National Education, as it would be then regularly inspected, and its efficiency more closely attended to in other ways ; and I am of opinion that one hour a day is quite sufficient time to allow for the instruction of the class of prisoners which frequent this gaol.

Employment on day of Inspection.

Industrial Labour.

	M.	F.						M.	F.
Mat-making, . . .	2	–	Mangling,	.	.	.		–	2
Tailoring.	2	–	Knitting.	.	.	.		–.	10
Weaving and Winding, .	5	–	Sewing,	.	.	.		–	8
Shoemaking, . . .	1	–							
Prison duties, . .	4	2	Total,		.	.		51	22
Stone-breaking, . .	37	–							

Summary.

							M.	F.
Industrial labour,	.	.	.	.	.		51	22
Sick, . .	.	.	:	:	:		1	1
Debtors (*unemployed*),	.	.	.	.	.		–	1
	Total in custody,	.	.	.			52	24

Amount received for Produce of Prisoners' labour disposed of outside the Gaol for the last three years.

1872, £44 10s. 11d. | 1873, . £38 0s. 6d. | 1874, . £61 13s. 1d.

Net average daily cost of Ordinary Diet for each Prisoner in the three preceding years.

1872, . 4d. | 1873, . 4d. | 1874, . 5d.

Net cost of Gaol, including Diet and Salaries, for the three preceding years.

1872, . £1,867 1s. 5d. | 1873, . £1,871 9s. 6d. | 1874, . £2,097 1s. 9d.

Total cost of Officers, including Clothing, Value of Rations, Washing, Gas, &c.

1872, . £964 2s. 6d. | 1873, . £1,018 17s. 6d. | 1874, . £1,003 6s. 0d.

Average cost of each Prisoner per annum in each of the last three years.

1872, . £31 1s. 0d. | 1873, . £34 13s. 0d. | 1874, . £30 7s. 10d.

Amounts repaid by the War Department for Military Prisoners, in each of the last three years.

1872, . £73 0s. 6d. | 1873, . £55 19s. 0d. | 1874, . £62 0s. 0d.

Amounts repaid from the Consolidated Fund for the maintenance, &c., of Prisoners during the years

1872, . £147 0s. 10d. | 1873, . £138 1s. 3d. | 1874, . £227 3s. 6d.

Stone-breaking is the most severe labour of any that is performed in this gaol, as there are no mechanical means for carrying out hard labour.

NORTH DISTRICT.

Armagh County Gaol.

I would draw the serious attention of the Board to the subject of labour in this gaol, as at present I do not consider it at all on a satisfactory footing. Sufficient distinction is not made between prisoners sentenced and those not sentenced to hard labour, and owing to the want of a sufficient number of stone sheds proper separation is not observed. The Governor endeavours as far as possible to separate prisoners while at labour, and to obtain as much work as possible from them, but so long as they are allowed to work in so desultory a manner as at present, hard labour cannot be considered to be carried out at all. I submit that a greater amount of labour should be carried on in the cells than at present. An hour is allowed for breakfast and an hour for dinner, during most of which time the prisoners are wholly idle, whereas they should be given a certain amount of oakum-picking or such work to perform during that period. I am strongly of opinion that if more attention were paid to this subject, and if a greater amount of labour were exacted from both male and female prisoners, that the old offenders in this district would not be so numerous

Discipline.

as they are at present. I also would suggest a stricter discipline to be enforced, and silence to be more observed throughout the prison than is the custom now ; for nothing is more calculated to instil terror into ordinary criminals than a perfect system of silence and strict discipline, whereas if talking in the gaol, even amongst the officers, is permitted an old offender will care little for the punishment inflicted, and a person convicted of a first offence will leave the prison probably more hardened than when he came into it. The industrial labour here consists of weaving, matmaking, shoemaking, tailoring, and other prison duties, and during this year I was glad to find that a good deal of painting had been performed by prison labour. As gas is provided in most of the cells industrial pursuits should be carried on both in winter and summer up to 8 o'clock in the evening, and I have no doubt that if these suggestions are attended to the amounts in future derived from the produce of prisoners' labour will

Expenditure.

be considerably increased. In the year 1874, however, the results from this source were larger than they had been for some time, being £61 13s. 1d., but this sum is very small having regard to the daily average number of prisoners in custody in that year, namely, 50 males and 18 females, as well as to the average cost of each prisoner per annum, which amounted in that year to £30 7s. 10d. The net cost of the gaol in 1874 was £2,097 1s. 9d., nearly the half of which sum was expended in the cost of officers, which, in proportion to the daily average number of prisoners in custody, is very large ; but pending the long expected alteration in our prison arrangements in Ireland I do not suppose the Board of Superintendence would be inclined to make any sensible reduction in the staff.

Contracts.

Bread, white, per lb., 1¼d.; ditto, brown, per lb., 1¼d.; oatmeal, per cwt., 14s. 6d.; potatoes, per cwt., 4s. 0d.; new milk, per gallon, 10½d.; salt, per cwt., 3s. 4d.; coal, per ton, 18s. 8d.; straw, per cwt., 3s.; gas, per 1,000 cubic feet, 6s. 8d.; candles, per lb., 5d.; soap, per cwt., £1 5s.

Provisions.

The contracts are all sanctioned by the Board, and are taken twice a year except that for milk, which is taken every twelve months. The samples of the provisions that I saw appeared excellent, but I observe that the Chaplains and Governor occasionally take exception to the quality of the bread provided during this year by the contractor. This is a matter that I am sure the Board will see the necessity of dealing with promptly. Every prisoner's portion is either weighed or measured in the presence of an officer before it is served out, and none of the prisoners in custody complained to me regarding their food or treatment in prison.

Officers and Salaries.

Non-Resident.	£	s.	d.	Resident.	£	s.	d.
John M'Kinstry, esq., Local Inspector,	100	0	0	John M'Cutcheon, Governor,	210	0	0
Rev. Chas. Faris, Irish Church Chaplain,	40	0	0	John Armstrong, . .	60	0	0
				Henry Jenkinson, *Weaver*,	50	0	0
Rev. Jackson Smyth, Presbyterian Chaplain, .	40	0	0	Robert Con'ter, . .	45	0	0
Rev. Hugh M'Oscar, Roman Catholic Chaplain, .	40	0	0	John M'Coy, . .	45	0	0
				Samuel M'Arthur, *Tailor*,	45	0	0
Alexander Robinson, esq., Surgeon, . . .	—			Asaph Moore, . .	48	0	0
				Thomas Stringer, . .	45	0	0
Joseph M. Palmer, esq., Apothecary, . .	30	0	0	Eleanor Hanna, Matron, .	45	0	0
				Mary M'Arthur, Assistant do.,	35	0	0
Alex. Briens, Schoolmaster,	50	0	0	Mary Anne Agnew, Hospital Nurse, . . .	30	0	0

Armagh County Gaol.

Vacancy in the staff since last Inspection, how caused, and how filled up.

Rev. Peter J. Byrne, Roman Catholic Chaplain, resigned, and the vacancy has been filled by the appointment of Rev. Hugh M'Oscar.

Visits paid by Officers.

	From 1st Jan. to 31st Dec., 1874.	From 1st Jan., 1875, to day of Inspection.
Number of times the Board of Superintendence met and discharged business,	12	6
Local Inspector to Gaol,	149	128
Do. each Bridewell,	*4	*4
Chaplain, Prot. Episcopal Church,	176	114
Presbyterian Chaplain, . . .	163	113
Roman Catholic Chaplain, . .	167	120
Surgeon, ...	119	81
Apothecary, ...	293	189

* Except Newtownhamilton, to which three visits were paid in 1874, and two in 1875.

The male subordinate officers' quarters here were clean and tidy. Two officers of the officers sleep in the male prison and take their food there, which is an objectionable practice, as no officer should have access to prisoners except when on duty. I would therefore recommend that quarters be provided for these officers either in the old debtor's prison which is not now required for debtors. The state of cleanliness and order of the prison, and the manner in which the books and accounts are kept reflects much credit on the Governor and his subordinates. He is a most painstaking officer, and his zeal and attention to the public service is most praiseworthy.

Hospitals.

	1872.		1873.		1874.		1875 (to day of Inspection).	
	M.	F.	M.	F.	M.	F.	M.	F.
No. of prisoners in hospital, .	63	17	82	16	93	28	—	
Average daily number in hospital, . . .	2·0	—	1·8	·4	3·6	1·3	—	
No. of prisoners prescribed for and treated out of hospital, . .	95	63	109	49	102	46	—	
Cost of Medicine, . .	£29 15s. 4d.		£32 3s. 9d.		£44 16s. 3d.		—	
Cost of diet for prisoners in hospital, . .	£18 0s. 11d.		£27 6s. 6d.		£43 15s. 7d.		—	

The arrangements with regard to the hospital are the same as at my Hospital. last inspection. I am clearly of opinion that a good deal of economy is required in this department. If trivial cases were treated in their cells, as is the case in a great number of prisons now, the hospital need very seldom be used, and the services of the hospital matron could be dispensed with, for at present this officer has no other duties to perform than those connected with the hospital which cannot occupy her whole time. I have

NORTH.
DISTRICT.

*Armagh
County
Gaol.*

Books.

also again to draw attention to the large cost of medicines here, amounting in the year 1874 to £44 16s. 3d. In addition to this the apothecary receives £30 a year salary, so that, as compared with some other gaols, the charges under this head here are I submit most extravagant.

The books of registry and finance are all kept by the Governor and clerk, and are daily supervised by the former, who devotes much time and attention to this as well as his other prison duties. I regret to find that the Local Inspector has not kept a journal, but he has now informed me that he will do so in future. As he is the principal officer of the gaol his remarks and observations thereon should certainly be recorded. The Governor's journal is carefully and well kept, showing clearly how attentive he is in all matters relating to his duties. The proper Work Ledger should be procured and regularly written up, and an account, as laid down in the proper form of Work Ledger, should be carefully kept of the profits derived from prisoners' labour. I am informed that prisoners occasionally get a gratuity on leaving the prison, but as no regular account is kept of their labour the 107th section of the Prisons Act is not complied with. The hospital books are carefully written up, but the authorized form of hospital book is not used. This should at once be procured. I also regret to find that the General Visitors' Book is not kept as it should be. These are matters to which I drew the attention of the Local Inspector and Governor, and I therefore trust that they will have the necessary forms procured and regularly kept.

Board of Superintendence.

Rt. Hon. Lord Lurgan, K.P.	John Hancock, esq.	Maxwell C. Close, esq.
Sir James M. Stronge, bart.	Joseph Atkinson, esq.	Stewart Blacker, esq.
Sir Capel Molyneux, bart.	Hugh Boyle, esq.	Colonel Cross.
Thomas A. Prentice, esq.	St. John Thos. Blacker, esq.	Major Craig.

Board.

The Board meets on the second Saturday of the month for the transaction of business, on which occasion cheques are signed for the different tradesmen, which are countersigned by the Local Inspector, and vouchers are produced on the following board day. All the officers are paid quarterly, and the accounts of the Board appear to be most carefully kept. I annex my tabular reports of the bridewells of the county, and now that the criminal quarter sessions at Markethill is to be discontinued, and that this town is connected by rail with Armagh, I certainly consider that the bridewell should be closed, and trust that steps will be taken for so doing at the coming assizes.

[BRIDEWELLS.

STATE OF BRIDEWELLS.

———	Ballybot.		Lurgan.	
No. of Committals in past year, . . .	M. 73	F. 28	M. 237	F. 100
Of whom were Drunkards, .	13	13	76	20
No. of Committals in the quarter preceding inspection, . .	38	9	60	14
Of whom were Drunkards, .	13	5	20	5
Petty Sessions and Transmittals, how often?	Petty Sessions weekly at Ballybot; and Borough Court on Fridays at Newry.		Once a fortnight, and at end of each quarter; only once in 3 weeks. Transmittals immediate; criminal Quarter Sessions four times a year.	
Committals, . . .	Regular.		Regular; but prisoners are still frequently detained here without any warrant to this bridewell, a matter I have before drawn attention to.	
Registry, . . .	Carefully kept.		Regularly kept.	
Repairs and Order, .	Not improved since last inspection.		Good.	
Security, . . .	Bad.		Good; but yards still low, and not yet pointed.	
Accommodation, .	Two cells for males, one for females, and a day-room for each sex.		Three cells for males, and two for females, upstairs; one for drunkards down; two day-rooms.	
Furniture, Bedding, and Utensils.	Sufficient; but some blankets are so much worn that extra ones should be given in cold weather.		Good, clean, and sufficient.	
Water, how supplied? .	By a force-pump.		By good pump.	
Sewerage, . . .	Privies, which are cleaned out, at rere of house.		Effective.	
Cleanliness, Dryness, and Ventilation, .	Ventilation bad; clean, but damp.		Clean, and well ventilated.	
Cost of Dietary, . .	6½d.		6½d. per day, which is too high, as it is only 4d. in Dungannon.	
Salary of Keeper, and whether he follows any other employment.	£25 per annum; and £14 for fuel and straw; £5 to daughter as matron. Is court-keeper at £5 a year.		£30; £14 for fire, light, and straw; wife £5. Is a pensioner from the R. I. Constabulary.	
Date of Inspection, .	September 28th, 1875.		October 1st, 1875.	
Remarks, . . .	No prisoner in charge.		No prisoner in custody. The cleanliness and order of this establishment reflects much credit on the keeper.	

NORTH DISTRICT.

STATE OF BRIDEWELLS—*continued.*

Armagh County.

Bridewells.

	Markethill.		Newtownhamilton.	
	M.	F.	M.	F.
No. of Committals in past year, . . .	33	15	36	8
Of whom were Drunkards, .	8	—	27	3
No. of Committals in the quarter preceding inspection, . . .	1	1	11	2
Of whom were Drunkards, .	—	1	5	1
Petty Sessions and Transmittals, how often?	Petty Sessions monthly; Criminal Quarter Sessions quarterly, but are about to be discontinued. Transmittals on the following day.		Petty Sessions monthly; no Criminal Quarter Sessions now. Transmittals immediate.	
Committals, . . .	Regular, but very few.		Regular, with one exception.	
Registry, . . .	Regularly kept.		Regular.	
Repairs and Order, .	Good.		Fair, but some painting much wanted.	
Security, . . .	Fair with care, except yards, which are very insecure.		Very bad.	
Accommodation, . .	Three cells for males, 3 for females—2 day-rooms.		Only one damp cell for each sex, and two day-rooms. Yards very small and insecure.	
Furniture, Bedding, and Utensils.	Good and sufficient.		Sufficient and good.	
Water, how supplied? .	By good pump on premises.		By good pump.	
Sewerage, . . .	Effective.		Only a cesspool cleaned out through the house.	
Cleanliness, Dryness, and Ventilation.	Clean, and well ventilated.		Damp and badly ventilated.	
Cost of Dietary, per head, per day.	6¼d. per head per day.		6¼d. per head per day.	
Salary of Keeper, and whether he follows any other employment.	£20, and wife £5; is Court-keeper at £5; £11 a year for fuel, light, and straw. Is a tailor by trade, and works at it.		£20, and wife £5; is Court-keeper, and has a small piece of land.	
Date of Inspection,	September 29th, 1875.		September 30th, 1875.	
Remarks, . . .	No prisoner in custody, and so few now that this bridewell should be closed, as it is only six miles from the county gaol.		No prisoner in custody.	

CHARLES F. BOURKE, *Inspector-General.*

CAVAN COUNTY GAOL, AT CAVAN, STATUTABLE INSPECTION, 17TH MAY, 1875.

NORTH DISTRICT.
Cavan County Gaol.

At the above date 29 males and 3 females were the total numbers in custody, 14 of whom were untried ; 7 were cases disposed of at quarter sessions and assizes, and the remaining 11 were summary convictions. Up to this period no juveniles were committed to this prison this year, but 8 cells are reserved in the male section for prisoners of this class, and I am informed that they are kept quite separate from adults. *Number in custody.* *Juveniles.*

Number of Prisoners of all classes in Gaol on the day of Inspection, and on the corresponding date in the three preceding years.

	M.	F.		M.	F.
1872,	39	6	1874,	22	8
1873,	37	11	1875 (day of Inspection),	29	3

Number of Returned Convicts in Gaol on day of Inspection, and during each of the three preceding years, and the expired portion of 1875.

	M.	F.		M.	F.
1872,	1	1	1875 (up to and including		
1873,	1	–	day of Inspection),	–	1
1874,	–	2	Day of Inspection,	–	–

Commitments.

CLASSES.	From 1st January to 31st Dec., 1874.		From 1st Jan., 1875, to day of Inspection.	
	M.	F.	M.	F.
Debtors,	6	–	–	..
Criminals,	199	24	80	7
Vagrants,	–	4	–	–
Drunkards,	114	57	21	16
Total,	319	85	101	23

Up to the time of my visit this year no debtor was committed here, and now that the law regarding debt has been altered, it is not likely that any more prisoners of this class will be committed here. Previous to my visit as many as 7 persons were committed here, charged with conspiring against or threatening life, and one of the latter was then in custody. With these exception, serious crime cannot be considered to be very prevalent in this county, as the commitments to this gaol are chiefly for assaults and drunkenness. The total number of commitments in 1874 was 319 of males and 89 females, against 101 of the former and 23 of the latter during the 4½ months of 1875 previous to my visit. *Commitments.*

[TABLE.

Number of Individual Prisoners (exclusive of Debtors) and number of times each had been committed during the following periods, distinguishing Adults from Juveniles.

NUMBER OF TIMES COMMITTED.	1874.				1875, to day of Inspection.			
	Juveniles.		Adults.		Juveniles.		Adults.	
	M.	F.	M.	F.	M.	F.	M.	F.
Once within the year,	3	1	222	35	–	–	76	11
Twice ,,	–	–	22	2	–	–	5	4
Thrice ,,	–	–	4	4	–	–	5	–
4 times ,,	–	–	4	2	–	–	–	1
5 ,, ,,	–	–	2	–	–	–	–	–
6 ,, ,,	–	–	1	1	–	–	–	–
8 ,, ,,	–	–	–	1	–	–	–	–
11 ,, ,,	–	–	–	1	–	–	–	–
Total,	3	1	255	46	–	–	86	16
No. of above who had not been in Gaol previous to 1st January in .	3	–	212	32	–	–	68	10

Number of Individual Prisoners, exclusive of Debtors, committed in the year 1874, and to the day of Inspection in 1875, who had been Once, Twice, Thrice, Four Times, Five Times, &c., &c., from their first commitment in any year, so far as can be ascertained, distinguishing Adults from Juveniles.

NUMBER OF TIMES COMMITTED.	1874.				1875, to day of Inspection.			
	Juveniles.		Adults.		Juveniles.		Adults.	
	M.	F.	M.	F.	M.	F.	M.	F.
Once only,	3	–	199	30	–	–	65	8
Twice,	–	1	19	3	–	–	6	3
Thrice,	–	–	11	2	–	–	4	–
4 times,	–	–	2	2	–	–	2	–
5 ,,	–	–	3	–	–	–	1	–
6 ,,	–	–	4	–	–	–	1	–
7 to 11 ,,	–	–	7	2	–	–	4	2
12 to 16 ,,	–	–	6	1	–	–	2	–
17 to 20 ,,	–	–	–	–	–	–	1	–
21 to 30 ,,	–	–	2	1	–	–	–	1
31 to 40 ,,	–	–	2	1	–	–	–	–
41 to 50 ,,	–	–	–	2	–	–	–	1
51 to 60 ,,	–	–	–	1	–	–	–	–
201 to 250 times,	–	–	–	1	–	–	–	–
251 to 252 ,,	–	–	–	–	–	–	–	1
Total No. of Individuals committed,	3	1	255	46	–	–	86	16
No. of commitments represented in foregoing,	3	2	559	533	–	–	189	352

Highest Number of Prisoners (exclusive of Debtors) in Gaol during each of the previous seven years, and up to day of Inspection in 1875.

3rd January, 1868,	49	22nd May, 1872,		45
17th June, 1869,	41	21st April, 1873,		44
8th December, 1870,	31	8th January, 1874,		45
11th May, 1871,	45	6th January, 1875,		43

Averages, and Highest and Lowest Numbers (exclusive of Debtors).

	From 1st January to 31st December, 1874.			From 1st January, 1875, to day of Inspection.		
	M.	F.	Date.	M.	F.	Date.
Average daily number of prisoners in custody, .	21	6	—	27	5	—
Highest number of prisoners at any one time,	45		8th Jan.	43		6th Jan. .
Lowest ditto, .	14		10th Oct.	18		6th April.
Highest number of males at any one time, .	36		16th June.	38		27th Feb.
Ditto of females, .	16		8th Jan.	10		6th Jan.
Lowest number of males at any one time, .	12		10th Oct.	13		6th April.
Ditto of females, .	1		29th Aug.	3		17th May.

The recommitments to this gaol, though not as numerous as in many other districts, are still kept up by a few individuals. In 1874 one female was committed here as often as 11 times; and during this year one prisoner of that sex had, even up to the time of my visit, been committed four times; but it may be observed that one of those confirmed bad characters who has been in gaol this year has as many as 252 convictions recorded against her. It is, in my opinion, quite superfluous for justices to sentence such offenders to short terms of imprisonment, and it would have a much better effect upon the prisoner herself, and upon others, for example's sake, if repeated offenders such as this person is, upon every occasion they were committed, received the full period of punishment permitted by law. The following figures show that the numbers in this gaol are kept up, almost entirely, by a few individuals:—In 1874, the total number of adult individuals committed here was 255 males and 46 females; 212 of the former and 32 of the latter had not previously been in gaol. Nevertheless, the commitments of those who had been more than once in prison, numbered 559 of males and 523 of females. Up to the period of my visit this year, the total number of individuals committed was 86 males and 16 females; 68 of the former and 10 of the latter had not previously been in prison, but the recommitments of those few who had been before in gaol were 189 of males and 352 of females. At one period, in 1874, only one female was in custody; and at one period this year, only 3 of that sex were in charge; while at no time in either years was the number of females in custody higher than 16. Nevertheless, the county is obliged to maintain a prison and a staff of officers almost for these few delinquents.

Re-com-mitments.

Accommodation.

	M.	F.		M.	F.
Wards, ...	4	3	School Room, . . .	1	—
Yards, ...	7	2	Workshops, . . .	3	—
Day Rooms, . . .	9	3	Kitchen, ...	1	—
Solitary Cells, . .	4	1	Store Rooms, . . .	6	2
Single Cells, not less than 9 feet long, 6 feet wide, and 8 feet high = 432 cubic feet, .	70	—	Laundry, ...	—	1
			Baths, with hot and cold water laid on, ...	1	1
Do. heated, and not furnished with bells, .	3	—	Privies, ...	6	—
Do. of smaller size not so furnished,	70	17	Water-closets, . . .	2	3
Cells to contain three persons, .	—	17	Fumigating Apparatus, .	1	—
Sleeping Rooms, . .	4	—	Reception Room or Cell,	1	—
No. of Beds in such Rooms,	4	—	Pumps, ...	2	1
Hospital Rooms, . .	2	1	Crank Pump, . . .	1	—
Chapel, ...	1	—	Wells, ...	2	1
			Tell-tale Clock, . . .	1	—

NORTH
DISTRICT.
———
Cavan
County
Gaol.

Reception.
Baths.

Lavatories.

Water.
Sewerage.

Heating and
gas.

Cells.

Chapel.

Laundry.

Fumigator.

Photo-
graphy.

Night-
watch.

Since my last visit here very little has been done to improve the structural condition of this prison. The same arrangements exist now as then in regard to the reception cells, but I regret to find that prisoners are still kept in these cells, in a filthy state, until they are seen by the doctor. I, therefore, again submit that all healthy prisoners should be at once bathed on admission; and, in the event of any being ill, the doctor should at once be sent for. A good bath is now provided in each prison, with hot and cold water laid on, so that prisoners are, I am informed, regularly washed on every Saturday during their imprisonment. In my last report I suggested that, as there were no lavatories in the gaol, a basin should be furnished in each cell; but this simple requirement has not yet been provided, so that prisoners are still obliged to wash themselves in the mornings in tubs in the yards. The water supply is the same as at my last inspection, and is ample for the requirements of the gaol. The sewerage is still very defective, as I had full testimony of when I was making my inspection. Water-closets are only provided to the hospital, the female prison, and to the male debtors' quarters, but there are privies in all the yards. No part of the prison, except the male solitary cells, is artificially heated, and gas is only provided in the corridors, in the day rooms, in the hospital, in the officers' quarters, in the laundry, and in the school, so that prisoners cannot be employed during the winter months for many hours of the day in their cells; but as the cells are of full size, the separate system should be thoroughly adopted during the summer months, and a full amount of labour should be performed in them. Three religious services are performed in the chapel, which has undergone no alteration since my last inspection; but it would be very much improved by being painted. Since my last visit the laundry has been divided into three stalls for washing, but fixed troughs have not yet been provided, and the washing is therefore done in ordinary tubs. I would recommend that three troughs be put up, with hot and cold water laid on to each, so that prisoners who are employed here may be kept in perfect separation. A day room is used as a drying room in winter. One fumigating apparatus is provided, in which all prisoners' clothing is purified. The kitchen arrangements here are the same as at my last visit; two boilers are provided, but are not as cleanly kept as they should be, and I regret to find that the prisoner who was employed here as cook was one of the most grave offenders in the gaol. Two other grave offenders were also selected for special duties, which, in my opinion, should always be allotted to prisoners committed for minor offences. This is a matter that I laid before the Board at the time of my visit, and which, I trust, the Governor will in future attend to, as it is a highly objectionable practice to select grave offenders and men sentenced to long periods of imprisonment with hard labour, for easy posts in the gaol. The provisions are kept by the Deputy Governor, and are served out to the cook-warder, who is also the schoolmaster-warder. The photography is also performed by this officer, who receives 9d. for each copy, and is provided by the Board with the apparatus and chemicals. The vigilance of the night watch is tested by means of one tell-tale clock, which is marked half-hourly, from 10 P.M. to 6 A.M. in summer, and to daylight in the winter. I would recommend that this clock be removed to a more distant part of the prison, so as to insure a more effective patrol of the gaol by the night watchman. The markings are taken every morning by the Deputy Governor, and are entered by him in the Morning State Book. Unlock takes place in summer at 6 A.M., and in winter at daylight; and lock-up at 6 P.M. throughout the year. The keys of the prison are taken to the Governor's bed-room every night, who, I am informed, goes round the gaol several times during the year at

uncertain hours of the night in order to test the vigilance of the night
watchman, and to see that all is correct. No improvement has been
made in the arrangements for visitors to prisoners since my last visit,
so that I must refer again to the remarks I made in my last report
on this gaol upon that subject. Since my last visit the boundary wall
has been thoroughly repaired, but some of the inside walls still require to
be pointed.

Stock at the time of Inspection.

	In Use.	In Store.	Male Clothing.		In Use.	In Store.	Female Clothing.		In Use.	In Store.
Blankets, pairs of,	95	27	Shirts,	.	51	39	Shifts,	.	12	11
Sheets, pairs of,	134	21	Jackets,	.	37	4	Jackets,	.	27	141
Rugs,	90	8	Vests,	.	32	–	Petticoats,	.	32	31
Bedticks,	94	38	Trowsers,	.	42	2	Aprons,	.	16	17
Bedsteads,	103	–	Caps,	.	37	–	Neckerchiefs,	.	16	18
			Shoes, Slippers,&				Caps,	.	20	24
			Clogs, pairs of,	47	32		Stockings,pairs of,	6	8
							Shoes, Slippers, &			
							Clogs, pairs of,	18	47

The general store of clothing is kept by the Deputy Governor who
issues articles as required from this store to the schoolmaster-warder and
matron, who each have a supply of the clothing in use throughout
the prison. I am informed that the Governor takes stock of all clothing
quarterly. Females are now provided with stockings, but I regret to find
that socks are not yet given to the males, and as they could easily be
knitted in the female prison, I am of opinion that this necessary should
be provided. The stores were all carefully and well kept and the clothing
tidily put away and arranged. All are made up by prison labour, except
the clogs for the men, which are got by contract. These I submit should
be made in the prison. The bedding was all clean and in good order—
the sheets being, as I am informed, changed every Saturday.

Number of Punishments for Prison Offences.

	From 1st January to 31st Dec., 1874.		From 1st Jan., 1875, to day of Inspection.	
	M.	F.	M.	F.
By Governor—				
Dark or Refractory Cells, . . .	6	2	3	1

Three cells are heated and arranged for the punishment of refractory
male prisoners, and there is one cell darkened in the top tier of the female
prison and reserved for the same purpose, but it is not heated, and neither
of these cells are provided with bells. I am strongly of opinion that no
prisoner should be put into a solitary cell without means of communicating with the officers on duty, and I therefore submit that the refractory
cells for both sexes should be fitted with the spiral bell, as this is now
found to be best adapted for this purpose.

Schools.

	From 1st Jan. to 31st Dec., 1874.		From 1st Jan., 1875, to day of Inspection.	
	M.	F.	M.	F.
Number of individual prisoners who attended school, ...	83	41	50	13
Average daily number of pupils, . .	15½	3½	16·61	4·65
Number of days on which school was held, .	298	290	111	110

School-hours.—Males, 5 to 6 o'clock; Females, 5 to 6 o'clock.

The male school is divided into 19 stalls, but the females are taught
only in a day-room. At the time of my visit both schools were held
from 4 to 6 P.M. daily, and I then suggested that an hour was sufficient to allow for the instruction of prisoners here, and that as gas is
provided in the school-room the school-hours should not interfere with
those of labour, so that it is now carried on from 5 to 6 o'clock. I am
happy to find that the school is now more regularly inspected by the

C

NORTH
DISTRICT.

*Cavan
County
Gaol.*

chaplains, especially as it is not connected with the National Board of Education, which I submit it should be.

Employment on day of Inspection.

	M.	F.
Hard Labour, ...	12*	2
Industrial Labour, ...	9	1
Sick, ...	2	–
Unemployed, ...	4	–
Discharged (before labour hours), . .	2	–
	—	—
Total in custody, . .	29	3

* Twelve men at hard labour return to stone-breaking at 12 o'clock noon.

Amount received for produce of Prisoners' Labour disposed of outside the Gaol for the last three years.

1872, . £10 5s. 8d. | 1873, . £16 7s. 0d. | 1874, . £9 19s. 6d.

Net average daily cost of Ordinary Diet for each Prisoner in the three preceding years.

1872, . 4d. | 1873, . 3½d. | 1874, . 4d.

Net cost of Gaol, including Diet and Salaries, for the three preceding years.

1872, . £1,456 11s. 5d. | 1873, . £1,547 10s. 9d. | 1874, . £1,461 0s. 9d.

Total cost of Officers, including Clothing, Value of Rations, &c.

1872, . £887 9s. 2d. | 1873, . £912 10s. 2d. | 1874, . £901 11s. 1d.

Average cost of each Prisoner per annum in each of the last three years.

1872, . £45 5s. 6d. | 1873, . £40 1s. 0d. | 1874, . £51 5s. 4d.

Amounts repaid by the War Department for Military Prisoners in each of the last three years.

1872, . £3 8s. 0d. | 1873, . £1 12s. 0d. | 1874, . £4 1s. 0d.

Amounts repaid by the Inland Revenue Department for Excise Prisoners for the last three years.

1872, . £10 15s. 2d. | 1873, . £2 13s. 7d. | 1874, . £3 2s. 8d.

Amounts repaid from the Consolidated Fund for the maintenance, &c., of Prisoners during the years

1872, . £102 2s. 5d. | 1873, . £79 18s. 10d. | 1874, . £90 0s. 3d.

Labour.

Men sentenced to hard labour are employed at the crank-pump for two hours a day, being absolutely on the mill 15 minutes and off for the same period. At the time of my visit separate stone-sheds were about to be put up, but not by prison labour. Such work as this should always be executed by prisoners under the direction of a carpenter-warder, by which means numerous improvements can be carried out at very little cost to the gaol. I do not consider that a sufficient amount of labour is exacted from prisoners here; more industry is required, and the officers supervising prisoners at work should be much more vigilant in the performance of their duty; for unless the officers are constantly spurring prisoners on to work, and that idleness or disobedience of orders is not at once reported to the Governor, it cannot be expected that a due amount of labour will be obtained. Women are chiefly employed at washing and needlework, but no washing other than that for the prison and for the officers is performed. I have in former reports called attention to the want of sufficient labour in this gaol and the consequent small amount received from the produce of prisoners' labour. This amounted in 1874 only to the small sum of £9 19s. 6d., whereas the average annual cost of a prisoner here for the same year came to the large sum of £51 5s. 4d. The net cost of the gaol for that year was £1,461 0s. 9d., but £901 11s. 1d. was expended in the cost of officers. It cannot be said that the subordinate officers in this gaol are too highly paid, but at the same time, having regard to the daily average numbers committed here, namely, 27 males and 5 females, the cost of officers is certainly extravagant; especially as so small a result is derived from the produce of the labour of the prisoners.

Contracts.

Bread, white, per 1-lb. loaf, 1¼d.; bread, brown, per 1-lb. loaf, 1d.; oatmeal, per cwt., 13s. 9d.; potatoes, per cwt., 3s. 5d.; meat, per lb., 10d.; new milk, per gallon, 8d.; buttermilk, per gallon, 2d.; salt, per cwt., 3s. 10d.; coal, per ton, £1 5s.; straw, per cwt., 1s. 10d.; gas, per 1,000 cubic feet, 10s. 6d.; candles, per lb., 5d.; soap, per cwt., £1 0s. 4½d.

The contracts for provisions and materials for clothing are all taken by the Board once a year, and the samples of the diet that I saw were excellent, with the exception of the milk, which was sour on the day of my visit, though I perceived by the Dietary Report books that the chaplains, as a rule, report favourably on its condition throughout the year, and I am glad to find that these gentlemen inspect the provisions regularly in their turn according to the requirements of the statute.

Provisions.

Officers and Salaries.

Non-Resident.		*Resident.*	
		William Wills, esq., Governor,	£200
Theophilus Thompson, esq., Local		Thomas M'Dowell, Head Warder,	60
Inspector,	£100	Robert West, *Carpenter*,	40
Rev. S. Shone, Protestant Chaplain,	30	William Beatty,	30
Rev. Edward Sheridan, Roman Catholic Chaplain,	30	Wm. Henry Lowry, *Schoolmaster*,	30
Rev. James Carson, Presbyterian Chaplain,	30	Hezekiah Mee, *Blacksmith*,	30
Andrew Mease, esq., Physician,	74	Miss Jane Simons, Matron,	40
Thomas O'Connor, Apothecary,	–	Miss Isabella Pratt, Assist.-Matron,	16
		Jas. M'Cormick, Night Watchman,	30

Vacancies in Staff since last Inspection, how caused, and how filled up, viz.

Miss Ellen Darby, Assistant-Matron, died; Miss Isabella Pratt, appointed.

Officers on Gaol Allowance.

All, except the Governor.

Visits paid by Officers.

	From 1st Jan. to 31st Dec., 1874.	From 1st Jan., 1875, to day of Inspection.
Number of times the Board of Superintendence met and discharged business,	9	4
Local Inspector to Gaol,	194	75
Do. to each Bridewell,	4	2
Chaplain, Protestant Epis. Church,	176	67
„ Presbyterian,	164	62
„ Roman Catholic,	159	65
Physician,	158	59

All the subordinate officers sleep within the gaol. Their quarters were all neatly and tidily kept, with the exception of one—the cook-warder, who I had also occasion to find fault with for want of cleanliness in the kitchen. During my inspection I had occasion to express disapprobation at some serious omissions of duty on the part of the subordinate officers, and would consequently suggest that a scale of fines be laid down by the Board—such as is in existence in other prisons, in order that the Governor may inflict punishment in this way upon subordinate officers for neglect of duty. I find that a prisoner is told off here daily to attend on the officers—a practice which is contrary to prison rule and very

Officers.

detrimental to discipline. The Governor is a most painstaking and attentive officer, but it is impossible that he can maintain discipline amongst his subordinates unless he is given some power to make his authority felt. The matron also deserves every credit for the clean and orderly condition of her prison. During my inspection no prisoner made any complaint to me regarding the treatment received here.

Hospitals.

	1872.		1873.		1874.		1875 (to day of Inspection).	
	M.	F.	M.	F.	M.	F.	M.	F.
No. of prisoners in hospital, .	2	–	–	–	–	–	–	–
Average daily number in hospital, ...	₁ᴬᴵ	–	–	–	–	–	–	–
No. of prisoners prescribed for and treated out of hospital,	110	20	82	13	108	7	–	–
No. of deaths in the gaol, .	–	–	1	–	–	–	–	–
Cost of medicine, . .	£18 3s. 11d.		£15 0s. 10d.		£13 15s. 7d.		—	
Cost of diet for prisoners in hospital, ...	£2 9s. 0d.		—		—		—	
Cost of all extra diet ordered by Medical Officer for prisoners not in hospital, .	—		£6 19s. 1d.		£3 0s. 11d.		—	

Hospital. The hospital arrangements are the same as at my last visit. The building consists of two wards—one for males and one for females; but the latter has not been used for over 6 years, and the former for 3 years. As the hospital is absolutely within the male prison, I would suggest that the room formerly used for master debtors should now be given over for the female hospital, as it is not likely again to be required for debtors. The present hospital wards are not supplied with bells. I therefore submit that these requirements should be put up. The medicines are procured from an apothecary in the town, whose bill is examined by the surgeon, and a legal declaration is made of its correctness before it is paid at every assizes. But I observe, notwithstanding these precautions, that the cost of medicines is still very high, as compared with other gaols, and the number of prisoners committed here—amounting in 1874 to £13 15s. 7d. I drew attention in my report of 1873 to this matter, and would again recommend that the medicines should either be procured from Dublin or from the County Infirmary, for where this custom is pursued their cost to the county is very small, indeed, as compared with what they come to otherwise.

Books. Most of the books of registry and finance are kept by the Governor, and some by the Deputy Governor, but the former officer carefully supervises them all, and devotes much of his attention to this part of his duty. The journals of the Local Inspector and Chaplains do not contain much information in regard to their respective duties, but that of the Governor is a full record of the duties performed by him. The Surgeon also keeps his journal carefully, as well as the hospital books required to be kept in gaols, from which I perceive that every attention is paid by him to his prison duties. All the prescribed forms are in use and appear to be free from error, with the exception of the Check Ticket Book, in which there were some mistakes, to which I drew the attention of the Governor, and I have no doubt he will see that it is correctly kept in future.

Board.

Board of Superintendence.

On the first Tuesday of the month the Board meet for the discharge of business, when cheques are drawn for the payment of current accounts, and receipts are produced by the Local Inspector at the following meeting of the Board. The officers receive their salaries on every second month. Annexed are my tabular reports on the three bridewells of the county.

NORTH DISTRICT.

Cavan County.

STATE OF BRIDEWELLS.

Bridewells.

	Ballyconnell.		Bailieborough.		Cootehill.	
	M.	F.	M.	F.	M.	F.
No. of Committals in past year,	5	1	16	3	17	7
Of whom were Drunkards,	1	—	6	1	14	1
No. of Committals in the quarter preceding inspection.	1	—	5	3	3	2
Of whom were Drunkards,	—	—	1	—	1	1
Petty Sessions and Transmittals, how often?	Fortnightly; transmittals direct.		Petty Sessions fortnightly. Transmittals direct.		Fortnightly; transmittals direct.	
Committals,	Only one this year. A prisoner kept here for 18 days on remand, signed by one justice, for periods beyond 3 days, and with no stamp.		Regular; only two this year.		Regular.	
Registry,	Regular.		Carefully kept.		Carefully kept.	
Repairs and Order,	Good.		Good.		Good, and improved since last visit.	
Security,	Fair, except yards, the walls of which are very low.		Fair, except the yards.		Improved, but the privy renders the yard still very insecure, and the lock has not yet been put to the door leading into the keeper's garden.	
Accommodation,	Two cells for males, 1 for females; 2 day-rooms.		Three cells for males, and 2 for females; two day-rooms.		Two cells for males, one for females; two day-rooms.	
Furniture, Bedding, and Utensils.	Good, clean, and sufficient.		Sufficient, good, and clean.		Good, except the blanket and sheet referred to by my colleague last year has not yet been replaced by new ones.	
Water, how supplied?	By pump in keeper's yard.		By pump on premises.		By a good pump on premises.	
Sewerage,	Said to be good.		Effective.		Effective.	
Cleanliness, Dryness, and Ventilation.	Clean, and well ventilated.		Clean, dry, and well ventilated.		Clean, and well ventilated.	
Cost of Dietary,	5½d. per day.		5d.		5d. a head per day.	
Salary of Keeper, and whether he follows any other employment.	£20, and £6 for fuel, straw, and light. Is Court-keeper at £10; no other employment.		£30; no other employment. Is a pensioner of the R.I.C.		£30 a year, and is a pensioner from the R.I.C.; is also Court-keeper, but with no salary.	
Date of Inspection,	18th May, 1875.		30th April, 1875.		21st May, 1875.	
Remarks,	No prisoner in custody, and only 1 this year, a male, detained for 18 days.		No prisoner in custody, and only 2 committed during this year.		No prisoner in custody.	

CHARLES F. BOURKE, *Inspector-General.*

DONEGAL COUNTY GAOL, AT LIFFORD.—STATUTABLE INSPECTION,
18TH AUGUST, 1875.

Juveniles.

The numbers in custody at the above date were considerably larger than they had been for some years, being forty males and three females. Of these, three were untried, twenty-five had been disposed of at quarter sessions or assizes, and the remaining fifteen were tried by summary jurisdiction. Four juveniles were in custody at the time of my visit, one a child of nine years of age, who was charged with placing a stone upon the railway. His father is alive, and is serving in the artillery, but his mother is dead. If, therefore, he is found guilty of the offence, he should, in my opinion, be transmitted to a reformatory school. Previous to my visit this year as many as twenty-two juveniles had been committed here, one only of these was sent to a reformatory, though three of them had been committed to the gaol during this year three times. I must remark that the number of juvenile offenders committed to this prison of late appears to be very large as compared with other gaols situated in country districts. I would, therefore, strongly urge upon the justices of this county the importance of dealing more seriously with juvenile offenders, for unless this class is shown early the error of their ways they are almost sure to grow up in crime, and continue through life constant inmates of our gaols and an expense to the country. In some districts, where justices' sentence juveniles as a rule to reformatory schools, this class of offender has of late been certainly on the decrease.

Number of Prisoners of all classes in Gaol on the day of Inspection, and on the corresponding date in the three preceding years.

	M.	F.		M.	F.
1872,	23	6	1874,	20	10
1873,	22	2	1875 (day of Inspection),	40	3

Number of Returned Convicts in Gaol on the day of Inspection, and during preceding years, and the expired portion of 1875.

	M.	F.		M.	F.
1872,	-	2	1875 (up to and including		
1873,	1	4	day of Inspection),	-	1
1874,	-	3	Day of Inspection,	-	-

Commitments.

CLASSES.	From 1st January to 31st December, 1874.		From 1st January, 1875, to day of Inspection.	
	M.	F.	M.	F.
Debtors,	5	1	1	-
Criminals,	214	35	291	27
Vagrants,	2	1	4	-
Drunkards,	50	17	43	11
Total,	271	54	339	38

Commitments.

The number of male prisoners in custody this year at the time of my inspection was nearly double that at the corresponding date during the preceding three years; but I am glad to find that during the year 1875 the only person in custody for an offence against life was one male charged with manslaughter. The great increase in crime this year seems to have been in assaults, and we have also a large increase in the number of military offenders committed here, but none of that class were in custody at the time of my visit, and having regard to the period of the

year at which my inspection is made, there is this, a very sad increase in
the offence of drunkenness as compared with the last two years. In fact,
even up to the above date the commitments of males for drunkenness this
year was equal to the entire number in the year 1873, and within seven
of those committed in 1875. There is also, I observe, a gradual increase of
commitments of females during the last three years for that offence. The
total number of commitments in 1874 was 271 of males and fifty-four of
females, but during the seven and a half months of 1875 previous to my
visit the commitments respectively numbered 339 and thirty-eight. It is
evident, therefore, that when the returns are made up at the close of this
year they will show a considerable increase of crime as compared with
the two previous years.

NORTH DISTRICT.

Donegal County Gaol.

*Number of Individual Prisoners (exclusive of Debtors) and Number of Times
each had been committed during the following periods, distinguishing
Adults from Juveniles.*

NUMBER OF TIMES COMMITTED.	1874.				1875, to day of Inspection.			
	Juveniles.		Adults.		Juveniles.		Adults.	
	M.	F.	M.	F.	M.	F.	M	F.
Once within the year, . . .	8	1	176	29	14	2	217	26
Twice ,, . . .	2	1	23	4	3	–	34	3
Thrice ,, . . .	–	–	8	3	–	–	8	–
4 times ,, . . .	–	–	2	1	–	–	1	1
5 ,, ,, . . .	–	–	–	–	–	–	1	–
Total, . . .	10	2	209	37	17	2	261	30
No. of above who had not been in Gaol previous to 1st January in	9	2	155	20	17	2	204	21

*Number of Individual Prisoners, exclusive of Debtors, committed in the
year 1874, and to the day of Inspection in 1875, who had been Once,
Twice, Thrice, Four Times, Five Times, &c., &c., from their first commitment in any year, so far as can be ascertained, distinguishing Adults
from Juveniles.*

NUMBER OF TIMES COMMITTED.	1874.				1875, to day of Inspection.			
	Juveniles.		Adults.		Juveniles.		Adults.	
	M.	F.	M.	F.	M.	F.	M.	F.
Once only, ...	8	1	139	18	14	2	177	18
Twice, ...	1	1	33	8	3	–	46	4
Thrice, ...	–	–	16	–	–	–	25	2
4 times	1	–	10	4	–	–	7	1
5 ,, ...	–	–	4	2	–	–	1	–
6 ,, ...	–	–	2	–	–	–	2	–
7 to 11 ,, ...	–	–	3	–	–	–	2	–
12 to 16 ,, ...	–	–	1	1	–	–	–	–
17 to 20 ,, ...	–	–	1	1	–	–	1	–
21 to 30 ,, ...	–	–	–	1	–	–	–	4
41 to 50 ,, ...	–	–	–	1	–	–	–	1
121 to 140 ,, ...	–	–	–	1	–	–	–	–
Total No. of Individuals committed,	10	2	209	37	17	2	261	30
No. of commitments represented in foregoing, . . .	14	3	382	290	20	2	422	180

*Highest Number of Prisoners (exclusive of Debtors), in Gaol during each
of the previous Seven years, and up to day of Inspection in 1875.*

27th June, 1868,	. . . 58	11th July, 1872,	. . . 55
6th July, 1869,	. . . 48	7th April, 1873,	. . . 49
3rd May, 1870,	. . . 53	16th July, 1874,	. . . 46
8th June, 1871,	. . . 48	15th June, 1875,	. . . 79

Averages, and Highest and Lowest Numbers (exclusive of Debtors).

—	From 1st January to 31st December, 1874.			From 1st January, 1875, to day of Inspection.		
	M.	F.	Date.	M.	F.	Date.
Average daily number of prisoners in custody,	24	5	—	41	3	—
Highest number of prisoners at any one time,	46		16th July.	79		15th June.
Lowest ditto, .	19		10th May.	22		4th Jan.
Highest number of males at any one time, .	41		26th Nov.	73		15th June.
Ditto of females,	13		16th July.	8		6th June.
Lowest number of males at any one time,	16		10th May.	19		4th Jan.
Ditto of females,	1		7th Nov.	–		7th March.

The total number of adult male individuals committed here in 1874 was
209, and of females thirty-seven; but even in the expired portion of
this year they numbered respectively 261 and thirty. During the whole
of the year 1874 no prisoner was in custody here more than four times,
whereas up to the time of my visit one male prisoner had been in charge
as often as five times during this year, and a male and female four
times. In 1874 one female had been in charge who had been over
121 times in prison from her first commitment; but this year up to the
time of my visit no prisoner had been in custody here who had previously
been more than fifty times in gaol. As compared with some of the other
gaols the recommitments here do not show a very great perversity in crime
amongst the inhabitants of this county who find their way to gaol; but it
will be seen by the previous tables that comparatively speaking the individuals committed are few as compared with the commitments they represent. This is to be remarked especially among the females. At one period
of this year there were none in gaol, while at one period in 1874 only one
prisoner of that sex was in custody, their highest number this year at any
time being eight, and thirteen in 1874. I regret to observe by the foregoing tables that the numbers in custody this year were higher than they
had been for the last eight years. For four months previous to my visit
no debtor had been in charge, and only one prisoner of that class had been
committed here this year, so that I hope that in future, owing to the alteration in the law regarding debt in Ireland, that we shall have no more
debtors committed to this gaol.

Accommodation.

	M.	F.		M.	F.
Wards, ...	8	3	Worksheds, . . .	4	–
Yards, ...	8	2	Kitchens, . . .	1	1
Day Rooms, . . .	10	4	Store Rooms, . . .	5	2
Solitary Cells, . .	3	1	Laundry, . . .	–	1
Single Cells, 9 feet long, 6 feet wide, and 8 feet high, or which contain 432 cubic feet,	-	-	Drying Room, . . .	–	1
			Lavatories, . . .	15	1
			Baths, with hot and cold water laid on, . . .	1	1
Single Cells of smaller size, .	64	19	Privies, . . .	9	–
Cells to contain three persons,	2	–	Waterclosets, . . .	5	3
Sleeping Rooms, . .	4	1	Fumigating Apparatus, .	2	1
No. of Beds in such Rooms,	4	1	Reception Rooms or Cells, .	1	1
Hospital Rooms, . .	2	1	Pump, . . .	1	–
Chapel, . . .	1	–	Crank Pump, . . .	1	–
School Room, . .	1	–	Tell-tale Clocks, . .	2	–
Workshops, . . .	4	–			

The structural condition of this prison has undergone no alteration since NORTH DISTRICT. my last visit, so that the defects so frequently pointed out still exist. I was glad, however, to find that, in accordance with suggestions, some new Donegal County Gaol. water-closets were being put up at the time of my visit. Good arrangements exist as to the reception ward; and all prisoners are at once bathed as they come in, and subsequently once a week, four good baths being Reception. provided in the male prison, one of which has hot and cold water laid on to it. There is also a bath in the female prison. There were two sets of Bath. lavatories in the male prison, but there are none of these requirements in the female section. No improvements have been effected in the sewerage Sewerage. since my last inspection, and the new water-closets will, I am informed, be emptied into cesspools on the premises, the soil from which will have to be emptied out through the prison. There is a full supply of water on Water. the premises, obtained from a reservoir about half a mile distant, also from a well in the gaol, from which the water is pumped by a two-handled crank-pump, at which men sentenced to hard labour work for one hour and a half daily. The prison is not artificially heated throughout, Heating. but there are fires in the day-rooms in the winter. However, I am glad to find that prisoners are not allowed to congregate in these rooms. A fumigating apparatus is provided in each prison, in which all clothing Fumigator. is cleansed before it is put away. The arrangements regarding the chapel Chapel. are the same as at my last visit; and neither the laundry nor kitchen Laundry & Kitchen. have undergone any alterations since then; but the kitchen in the female prison is not now used, except when prisoners of this sex in custody exceed six in number. I would strongly recommend that the kitchen in the male prison be done away with, and that the whole of the culinary duties of the prison be transferred to the female prison, by which means the labour of one man could be turned throughout the year to greater advantage. The ventilation in the drying-room should be altered, as at present it is very defective. No gas has yet been introduced into the prison, oil lamps Gas. being still used in the corridors, so that prisoners cannot be employed during the winter months after dark. The photography is still carried Photography. on by the clerk under the same arrangements as at my last inspection, this officer being allowed 10d. for each copy, and supplies his own chemicals. Every care is taken by the Governor to photograph suspected prisoners, and to trace out their previous history as far as he is able, a course which is found most useful in the detection of crime, and has a very wholesome deterrent effect upon old offenders. Visitors to pri- Visitors. soners are received under the same rules as were in existence at the time of my last visit, and sufficient precautions are taken to prevent the introduction of any prohibited articles into the prison. A member of the Board of Superintendence or the Local Inspector gives orders for the admission of visitors to prisoners—the convicted prisoners being allowed a visit once in three months, the untried twice a week, or oftener if necessary for the purposes of their trial—and all visitors to prisoners are searched. Two new tell-tale clocks have been provided since my last visit, and are now marked hourly by the night-watch, from 10 P.M. to 6 A.M. This Night-watch duty is performed by the the night watchman, and the state of the clocks is ascertained by the Governor, who examines them every morning, and enters the markings both in the Lockings Book and his journal, and also notes in the Officers' Conduct Book any omissions in the marking of the clock. I would recommend that one of the clocks be moved to a greater distance from the other, and outside the buildings, in order to ensure a more perfect patrol of the prison during the night. The clocks are protected by Chubbs' patent locks, the keys of which are kept by the Governor. Unlock takes place in the summer at 6 A.M. and in the winter at 7 o'clock. In the former season lock-up is at 6 P.M. and in the latter at dark, after which time no employment is carried on in the

NORTH DISTRICT.

Denegal County Gaol.

cells. I would suggest that all prisoners he required to pick oakum during the summer months as long as it is daylight, or up to eight o'clock.

Stock at the time of Inspection.

	In Use.	In Store.		In Use.	In Store.		In Use.	In Store.
			Male Clothing.			**Female Clothing.**		
Blankets, pairs of,	112	58	Shirts,	80	50	Shifts,	6	19
Sheets, pairs of,	114	48	Jackets,	36	50	Jackets,	6	17
Rugs,	108	51	Vests,	36	70	Petticoats,	6	21
Bed-ticks,	98	40	Trowsers,	36	44	Aprons,	6	30
Bedsteads,	98	7	Caps,	36	44	Neckerchiefs,	6	30
			Stockings, or Socks, pairs of,	36	47	Caps,	6	24
			Shoes, Slippers, & Clogs, pairs of,	36	47	Stockings, pairs of,	6	16
						Shoes, Slippers, & Clogs, pairs of,	3	21

Stores.

The general store of prison clothing and bedding is kept by the store-keeper, who also has charge of the store of male clothing in use, and the Matron has charge of the female clothing. All the prison clothing is made up within the gaol, but none of the materials are manufactured here. Stock is taken of all prison property twice a year by the Governor and Local Inspector, and the stores are kept in the most orderly and regular manner. The bedding throughout the prison was in excellent repair, abundant, and clean, testifying clearly that proper precautions are taken for the cleansing and washing of all prisoners on being committed, without which precaution it cannot be expected that the clothing and bedding of the prison can be in a proper state of cleanliness.

Punishments.

Number of Punishments for Prison Offences.

	From 1st Jan. to 31st Dec., 1874.		From 1st Jan., 1875, to day of Inspection.	
	M.	F.	M.	F.
By Magisterial authority,	–	–	1	–
By Governor—				
Dark or Refractory Cells,	12	–	37	1
Other Punishments,	3	–	–	–
Total,	15	–	38	1

Nature of the Punishments included under "Other Punishments," viz.:—Being confined in their sleeping cells on Sunday for a certain number of hours, but on the ordinary prison diet.

There are three solitary cells for males and one for females, one for each sex being provided with bells, and one of those for males is artificially heated, but the female solitary is not heated. However, as very few women are ever sentenced to solitary confinement in this gaol, the cell for that purpose is seldom required ; and I find that prisoners are all given their beds at night when in solitary—an indulgence which, I submit, would be better dispensed with ; and, if this were the case, I have no doubt that it would be found necessary much less frequently to punish male prisoners than at present for breach of prison rule. I find that more prisoners have been committed to solitary up to the time of my visit this year than during the whole of 1874 ; and on one occasion it was found necessary this year to call in magisterial authority for the punishment of a refractory prisoner. Under these circumstances, I consider it would be more advisable to make the punishment of refractory prisoners more felt than it is at present.

Employment on day of Inspection.

	M.	F.
Hard Labour,	31	2
Industrial Labour,	6	1
Discharged (before labour hours),	2	–
Cook,	1	–
Total in custody,	40	3

Amount received for produce of Prisoners' Labour disposed of outside the Gaol for the last three years.

1872, . £22 5s. 5d. | 1873, . £18 0s. 2d. | 1874, . £12 9s. 0d.

Net average Daily Cost of Ordinary Diet for each Prisoner in the three preceding years.

1872, . . 5d. | 1873, . . 6d. | 1874, . . 5d.

Net Cost of Gaol, including Diet and Salaries, for the three preceding years.

1872, . £1,752 0s. 2d. | 1873, . £1,912 6s. 8d. | 1874, . £1,867 18s. 3d.. '

Total Cost of Officers, including Clothing, Value of Rations, &c.

1872, . £1,013 13s. 10d. | 1873, . £1,014 1s. 2d. | 1874, . £1,020 12s. 6d.

Average Cost of each Prisoner per annum in each of the last three years.

1872, . £54 0s. 2d. | 1873, . £58 11s. 1d. | 1874, . £62 5s. 3d.

Amounts repaid by the War Department for Military Prisoners in each of the last three years.

1872, . £18 16s. 0d. | 1873, . £10 18s. 0d. | 1874, . £10 9s. 0d.

Amounts repaid by the Inland Revenue Department for Excise Prisoners for the last three years.

1872, . £33 1s. 6d. | 1873, . £50 5s. 8d. | 1874, . £38 0s. 6d.

Amounts repaid from the Consolidated Fund for the Maintenance, &c., of Prisoners during the years

1872, . £90 13s. 9d. | 1873, . £64 12s. 1d. | 1874, . £76 1s. 11d.

Men sentenced to hard labour are, I am informed, required to break 12 cwt. of stones daily, or, in the winter, a bushel of bones; while those not so sentenced are required to break 8 cwt. of stones and half a bushel of bones; and in addition to this a certain number of men are required to work a crank-pump daily. The labour at which women are employed is chiefly washing, sewing, and knitting, while the drunkards are required to pick coir. A large quantity of broken stones was on hands at the time of my inspection, which the Governor informed me he was about immediately to dispose of. Tradesmen are required to work at their several trades, and the Governor is careful to take advantage of those committed, for the purpose of making up the clothing and necessaries of the prison. Although the time of prisoners here is fairly occupied during the day, yet as no work is carried on in their cells the return for labour here is still but small, amounting in 1874 only to £12 9s. This, I submit, is a very inadequate return for the industry of a daily average number of twenty-four males and five females, which was the average in custody here during that year. The net cost of the gaol in 1874 amounted to £1,867 18s. 3d., but the greater part of this sum is expended upon officers, who cost the county in that year £1,020 12s. 6d. Owing principally to this large charge, and to the want of any adequate profits to counterbalance it, in the way of the produce of prisoners' labour, the average cost of each prisoner per annum here is extremely large, amounting in 1874 to £62 5s. 2d. Independent of extern officers, eleven discipline officers are still maintained, which, I submit, is in excess of the requirements of this prison, having regard to the daily average number of prisoners confined. As I have already observed, the females are never numerous, and at some periods of the year there are none in custody, but, nevertheless, three female officers are maintained.

Labour.

Expenditure.

NORTH DISTRICT

Donegal County Gaol.

Officers and Salaries.

Non-Resident.	£	s.	d.		£	s.	d.
Captain James F. Stewart, Local Inspector,	150	0	0	John Browne, Clerk & Store-keeper, and *superintends trades*,	64	0	0
Rev. John Saml. M'Clintock, Chaplain Protestant Episcopal Church,	40	0	0	Geo. Walker, Schoolmaster and Turnkey,	49	0	0
Rev. Wm. A. Russell, Chaplain Presbyterian Church,	40	0	0	James Baird,	34	0	0
				John Vance, *Shoemaker*,	44	0	0
Rev. Wm. Hagarty, Chaplain Roman Catholic Church,	40	0	0	William Neely,	39	0	0
				Robert Longmore,	34	0	0
Robert Little, esq., M D., Physician and Surgeon,	—			Archibald Allen, Night-Watch,	34	0	0
James Gillespie, Apothecary,	30	0	0	Eleanor Shields, Matron,	44	0	0
Resident.				Mary Jane Hetherington, Assistant Matron,	29	0	0
Samuel Searle, esq., Governor,	225	0	0	Eliza Baird, Nursetender,	20	0	0

Vacancies in the Staff since last Inspection, how caused, and how filled up.

Robert Keatley, Turnkey, was appointed Bridewell-Keeper at Donegal; Robert Longmore, Night-Watch, was promoted Turnkey, and Archibald Allen was appointed Night-Watch in his place. Jane Ashe, Matron of Gaol, died, and Eleanor Shields was appointed to fill the vacancy.

Visits paid by Officers.

	From 1st Jan. to 31st Dec. 1874.	From 1st Jan., 1875, to day of Inspection.
Number of times the Board of Superintendence met and discharged business,	12	9
Local Inspector to Gaol,	162	129
Ditto, to each Bridewell,	4	2
Chaplain, Protestant Episcopal Church,	190	114
Presbyterian Chaplain,	174	109
Roman Catholic Chaplain,	174	112
Physician and Surgeon,	158	90
Apothecary,	375	237

Officers.

The quarters of the subordinate officers are regularly inspected by the Governor, and were at the time of my visit clean and well kept. They are provided with a mess-room, and all single men take their meals in the prison; but I regret to find that a prisoner is still allowed to wait upon these officers, which is a system very detrimental to discipline, and which, I again submit, should not be permitted. Since my inspection of this prison serious charges were brought by the Assistant Matron, and also by a prisoner, against the Matron, which were carefully investigated by the Board, on oath, and resulted in the Matron being called upon to resign, which she ultimately did, and another has been appointed in her place.*

Hospital.

	1872.		1873.		1874.		1875 (to day of Inspection).	
	M.	F.	M.	F.	M.	F.	M.	F.
No. of prisoners in hospital,	8	1	11	–	5	1	5	–
Average daily number in hospital,	·3	·1	·3	–	·1	··1	·39	–
No. of prisoners prescribed for and treated out of hospital,	63	25	69	11	60	25	30	7
No. of deaths in the Gaol,	–	–	–	–	–	–	–	–
Cost of medicine,	£1 12s. 0d.		£1 10s. 10d.		£0 17s. 4d.		£8 13s. 4d.	
Cost of diet for prisoners in hospital,	£2 4s. 8d.		£2 1s. 0d.		£1 0s. 1d.		£1 11s. 10d.	
Cost of all extra diet ordered by Medical Officer for prisoners not in hospital,	£0 9s. 10d.		£1 10s. 10d.		£0 7s. 10d.		£0 4s. 3d.	

* Since this has passed through the press, I learn from the Governor that the Board having considered three female officers unnecessary, promoted the nurse to the office of Matron, so that the number of officers has now been reduced by one.

The hospitals, both male and female, are suitably arranged, but are very seldom used, as fortunately the health of the prison has been for a long time very good. Two male officers have apartments in the male hospital, but a nurse attends to the sick here during the daytime, though she does not sleep in the male wing. A store of medicines is kept here, which are procured from Dublin, and are compounded by the apothecary of the town, which is an excellent and economical system, for it will be seen by the reports of Inspectors-General that where medicines are procured in the different localities their cost to the county is sometimes very extravagant, but I find that during the whole of the year 1874 the cost of medicines here only came to 17s. 4d. However, a supply was laid in this year, which, I am informed, will be sufficient to last for some years to come, the bill for which amounted to £8 13s. 4d.

(marginal notes: North District. Donegal County Gaol. Hospital. *)*

Schools.	From 1st Jan. to 31st Dec., 1874.		From 1st Jan., 1875, to day of Inspection.	
	M.	F.	M.	F.
Number of individual prisoners who attended school,	185	31	195	19
Average daily number of pupils,	18	3	31	2
Number of days on which school was held,	242	251	143	159

School-hours—Males, 10 to 3 o'clock; Females, 12 to 1 o'clock.

No regular school-room has yet been provided here, so that prisoners are still taught in batches in a day-room, and the time of the schoolmaster is occupied for four hours a day in the performance of this duty, whereas if a properly stalled school-room was provided the secular instruction of male prisoners need not occupy him more than an hour. At the time of my visit no school was carried on at the female prison, and, as will be seen by the above table, very few women receive secular instruction during the year. The school is inspected by the Chaplains, but most regularly so by the Presbyterian Chaplain, and although I am informed the Protestant Chaplain performs this duty, he has omitted so far to enter his remarks in the school registry; but I have had the pleasure of an interview with this gentleman, and I trust he will comply with this rule in future. As the schools are not in connexion with any educational body, it is all the more important that they be regularly supervised by the Chaplains. *(marginal note: School.)*

Contracts.

Bread, white, per 4-lb. loaf, 8d.; oatmeal, per cwt., 14s.; Indian meal, per cwt., 9s. 6d.; potatoes, per cwt., 2s. 4d.; new milk, per gallon, 9d.; buttermilk, per gallon, 5d.; salt, per cwt., 2s. 0d.; coal, per ton, £0 19s. 0d.; straw, per cwt., 2s. 9d.; candles, per lb., 5½d.; soap, per cwt., £1 1s. Other contracts—whinstone, per ton, 1s. 8d.; heath brooms, per dozen, 2s. 6d.; leather, upper, per lb., 2s. 2d.; leather, sole, per lb., 1s. 10d.; sweeping chimneys, per annum, £2 10s.

The contracts both of provisions and materials are taken yearly, and are always sanctioned by the Board of Superintendence. The samples of the diet that I saw appeared to be excellent, and none of the prisoners complained to me of their treatment, or of their food. The provisions are kept by the storekeeper, who weighs out each portion before it is issued, and gives over the meal for breakfast every night to the watchman, which latter officer sees the stirabout made in the morning. They are regularly inspected by the Chaplains alternately three times a week, in accordance with the statute relating to this matter; but I regret to observe that the duties of the Roman Catholic Chaplain are chiefly performed by substitute not legally or regularly appointed, and who, therefore, has no legal status in the gaol. *(marginal note: Provisions.)*

The Governor, assisted by the clerk, keeps the books of registry and finance, which are all very carefully and regularly written up, and the prescribed forms duly observed, for which every credit is due to those officers. The Governor keeps an excellent journal; but he is the only *(marginal note: Books.)*

NORTH
DISTRICT.
___
Donegal
County
Gaol.

superior officer who does so, as that of the Local Inspector is very meagre, and so are those of the Chaplains. The Surgeon's journal is regularly written up, but contains very little information regarding his duties. However, I am informed that he is most attentive to the sick when any are in his charge, and the hospital books are carefully kept, with the exception of the Prescription Book, which should be written up by the Medical Officer himself, for obvious reasons. The prisoners so entitled are, I am informed, given about one-third of the profits of their labour, and a careful account is kept of the same. I cannot close this report without bearing testimony to the close attention to duty of the Governor, which is clearly shown by the discipline, order, and regularity, and cleanliness existing throughout the whole gaol.

Board of Superintendence.

Sir James Stewart, bart.	Wm. H. M. Style, esq.	John Cochrane, esq.
Francis Mansfield, esq.	Major R. G. Montgomery.	William Young, esq.
William Sinclair, esq.	Geo. Spence Fenton, esq.	Robert M'Clintock, esq.
T. W. D. Humphreys, esq.	James G. Grove, esq.	Richard Doherty, esq., M.D.

Board.

The second Thursday of the month is the day appointed for the Board to meet, on which occasions accounts are settled, and the officers are paid by separate cheques, the Local Inspector producing the receipts at the following meeting of the Board. I annex my tabular reports on the several bridewells of this county.

Bridewells.

STATE OF BRIDEWELLS.

	Buncrana.		Donegal.	
	M.	F.	M.	F.
No. of Committals in past year, . . .	28	4	34	13
Of whom were Drunkards, . . .	13	1	3	4
No. of Committals in the quarter preceding Inspection, . . .	8	1	18	2
Of whom were Drunkards, . . .	–	1	1	1

	Buncrana.	Donegal.
Petty Sessions and Transmittals.	Petty Sessions fortnightly; transmittals on following day.	Petty Sessions every third week, on Wednesdays; transmittals direct. Criminal Quarter Sessions four times a year.
Committals, . . .	Regular.	Regular, with one exception.
Registry, . . .	Regular.	Carefully kept.
Repairs and order, . .	Good.	Good.
Security, . . .	Fair, with care, but cells look into street.	Fair, except in yards, and that the male cells look on the street.
Accommodation, . .	Four cells, and two day-rooms.	Three cells; one day-room—very small.
Furniture, Bedding, and Utensils.	Good and sufficient.	Good, clean, and sufficient.
Water, how supplied? .	None but rain water.	None on premises except what is caught from roofs.
Sewerage, . . .	Good.	Said to be effective.
Cleanliness, Dryness, and Ventilation.	Clean, and well ventilated.	Clean, but cells very damp and badly ventilated.
Cost of Dietary, . .	6d. per head per day	6d. per head per day.
Salary of Keeper, and whether he follows any other Employment?	£30; £7 a year for fuel; a suit of clothes; is Court-keeper at £4.	£30 a year; wife £5; £7 for fuel and light. Is Court-keeper at £4. and has to supply the Court with fire out of that.
Statutable Inspection, .	17th August, 1875.	19th August, 1875.
Remarks, . . .	No prisoner in custody.	No prisoner in charge.

STATE OF BRIDEWELLS —*continued.*

—	Letterkenny.		Glenties.	
	M.	F.	M.	F.
No. of Committals in past year, . . .	62	8	16	2
Of whom were Drunk-ards, . . .	41	7	11	–
No. of Committals in the quarter preceding Inspection, . . .	13	4	1	1
Of whom were Drunk-ards, . . .	5	2	1	–
Petty Sessions and Transmittals, how often?	Petty Sessions every alternate week; transmittals immediate. Criminal Quarter Sessions are held here twice a year.		Monthly at Glenties, Ardara, Dunlow, Arranmore. No Criminal Quarter Sessions in this district.	
Committals, . . .	Some irregular, being signed by only one justice for periods beyond 3 days.		Regular.	
Registry, . . .	Correctly kept.		Carefully kept.	
Repairs and order, .	Good, and regularly kept.		Good.	
Security, . . .	Fair, with care.		Fair, but yard still very insecure, and cells look out on road.	
Accommodation, .	Two cells and a day-room for each sex; in all 12 beds.		Three cells and two day-rooms.	
Furniture, Bedding, and Utensils.	Clean, good, and sufficient.		Clean and sufficient	
Water, how supplied? .	By a pump, now in good order.		None on the premises, but procured from river.	
Sewerage, . . .	Much improved, and now effective. M'Farlane's water-closets have been put up in each yard.		A cesspool.	
Cleanliness, Dryness, and Ventilation.	Clean, fairly ventilated, but one cell damp; keeper's sitting room also damp.		Clean, and well ventilated.	
Cost of Dietary, .	4½d. per head per day.		5d. a head per day.	
Salary of Keeper, and whether he follows any other Employment?	£30; wife allowed £5 now; and £7 for fuel and candles; gas is supplied. Is Court-keeper at £4.		£30, and wife £5; £7 for fuel and light. Is Court-keeper at £4 a year, and clerk in the church.	
Date of Inspection, .	16th August, 1875.		19th August, 1875.	
Remarks, . . .	No prisoner in custody. Militiamen are still imprisoned here, some for 7 days.		No prisoner in custody, and very few throughout the year.	

CHARLES F. BOURKE, *Inspector-General.*

DOWN COUNTY GAOL, AT DOWNPATRICK.—STATUTABLE INSPECTION, 9TH OCTOBER, 1875.

Forty-seven males and 29 females formed the total number of prisoners in custody at the above date. Ten were untried, 6 were cases disposed of at quarter sessions or assizes, and the remainder were disposed of summarily. Five male prisoners were in custody this year charged with offences against life, only one of whom was in gaol at the date of my inspection. The crimes for which prisoners are chiefly committed here are assaults and riots arising from drunkenness. I regret to observe that the number of juveniles committed to this prison is large in comparison with those in other localities, 16 having been committed to this gaol during the year up to the time of my inspection. Four of these had been twice imprisoned from their first conviction, and 2 had been committed twice within the year. Five were sent to reformatories this year; but 2 of these were so sentenced in 1874, but only removed in January, 1875. At the time of my visit a youth aged seventeen years was in custody (T. M'K.) for an indecent assault upon an old woman. His conduct was so disorderly, that up to the time of my visit he had been altogether 114 days in solitary, including two periods of thirty days each, one of fourteen, and one of seven days, and I was informed, that even these severe measures had had little effect upon him for good. I fear therefore, that this youth will soon find his way back to gaol, unless he leaves the district, and that his disposition improves. I am decidedly of opinion, that there should be power to call in a justice to sentence such obstreperous prisoners to corporal punishment, as it is the only means known of dealing with such characters, and of bringing them to reason. Having regard to the disposition of this youth, and to the severity of the punishment he received while in gaol, I have little doubt that at the expiration of his sentence he will have left the prison a more hardened, and more incorrigible offender than when committed, whereas, if he had received a sharp corporal punishment he would, I have no doubt, at any rate have left the gaol with a wholesome dread thereof.

Number of Prisoners of all classes in Gaol on the day of Inspection, and on the corresponding date in the three preceding years.

	M.	F.		M.	F.
1872,	30	12	1874,	35	27
1873,	38	39	1875 (day of Inspection),	47	29

Number of Workhouse Offenders in Gaol on the day of Inspection, and on the corresponding date in the three preceding years.

	M.	F.		M.	F.
1872,	—	—	1874,	—	—
1873,	—	—	1875 (day of Inspection),	—	1

Number of Vagrants in Gaol on the day of Inspection, and on the corresponding date in the three preceding years.

	M.	F.		M.	F.
1872,	—	—	1874,	—	—
1873,	—	—	1875 (day of Inspection),	1	—

Number of Returned Convicts in Gaol on the day of Inspection, and during each of the three preceding years, and the expired portion of 1875.

	M.	F.		M.	F.
1872,	4	3	1875 (up to and including		
1873,	1	4	day of Inspection),	—	4
1874,	1	2	Day of Inspection,	—	3

Commitments.

CLASSES.						From 1st January to 31st Dec., 1874.		From 1st Jan., 1875, to day of Inspection.	
						M.	F.	M.	F.
Debtors,	·	·	·	·	·	5	–	–	–
Criminals,	·	·	·	·	·	248	130	204	84
Vagrants,	·	·	·	·	·	8	–	11	–
Drunkards,	·	·	·	·	·	29	34	47	54
Total,	·	·	·	·	·	290	164	262	138

Up to the time of my inspection this year the commitments numbered 262 of males and 138 of females, against 290 of the former and 164 of the latter in the previous year. No debtors were in custody this year, so that I may hope that this class of prisoners has ceased to frequent this gaol ; but I regret to observe, that even up to the time of my visit, the commitments for drunkenness this year were very nearly twice as many as in 1874. Several women of weak intellect were in charge at the above date, who appeared to me to be more subjects for an asylum than a gaol, as they were evidently not accountable for their own actions. As the legislature provides asylums for such afflicted individuals, I submit, that advantage should be taken of such institutions, and that these unfortunate creatures should be sent where there are proper means for taking care of them. I also found here a very distressing case of a woman having been committed to gaol from the workhouse for refusing to work there. She informed me that she was quite unable to do so, and her statement was borne out by the Medical Officer of the prison, who saw her on the day that she arrived in gaol, and considered her in such a weak state that he at once exempted her from labour, gave her extra diet, allowed her to remain in bed, and considered her weakness probably to arise from her nursing a large and very strong child. Under these circumstances I must submit that this woman should not have been sent to gaol, and that some serious mistake must have been committed in sending her here.

Number of Individual Prisoners (exclusive of Debtors) committed in the year 1874, and to the day of Inspection in 1875, who had been once and oftener committed from their first Commitment in any year, so far as can be ascertained.

NUMBER OF TIMES COMMITTED.	1873.				1874, to day of Inspection.			
	Juveniles.		Adults.		Juveniles.		Adults.	
	M.	F.	M.	F.	M.	F.	M.	F.
Once only, · · ·	13	2	186	44	10	–	156	45
Twice, · ·	–	–	15	9	4	–	15	4
Thrice, · ·	1	–	14	7	–	–	9	7
4 times, · ·	–	–	5	3	–	–	6	3
5 ,, · ·	–	–	4	3	–	–	5	5
6 ,, · ·	–	–	3	1	–	–	1	2
7 to 11 ,, · ·	–	–	7	8	–	–	9	8
12 to 16 ,, · ·	–	–	4	4	–	–	1	3
17 to 20 ,, · ·	–	–	2	1	–	–	6	1
21 to 30 ,, · ·	–	–	1	5	–	–	–	3
31 to 40 ,, · ·	–	–	1	3	–	–	1	4
41 to 50 ,, · ·	–	–	–	8	–	–	–	5
51 to 60 ,, · ·	–	–	–	–	–	–	–	2
61 to 70 ,, · ·	–	–	–	1	–	–	–	2
Total No. of Individuals committed,	14	2	242	97	14	–	209	93
No. of Commitments represented in foregoing, · ·	16	2	532	940	18	–	501	1041

D

Number of Individual Prisoners (exclusive of Debtors) and number of times each had been Committed during the following periods.

NUMBER OF TIMES COMMITTED.	1874.				1875, today of Inspection.			
	Juveniles.		Adults.		Juveniles.		Adults.	
	M.	F.	M.	F.	M.	F.	M.	F.
Once within the year,	14	2	222	66	12	–	187	69
Twice ,	–	–	14	9	2	–	13	13
Thrice ,	–	–	4	11	–	–	5	5
4 times ,	–	–	1	4	–	–	2	4
5 , ,	–	–	1	3	–	–	2	1
6 , ,	–	–	–	2	–	–	–	–
7 , ,	–	–	–	–	–	–	–	1
Total,	14	2	242	97	14	–	209	93
No. of above who had not been in Gaol previous to 1st Jan. in	13	2	189	47	12	–	158	47

Highest Number of Prisoners (exclusive of Debtors) in Gaol during each of the previous seven years, and up to day of Inspection in 1875.

1868,	. . . . .	100	1872,	. . . . .	63
1869,	. . . . .	87	1873,	. . . . .	83
1870,	. . . . .	84	1874,	. . . . .	79
1871,	. . . . .	67	1875,	. . . . .	76

Averages, and Highest and Lowest Numbers (exclusive of Debtors).

—	From 1st January to 31st December, 1874.			From 1st January, 1875, to day of Inspection.		
	M.	F.	Date.	M.	F.	Date.
Average daily number of prisoners in custody,	35	25	—	34	23	—
Highest number of prisoners at any one time,	79		7th Sept.	76		9th Oct.
Lowest ditto,	38		20th Jan.	40		21st Aug.
Highest number of males at any one time,	46		30th Oct.	47		9th Oct.
Ditto, of females,	35		11th July	32		17th Feb.
Lowest number of males at any one time,	21		15th Jan.	23		14th Aug.
Ditto, of females,	16		23rd Jan.	15		21st Aug.

Re-commitments.

Seven was the greatest number of times that any individual prisoner was in custody here this year up to the time of my inspection, whereas, in 1874 no individual was in charge here more than six times, and of the 242 adult males and 97 adult females in custody in 1874, 189 and 47 respectively had not previously been in gaol up to the day of inspection. In 1875 the total number of adult individuals committed was 209 males and 93 females, but of these 158 and 47 respectively were first commitments. During the years 1874 and 1875, three females had been in gaol who had over sixty committals recorded against them from their first imprisonment, and 9 males who had over thirty committals recorded against them; and it will be observed by one of the previous tables, that in proportion to the number of individuals committed, the re-commitments here are very numerous.

Accommodation.

	M.	F.		M.	F.
Wards,	R	3	Store Rooms,	8	4
Yards,	9	2	Laundry,	–	1
Day Rooms,	7	2	Drying Room,	–	1
Solitary Cells,	16	1	Lavatories,	6	2
Single Cells, 9 feet long, 6 feet wide, and 8 feet high, or which contain 432 cubic feet,	162	59	Baths, with Hot and Cold Water laid on,	1	1
			Privies,	6	2
Do. heated, and furnished with bells,	53	47	Waterclosets,	18	15
Cells to contain three persons,	2	–	Fumigating apparatus,	1	–
Hospital Rooms,	4	2	Reception Rooms or Cells,	4	4
Chapel,	1	–	Pumps,	1	1
Workshops,	15	–	Capstan Mill,	1	–
Worksheds,	24	–	Other machines for hard labour— Shot, 9 lbs. weight, for shot drill.		
Kitchen,	1	–	Tell-tale Clocks,	3	–
Bakery,	1	–			

The structural condition of this gaol has undergone little or no alter- Cells. ations since my last visit. The inhabited cells are all comfortably heated, and provided with bells and gas, with the exception of the four reception cells. The gas, however, is extinguished at 6 P.M., and is not lighted in Gas. the winter mornings before daylight, as no labour is carried on before that time or after 6 P.M. during the winter months. Baths with hot Baths. and cold water are provided in both prisons, and all prisoners are washed immediately on being committed, and subsequently weekly during imprisonment. The water supply of the prison is abundant, and is supplied Water. to the cells for ablutionary purposes. The sewerage is now reported to Sewerage. be good, the two cess-pools having been cleaned out during last summer. There is an ample supply of water-closets and privies throughout the prison, a new W.C. having been put up lately in the female exercise yard. The arrangements of the chapel and laundry have not been altered since my last Chapel. visit, and I regret to find that only prison washing is performed in the laundry, as it is amply provided with all the requirements for carrying on Laundry. large washing contracts. The clothing of the prisoners is all purified by Fumigator. means of a good fumigator, which is placed in the male hospital. Photo- Photo- graphy is carried on by one of the warders who receives 6d. for each nega- graphy. tive, the Board supplying the chemicals. The kitchen arrangements are the same as at my last visit, and on days on which potatoes are used two Kitchen. male prisoners are employed here, but they are also required to carry coals, &c., throughout the prison. Excellent bread is baked in the prison for which duty two other prisoners are told off. I submit that these duties should be performed by one prisoner as they are not heavy, for under the present arrangements too much association is permitted. The night-watch is required to mark three tell-tale clocks half-hourly from Night- 9 P.M. to 6 A.M. This duty is performed by two warders each night. watch. The markings are taken in the morning by the Deputy-Governor, and entered by him in the Morning State Book, and the turnkeys on night duty make their entries relating to the clock in the Lockings Book. Lock- up takes place at 9 P.M. in the summer, and 4·30 P.M. in winter, and unlock at 6·30 A.M. and 7 A.M. respectively. After lock-up the keys of the cells are taken to the office, and at 10 P.M. they are finally locked up there; but the Governor only takes the key of the outside gate to his room at night. I am of opinion that all the keys of the prison should be in his custody during the night, except the keys of the interior of the female prison which might be left as at present with the matron. The same arrangements exist as at my last inspection for visitors to prisoners, and I regret to find that the wire then recommended to be placed on the top of the visiting place has not been yet procured.

NORTH
DISTRICT.

*Down
County
Gaol*

Stores.

The principal stores are kept by the Deputy-Governor who issues them under the Governor's order to the head-turnkey and matron, these latter officers being responsible for the clothing of the prisoners of the different sexes. The head-turnkey being a tailor, superintends the cutting out of the male clothing, which is all made within the prison with the exception of the clogs and shoes, and these are procured by tender. I submit that shoes should certainly be made in the prison, as when this is done they are always found to be of better quality, and to last longer than when they are obtained by contract. The supply of clothing and bedding throughout the prison was abundant, and was carefully and tidily stored. The sheeting is changed fortnightly, and was all clean and well kept. I had occasion during my inspection to draw the attention of the Governor to some carelessness on the part of the warders in fitting the male clothing for which there was no excuse.

Number of Punishments for Prison Offences.

	From 1st Jan. to 31st Dec., 1874.		From 1st Jan ,1875, to day of Inspection.	
	M.	F.	M.	F.
By Magisterial authority.	~	-	4	-
By the Governor—.				
Dark or Refractory Cells, .	74	4	72	2
Stoppage of Diet, . .	32	-	56	-
Other punishments, .	2	-	-	-
Total, . .	108	4	132	2

Punish-
ments.

Up to the time of my inspection the number of punishments that had been inflicted for the breach of prison rules on male prisoners was larger than usual, owing chiefly to the number of times that the boy already referred to had been sentenced to solitary, for during his imprisonment there were ninety offences recorded against him, and he had been twenty-five times in the punishment cells. The male solitary cell is properly heated and provided with a bell, and a guard bed, and a rug is given to the prisoner at night. The solitary cell for females is not heated nor provided with a bell, but prisoners are not left in it at night, and as will be perceived from the above table it is seldom found necessary to have recourse to the punishment of females in this prison.

Schools.

	From 1st Jan. to 31st Dec., 1874.		From 1st Jan. 1875, to day of Inspection.	
	M.	F.	M.	F.
Number of individual prisoners who attended school, ...	19	56	34	44
Average daily number of pupils, .	4	4	7	5
Number of days on which school was held, . . .	82	230	67	190

School-hours.—Males, 12 to 1.   Females, 12 noon to 2.

School.

Only juveniles and youths are permitted to go to school. This is a matter that I have repeatedly drawn attention to, and as the 106th sec. provides, that all poor prisoners who are capable of learning should receive secular instruction, I submit that this statute should be strictly adhered to, and that a regular stalled school-room should be established in both prisons. The males are taught by one of the turnkeys, and the females by the assistant matron; but the preceding table will show, that as compared with the number of prisoners committed here during the year, very few have received any instruction. I also regret to find that no attempt is made to teach prisoners trades.

Employment on day of Inspection.

	M.	F.			M.	F.	
Shot Drill,	23	–	Cleaning prison,		–	1	Down
Breaking stones,	9	–	Nursing,		–	3	County
Breaking freestone,	1	–	Sick,		2	–	Gaol.
Shoemaking,	1	–	Unemployed,		1	1	
Tailoring,	1	–	Discharged (before labour				
Labouring,	2	–	hours),		1	1	
Cooking,	2	–	Committed,		1	–	
Sewing work,	–	4	In Court-house for trial,		3	1	
Flowering,	–	7			—	—	
Washing,	–	2	Total in custody,		47	29	
Picking oakum,	–	9					

Amount received for produce of Prisoners' Labour disposed of outside the Gaol.

1872, . £13 7s. 7d. | 1873, . £13 6s. 8d. | 1874, . £6 3s. 4d.

Net average daily cost of Ordinary Diet for each Prisoner.

1872, . 4d. | 1873, . 4d. | 1874, . 4d.

Net cost of Gaol, including Diet and Salaries.

1872, . £1,765 6s. 9d. | 1873, . £1,836 1s. 2d. | 1874, . £2,013 4s. 8d.

Total cost of Officers, including Clothing, Value of Rations, &c.

1872, . £1,020 8s. 5d. | 1873, . £1,049 2s. 7d. | 1874, . £1,053 15s. 3d.

Average cost of each Prisoner per annum.

1872, . £32 6s. 5d. | 1873, . £32 8s. 8d. | 1874, . £32 9s. 5d.

Amounts repaid by the War Department for Military Prisoners.

1872, . £1 11s. 0d. | 1873, . £19 6s. 9d. | 1874, . £1 19s. 0d.

Amounts repaid from the Consolidated Fund for the maintenance, &c., of Prisoners.

1872, . £140 7s. 1d. | 1873, . £130 4s. 10d. | 1874, . £217 5s. 5d.

The hard labour performed here is chiefly by shot drill, at which Labour. prisoners are employed for about three hours a day, they also are required to break stones, there being twenty-two separate stone sheds provided; and tradesmen such as carpenters and tailors, are employed as required in separate cells. There is also a certain amount of oakum-picking performed. In winter there is no work done after 6 o'clock P.M., but in summer prisoners are required to work up to 8 P.M. This is a subject to which I have previously drawn attention to, and am clearly of opinion, that a greater amount of labour should be performed here than is at present carried on. The profits received for the produce of prisoners' labour here in 1874, was less by half than that of each of the two preceding years, being but £6 3s. 4d. This I submit is a miserable return from the industrial labour of a daily average of 35 males and 25 females, which was the number in the year 1874. Situated as this prison is, so close to the most prosperous and industrious town in Ireland, I cannot but think that if Expendi- proper steps were taken large returns should accrue from the produce ture. of the prisoners' labour in this gaol. The average annual cost of a prisoner in the year 1874, was £32 9s. 5d., whereas, in Belfast gaol, where the returns from industrial labour are large, it only amounted that year to £16 4s. 7d. The net cost of this gaol in the same year came to £2,013 4s. 8d.; but from that sum the cost of officers amounted to £1,053 15s. 3d., so that the entire cost of the gaol—minus the officers— was less than the absolute cost of the officers. Although it is not to be supposed, that prisoners could be kept in this gaol under its present arrangements, so economically as in large well arranged gaols, such as Belfast, yet I am of opinion, that the annual cost of a prisoner should be much less than it is at present, under improved management and with more careful attention to industrial labour.

Contracts.

Bread, white, per 1 lb. loaf, 2*d*.; ditto, brown, per 1 lb. loaf, 1½*d*.; oatmeal, per cwt., 14*s*. 6*d*.; Indian meal, per cwt., 10*s*.; potatoes, per cwt., 2*s*. 4*d*.; new milk, per gallon, 8*d*.; buttermilk, per gallon, 1*d*.; salt, per cwt., 2*s*.; coal, per ton, 19*s*.; turf, per load, 6*s*.; straw, per cwt., 3*s*. and 4*s*.; gas, per 1,000 cubic feet, 8*s*. 4*d*.; candles, per lb., 6½*d*.; soap, per cwt., £1 6*s*. and £1 4*s*.; wheatmeal, per cwt., 13*s*.

Provisions

All materials and provisions are obtained by contract, and are sanctioned by the Board of Superintendence, generally in the month of November. The samples of the diet that I saw appeared to be excellent, and none of the prisoners complained to me of its quality, and both the Chaplains and Governor generally report favourably thereon.

Officers and Salaries.

Non-Resident.	£	s.	d.				£	s.	d.
B. N. Johnson, Local Inspector,	100	0	0	Turn-keys.	George Gordon,	.	37	10	0
					John Boyd, .	.	37	10	0
Rev. T. B. Price, Protestant Chaplain,	40	0	0		Thomas Robinson,	.	37	10	0
Rev. Wm. White, Presbyterian Chaplain,	40	0	0		Joseph Lawson,	.	37	10	0
					Resident.				
Rev. P. O'Kane, Roman Catholic Chaplain,	40	0	0		Major L. Thompson, Governor,	.	200	0	0
John K. Maconchy, Surgeon,	—				John Waterworth, Deputy Governor,	.	120	0	0
Dr. E. F. Nelson, Apothecary,	27	13	10		John Skillen, Turnkey,	.	37	10	0
Turn-keys.	Elisha Jackson, Tailor,	60	0	0		Eliza Davidson, Matron,	.	32	10	0
	J. C. M'Cartney, Schoolmaster & Photographer,	47	10	0		Harriet E. Jackson, Assistant Matron,	.	32	10	0

Vacancies in the staff since last inspection, how caused, and how filled up.

Thomas West, Turnkey, resigned; James Thompson appointed. James Thompson, Turnkey, resigned; Joseph Lawson appointed.

Officers on Gaol Allowance.

No food rations are given; the resident officers are allowed fuel and gas. The turnkeys are supplied with one suit each of clothing yearly.

Visits paid by Officers.

	From 1st Jan. to 31st Dec., 1874.	From 1st Jan., 1875, to day of Inspection.
Number of times the Board of Superintendence met and discharged business,	12	9
Local Inspector to Gaol,	142	141
Do. to each Bridewell,	4	3
Chaplain, Protestant Episcopal Church,	271	217
,, Presbyterian,	300	241
,, Roman Catholic,	229	176
Surgeon,	157	134
Apothecary,	169	162

Officers.

One turnkey always sleeps in the male prison, and the arrangements with regard to the officers on duty during the night are the same as at my last visit. The quarters of the subordinate officers were as a rule tidy and well kept. At the time of my inspection I had occasion to draw the attention of the Board to a statement made by one of the prisoners, with regard to not being visited by the Roman Catholic Chaplain. My remarks have resulted in correspondence with that gentleman, who appears to be under a misapprehension as to the mode in which his duties should be performed. I have drawn the attention of the Board to this subject, and trust that in future the Chaplain will visit the prisoners in accordance with the requirements of the 72nd sec. of the "Prisons Act," which is clear and unambiguous, and should be strictly adhered to by those officers. The appointment of substitutes should be regulated by the 11th sec. of 19th & 20th Vic., chap. 68, as it is obvious that little good can arise unless the Chaplain becomes acquainted with the several prisoners committed to his charge.

Hospital.

	1872.		1873.		1874.		1875 (to day of Inspection).	
	M.	F.	M.	F.	M.	F.	M.	F.
No. of prisoners in hospital,	14	2	7	4	7	2	6	1
Average daily No in hospital,	1·2	·1	·3	·3	1	·25	·34	–
No.of prisoners prescribed for and treated out of hospital,	63	28	11	2	16	5	20	14
No. of deaths in the gaol,	·1	·	1	–	1	·–	–	1
Cost of medicine,	£5 11s. 4d.		—		—		£7 7s. 7d.	
Cost of Diet, &c., for prisoners in hospital,	—		—		£3 1s. 3d.		—	

No alteration has taken place in the hospital building since my last visit. The services of the nurse have been discontinued, and the hospital is now taken charge of by the matron ; but I object very much to the custom prevailing here, of having two male prisoners to take charge of a sick prisoner. This is open to such obvious objections, and to so many abuses, that I trust it will he discontinued. In the event of a male prisoner being sent to hospital, he should in future be looked after by one of the warders. Trivial cases could he treated in the cells. The health of the gaol throughout the year seems to have been most satisfactory, as up to the time of my inspection only 6 males and 1 female were sent to hospital in 1875, and 7 males and 2 females during the whole of 1874. The medicines are procured from Dublin when required, and are compounded by the apothecary, who is, I am informed, surgeon to the workhouse.

Books and Journals.

The registries and books of finance are chiefly kept by the Deputy-Governor, who also acts as clerk, and keeps these books with great care and regularity. The Local Inspector's Journal is fully written up and well kept, and this officer adopts a very useful plan of writing a summary of his journal for the Board monthly. The Governor also writes a useful journal from which it is evident, that his duties are carefully and regularly performed, which is fully borne out by the discipline, order, and regularity, which I perceived throughout the prison. The Chaplains also keep journals, but that of the Presbyterian was the fullest and most explicit of the three. The books are supervised by the Governor, who, I am informed, goes through the Dietary Book once a month, and through the other books daily. The weekly earnings of the prisoners should be carefully entered in the Daily Employment Book, and the 107th sec. of the "Prisons Act" having reference to this subject should be observed. I also would request that the General Visitors Book be procured, and regularly written up, as it is one of those laid down by authority to be kept in all gaols.

Board of Superintendence.

Major Andrew Nugent.	Major R. P. Maxwell.	Capt. The Hon. S. Ward.
Robert Heron, esq.	Samuel Murland, esq.	William Boyd, esq.
Colonel Forde.	Major James Baillie.	Lord de Ros.
Robert Gordon, esq.		

NORTH
DISTRICT.
———
*Down
County.*

The meetings of the Board take place on the last Saturday of the month, when cheques are handed to the Local Inspector for the payment of the subordinate officers' salaries and small accounts, the vouchers being produced at the following meeting of the Board. The salaries of the Chaplains are paid half-yearly at assizes, and those of the Local Inspector, Governor, and Deputy-Governor quarterly.

I annex my report on the bridewells of Newtownards and Newry.

Bridewells.

STATE OF BRIDEWELLS.

—	Newtownards.		Newry.	
	M.	**F.**	**M.**	**F.**
No. of Committals in past year, . .	36	3	71	34
Of whom were Drunkards, . . .	2	2	21	16
No. of Committals in the quarter preceding Inspection, .	9	1	18	10
Of whom were Drunkards, . . .	—	—	9	3
Petty Sessions and Transmittals, how often ?	Petty Sessions fortnightly ; transmittal direct ; no Criminal Quarter Sessions.		Petty Sessions weekly, and Borough Court on every Friday.	
Committals, whether regular ?	Regular.		Regular ; but a lunatic lately in charge, though not committed as such ; she should have been transmitted direct to the Asylum.	
Registry, . . .	Correctly kept.		Carefully kept.	
Repairs and Order, .	Good.		Good.	
Security, . . .	Good.		Good.	
Accommodation, . .	Good ; four cells and a day-room for each sex.		Seven cells and a day-room for each.	
Furniture, Bedding, and Utensils.	Good, clean, and sufficient.		Good and sufficient.	
Water, how supplied ? .	By good force-pump.		From town main.	
Sewerage, . . .	Effective.		Good.	
Cleanliness, Dryness, and Ventilation.	Clean and well ventilated.		Clean, dry, and well ventilated.	
Cost of Dietary per head per day.	$6\frac{1}{4}d$. for males; $5\frac{1}{4}d$. for females.		$5\frac{1}{4}d$. for males; $4\frac{1}{4}d$. for females.	
Salary of Keeper, and whether he follows any other employment.	£40; wife, £8; fire and light ; is Court-keeper, at £8.		£30, and matron £8 a year ; keeper has no other employment.	
Statutable Inspection, .	6th October, 1875.		28th September, 1875.	
Remarks, . . .	No prisoner in custody.		—	

CHARLES F. BOURKE, *Inspector-General.*

County of the City of Dublin Prison, for Males—Richmond Bridewell—Statutable Inspection, 20th, 22nd, and 28th December, 1875.

North District.

County of City of Dublin Gaol for Males.

Juveniles.

Classes, &c., of Offenders.	In custody on the day of Inspection.				From 1st January to day of Inspection.			
	12 years old and under.		Above 12 and not exceeding 16 years.		12 years old and under.		Above 12 and not exceeding 16 years.	
	M.	F.	M.	F.	M.	F.	M.	F.
Convicted at Quarter Sessions,	—	—	—	—	—	—	14	—
" Summarily,	1	—	—	—	10	—	130	—
Committed for Trial,	—	—	—	—	12	—	85	—
Total,	1	—	—	—	22	—	229	—
Number sent to Reformatories,	—	—	—	—	10	—	84	—

The tables in this report are taken from the gaol returns on the first of the above days, when the total number in custody was 258. Thirty-seven of these were untried. One hundred and twenty-five were disposed of at the Recorder's or Commission courts; 10 were Courts-martial prisoners, and 86 were summarily convicted.

Although but 1 juvenile was in custody at this date, 252 had been committed here throughout the year; 35 of whom were sentenced to reformatories. The child in custody was only nine years of age, and was sentenced to five years in a reformatory for larceny. His mother was living, but he told me that his father was dead.   *Juveniles.*

For some years Inspectors-General have, in their annual reports, drawn attention to the very large number of juveniles committed to this prison, as compared with the commitments of that class throughout the rest of Ireland.

In 1872 the commitments of juveniles here, were 296; in 1873, 256; in 1874, 319; and in 1875, 251. So that it is pleasing to observe that there is somewhat of a diminution in their numbers this year as compared with last; but the numbers are still very large, and call for serious consideration. For no one can walk through the streets of Dublin without observing the large number of children at all times of the day, and even at night, who appear to have no means of employment, who attend no schools, and whose parents appear to have no control for good over them. In my two last reports on this prison, namely, that for 1873 and 1874, I remarked on the numbers of this class committed here as compared with the total number of prisoners, as well as with the commitments of juveniles in other places, and I would again remark with regret, that Dublin still furnishes a preponderating proportion of the juvenile offenders of the whole of Ireland. In Belfast gaol, for example, which receives prisoners not only from that large and populous town, but also from the whole of the county of Antrim, the number of individual male juveniles committed in 1874 was 65, and in Cork city and county, 101; but, as I have already

NORTH
DISTRICT.

*County of
City of
Dublin
Gaol for
Males.*

Juveniles.

pointed out, they numbered in that year in the city of Dublin alone, 319.

In my report of 1873 I pointed out that this deplorable state of depravity of the juvenile class of this city, must result in the training of a certain number of individuals to a profession of crime, and I greatly fear that this is now proving too true; for at the time of my inspection this year, I was so struck by the youthful appearance of the majority of the prisoners then in custody, that I requested to be furnished with a table of their ages, which I here append, from which it will be seen how numerous were those in custody under thirty years of age.

Six of the juveniles committed here this year were for the offence of drunkenness, but unfortunately, as the law now stands, these offenders cannot be sent to a reformatory school; for in all sentences for drunkenness alone, the law allows the option of a fine. This is a matter that has been referred to in the General Report of the Inspectors-General of last year, as both my colleague and I are of opinion that it would be a wise provision to give the committing justice power to inflict the punishment of imprisonment for drunkenness without the option of a fine, especially in the case of juveniles. One of the above number was only ten years of age, and another twelve, and they were nearly all sentenced to seven days; so that I fear they will have derived little good from their prison experience.

At the time of my visit the juvenile class was partly occupied by adult prisoners, as the gaol was somewhat crowded; but I was informed that the former were always exercised alone, and not allowed to associate with adults at any time. I cannot too strongly urge the importance of dealing with this class of prisoner with the utmost strictness and care, for if a wholesome horror of prison life is established during a first committal, upon a youthful mind, it will, in most cases, effect a greater reformation of character than numberless subsequent imprisonments. Youths committed here should be required to perform as much labour in separation as possible; they should be taught trades, and required to attend school for two hours daily, except those sentenced to reformatories.

Return showing the Ages of Prisoners locked up on the night of the 22nd December, 1875.

Under 12 years (9 years), . . . : 1
16 to 21 ,, ... 74
21 to 30 ,, ... 121
31 to 40 ,, ... 38
41 and above, ... 24

Total, . . . 258

Twelve prisoners were committed here this year up to the day of my visit, who were known to have been previously in reformatories, and 29 in the previous year.

Number of prisoners of all classes in gaol on the day of inspection, and on the corresponding date in the three preceding years.

	M.		M.
1872, ...	269	1874, ...	237
1873, ...	291	1875 (day of inspection), .	258

Number of returned convicts in gaol on the day of inspection, and during each of the three preceding years, and the expired portion of 1875.

	M.		M.
1872, ...	28	1875 (up to and including day	
1873, ...	37	of inspection), . .	28
1874, ...	34	Day of inspection, . .	2

Commitments.

CLASSES.			From 1st Jan. to 31st December, 1874.	From 1st January, 1875, to day of inspection.
Criminals,	.	.	3,221	1,760
Vagrants,	.	.	18	–
Drunkards,	.	.	1,800	9
Total,	.	.	5,039	1,769

Number of Individual Prisoners (exclusive of Debtors), and number of times each had been committed during the following periods, distinguishing Adults from Juveniles.

NUMBER OF TIMES COMMITTED.	1874.				1875, to day of Inspection.			
	Juveniles.		Adults.		Juveniles.		Adults.	
	M.	F.	M.	F.	M.	F.	M.	F.
Once within the year,	298	–	3,162	–	209	–	1,369	–
Twice "	17	–	465	–	21	–	71	–
Thrice "	4	–	122	–	–	–	1	–
4 times "	–	–	32	–	–	–	1	–
5 " "	–	–	12	–	–	–	–	–
6 " "	–	–	2	–	–	–	–	–
7 " "	–	–	4	–	–	–	–	–
9 " "	–	–	1	–	–	–	–	–
Total,	319	–	3,800	–	230	–	1,442	–
No. of above who had not been in gaol previous to 1st January in	303	–	2,283	–	214	–	781	–

Number of Individual Prisoners (exclusive of Debtors), committed in the year 1874, and to the day of Inspection in 1875, who had been Once, Twice, Thrice, Four Times, Five Times, &c., &c., from their first Commitment in any year, so far as can be ascertained, distinguishing Adults from Juveniles.

NUMBER OF TIMES COMMITTED.	1874.				1875, to day of Inspection.			
	Juveniles.		Adults.		Juveniles.		Adults.	
	M.	F.	M.	F.	M.	F.	M.	F.
Once only, .	285	–	2,157	–	201	–	761	–
Twice,	25	–	650	–	28	–	259	–
Thrice,	5	–	284	–	1	–	115	–
4 times,	3	–	178	–	–	–	77	–
5 "	1	–	160	–	–	–	42	–
6 "	1	–	65	–	–	–	36	–
7 to 11 "	–	–	200	–	–	–	82	–
12 to 16 "	–	–	61	–	–	–	32	–
17 to 20 "	–	–	49	–	–	–	17	–
21 to 30 "	–	–	41	–	–	–	4	–
31 to 40 "	–	–	10	–	–	–	5	–
41 to 50 "	–	–	3	–	–	–	4	–
51 to 60 "	–	–	1	–	–	–	–	–
61 to 90 "	–	–	–	–	–	–	1	–
91 to 100 "	–	–	1	–	–	–	–	–
101 to 120 "	–	–	–	–	–	–	1	–
Total No. of individuals committed,	319	–	3,800	–	230	–	1,442	–
Number of commitments represented in foregoing,	369	–	11093	–	260	–	4,402	–

NORTH DISTRICT.

County of City of Dublin Gaol for Males.

Averages, and Highest and Lowest Numbers (exclusive of Debtors).

—	From 1st January to 31st December, 1874.		From 1st January, 1875, to day of Inspection.	
	M.	Date.	M.	Date.
Average daily number of prisoners in custody,	321	—	243	—
Highest number of males at any one time,	429	3rd September.	270	24th April.
Lowest number of males at any one time,	236	25th December.	218	7th March.

Highest number of prisoners (exclusive of debtors), in gaol during each of the previous seven years, and up to day of inspection in 1875.

18th August, 1868,	. . 309	19th September, 1872, .	. 317
3rd May, 1869,	. . 290	29th July, 1873, . .	. 330
26th July, 1870, .	. . 341	29th September, 1874, .	. 429
17th July, 1871, .	. . 317	24th April, 1875, .	. . 270

Commitments. One of the previous tables shows a considerable reduction in the numbers of commitments this year as compared with last, as well as a remarkable diminution in the number of drunkards; but it must be borne in mind that since October, 1874, a wing of Grangegorman Prison has been occupied by male prisoners, whose sentence does not exceed one month, so that the drunkards and minor offenders are now sent there; and in addition, owing to the excess of the numbers in Richmond over the accommodation provided, it has been necessary, from time to time, to transfer other prisoners to Grangegorman. To form a fair comparison, therefore, of the number of commitments of males in the city, during this and the previous year, the commitments of that sex to Grangegorman should be considered.

Re-commitments. Notwithstanding the removal from this prison of the short commitments, it will be observed that there was a prisoner in charge here this year who had been between 100 and 120 times committed, whereas in 1874, no prisoner was in custody here who had been more than 100 times in gaol. The number of male prisoners committed to this and to Grangegorman Prison for drunkenness in 1874, amounted together to 2,193; and in this year, up to the time of my inspection of both prisons, to 2,357. Thus showing that this deplorable evil is still steadily on the increase; but large as these figures are, they do not represent the full number of persons committed through drunkenness, for a very large per-centage of the other commitments to this gaol may be truly attributed to that evil.

Accommodation.

	M.		M.
Wards, ...	15	Kitchens, . . .	2
Yards, ...	17	Store Rooms, . . .	24
Day Rooms, . . .	34	Laundry, . . .	1
Solitary Cells, . .	9	Drying Room, . .	1
Single Cells, not less than 9 feet long, 6 feet wide, and 8 feet high=432 cubic feet, .	147	Lavatories, . . .	16
Do. heated and furnished with bells, . .	267	Baths, with Hot and Cold Water laid on. . . .	5
		Water-closets, . .	45
Cells to contain three persons, .	115	Fumigating Apparatus, .	1
Hospital Rooms, . . .	6	Reception Room or Cell, .	1
Chapels, . . .	2	Pumps, . . .	2
School Room, . . .	1	Wells, . . .	2
Workshops, . . .	10	Tread-wheels, . .	2
Worksheds, . . .	48	Tell-tale Clocks, . .	7

In my report of 1873, I announced the intention of the Board to re- NORTH
model and to make some additions to this prison, by which 72 cells were DISTRICT.
to be added to the accommodation; but I regret to say, notwithstanding County of
that £7,000 had been advanced by the Treasury, and that all the prelimin- City of
ary arrangements were made to commence the work, the Town Council Dublin
ultimately refused to commence the works, as stated in the report of my Gaol for
colleague of last year. I therefore fully concur in his remarks on this Males.
subject, and with him regret that the opportunity of making this a Accommo-
suitable place of confinement has been neglected. dation.

The cost of the alterations not having been properly estimated at the
outset, is stated to be the cause of the abandonment of the work; but, as
has frequently been pointed out by Inspectors-General, so long as the
building is allowed to remain in its present unsuitable and faulty condition, the expense of heating and supervision must be enormous. Discipline cannot be properly carried out, nor can either punitive or
reproductive labour be sufficiently enforced.

I pointed out in my last report that there is an insufficient number of Baths.
baths provided for the requirements of the gaol, and that prisoners
should all be bathed on admission; but neither of these suggestions have
been carried out, nor indeed has any improvement been effected, with
the exception that the solitary cells near the Protestant Chapel has
been provided with spiral bells.

There are 15 cells in the reception ward, in which prisoners are placed Reception
at night, just as they come in from the Courts in all their filth, and are as ward.
a rule, not bathed until morning. This is a system that I have endeavoured, but unsuccessfully, to have altered for some years; and now that
the short sentences are sent to Grangegorman, there should be no difficulty in carrying it out. As this ward is frequently also used for the
untried, owing to the overcrowded state of the gaol, it would be
all the more desirable to keep it in as cleanly a condition as possible.
I am glad to learn that the prisoners are now all seen by the Medical
Officer before they are passed into their proper wards, as required by
statute. The number of water-closets and lavatories is the same as at my
last inspection, and they were all clean and in good order. Some of the
sewerage has lately been cleared, and was reported to me to be effective. Sewerage.
The supply of water is abundant, and the heating apparatus are in good Heating.
repair. I would, however, observe on the danger of having some of the
pipes in the cells of the lower prison placed over head, affording as they
do a facility to prisoners to commit suicide. All the cells in the prison
are provided with bells, and are of the size required for separate confinement. Their condition of order and cleanliness on the above date was,
as a rule, very satisfactory.

Both of the chapels are neatly and well kept; that for R.C. worship Chapels.
having lately been painted.

Although there is a good laundry here it is very seldom used, and the Laundry.
suggestions I made on this subject in my last report have not been
adopted. It is in my opinion, a pity not to employ men in such labour
when such suitable appliances are at hand, and especially as there is in this
prison a lack of means for carrying on a full amount of labour.

Gas is provided to all the cells, and is lighted until 7.30 P.M. in the Gas.
winter months. It is procured from the town main, at a cost of £250
per annum. This is an item in which a considerable saving could be
effected, if the gas were made on the premises, as is done in some gaols.

The arrangements in the kitchen are the same as at my last inspection, Kitchen.
and at the time of my last visit it was clean and in good order; but I
found that three men are employed here daily, and was informed that
the reason for having so many there was for the purpose of cutting and

weighing the different portions of bread. This would not be necessary if the baker were required to send the bread in, as is usual, in small loaves of the required weight. One male prisoner should, I submit, be quite sufficient to perform all the culinary duties of this prison. In Londonderry gaol it is all done by one female.

Seven tell-tale clocks are provided, being placed in different parts of the building; they are marked by the night watchmen hourly, from 7 P.M. to 6 A.M. Up to 10 P.M. three warders are on duty as watchmen, and after this hour two perform this duty.

There are in addition three men on reserve during the night, who can be roused at once in the event of necessity. The markings of the clocks are taken by the chief warder every morning, and are entered in the Lockings Book ; and in the event of an omission of duty on the part of the night-guard, there is a fine of 1*s*. inflicted for the first offence, and 5*s*. for the second ; so that, as a rule, the clocks are regularly pegged.

Unlock in summer takes place at 6.30 A.M., and at 7 A.M. in winter ; and lock-up is at 6 P.M. the whole year round, at which hour all the cell keys are shut up in a safe in the office, the key of which is kept by the Governor during the night. I here repeat my opinion that unlock should certainly not be later than 6 o'clock A.M. all the year round, as prisoners should be at work as soon after that hour as possible.

The photography is done by the schoolmaster warder under the same arrangements as at my last inspection, care being taken to photograph all prisoners, as provided by the Crimes Prevention Act, as well as suspected ones who are for trial, unless they object. The clerk is allowed 7*d*. for each copy, he finding his own chemicals.

In former reports I have suggested that the person who performs the photography should register them, as he would then conduct the entire business in connexion with the habitual offenders and suspected persons, but this duty is still divided between two officers.

Notwithstanding that I have in my three last reports drawn attention to the very faulty arrangements in the place apportioned for visitors to prisoners, no alteration has yet been made in furtherance of the suggestions I have made. The untried are allowed a visit twice a week, or oftener if necessary for the preparation of their defence ; and convicted prisoners are allowed a visit once in three months, but the Governor and Local Inspector have power to permit a visit at any time, if they consider the case urgent. None of the prisoners in custody preferred any complaints to me worth recording. They appeared all kindly treated, well fed, and clothed. A professional thief, J. M., asked me to get the prison authorities to send him to Liverpool on his discharge, as he had no means here of earning a living except by thieving, and told me that if he were turned out of the gaol unprovided for that he would at once return to his old practices. He had been leading a dishonest life for fifteen years, and did not appear inclined to reform. I requested the Governor to lay this case before the Board, with a view to his being transmitted to Liverpool ; but I trust that in the event of his being found guilty of any crime again in this country, that he will be sentenced to penal servitude.

I would here remark on the impropriety and hardship of keeping Protestant prisoners idle on Roman Catholic holidays, and submit that there is no authority or justification for such a proceeding.

The law acknowledges a certain number of holidays in the year, and only these should be observed as such, at any rate by the Protestant prisoners. I am informed that besides Christmas Day and Good Friday, and Sundays, there are eleven days in the year which are kept as holidays in this gaol, when the prisoners are not compelled to work, and which are kept as Sunday.

(margin notes)
NORTH DISTRICT.

County of City of Dublin Gaol for Males.

Tell-tale clocks.

Unlock.

Photography.

Visitors to prisoners.

Holidays.

Stock at the time of Inspection.

	In Use.	In Store.			In Use.	In Store.
Blankets, pairs of,	361	–	Shirts,		526	15
Sheets, pairs of,	557	5	Jackets,		434	23
Rugs,	337	17	Vests,		327	30
Hammocks or Cots,	239	18	Trowsers,		375	35
Bed-ticks,	293	64	Caps,		300	20
			Shoes, Slippers, and Clogs, pairs of,		467	236

The general store of new clothing and materials is kept by the store-keeper, who sees all articles cut out by the master tailor, and issues nothing from this store except by the order of the Governor. *Clothing, &c.*

The reception warder has charge of all clothing in use, and is responsible for them to the store-keeper. The shirts and sheets are now made up at Grangegorman female prison, a proper account being kept of the materials issued for this purpose. I am pleased to find that all the shoes for both the male and female city prisons are now made here; 262 pair having been made this year for this, and 251 for Grangegorman, at an estimated cost of 5s. 9d. a pair for the males, and 4s. 6d. for the females. I am informed that in calculating the profits of this prison, credit is taken in the accounts for 1s. 9d. a pair for men's shoes, and 1s. 6d. for females', and also, that certain things made here for Grangegorman prison are returned as profits. Inasmuch as both prisons are under one management, and that the rates are levied for both from the same sources, I submit that such returns are only calculated to mislead the public, and are in fact not profits at all. In addition to the store of clothing, the store-keeper has charge of all the raw material for the manufactory department, which is now very extensive, as mats and matting of various description are made here by prison labour; and I am bound to say that this officer is most regular in his accounts and attentive to his duties.

The clothing of the warders is obtained by contract, but I see no reason why it should not be made up here quite as well, and at a much cheaper rate.

The clothing and bedding throughout the prison was generally in good repair and clean. The sheets of the untried prisoners are changed fortnightly, but those of the tried only monthly, so that the latter could not be as clean as the former. I would certainly recommend that all the sheets be changed at least once a fortnight. *Bedding.*

The prisoners' own clothes are all fumigated before they are put away, and are properly labelled; a correct account being kept of each article, and a receipt taken from the prisoner for the return of the same to him when he is leaving. *Prisoners' clothes.*

Punishments for Prison Offences.

	From 1st January to 31st December, 1874.	From 1st January, 1875, to day of Inspection.
	M.	M.
By Magisterial authority,	4	2
By Governor—Dark or Refractory Cells, Stoppage of diet,	584	479
Total,	588	481

The punishments inflicted this year for breach of prison rules are naturally not so numerous as in previous years, owing to the large number of prisoners now sent to Grangegorman, who are generally of a most troublesome class. *Punishments.*

NORTH
DISTRICT.
——
County of
City of
Dublin
Gaol for
Males.
——
Heating
pipes.

I would here refer to the observation I made in my last report on this prison, in regard to the danger of piping running over head in some of the solitary cells.

School.

	From 1st Jan. to 31st Dec., 1874.	From 1st Jan., 1875, to day of Inspection.
Number of individual prisoners who attended school,	178	108
Average daily number of pupils,	27	20
Number of days on which school was held,	262	265

School-hours—11 o'clock, A.M., to 12½ o'clock, P.M.

Schools

The school is divided into 41 separate stalls, but I regret to find that the daily average number of pupils this year was only 20, although the daily average number in custody was 248; and it will be seen by the preceding table that the number of prisoners who attended the school during this year was only 108. This arises from the age of those allowed to go to school being limited to twenty-five, which I again submit does not meet the requirements of the 106th sec. of the Prisons Act. The school is held on five days in the week, and is regularly inspected by the chaplains, who make their remarks thereon in the school registry. But although it is in connexion with the National Board, I find it was only once inspected during this year by one of their officers, namely, in July. On one day of the week the Roman Catholic prisoners are assembled in the school for religious instructions by their Chaplain.

Summary of Employment on day of Inspection.

Hard labour,	109
Industrial labour,	118
Sick,	11
Unemployed,	20
	——
Total in custody,	258

Amount received for produce of prisoners' labour disposed of outside the gaol—for the last three years.

1872, £493 11s. 1d. | 1873, £414 12s. 6d. | 1874, £410 1s. 2d. | 1875, £526 6s. 1d.

Employment.
Hard
Labour.

Since my last report on this prison no improvement has been made in the mode of carrying out hard labour, and owing to the excess of the numbers so sentenced to the means of enforcing hard labour, it is found impossible to carry out the sentence of the law fully in this respect, for a man is seldom on the tread-mill for more than a month, although he may be sentenced to two years with hard labour. Only 30 men can be employed at the mill at a time, who must therefore, in rotation, make way for new comers. The tread-wheel is used for pumping the water from the canal into the cistern over the prison, and is worked for five hours a day in summer, and four in winter, and there is half an hour of that time allowed as a total suspension of labour; this I consider quite unnecessary, as prisoners are only absolutely on the mill twenty minutes at a time, and then have an interval of ten minutes for rest. The other chief employment of prisoners is in stone breaking, and the manufacture of mats, matting, and different articles for the use of the prison, under the superintendence of officers. It is estimated that a man breaks from eight to ten cwt. of stones a day. Twenty-seven looms are provided in separate compartments, at which men are constantly employed, and this labour is considered very irksome; but until more punitive labour is carried out, the sentence of hard labour cannot be said to be duly enforced, nor will the punishment inflicted in this prison have a deterrent effect on the many hardened offenders who frequent this city. Having regard therefore to the steady increase in crime in Dublin for some years past, I cannot too strongly urge the importance of providing adequate means for carrying out the sentence of the law, and of requiring more punitive labour to be maintained than at present.

It will be observed by the foregoing table that the amount received this year on account of prisoners' labour, came to £526 6s. 1d., which is an increase on the two previous years. This increase is chiefly to be attributed to a more constant employment of prisoners at industrial pursuits, for which every credit is due to the Governor and the different officers superintending the works ; but still, in my opinion, it is far from being sufficient.

In 1874, the daily average number of prisoners in this gaol was 321, and in the county Antrim prison it was 389 ; yet the profits on works in the latter gaol for that year was £1,102, while in the former it only came to £410. And now that none of the very short sentences are sent to Richmond, and that the time of the officers can be more devoted to superintending and enforcing labour, I am of opinion that a proportionate increase should be made in the profits of prison labour.

Contracts.

Bread, white, per 4 lb. loaf, 6d. ; brown, per 4 lb. loaf, 5½d. ; oatmeal, per cwt., 17s. 6d. ; potatoes, per cwt., 4s. ; meat, per lb., 6½d. ; new milk, per gallon, 9d. ; buttermilk, per gallon, 2d. ; salt, per cwt., 4s. ; coal, per ton, 17s. ; gas, per 1,000 cubic feet, 5s. 1d. ; candles, per lb., 5d. ; soap, per cwt., £1 9s. ; buckets, 3s. ; blankets, per lb., 2s. 4d. ; frieze, per yard, 5s. 9d. ; rugs, each, 6s.

The contracts for provisions and clothing are all taken about the close of the year, and are sanctioned and approved of by the Board.

The Chaplains, as a rule, report favourable of the quality of the diet which they inspect frequently, but not by alternate weeks as required by statute. The samples that I saw were excellent, and none of the prisoners in custody complained of the quality of the diet. The meal for the stirabout is served out by the store-keeper every morning to the cook warder, and each prisoner's portion is weighed or measured.

Net average daily cost of ordinary diet for each prisoner in the three preceding years.

1872, . 5d. | 1873, . 5d. | 1874, . 5d. | 1875, . 5·2d.

Net cost of gaol, including diet and salaries, for the three preceding years.

1872, £7,300 2s. 3d. | 1873, £7,559 17s. 5d. | 1874, £8,465 6s. 6d. | 1875, £7,843 10s.

Total cost of officers, including clothing, value of rations, washing, gas, &c.

1872, £3,304 19s. 5d.| 1873, £3,177 14s. 4d.| 1874, £3,231 13s. 1d.| 1875, £3,064 2s. 10d.

Average cost of each prisoner per annum in each of the last three years.

1872, £27 19s. 5d. | 1873, £28 12s. 8d. | 1874, £26 6s. 6d. | 1875, £30 16s. 5d.

Amounts repaid by the War Department for Military prisoners in each of the last three years.

1872, . £53 2s. | 1873, . £15 14s. | 1874, . £7 1s. | 1875, . £6 10s.

Amounts repaid by the Admiralty Department for Naval Prisoners in each of the last three years.

1872, . £15 11s. | 1873, . £52 5s. | 1874, . £19 4s. | 1875, . £27 10s.

E

NORTH DISTRICT.

Amounts repaid from the Consolidated Fund for the maintenance, &c., of prisoners during the years—

County of City of Dublin Gaol for Males.

1872, £741 6s. 7d. | 1873, £677 12s. 9d. | 1874, £1,010 18s. 10d. | 1875, £1,254 13s. 11d.

Expenditure.

In my last report on this prison, I expressed a hope that the remodeling of the buildings that was then proposed, would cause a reduction of the expenditure ; but as this very necessary improvement has been abandoned, so far from the cost of the prison being reduced, it will be seen by the foregoing tables, that it has increased as compared with 1873, amounting in 1875, to £7,643, whereas in 1873 it was £7,559, and owing to the diminution this year in the number of commitments, and no corresponding reduction of the staff having taken place, the annual average cost of a prisoner here in 1875 was more than £4 per head in excess of the previous year. It would, therefore, be my duty to recommend a reduction of the present staff, but that I am in hopes that a prisons bill will this session be introduced and become law, which will altogether alter and revise our whole prison system, under which the county and borough gaols will be conducted with more efficiency and at a considerable saving to the country at large.

Hospital.

	1872.	1873.	1874.	1875 [to day of Inspection].
No. of prisoners in hospital, . .	283	318	316	257
Average daily number in hospital, .	10·6	10	16	16
Number of prisoners prescribed for and treated out of hospital, . .	4,152	3,950	5,948	5,927
No. of deaths in the gaol, . . .	4	2	2	1
Cost of medicine, ...	£80	£70	£80	£75
Cost of diet, &c., for prisoners in hospital, ...	—	£130 4s. 2d.	£160 9s. 8d.	£135 2s. 4d.

Cost of all extra diet ordered by Medical Officer for prisoners not in hospital, £20 17s. 11d. £15 10s. 11d. £32 2s. 10d. £24 5s. 9d.

Hospitals.

The hospital arrangements have undergone no change since my last inspection. Full particulars of these are given in my report of 1873. They are now very complete and well ordered, the officers in charge having a full supervision of the patients both by day and night, and being also provided with means of immediate communication with the night watch and Governor, should necessity for such arise. At the time of my visit 11 patients were in hospital, several of whom were in association and appeared to be but little ailing. As there are a certain number of separate cells attached to the hospital for the treatment of the sick, I would strongly urge the Medical officers not to allow any prisoners to be in association whom they can treat with equal success in separation, for the mere fact of their being in association is a strong inducement to practised hands to feign sickness.

Medicines.

In previous reports on this prison, I have felt it my duty to compare the cost of medicines here, as well as the salaries of the Medical Officers, with those of other large gaols, and showed that the cost to the ratepayers here under both those heads was proportionally much larger than in any other county or borough in Ireland ; but nevertheless I find since my last report that the salaries of both Medical Officers have been raised by £25 a year, while the cost of medicines has been reduced only by £5 yearly. In Belfast gaol, where there is but one Medical Officer, who attends at the prison generally twice a day, and examines all newly committed prisoners every evening, and who devotes much of his valuable time to prison duties, his salary is £75 a year, and the cost of medicines in 1874 was £21 14s. 11d.; but in the city of Dublin prisons it is considered necessary to have two Medical Officers, who only visit each prison on alternate days, and whose present salaries amount to £550

Medical Officers.

a year, while the cost of medicines came to the large sum of £75 a year. The cost for oxtra diet in Belfast gaol in 1874 was £59 0s. 10d.; but in Richmond Bridwell alone it amounted to £192 12s. 6d., in Grange-gorman to £246 13s. 11d.

I therefore must again point out that the system pursued in the city of Dublin prisons in regard to these matters and the division of responsibility of the Medical Officers, is by no means economical nor as effective as if the duties were performed by one officor.

It will be seen by the annexed return that there is a considerable difference in the quantity of extra diet ordered by the two Medical Officers, also that numbers exempted from hard labour by the Surgeon are much larger than those by the Physician, showing what bad effects arise from the different views taken by those gentlemen.

Number of prisoners taken off the treadmill, in 1875, by order
  of the Surgeon, ... 90
  Ditto of ditto, by order of Physician, ... 17

Cost of extra diet ordered by the Surgeon and Physician to prisoners out of Hospital, in 1875, £24 5s. 9d. (being £10 0s. 7d. by Physician, and £14 5s. 2d. by Surgeon.)*

Officers and Salaries.

Extern.	£	s.	d.		£	s.	d.
William Ormsby, esq., Local Inspector,	150	0	0	Chas. Mills, 2nd Class Warder,	36	0	0
H. Minchin, esq., Surgeon,	150	0	0	John Clarke, do.	36	0	0
J. G. Burne, esq., Physician,	125	0	0	Patrick Hayden, do.	36	0	0
Rev. J. S. MacNeill, Protestant Chaplain,	50	0	0	Chas. O'Sullivan, do.	36	0	0
Rev. John Norris, Roman Catholic Chaplain,	100	0	0	John R. Jones, do.	36	0	0
				Michael M'Gann, do.	36	0	0
Rev. Joseph Hunter, Presbyterian Chaplain,	33	6	8	Patrick Crimmins, do.	36	0	0
				Michael M'Grath, Schoolmaster & Assistant Clerk,	96	0	0
Intern.				John Gardiner, Storekeeper,	60	0	0
Richard Boyd,esq.,Governor,	350	0	0	John Molloy, Master of Works,	55	0	0
Edward Rothe, Chief Clerk and Registrar,	150	0	0	Joseph Greer, Wearing Warder,	57	0	0
Geo. W. Hill, Chief Warder,	80	0	0	Philip Bryan, 2nd Class Warder,	45	0	0
Jno. M'Cormack, Gate-keeper,	60	0	0	James Campbell, do.	40	0	0
Ambrose O'Connor, 1st Class Warder,	59	0	0	John Allen, do.	39	0	0
Bernard M'Darby, do.,	59	0	0	John Hoey, do.	38	0	0
James Desmond, Hall Porter,	45	0	0	William Foster, do.	38	0	0
Michael Barron, Hospital Superintendent,	43	0	0	Phelim Redmond, do.	38	0	0
				Patrick Boggin, do.	37	0	0
				John Blair, do.	37	0	0
				Robert Connolly, do.	36	0	0
				Michael Grant, do.	36	0	0
				William Beattie, do.	36	0	0
				Bridget Magee, Cook & Servant,	15	0	0

Vacancies in the Staff since last inspection, how caused, and how filled up.

Rev. Charles J. Malone, Roman Catholic Chaplain, resigned; Rev. J. Norris appointed thereto. George W. Hill appointed Chief Warder, vice Sleith, super-annuated. Matthew Kennedy and W. Dunne returned unfit by Medical Officers. Thomas Gannon and Charles Kelly not passed by Civil Service Commissioners. John O'Connor resigned. James Carey retired on compensation. P. Hayden promoted from Carter and Messenger to be Warder. H. O'Loughlin and Michael Grant appointed Shoemaker Warders; the former resigned. Charles O'Sullivan, W. Beattie, J. R. Jones, Michael M'Gann, and Patrick Crimmins, appointed Warders. Charles Walker appointed Warder, and resigned.

Officers on Gaol Allowance.

All the officers, from the Governor down, receive an allowance of bread, milk soap, candles, and fuel.

All married officers who reside outside receive five tons of coal each at their residence annually.

* The book containing names, &c., of prisoners on extra and change of diet is signed alternately each week by Surgeon and Physician.

NORTH
DISTRICT.

*County of
City of
Dublin
Gaol for
Males.*

Visits Paid by Officers.

	From 1st Jan. to 31st Dec., 1874.	From 1st Jan. 1875, to day of Inspection.
Number of times the Board of Superintendence met and discharged business,	36	32
Local Inspector to Gaol,	122	114
Chaplain, Protestant Episcopalian Church,	193	244
Presbyterian Chaplain,	90	93
Roman Catholic Chaplain,	361	337
Physician,	209	222
Surgeon,	205	175

Cost of
staff.

There are 37 paid officers attached to the prison, 27 of whom are discipline officers, so that about 1 officer is considered necessary for the safe keeping and management of about every 9 prisoners in custody of the daily average number in charge last year—making every allowance for the difficulty of supervision here owing to the faulty construction of the building, I am of opinion that the staff is somewhat too numerous, more especially as the daily average in custody is now reduced owing to the short sentences being sent to Grangegorman. In 1874 there was a daily average number in custody here of 321 ; but during 1875 it was only 248, and at one time in the former year 429 prisoners were in charge here, while in the latter the numbers were never higher than 270. Under these circumstances there should be made some proportionate reduction in the staff. At the time of my visit, the quarters of the subordinate officers were all clean and well kept. Eight warders have rooms in the prison, and are provided with a comfortable mess-room and kitchen; the Board also provides a female servant to cook for them. The chief warder, the chief clerk, and gate-keeper also have apartments within the prison. The married warders, 14 in number, sleep out of the gaol. Owing to the difficulty in supervision in this prison by the superior officers, it is not easy for the Governor to maintain a proper amount of discipline amongst the warders. Several instances of irregularity have occurred amongst them during the year, and I do not think that any benefit to the service has arisen by the Lord Lieutenant having ceded his right of appointing directly to the vacancies amongst the subordinate officers of the city prisons. The Governor has an onerous task to perform in carrying out discipline and order, and I am bound to bear testimony, as I have in former reports, to his close attention to business, and to his zeal in the execution of the many duties connected with the office.

Books of
accounts,
&c.

Books and Journals.

The chief clerk keeps most of the books of finance and the registries, and deserves much credit for the regular and careful manner in which they are kept. He is assisted by the school warder, who is also a painstaking officer. All these prison books are very regularly and carefully inspected by the Governor, but I am still of opinion that too many registries are kept, entailing an amount of labour and clerks' work that is quite unnecessary. Most of the prescribed forms are in use, but the proper work ledger is not kept. The Governor keeps the Punishment book, which he lays before the Board at their meetings. An account is kept of the progress of prison labour, and those not sentenced to hard labour are, I am informed, allowed on discharge one-third of the profits of such labour, as laid down by statute. The Governor keeps a full and useful journal, in which he writes all matters of note connected with his office and relating to the discipline of the prison ; and from it I was made acquainted with many occurrences of interest and importance. The Roman Catholic Chaplain's journal is regularly written up, and is a useful record of the duties con-

<sub>

nected with his office ; hut I regret that the journals of the other Chaplains contain few comments or observations relating to their duties. The regular Presbyterian Chaplain has not done duty here for nearly five years ; hut I am informed that the few Presbyterian prisoners who usually are sent here are carefully attended to by his assistant.

Both the Medical Officers are careful to enter in their journals their remarks on the performance of their duties, noting therein all cases of importance that comes under their notice. The hospital books and registry are also well kept, and supervised hy those gentlemen.

NORTH DISTRICT.

County of City of Dublin Gaol for Males.

Board of Superintendence.

Board.

Alderman Joseph Manning, J.P.	Alderman John Draper.
Alderman Sir J. W. Mackey, J.P.	Councillor P. W. Long, M.D.
Councillor Sir J. Burrington, D.L., J.P.	Councillor James Reilly.
Councillor Thomas Fry, J.P.	Councillor P. T. Bermingham.
Councillor Cornelius Dennehy, J.P.	Councillor W. Campbell.
Councillor G. B. Owens, M.D., J.P.	Councillor E. H. Carson, C.E.

The Board met twelve times in this prison during this year, ten at Grangegorman, and I am informed twelve times in the City Hall for the transaction of prison business.

CHARLES F. BOURKE, *Inspector-General.*

COUNTY OF THE CITY OF DUBLIN GAOL—FOR MALES UNDER SHORT SENTENCES, AND FOR ALL THE FEMALES OF THE ABOVE JURISDICTION. —4TH AND 16TH DECEMBER, 1875.

County of City of Dublin Gaol for Males and Females.

Although my official inspections were made on different days in the month of December, the following tables are made up to the 16th of the month, on which day I visited the principal part of the male prison. On the 4th, I spent most of the day in the female section.

On the first of the above dates the numbers in custody were 77 males and 153 females.

State.

Denomination of Class.	No. in each Class.			No. of whom were Sick in Hospital.		
	M.	F.	Total.	M.	F.	Total.
UNTRIED.						
For Larceny,	–	2	2	–	–	–
For further Examination,	–	9	9	–	–	–
TRIED.						
Cases disposed of at Assizes and Quarter Sessions.						
Of Felony or Larceny :—						
To Penal Servitude,	–	1	1	1	–	
To Imprisonment,	8	16	24	1	3	4
Of Misdemeanors, &c., .	2	19	21	–	2	2
Disposed of Summarily.						
For Larceny,	11	8	19	–	3	3
Offences under Larceny Act,	2	14	16	1	2	3
In default of Bail,	5	2	7	–	–	–
Non-payment of Fines and Penalties,	15	22	37	–	3	3
Other Misdemeanors,	10	24	34	–	–	–
Under Poor Law Act,	1	–	1	–	–	–
Vagrants,	–	4	4	–	–	–
Drunkards,	23	32	55	1	3	4
Total in Custody,	**77**	**153**	**230**	**3**	**16**	**19**

NORTH DISTRICT.

County of City of Dublin Gaol for Males and Females.

It will he observed by the foregoing table that most of the males in custody were summary convictions, inasmuch as only those sentenced to a month and under are committed to this prison. But owing to the crowded state of Richmond Bridewell, it is found necessary at times to transfer some of the prisoners from that to this gaol.

Juveniles.

CLASSES, &c., OF OFFENDERS.	In custody on the day of Inspection.				From 1st January to day of Inspection.			
	12 years old and under.		Above 12 and not exceeding 16 years.		12 years old and under.		Above 12 and not exceeding 16 years.	
	M.	F.	M.	F.	M.	F.	M.	F.
Convicted at Assizes,	–	–	–	–	–	–	→	1
,, Quarter Sessions,	–	–	–	–	–	1	–	5
,, Summarily,	–	–	2	3	–	4	18	57
Committed for Trial,	–	–	–	–	–	4	–	9
Total,	–	–	2	3	–	9	18	72
Number sent to Reformatories,	–	–	–	1	–	5	–	12

Juveniles.

As there is no proper provision in this prison for male juveniles, they should all be sent to Richmond Bridewell, as was arranged when this prison was opened for males; but during the year some have been sent here who had stated their ages to be over sixteen at the different courts, but who were subsequently discovered by the Governor of the gaol to be under that age, and were then classed as juveniles. I observed here the same lamentable circumstance as at Richmond in regard to the extreme youth of the greater number of males in custody at the above date. They were mostly under thirty years of age, and I am informed that the average age of those was twenty-two. As I have remarked more fully on the subject in my report on Richmond Bridewell, it is not here necessary to repeat those observations. In my report of 1873, I drew attention to the large number of female juvenile offenders committed here, compared with those throughout the rest of Ireland. Those committed here for that year numbered 93, in 1874, 83, and this year, up to the day of my visit, 81; of the latter only 17 were sent to reformatories. One of the girls in custody at the time of my visit had eleven commitments against her for drunkenness, 1 ten, 1 nine, and 1 seven, none of whom were sentenced to reformatories—for under the present law the option of a fine is always given where the offence is drunkenness alone, hence it is that magistrates do not commit those children to reformatories. The result is that there is no hope of effecting any reform in them, for little good results can be expected during their short term of imprisonment, and the oftener these short periods of imprisonment are repeated, the less likely are they to have any effect for good on them. I therefore submit, that justices should have the power to inflict imprisonment for drunkenness, with or without a fine according as they may think right. In this event, these girls could be sent to reformatories, and would probably become respectable members of society. The total number of female juveniles committed to gaol in Ireland in 1874, was 186, so that it will be seen that those from the city of Dublin formed a very large proportion of the whole number, whereas the county Antrim, including the large and populous town of Belfast, only contributed 9, and the county and town of Cork 23. It is, therefore, clearly the duty of the authorities in Dublin who have the power to deal with the prevailing depravity of a certain class of the juvenile inhabitants of this town to endeavour to meet it with as firm a hand as possible, in order to put a stop to the rearing up in our midst a large number of unfortunate creatures, whose life must be one of crime and debauchery, and as the parents of youthful offenders are in most cases to blame, either through neglect or worse causes, for the early delinquencies of their children, they should, in my opinion, be compelled as far as possible to contribute to the support of the institution, whether it be an industrial or reformatory school to which the young offender is sent.

Three males and 8 females committed here this year were known previously to have been in reformatories.

Number of prisoners of all classes in gaol on the day of inspection, and on the corresponding date in the three preceding years.

	M.	F.		M.	F.
1872, ...	–	133	1874, ...	60	207
1873, ...	–	184	1875 (day of inspection),	77	153

Number of returned convicts in gaol on the day of inspection, and during each of the three preceding years.

	M.	F.		M.	F.
1872, ...	–	34	1875 (up to and including		
1873, ...	–	36	day of inspection), .	11	40
1874, ...	–	42	Day of inspection, .	1	3

Commitments.

CLASSES.		From 1st January to 31st December, 1874.		From 1st January, 1875, to day of Inspection.	
		M.	F.	M.	F.
Criminals,	. .	242	2,723	1,667	2,586
Vagrants,	. .	5	63	27	77
Drunkards,	. .	393	2,289	2,253	2,348
Total,	. .	640	5,075	3,947	5,011

Having regard to the date on which these tables are made up to this year, they do not show any great difference in the number of females committed here as compared with last year, and in comparing the number of males committed here in 1874, with those committed this year, it must be remembered that this prison was not open to males until October, 1874.

It will, however, be seen by the foregoing table, that even up to my visit this year the number of females committed for drunkenness and vagrancy, is much larger than during the whole of the previous year, though the criminal commitments are not so numerous; but I fear when the total number is made up for the entire year, it will show an increase in the numbers committed in 1875 over those of 1874. Even during the last three years it is truly lamentable to see to what an alarming extent the offence of drunkenness has increased amongst the females of this city. In 1873, 875 was the number of commitments of females to this gaol for being drunk; but the above table shows that these numbers increased in 1874 to 2,289, and up to the 16th of December this year to 2,348. It is then not surprising that with these examples before them, that a certain class of the youth of this city is neglected, and that they are following in the disgraceful and ruinous footsteps of such unworthy parents. My report on Richmond Bridewell contains a statement of the number of the male drunkards committed to the city prisons, which I regret to observe shows a no less disgraceful state of things amongst that sex.

NORTH DISTRICT.

Averages, and Highest and Lowest Numbers (exclusive of Debtors).

County of
City of
Dublin
Gaol for
Males and
Females.

	From 1st January to 31st December, 1874.			From 1st January, 1875, to day of Inspection.		
—	M.	F.	Date.	M.	F.	Date.
Average daily number of prisoners in custody,	65	184	—	92	181	—
Highest number of prisoners at any one time,	318	—		375		9th Oct.
Lowest ditto,	125	—		136		26th Dec.
Highest number of males at any one time,	99		11th Nov.	148		18th May.
Ditto of females,	259		22nd Sept.		250	25th Sept.
Lowest number of males at any one time,	10		20th Oct.	50		23rd Dec.
Ditto of females,	125		5th April.		85	26th Dec.

Highest number of prisoners (exclusive of Debtors) in gaol during each of the previous seven years, and up to day of inspection in 1875.

16th March, 1868,	.	.	190	12th September, 1872,	.	.	234
13th October, 1869,	.	.	161	18th October, 1873,	.	.	254
12th July, 1870,	.	.	178	22nd September, 1874,	.	.	259
26th September, 1871,	.	.	181	9th October, 1875,	.	.	375

Number of Individual Prisoners (exclusive of Debtors), and Number of Times each had been committed during the following periods, distinguishing Adults from Juveniles.

NUMBER OF TIMES COMMITTED.	1874.				1875, to day of Inspection.			
	Juveniles.		Adults.		Juveniles.		Adults.	
	M.	F.	M.	F.	M.	F.	M.	F.
Once within the year,	—	56	556	1944	18	53	2525	1597
Twice ,,	—	16	26	377	—	7	375	325
Thrice ,,	—	8	4	176	—	3	98	153
4 times ,,	—	1	5	77	—	—	43	101
5 ,, ,,	—	1	—	64	—	1	20	54
6 ,, ,,	—	—	—	36	—	—	8	49
7 ,, ,,	—	—	—	23	—	—	3	37
8 ,, ,,	—	1	—	15	—	—	1	25
9 ,, ,,	—	—	—	11	—	—	1	27
10 ,, ,,	—	—	—	11	—	—	—	10
11 ,, ,,	—	—	—	4	—	—	—	7
12 ,, ,,	—	—	—	6	—	—	—	4
13 ,, ,,	—	—	—	6	—	—	—	3
14 ,, ,,	—	—	—	7	—	—	—	7
15 ,, ,,	—	—	—	1	—	—	—	2
16 ,, ,,	—	—	—	2	—	—	—	2
17 ,, ,,	—	—	—	1	—	—	—	3
18 ,, ,,	—	—	—	1	—	—	—	1
19 ,, ,,	—	—	—	—	—	—	—	1
20 ,, ,,	—	—	—	—	—	—	—	2
Total,	—	83	591	2764	18	64	3075	2410
No. of above who had not been in gaol previous to 1st January in	—	63	272	907	15	61	1621	793

Number of Individual Prisoners (exclusive of Debtors), committed in the year 1874, and to the day of Inspection in 1875, who had been Once, Twice, Thrice, Four Times, Five Times, &c., &c., from their first Commitment in any year, so far as can be ascertained, distinguishing Adults from Juveniles.

NORTH DISTRICT.

County of City of Dublin Gaol for Males and Females.

NUMBER OF TIMES COMMITTED.	1874.				1875, to day of Inspection.			
	Juveniles		Adults		Juveniles		Adults	
	M.	F.	M.	F.	M.	F.	M.	F.
Once only,	–	56	253	773	15	42	1656	793
Twice,	–	16	190	716	3	12	631	389
Thrice,	–	8	35	225	–	5	300	208
4 times,	–	1	20	136	–	3	139	137
5 „	–	1	18	96	–	–	76	84
6 „	–	–	20	75	–	–	67	75
7 to 11 „	–	1	35	232	–	2	123	246
12 to 16 „	–	–	12	152	–	–	46	119
17 to 20 „	–	–	5	66	–	–	12	58
21 to 30 „	–	–	3	120	–	–	12	124
31 to 40 „	–	–	1	54	–	–	6	66
41 to 50 „	–	–	1	40	–	–	2	31
51 to 60 „	–	–	1	21	–	–	1	23
61 to 70 „	–	–	–	16	–	–	–	18
71 to 80 „	–	–	–	11	–	–	1	6
81 to 90 „	–	–	–	7	–	–	–	7
91 to 100 „	–	–	–	4	–	–	–	7
101 to 120 „	–	–	–	4	–	–	1	9
121 to 140 „	–	–	–	2	–	–	–	4
141 to 160 „	–	–	–	3	–	–	–	2
161 to 180 „	–	–	–	1	–	–	–	–
181 to 200 „	–	–	–	–	–	–	–	1
201 to 250 „	–	–	–	1	–	–	–	1
Total Number of Individuals committed,	–	83	591	2764	18	64	3075	2410
No. of Commitments represented in foregoing,	–	129	1795	22256	21	111	7897	21641

It will be observed from the foregoing tables, that the number of re-commitments of both sexes is very large, and that some individuals appear almost to spend their lives in gaol. Re-commitments.

Two females were this year in custody as often as twenty times up to the day of my visit, and one who was in custody this year had been in charge between 200 and 250 times, and several over 100 times. There was also one male in charge this year who had between 100 and 120 commitments recorded against him. The total number of adult individuals committed in 1874 was 591 males, and 2,764 females, whose commitments since their first offence numbered 1,795 and 22,256, respectively. In 1875, up to the day above named, the adult individuals committed were 3,075 males, and 2,410 females, whose previous commitments were respectively 7,897 and 21,641. It will thus be seen that short periods of imprisonment have little effect for good on the majority of those committed here, and that the punishment inflicted is such as not to deter them from their evil ways, for out of the total number of the above committed this year, only 1,821 of the males, and 793 of the females, *had not* been previously in gaol.

NORTH
DISTRICT.

County of
City of
Dublin
Gaol for
Males and
Females.

Accommodation.

	M.	F.		M.	F.
Yards, . . .	9	14	Kitchen, . . .	–	1
Solitary Cells, . .	3	8	Store Rooms, . .	1	5
Single Cells, not less than 9			Laundries, . . .	–	2
feet long, 6 feet wide, and			Drying Rooms, . .	1	2
8 feet high=432 cubic feet,	120	126	Lavatories, . . .	1	6
Do. heated and furnished			Baths, with Hot and Cold		
with bells, . .	120	126	Water laid on, . .	5	4
Hospital Rooms, . .	1	6	Water-closets, . .	21	28
Chapels, . . .	–	2	Fumigating Apparatus, .	1	1
School Room, . .	–	1	Reception Rooms or Cells, .	1	1
Workshop, . . .	–	1	Pump, . . .	–	1
Workshed, . . .	–	1	Tell-tale Clocks, . .	2	5

Alterations.

Since my inspection of this gaol in 1873, the female prison has been enlarged by twenty-seven cells, and the north wing of the prison, which for some years was disused, has been converted into a prison for males, containing 120 cells, which are all well ventilated, heated, and lighted with gas ; but the building is not suited for the carrying out of long sentences, and is so constructed as to make supervision and the maintenance of discipline very difficult and expensive, owing to the number of officers required. The entire cellular accommodation of the prison now consists of 120 cells for males, and 179 for females. The new twenty-seven cells in the female prison, are set apart for reception. Four baths are provided in each reception ward, where all prisoners are washed at once as they come in, and subsequently the females weekly, and the males once a fortnight, during imprisonment. They are all examined by the Medical Officers before they are passed into their proper wards.

Baths.

I should certainly recommend the male as well as the female prisoners to be bathed weekly, and as I remarked at the time of my visit, the females had a much less cleanly appearance than the males, I would suggest that more cleanly habits be instilled into the former, and that the matrons pay more attention to this matter. As the baths in the reception ward are the only ones in the female section, I am still of opinion, that at least two more should be put up in the large female prison. All the cells are artificially heated, and are furnished with gas and bells ; but the water pipes running over head, through the cells in the long hall are dangerous, affording a facility to those so inclined, to commit suicide. They should be sheeted over with wood. At the time of my visit I remarked on the dangerous position of the gas burners, and suggested an alteration in them, which I have since learned the Board have consented to have made.

Heating and gas.

The cells throughout both prisons presented a clean and tidy appearance ; though the twenty-seven new reception cells for females require painting ; but I have no doubt this will be accomplished before long, as the Governor has already done a good deal of painting this year by prison labour. The long hall of the female prison is well provided with lavatories, which I hope in future will be made more use of, and would recommend that the cells in the other parts of the prison be provided with a basin and water, and that prisoners be required to cleanse themselves before going to bed, and on getting up in the morning, by which means the clothing and bedding would be much cleaner than it now is.

Sewerage.

The sewerage is said to be in excellent order, and there is an ample supply of water-closets and privies throughout the gaol, all in good repair.

Water.

There is always an abundant supply of Vartry water in the gaol, for which £75 a year is paid.

Chapels.

The arrangements as to the Protestant and Roman Catholic services are very suitable, and the Chapels are both neatly kept. No Presbyterian service was performed in the gaol this year, there being seldom more than a daily average of more than one prisoner of that persuasion in custody.

The laundry in the female prison is well adapted for the carrying out of a large business in washing, being provided with forty separate stalls, with hot and cold water laid on; but with the exception of a small contract from one of the hospitals, and the washing of both this and the other city prison, very little of this labour is carried on. However, the Governor informs me that he has now entered into a contract for washing, which I trust will be the means of providing an abundance of this most suitable and remunerative employment for the class of females committed here. The clothing is all fumigated before it is sent to the laundry, as well as the prisoners' own clothing, which latter is now all carefully labelled before it is put away.

The kitchen arrangements are now very convenient, and this department is conducted by the females. The head matron issues the meal and bread to the cook matron, who is then responsible for both the stirabout and bread, all the portions being weighed or measured. Five prisoners are employed in the kitchen, which I consider is beyond the requirements, considering that so little cooking is required, and that the daily average to be served is not 200. I therefore submit that at least two of these cooks should be more profitably employed.

The chief warder is charged with the duty of taking the photographs of certain classes of prisoners, for which he receives 7d. per copy. All the photographs are registered, and are kept in a book on a form similar to that sent to the Habitual Criminals Office.

Five tell-tale clocks are provided in the female, and two in the male prison. They are marked hourly from 7 P.M. to 6 A.M. The head matron takes the markings in the female prison, and the chief warder in the male prison, which are afterwards checked by the Governor, and entered by him in the Lockings Book. The officers are fined for all neglect of this duty, and each default is noted in the Conduct Book. The male subordinate officers perform the duty of night watch by rotation, and in the female prison this duty is performed by the junior matron. The Governor, the Superintendent, and the principal matron attend the respective lockings, the keys of the female prison being kept by the Superintendent at night, and those of the male, together with those of the extern doors, by the Governor.

No alteration has taken place as to the rules for visitors to prisoners of late, there being convenient arrangements in both prisons in this respect; but as the sentences of males sent here are generally so short, very few of that sex receive visits. Under the by-laws a convicted prisoner can receive a visit. and a letter once in three months, and an untried prisoner twice in the week.

During the year much work has been performed in the male prison, under the superintendence of the Governor, and many important improvements have been effected by prison labour, by which means a large outlay has been saved, and the work has been done in the most satisfactory manner. An iron gallery has been removed from one of the yards, and sold for £45. Four of the old exercise yards have been turned into vegetable gardens for the use of the prison, and a great deal of carpentering and joinery and other work has been performed, which would have run up large bills had free labour been employed, or had the Governor shown less zeal in the performance of his duties. There are, however, some matters of importance still to be carried out, to which I called attention at the time of my visit, and which, I have no doubt, will not escape the attention of the Governor.

In my last report on this prison I recommended that no children over

(marginal notes:)
North District.
County of City of Dublin Gaol for Males and Females.
Laundry.
Fumigator.
Kitchen.
Photography.
Night-watch.
Visitors.
Improvements.

NORTH DISTRICT.
County of City of Dublin Gaol for Males and Females.

twelve months of age should be admitted with their mothers, as they create much noise, confusion, and unpleasantness in the gaol, and the Medical Officers considered that in a sanitary point of view the presence of infants shut up with their mothers in small cells was very objectionable. It is also impossible to obtain any employment from the mothers while they are thus hampered with their children. I would, therefore, again recommend that the above suggestion be adopted.

Infants.

Stock at the time of Inspection.

	In Use.	In Store.	Male Clothing.	In Use.	In Store.	Female Clothing.	In Use.	In Store.
Blankets, pairs of,	F. 366 / M. 130	21 / 47	Shirts,	180	91	Shifts,	434	113
Sheets, pairs of,	F. 333 / M. 160	62 / 40	Jackets,	75	3	Jackets,	378	158
			Vests,	89	15	Gowns,	4	-
Rugs,	F. 209 / M. 130	84 / 43	Trowsers,	90	37	Petticoats,	505	124
			Caps,	90	12	Aprons,	392	386
Hammocks or Cots,	F. 126 / M. -	- / -	Shoes, Slippers, & Clogs, pairs of,	109	105	Neckerchiefs,	446	265
Bed-ticks,	F. 135 / M. 130	25 / 13				Caps,	445	354
Bedsteads,	F. 97 / M. 130	- / -				Stockings, pairs of,	428	534
						Shoes, Slippers, & Clogs, pairs of,	307	272

Stores.

The stores in both prisons were well provided with clothing, bedding, and other requirements, at the time of my visit. In the male prison the chief warder has charge of the general store, and the reception warder that of the things in use. In the female prison the general store is kept by the head matron, and the reception matron keeps the store of things in use, and dresses the females as soon as they come in. She is also responsible for the fumigating and the keeping of the private clothing of the females. Since my last inspection, a new room has been fitted up as a store at the reception ward in the female prison, and the order and regularity here was more creditable than on that occasion. Stock is taken four times a year by the Governor of all prison property, but I was unable to ascertain that this important matter is attended to by the Local Inspector, although he is the officer statutably responsible for the supply of clothing to the prison. The clothing and sheeting, and shirts, are all made up in the prison, and this year a number of the shoes have been made here by the male prisoners, whereas it was formerly necessary to buy about 400 pairs a year for this prison. I see no reason why all the shoes required should not be made up either here or at Richmond. I was sorry to find that the bed-ticks, which were cut out and made up in the female prison, are much too short for the beds in the male cells, denoting much carelessness on the part of those whose duty it was to superintend this matter.

The bedding throughout the prison was clean and in good repair; the sheets being changed fortnightly, but new prisoners are not supplied with a clean pair. This rule for obvious reasons should be altered, for, unless in the case of known habitual drunkards, or constant offenders, no prisoner should be required to sleep in sheets that have already been used.

Number of Punishments for Prison Offences.

	From 1st January to 31st December, 1874. M.	F.	From 1st January, 1875, to day of Inspection. M.	F.
By Magisterial authority,	-	-	-	2
By Governor—				
Dark or Refractory Cells,	-	1	-	-
Stoppage of Diet,	-	191	190	131
Total,	-	192	190	133

Four out of the 8 solitary cells for females have now been fitted with spiral bells, and those for males, three in number, are also so arranged. All are artificially heated. A mattress and bedding are given to females in solitary at night, an indulgence which I do not consider is at all advisable, as I have no doubt that the less comforts *allowed* to prisoners under such circumstances, the more likely are they to be well behaved.

NORTH
DISTRICT.

County of
City of
Dublin
Gaol for
Males and
Females.

Punish-
ments.

Summary of Employment on day of Inspection.

	M.	F.
Hard Labour,	14	23
Industrial Labour,	45	77
Sick,	3	16
Unemployed,	10	20
Nurses,	–	8
Infirm,	–	9
In Solitary Confinement,	5	–
Total in custody,	77	153

Amount received for produce of prisoners' labour disposed of outside the gaol for the last three years.

1872, . £75 15s. 7d. | 1873, . £110 4s. 8d. | 1874, . £108 5s. 4d | 1875, . £110 4s. 8d

Net average daily cost of ordinary diet for each prisoner in the three preceding years.

1872, . 4·7d. | 1873, . 4·5d. | 1874, . 4·4d. | 1875, . 4·5d.

Net cost of gaol, including diet and salaries, for the three preceding years.

1872, £4,942 14s. 0d. | 1873, £5,526 0s. 2d. | 1874, £6,726 12s. 7d. | 1875, £7,633 16s. 2d.

Total cost of officers, including clothing, value of rations, washing, gas, &c.

1872, £2,108 6s. 3d. | 1873, £2,140 6s. 4d. | 1874, £2,274 18s. 7d. | 1875, £2,870 9s. 11d.

Average cost of each prisoner per annum in each of the last three years.

1872, . £38 12s. 3d. | 1873, . £33 12s. 8d. | 1874, . £33 12s. 1d. | 1875, . £27 17s. 2d.

Amounts repaid by the Consolidated Fund for the maintenance, &c., of prisoners during the years

1872, . £88 5s. 3d. | 1873, . £346 0s. 1d. | 1874, . £514 19s. 10d. | 1875, . £493 16s. 5d.

The females are chiefly employed in washing, sewing, and oakum-picking, and the males at matmaking, trades of different sorts, oakum-picking, and stone-breaking; males sentenced to hard labour are kept chiefly to the latter employments, as there is neither tread-wheel nor crank available here.

After stone-breaking is over, men are compelled to pick one pound of oakum daily, at which they are employed up to 7 P.M., and in the winter the gas is extinguished in the cells at 7.30 in both prisons. Now that the arrangements in the male prison are nearly completed, men will be more available for reproductive labour, so that I trust those sentenced to hard labour will be required to perform a given quantity of work daily, and a greater amount than those not so sentenced, and that every effort will be made to carry out a full amount of industrial labour. In my previous reports on this prison I have endeavoured to point out the importance of enforcing more labour amongst the females, and am still of opinion that women are not sufficiently employed here.

Those who are employed in the laundry do not commence work until 10 A.M., and are not required to perform any labour in their cells after lock-up, though the other women are supposed to pick one pound of oakum after that time, but I fear even this is not always insisted on, and that no strict rule is enforced in this regard. They should be at work much earlier than they now are, and should be kept constantly employed up to 8 o'clock every evening.

NORTH DISTRICT.

County of City of Dublin Gaol for Males and Females.

Having regard to the large increase of female commitments here of late years, and to the number of times that some have been in gaol, I believe it to be the duty of all prison authorities to endeavour as far as possible to deter these constant offenders in their evil ways, and to make prison life as irksome to them as possible, affording to them at the same time every possible means of reforming. But so long as old offenders are allowed to spend their time in gaol in comparative ease and comfort, there can be no hope of deterring them from a life of crime and disorder.

The consequence of the little labour followed in this prison up to this is that the amount received from that source in 1874 was only £108 5s. 4d., whereas the total cost of the gaol came to the large sum of £6,726 12s 7d. From this the cost of officers was £2,274 18s. 7d., making the average annual cost of a prisoner confined there for that year come to £33 12s. 1d.

But this year, although the cost of the prison, together with that of the officers was higher than in 1874, yet, owing to the increase in the numbers confined, the average annual cost per head in 1875 is nearly £6 under that of the previous year. The amount received from prisoners' labour this year is very little more than it was in 1874, namely, £110 4s. 8d.

Yet as the labour of many of the male prisoners, whose time was occupied in the alterations and improvements of the gaol, is not herein computed, the profits from this source this year may very fairly be estimated as much higher than the above sum.

School.

	From 1st Jan. to 31st Dec., 1874. F.	From 1st Jan., 1875, to day of Inspection F.
Number of individual prisoners who attended school,	574	499
Average daily number of pupils,	24	26
Number of days on which school was held,	242	253

School-hours—From 10 A.M. to 1.30 P.M.

School.

No school is held in the male prison, as the commitments are for so short a period that it is not considered possible to impart secular instruction in so limited a time.

Females under thirty, and whose term of imprisonment is over seven days, are sent to school. They are divided into two classes; the first offences being kept apart from the others.

I regret, however, to find that women employed in the laundry do not partake of the benefits of the school. I cannot think that this is a good or fair arrangement, and submit that a certain number of these should be sent to school in their turn daily. I am informed that the chaplains visit the school frequently, but with the exception of the Presbyterian, their remarks in the school registry are not full or frequent enough. Women are taught needlework for one hour a day, which is very necessary, as many of those committed are quite unable to do the commonest sewing, exemplifying in what ignorance and idleness they must be brought up.

Contracts.

Bread, white, per 4 lb. loaf, 6d.; brown, per 4 lb. loaf, 5¼d.; oatmeal, per cwt., 17s. 6d.; Indian meal, per cwt., 8s. 10¼d.; potatoes, per cwt., 4s.; meat, per lb., 6¼d.; new milk, per gallon, 9d.; buttermilk, per gallon, 2d.; salt, per cwt., 4s.; coal, per ton, house, 18s. 1d., furnace, 17s. 6d.; straw, per cwt. (at market prices); gas, per 1,000 cubic feet, 5s. 4d.; candles, per lb., 5d.; soap, per cwt., £1 9s.; tea, per lb., 2s. 4d.; sugar, per lb., 3d.; port and sherry, per doz., £1 7s.; whisky, per quart, 4s.; women's shoes, per pair, 6s. and 5s.; Irish blankets, per lb., 2s. 4d.

Contracts and diet.

All the contracts are taken by tenders sanctioned by the Board. The samples of the provisions that I saw were excellent, and are generally reported to be so by the chaplains, who inspect them frequently, but not

by "alternate weeks," as required by the statute. At the time of my
visit I found that the dietary scale was not strictly adhered to, and that
some prisoners were receiving a rather better diet than others. I consequently brought the whole matter before the Board, who have now
very properly ordered that a uniform scale shall in future be followed
throughout both prisons. This will, I trust, help to simplify the keeping
of the accounts, and have beneficial results in other ways.

NORTH
DISTRICT.

*County of
City of
Dublin
Gaol for
Males and
Females.*

Officers and Salaries.

Extern Officers.	£	s.	d.		£	s.	d.
Wm.Ormsby, Local Inspector,	150	0	0	Maria T. Kelly, Class Matron,	83	0	0
Rev. William Maturin, Pro-				Teresa Darcy, do.	32	0	0
testant Chaplain, . .	75	0	0	Alice Kelly, do.	31	0	0
Rev. James Murphy, Roman				Elizabeth Jones, do.	31	0	0
Catholic Chaplain, . .	200	0	0	Mary Power, do.	31	0	0
Rev. S. G. Morrison, Presby-				Sarah Croese, do.	31	0	0
terian Chaplain, . ,	56	6	8	Anne M. Healy, do.	30	0	0
Humphrey Minchin, Surgeon,	150	0	0	3 Female House Servants at £15 each.			
Joseph G. Burne, Physician,	125	0	0	Lorenzo Lyons, Registrar and			
				Chief Clerk, . .	110	0	0
Resident Officers.				Michael Meagher, Chief			
Henry Philpotts, Governor, .	220	0	0	Warder, &c., . .	90	0	0
Helena M. Worthy, Super-				Edward Ternan, Gate-			
intendent, ...	130	0	0	keeper, . . .	65	0	0
Alice Keshan, Principal Ma-				Joseph Coffey, Guardsman, .	45	0	0
tron, ...	80	0	0	Thomas M'Kinney, Hospital			
Eliza Dillon, Hospital Matron,	60	0	0	Superintendent, . .	38	0	0
Maria Hitchcock, Work Matron,	55	0	0	James Forde, Warder, .	38	0	0
Mary E. Carey, Court				George Mills, do.	37	0	0
Matron, . . .	50	0	0				
Mary Jane Larkin, School do.	46	0	0	*Non-resident Officers.*			
Eliza Conry, Kitchen Matron,	43	0	0	John M'Manus, Warder, .	38	0	0
Eliza Sullivan, Class Matron,	34	0	0	James C. Carr, do.	37	0	0
Anne Hickey, Class Matron,				James Thayne, do.	37	0	0
at the rate of 1s. per diem				Henry Kelly, Night Watchman,	37	0	0
Jane Redmond, Class Matron,	32	0	0				

Vacancy in the Staff since last inspection, how caused, and how filled up.
John Shea, Apothecary, died, succeeded by Charles Harrison.

Officers on Gaol Allowance.
All intern officers, from the Governor downwards, receive rations of bread, milk,
coals, and soap ; candles to officers who have not the use of gas. 15 Sub-Matrons
are provided with uniform dress.

Visits paid by Officers.

	From 1st Jan. to 31st Dec., 1874.	From 1st Jan., 1875, to day of Inspection.
Number of times the Board of Superin-tendence met and discharged busi-ness, ...	9	10
Local Inspector to Gaol, . .	123	115
Chaplain, Protestant Episcopalian Church, .	157	163
Presbyterian Chaplain, . .	158	161
Roman Catholic Chaplain, : . .	483	454
Physician, ...	158	190
Surgeon, ...	332	275

On this, as on former inspections of this prison, I have to express my
approval of the care and attention evinced by the Governor, Superintendent,
and their assistants, in the performance of their several duties. The
addition of the male wing to this prison has added considerably to
the duties and the responsibilities of the Governor, who has conduced
largely, by his foresight and activity, to the carrying out of all the alterations
and additions consequent on converting a portion of this into a male prison.
Some of the married warders complained to me of what they con-

NORTH DISTRICT.

County of City of Dublin Gaol for Males and Females.

sidered insufficient pay and want of lodging allowance; but pending expected legislation on our entire prison system, I did not feel justified in recommending their claims to the Board. Half of the subordinate staff go out every evening after lock until 10·30, and are fined if they are not in by that hour.

Hospital.

	1872.	1873.	1874.	1875 (to day of Inspection). M. F.
Number of prisoners in hospital,	326	412	361	–
Average daily number in hospital,	15	15	18	–
Number of prisoners prescribed for and treated out of hospital,	4,323	5,997	7,280	651 8,850
Number of deaths,	2	2	1	1 2
Cost of medicine,	£80	£71 6s. 3d.	£80	£77 10s.
Cost of diet, &c., for prisoners in hospital,	£229 3s. 9d.;	£207 4s. 10d.;	£217 4s. 9d.	
Cost of all extra diet ordered by medical officer for prisoners not in hospital,	£18 3s. 3d.;	£25 13s. 0d.;	£28 9s. 2d.	–

Hospital.

The arrangements in the female hospital are the same as at my last inspection in 1873. The regularity, order, and cleanliness of this department reflect much credit on the hospital matron. Sixteen females and 3 males were in the hospital at the time of my visit. In my report on Richmond Bridewell this year, I have pointed out how undesirable it is to order prisoners to hospital, and consequently into association, if they can be treated in their cells equally well; and in my last report on this prison I also observed on this subject; and I would here again impress upon the Medical Officers the importance of not sending any prisoners to hospital except those who are really ailing.

The new hospital for males is properly arranged, the hospital warder being able to see into the ward at night from his room. This ward was clean and well ventilated, and contains ten beds; in addition there are seven cells adjoining used for cases which can be treated in separation. I trust, therefore, that most of those sent to hospital will be thus treated, and if this rule be followed, I have no doubt that the male hospital will not be much frequented.

As I have, in my report on Richmond Bridewell, shown what a want of economy there is in the hospital service of the city prisons, as compared with others in the country, I need not go further into this matter here, but must again enter my protest against the system of divided responsibility of the medical officers attached to the city prisons, who only visit each of the prisons on alternate days, and who, I am informed, have each their separate patients to attend to. In many gaols extra diet is not now considered necessary for prisoners out of hospital, in consequence of the improved dietary scale; but the medical officers here still continue to order it, the cost of which this year came to £39 1s.: in justice however to the physician it is right to state that the extra diet ordered by him only came to £1 8s., the remainder, amounting to £27 13s., having been ordered by the surgeon.

Books.

The clerk, assisted by the chief and hospital warder, keeps most of the books of registry and finance, which are supervised by the Governor, and for the most part are kept with much care and precision. I had, however, to call the attention of the Board to some errors and omissions in the Dietary Book of the female prison, which I have since learned have been looked into and corrected, so that I am in hopes they will not occur again. At present the accounts and expenditure of males and females are kept quite apart and in separate books, which entails an enormous amount of unnecessary labour. Some of the officers also keep separate journals for each prison, which is also unnecessary and inconvenient. I would, therefore, strongly advise the number of such books and accounts to be reduced, as all such labour causes useless expense, and if the forms recommended by the Inspectors-General be properly observed, such errors in the accounts as I have referred to could not occur without gross negligence and want of supervision.

The journals of the Governor and Superintendent are full, and are useful records relating to their several duties and the discipline of the prisons. The Medical Officers' journals are regularly and carefully written up, and the hospital books are kept in accordance with the prescribed forms. The Chaplains also have journals, in which they record the performance of their different duties, and their remarks thereon. I was sorry to learn that through ill health the Protestant Chaplain has not been able to attend to either prison this year, but his duties have been carefully and regularly performed by his curate.

Board of Superintendence.

Alderman Joseph Manning, J.P.	Councillor James Reilly.
Councillor George B. Owens, M.D., J.P.	Alderman John Draper.
Councillor Thomas Fry, J.P.	Councillor Patrick T. Bermingham.
Alderman Sir James W. Mackey, J.P.	Councillor Edward H. Carson, C.E.
Councillor Sir John Barrington, D.L., J.P.	Councillor Peter W. Long, M.D.
Councillor Cornelius Denneby, J.P.	Councillor William Campbell.

The particulars regarding the meetings of the Board are to be seen in my report on Richmond Bridewell.

CHARLES F. BOURKE, *Inspector-General.*

FERMANAGH COUNTY GAOL, AT ENNISKILLEN.—STATUTABLE INSPECTION, 11TH AUGUST, 1875.

State.

Denomination of Class.	No. in each Class.			No. of whom were Sick in Hospital.		
	M.	F.	Total.	M.	F.	Total.
UNTRIED.						
For further Examination,	1	–	1	–	–	–
TRIED.						
Cases disposed of at Assizes and Quarter Sessions.						
Of Felony or Larceny—						
To Imprisonment,	2	–	2	–	–	–
Of Misdemeanors, &c.,	9	–	9	–	–	–
By Court-Martial.						
Military and Naval Offenders,	6	–	6	–	–	–
Disposed of Summarily.						
Offences under Larceny Act,	–	1	1	–	–	–
Non-payment of Fines and Penalties,	2	–	2	–	–	–
Other Misdemeanors,	6	–	6	–	–	–
Under Revenue Laws,	1	–	1	–	–	–
Drunkards,	2	2	4	–	–	–
Total in custody,	29	3	32	–	–	–

The numbers in custody at the above date were 29 males and 3 females. Eleven of whom were cases disposed of at quarter sessions or assizes; 14 were disposed of summarily; 6 were military offenders, and one was untried. At the time of my visit only one juvenile was in charge—

F

a male, being the only prisoner of this class committed here this year; and I am informed by the Governor that since it has been the custom to send juveniles to reformatories, very few have been committed here whose offences were sufficiently grave to be sent to these institutions. Care is taken here, when any juveniles are in custody, to keep them apart from adult prisoners, both while at work and otherwise. I was glad to learn that no debtors had been committed here for the last eighteen months.

Number of Prisoners of all classes in Gaol on the day of Inspection, and on the corresponding date in the three preceding years.

	M.	F.		M.	F.
1872,	17	5	1874.	13	3
1873,	11	6	1875 (day of Inspection),	29	3

Number of Returned Convicts in Gaol on the day of Inspection, and during each of the three preceding years, and the expired portion of 1875.

	M.	F.		M.	F.
1872,	1	2	1875, up to and including		
1873,	-	1	day of Inspection,	1	1
1874,	1	1	Day of Inspection,	1	1

Commitments.

CLASSES.	From 1st January to 31st December, 1874. M.	F.	From 1st January, 1875, to day of Inspection. M.	F.
Criminals,	123	32	85	14
Vagrants,	1	-	11	2
Drunkards,	77	31	41	19
Total,	201	63	137	35

At the above date the male prisoners were more numerous than they had been for some years, on the day of inspection, which I was informed was owing to the great increase in drunkenness, riots, and party factions. As drunkenness is certainly on the increase throughout the whole country, I would strongly recommend that it be treated invariably with the utmost severity, as it is the cause of the greater part of the crime in Ireland; and, without it, most of our gaols would be, comparatively speaking, empty. The total number of committuents in 1874 was 201 of males and 63 of females, against 137 of the former and 35 of the latter previously to my visit in 1875.

Number of Individual Prisoners (exclusive of Debtors) and number of times each had been Committed during the following periods, distinguishing Adults from Juveniles.

NUMBER OF TIMES COMMITTED.	1874. Juveniles. M.	F.	Adults. M.	F.	1875, to day of Inspection. Juveniles. M.	F.	Adults. M.	F.
Once within the year,	3	2	129	41	1	-	94	18
Twice "	-	-	17	5	-	-	7	2
Thrice "	-	-	5	1	-	-	4	3
Four times "	-	-	2	-	-	-	4	1
Six " "	-	-	2	-	-	-	-	-
Seven " "	-	-	-	1	-	-	-	-
Total,	3	2	155	48	1	-	109	24
No. of above who had not been in Gaol previous to 1st Jan. in	3	2	116	22	1	-	81	16

Number of Individual Prisoners, exclusive of Debtors, committed in the year **North**
1874, and to the day of Inspection in 1875, who had been once and **District.**
oftener committed from their first Commitment in any year, so far as can **Fermanagh**
be ascertained. **County Gaol.**

NUMBER OF TIMES COMMITTED.	1874.				1875, to day of Inspection.			
	Juveniles.		Adults.		Juveniles.		Adults.	
	M.	F.	M.	F.	M.	F.	M.	F.
Once only, ...	3	2	110	19	1	—	78	13
Twice, ...	—	—	5	7	—	—	7	2
Thrice, ...	—	—	9	6	—	—	5	1
Four times, ...	—	—	8	3	—	—	2	2
Five „	—	—	5	4	—	—	4	—
Six „	—	—	3	2	—	—	2	3
7 to 11 times, . . .	—	—	12	4	—	—	6	1
12 to 16 „ . . .	—	—	3	2	—	—	2	1
17 to 20 „ . . .	—	—	1	—	—	—	1	—
21 to 30 „ . . .	—	—	2	1	—	—	—	1
41 to 50 „ . . .	—	—	1	—	—	—	1	—
131 to 140 „ . . .	—	—	1	—	—	—	1	—
Total No. of individuals committed,	3	2	155	48	1	—	109	24
No. of commitments represented in foregoing, . . .	3	2	586	183	1	—	421	95

Averages, and Highest and Lowest Numbers (exclusive of Debtors).

—	From 1st January to 31st December, 1874.			From 1st January, 1875, to day of inspection.		
	M.	F.	Date.	M.	F.	Date.
Average daily number of prisoners in custody,	18	4	—	21	4	—
Highest number of prisoners at any one time,	33		12th April.	37		4th July.
Lowest ditto.	12		20th July.	14		14th Jan.
Highest number of males at any one time, .	27		4th May.	30		12th May.
Ditto, of females,	10		15th Nov.	9		15th July.
Lowest number of males at any one time, .	9		20th July.	10		14th Jan.
Ditto, of females,	1		24th June.	—		3rd May.

*Highest number of Prisoners (exclusive of Debtors) in Gaol during each
of the previous seven years, and up to day of Inspection in 1875.*

28th January, 1868,	.	. 33	5th June, 1872,	. .	. 36
14th October, 1869,	.	. 28	4th March, 1873,	. .	. 53
2nd July, 1870,	.	. 27	12th April, 1874,	. .	. 33 .
1st May, 1871,	.	. 32	4th July, 1875,	. .	. 37

Up to the time of my visit four was the greatest number of times that **Re-commit-**
any individual was committed to this prison this year, and seven during **ments.**
the whole of last year; but during both years one individual—a male
—was in custody here who had been over 121 times in gaol since his
first commitment; and females had been in this prison in both years
who had been over twenty times in gaol. As compared with other
districts, this, however, does not represent a very large number of re-
commitments of females. Indeed, the female class who become amenable
to justice in this county are, comparatively speaking, few. The

F 2

NORTH DISTRICT.

Fermanagh County Gaol.

total number of adult individuals committed in 1874 was 155 of males and 48 of females, who were known to have been in gaol 586 and 183 times respectively ; but of these 116 males and 22 females had not previously been known to have been in gaol. In the expired portion of 1875, 109 adult individual males and 24 adult individual females were committed here. These had as many as 421 and 95 re-commitments respectively registered against them ; but when one finds that 81 males and 16 females of these had not previously been in gaol, it will be seen that crime in this district is confined to comparatively few individuals. The daily average this year of males was higher by three than last, but the daily average number of females in custody was the same in both years. At one period in 1875 there was no female in custody here at all, while at a certain period in 1874 only one was in charge, and at no period in either years was the number of females in custody higher than ten.

Accommodation.

	M.	F.		M.	F.
Wards,	7	2	Worksheds,	20	–
Yards,	5	3	Kitchen,	1	–
Day Rooms,	3	1	Store Rooms,	3	1
Solitary Cells,	1	1	Laundry,	–	1
Single Cells, 9 feet long, 6 feet wide, and 8 feet high, or which contain 432 cubic feet,	66	36	Drying Room,	–	1
			Lavatory,	–	1
Ditto, heated and furnished with bells,	66	36	Baths, with hot and cold water laid on,	4	2
Sleeping Rooms,	5	2	Privies,	6	2
No. of Beds in such Rooms,	5	2	Water-closets,	14	2
Hospital Rooms,	4	4	Fumigating Apparatus,	1	1
Chapel,	One.		Reception Rooms or Cells,	1	1
Workshop,	1	–	Pumps,	2	–
			Tell-tale Clock,	One	

Reception.

Since my last visit some cells have been very properly set apart in the female prison for a probationary ward, but the old female reception cells at the gateway are still made use of in the day time, where the prisoners of that sex are bathed before they are brought into the prison. The male reception ward is also at the gateway, and the arrangements here are the same as at my last visit. I found a man here who had been in custody more than two days, and who should have been sooner passed into his proper ward by the Medical Officer. This man complained to me that four days ago he had asked to see the doctor, but had not succeeded in doing so up to the time of my visit. I am of opinion that such matters as these should be more promptly attended to by this officer, as he is bound under the 72nd section of the Prisons Act to visit the prison twice at least in every week, and oftener if necessary ; and also under the 20th rule of the 109th section of the Prisons Act the Medical Officer is required to examine every prisoner who is brought into the prison, before he or she

Baths.

shall have been passed into the proper ward. Since my last visit a bath has been put up in the male prison, and all prisoners are now washed as they come in, but no fixed time is arranged for subsequently bathing them during imprisonment. I submit that this should be done at least once a week, as it is impossible to keep the bedding and clothing clean otherwise. Tin basins are now supplied to all the cells, but at the time of my visit no

Water.

stands were provided for them in the cells for females. There is an ample supply of water-closets in the male prison, but as I stated in my last report there is not a sufficient number in the female prison. Since my last inspection two new cisterns have been put up, at a cost of £100, and there is an abundance of water now in the prison, which is

obtained from the town main. The sewerage is said to be effective, and
is emptied into the lake. The heating of the male prison has been improved since my last visit, and all the cells there are provided with bells, but
the heating of the female prison is still defective. However, there are a
certain number of the cells close to the heating apparatus which are
warmed and are generally sufficient for the numbers in custody. The
laundry and drying-room have undergone no alteration since my last
visit. Only the prison washing is done here, together with the sheets
and blankets for the officers. As nothing has been yet done to improve
the chapel, I have merely to refer to the suggestions made by my
colleagues and myself on this subject for many years in our reports. Two
fumigators are provided, which were in good order at the time of my
inspection. As gas has not yet been introduced into the cells, labour
cannot of course be carried on here after dark in the winter; but now
that other parts of the gaol is lighted by gas, I would again strongly
recommend that it be made use of in the cells, in order that industrial
labour may be properly pursued. The kitchen arrangements have not
been altered since my last visit, except that I am informed the prisoner
employed here is now required to break some stones in addition to his
work in the kitchen. But this labour is not performed regularly. I would,
therefore, again recommend that the culinary department be removed into
the female prison, as the time of a male prisoner should then be more
profitably employed throughout the entire year. The photography is
done by the schoolmaster, and seems efficiently carried on. Copies
of all persons photographed are kept in a book, attached to which
there is a duplicate of the Form sent to the Habitual Criminals Office,
and the Governor appears careful to photograph old offenders for the
purpose of detection. As already stated in former reports, the arrangements here for visitors to prisoners are by no means good. I
would therefore again recommend that the rules existing on this subject
in Londonderry and other such well-managed gaols be here adopted, and
also that a visiting place be fitted, such as exists in that prison, so as to
prevent any prohibited articles being introduced. When certain restrictions exist with regard to the visitors, as well as in the privilege of
being allowed to receive and write letters, the conduct of prisoners is
very much influenced by such rules, for if constant frequenters of gaols are
permitted to receive visits and to write letters to their own friends constantly,
the inconvenience of imprisonment will have very little effect upon them.
One man complained to me of having been permitted to write only three
letters in seven months, whereas, by the by-laws, it appears that he is
entitled to do so once a month. But, as there was no proper registry kept
of the letters written, I was unable to ascertain whether his statements
were true. A telltale clock is provided, and marked half-hourly from 9
P.M. to 6 A.M. Five turnkeys in rotation perform the duties of the night
watch. The markings of the clock are taken by the Governor every
morning, and are entered in the Morning State Book and in his journal,
and all omissions are recorded in the Officers' Conduct Book against
the defaulting officer. In addition there is a book kept purposely
for recording the markings of the clock, which is laid before the
Board of Superintendence at their meetings. Besides which, the
Governor has visited the gaol during the year 54 times at late and
unexpected hours during the night. Lock-up takes place in summer at 6
P.M., and in winter at dusk. Unlock in summer is at 6 A.M., and at 7
o'clock in winter. At 10 P.M. all the keys of the prison are taken by
the Governor to his bedroom, and are kept there during the night. The
locks of the prison are reported to be in a satisfactory condition.

NORTH
DISTRICT.

*Fermanagh
County
Gaol.*

Stock at the time of Inspection.

	In Use.	In Store.	Male Clothing.	In Use.	In Store.	Female Clothing.	In Use.	In Store.
Blankets, pairs of,	75	19	Shirts,	56	15	Shifts,	10	31
Sheets, pairs of,	91	35	Jackets,	25	18	Jackets,	5	16
Rugs,	65	13	Vests,	25	4	Gowns,	6	12
Bed-ticks,	69	10	Trowsers,	24	19	Petticoats,	8	13
Bedsteads,	120	—	Caps,	24	5	Aprons,	7	9
			Stockings or Socks,			Neckerchiefs,	6	11
			pairs of,	36	9	Caps,	7	5
			Shoes, Slippers, &			Stockings, pairs	6	5
			Clogs, pairs of,	25	13	Shoes, Slippers, &		
						Clogs, pairs of,	3	6

Store.

The general store of male clothing is kept by the Governor, who issues a certain number of articles of male apparel to one of the warders. All prisoners sentenced to longer periods than one month are given a new suit of clothes. The stock in store was sufficient and abundant for the requirements of the prison. Stock of all prison property is taken by the Governor quarterly, and I am informed that the Local Inspector performs this duty twice a year. The female clothing is kept by the matron, who is responsible to the Governor for all in her charge. The prisoners' own clothing is all fumigated before it is put away, but it is not properly labelled. Each bundle should have attached to it a label such as is now in use in other gaols, enumerating all articles the property of a prisoner, which label should be signed by the store-keeper as having received the property, and also by the prisoner on leaving the gaol as having had the articles returned to him; so that no difficulty can arise under this system in case a prisoner may claim from the Governor more property than he brought into prison with him. All the bedding was clean, and in good repair, and I was glad to find that sheets are, as a rule, changed every Saturday, and that all prisoners now, on being committed receive a clean pair.

Number of Punishments for Prison Offences.

	From 1st January to 31st December, 1874.		From 1st January, 1875, to day of Inspection.	
	M.	F.	M.	F.
By Magisterial authority,	—	—	1	—
By Governor—				
Dark or Refractory Cells,	19	1	3	—
Total,	19	1	4	—

Punishments.

One solitary cell is provided in each prison—that for the males being heated and boarded. Prisoners of this sex are left in solitary during the night-time, but are given their bedding—a privilege which, I submit, should not be permitted to prisoners undergoing punishment, as it is not allowed to prisoners in solitary either in the army or navy. On one occasion this year it was found necessary to have recourse to magisterial authority for the punishment of an obstreperous male prisoner, but up to the time of my visit this year no female and only three males had been sentenced to solitary.

Schools.

	From 1st Jan. to 31st Dec., 1874.		From 1st Jan., 1875, to day of Inspection.	
	M.	F.	M.	F.
Number of individual prisoners who attended school,	121	38	83	14
Average daily number of pupils,	12	3	15	1
Number of days on which school was held,	313	313	191	191

School-hours.—Males—From 9.30 to 11, A.M.   Females—From 11 to 12, A.M.

The school for males is held for an hour and a-half daily, and for females for an hour. The former are now instructed by the schoolmaster and turnkeys in the hall of the male prison. All who are willing and who are capable of learning are sent to school. The schoolmaster warder also instructs the females, in the presence of the matron. This officer is a trained teacher, but I regret to state that the school is not in connexion with any educational body, nor is it properly inspected by the chaplains, although the by-laws direct those officers to inspect the school on each occasion of their visit to the gaol; yet I could only find that this duty is performed by the Presbyterian Chaplain three times during the year up to the date of my visit, and there is no record in the school registry of any other visit of the chaplains to the school during 1875. This is a matter that I have referred to in former reports, but which I regret to say has not yet induced these gentlemen to perform this simple duty in accordance with the rules of the prison.

NORTH DISTRICT.

Fermanagh County Gaol.

School.

Employment on day of Inspection.

	M.	F.			M.	F.
Hard Labour,	22	–	Prison duties,		2	1
Industrial Labour,	3	2				
Unemployed,	2	–	Total in custody,		29	3

Amount received for produce of Prisoners' Labour disposed of outside the Gaol for the last three years.

1872, . £18 12s. 1d. | 1873, £25 19s. 10d. | 1874, . £26 7s. 9d.

Net average daily cost of Ordinary Diet for each Prisoner in the three preceding years.

1872, . 4·5d. | 1873, . 5·6d. | 1874, . 6d.

Net cost of Gaol, including Diet and Salaries for the three preceding years.

1872, . £1,090 12s. 4d. | 1873, . £1,146 0s. 5d. | 1874, . £1,172 19s. 10d.

Total cost of Officers, including Clothing, value of Rations, Washing, Gas, &c

1872, . £735 9s. 10d. | 1873, . £728 14s. 6d. | 1874, . £724 2s. 1d.

Average cost of each Prisoner per annum in each of the last three years.

1872, . £51 16s. 0d. | 1873, . £53 6s. 0d. | 1874, . £53 6s. 4d.

Amounts repaid by the War Department for Military Prisoners in each of last three years.

1872, — | 1873, . £18 0s. 0d. | 1874, . £11 17s. 0d.

Amounts repaid from the Consolidated Fund for the Maintenance, &c., of Prisoners during the years

1872, . £65 4s. 7d. | 1873, . £51 1s. 3d. | 1874, . £55 5s. 10d.

The hardest labour carried on here for males is stone-breaking, eight separate sheds being provided for that purpose in one yard, but as no specified task is exacted or any difference made in the labour performed by prisoners sentenced or not sentenced to hard labour it cannot be considered that the law in regard to hard labour is carried out here. Little or no industrial labour is performed by any of the prisoners in their cells, as no oakum-picking is done, nor is any such remunerative employment followed as is now pursued in all well-managed gaols. Prisoners are, consequently, for a great number of hours during the twenty-four unemployed and idle. The result is that the amount received as the produce of prisoners' labour here is not as much as half the average annual

Labour.

Expenditure.

NORTH DISTRICT.

Fermanagh County Gaol.

cost of a prisoner. In 1874 the results derived from prisoners' labour disposed of outside the gaol was only £26 7s. 9d., whereas the average annual cost of a prisoner here in that year was £53 6s. 2d. The net cost of the gaol during that year was £1,172 19s. 10d., but of that sum the cost of officers amounted to £724 2s. 11d. Having regard to the requirements of the gaol as at present circumstanced, and to the difficulty of supervision here, I do not now recommend any reduction in the staff, especially as I have every hope that Parliament will this year deal with the whole of our prison system in Ireland.

Contracts.

Bread, white, per 4-lb. loaf, 6d.; oatmeal, per cwt., 12s. 10½d.; new-milk, per gallon, 1s.; butter-milk, per gallon, 4d.; coal, per ton, £1 2s. 4d.; gas, per 1,000 cubic feet, 7s. 6d.; candles, per lb., 5½d.; soap, per cwt., £1 9s. 10d.; calico, per yard, 6d.; frieze, per yard, 3s. 6d.; turpentine, per gal., 4s.; prepared oil, per gal., 3s. 2d.

Provisions.

The contracts of provisions and materials are all laid before the Board and are sanctioned by them yearly. The Governor serves out the meal daily, and the Deputy Governor keeps the store of bread and milk. The samples of the provisions that I saw were excellent and are generally reported on favourably by the chaplains, one prisoner, however, complained to me of the milk being frequently sour, but I was unable to find out whether such was the case. The chaplains inspect the provisions by alternate weeks, the Roman Catholic and Protestant Episcopalian chiefly by deputy, not legally appointed. I therefore submit that as these gentlemen have no legal status in the gaol they cannot properly perform the duties of chaplain. This is a matter that I have previously laid before the Board of Superintendence, and which I regret has not yet been corrected. It is, though, only fair to remark that the Presbyterian Chaplain is most careful to perform his duties according to the requirements of the statute.

Officers and Salaries.

	£	s.	d.		£	s.	d.
Non-Resident.				Joseph Masterson, Warder, Cooper,	42	0	0
Samuel Clarke, esq., Local Inspector,	90	0	0	Robt. Patterson, Schoolmaster, Warder,	89	4	0
Rev. Samuel Grear, Protestant Chaplain,	30	0	0	John Gough,	34	4	0
Rev. A. C. Maclatchy, Presbyterian Chaplain,	30	0	0	Edward Armstrong,	34	4	0
Very Rev. James M'Meel, Roman Catholic Chaplain,	30	0	0	John Moore,	29	0	0
				Matilda Beacom, Matron,	35	0	0
Resident.				Catherine Granlieze, Hospital Nurse,	28	16	0
James Jeffers, Governor,	200	0	0				

Vacancies in the Staff since last Inspection, how caused, and how filled up.

Hamilton Morrison, Deputy-Governor, superannuated; Benjamin Robinson appointed Turnkey; Benjamin Robinson, Turnkey, resigned, and was succeeded by John Moore.

Visits paid by Officers.

	From 1st Jan. to 31st Dec., 1874.	From 1st Jan., 1875, to day of Inspection.
Number of times the Board of Superintendence met and discharged business,	11	6
Local Inspector to Gaol,	125	80
Do. to each Bridewell,	4	—
Chaplain, Protestant Episcopal Church,	263	160
,, Presbyterian,	203	131
,, Roman Catholic,	215	129
Physician, Surgeon, Apothecary,	107	75

Officers.

No improvement has been made since my last visit as to the officers quarters. They all sleep within the gaol, but their rooms are situated in different parts of the male prison, which is very objectionable, as it should not be possible for any officer to have access to prisoners except when on duty. I therefore submit that provision should be made elsewhere than in the prison for the male officers, and that a suitable mess-room be provided for their use. Their quarters were on the day of my visit fairly tidy, but not as well kept as they should be. These rooms should be constantly inspected by the Local Inspector and Governor, and the subordinate officers should be required to keep their rooms as tidy and clean as are those of the prisoners, but as the warders are obliged to take their meals in these rooms, it could hardly be expected that they should be as well kept as if they were provided with a mess-room.

Hospital.

	1872.		1873.		1874.		1875 (to day of Inspection).	
	M.	F.	M.	F.	M.	F.	M.	F.
No. of prisoners in hospital,	8	2	5	3	5	4	4	1
Average daily number in hospital, . . .	·8	·04	·5	·8	·2	·4	·3 .	·06
Number of prisoners pre-scribed for and treated out of hospital, . .	14	3	.18	8	18	7	9	5
Cost of medicine, . .	£3 3s. 7d.		£3 0s. 2d.		£3 3s. 1d.		—	
Cost of diet for prisoners in hospital, . . .	£1 6s. 3d.		£5 18s. 7d.		£6 14s. 4d.		—	
Cost of all extra diet ordered by Medical Officer for pri-soners not in hospital, .	£0 19s. 6d.		—		£0 17s. 7d.		—	

No alteration has taken place in the hospital since my last inspection. There is ample accommodation here for many more invalids than are usually found in this prison. The wards are still kept on the upper story —an inconvenient arrangement which I have already pointed out in former reports. The whole of this building was very much in need of paint-ing, but as some painting had lately been done in the prison, I am in hopes that the Governor will take an early opportunity of employing a prisoner to paint the wood-work of the hospital. The medicines are pro-cured from the County Infirmary, by which means they are obtained at much less cost than in a great number of other gaols.

The registries and books of finance are kept by the Governor and the schoolmaster-warder, and all are also supervised and checked by the former. I am informed that the Local Inspector also looks over them from time to time. The journal of this officer is very meagre. As he is the principal officer of the gaol and should duly enter in his journal all the principal events occurring therein. The journal of the Episcopalian Chaplain is better kept than that of the Roman Catholic Chaplain, but as this latter officer seldom does his own duty the remarks in his journal are almost useless. As I have already remarked, the Presbyterian Chaplain performs his own duty in person, and writes a regular journal, but as he seldom has any prisoners of his persuasion in the gaol his religious duties are not onerous. The journal of the Governor is fuller than those of any of the other officers, and is regularly written up, but it contains very few matters of importance or interest. However, this officer is most attentive to his duties, and displays much zeal and diligence in the public service. He also deserves every credit for the clean and orderly condition of the entire prison. The Medical Officer's journal should, I submit, contain much more information regarding his duty, having regard to the requirements of the statute relating to this subject.

Hospital.

Books.

NORTH DISTRICT.

Fermanagh County Gaol.

Board.

Bridewell.

Board of Superintendence.

Lord Belmore.	Lieut.-Col. J. G. Irvine.	Colonel Archdale.
Robert Archdall, esq.	John Brady, esq.	Capt. J. A. M. Richardson.
Maurice C. Maude, esq.	John A. Wood, esq.	Edward Smyth, esq.
Matthew H. Sankey, esq.	John A. Pomeroy, esq.	John G. V. Porter, esq.

The Board meets on the first Thursday of the month, on which occasion the salaries of the subordinate officers and small accounts are paid, the Governor receiving a cheque for the amount, for which he produces receipts at the following meeting. The salaries of the superior officers and the contractors' accounts are settled half-yearly at assizes, at which time the committee of the grand jury look over the accounts of the gaol. I annex my report on the bridewell of Newtownbutler, to which I would draw the serious attention of the Board. On my visit on the 10th of May I found it in a most disorderly state. The registry was not written up, although only 3 prisoners had been committed there up to that time during this year, and the keeper was unable to inform me on what day one of these prisoners were released, and, as far as I could find there was no legal authority for releasing this prisoner. I visited this bridewell again in August, and found it much in the same condition as at my previous visit. Under these circumstances I must again submit that it be closed, and if steps are not taken in this direction at the next assizes, I shall feel it to be my duty to recommend the Lord Lieutenant to exercise the peremptory power vested in him of closing this bridewell. I find that the legally-prescribed dietary form is not carried out in this bridewell. This is a matter that the Local Inspector should attend to.

STATE OF NEWTOWNBUTLER BRIDEWELL.

	M.	F.
No. of Committals in past year, .	3	–
Of whom were Drunkards, . .	3	–
No. of Committals in the quarter preceding inspection, . .	2	–
Of whom were Drunkards, . .	1	–

Petty Sessions and Transmittals, .	Fortnightly. Transmittals sometimes not till following day.
Committals, whether regular, .	Only 3 this year; regular, but are badly drawn.
Registry, . . .	Badly kept. One of the three committals not fully entered; and no authority for the dismissal of the prisoner before his time, which was done, I am informed.
Repairs, ...	Bad, and untidy.
Security, . . :	Fair, with care, except yards.
Accommodation, . .	2 cells for females, and 3 for males; 2 day-rooms very untidy.
Furniture, Bedding, and Utensils, .	Bedding badly kept, but sufficient.
Water, how supplied, . .	By pumps—in repair.
Sewerage, . . .	Only cesspools.
Cleanliness, Dryness, and Ventilation, .	Well ventilated, but cells dirty.
Cost of Dietary, . . .	6d. per day; but dietary scale not followed.
Salary of Keeper, and whether he follows any other employment.	£20; is allowed fuel and light; is Courthouse-keeper and Petty Sessions Clerk.
Date of Inspection, . .	May 17, 1875.
Remarks, . . .	No prisoners in custody. This Bridewell should be closed. I paid another visit to it in August and found it in quite as great a state of disorder as at my previous visit.

CHARLES F. BOURKE, *Inspector-General.*

ᴄ

LEITRIM COUNTY GAOL, AT CARRICK-ON-SHANNON—STATUTABLE
INSPECTION, 5TH MAY, 1875.

Sixteen males and 5 females was the total number of prisoners in this gaol at the above date. Six were cases disposed of at quarter sessions and assizes, 2 were untried, 1 was a military prisoner, and the remainder were summary convictions. No juvenile was in custody at the time of my visit, and only two had been committed previously this year. I was informed that care was taken to keep this class of prisoner separate from adults, and all have hitherto been sent to the school. But I recommend in future that those sentenced to reformateries should be kept altogether in punishment, and not permitted the indulgence of school during the short periods of their imprisonments previous to their being sent to one of these institutions, as it is most desirable that their sojourn in prison should be made as irksome to them as possible.

Number of prisoners of all classes in gaol on the day of inspection, and on the corresponding date in the three preceding years.

	M.	F.		M.	F.
1872, ...	12	3	1874, ...	15	3
1873, ...	11	2	1875 (day of inspection),	16	5

Commitments.

CLASSES.						From 1st January to 31st Dec., 1874.		From 1st Jan., 1875, to day of Inspection.	
						M.	F.	M.	F.
Debtors,	.	.	.	.	.	2	–	–	–
Criminals,	.	.	.	.	.	139	22	74	10
Vagrants,	.	.	.	.	.	3	–	1	–
Drunkards,	.	.	.	.	.	26	18	18	8
Total,		.	.	.	.	170	40	93	18

Up to the time of my inspection this year the number of commitments was 93 of males and of 83 females, against 170 of the former and 40 of the latter during the whole of the previous year. No debtor was in custody during 1875, and only 2 during the previous year, so that part of their quarters have now been given up to the Deputy Governor, part turned into a photography-room, and part into a store-room. There is also one of these rooms used as a reception class for males. Having regard to the time my inspection was made this year, and to the numbers in the preceding table, I am greatly afraid that at the close of the year the number of commitments will be in excess of those of last year.

Number of Individual Prisoners (exclusive of Debtors), and Number of Times each had been Committed during the following periods, distinguishing Adults from Juveniles.

NUMBER OF TIMES COMMITTED.	1874.				1875, to day of Inspection.			
	Juveniles.		Adults.		Juveniles.		Adults.	
	M.	F.	M.	F.	M.	F.	M.	F.
Once within the year,	3	1	134	27	2	–	69	11
Twice ,,	1	–	8	3	–	–	9	1
Thrice ,,	–	–	3	2	–	–	–	–
4 times ,,	–	–	1	–	–	–	1	–
5 ,, ,,	–	–	–	–	–	–	–	1
Total,	4	1	146	32	2	–	79	13
No. of above who had not been in Gaol previous to 1st Jan. in .	3	1	116	22	2	–	62	6

Number of Individual Prisoners (exclusive of Debtors) committed in the year 1874, and to the day of Inspection in 1875, who had been Once, Twice, Thrice, Four Times, Five Times, &c., &c., from their first Commitment in any year, so far as can be ascertained, distinguishing Adults from Juveniles.

NUMBER OF TIMES COMMITTED.	1874.				1875, to day of Inspection.			
	Juveniles.		Adults.		Juveniles.		Adults.	
	M.	F.	M.	F.	M.	F.	M.	F.
Once only, .	3	1	108	21	2	–	54	6
Twice,	–	–	19	3	–	–	18	1
Thrice,	1	–	10	2	–	–	2	–
4 times,	–	–	1	2	–	–	3	–
5 ,,	–	–	5	–	–	–	–	1
6 ,,	–	–	–	–	–	–	1	–
7 to 11 ,,	–	–	2	2	–	–	1	3
12 to 16 ,,	–	–	..	2	–	–	–	2
17 to 20 ,,	–	–	1	–	–	–	.–	–
Total No. of Individuals committed,	4	1	146	32	2	–	79	13
No. of commitments represented in foregoing, .	6	1	239	83	2	–	122	64

Averages, and Highest and Lowest Numbers (exclusive of Debtors).

—	From 1st January to 31st December, 1874.			From 1st January, 1875, to day of Inspection.		
	M.	F.	Date.	M.	F.	Date.
Average daily number of prisoners in custody,	14	3	—	21·26	4·93	—
Highest number of prisoners at any one time,	30		15th Nov.	37		24th Jan.
Lowest ditto, .	10		9th April.	15		1st Jan.
Highest number of males at any one time, .	24		15th Nov.	31		23rd Jan.
Ditto, of females,	7		28th June.	7		24th Jan.
Lowest number of males at any one time, .	8		9th April.	11		1st Jan.
Ditto, of females,	1		25th March.	3		24th Feb.

Highest number of prisoners (exclusive of debtors) in gaol during each of the previous seven years, and up to day of Inspection in 1875.

17th January, 1868,	.	.	44	28th November, 1872,	.	.	31
25th October, 1869,	.	.	25	21st November, 1873,	.	.	38
4th March, 1870, .	.	.	67	15th November, 1874,	.	.	30
28th February, 1871,	.	.	28	24th January, 1875,	.	.	37

Four was the greatest number of times that any person was committed to this gaol in 1874, but even up to the time of my visit this year 1 individual had been committed as often as five times. However, the previous tables do not denote any very great perversity in crime in this district, for it will be observed that from 17 to 20 was the greatest number of commitments recorded against any individual imprisoned here during the last two years from their first offence. The total number of adult individuals committed in 1874 was 146 males and 32 females, and the commitments recorded against these since their first offence numbered respectively 239 and 83; but when one considers that 116 of those males and 22 of these females had not previously been in gaol it will be seen that crime in this district is confined to a very few individuals. In 1875, up to the time of my visit, 79 adult males and 13 adult females were committed here whose previous convictions numbered respectively 122 and 64, but 62 of these males and 6 of the females had not previously been in gaol. The daily average number in custody this year, both of males and females, was, I regret to say, in excess of last; and at one period in 1875 there was a greater number of prisoners in custody than at any time during the last five years. *Re-committments.*

Accommodation.

	M.	F.		M.	F.
Wards, . . .	5	3	Kitchen, . . .	1	—
Yards, . . .	9	5	Store Rooms, . .	2	2
Day Rooms, . .	13	3	Laundries, . . .	—	2
Solitary Cells, . .	5	2	Lavatories, . . .	1	1
Single Cells, 9 feet long, 6 feet wide, 8 feet high=432 cubic feet. . .	58	19	Bath, with Hot and Cold Water laid on, . .	1	2
Cells to contain 3 persons, .	—	2	Privies, . . .	17	4
Sleeping Rooms, . .	7	—	Water-closet, . .	1	—
No. of Beds in such Rooms,	12	—	Fumigating Apparatus, .	1	—
Hospital Rooms, . .	5	3	Reception Rooms or Cells, .	1	1
Chapel, . . .	1	—	Pump, . . .	1	—
School Rooms, . .	1	1	Well, . . .	1	—
Workshops, . .	2	—	Tread-wheel, . .	1	—
Worksheds, . .	22	—	Crank Mill (Flax Mill), .	1	—
			Tell-tale Clock, . .	1	—

One room in each prison is now reserved for reception class, in which prisoners are kept during the daytime until seen by the Doctor, but no cells are yet set apart for that class, so that in case the Doctor does not visit the prison in the daytime prisoners are necessarily sent to the ordinary cells at night. This is a matter referred to in former reports, and is in contravention of the 20th rule of the 109th section of the Prisons Act. A bath is now provided for both male and female prisoners, with water laid on; but in summer the male prisoners are washed in the old flagged bath, which is very unsuitable for this purpose. I therefore submit that they should be washed in warm water as they come in, for unless such precautions are taken it is impossible that they can be properly cleansed. All prisoners are, I am informed, now required to take a bath once a week during imprisonment. One lavatory is placed in the yard of each prison. As there is abundant room for these requirements in the old day-rooms, I submit that they be removed there pend- *Reception.*

Baths.

NORTH DISTRICT.

Leitrim County Gaol.

Water and sewerage.

Gas and heating.

Kitchen.
Chapel.
Laundry.

Fumigator.

Photography.

Night watch.

Visitors.

Improvements required.

ing better arrangements. The water is procured from the Shannon, and is pumped by the tread-wheel into the cisterns in the same manner as at my last visit. The sewerage is reported to be effective, and runs off into the river, but the only means of flushing the sewers is by buckets. There are no water-closets in the prison, but privies were provided in all the yards, and five effluvia traps have lately been placed in the sewers. None of the cells as yet have been artificially heated or provided with gas, nor are there bells attached, but cards descriptive of prisoners and their crimes have now been attached to all the doors. The floors of all the cells are bricked, but at the time of my visit some were much broken and required mending. No alteration has been made as to the kitchen, chapel, or laundry since my last visit. The sexes are properly separated in the chapel, and it is otherwise suitably arranged for divine service. The laundry has not yet been stalled, nor is hot water laid on to the washing troughs. The cooking is still carried on by means of one small fire, the large boilers not being required for the few prisoners usually in custody. Every prisoner's portion is weighed or measured before being served out, and the dinners are usually inspected by the Governor. Only one fumigating apparatus is provided, which was not in good repair at the time of my visit. I was informed that all clothing is, as a rule, fumigated before being put away ; but as that belonging to prisoners whose sentence does not exceed a month is not subjected to this operation, and as it is sometimes in a very filthy condition, I would recommend that this clothing also be carefully fumigated. Photography is performed by the Deputy Governor, who takes excellent likenesses, and is careful to photograph not only those prisoners required to be photographed under the Crimes Prevention Act but also all prisoners for trial who are suspected to be old offenders ; and it frequently occurs that former convictions are obtained against prisoners committed here by means of this art. Since my last visit I am glad to find that the tell-tale clock has been removed from the guard-room to the cook-house, by which means the night patrol is compelled to perform more lengthy circuits of the gaol than heretofore. The clock is marked hourly from dark to daylight, and is examined by the Deputy Governor every morning. Its condition is noted in the Morning State Book and in the Governor's journal, and all omissions of duty on the part of the night-watchman are recorded against him in the Officers' Conduct Book, as suggested in previous reports. Unlock takes place in summer at 6 A.M. and in winter at daylight, and prisoners are locked up at 6 P.M. all the year round. The Governor, I am informed, takes all the keys of the prison to his bedroom at 10 o'clock at night. Prisoners are permitted to see their friends through a trap at the gate with a turnkey at each side. Convicted prisoners may receive a visit once a month by order of the Local Inspector or members of the Board of Superintendence, the untried twice a week, and debtors daily. Although some of the suggestions of Inspectors-General have been carried out yet there are still many improvements required. At the time of my visit the prison garden was very much out of order; and although some painting had been lately performed a good deal more was required to be done. I am informed that a great number of holydays are kept in this prison, during which time the prisoners are allowed to remain in association in the day-room in utter idleness. This is a subject to which I would draw the attention of the Board, as it is highly objectionable that such a state of things should be permitted ; and I would therefore recommend that the holydays be more limited, and that on those days prisoners should be kept altogether in their cells except during the time allowed for exercise, which should be performed in a ring in one of the yards in the presence of an officer. As the cells

are not heated, prisoners, during the winter months, might be allowed, NORTH
one at a time, to the fire in the day-rooms. DISTRICT.

Leitrim
County
Gaol.

Stock at the time of Inspection.

	In Use.	In Store.	Male Clothing.	In Use.	In Store.	Female Clothing.	In Use.	In Store.
Blankets, pairs of,	84	–	Shirts,	63	12	Shifts,	10	23
Sheets, pairs of,	100	22	Jackets,	24	16	Jackets,	9	33
Rugs,	72	4	Vests,	22	19	Petticoats,	17	7
Hammocks or Cots,	1	6	Trowsers,	23	36	Aprons,	5	9
Bed-ticks,	102	8	Caps,	17	21	Neckerchiefs,	4	6
Bedsteads,	131	12	Shoes, Slippers, &			Stockings, pairs of,	8	–
			Clogs, pairs of,	17	45	Shoes, Slippers, &		
						Clogs, pairs of,	2	10

The general store of male clothing is kept by the Deputy Governor, Store.
and that for females by the Matron, but the male clothing in use is kept
by one of the warders, who is responsible to the Deputy Governor
for it, and who superintends the dressing of the prisoners of that sex.
The male prisoners' own private clothing is labelled before it is put
away, that for females is not. I was, however, informed that in future
care would be taken to carry out the same rule in the female as in the
male prison in this regard. Stock is taken by the Governor and Local
Inspector twice a year. At the time of my visit some few pairs of stockings were in use for females, but no socks had up to that time been
provided for male prisoners—an omission to which attention has been
called in former reports. The bedding throughout the prison was, as a
rule, clean, and the supply sufficient. The sheets are changed fortnightly, but prisoners when they come in are not given a clean pair. I
observed that some of the male clothing in use was by no means so clean
or in as good repair as it should have been. These are matters which,
I submit, the Governor should pay greater attention to. All the clothing
used in the gaol is made up by prison labour.

Number of Punishments for Prison Offences.

	From 1st January to 31st December, 1874.		From 1st January, 1875, to day of Inspection.	
	M.	F.	M.	F.
By Governor— Dark or Refractory Cells,	9	1	6	2

Two solitary cells are provided in each prison; but, as they are neither Punish-
artificially heated nor provided with bells, prisoners are not kept in them ments.
at night; therefore the punishment of being sentenced to refractory cell
here can have very little effect upon obstreperous characters. As it is
provided by the 6th section of the Prisons Act that every prison shall
have a competent number of cells adapted to solitary confinement of
refractory prisoners, I submit that cells of this description, properly
heated, and provided with bells, should be at once put up here, without
which the sentences imposed by law cannot frequently be carried out.

Summary of Labour on day of Inspection.

	M.	F.
Hard Labour,	9	–
Industrial Labour,	6	4
Sick,	1	1
Total,	16	5

NORTH
DISTRICT.

Leitrim
County
Gaol.

Amount received for produce of prisoners' labour disposed of outside the Gaol for the last three years.

1872, . £3 9s. 8d. | 1873, . £8 17s. 4d. | 1874, . £3 13s. 4d.

Net average daily cost of ordinary diet for each prisoner in the three preceding years.

1872, . . 4d. | 1873, . . 5d. | 1874, . . 5d.

Net cost of gaol, including diet and salaries, for the three preceding years.

1872, . £1,352 8s. 5d. | 1873, . £1,433 4s. 6d. | 1874, . £1,406 7s. 8d.

Total cost of officers, including clothing, value of rations, washing, gas, &c.

1872, . £811 1s. 0d. | 1873, . £845 17s. 0d. | 1874, . £828 14s. 7d.

Average cost of each prisoner per annum in each of the last three years.

1872, . £67 17s. 11d. | 1873, . £71 6s. 3d. | 1874, . £78 2s. 8d.

Amounts repaid by the War Department for military prisoners in each of the last three years.

1872, . £1 5s. 0d. | 1873, . £2 17s. 0d. | 1874, . £4 8s. 0d.

Amounts repaid from the Consolidated Fund for the Maintenance, &c., of Prisoners during the years

1872, . £67 13s. 10d. | 1873, . £58 8s. 3d. | 1874, . £69 2s. 4d.

Labour.

Since my last visit to this prison there has been a considerable improvement in the amount of labour exacted from male prisoners. The treadwheel has lately been repaired, and men sentenced to hard labour are now required to work at the mill for three hours a day, being ten minutes on at a time and five minutes off. The wheel is partitioned and some relief boxes are provided, but during the periods of relief prisoners are not required to pick oakum or perform any other industry. Prisoners are also compelled to break stones for four hours a day and are required to break about a barrel full per hour. Tradesmen sentenced to hard labour now perform their work on the mill daily, after which they are set to work at their different trades for the rest of the day. I was informed that during this year one shoemaker was imprisoned here who made as many as twenty-eight pairs of shoes. Mat-making was also about to be established by the Governor, and he expects to have a ready sale here for these articles. Women are chiefly employed in washing and making their own clothes. Having regard to the above facts, I am in hopes that by the exertions of the new Governor the returns received from the produce of prisoners' labour will in future be much larger than has usually been the case in this prison, for during the whole of the year 1874 the receipts from the produce of prisoners' labour only amounted to £3 13s. 4d., which is a very wretched result of the labour of a daily average of 14 males and 3 females, that being the number confined here during that year. Owing to the large expenditure in this gaol in proportion to the prisoners committed, and to the want of any sufficient returns from reproductive labour, the average cost of a prisoner here per annum is, with one exception, larger than in any other gaol in Ireland, amounting in the year 1874 to £78 2s. 8d. The net cost of the gaol for that year was £1,406 7s. 8d., but from this sum the cost of officers came to £828 11s. 7d. As I have already pointed out in former reports, the number of discipline officers maintained here is nine, quite out of proportion to the daily average number of prisoners; but as I entertain every hope that Parliament will take into consideration, during this

Expenditure.

session, our prison system in Ireland, I do not now recommend such steps to be taken as would disturb the existing arrangements of the staff.

Schools.

	From 1st Jan. to 31st Dec., 1874.		From 1st Jan., 1875, to day of Inspection.	
	M.	F.	M.	F.
Number of individual prisoners who attended school, ...	94	2	65	2
Average daily number of pupils, . .	9	1	11·4	1·16
Number of days on which school was held,	270	61	100	37

School-hours.—Males, 10 A.M. to 11 A.M.; females, 10 A.M. to 11 A.M.

As stated in my last report the male school is stalled, but that for females is not. Prisoners are taught for an hour a day, but only those whose sentence is over a fortnight, and who are under thirty years of age, are allowed to go to school. This, I submit, is a mistake, as short sentence prisoners who constantly frequent the gaol are, by this rule, debarred from receiving instruction and there are many prisoners over thirty years of age who are capable of being taught to read and write. I therefore submit that all prisoners capable of learning should be sent to school if well behaved. The male school is taught by the Deputy Governor and the female by the Matron, who both appear competent to perform this duty; but I regret to say that the school is not connected with any educational body; and I have again to draw attention to the neglect on the part of the Chaplains in regard to the inspection of the schools. *Schools.*

Contracts.

Bread, white, per lb., 1½d.; bread, brown, per lb., 1¼d.; oatmeal, per cwt., 14s. 9d.; Indian meal, per cwt., 10s. 9d.; potatoes, per cwt., 4s. 6d.; meat, per lb., 9d.; new milk, per gallon, 8d.; salt, per cwt., 4s.; coal, per ton, 17s. 5d.; turf, per box, 1s. 4d.; straw, per cwt., 2s. 8d.; candles, per lb., 5¼d.; soap, per cwt., £1 12s.

All the contracts are sanctioned by the Board, and are generally taken by that body once a year. The provision stores are kept by the cook-warder, and the samples which I saw were good; but I observe from the Inspection of Provisions Book that the Protestant Chaplain has on several occasions this year found fault with the quality of the milk. As that is the only animal diet permitted to prisoners in Ireland under the ordinary dietary scale, it certainly should be of the best quality. I therefore trust that the Board will insist on the milk contractor providing as good milk as can be procured in the district. The provisions are only inspected twice a week by the Chaplains, notwithstanding that the by-laws require this duty to be performed by these gentlemen three times a week. *Provisions.*

Officers and Salaries.

Non-Resident.	£	s.	d.		£	s.	d.
John A. Percy, esq., Local Inspector, . . .	100	0	0	F. J. M'Kenna, Deputy Governor, Clerk, and Schoolmaster, . . .	50	0	0
Rev. S. H. Lewis, Church of Ireland Chaplain, .	30	0	0	John Irwin, Porter, *Shoemaker,*	40	0	0
Rev. Thos. Fitzgerald, Roman Catholic Chaplain, . .	30	0	0	Robert M'Corduck, Assistant Schoolmaster, .	40	0	0
Robert Bradshaw, esq., surgeon, *ex-officio,* . .	—			Thomas Elliott, . .	35	0	0
A. C. Swayne, esq., Physician,	45	0	0	Thomas Murray, *assists in School,* . .	35	0	0
Mr. Wm. Hely, Apothecary,	20	0	0	Joseph Doherty, . .	35	0	0
Resident.				Miss M. A. Bourns, Matron,	40	0	0
Captain J. N. Croke, Governor, ...	100	0	0	Bridget Farrelly, Nurse-tender	20	0	0

G

Vacancies in the staff since last inspection, how caused, and how filled up.

Hyacinth Dickson, esq., Governor, superannuated; Captain J. N. Croke, appointed Governor, *vice* H. Dickson, esq.

Officer on Gaol Allowance.

Bridget Farrelly, nursetender.

Visits paid by Officers.

	From 1st Jan. to 31st Dec., 1874.	From 1st Jan., 1875, to day of Inspection.
Number of times the Board of Superintendence met and discharged business, ...	8	3
Local Inspector to Gaol, . .	170	49.
Do. each Bridewell,	4	1
Chaplain, Protestant Episcopal Church, ...	110	41
Chaplain, Roman Catholic, .	137	41
Physician, ... ,	208	57
Surgeon, ...	–	1
Apothecary, . . .	86	42

Owing, I greatly fear, to the laxity of discipline permitted by the late Governor, the staff of this prison is, I regret to observe, very much wanting in discipline ; but I am in hopes that the new Governor will endeavour to draw a closer rein and have more control over the subordinate officers. I visited their rooms, some of which were by no means as clean as they should be ; and I find that warders here do not parade regularly for the Governor or twice a day, as is the case in all well regulated gaols. As the duties of the hospital matron must be very light, I submit that she should be required to assist the Matron in the female prison, in order that a greater amount of separation and discipline be maintained here ; for at present, owing to there being only one matron in the female prison, prisoners of that sex who are for trial and those convicted are all mixed up together, which is extremely undesirable. I am glad to find that the Deputy Governor has been given a more suitable apartment for his own use, as this officer is always most attentive to duty and is worthy of the consideration of his superiors. I would suggest that as he has now charge of the photography, and performs both the duties of clerk and schoolmaster, that some small increase of salary be granted him.

Hospital.

	1872.		1873.		1874.		1875 (to day of Inspection).	
	M.	F.	M.	F.	M.	F.	M.	F.
No. of prisoners in hospital,	27	8	29	12	20	7	15	1
Average daily number in hospital, ...	·08	·01	·08	·03	·07	·02	·12	·00
No. of prisoners prescribed for and treated out of hospital, . . .	119	54	127	49	101	63	44	31
Cost of medicine, . .	£7 9s. 2d.		£7 1s. 0d.		£6 4s. 2d.		£1 18s. 11d.	
Cost of diet for prisoners in hospital, . . .	£18 18s. 11d.		£22 15s. 7d.		£9 2s. 8d.		£4 2s. 5d.	
Cost of all extra diet ordered by Medical Officer for prisoners not in hospital, .	£3 1s. 10½d.		£10 8s. 11d.		£8 14s. 6d.		£0 16s. 3d.	

No alterations have taken place in the hospital arrangements here since my last visit; and this department did not appear as clean as it should be, at the time of my inspection, for which I found no excuse, as the hospital matron has very little to do, and should therefore be required to keep her department in better order. A prisoner wardsman was employed in the male hospital, but his occupation was very light, indeed so much so that I consider his duties should have been performed by the matron. The medicines are procured from Dublin, and up to the time of my visit this year cost only £1 18s. 11d. I was glad to find that the Medical Officer has discontinued the practice of ordering tobacco to prisoners in this gaol, and that the requirements of the 109th section of the Prisons Act in this respect are now carried out.

Books and Journals.

The registries and books of finance are kept by the Deputy Governor, and some of the more important ones are examined daily by the Governor, who should of course be responsible for the proper keeping of all the books in the gaol, and should supervise them regularly. The Local Inspector, I am informed, inspects some of the books, chiefly those of finance. His journal is carefully and regularly kept, and he appears to note in it all matters of importance relating to the gaol. Indeed, as I have on former occasions had the pleasure to remark, this officer devotes much attention to his prison duties, and spares no time or pains in the fulfilment of them. The Governor's journal was not very full; but, as he was so lately appointed, this officer could not be expected to write such a journal as should be kept by the governor of a gaol. He appears anxious to perform his duties, so that I am in hopes in future the prison will be very differently managed to what it has been for some years. The Medical Officer keeps an excellent journal, and notes all matters of importance therein relating to his department. Some of the hospital books, however, were not kept quite as they should be, but I requested the Local Inspector to explain this matter to the Medical Officer, who, I have no doubt, in future will give it his attention. The journals of the Chaplains contain very little information and I have again to remark upon the impropriety of allowing both of these gentlemen to have substitutes not legally appointed, and would request a compliance with the 11th section of the 19th and 20th Victoria, chap. 68, in this regard. I greatly regret to have so frequently to draw attention to the non-compliance of duty, according to the requirements of the statute and by-laws, by these gentlemen, as it would be thought that they would be the first to show an example to others in the strict performance of their duty.

Board of Superintendence.

Lieut.-Colonel Birchall.	John A. La Touche, esq.
Hugh O'Beirne, esq.	A. L. Tottenham, esq.
John R. Dickson, esq.	William Peyton, esq.
Major-General Pottinger, c.b.	H. L. Montgomery, esq.
John T. Byrne, esq.	Francis La Touche, esq.
W. R. Ormsby Gore, esq., m.p.	C. C. B. Whyte, esq.

The Board of Superintendence meets once a month; on which occasion they hand the Local Inspector a cheque for the payment of current accounts, and also pay the salaries of all the officers—except that of the Medical Officer, who is paid half yearly at assizes; at which time also the prison accounts are audited by the Board of Superintendence. I annex my reports upon the two bridewells of the county.

[BRIDEWELLS.

STATE OF BRIDEWELLS.

	Manorhamilton.		Ballinamore.	
	M.	F.	M.	F.
No. of Committals in past year,	19	4	15	2
Of whom were Drunkards, .	–	–	1	–
No. of Committals in the quarter preceding Inspection, .	7	–	9	1
Of whom were Drunkards, .	–	–	1	–

	Manorhamilton.	Ballinamore.
Petty Sessions and Transmittals, how often?	Petty Sessions fort-nightly; transmittals on day following.	Fortnightly, on Satur-days; transmittals on following Monday.
Committals, ...	Regular, except one, un-der which a prisoner was committed here for "appearing to be of unsound mind."	Many quite illegal; and prisoners are detained here sometimes for trial without an order from any justice.
Registry, ...	Regular.	Regular.
Repairs and Order, . . .	Fair; but some doors and windows want mending, and the iron and wood-work should be painted.	Painting very much wanted throughout.
Security, ...	Fair, except in exercise yards.	Yards still very insecure, and a tree overhanging the female exercise yard that should be removed.
Accommodation, . . .	Three cells for males, with ten beds; one for females, with three; two day-rooms.	Two cells for males, one for females; two day-rooms.
Furniture, Bedding, and Utensils,	Good and sufficient.	Clean, good, and suffi-cient.
Water, how supplied? . .	By force-pump.	By pump in good repair.
Sewerage, ...	Effective; but no seat to male privy, and that for females is broken.	Said to be effective.
Cleanliness, Dryness, and Venti-lation.	Clean, and well venti-lated.	Clean, and well venti-lated.
Cost of dietary, ...	4d. for males, and 3½d. for females.	Males 4½d., females 3½½d.
Salary of Keeper, and whether he follows any other employment.	£40 a year, also fuel and light. Is Court-keeper without pay for it.	£40, fuel, and a suit of clothes. Is Court-keeper also, but no salary.
Date of Inspection, . . .	7th May, 1875.	18th May, 1875.
Remarks, ...	No prisoner in custody, and only 7 individuals committed this year.	No prisoner in custody.

CHARLES F. BOURKE, *Inspector-General.*

LONDONDERRY COUNTY GAOL, AT LONDONDERRY.—STATUTABLE
INSPECTION, 17TH AUGUST, 1875.

NORTH
DISTRICT.

London-
derry
County
Gaol.

At the above date 36 males and 25 females formed the total number of prisoners in custody here. Fourteen were cases disposed of at assizes or quarter sessions. Two were military offenders, one was untried, and the remaining cases were all disposed of by summary jurisdiction; so that it will be seen that although the numbers were large, yet the cases which were serious enough to be sent to assizes or quarter sessions were not very numerous. Seven juveniles in all were in custody this year, one of whom was sent to a reformatory—A. H., from Coleraine, a girl eight years of age, supposed to be illegitimate, and was abandoned by her parents. One boy was committed here this year twice who had been in gaol on two different occasions. This class of prisoner is, I am informed, now kept altogether separate from adults, both in their cells and during exercise. Four prisoners were in custody this year who were known to have been previously in reformatories.

Number of Prisoners of all classes in Gaol on the day of Inspection, and on the corresponding date in the three preceding years.

	M.	F.		M.	F.
1872,	30	15	1874,	71	13
1873,	57	22	1875 (day of Inspection),	36	25

Returned Convicts in Gaol on the day of Inspection, and during each of the three preceding years, and the expired portion of 1875.

	M.	F.		M.	F.
1872,	1	4	1875 (up to and including		
1873,	4	4	day of Inspection),	2	2
1874,	4	3	Day of Inspection,	1	—

Commitments.

CLASSES.	From 1st January to 31st December, 1874.		From 1st January, 1875, to day of Inspection.	
	M.	F.	M.	F.
Debtors,	5	—	1	—
Criminals,	327	91	165	65
Vagrants,	5	6	2	—
Drunkards,	173	303	93	181
Total,	510	400	261	246

Up to the above date the total number of commitments here was 261 of males and 246 of females, against 510 of the former and 400 of the latter sex during the whole of the previous year. Only one debtor was in custody during 1875, and at the time of my visit no prisoner of that class was in charge, so that I am in hopes in future debtors will not be committed to this prison. In proportion to the total number of prisoners, the drunkards committed to this gaol are extremely numerous, the commitments for this offence numbering in the year 1874 103 males and as many as 303 of females, and during the eight and a half months previous to the date of my inspection this year the numbers committed for that offence were 93 and 181 respectively. It will thus be seen that the females committed for drunkenness in this jurisdiction is very much larger than the males. This is a matter which, I submit, is worthy of the serious attention of the local authorities, as it is evident from these figures, and from those which I shall deal with further on, that repeated short imprisonments have little or no effect for good upon females of this class, as it frequently occurs that these women absolutely return to gaol within a few hours after being released. I would, therefore, strongly recommend that in every case when a prisoner is brought up before the magistrate, who is known to be of dissolute habits and a drunken character, that the full penalty of the law be imposed, this being, in fact, a much more humane course than that of allowing these unfortunate women to spend their lives in drunkenness, and in short periods of imprisonment.

Averages, and Highest and Lowest Numbers (exclusive of Debtors).

	From 1st January to 31st December, 1874.			From 1st January, 1875, to day of Inspection.		
	M.	F.	Date.	M.	F.	Date.
Average daily number of prisoners in custody,	50	20	—	38	19	—
Highest number of prisoners at any one time,		97	28th August.	68		25th July.
Lowest ditto,		50	23rd Dec.	44		22nd April.
Highest number of males at any one time,		82	23rd August.	48		7th March.
Ditto of females,		35	7th March.	30		20th June.
Lowest number of males at any one time,		30	6th March.	27		26th April.
Ditto of females,		10	12th August.	11		11th May.

Number of Individual Prisoners (exclusive of Debtors), and Number of Times each had been Committed during the following periods, distinguishing Adults from Juveniles.

NUMBER OF TIMES COMMITTED.	1874.				1875, to day of Inspection.			
	Juveniles.		Adults.		Juveniles.		Adults.	
	M.	F.	M.	F.	M.	F.	M.	F.
Once within the year,	23	4	313	81	2	2	153	38
Twice „	··	—	37	20	1	—	23	14
Thrice „	··	—	15	8	—	—	8	12
4 times „	—	—	5	5	—	—	2	10
5 „ „	—	—	2	3	—	—	2	3
6 „ „	—	—	2	5	—	—	—	2
7 „ „	—	—	—	2	—	—	1	4
8 to 10 „ „	—	—	1	3	—	—	1	5
11 to 15 „ „	—	—	—	9	—	—	—	—
17 „ „	—	—	—	1	—	—	—	—
19 „ „	—	—	—	1	·	—	—	—
Total,	23	4	375	138	3	2	190	88
No. of above who had not been in Gaol previous to 1st January in	23	4	251	54	2	2	100	41

Number of Individual Prisoners (exclusive of Debtors) committed in the year 1874, and to the day of Inspection in 1875, who had been once, twice, thrice, four times, five times, &c., from their first Commitment in any year, so far as can be ascertained, distinguishing Adults from Juveniles.

NORTH DISTRICT.

London-derry County Gaol.

NUMBER OF TIMES COMMITTED.	1874.				1875, to day of Inspection.			
	Juveniles.		Adults.		Juveniles.		Adults.	
	M.	F.	M.	F.	M.	F.	M.	F.
Once only,	21	4	244	46	1	2	95	34
Twice,	1	–	55	16	2	–	34	9
Thrice,	1	–	11	8	–	–	24	5
4 times,	–	–	11	5	–	–	7	5
5 ,,	–	–	9	3	–	–	4	4
6 ,,	–	–	6	4	–	–	4	2
7 to 11 ,,	–	–	19	10	–	–	6	4
12 to 16 ,,	–	–	5	7	–	–	3	4
17 to 20 ,,	–	–	3	–	–	–	6	4
21 to 30 ,,	–	–	2	15	–	–	3	4
31 to 40 ,,	–	–	7	10	–	–	3	2
41 to 50 ,,	–	–	1	5	–	–	1	3
51 to 60 ,,	–	–	–	1	–	–	–	2
61 to 70 ,,	–	–	–	2	–	–	–	1
71 to 80 ,,	–	–	1	5	–	–	–	1
81 to 90 ,,	–	–	–	–	–	–	–	2
91 to 100 ,,	–	–	–	–	–	–	–	1
121 to 140 ,,	–	–	–	–	–	–	–	1
141 to 160 ,,	–	–	–	1	–	–	–	–
Total No. of Individuals committed,	23	4	375	138	3	2	190	88
No. of Commitments represented in foregoing,	26	4	1,238	2,070	5	2	741	1321

Highest Number of Prisoners (exclusive of Debtors) in Gaol during each of the previous seven years, and up to day of Inspection in 1875.

24th November, 1868,	. .	58	31st January, 1872, . .	62
20th March, 1869,	. .	68	24th August, 1873, . .	82
5th July, 1870,	. .	67	26th August, 1874, . .	97
27th September, 1871, .	.	77	25th July, 1875, . .	68

During the year 1874 one female was committed here as often as 19 times, and up to the time of my inspection this year one male and five females were committed here from 8 to 10 times. In the latter year one female had been in charge whose former convictions were over 120, and in 1874 a female had been in charge whose former convictions exceeded 140; and I was informed that there was a prisoner in custody on the day of my inspection whose previous convictions numbered 151, yet I find her sentence was identical with that of another woman who had only 2 previous convictions recorded against her. The total number of adult male individuals committed during 1874 was 375, and of females 138, but 251 of the former and 54 of the latter had not previously been in gaol. However, the recommitments of the remainder numbered respectively as many as 1,238 males and 2,070 of females. Up to the time of my visit this year the number of adult male individuals committed here was 190, and of females 88. One hundred of the former and 41 of the latter had not previously been in gaol; but, notwithstanding this, the recommitments of those who were known to have been previously in prison numbered respectively 741 and 1,321, showing clearly how little effect short imprisonments have upon hardened offenders, and how few are the number of individuals committed here as compared with the total number

Re-commitments.

NORTH DISTRICT.

Londonderry County Gaol.

of commitments to the prison. Up to the time of my inspection this year the daily average number of male prisoners was considerably less than last year; but I regret to find that the daily average of females was only 1 less this year than in 1874, and at no time in 1875 were the number of females so low as at one period in 1874. However, I am in hopes that when the returns are made up to the end of the year the total number committed this year will be less than during the last two years.

Accommodation.

	M.	F.		M.	F.
Wards, . . .	11	–	Store Rooms, . .	4	2
Yards, . . .	13	2	Laundry, . . .	–	1
Day Rooms, . . .	5	–	Drying Room, . .	–	1
Solitary Cells, . .	10	2	Lavatories, . . .	2	3
Single Cells, 9 feet long, 6 feet wide, and 8 feet high, or which contain 432 cubic feet,	136	34	Baths, with Hot and Cold Water laid on, . .	3	1
			Privies, . . .	5	–
Do., heated and furnished with bells, . . .	57	34	Water-closets, . .	16	7
Sleeping Rooms, . .	5	2	Fumigating Apparatus, .	1	–
No. of Beds in such Rooms, .	16	4	Reception Rooms or Cells, .	1	1
Hospital Rooms, . .	3	3	Pump, . . .	1	–
Chapel, . . .	1	–	Well, . . .	1	–
School Rooms, . .	1	1	Other Machines for Hard Labour, viz.—		
Workshops, . . .	2	–	Heavy Looms for Weaving		
Worksheds, . . .	49	–	Mats and Matting, . .	8	–
Kitchen, . . .	1	1	Tell-tale Clocks, . .	3	–

Reception. Since my last visit here 8 reception cells have been fitted up for males, and all prisoners are washed immediately on being admitted, and subsequently once a week during imprisonment. I would suggest that 6 cells in the female prison be also set apart for the reception class; and, in compliance with the 20th rule of the 109th section of the Prisons Act, that no prisoner be removed from this class until they are inspected by **Sewerage.** the Medical Officer. The sewerage is reported to be in good order, and is carried into the main sewer of the town, and there is a sufficient number of water-closets and lavatories. Owing to an accident, on the day of my **Water.** visit there was a scarcity of water in the gaol, but I am informed there is usually a good supply, which is procured from the town main at a cost of £30 a year. There is also a good well upon the premises, from which water can also be driven into the tanks in case of the failure of the supply from the **Fumigator.** town. A fumigating apparatus is provided in the male, but none in the female prison. I submit that one of these requirements should also be provided for the female prison, and that all clothing be at once fumigated on the prisoner's admission, for I am astonished to learn that it is the custom here not to fumigate the clothing of females committed for drunkenness. This is an omission which I trust will be in future corrected, as it is evident that infection is as likely to be introduced **Chapel.** by one class of prisoner as by another. The arrangements of the chapel have not been altered since my last visit, except that a door has been opened from the female prison, by which means prisoners of that sex enter the chapel now without being seen by the males. All three services are performed here on Sundays, and I am informed that all healthy **Kitchen and** prisoners are required to attend. The laundry and kitchen departments **Laundry.** here are very complete, and much economy of labour and fuel is consequently effected. One stove serves to heat the water for the bath in the female prison, for the laundry, for the cooking apparatus, and also the drying-closet; and one female performs all the culinary duties of the prison, and washes up all the utensils. Both of these departments were in their usual orderly and cleanly condition, and are evidently efficiently supervised by the Matron. Fifty-seven cells in the male prison and 34 in the female are artificially heated, and provided with gas and bells. They were all clean and in good order at the time of my inspection. The photography is performed by the clerk, who receives £3 per annum in addition to his salary for carrying on this duty; and I am informed that owing to the careful attention to trace prisoners by means of this art old offenders are constantly being recognised and brought to justice. Three tell-tale clocks are provided in the prison, and are marked half-hourly, from 6.30 P.M. to 9.30 by the evening guard, but two only are marked from the latter hour to 5 A.M. The markings are taken by the clerk, and are entered into the Lockings Book, and all omissions on the part of the night watchman are noted in the Officers' Conduct Book. The Governor also, I am informed, verifies the markings of the clock, and besides this, he occasionally visits the prison at unexpected hours of the night. Look-up takes place all the year round at 6 P.M., except on Sundays, when it is at 4 P.M. Unlock in summer is at 6 A.M., and in winter at 7 A.M. The keys of the prison are given up to the Governor at 10 P.M., and those of the cells and corridors at 6 P.M., and are locked up in his bedroom during the night. I am bound to say that every reasonable precaution is taken in this prison for the safe keeping of the prisoners at night. The arrangements for visitors to prisoners here are, as I have stated in former reports, quite satisfactory, being such that it would become almost impossible for a visitor to a prisoner to introduce prohibited articles into the gaol without the connivance of the officers on duty. At the time of my visit some repairs were being done to the slating of the roof, as the slates were frequently falling off.

Stock at the time of Inspection.

	In Use.	In Store.	Male Clothing.	In Use.	In Store.	Female Clothing.	In Use.	In Store.
Blankets, pairs of,	270	50	Shirts, .	160	32	Shifts, .	80	—
Sheets, pairs of,	283	97	Jackets, .	196	70	Jackets .	78	—
Rugs, .	30	—	Vests, .	140	100	Gowns, .	97	—
Hammocks or Cots, .	40	18	Trowsers, .	201	139	Petticoats, .	97	—
Bed-ticks, .	87	97	Caps, .	100	—	Aprons, .	72	—
Bedsteads, .	86	84	Stockings or Socks, pairs of,	150	—	Neckerchiefs, .	109	—
			Shoes, Slippers, & Clogs, pairs of,	140	—	Caps, .	77	—
						Stockings, pairs of,	40	20
						Shoes, Slippers, & Clogs, pairs of,	33	—

The stock of clothing and bedding in store here at the time of my inspection was sufficient, and of good quality. The hospital warder is responsible for the clothing in use for male prisoners, and also dresses them as they come in. The first turnkey has a store of extra bedding, for which he and the hospital warder are responsible. The female clothing is all kept by the Matron, as also the shirts in use for males; and I saw some excellent petticoats made up out of old blankets. The stores of articles not issued are kept by the Governor; but I would recommend that these stores be more concentrated, and better arranged than they are at present. The Governor receives an account of all the clothing in use from the hospital warder and Matron about twice a year, but I could not ascertain that this duty was done sufficiently systematically. I would therefore recommend that stock be taken regularly by the Governor and Local Inspector quarterly; for it is not right that so large a quantity of prison property should be left so entirely to the care of subordinate officers, as is now the case. At the time of my visit all the sheets and bedding of the prison were clean and in good order, the former being changed once a week, and some new blankets had lately been procured.

*Number of Prisoners sentenced to Solitary Confinement, by order of Court
from 1st January to 31st December, 1874.*

13 males.

Number of Punishments for Prison-Offences.

	From 1st January to 31st December, 1874.		From 1st January, 1875, to day of Inspection.	
	M.	F.	M.	F.
By Magisterial authority,	–	1	2	3
By Governor—				
Stoppage of Diet,	47	14	26	14
Total,	47	15	26	17

Five solitary cells are provided for males and two for females. Three
of the former and both of the latter are properly heated, and provided
with spiral bells. The number of punishments recorded in the foregoing
table appears large, but it must be borne in mind that 13 of these were
sentences being carried out by order of the captain of a man-of-war on
sailors for misconduct at sea. However, it was found necessary on five
occasions this year to have recourse to magisterial authority for the
punishment of ordinary prisoners in this gaol for breach of prison rule;
the remainder of the punishments were inflicted by the Governor, who
takes care to lay the Punishment Book before the Board of Superintendence at their monthly meetings.

Employment on day of Inspection.

Summary.

	M.	F.
Hard labour,	13	–
Industrial labour,	22	24
Discharged (before labour hours),	1	–
Cook,	–	1
Total in custody,	36	25

*Amount received for produce of Prisoners' labour disposed of outside the Gaol
for the last three years.*

1872, . £150 9s. 6d. | 1873, . £169 7s. 3d. | 1874, . £209 0s. 10d.

There is no mechanical appliance in this gaol by which hard labour
can be carried on, and at the time of my visit there was no stone-breaking
provided, so that the most severe labour for males consisted of mat-making
and oakum-picking. I was informed that men sentenced to hard labour
when not working at the looms were required to pick 4 lbs. of oakum
daily, and those not so sentenced 3 lbs. All women sentenced to hard
labour were required to pick 3 lbs. of oakum a day. In my former reports
of this gaol I have drawn attention to the insufficient quantity of labour
performed here, and I am still of opinion that a greater amount of industry
should be carried out, and that prisoners should be required to work for a
greater number of hours in the day than at present, especially as gas is
provided in the cells, in which all prisoners should be employed up to 8
o'clock in the evening and as soon as the prison is open in the morning.
The gaol is abundantly provided with separate working cells and stone-
sheds where trades could be carried on, and where labour can be performed
in separation. I, therefore, would strongly urge upon the Board the
necessity of requiring a greater amount of labour to be undertaken here
than is now the case. The amount received for the produce of prisoners'
labour disposed of outside the gaol in 1874 was £209 0s. 10d., but having
regard to the daily average number of prisoners committed here, namely,
50 males and 20 females in that year, and of the class of prisoners who

are usually inmates of this gaol, I am certainly of opinion that such is not a sufficient result to receive from those numbers.

Schools.

	From 1st Jan. to 31st Dec., 1874.		From 1st Jan., 1875, to day of Inspection.	
	M.	F.	M.	F.
Number of individual prisoners who attended school, ...	304	56	163	35
Average daily number of pupils, . .	46	6	28	6·43
Number of days on which school was held,	228	208	142	134

School-hours.—Males—11.30 to 12.30. Females—10.30 to 11.30.

The male school is properly stalled, but I regret to find that females **School.** are not yet taught in separation, as recommended in my last report. I find that only females sentenced to a month and upwards are permitted to go to school, so that many of the repeated offenders, who form the great majority of the females in this prison, are not allowed to take advantage of the school. I submit that, under the 106th section of the Prisons Act, all prisoners who are capable of learning, and who are well behaved, should be sent to school, with the exception of those who are already sufficiently well instructed in reading, writing, and arithmetic, for, as a rule, schools in gaols are not meant to instruct prisoners in the higher educational subjects. I am of opinion that the remarks on the school by the Chaplains are not sufficiently full, and that they are not made in the School Registry as required. As the duty of the inspection of the schools is more specially laid down in the by-laws to the Chaplains, I would recommend that these officers be requested in future to note their remarks more fully in the School Registry than they have hitherto done.

Contracts.

Bread, brown, per 4 lb. loaf, 7¼d.; oatmeal, per cwt., 15s. 3d.; potatoes, per cwt., 4s. 10d.; new milk, per gallon. 11d.; buttermilk, per gallon, 11d.; coal, per ton, 13s. 9d.; gas, per 1,000 cubic feet, 5s. 10d.

The provisions are obtained by contract sanctioned by the Board, **Provisions.** and are kept by the clerk, who issues the meal every night to the Matron, bread and milk being issued a little before meal hours. The samples of the diet that I saw were excellent, and none of the prisoners made any complaint to me in regard to their food, except one man (W.A.), an Englishman, who complained of receiving an insufficient quantity, but I found that he had always received his full allowance, and that he was in excellent health. All the portions of food are weighed out before they are issued. I regret to be obliged to call attention to the irregularity on the part of the Chaplains in the performance of their duty in respect to the inspection of provisions. There was no entry in the Inspection Provisions Book by any Chaplain from the 6th to the 17th of August, and the duty of inspecting provisions is not done, as required by the statute, by alternate weeks. This is a matter that I have referred to before in previous reports.

Net average Daily Cost of Ordinary Diet for each Prisoner in three preceding years.

1872, . 5d. | 1873, . 5¼d. | 1874, . 5¼d.

Net cost of Gaol, including Diet and Salaries, for the three preceding years.

1872, . £2,183 19s. 4d. | 1873, . £2,372 8s. 9d. | 1874, . £2,473 11s. 11d.

Total cost of Officers, including Clothing, Value of Rations, Washing, Gas, &c.

1872, . £1,152 1s. 9d. | 1873, . £1,147 6s. 11d. | 1874, . £1,114 11s. 3d.

NORTH
DISTRICT.
———

London-
derry
County
Gaol.

Average cost of each Prisoner per annum in each of the last three years.

1872, . £45 8s. 8d. | 1873, . £39 9s. 6d. | 1874, . £34 7s. 1d.

Amounts repaid by the War Department for Military Prisoners in each of the last three years.

1872, . £5 4s. 6d. | 1873, . £21 2s. 0d. | 1874 . £1 10s. 0d.

Amounts repaid by the Admiralty Department for Naval Prisoners in each of the last three years.

1872, . £8 5s. 0d. | 1873, . . £3 9s. 0d. | 1874, . —

Amounts repaid from the Consolidated Fund for the maintenance, &c., of Prisoners during the years

1872, . £127 6s. 3d. | 1873, . £162 0s. 5d. | 1874, . £300 2s. 0d.

Expendi-
ture.

Since my last inspection of this gaol in 1873 there has, I am happy to find, been some reduction in the annual average cost of a prisoner here, for in 1872 the charge under this head was £45 8s. 8d., whereas in 1874 it was reduced to £34 7s. 1d., but the net cost of the gaol in the latter year was higher than it was during the two previous years, amounting to £2,473 11s. 11d., from that sum the total cost of the officers was £1,114 11s. 3d., so that this latter charge forms very nearly half the entire cost of the gaol.

Officers and Salaries.

Non-Resident.	£	s.	d.		£	s.	d.
Thos. Chambers, esq., Local Inspector,	150	0	0	Marcus Mooney, Clerk,	79	0	0
Rev. Charles Boyton, Episcopalian Chaplain,	46	3	1	James Boyle, Schoolmaster,	44	0	0
Rev. Robt. Ross, Presbyterian Chaplain,	46	3	1	Benjamin Wilson, Hospital Warder, teaches Mat-making and weaving,	44	0	0
Rev. Michael Treacey, Roman Catholic Chaplain,	46	3	1	Robert Mortimer,	44	0	0
Wm. Miller, esq., Surgeon,	—			Alexander Foster,	46	0	0
				Thomas Boyd,	36	0	0
Resident.				Thomas Burnside,	34	0	0
Captain Stewart H. Bruce, Governor,	184	0	0	William Sinnott, Night Watchman,	34	0	0
				Matilda Stirling, Matron,	56	0	0
Thomas Lecky, Gate Porter and Deputy-Governor, a Stone-mason,	104	0	0	Matilda Barbour, Assistant Matron,	44	0	0
				Letitia Wilson, Hospital Nurse,	26	0	0

(Turn-keys.)

Visits paid by Officers.

	From 1st Jan. to 31st Dec, 1874.	From 1st Jan., 1875, to day of Inspection.
Number of times the Board of Superintendence met and discharged business,	12	6
Local Inspector to Gaol,	216	151
Do., to Bridewells, { Magherafelt,	7	4
Coleraine,	8	3
Limavady,	5	2
Chaplain, Protestant Episcopal Church,	157	103
Presbyterian Chaplain,	151	102
Roman Catholic Chaplain,	139	91
Surgeon,	288	171

Officers

At the time of my visit, I regret that I was not fortunate enough to see the Governor, as he was on leave, but I was accompanied in my inspection by the Local Inspector and Clerk. The Deputy Governor, being a very old man and a long time in the service, should, in my opinion, be superannuated, as he is physically unable to perform the duties efficiently of a Deputy Governor. Another officer need not be appointed in his place, as the present Clerk could easily fulfil the duties of Deputy Governor in addition to those of Clerk ; and the gate, which is now kept by the Deputy Governor, could be kept by one of the turnkeys, or by the turnkeys in rotation. So long as the numerous and expensive staff that exists here is kept up, I fear that there can be little hope of reducing the very large expenditure under the head of officers in this prison. The quarters of the subordinate officers were, at the time of my visit, clean and well kept, and are regularly inspected by the superior officers. Most of the subordinate officers, I find, take their meals out of doors, but, there is a good mess-room provided within the gaol. Although the Governor was absent on leave, as I have already stated, there was abundant proof brought before me during my inspection of his close attention to business, which was borne out by the cleanliness and order prevailing throughout the whole establishment; and I have again to bear testimony to the zeal and care evinced by the Local Inspector in the performance of his prison duties.

North District.

London-derry County Gaol.

Hospitals.

	1872.		1873.		1874.	
	M.	F.	M.	F.	M.	F.
No. of prisoners in hospital,	9	14	13	14	3	
Average daily number in hospital, . . .	·3	·6	·6	·8	·1	·1
Number of prisoners prescribed for and treated out of hospital, . .	63	22	89	36	108	47
Number of deaths, . .	–	–	–	–	–	1
Cost of medicine, . .	£20 15s. 2d.		£21 18s. 10d.		£27 17s. 7d.	
Cost of diet for prisoners in hospital, . . .	17s. 4d.		£14 0s. 1d.		£1 14s. 1d.	

No alteration has taken place in the hospital since my last visit. Two wards are provided for each sex, and are fully supplied with water-closets and baths. I must, however, again call attention to what I consider very great extravagance in the cost of medicines here as compared with some other gaols. They are procured from the town—a system which is always found more expensive than when the medicines are either got from the County Infirmary or from Dublin. In the County Donegal Gaol the cost under this head in 1874 came only to 17s. 4d., and in Fermanagh to £3 3s. 1d.; in the former county the hospital medicines are procured from Dublin, and in the latter they are got from the County Infirmary. But I find that the cost of medicines in this gaol in 1874 amounted to the large sum of £27 17s. 7d., which, I submit, is excessive, considering that the number of prisoners in hospital during that year was but five. I, however, observe with pleasure that the Medical Officer here very seldom orders extra diet to prisoners, which in some prisons is a very great source of expense, frequently causing discontent, and, in my opinion, is sometimes very much abused.

Hospital.

Books and Journals.

The Registries and Books of Finance are very regularly and carefully kept by the clerk, and are supervised periodically by the Governor, and by the Local Inspector occasionally. I, however, do not consider that the General Registry is a good one, and would recommend a different form, such as I explained to the clerk, should be procured. Some of the prescribed forms are not in use. These should be all got, and should be regularly written up with the other books. The Local Inspector keeps a journal in which he notes matters of importance. The Governor keeps a journal according to a printed form of daily duties, but seldom notes anything but those matters referred to in the printed form. This is a system that I cannot approve of, as many things must occur daily in the prison which cannot be foreseen, and which, therefore, no form can

Books.

NORTH
DISTRICT
—
Londonderry
County
Gaol.

provide for. I perceive by his journal that he generally goes round the prison at lockings, and also at 10 P.M., and in other respects appears most regular in the performance of his duties. The chaplains also keep journals, in which they record the performance of their duties; but I failed to observe in the journal of the Protestant Chaplain that he complies with the 11th section of the 19th and 20th Vic., chap. 68, as to the appointment of a substitute. I would also request that the attention of the Medical Officer be drawn to the requirements of the 77th section of the Prisons Act in regard to his journal, which should be written up upon every occasion of his visit, and I submit that all the Doctor's prescriptions should he signed or initialled by him, as he alone is responsible for them. It is, however, right to remark that this officer is always most attentive to the sick, and is most regular in the performance of his prison duties, although he receives no salary for his services in the prison. The Officers' Conduct Book being in possession of the Governor I had not an opportunity of seeing it. As no improvement has been made since my last visit in regard to the Police Lock-up, and as it was in the same very disgraceful state as in 1873, I again brought the matter before the Executive on my return to Dublin. It appears that on the 20th of February au officer of the Board of Works made inquiries from the Board of Superintendence as to on what terms it would consent to take possession of the lock-up. The reply of the Board was to the effect that, on the Government giving up to that body those premises, they would pay the Government the sum of £200, provided that possession of the lock-up be given up before the 1st of July, 1876. Since then I am not aware that any steps have been taken to carry out this proposition, so that this very disgraceful place of detention still remains in the same condition as it was when first brought under the notice of the Government some three years ago.

Board of Superintendence.

The Mayor of Derry.	Conolly T. M'Causland, esq.	S. M. Alexander, esq.
Sir H. H. Bruce, bart.	Hon. A. C. C. Plunket.	Major George Knox.
Sir F. W. Heygate, bart.	William C. Gage, esq.	Major W. E. Scott.
John B. Beresford, esq.	George Skipton, esq.	Major Alex. Shuldham.

Board.

On the second Wednesday of each month the Board meets for the discharge of business, on which occasion the salaries of the subordinate officers and current accounts are paid. The contractors accounts are settled, together with the salaries of the superior officers half-yearly at assizes, and the Governor receives his salary quarterly. In 1874 the Board met for the discharge of business 12 times, and this year 6 times up to the time of my inspection. I annex my reports upon the three bridewells of the county.

[BRIDEWELLS.

STATE OF BRIDEWELLS.

	Coleraine.		Magherafelt.	
	M.	F.	M.	F.
No. of Committals in past year, . .	49	19	39	9
Of whom were Drunkards, .	19	12	16	6
No. of Committals in the Quarter preceding Inspection,	32	7	7	1
Of whom were Drunkards, .	12	7	2	1

	Coleraine.	Magherafelt.
Petty Sessions and Transmittals, how often?	Petty Sessions every second Friday. Transmittals as soon as possible. Criminal Quarter Sessions quarterly.	Petty Sessions once a quarter. Transmittals direct. Criminal Quarter Sessions once a quarter.
Committals, . .	Regular.	Two irregular. One signed by one Justice for four days; one of a dangerous lunatic who was kept here for two days, and died in two days after removal to the asylum.
Registry, . .	Well kept.	Correctly kept.
Repairs and Order, .	Good.	Fair.
Security, . . .	Fair, except in yards, which is still very bad.	Fair, with care.
Accommodation,	Nine cells in use; two day-rooms.	Three cells for males; one for females; two day-rooms; two of cells very damp.
Furniture, Bedding, and Utensils.	Clean and sufficient.	Good and sufficient.
Water, how supplied?	By two pumps and a well on premises.	By pump on premises.
Sewerage, . .	Effective and clean.	Fair.
Cleanliness, Dryness, and Ventilation.	Clean and well ventilated.	Clean, but lower cells damp.
Cost of Dietary, .	6d. per head per day.	6d. per day.
Salary of Keeper, and whether he follows any other employment.	£25; wife, £5; a suit of clothing; £8 for straw, fuel, and light.	£25; a suit of clothing; wife £5. Is court-keeper at £4. No other employment.
Date of Inspection, .	October 2nd, 1875.	October 4th, 1875.
Remarks, . .	One prisoner in custody.	No prisoner in custody.

STATE OF BRIDEWELLS—*continued.*

London-
derry
County.

Bridewells.

	Limavady.	
	M.	F.
No. of Committals in past year, .	18	10
Of whom were Drunkards, .	7	6
No. of Committals in the Quarter preceding Inspection, . .	11	5
Of whom were Drunkards, .	2	5

Petty Sessions and Transmittals, how often?	Petty Sessions fortnightly, on Tuesdays. Transmittals direct. No Criminal Quarter Sessions held here now.
Committals, ...	Regular.
Registry, ...	Carefully kept.
Repairs and Order, . . .	Good.
Security, ...	Fair, with care.
Accommodation, ...	Two cells for males and one for females; two day-rooms, which have beds in them; altogether six beds for males and four for females.
Furniture, Bedding, and Utensils,	Clean, good, and sufficient.
Water, how supplied? . . .	From town reservoir in abundance.
Sewerage, ...	Effective.
Cleanliness, Dryness, and Ventilation.	Very clean, well kept, and dry.
Cost of Dietary, ...	3d. for each meal; but the dietary formula is not strictly adhered to.
Salary of Keeper, and whether he follows any other employment?	£25 a year; wife £5, with £8 for fuel. Keeper is court-keeper at £4.
Date of Inspection, . . .	August 8th, 1875.
Remarks, ...	No prisoner in custody, and only one this quarter. The keeper and his wife deserve every credit for the tidy way they keep this Bridewell. This Bridewell is so little used, and being connected with the county town by rail, should be closed.

CHARLES F. BOURKE, *Inspector-General.*

LONGFORD COUNTY GAOL, AT LONGFORD.—STATUTABLE INSPECTION, 10TH MAY, 1875.

Number in
custody.

Juveniles.

Twenty-one males and 10 females formed the total number of prisoners in custody at the above date; 2 were military offenders, 3 were cases disposed of at quarter sessions or assizes, and the remainder were summary convictions. Previous to my visit, this year 6 juveniles were committed here, 1 of whom was in custody at the date of my visit—a boy of thirteen years of age who was awaiting trial; and I regret to state, that contrary to prison rules and to repeated remonstrances on the part of my colleague and myself, as regards juveniles, this boy was kept in association not only with adult prisoners but with a returned convict. I cannot too strongly reprobate the conduct of the Governor in this matter, as he must be aware how important it is that juveniles should be kept altogether separate and free from the contamination of adult prisoners. At the time of my visit I recommended that this child (who appeared to be of weak mind, and was committed for attempting suicide in the workhouse), should be sent to a reformatory, as it was evident if he were allowed to go back to the workhouse, his only home, he would gradually return to crime, and I am happy to say, that I have since learned that he has been sent to a reformatory school.

Number of Prisoners of all classes in Gaol on the day of Inspection, and on the corresponding date in the three preceding years.

	M.	F.		M.	F.
1872,	14	3	1874,	25	4
1873,	25	6	1875 (day of Inspection),	21	10

Number of returned convicts in Gaol on the day of Inspection, and during each of the three preceding years, and the expired portion of 1875.

	M.	F.		M.	F.
1872,	—	2	1875 (up to and including		
1873,	4	1	day of Inspection),	2	1
1874,	3	2	Day of Inspection,	1	1

Commitments.

Classes.	From 1st January to 31st Dec., 1874.		From 1st Jan., 1875, to day of Inspection.	
	M.	F.	M.	F.
Debtors,	1	—	—	—
Criminals,	214	54	69	21
Vagrants,	19	—	26	—
Drunkards,	106	23	19	4
Total,	340	77	114	25

It will be seen from the foregoing table that several returned convicts have been inmates of this gaol during the last three years, and that 2 were in custody on the day of my inspection. This fact alone does not speak well for the discipline of the prison, as those old hands are quite aware how all gaols are managed, and scrupulously avoid the districts in which gaols are situated in which discipline and punishment are strictly enforced. At the time of my visit, a female returned convict, was in custody, whom I was surprised to find was in bed in her cell, and I was informed that she stated she was ill; but this was evidently an excuse which the Matron should not have received, as I subsequently requested the Doctor to visit her and he ordered her at once into her class. This woman had sixty-six committals recorded against her—sixteen in Longford, nine in Kildare, thirty-five in Dublin, and six in Westmeath. Notwithstanding this, she managed to impose upon the apparent simplicity of the Matron of this prison, who, I submit, should always insist upon prisoners rising in the morning at their proper time unless she is fully convinced they are ill, in which case the Medical officer should at once be sent for. The total number of committals this year up to the time of my inspection, was 114 of males and 25 of females against 340 of the former and 77 of the latter during the whole of 1874. No debtor was committed here this year, and part of the quarters allotted to this class of prisoners, has now very properly been turned into stores as it is not

H

probable that any such in future will be committed here. My inspection was made at so early a period of the year, that it is difficult to compare the number of commitments this year with last; but up to the time of my visit the number of commitments for vagrancy had exceeded by 7 those of the whole of last year; and judging from the figures in the preceding table, it is to be hoped that the numbers committed for drunkenness in 1875, will, when computed, be found to be less than those committed for that offence last year.

Number of Individual Prisoners, exclusive of Debtors, committed in the year 1874, and to the day of Inspection in 1875, who had been Once, Twice, Thrice, Four Times, Five Times, &c., &c., from their first Commitment in any year, so far as can be ascertained, distinguishing Adults from Juveniles.

NUMBER OF TIMES COMMITTED.	1874.				1875, to day of Inspection.			
	Juveniles.		Adults.		Juveniles.		Adults.	
	M.	F.	M.	F.	M.	F.	M.	F.
Once only, ...	5	3	148	19	3	1	50	7
Twice, ...	2	–	45	7	–	–	13	4
Thrice, ...	1	–	16	3	–	–	7	1
4 times, . . .	–	–	15	1	–	–	4	–
5 ,, . . .	–	–	5	–	–	–	3	2
6 ,, . . .	–	–	7	1	–	–	2	1
7 to 11 ,, . . .	–	–	17	3	–	–	8	1
12 to 16 ,, . . .	–	–	6	5	–	–	2	1
17 to 20 ,, . . .	–	–	3	2	–	–	1	1
21 to 30 ,, . . .	–	–	2	1	–	–	–	–
31 to 40 ,, . . .	–	–	–	2	–	–	–	1
51 to 60 ,, . . .	–	–	2	–	–	–	–	–
61 to 70 ,, . . .	–	–	1	–	–	–	1	1
Total No. of Individuals committed,	8	3	264	44	3	1	91	20
No. of commitments represented in foregoing, . . .	12	3	907	300	3	1	318	180

Number of Individual Prisoners (exclusive of Debtors), and number of times each had been Committed during the following periods, distinguishing Adults from Juveniles.

NUMBER OF TIMES COMMITTED.	1874.				1875, to day of Inspection.			
	Juveniles.		Adults.		Juveniles.		Adults.	
	M.	F.	M.	F.	M.	F.	M.	F.
Once within the year, . .	6	3	221	30	3	1	75	16
Twice ,, . .	2	–	26	5	–	–	12	4
Thrice ,, . .	–	–	12	5	–	–	4	–
4 times ,, . .	–	–	1	3	–	–	–	–
5 ,, ,, . .	–	–	1	1	–	–	–	–
6 ,, ,, . .	–	–	–	1	–	–	–	–
7 ,, ,, . .	–	–	1	–	–	–	–	–
Total, . .	8	3	264	44	3	1	91	20
No. of above who had not been in Gaol previous to 1st Jan. in .	7	3	158	22	3	1	54	9

Averages, &c. (exclusive of Debtors).

—	From 1st January to 31st December, 1874.			From 1st January, 1875, to day of Inspection.		
	M.	**F.**	**Date.**	**M.**	**F.**	**Date.**
Average daily number of prisoners in custody,	24	5	—	28	4	—
Highest number of prisoners at any one time,	45		29th Oct.	45		16th & 17th February.
Lowest ditto, .	16		30th May.	21		22nd March.
Highest number of males at any one time, .	37		12th Jan., 23rd April, 26th & 29th Oct., and 1st Nov.	45		16th Feb.
Ditto of females, . .	11		26th June.	11		6th and 7th May.
Lowest number of males at any one time, .	12		29th May, 1st June, 18th & 19th July, 26th & 27th Aug.	19		22nd Mar.
Ditto of females, . .	1		6th to 10th Jan., 24th Mar. to 5th April, 26th and 30th April, 20th to 31st Dec.	Nil.		13th to 15th Jan., 3rd to 6th, & 9th to 16th Feb.

Highest number of prisoners (exclusive of debtors) in gaol during each of the previous seven years, and up to day of Inspection in 1875.

15th July, 1868, ...	49	4th November, 1872, . . .	36
20th and 22nd April, 1869, . .	52	1st August, 1873, . . .	36
6th May and 4th July, 1870, .	41	29th October, 1874, . . .	45
23rd June, 1871, ...	43	16th and 17th February, 1875, .	45

Up to the time of my visit no individual was committed here this **Re-commit-** year more than three times; but 1 male was in custody here during 1874 **ments.** as often as seven times, and in both years there were individuals in charge who had been from sixty to seventy times in custody since their first offence. The total number of adult individuals committed in 1874, was 264 males and 44 females, whose previous commitments from their first offence numbered respectively 907 and 300. Up to the time of my visit in 1874 the number of adult individuals committed was 91 males and 20 females, whose previous commitments since their first offence amounted respectively to 318 and 181. Of those committed in 1874, 158 males and 22 females had not been previously in gaol, and of those committed up to the time of my inspection in 1875, 54 males and 9 females had not previously been committed to prison, so that these figures reduce the numbers of old offenders to comparatively few individuals; and I have no doubt that under an improved management these few individuals who constantly frequent this gaol could be still further very much reduced in numbers.

NORTH
DISTRICT.

Longford
County
Gaol.

Accommodation.

	M.	F.		M.	F.
Wards,	8	1	Worksheds,	16	-
Yards,	8	3	Kitchen,		One.
Day Rooms,	8	-	Store Rooms,	4	1
Solitary Cells,	3	1	Laundry,	-	1
Single Cells, 9 ft. long, 6 ft. wide, and 8 ft. high, or which contain 432 cubic feet,	-	-	Drying-Room,	-	1
			Lavatories,	5	5
Single Cells of larger size, heated and furnished with bells,	-	4	Baths, with hot and cold water laid on,	1	1
			Ditto, moveable,	1	1
Single Cells of smaller size, do.,	-	12	Privies,	8	2
Ditto, not so furnished,	48	-	Water-closets,	5	4
Cells to contain three persons,	2	-	Fumigating Apparatus,	1	-
Sleeping Rooms,	6	2	Reception Rooms, or Cells,	1	1
No. of Beds in such Rooms,	5	-	Pumps,	1	1
Hospital Rooms,	2	1	Well,	1	-
Chapel,		One.	Tread-wheel,	1	-
School Rooms,	1	1	Tell-tale Clocks,	2	-
Workshops,	5	-			

Receptions.

Little or no alteration has taken place in the structural condition of this prison since my last visit. I have repeatedly called attention to the want of proper ablutionary arrangements, by which prisoners should be properly cleansed on admission, and I have no hesitation in saying, that the bedding in the male reception class here is a disgrace to any establishment, being filthy dirty, and full of vermin. Notwithstanding the frequent recommendations of Inspectors-General, male prisoners are not bathed or washed immediately on entering into prison, but are allowed to remain in all their filth and dirt in the reception class until inspected by the Doctor, which may not be perhaps for a day or two. I therefore again repeat, that all healthy prisoners should be at once bathed on admission, their clothes taken from them and fumigated, for under no other system can the bedding or clothing or the persons of the prisoners be kept in a decent state

Baths.

of cleanliness. I am glad, however, to find that the Matron has adopted our suggestions, and that females are now bathed immediately they come in and subsequently weekly. Only a moveable tin bath is provided in the male reception class. A good permanent fixed bath, with hot and cold water laid on is very much required here, and I submit, should be provided. The cells in the female prison are artificially heated; but those in the male are not, and none are of the required size for separate confinement, but contain about 418 cubic feet. Three lavatories are provided in the female prison, and there are some stalled ones in the exercise yard of the male prison; but so much association is permitted in this gaol, that stalled lavatories are of very little use at present. No alteration has

Sewerage.
Water.

been made since my last visit in the sewerage or the supply of water-closets and privies throughout the gaol. The water is provided from the same source as when I last inspected here, and the main sewer of the prison still runs close by the well, although this matter has been frequently brought under the notice of the Board of Superintendence in our reports. During my visit I perceived in many places throughout the gaol a very disagreeable smell from the sewers which are not properly trapped or ventilated, and I regret to find that my recommendations with regard to the running of the rain water by means of down pipes into the sewers has not yet been adopted. If this improvement were made the sewerage would be more effective, and the lower tier of the prison, which is still very damp,

Chapel.

would be much improved. The arrangements of the chapel are the same as at my last visit, and this apartment was clean and neatly kept, the sexes being also properly separated. Gas is provided in twenty-six of the

Gas.

male cells, but in none of those for females; but as no labour is performed after six o'clock little profit would be derived by providing the cells with gas. Hot and cold water is laid on to three separate stalls in the laundry, which department has undergone no alteration since my last visit. The kitchen was clean and well arranged; but I was surprised to find employed there a man sentenced to twelve months' imprisonment with hard labour for manslaughter, he being about the most serious offender in the gaol. He was exempt from hard labour by the Medical Officer; but at the same time, I do not consider this a sufficient excuse for so grave an offender being selected for employment in the kitchen. At the time of my visit this man had only put in two months of his sentence, so that being already exempt from hard labour and being selected for employment in a comfortable post in the prison, he will have passed his time in this gaol rather more comfortably than was the intention, I have no doubt, of the judge who passed sentence on him. Photography was still done by an artist from the town who was paid 2s. 6d. for four copies; but I am informed that the Board has arranged that the Deputy Governor shall be taught this art, so that I am in hopes by this time that this officer is able to take the photographs of prisoners in this gaol. Care is taken here to photograph all suspected prisoners, as well as those who are required to be photographed under the "Crimes Prevention Act," which is a most useful assistance to the detection of crime, and the hunting up of old offenders. One fumigating apparatus is provided, but at the time of my visit it was out of order, and consequently the clothing could not be properly disinfected. This is a simple matter which I should have imagined would have been corrected by the Governor of his own accord. Two tell-tale clocks are provided which are both situated in the corridor of the prison; they are marked half-hourly from half-past six P.M. to unlock in the morning, and the night-watch is fined 6d. for each omission. The markings are entered in the Lockings Book, and are taken by the Deputy Governor every morning, and in the event of there being any omissions in the markings of the clock the fact is noted against the night-watchman in the Officers' Conduct Book. In the summer unlock takes place at 6.30 A.M., in winter at 7 o'clock, and lockings is at 6 P.M. all the year round. I am of opinion that if the prisoners were properly employed, that unlock should not take place later than 5.30 A.M. in summer and 6 in winter, especially as gas is provided to the male cells, by which means the prisoners of that sex could be profitably employed during the winter mornings. The keys of the prison are locked up by the Governor, or in his absence by the Deputy Governor, at 10 o'clock at night, in an iron safe, the key of which is kept by the Governor. The arrangements for visitors to prisoners here are the same as at my last inspection, and are effective for the prevention of too close intercourse between the prisoner and the visitor. All visits to prisoners are on the authority of the Governor, under a rule sanctioned by the Board of Superintendence. I find that all the classes in this prison are in association, and although a certain amount of assembling of prisoners cannot be avoided here, yet I am clearly of opinion, that a great deal too much idleness, lolling about, and association is permitted. The prisoners now take their meals in the day-rooms, whereas they should be sent to their cells for that purpose, as well as for breakfast, as is now the case. I found one man in custody who was sentenced to two months' imprisonment; but at the time of my visit, although he had been in four days, he was not yet dressed in prison clothing. These are some of the matters which I regret to have to draw attention to, as they denote great negligence —want of care or zeal for the service on the part of the Governor. A grating has not yet been put upon the forge window, as suggested in my last report; if this were done a prisoner might be employed here with only the occasional supervision of an officer.

NORTH DISTRICT. Longford County Gaol. Laundry. Kitchen. Photography. Night-watch. Visitors. Association.

NORTH
DISTRICT.

*Longford
County
Gaol.*

Stock at the time of Inspection.

	In Use.	In Store.	Male Clothing.	In Use.	In Store.	Female Clothing.	In Use.	In Store.
Blankets, pairs of,	115	6	Shirts, .	88	–	Shifts, .	42	–
Sheets, pairs of, .	125½	1	Jackets, .	55	17	Jackets, .	53	–
Rugs, .	106	12	Vests, .	50	13	Petticoats, .	47	–
Hammocks or Cots,	48	17	Trowsers, .	47	24	Aprons, .	37	–
Bed-ticks, .	99	23	Caps, .	55	10	Neckerchiefs, .	37	–
Bedsteads, .	49	–	Socks, pairs of,	56	41	Caps, .	10	–
Pillows, .	102	6	Clogs, pairs of,	51	21	Stockings, pairs of,	10	22
			Overcoats (for prisoners' use),	2	2	Shoes, pairs of,	10	8
						Cloaks (for prisoners' use), .	1	2

Stores.

The general store of clothing and bedding is kept by the Deputy Governor who issues articles from it to the schoolmaster-warder under the written order of the Governor, the former officer being responsible for the prison clothing in use, and for the dressing of male prisoners as they come in. The Matron keeps the store of female clothing, and is herself responsible to the Governor for it. I was informed that the Governor takes stock of all prison stores about three times a year. This is a department that should be closely supervised and attended to by the Local Inspector. The store of prisoners' private clothing should be kept in a different place to that of the prison clothing, and I regret to say, that some of the male prisoners' own clothing was not properly labelled before being put away, nor, as I have already pointed out, was it thoroughly fumigated. All the clothing is now made up by the prisoners, with the exception of the clogs which are generally made outside the gaol. The female clothing is for the most part made up in the prison under the superintendence of the Matron, with the exception of the shoes. As many as 23 shoemakers have been committed here during this year, I, therefore, cannot understand why the Governor should not have taken advantage of their skill in order to get a sufficient quantity of shoes and clogs made up for the use of the prison. Since my inspection an addition has been made to the store of clothing and bedding, and there is now an abundant supply in the prison, with the exception of the bedding already referred to in the reception ward, it was as a rule all clean and in good order throughout the prison, especially that in the female department.

Number of Punishments for Prison Offences.

	From 1st January to 31st Dec., 1874.		From 1st Jan., 1875, to day of Inspection.	
	M.	F.	M.	F.
By Governor—				
Dark or Refractory Cells, . . .	10	4	19	–
Stoppage of Diet, ...	10	–	10	–
Other punishments, ...	3	–	4	–
Total, ...	23	4	*33	–

* In the year 1875 one was punished 8 times, one 6 times, one 5 times, one 3 times, and one twice.

Punishments.

On no occasion this year or last was it considered necessary to have recourse to magisterial authority for the punishment of any prisoner here for the breach of prison rules. The female solitary cell is properly heated and provided with a bell; but that for the males is not heated, and all prisoners are permitted to return to their own cells at night while undergoing punishment. I submit that as the female solitary cell is properly furnished and heated, prisoners should not be removed from it at night, and this rule might also apply to males during the summer months, for if it is necessary to punish a prisoner, it should he done so as to make the punishment felt. Where this rule is carried out there is generally very little breach of discipline amongst the prisoners.

NORTH DISTRICT.

Longford County Gaol.

Schools.

	From 1st Jan. to 31st Dec., 1874.		From 1st Jan., 1875, to day of Inspection.	
	M.	F.	M.	F.
Number of individual prisoners who attended school, ...	126	23	51	8
Average daily number of pupils, . .	11·9	4·35	11·2	5·23
Number of days on which school was held, .	193	80	63	13

School-hours.—Males, 10 to 11 A.M.; females, 10 to 11 A.M.

School is held for an hour daily; but for some time previous to my visit, I find that females have not been taught, for which there is no excuse. The schoolmaster and schoolmistress both appear efficient though not regularly trained teachers, and the school is now, I am glad to learn, placed in connexion with the Board of National Education. Up to the time of my visit this year the Roman Catholic Chaplain had only inspected the school twice, the Presbyterian once; and there was no visit recorded by the Protestant Chaplain in the School Registry. As it is the duty of the Chaplains to constantly visit the schools, and as it is laid down by the by-laws, that they should do so at least once a week, I submit that this duty should be more regularly and carefully performed by these gentlemen.

Schools.

Employment on day of Inspection.

	M.	F.
Hard Labour, ...	*7	—
Industrial Labour, ...	11	6
Sick in hospital, ...	—	1
Unemployed, ...	2	—
Discharged (*before labour hours*), . . .	1	1
Sick report, ...	—	1
Nursing child, ...	—	1
Total in custody, . .	21	10

* Six of these were employed cleaning and dressing yards; the other assisted in kitchen.

Amount received for produce of Prisoners' labour disposed of outside the Gaol for the last three years.

1872, . £0 16s. 3d. | 1873, . £7 14s. 4d. | 1874, . £9 3s. 1d.

Net average daily cost of Ordinary Diet for each Prisoner in the three preceding years.

1872, . 4d. | 1873, . 5d. | 1874, . 5d.

Net cost of Gaol, including Diet and Salaries, for the three preceding years.

1872, . £1,631 14s. 6d. | 1873, . £1,701 0s. 3d. | 1874, . £1,765 13s. 10d.

Total cost of officers, including clothing, value of rations, washing, gas, &c.

1872, . £928 15s. 9d. | 1873, . £955 12s. 0d. | 1874, . £989 13s. 7d.

Average cost of each prisoner per annum in each of the last three years.

1872, . £76 16s. 6d. | 1873, . £71 19s. 8d. | 1874, . £61 10s. 5d.

Amounts repaid by the War Department for Military Prisoners in each of the last three years.

1872, . £4 2s. 0d. | 1873, . £1 14s. 0d. | 1874, . £14 13s. 8d.

NORTH DISTRICT.

Longford County Gaol.

Labour.

Hard labour is carried on here by means of a tread-wheel, at which prisoners so sentenced are employed for three hours a day. Men are absolutely on it for ten minutes at a time, and have five minutes intervals of rest, but are not given any oakum-picking or fibre-teasing to do during those periods, as should be the case. Little or no other labour was being carried on at the time of my visit with the exception of some painting that was being done by one prisoner, as I was informed that stones could not be procured and no other industry was followed; and I was surprised to find that the hard labour above mentioned was not always carried out, as for instance, on the days on which coals are delivered, hard labour is suspended. This is a departure from prison rule which, I submit, the Governor is not authorised to sanction or to order. If a prisoner is sentenced to hard labour it is the duty of a Governor to carry out that sentence daily, except under medical prohibition. I regret to have to report that in no gaol in Ireland, as far as I am aware, is so much idleness, loitering, and association permitted as I witnessed here at the time of my inspection. The consequence is that the burden to the ratepayer of this gaol is very large, and punishment as carried on here can have very little effect for good on the prisoners committed. As there is abundant accommodation here there is no excuse for not employing prisoners, and instructing them in different trades; and, in addition, prisoners should be required to pick a certain amount of oakum daily in their cells. I regret to find that my suggestions in my last report with regard to the alteration of the stone-sheds have not yet been carried out. This could easily be done by prison labour, at little or no cost to the gaol, and I have no doubt that if such requirements were properly represented to the Board that that body would willingly sanction such inexpensive improvements. As will be seen from the foregoing table the entire amount received from the produce of prisoners' labour in 1874 was only £9 3s. 1d., which is but a miserable return from the daily average number during that year of 24 males and 5 females, together with a large and expensive staff of 11 intern officers, independent of Local Inspector,

Expenditure.

Chaplains, and Surgeon. The net cost of the gaol for that year was £1,765 13s. 10d., and from that sum the cost of officers came to £989 13s. 7d., so that the cost of the gaol exclusive of officers only amounted to £776 0s. 3d., and the result of this large expenditure and small profits from prisoners' labour in the gaol is, that the cost of a prisoner per annum here amounts to the large sum of £61 10s. 5d. This is a matter that I have already reported on on former occasions; but I regret to say with very little result for good, and I fear that so long as so little attention is paid to reproductive labour, and to carrying out suggestions made by experienced and competent authority, that very little economy or improvement can be expected. However, I trust that such legislation will soon take place as will rectify our present very faulty prison system in Ireland.

Contracts.

Bread, white, per 4-lb. loaf, 6d.; brown, per 4-lb. loaf, 5¼d.; oatmeal, per cwt., 14s. 8d.; Indian meal, per cwt., 10s. 3d.; potatoes, per cwt., 5s. 0d.; meat, per lb. 9d.; new milk, per gallon, 10d.; salt, per cwt., 4s. 4d.; coal, per ton, £1 8s. 9d.; turf, per 100 boxes, 6s. 10d.; straw, per cwt., 2s. 4d.; gas, per 1,000 cubic feet, 8s. 9d.; candles, per lb., 5¼d.; soap, per cwt., £1 1s. 6d.

Provisions.

The samples of the diet that I saw appeared to be good, and none of the prisoners made any complaint to me of it. The provisions are carefully and regularly inspected by the Chaplains, who report on their condition as a rule most favourably. All articles for consumption are obtained by contracts, sanctioned by the Board of Superintendence; but there is no contract for the materials for clothing, which are procured by the Governor with the sanction of the Board.

Officers and Salaries.

	£	s.	d.
Non-Resident.			
Alex. C. Kingstone, esq., J.P., Local Inspector,	90	0	0
Rev. Henry M. West, Prot. Episcopal Chaplain,	36	18	6
Rev. Samuel M'Cutcheon, Presbyterian Chaplain,	36	18	6
Rev. John O'Reilly, Roman Catholic Chaplain,	36	18	6
Henry Edgeworth, esq., Surgeon (County Infirmary),	—		
Resident.			
Thomas Lucas Murphy, esq., Governor,	200	0	0

	£	s.	d.
Mr. Geo. Robinson, Deputy Governor,	73	0	0
Patk. M'Grath, Schoolmaster,	46	0	0
John Bruen, Gate,	41	0	0
John M'Creddon,	41	0	0
Robert Palmer,	41	0	0
Thomas Hackett,	35	0	0
Patrick Murphy,	35	0	0
Patrick Lalor, *Carpenter*,	40	0	0
Miss Elizabeth Robinson, Matron,	45	0	0
Mrs. Emily Murphy, Assistant Matron,	32	0	0

(Warders: John Bruen, John M'Creddon, Robert Palmer, Thomas Hackett, Patrick Murphy, Patrick Lalor.)

Vacancies in Staff since last Inspection, how caused, and how filled up.

Hamilton Fellowes, Temporary Watchman, discontinued; Patrick Lalor, Carpenter Warder, appointed. Rev. M. N. Kearney, Prot. Chaplain, resigned; Rev. H. M. West, Prot. Chaplain, appointed. James H. Dopping, esq., Local Inspector, dismissed; Alex. C. Kingstone, esq., J.P., Local Inspector, appointed.

Officers on Gaol Allowance.

Resident officers receive fuel and light only.

Officers' Visits.

	From 1st Jan. to 31st Dec., 1874.	From 1st Jan., 1875, to day of Inspection.
Number of times the Board of Superintendence met and discharged business,	12	7
Local Inspector,	141	75
Chaplain, Protestant Episcopal Church,	204	71
,, Presbyterian,	170	57
,, Roman Catholic,	235	81
Surgeon,	274	126

The subordinate officers' quarters were at the time of my visit clean and orderly with one exception; but I should recommend their being given a little extra furniture in order to make their rooms more comfortable. The staff here in proportion to the number of prisoners is large; and I regret to find that there is only one tradesman amongst them, namely, a carpenter-warder. An extra duty has lately been imposed upon the officers of this gaol by the constabulary refusing to escort prisoners to petty and quarter sessions. This is a matter complained of now throughout the country, and will, if persisted in, entail considerable expense on the counties, whereas it does not relieve the constabulary of any duty. I therefore trust, that as the matter has been brought under the notice of the Chief Secretary, remedial measures will be adopted in the next session of Parliament on this subject. At the time of my visit a new Local Inspector had just been appointed, whom I regret to say, I had not the opportunity of seeing as his residence is some distance from the gaol. As the dismissal of the late Local Inspector has already been prominently brought before the public, and the circumstances relating to it having been published, I do not consider it necessary further to refer to this painful matter. A lengthy correspondence has taken place during this year between the Inspectors-General and the Governor of this gaol, owing to neglect on his part in remitting fines to the clerk of petty sessions, and I regret to state that my colleague and I were obliged to lay the matter before the Board before the Governor could be compelled

NORTH
DISTRICT.

Longford
County
Gaol.

to settle this matter satisfactorily. As the whole correspondence has been laid before the Government, and as the Governor has been reprimanded for his conduct in this matter I shall refrain from further comment here on this unpleasant subject. At the time of my visit the Deputy Governor complained to me of having been reprimanded by the Board concerning a matter of which he declares he had no knowledge. I laid his case before the Board of Superintendence at the time of my visit, and I feel sure that that body (who I regret to state, have had some very disagreeable duties to perform lately in regard to some of their officers), will uphold the Deputy Governor if they feel that they can justly do so. This officer has been in the service over twenty years, and I am bound to state here, that both my colleague and I have always had a high opinion of him.

Hospitals.

	1872.		1873.		1874.		1875 (to day of Inspection).	
	M.	F.	M.	F.	M.	F.	M.	F.
No. of prisoners in hospital,	29	2	29	7	39	8	–	–
Average daily number in hospital, . . .	1·5	·03	·1	·04	·94	·5	–	–
No. of prisoners prescribed for and treated out of hospital,	57	2¾	46	12	83	23	–	–
No. of deaths in the gaol, .	–	–	–	–	–	–	–	–
Cost of medicine, . .	£18 8s. 2d.		£18 9s. 7d.		£17 5s. 11d.		—	
Cost of diet for prisoners in hospital, . . .	£15 14s. 11d.		£14 5s. 7d.		£15 10s. 4d.		—	
Cost of all extra diet ordered by Medical Officer for prisoners not in hospital, .	£1 7s. 1d.		£2 16s. 8d.		£2 18s. 3d.		—	

Hospitals.

The arrangements of the female hospital are now considerably improved, consisting of two wards containing five beds. The hospital accommodation also for males is sufficient, but no bell is attached to these wards nor from the warders' room. I submit that a bell should be put up from the wards into the officer's room, and that he also be provided with a bell in order that he may if necessary communicate with the night-watchman. The medicines are procured from the town and made up by the apothecary there. Their cost in 1874 amounted to £17 5s. 11d., and the extra diet in that year to £2 18s. 3d. Having regard to the number of prisoners treated here, I am of opinion that these charges are excessive as compared with other gaols where medicines are procured either from the county infirmary or from Dublin.

Books and Journals.

Books.

Most of the registries and books of finance are kept by the Deputy Governor except the dietary books which are kept by the schoolmaster, and all are checked daily by the Governor. In the absence of the Local Inspector I was not able to see his journal; but the Governor's is full and carefully written up. By it I perceive that he visits the gaol frequently at uncertain hours in the night. The Chaplains' journals are all regularly and well kept. The journal of the Medical Officer is full, recording all his orders and other matters relating to his duties. As other books are kept for his orders, I would suggest that his journal should be reserved for his remarks and records of his visits to the gaol. It is evident by the perusal of this book that he is most attentive to his duties here and that he visits frequently. I am informed that the Punishment Book is always laid before the Board of Superintendence at their monthly meetings. None of the subordinate officers leave the gaol without passes during the business hours, and these passes the Governor compares every day with the Gate Book.

Board of Superintendence.

Anthony Lefroy, esq., D.L.	Capt. E. R. King-Harman, J.P.	Jas. W. Bond, esq., J.P.
Henry Dopping, esq., J.P.	Tobias H. Peyton, esq., J.P.	Edwd.M.O'Ferrall, esq.,J.P.
Chas. S. Dudgeon, esq.,J.P.	Right Hon. the Earl of Granard, K.P., J.P.	Ambrose Bole, esq., J.P.
Patrick Rhatigan, esq.		St. Geo. R. Johnstone, esq., J.P.

The first Saturday of the month is the day appointed for the Board to meet, on which occasion the intern officers' salaries and current accounts are paid, and the receipts are laid before the Board at the following meeting by the Local Inspector. The extern officers receive their salaries half-yearly at assizes. *Board.*

CHARLES F. BOURKE, *Inspector-General.*

LOUTH COUNTY GAOL, AT DUNDALK.—STATUTABLE INSPECTION, 2ND SEPTEMBER, 1875.

Louth County Gaol.

State.

Denomination of Class.	No. in each Class.			No. Sick in Hospital.		
	M.	F.	Total.	M.	F.	Total.
UNTRIED.						
For Felony,	1	—	1	—	—	—
For Misdemeanors,	3	—	3	—	—	—
Deserters,	2	—	2	—	—	—
For further Examination,	1	—	1	—	—	—
TRIED.						
Cases disposed of at Assizes and Quarter Sessions.						
Of Felony or Larceny—						
To Imprisonment,	—	1	1	—	—	—
Of Misdemeanors, &c.,	3	—	3	—	—	—
By Courts-Martial.						
Military and Naval Offenders,	26	—	26	—	—	—
Disposed of Summarily.						
For Larceny,	—	2	2	—	—	—
Other Misdemeanors,	8	5	13	—	—	—
Vagrants,	2	—	2	—	—	—
Drunkards,	2	—	2	—	—	—
Total in Custody,	48	8	56	—	—	—

Number of Commitments of Juveniles from 1st January to day of Inspection, 1875.

	12 years old and under.		Above 12 and not exceeding 16 years.	
	M.	F.	M.	F.
Convicted Summarily,	2	—	5	—
Committed for Trial,	2	—	1	—
Total,	4	—	6	—
Number sent to Reformatories,	1	—	—	—

Fifty-six prisoners formed the total number in custody at the above date, 48 of whom were males and 8 females. Nineteen were disposed of summarily, and 4 at assizes or quarter sessions, 7 were tried, and the remaining 26 were military or naval offenders. There were no *Number in custody.*

NORTH
DISTRICT.

Louth
County
Gaol.

Juveniles.

juveniles in charge at this time, but 10 were committed here previous to my inspection this year, one only of whom was sent to a reformatory. One juvenile in charge here this year had been over 7 times in gaol, and another 4 times, so that it would appear that these would he proper subjects for reformatory schools. The quarters for debtors were not occupied, nor was there any prisoner of that class in custody this year.

Number of Prisoners of all Classes in Gaol on the day of Inspection, and on the corresponding date in the three preceding years.

	M.	F.		M.	F.
1872,	43	7	1874,	38	8
1873,	61	7	1875 (day of Inspection),	48	8

Commitments.

CLASSES.	From 1st January to 31st December, 1874.		From 1st January, 1875, to day of Inspection.	
	M.	F.	M.	F.
Debtors,	1	–	–	–
Criminals,	204	50	171	33
Vagrants,	1	2	11	2
Drunkards,	70	78	35	55
Total,	276	130	217	90

Commitments.

At the time of my visit in 1873 the numbers were then unusually large caused by some prisoners that were transferred here from the City of Dublin Prison, and this year the large number of military prisoners in custody— 26, as already stated—formed nearly the half of those in custody at the above date, so that it will be seen that the number of prisoners actually belonging to the county is by no means excessive. The total number of commitments to this prison this year up to the time of my visit was 217 males and 90 females, against 276 males and 130 females during 1874, so that it may he fairly surmised that the total number of commitments in 1875 will be somewhat less than in the previous year.

Number of Individual Prisoners (exclusive of Debtors), and Number of Times each had been committed during the following periods.

NUMBER OF TIMES.	1874.				1875, to day of Inspection.			
	Juveniles.		Adults.		Juveniles.		Adults.	
	M.	F.	M.	F	M.	F.	M.	F.
Once within the year,	8	2	152	42	5	–	155	17
Twice „	–	–	25	16	1	–	13	10
Thrice „	1	–	9	2	1	–	4	3
Four times „	–	–	4	3	–	–	2	3
Five times „	–	–	2	1	–	–	–	4
Six times „	–	–	–	–	–	–	1	2
Seven times „	–	–	–	2	–	–	–	–
Eight times „	–	–	–	1	–	–	–	–
Nine times „	–	–	–	1	–	–	–	–
Ten times „	–	–	1	–	–	–	–	–
Total,	9	2	193	68	7	–	175	39
No. of above who had not been in Gaol previous to 1st Jan. in	8	2	148	32	5	–	146	15

Number of Individual Prisoners (exclusive of Debtors) committed in the year 1874, and to the day of Inspection in 1875, who had been once and oftener committed from their first commitment in any year, so far as can be ascertained.

NORTH DISTRICT.

Louth County Gaol.

NUMBER OF TIMES.	1874.				1875, to day of Inspection.			
	Juveniles		Adults.		Juveniles		Adults.	
	M.	F.	M.	F.	M.	F.	M.	F.
Once only, ...	8	2	126	30	5	-	132	11
Twice, ...	-	-	28	9	-	-	20	6
Thrice, ...	-	-	10	2	-	-	4	3
4 times, ...	-	-	10	2	1	-	4	-
5 ,, ...	1	-	6	1	-	-	4	1
6 ,, ...	-	-	3	-	-	-	-	-
7 to 11 ,, ...	-	-	5	6	1	-	6	4
12 to 16 ,, ...	-	-	5	7	-	-	2	3
17 to 20 ,, ...	-	-	-	2	-	-	1	2
21 to 30 ,, ...	-	-	1	3	-	-	1	3
31 to 40 ,, ...	-	-	-	1	-	-	-	1
51 to 60 ,, ...	-	-	1	-	-	-	1	-
81 to 90 ,, ...	-	-	-	1	-	-	-	1
141 to 160 ,, ...	-	-	-	2	-	-	-	2
161 to 180 ,, ...	-	-	-	1	-	-	-	1
251 to 276 ,, ...	-	-	-	1	-	-	-	1
Total No. of Individuals committed,	9	2	193	68	7	-	175	39
No. of Commitments represented in foregoing, ...	14	2	488	1,187	17	-	393	1114

The former of the two last tables shows somewhat of an improvement in the conduct of the habitual offenders of this district during this year as compared with last, for it will be observed that in 1874 one male was committed as often as 10 times, and one female 9 times, whereas during this year six was the greatest number of times that any individual was committed to this gaol, but it will be seen by the foregoing table that there is a certain class of female in this district who almost spend their lives in gaol. In both the last two years one female has been in charge who has been committed over 161 times, two over 120 times, and one as often as 276 times from their first commitment. The total number of individuals committed in 1874 was 193 males and 68 females whose commitments altogether since their first offence numbered 488 and 1,187 respectively. Up to the date of my inspection in 1875 the number of individuals committed was 175 of males and 39 females, whose previous commitments numbered respectively 393 and 1,114, and it should be borne in mind that the numbers of recommitments of males would be even greater than they are here represented in proportion to the number of individuals of that sex committed, were it not for the military offenders who are imprisoned here, for these are nearly all, as far as we are aware, first commitments.

Re-commitments.

Highest number of prisoners (exclusive of debtors) in gaol during each of the previous seven years, and up to day of Inspection in 1875.

31st January, 1868, . . 52	19th October, 1672, . . 53
3rd November, 1869, . . 51	3rd October, 1873. . . 56
9th December, 1870, . . 50	9th January, 1874, . . 61
27th June, 1871, . . . 51	30th August, 1875, . . 62

Averages, and Highest and Lowest Numbers (exclusive of Debtors).

Louth County Gaol.

—	From 1st January to 31st December, 1874.			From 1st January, 1875, to day of Inspection.		
	M.	F.	Date.	M.	F.	Date.
Average daily number of prisoners in custody,	45	9	—	36	9	—
Highest number of prisoners at any one time,	61		9th Jan.	62		30th Aug.
Lowest ditto, .	25		6th Dec.	31		16th April.
Highest number of males at any one time, .	58		27th June.	50		30th Aug.
Ditto, of females,	13		2nd Aug.	15		21st Aug.
Lowest number of males at any one time, .	25		26th Feb.	22		16th April.
Ditto, of females,	5		20th May.	2		23rd Mar.

The foregoing tables show that at certain periods of the year the number of females committed are very low, and at no time during the last two years have they exceeded 15 while at one time in 1874 the males numbered 58. They were at no time during the last two years lower in number than 22.

Accommodation.

	M.	F.		M.	F.
Wards, ...	3	1	Kitchen, ...	. one.	
Yards, ...	5	13	Store Room, . . .	. one.	
Day Rooms, . . .	1	1	Laundry, ...	. one.	
Solitary Cells, . . .	2	1	Drying Room, . . .	. one.	
Single Cells, 9 feet long, 6 feet wide, and 8 feet high, or which contain 432 cubic feet, .	83	21	Lavatories—prisoners wash in cells.		
Ditto, heated and furnished with bells, ...	83	21	Baths, with hot and cold water laid on, ...	1	1
Sleeping-rooms, . . .	2	1	Privies, ...	. eight.	
Hospital Rooms, . . .	4	3	Water-closets, . . .	. seven.	
Chapel, ...	one.		Fumigating apparatus, .	. one.	
School—in Chapel.			Reception Rooms or Cells,	8	3
Workshops—prisoners work in cells.			Pump, ...	. one.	
			Crank do., . . .	. one.	
Worksheds, . . .	24	-	Wells, ...	. two.	
			Tell-tale Clock, . . .	. one.	

Since my last inspection here very few improvements have been effected in this prison, and the recommendations of my colleague and myself have been of little avail. I was informed by the Local Inspector that the Board, pending the long expected legislation regarding our prisons, are unwilling to go to any expenditure, or to lay out money upon the gaol, so that I fear under these circumstances there is very little use in drawing further attention to any requirements that may be necessary. The

Reception. two cells that are apportioned to the reception class in the female prison are damp. I therefore would suggest that others on the upper tier be

Ventilation. used for this purpose, as there is abundant room there. The ventilation of the cells is by no means effective, as the windows do not open sufficiently to admit the air, and at the time of my visit, owing to a deficiency

Water. of water on the premises, the smell in some of the cells was very objectionable, as they are all provided with a water-closet, and there was not enough water to flush the pipes effectively. This state of things had

Heating. existed for two months previous to my visit. The heating of the cells, to which I called attention in my reports of 1869, 1871, and 1873, is still defective, but is somewhat improved since last year. No additional baths Noarn have yet been put up in the male prison, and none at all are provided in the female prison, so that prisoners of that sex are not properly washed or cleansed, and the 9th rule of the 109th section of the Prisons Act is not complied with in regard to them. Two baths are provided in the base- ment in which male prisoners are said to be washed as they come in, and fortnightly during imprisonment, but I am bound to remark that some of the prisoners in custody had anything but a cleanly appearance. The kitchen department is still in the male prison, and I have again, as at my last inspection, to complain of the custom of employing a male prisoner here, sentenced to hard labour, and who is thereby improperly exempted from a portion of his sentence. An excellent steam boiler is provided, which cooks the stirabout, heats the water for the laundry, for the bath, and provides the steam for the disinfection of the clothing. The recom- mendation of my colleague with regard to the shed being put up over the potato boiler and steam purifier has not been adopted. This is such an inexpensive and simple matter that if it were only to protect the potato boiler from rust one would imagine that a simple shed would have been before this erected here. The recommendations of Inspectors-General as regards the alteration of both the chapel and school have not yet been carried out. The school is still held in the chapel in contravention of the 6th section of the Prisons Act. The clothing of the prisoners is purified by means of steam, but this process is not so effective as when clothes are fumigated by sulphur. The laundry is fitted with six washing stalls with hot and cold water laid on, and a drying-room with a stove, surrounded by wooden horses is provided. The only washing done is that for the prison, so that the principal source of profit in some gaols, namely, that of washing for the public, is not yet taken advantage of here. Gas is pro- vided to all the cells, and is left lighting in winter up to 8 o'clock in the evening in order to allow the prisoners sentenced to hard labour to pick oakum up to that hour. The photography is performed by the chief warder and Governor, and 6d. is allowed for each copy, the chemicals being provided by the officers, but the apparatus is the property of the Board. There are 25 stone sheds in the yard in which stone-breaking is carried on, and several cells on the basement floor are employed as workshops. The vigilance of the night watch is tested by means of a tell-tale clock which is marked half-hourly from 6, P.M., to 6, A.M. Three warders perform this duty each night, one being on from 6, P.M., to 10, P.M., another from 10, P.M., to 2, A.M., and the third from 2, A.M., to 6, A.M. The markings are taken every morning by the chief warder, who enters them in the Lockings Book, and all omissions of duty in marking the clock are noted in the Conduct Book. The lock-up takes place at 6, P.M., throughout the year, and unlock in summer at 6, A.M., and in winter at 7, A.M. All the keys are taken by the Governor to his room at night, and both this officer and the chief warder visit the gaol during the night from time to time at uncertain hours. Excellent arrangements exist here for visiters to prisoners, and as they are the same as noted in my report of 1873 there is no need of my repeating them here. I regret to find that the screen has not yet been put up between the male and female prison as recommended at the time of my last visit. This suggestion would entail, if carried out, very little expense, and it should I submit be at once adopted. As at present it is necessary in order to obtain access to the top tier of the female prison, to take prisoners outside that section, I would suggest that proper communication between the basement and the top tier of the female prison be erected. The handles of the bells to the cells are dangerously high, and afford facilities for prisoners so inclined to commit suicide.

Marginal notes: North District. Louth County Gaol. Baths. Kitchen. Chapel and school. Fumigator. Laundry. Gas. Photography. Night watch. Improvements required.

NORTH.
DISTRICT.

Stock at the time of Inspection.

Louth
County
Gaol.

	Male Clothing.		Female Clothing.	
In Use. In Stere.		In Use. In Store.		In Use. In Store.
Blankets, pairs of, 56 28	Shirts, . . 47 59	Shifts, . . 8 16
Sheets, pairs of, . 56 27½	Jackets, . . 41 32	Jackets, . . 8 13
Rugs, . . . 56 59	Vests, . . 41 42	Petticoats, . . 8 62
Hammocks or Cots, 104	Trowsers, . . 41 44	Aprons, . . 8 13
Bed-ticks, . 56 34	Caps, . . 41 21	Neckerchiefs, . 8 20
Bedsteads, . . 17	Stockings or Socks,	Caps, . . 8 15
	pairs of, . . 48 118	Stockings, pairs of, 8 82
	Shoes, Slippers, &	Shoes, Slippers, and
	Clogs, pairs of, 41 52	Clogs, pairs of, 8 25

Stores.   The stock of clothing and bedding in store and in use at the time of my
inspection was abundant, and in good repair. I find that the sheeting in
the male prison is only changed once a month, but all females on admission get clean sheets. This latter rule is not strictly carried out in the
male prison. I am of opinion that no prisoner should be required to sleep
in sheets that have already been used, and again submit that all sheets
in the gaol should be changed at least once a fortnight. All the linen and
sheeting is in charge of the matron, and the principal store of male
clothing is kept by the chief warder who issues from his store only by
the order of the Local Inspector to the basement warder, whose duty it is
to see to the clothing of all prisoners as they come in. All the prison
clothing is made up in the gaol by prison labour, and the chief warder
superintends this department with much care and efficiency. The matron
has charge of all the female clothing, and both she and the chief warder
are accountable for all prison property in their charge to the Local Inspector and the Governor. I submit that a small neckcloth should be
provided for the male prisoners, as numbers of those who are committed
are accustomed to such requirement, and are now permitted to wear their
own, to which there is an obvious objection.

Number of Punishments for Prison Offences.

	From 1st January to 31st December, 1874.		From 1st January, 1875, to day of Inspection.	
	M.	F.	M.	F.
By Magisterial authority, . .	1	–	–	–
By Governor—				
Dark or Refractory Cells, . .	21	4	8	2
Stoppage of Diet, . .	28	–	13	–
Total, . . .	50	4	21	2

Punish-
ments.

On no occasion this year was there any prisoner punished by magisterial
authority for breach of prison rule, but at the time of my visit I found
two men in custody who had attempted or threatened to attempt suicide.
They were evidently "scheming," and were each placed in association with
two other prisoners to watch them, pending the decision of the Board before
whom they were subsequently brought; one was sentenced by that body to
seven days' solitary; the other was dealt with by the Governor, who gave
him three days' solitary, a punishment in my opinion quite inadequate to
the offence. Such cases as these require to be dealt with immediately
by the Governor, who should of course consult the Medical Officer, and if
necessary call in a magistrate for the punishment of such serious offences.
Two solitary cells are provided for each sex, and are heated and furnished
with bells, but as prisoners are allowed bedding at night such mild punishment as this can have very little effect upon hardened offenders.

Employment on day of Inspection.

	M.	F.
Stone-breaking,	22	—
Picking oakum,	15	1
Tailoring and Sewing,	1	4
Cooking and Cleaning,	3	1
Matmaking and Weaving,	2	—
Shoemaking,	1	—
Working at Coal,	3	—
Cleaning Walk,	1	—
Knitting,	—	2
Total in custody,	**48**	**8**

NORTH DISTRICT.

Louth County Gaol.

Juveniles.

Amount received for produce of Prisoners' Labour disposed of outside the Gaol.

1872, . £70 3s. 9d. | 1873, . £79 8s. 11d. | 1874, . £80 12s. 6d.

Hard labour here is usually carried on by means of a crank-pump, but at the time of my inspection, owing to a deficiency of water, the crank could not be used, so that stone-breaking was the most severe labour performed. Men were employed at this work for about five hours a day, but no specified quantity was given, and I was surprised to find that notwithstanding that stone-breaking is carried on in the open air, men so employed were allowed two hours walking exercise daily, besides one hour at school, and as one hour is also allowed for breakfast and another for dinner, the hours for labour in the short days of the winter are consequently very limited. It is in my opinion quite unnecessary to allow men who are working in the open air, to walk about doing nothing for two hours a day; but tradesmen and men employed at sedentary occupations indoors are of course entitled to the prescribed periods of exercise in the open air. Men sentenced to hard labour are, I am informed, required to pick ½ lh. of oakum in the morning from seven till nine o'clock, and another ¼ lb. in the evening from six to eight o'clock, but men not so sentenced are not compelled to pick oakum, but are allowed to remain idle in their cells during those periods. I would suggest that no prisoner should be allowed to remain idle in his cell any portion of the day between unlock and final lock-up; but the oakum required to be picked by prisoners not sentenced to hard labour should be prepared and made somewhat easier for them than that given to prisoners so sentenced. The total amount of prisoners' labour disposed of outside the gaol in 1874 was a trifle larger than the previous year; but I regret to find that the average cost of each prisoner per annum in that year was higher than in 1873. Unless every possible exertion is made to keep prisoners continually and profitably employed the cost of their maintenance must of course increase, for the greater the amount of the profits that are received from their labour, the greater will be the reduction of the average cost of each prisoner per annum. I cannot therefore too strongly urge upon the authorities of this gaol to endeavour to establish a greater amount of profitable labour amongst the prisoners than is now carried on.

Net average daily cost of Ordinary Diet for each Prisoner.

1872, . . 4·6d. | 1873, . . 5·0d. | 1874, . . 6·0d.

Net cost of Gaol, including Diet and Salaries.

1872, . £1,594 5s. 4d. | 1873, . £1,924 10s. 3d. | 1874, . £1,903 16s. 2d.

Total cost of Officers, including Clothing, Value of Rations, &c.

1872, . £834 1s. 6d. | 1873, . £897 17s. 4d. | 1874, . £1,006 0s. 2d.

I

NORTH
DISTRICT

Louth
County
Gaol.

Average cost of each Prisoner per annum.

1872, . £40 3s. 0d. | 1873, . £36 6s. 8d. | 1874, . £37 11s. 1d.

Amounts repaid by the War Department for Military Prisoners.

1872, £257 2s. 0d. | 1873, £380 13s. 0d. | 1874, £402 16s. 6d. | 1875, £178 6s. 0d

Amounts repaid by the Admiralty Department for Naval Prisoners.

1872, . £2 7s. 0d. | 1873, — | 1874, —

Amounts repaid by the Inland Revenue Department for Excise Prisoners.

1872, — | 1873, — | 1874, £5 3s. 6d. | 1875, —

*Amounts repaid from the Consolidated Fund for the maintenance, &c.,
of Prisoners.*

1872, . £79 15s. 6d. | 1873, . £128 11s. 10d. | 1874, . £122 11s. 2d.

Expenditure

The net cost of the gaol in 1874 amounted to £1,903 16s. 2d.; but from that sum the cost of officers came to £1,006 0s. 2d. Having regard to the daily average number of prisoners in custody here throughout the year, namely 45, this expenditure certainly appears very extravagant; but in the unsettled state of the law regarding prisons at present, I cannot recommend any steps being taken now for the reduction of the staff, but I have every hope that another session of Parliament will not pass without legislation taking place on our prison system.

School.

	From 1st Jan. to 31st Dec., 1874.		From 1st Jan., 1875, to day of Inspection.	
	M.	F.	M.	F.
Number of individual prisoners who attended school,	63	50	61	43
Average daily number of pupils,	20	5	20	6
Number of days on which school was held,	237	186	149	89

School hours :—Males—from 10 to 11 o'clock; Females—from 11 to 12 o'clock.

School.

The school is held for an hour each day for each sex, and at the time of my visit had recently been painted. All prisoners who are capable of learning and cannot read and write properly are sent to school. The assistant matron teaches the females and the clerk the males, and both teachers, though not certified trained teachers are fully competent to impart the knowledge required from them. The school is not connected with any educational body, but is now, I am happy to find, properly inspected by the Chaplains.

Contracts.

Bread, brown, per 1 lb. loaf, 1¼d.; oatmeal, per cwt., 15s.; Indian meal, per cwt., 9s.; potatoes, per cwt., 4s.; new milk, per gallon, 10d.; buttermilk, per gallon, 2d.; salt, per cwt., 3s.; coal, per ton, 16s. 3d.; straw, per cwt., 4s. 9d.; gas, per 1,000 cubic feet, 5s. 8d.; candles, per lb., 5½d.; soap, per cwt., £1 5s.; lime, per barrel, 3s. 6d.

Provisions.

The contracts for provisions are all sanctioned by the Board twice a year, and the materials for the clothing, &c., are procured by the Local Inspector as required; the officers' clothing is obtained by contract. The samples of the diet that I saw were good, with the exception of the bread, which I did not think was as good as it should be; however, the Chaplains usually report favourably upon the prison diet, which they inspect in their turn by alternate weeks.

Officers and Salaries.

Non-Resident.	£	s.	d.
Edward Tipping, esq., Local Inspector,	100	0	0
Rev. J. G. Rainsford, Protestant Chaplain,	36	18	6
Rev. Robert Black, Presbyterian Chaplain,	36	18	6
Rev. Thomas Hardy, Roman Catholic Chaplain,	36	18	6
E. G. Brunker, esq., Surgeon,	—		
Mr. Fras. Scott, Apothecary,	20	0	0
Mr. Alexander Shekleton, Secretary to the Board of Superintendence,	25	0	0

Resident.	£	s.	d.
Mr. Henry Noble, Governor,	150	0	0
John M'Dowell, Chief Warder, Tailor,	50	0	0
Hugh Davidson, Schoolmaster and Clerk,	35	0	0
Michael Heeney, Gate Warder,	35	0	0
Sub-Warders — Jas. Nesbitt, Shoemaker,	35	0	0
John Woods,	35	0	0
Alexander Wilson,	35	0	0
William Boyle,	35	0	0
Eleanor Owen, Matron,	35	0	0
Annie Wiseman, Assistant Matron,	30	0	0

Vacancies in the Staff since last Inspection, how caused, and how filled up, viz. :—

Gate-Warder Richard Ruth superannuated. Sub-Warder James M'Mahon resigned; vacancy filled up by the Board of Superintendence.

Officers on Gaol Allowance.

Governor, £25; Chief Warder, Schoolmaster, and Gate Warder, £18; one Sub-Warder, £15; Matron, Assistant Matron, and one Sub-Warder, £12; and two Sub-Warders £8 per annum.

Visits paid by Officers.

	From 1st January to 31st Dec., 1874.	From 1st Jan., 1875, to day of Inspection.
Number of times the Board of Superintendence met and discharged business,	12	8
Local Inspector to Gaol,	100	68
Do. to each Bridewell,	3	2
Chaplain, Protestant Episcopal Church,	193	130
Presbyterian Chaplain,	187	106
Roman Catholic Chaplain,	253	159
Surgeon,	289	193
Apothecary,	331	222

The intern officers have comfortable apartments inside the gaol, and are provided with a mess-room, but as they chiefly take their meals separately this room is little used. The Governor is a painstaking officer, and deserves every credit for the cleanly condition of the gaol. The chief warder and the subordinate officers are as a rule attentive to duty, and the former deserves much credit for the careful manner in which he performs his duties. I spoke to the Local Inspector regarding the matron who has been appointed within the last three years, and who, although I believe to be thoroughly respectable, is rather advanced in age for prison service. Both Protestant and Roman Catholic Chaplains have substitutes who are not legally appointed, but who are sanctioned by the Board; however, I submit that that body should be governed in this matter by the 11th sec. of the 19th & 20th Vic., chap. 68.

Officers.

Hospital.

	1872.		1873.		1874.		1875 (to day of Inspection).	
	M.	F.	M.	F.	M.	F	M.	F.
Number of prisoners prescribed for and treated out of hospital,	65	21	106	15	208	22	117	18
Number of Deaths,	—	—	—	—	1	—	—	—
Cost of medicine,	£4 4s. 11d.		£2 18s. 5d.		£5 4s. 4d.		—	

Owing to some damp in the hospital wards this building has not been used for some time; but when I made my inspection it seemed quite dry

Hospital.

NORTH
DISTRICT.

*Louth
County
Gaol.*

enough to be used if required ; sick persons are therefore usually treated in their cells, but very few cases of any importance have fortunately lately arisen in the gaol. Up to the time of my inspection this year, 117 males and 18 females had been prescribed for by the Doctor. The medicines are procured from an apothecary in the town who compounds them according to the Doctor's prescriptions. Their cost in 1874 amounted to £5 4s. 4d. In gaols where medicines are procured from the county infirmary much saving is effected, and as this institution is so close to the gaol here I would recommend that system to be adopted. In the event of any infectious disease taking place, I consider that it should be at once removed to hospital, as this building is now perfectly fit for use.

Books and Journals

Books.

The registries and books of finance are chiefly kept by the clerk, the chief warder keeping the Lockings Book. All are said to be supervised by the Governor daily, and the Local Inspector looks over them occasionally. The journal of the Local Inspector is not as full as it might be—that of the Governor is well and carefully written up, and contains much information regarding the management of the prison. The Surgeon does not observe the requirements of the 77th sec. of the "Prisons Act," with regard to his journal, which should be written up on every occasion of his visit ; but it is right to state, that although this officer does not receive pecuniary compensation for his attendance in the prison, he is most careful to perform his duties to those entrusted to his care here, and spares no time or trouble in the execution of them. The Chaplains do not perform their duties in accordance with the requirements of the statute regulating them, for I find that they do not visit the prisoners except they are asked for ; but the Protestant Chaplain assembles the prisoners of his persuasion once a week for religious instruction. I observe by the Work Ledger that no account is kept of the value of prisoners' labour, and consequently that prisoners do not receive the proportion of the profits of their labour to which they are legally entitled. I consider that this account should be carefully kept, and that the provisions of the 107th sec. of the "Prisons Act," relative to the profits of labour should be complied with.

Miscellaneous.

Scarcity of water.

Owing to the scarcity of water, and to the want of proper means of carrying out hard labour in this prison at the time of my inspection, together with other circumstances that were brought to my notice, I felt it to be my duty to recommend to the Executive for the present not to send any more military prisoners here. I received orders from the Government to report again upon the state of the prison, and consequently visited it a second time on the 25th of November, when I was glad to find that the supply of water was abundant owing to the heavy rains that had lately fallen ; but as no other improvement had taken place, I cannot yet recommend that military prisoners be permitted to be im-

Escape.

prisoned here. An escape of a prisoner took place here in June last, which denoted a serious neglect of duty, and great laxity of discipline on the part of the Governor and the officers concerned. A very careful investigation was held into the subject by the Board of Superintendence, which ultimately resulted in that body administering to the Governor a severe reprimand. The prisoner has not since been retaken or made amenable to justice. I have again to remark on the anomaly of a gentleman being employed here, other than a prison official, to act as secretary to the Board of Superintendence, this duty being usually performed by the Local Inspector,

Board of Superintendence.

Right Hon. Lord Clermont.	John Murphy, esq.	Fredk. J. Foster, esq.
Sir John S. Robinson, Bart.	John George Coddington,	John Coleman Kieran,
Lieut.-Colonel J. C. W.	esq.	esq.
Fortescue.	John A. Haig, esq.	John Jas. E. Bigger, esq.
William Ruxton, esq.	Michael Kelly, esq.	Burton Brabazon, esq.

The first Friday of each month is the day appointed for the Board to **Board.** meet, at which time the salaries of the subordinate officers and minor accounts are settled. The superior officers receive their salaries half-yearly at assizes, at which time also the contractors are paid. The Board also make a careful examination of the prison and the accounts each quarter. Annexed is my report of the Bridewell of Ardee.

STATE OF ARDEE BRIDEWELL.   *Bridewell.*

	M.	F.
No. of Committals in past year,	141	18
Of whom were Drunkards,	129	15
No. of Committals in the quarter preceding inspection,	31	5
Of whom were Drunkards,	29	4

Petty Sessions and Transmittals, how often ?	Petty Sessions fortnightly; transmittals regular.
Committals, whether regular ?	Correct.
Registry,	Carefully kept.
Repairs and order,	Good.
Security,	Good.
Accommodation,	Three cells for males, two for females, and two day-rooms.
Furniture, Bedding, and Utensils,	Clean, good, and sufficient.
Water, how supplied ?	By pipes to each ward from cistern, which is supplied by the force-pump.
Sewerage,	Effective.
Cleanliness, Dryness, and ventilation,	Clean and well ventilated.
Cost of Dietary, per head, per day,	5d. for males ; 4½d. for females.
Salary of Keeper, and whether he follows any other employment,	£50 with uniform, and £8 a year in lieu of rations. Has no other employment.
Official Inspection,	30th April, 1875.
Remarks,	One prisoner in custody. I find that prisoners are committed here while in a state of drunkenness, which is quite irregular, and should be discontinued.

CHARLES F. BOURKE, *Inspector-General.*

North
District.
———
*County of
the Town of
Drogheda
Gaol.*

DROGHEDA GAOL, COUNTY OF THE TOWN OF, AT DROGHEDA.—
STATUTABLE INSPECTION, 27TH NOVEMBER, 1875.

State.

Denomination of Class.	No. in each Class.			No. Sick in Hospital.		
	M.	F.	Total.	M.	F.	Total.
UNTRIED. For Misdemeanors, . . .	1	–	1	–	–	–
Disposed of Summarily. Offences under Larceny Act, . .	1	1	2	–	–	–
Other Misdemeanors, . . .	3	–	3	–	–	–
Total in Custody, . .	5	1	6	–	–	–

*Number of Commitments of Juveniles from 1st January to day of
Inspection,* 1875.

	12 years old and under.	Above 12 and not exceeding 16 years.
	M.	M.
Convicted Summarily, . .	1	2

At the above date 6 was the total number of prisoners in custody, 5
being males and 1 female, all of whom were cases disposed of summarily,
except 1 male who was untried. This latter was in bed, and under the
care of the doctor, suffering from the effects of a kick on his leg, received,
as he informed me, from a workhouse official, with whom he appears to
have had a serious *fracas*, and was in consequence arrested and committed
for trial at quarter sessions. Only 3 juveniles were committed here
during the year, and none were in custody at the time of my visit, but I
was informed by the Governor that care is taken to separate them from
adult prisoners. One of these youths, a male, had been already three
times in gaol, but was nevertheless not sentenced to a reformatory school,
nor were either of the others who were in custody this year so sentenced.

*Number of Prisoners of all Classes in Gaol on the day of Inspection, and
on the corresponding date in the three preceding years.*

	M.	F.		M.	F.
1872, ...	7	10	1874, ...	7	6
1873, ...	10	7	1875 (day of Inspection),	5	1

*Number of Returned Convicts in Gaol on the day of Inspection and during
each of the three preceding years, and the expired portion of* 1875.

	M.	F.		M.	F.
1872, ...	–	–	1875 (up to and including day of Inspection), . .	–	–
1873, ...	1	–			
1874, ...	4	1	Day of Inspection, . .	–	–

Commitments.

CLASSES.	From 1st January to 31st December, 1874.		From 1st January, 1875, to day of Inspection.	
	M.	F.	M.	F.
Debtors, ...	–	–	–	–
Criminals, . . .	93	39	108	48
Vagrants, . . .	1	2	5	2
Drunkards, . . .	75	24	80	40
Total, . .	169	65	193	90

It will be seen by the preceding tables how very few were the numbers committed to this prison during the last four years, and now that imprisonment for debt is practically abolished the quarters allotted to this class of prisoner are unoccupied, except by a warder, who is permitted to make use of one of these rooms. The last debtor committed here was discharged in February, 1873. The total number of commitments to this prison during the year 1875 was 193 males and 90 females, against 169 of the former and 65 of the latter in the previous year, the increment being chiefly in the commitments of drunkards, as will be seen by the previous tables; and as the principal portion of the criminal commitments here are for riot and assaults, drunkenness may also be attributed to cause the majority of offences committed by those classed as criminals.

Individual Prisoners (exclusive of Debtors), and Number of Times each had been committed during the following periods.

NUMBER OF TIMES COMMITTED.	1874.				1875, to day of Inspection.			
	Juveniles.		Adults.		Juveniles.		Adults.	
	M.	F.	M.	F.	M.	F.	M.	F.
Once within the year,	6	—	116	34	3	—	121	38
Twice "	—	—	16	6	—	—	19	8
Thrice, "	—	—	2	2	—	—	6	3
Four times ",	—	—	1	2	—	—	2	4
Five times "	—	—	1	1	—	—	1	1
Six times "	—	—	—	—	—	—	—	1
Total,	6	—	136	45	3	—	149	55
No. of above who had not been in Gaol previous to 1st Jan. in	6	—	163	65	3	—	190	90

Individual Prisoners (exclusive of Debtors) committed in the year 1874, and to the day of Inspection in 1875, who had been Once and oftener committed from their first Commitment in any year.

NUMBER OF TIMES COMMITTED.	1874.				1875, to day of Inspection.			
	Juveniles.		Adults.		Juveniles.		Adults.	
	M.	F.	M.	F.	M.	F.	M.	F.
Once only,	5	—	86	20	2	—	85	23
Twice,	1	—	22	4	—	—	21	5
Thrice,	—	—	6	2	1	—	9	4
Four times,	—	—	5	2	—	—	12	2
Five times,	—	—	4	4	—	—	4	2
Six times,	—	—	3	—	—	—	4	4
7 to 11 times,	—	—	4	6	—	—	8	4
12 to 16 ",	—	—	3	3	—	—	2	6
17 to 20 ",	—	—	1	2	—	—	2	3
21 to 30 ",	—	—	2	1	—	—	1	1
31 to 40 ",	—	—	—	—	—	—	1	1
51 to 60 ",	—	—	—	1	—	—	—	—
Total No. of Individuals committed,	6	—	136	45	3	—	149	55
No. of commitments represented in foregoing,	7	—	335	275	5	—	434	318

NORTH
DISTRICT.

*County of
the Town of
Drogheda
Gaol.*

Re-com-
mitments.

Six was the greatest number of times that any individual prisoner was committed here during this year up to the time of my inspection, but it will be seen by the previous tables that both a male and a female were in custody in 1875 who had been committed to gaol from 31 to 40 times from their first commitment, and in the previous year 1 female was in custody who had been over 5 times in prison. The total number of individuals committed in 1874 was 136 males and 45 females, and the number of commitments from the first offence was 335 and 275 respectively. Of the 149 males and 59 females committed up to my inspection this year their recommitments numbered respectively 434 and 318. Having regard to these figures I regret to state that it cannot be argued that much improvement in the disposition of old offenders is effected by the reformatory or deterrent system of this gaol.

Averages, and Highest and Lowest Numbers (exclusive of Debtors).

—	From 1st January to 31st December, 1874.			From 1st January, 1875, to day of Inspection.		
	M.	F.	Date.	M.	F.	Date.
Average daily number of prisoners in custody,	8	6	—	10	6	—
Highest number of prisoners at any one time,	40		13th Aug.	28		15th Aug.
Lowest ditto,	7		24th Mar.	6		22nd Nov.
Highest number of males at any one time,	30		13th Aug.	22		15th Aug.
Ditto, of females,	11		15th Jan.	13		13th Jan.
Lowest number of males at any one time,	2		13th July.	3		1st Feb.
Ditto, of females,	2		24th Mar.	1		22nd Nov.

Highest Number of Prisoners (exclusive of Debtors) in Gaol during each of the previous Seven Years, and up to day of Inspection in 1875.

21st November, 1868,	.	25	29th June, 1872, . .	26
25th October, 1869,	.	19	3rd July, 1873, . .	28
7th September, 1870,	.	25	13th August, 1874, .	40
25th September, 1871,	.	21	15th August, 1875, .	30

Although the daily average number of prisoners in custody this year was higher than last, at no time during 1875 were the numbers so large as in the previous year, and it will be seen that in both years, at different periods, there were but one or two females in custody. It may be observed from the foregoing table that there has been a gradual increase in the number of prisoners committed here during the last five years, and at no time during the last eight years were the numbers so high as at one period in 1874. This I attribute chiefly to a gradual increase in the shipping business of this town, and to the increase of wages amongst all classes, the result being a lamentable increase of drunkenness and of crimes consequent thereon.

Accommodation.

	M.	F.		M.	F.
Wards, ...	2	1	Worksheds, . . .	6	-
Yards, ...	3	2	Kitchen, . . .	-	1
Solitary Cells, . . .	1	1	Store Rooms, . . .	3	-
Single Cells, not less than 9 feet long, 6 feet wide, and 8 feet high = 432 cubic feet, heated, and furnished with bells, . .	23	16	Laundry, . . .	-	1
			Lavatories, . . .	2	1
			Baths, with hot and cold water laid on, . .	1	1
Sleeping Rooms, . .	2	1	Privies, . . .	3	2
Number of Beds in such rooms,	2	1	Water-closets, . .	3	1
Hospital Rooms, . .	1	1	Fumigating Apparatus, .	1	-
Chapel, . . .	1	-	Reception Rooms or Cells, .	2	1
School-room, . . .	1	-	Pumps, . . .	1	1
Workshop, . . .	1	-	Shot Drill, . . .	1	-

Since my last visit to this prison some of the suggestions of Inspectors-General have been adopted. A new iron railing was at the time of my visit being placed in front of the gaol. *Chevaux de frise* have been erected on the corners of the walls as recommended some years ago, and the kitchen department is now transferred to the female prison, by which means the labour of a male prisoner is more profitably employed. But other matters of improvements recommended by my colleague and myself have not yet been sufficiently attended to. Although the condition of cleanliness and order of the cells and the buildings throughout was satisfactory, yet I have again to call attention to the want of cleanliness of some of the bedding, and to the thinness of some of the blankets. Some of the sheets were quite dirty, and others very insufficiently and badly washed, and I regret to find that prisoners are still required to sleep in sheets that have already been occupied by others, although I was informed that the sheets are all changed weekly, but I have reason to know that the matron is not sufficiently particular about this matter. No alteration since my last visit has taken place in the number of the cells, there being 25 for males and 18 for females, all heated and provided with bells, and also furnished with gas, with the exception of 13 in the centre of the range. There is an ample supply of water-closets, lavatories, and baths throughout the gaol, and all prisoners receive a bath on admission, and once a week during imprisonment. There is also a good supply of water on the premises, and since my last visit the sewerage has been improved, and the offensive smell then complained of no longer exists. A fumigating apparatus is provided in which all clothing is purified before being put away. No alteration has been made in the arrangements for photographing prisoners since my last visit except that the charge is now 4s. 6d. instead of 4s. for four copies. It is therefore still more important that my recommendation as regards an officer being taught to perform this duty should be carried out. No change has been made in the laundry since my last visit, and the defects mentioned in my last report still exist in this department. Both Protestant and Roman Catholic worship are performed in the chapel, which is suitably and well arranged. No alteration has been carried out in the arrangements for visitors to prisoners since my last inspection. Convicted prisoners are allowed one visit a month, and the untried weekly, and all visitors are searched at the gate before being admitted, and visits always take place in presence of an officer. There is still no tell-tale clock in the night-prison, nor is there any night watch after 10 o'clock in the evening, but the Governor's apartments and those of the matron are close by, and it would be difficult for any prisoner to escape without their hearing them. Lock-up takes place at 6, P.M., and unlock at half-past 6, A.M., both in summer and winter, and the Governor takes charge of all the keys at lock-up, with the exception of the key of the outer door, which is given up to him at 10 o'clock, P.M., and all the keys are kept by him in his bedroom during the night.

(margin notes:) NORTH DISTRICT. — County of the Town of Drogheda Gaol. — Improvements. — Want of Cleanliness. — Cells. — Baths, Lavatories, &c. — Water. — Photography. — Laundry. — Chapel. — Visitors. — Night-watch.

Stock at the time of Inspection.

	In Use.	In Store.	Male Clothing.	In Use.	In Store.	Female Clothing.	In Use.	In Store.
Blankets, pairs of,	30	13	Shirts,	20	24	Shifts,	10	30
Sheets, pairs of,	30	24	Jackets,	10	14	Jackets,	10	14
Rugs,	30	18	Vests,	20	14	Petticoats,	10	14
Hammocks or			Trowsers,	10	26	Aprons,	10	14
Cots,	26	–	Caps,	10	14	Neckerchiefs,	10	14
Bed-ticks,	30	13	Stockings or Socks,			Caps,	10	14
Bedsteads,	19	–	pairs of,	10	14	Stockings, pairs of,	10	14
			Shoes, Slippers, &			Shoes, Slippers, &		
			Clogs, pairs of,	10	30	Clogs, pairs of,	10	18

NORTH
DISTRICT.

*County of
the Town of*
Drogheda
Gaol.

STORES.

As at my last inspection the stores are carefully kept, and supervised by the Governor, who takes care of and issues therefrom all the materials before they are made up. The females' clothing is now more tidily kept, presses having been put up at the end of the corridor, in which they are now stored as recommended. The stock of clothing and bedding at the time of my visit was abundant for the use of the prison, and is all made up by prison labour. The Governor also takes advantage of tradesmen committed to this gaol, and has tins, brushes, and mats all manufactured here.

Number of Punishments for Prison Offences.

	From 1st January to 31st December, 1874.		From 1st January, 1875, to day of Inspection.	
	M.	F.	M.	F.
By Governor—				
Dark or Refractory Cells,	8	6	19	11

Two of the ordinary cells are darkened, and used for the punishment of refractory prisoners, their bedding being given to them at night. On no occasion has it been necessary to punish a prisoner by magisterial authority for breach of prison rule, but as many as 19 males and 11 females were sentenced this year to refractory cells by the Governor. I cannot but think if prisoners were deprived of their bedding while in solitary, that punishment would have a much more salutary effect on them, and the consequence would be that it would be found necessary to punish them less often than at present.

Amount received for produce of Prisoners' Labour disposed of outside the Gaol.

1872, . £25 7s. 10d. | 1873, . £29 1s. 7d. | 1874, . £26 10s. 3d.

There being no tread or crank wheel here it is difficult to carry on purely hard labour for any definite time, but I am informed that men so sentenced are required to break 12½ cwt. of stones daily, and to pick 2 lbs. of hard oakum—if they are considered capable of so doing. No shot drill is now carried on, but all prisoners work in their cells at oakum-picking up to eight o'clock at night, and some cells are used as work-cells in which trades are carried on during the day. At the time of my visit I was surprised to find that prisoners were employed outside the gaol walls filling carts with broken stones. As this practice is quite illegal I requested the Governor to discontinue it at once. Although the amount received from the produce of prisoners' labour disposed of outside the gaol in 1874 is smaller than that received in the previous year, it should be borne in mind that a good deal of the time of the prisoners has during these past years been taken up by improvements in the prison, and in cultivating the different yards with vegetables for the use of the prison, which labour although a saving to the gaol is not computed as profits, at the same time I am far from thinking that the labour of prisoners here could not be turned to greater advantage than it is, for in proportion to the number of prisoners committed the results of the profits of their labour are still very diminutive.

Schools.

	From 1st Jan. to 31st Dec., 1874.		From 1st Jan., 1875, to day of Inspection.	
	M.	F.	M.	F.
Number of individual prisoners who attended school,	65	37	67	30
Average daily number of pupils,	6	4	8	4
Number of days on which school was held,	282	272	260	251

School-hours—Males, 12 to 1 in summer, and from 5 to 6, P.M., in winter. Females, 1 to 2 in summer, and 10 to 11, A.M., in winter.

The same arrangements exist with regard to the school as at my last inspection. The sexes are each taught separately for an hour, one of the turnkeys having charge of the males, and the females are taught by the matron. The school is not yet placed in connexion with any educational body. I have again, I regret to say, to draw attention to the irregularity on the part of the Protestant Chaplain in regard to the inspection of the school, for I was unable to find from the school registry that he had complied with the requirements of the by-laws at any time during this year, in regard to the visiting of the school ; but I am glad to find that this duty has been performed on several occasions this year by the Roman Catholic Chaplain.

Contracts.

Bread, white, per 20 lbs., 2s. 8d. ; ditto, brown, per 20 lbs., 2s. 1½d. ; oatmeal, per cwt., 16s. 6d. ; Indian meal, per cwt., 9s. ; potatoes, per cwt., 5s. ; meat, per lb., 10d. ; new milk, per gallon, 10d. ; buttermilk, per gallon, 2½d. ; salt, per cwt., 2s. 2d. ; coal, per ton, 19s. ; straw, per load, 10s. ; gas, per 1,000 cubic feet, 5s. 10d. ; candles, per lb., 6d. ; soap, per cwt., £1 12s.

The provisions are issued and weighed by the Governor daily, and are regularly inspected by the Chaplains, who as a rule report favourably thereon ; but on the day of my visit I considered the milk so poor that I requested it to be analysed, and have since learned that it contained 10 degrees of water. I have drawn the attention of the Board to the matter, who I trust will now require the contractor to be more particular in future in serving good milk. The bread and the milk are obtained by contract, but the other provisions are got in by the Governor by tender on the best terms he can make, and up to the time of my inspection the supply of potatoes grown on the premises was sufficient for the use of the prison during this year. The arrangements connected with the new kitchen are very complete and economically arranged, and are very adequate for the requirements of the prison.

Net average daily cost of ordinary diet for each prisoner.

1872, . 4d. | 1873, . 4d. | 1874, . 4d.

Net cost of gaol, including diet and salaries.

1872, . £454 19s. 1d. | 1873, . £524 3s. 6d. | 1874, . £519 12s. 6d.

Total cost of officers, including clothing, value of rations, &c.

1872, . £332 13s. 2d. | 1873, . £370 2s. 6d. | 1874, . £403 3s. 1d.

Average cost of each prisoner per annum in each of the last three years.

1872, . £29 13s. 2d. | 1873, . £28 12s. 10d. | 1874, . £37 2s. 4d.

Amounts repaid by the War Department for military prisoners.

1872, . £1 9s. 0d. | 1873, . £8 5s. 0d. | 1874, . £9 0s. 0d.

Amounts repaid from the Consolidated Fund for the maintenance, &c., of prisoners.

1872, . £45 1s. 3d. | 1873, . £37 1s. 5d. | 1874, . £27 7s. 11d.

In former reports I have called attention to the large cost of this gaol in proportion to the number of prisoners committed, but I regret to find that in 1874 the average cost of each prisoner per annum was higher than it has been for many years, amounting to £37 2s. 4d., the total cost of the gaol being for that year £519 12s. 6d. ; but of this sum the cost of officers came to £403 3s. 1d., so that the absolute cost of the maintenance of the prison, rates, taxes, &c., only amounted to £116 9s. 5d. So long as the present expensive and unnecessary staff of superior officers

NORTH DISTRICT.
___
County of the Town of Drogheda Gaol.

is kept for so small a gaol as this is, I fear there is very little hope of reducing its expenditure. However I trust that the long expected legislation on our prison system will take place next session, and that this and other minor prisons will then be more economically managed.

Officers and Salaries.

Non-Resident.

	£
George Delahoyde, esq., Local Inspector,	10
Rev. John G. Eccles, Protestant Episcopal Chaplain,	30
Rev. Thomas J. Murphy, Roman Catholic Chaplain,	30
John L. Kealy, esq., Surgeon,	35

	£
Robert J. Kelly, esq., Apothecary,	—
Resident.	
Patrick Murtagh, Governor,	100
Richard Bourke, Turnkey,	50
Nicholas Furlong, do.	35
Margaret Bourke, Matron,	20

Officers on Gaol Allowance.

All the intern officers receive rations of bread and milk, and an allowance of coal, soap, and gas-light.

Officers' Visits.

	From 1st Jan. to 31st Dec., 1874.	From 1st Jan., 1875, to day of Inspection.
Number of times the Board of Superintendence met and discharged business,	11	10
Local Inspector,	107	99
Chaplain, Protestant Episcopal Church,	156	97 } 114
Do., by substitute,	–	17 }
Chaplain, Roman Catholic,	177	69 } 149
Do., by substitute,	–	80 }
Surgeon,	105	97

Officers.

Since my last visit the gatekeeper has been abolished, and the office has not been filled up. The turnkeys take this duty now in rotation, for the number of prisoners is so small, that one turnkey at a time with the assistance of the Governor should be quite sufficient to superintend the prisoners in custody during the day time. I had reason at the time of my visit to complain of the untidy condition of the subordinate officers, and the want of cleanliness in their dress, and was informed that their pay is so small that they are unable to dress themselves decently. I would therefore submit that both the turnkeys and the matron should be allowed one suit of uniform yearly, and that they be then required to dress themselves properly. In most gaols warders are provided with uniform which can be made up with prison labour at very little expense. I submit that as the matron is the only female officer of the prison, that she should take her meals in the female prison, and not absent herself therefrom except by the permission of the Governor.

Hospital.

	1872.		1873.		1874.		1875 (to day of Inspection).	
	M.	F.	M.	F.	M.	F.	M.	F.
No. of prisoners prescribed for and treated out of hospital,	13	6	14	7	9	7	—	
Cost of medicine,	£8 1s. 9d.		£7 13s. 2d.		£5 12s. 4d.		—	
Cost of all extra diet ordered by Medical Officer for prisoners not in hospital,	£0 18s. 0d.		£2 1s. 1d.		£0 14s. 11d.		—	

Hospital.

The health of this gaol is usually so good, that no prisoner has been sent to hospital since the year 1867, trivial complaints being treated in cells; 9 males and 7 females have been prescribed for out of hospital during the year 1874. Although the cost of medicines is now less than it has been for some time, yet in proportion to this charge in other small gaols, and to the number of prisoners committed, it is in my opinion still large.

The books are chiefly kept by the Governor who is assisted by the schoolmaster-warder, and the manner in which they are kept reflects much credit upon those officers, indeed the Governor deserves every praise for his unremitting attention to duty, and his zeal for the public service. His journal is full and well kept ; but I regret to find that of the Local Inspector contains little or no information with regard to his important duties, and has almost always the same entry for each day. The Chaplains do not visit the prisoners as required by the 79th sec. of the Prisons Act, but merely go to them when they are sent for, and the Roman Catholic Chaplain has two substitutes not appointed in accordance with the requirements of the 11th sec. of the 19 & 20 Vic., chap. 68. I had occasion to draw the attention of the Medical Officer at the time of my inspection to an order of his, prohibiting a prisoner to receive exercise such as he is legally entitled to. I submit that this officer has no power to deprive a prisoner of his exercise in the open air except on medical grounds, and on those occasions his reasons should be stated in his journal. I find that the weekly earnings of prisoners not sentenced to hard labour is not given in the work ledger. This is a matter that should be carefully attended to, as all prisoners not so sentenced are, under the 106th sec. of the Prisons Act, entitled to a portion of their weekly earnings, which should be handed to them on their leaving the gaol.

NORTH DISTRICT.

County of the Town of Drogheda Gaol.

Books.

Miscellaneous.

I drew the attention of the Governor at the time of my inspection to some scribbling on doors in the cells which should not be allowed, and which denotes great carelessness on the part of the subordinate officers, for all such matters should be detected and reported to the Governor immediately. At the time of my visit the Governor very naturally complained of being now obliged to send an officer both to petty sessions and to the Mayor's court with the police and prisoners, the consequence is, that the time of one of these officers is engaged for some hours daily in this duty, and I fear if the constabulary continue to insist upon this unnecessary escort, that the Board will be obliged to go to the expense of appointing an extra officer to the prison.

Board of Superintendence.

Nicholas Leech, esq., Mayor, Chairman.
Patrick Casey, esq., J.P.
Robert B. Daly, esq., J.P.
George Harpur, esq., J.P.

Jas. D. Mathews, esq., J.P.
Patrick Ternan, esq., J.P.
William Boylan, esq.
James A. Flanagan, esq.

George Knaggs, esq.
Laurence Moore, esq.
John O'Neill, esq.
Patrick Reilly, esq.

The first Friday of each month is the day appointed for the Board to meet, on which occasion the accounts of the different creditors are paid by separate cheques if they come to any sum exceeding £2 ; for accounts under that amount a separate cheque is given to the Governor, who produces receipts at the next meeting. The officers' salaries are paid half-yearly at assizes, at which time the committee of the Grand Jury audits the prison accounts.

Board.

CHARLES F. BOURKE, *Inspector-General.*

NORTH DISTRICT.

MAYO COUNTY GAOL, AT CASTLEBAR.—STATUTABLE INSPECTION, 27TH AUGUST, 1875.

Mayo County Gaol.

Number in custody.

Forty formed the total number of individuals committed here up to this date; 11 of whom were untried, 9 were cases disposed of at quarter sessions or assizes, and the remainder were summary convictions. Only one juvenile (a female) was in custody at the time of my visit; but 14 of that class were committed here during this year up to that time, and 2 of these were sent to reformatories. In my report of 1873 I particularly observed on the necessity of keeping juvenile separate from adult prisoners; but on my recent visit I found that my suggestions in this respect were entirely disregarded, a child being then in gaol, who was sentenced to a reformatory, and allowed to be in association with convicted adult prisoners. For this breach of prison rule there was no valid excuse. Four of the juveniles who were committed here this year had been twice previously in prison.

Number of prisoners of all classes in gaol on the day of inspection, and on the corresponding date in the three preceding years.

	M.	F.		M.	F.
1872,	40	11	1874,	32	11
1873,	30	13	1875 (day of Inspection),	30	10

Number of returned convicts in gaol on the day of inspection, and during each of the three preceding years, and the expired portion of 1875.

	M.	F.		M.	F.
1872,	3	3	1875 (up to and including		
1873,	2	4	day of Inspection),	1	2
1874,	3	1	Day of Inspection,	1	2

Commitments.

CLASSES.	From 1st January to 31st Dec., 1874.		From 1st Jan., 1875, to day of Inspection.	
	M.	F.	M.	F.
Debtors,	1	–	–	–
Criminals,	389	106	238	57
Vagrants,	6	1	8	6
Drunkards,	110	50	72	40
Total,	506	157	318	103

Commitments.

Only 1 prisoner was committed here this year—a male—charged with murder, though 5 were in custody during the year charged with manslaughter. The total number of commitments in 1874 were 560 males and 157 females, against 318 of the former and 103 of the latter in the expired portion of 1875. Having regard, however, to the time of the year when my inspection was made, I fear that when the returns are made up at the end of the year, the number of drunkards committed here in 1875 will exceed those of the previous year. There having been no debtor in gaol here for nearly two years, the quarters allotted to this class are now unoccupied, except by the Deputy Governor, who, I find, is still allowed a prisoner to attend upon him in his quarters. I must again repeat that this custom is quite irregular, and open to such grave abuse that I consider the Board should not permit it. The upper rooms in the debtors' quarters might, with very little improvement, be adapted to the separate system, as the rooms are large enough for that purpose. I would therefore recommend that these rooms be converted into quarters for criminal prisoners, so that a greater amount of separation be maintained than is now enforced in the prison; for I am of opinion that the want of a due amount of separation here is one of the chief defects in the management of this gaol, and is subversive of good discipline and order.

Number of Individual Prisoners (exclusive of Debtors), and Number of Times each had been committed during the following periods, distinguishing Adults from Juveniles.

NUMBER OF TIMES COMMITTED.	1874.				1875, to day of Inspection.			
	Juveniles.		Adults.		Juveniles.		Adults.	
	M.	F.	M.	F.	M.	F.	M.	F.
Once within the year,	20	4	393	109	11	1	237	63
Twice ,,	–	–	22	5	2	–	16	7
Thrice ,,	–	–	6	1	–	–	3	1
4 times, ,,	–	–	1	–	–	–	2	1
5 ,, ,,	–	–	–	2	–	–	1	1
6 ,, ,,	–	–	1	2	–	–	–	1
7 ,, ,,	–	–	1	–	–	–	–	1
8 ,, ,,	–	–	–	–	–	–	1	–
9 ,, ,,	–	–	–	1	–	–	–	–
13 ,, ,,	–	–	1	–	–	–	–	–
Total,	20	4	425	120	13	1	262	75
No. of above who had not been in Gaol previous to 1st January in .	19	4	346	95	12	–	204	50

Number of Individual Prisoners (exclusive of Debtors) committed in the year 1874, and to the day of Inspection in 1875, who had been Once, Twice, Thrice, Four Times, Five Times, &c., &c., from their first Commitment in any year, so far as can be ascertained, distinguishing Adults from Juveniles.

NUMBER OF TIMES COMMITTED.	1874.				1875, to day of Inspection.			
	Juveniles.		Adults.		Juveniles.		Adults.	
	M.	F.	M.	F.	M.	F.	M.	F.
Once only,	19	4	337	95	10	–	195	48
Twice,	1	–	30	5	3	1	28	5
Thrice,	–	–	26	2	–	–	16	5
4 times,	–	–	8	–	–	–	7	1
5 ,,	–	–	7	4	–	–	3	–
6 ,,	–	–	5	2	–	–	2	1
7 to 11 ,,	–	–	6	7	–	–	5	7
12 to 16 ,,	–	–	1	1	–	–	1	2
17 to 20 ,,	–	–	–	–	–	–	–	2
21 to 30 ,,	–	–	1	2	–	–	1	3
31 to 40 ,,	–	–	–	2	–	–	1	1
41 to 50 ,,	–	–	–	–	–	–	–	1
51 to 60 ,,	–	–	–	–	–	–	–	–
61 to 70 ,,	–	–	1	–	–	–	1	–
71 to 80 ,,	–	–	–	–	–	–	1	–
Total No. of Individuals committed,	20	4	425	120	13	1	262	75
No. of commitments represented in foregoing,	21	4	783	332	16	2	604	334

NORTH
DISTRICT.

Mayo
County
Gaol.

Averages, and Highest and Lowest Numbers (exclusive of Debtors).

	From 1st January to 31st December, 1874.			From 1st January, 1875, to day of Inspection		
	M.	F.	Date.	M.	F.	Date.
Average daily number of prisoners in custody,	34	12	—	33	13	—
Highest number of prisoners at any one time,	62		12th July.	60		10 & 11 Feb.
Lowest ditto,	33		6, 7 & 8 June.	35		18th July.
Highest number of males at any one time,	46		24th Nov.	51		18th Feb.
Ditto, of females,	22		6th Oct.	19		14 & 15 Aug.
Lowest number of males at any one time,	23		18 & 19 Mar.	21		19, 20, and 22 July.
Ditto, of females,	5		16, 17, and 18 Dec.	6		1, 2, 3, 4, & 5 Jan.

Highest Number of Prisoners (exclusive of Debtors) in Gaol during each of the previous seven years, and up to day of Inspection in 1875.

22nd February, 1868,	.	.	64	22nd February, 1872,	. . .	69
4th February, 1869,	.	.	62	1st April, 1873,	. . .	70
15th March, 1870,	.	.	69	12th July, 1874,	. . .	62
29th September, 1871,	.	.	70	10th February, 1875,	. . .	60

Re-com-
mitments.

Four hundred and twenty-five adult males and 120 adult females were committed here in 1874 whose previous convictions numbered respectively 783 and 339; but 346 of the former and 95 of the latter had not previously been in gaol. In the expired portion of 1875, 262 adult individual males and 75 females were committed here, who had been in gaol respectively as many as 604 and 334 times; but 204 of the former and 50 of the latter sex had not previously been in gaol; so that, as may be observed by the previous tables, the recommitments here are confined to a few individuals. For example, in 1875 there was a male in custody who had been between 70 and 80 times in gaol from his first commitment, and one who had been even 8 times committed during the seven months previous to my visit in that year ; it may, therefore, be concluded from those figures that short imprisonments in an associated gaol, as this is, has very little effect for good upon habitual offenders. In most of our county and borough prisons the recommitments are much more numerous amongst females than amongst males ; but this rule is reversed here, which would show that there are men in this district who appear to spend their lives in crime and dissolute habits.

Accommodation.

	M.	F.		M.	F.
Wards, ...	8	3	Store Rooms, . . .	3	1
Yards, ...	8	3	Laundry, ...	—	1
Day Rooms, . . .	7	3	Drying-room, . . .	—	1
Solitary Cells, . .	3	3	Lavatories, . . .	7	1
Single Cells, not less than 9 feet long, 6 feet wide, and 8 feet high=432 cubic feet, .	—	—	Bath, with Hot and Cold Water laid on, . . .	1	—
Single Cells of smaller size,	91	30	Baths, with Cold Water laid on,	7	2
Cells to contain three persons,	14	6	Privies, ...	12	5
Sleeping Rooms, . .	4	2	Water-closets, . . .	2	1
No. of Beds in such Rooms,	8	4	Fumigating Apparatus, .	1	1
Hospital Rooms, . .	2	2	Reception Rooms or cells,	9	1
Chapels, ...	Two.		Pump, ...	1	—
School Rooms, . .	1	1	Well, ...	1	—
Workshop, . . .	1	—	Tread-wheel, . . .	1	—
Worksheds, . . .	28	—	Other Machines for hard labour—9 lb. Shot.		
Kitchen, ...	1	—	Tell-tale Clocks, . .	2	—

In looking over the past reports of Inspectors-General on this prison, I am sorry to have to state that for many years almost the same defects have been pointed out by my colleague and myself, and that very few steps have been taken to adopt our recommendations; so that the structural defects of the gaol are much the same as they have been for the last ten years. The arrangements here in the reception class are good; and I am glad to find that prisoners are now all washed as they come in, and subsequently once a week—three good baths being provided in the male and one in the female prison; but hot water is only laid on to one of those in the male prison. None of the cells are artificially heated, nor are they provided with bells or gas, and most of them are of too small a size for separate confinement, with the exception of those I have already pointed out in the debtors' quarters. There is an ample supply of water in the prison, laid on to all the yards, and it is pumped into a large cistern by means of a tread-wheel; small lavatories are also put up at the end of each range of buildings. There are no water-closets provided in the prison, but there is an earth-closet in each of the exercise yards; and no improvement has been made in the sewerage since my last visit. Two chapels are now provided, in which the sexes are properly separated from each other's view. In most gaols divine service is performed for all religious persuasions in one chapel. I am therefore at a loss to perceive the necessity of two in this prison. No alteration has yet been made in the laundry since my last visit; nor have the laundry operations been extended in accordance with the recommendations I then made. The kitchen is still in the male prison; consequently the labour of a male prisoner and portion of the time of an officer is spent here during the whole day, whereas if this department were removed into the female prison the labour of a male prisoner could be turned to great advantage, and the continuous supervision of a warder would be saved; and, in addition to these advantages, I have no doubt that the culinary department would be carried on more efficiently by females than by males. The photography is performed by the clerk, who receives 6d. for each copy—the Board supplying the chemicals. This duty is efficiently performed, and the photographs are carefully registered. The Governor is also very attentive in tracing out former convictions of prisoners by means of photography. A fumigating apparatus is provided in each prison, in which all prison clothes are now purified before being put away. Two tell-tale clocks are used in order to test the vigilance of the night watchman, and are marked ten times during the night, from 10 P.M. to 6 A.M. The markings are taken by the Governor every morning, and are entered by him into the Lockings Book; and in case there are any omissions they are recorded against the defaulting officer in the Officers' Conduct Book. It is, however, right to say that there are very few omissions of this duty during the year; for, as a rule, the clocks are regularly and carefully marked. Unlock takes place in summer at 6 A.M., and in winter at 6.45 A.M.; and lock-up in the former season between 6 and 7, and in the latter season between 5 and 6 o'clock P.M., after which hour no labour is carried on.

Untried prisoners are permitted to see their friends, under the by-laws, twice a week; and the visits to convicted prisoners are regulated by the Local Inspector, who, I am informed, limits them now as much as possible. Inasmuch as visits to prisoners are very detrimental to discipline, I am certainly of opinion that they should be restricted to as few as possible; and further, that no convicted prisoner should receive a visit until the expiration of three months of his term of imprisonment. Where this rule is strictly enforced it has a most excellent deterrent effect upon habitual offenders; for they do not like being entirely isolated for that

K

Marginal notes: North District. Mayo County Gaol. Reception. Baths. Cells. Water. Sewerage. Chapels. Laundry. Kitchen. Photography. Fumigator. Night-watch. Visitors.

NORTH
DISTRICT.

*Mayo
County
Gaol.*

Stores.

length of time from the outer world. The place for visiting is through a latticed door, and I am informed that all visitors to prisoners are searched before being admitted. The general store of prison clothing and bedding is kept by the Governor, and there was an ample supply at the time of my visit. He issues articles from this store both to the matron and the reception warder, who respectively have charge of the prison property in use, and who are responsible for the dressing of the prisoners as they come in. All the stores are tidily and regularly kept; and the prisoners' own clothing is carefully put away in bundles, being properly labelled and signed previously. All prison clothing is made up within the gaol, with the exception of clogs; and all materials are procured by contract sanctioned by the Board. The cells and the bedding were all clean and in good order at the time of my visit, with the exception of some of the bedding in the reception class, which was slightly torn. No school has been carried on here for the last five years, notwithstanding repeated remonstrances on this subject by Inspectors-General.

Punishments for Prison Offences.

	From 1st January to 31st Dec., 1874.		From 1st Jan., 1875, to day of Inspection.	
	M.	F.	M.	F.
By Magisterial authority, . . .	1	1	—	—
By Governor—				
Dark or Refractory Cells, . .	21	5	19	6
Total, . . .	22	6	19	6

On no occasion this year was it found necessary to have recourse to magisterial authority for the punishment of any prisoner for the breach of prison rule; but up to the time of my visit 19 males and 6 females had been sentenced to solitary by the Governor. Inasmuch as these cells are not artificially heated, the prisoners are not left in them during the night; therefore such punishment can have very little effect upon obstreperous prisoners. Under these circumstances, I submit that the requirements of the section of the Prisons Act in regard to the punishment cells should be carried out here, and that two properly heated and fitted up refractory cells should be provided in which prisoners undergoing punishment could remain during the whole period of such sentence.

Summary of Employment on day of Inspection.

	M.	F.
Hard Labour, ...	11	2
Industrial Labour, ...	17	8
Sick, ...	1	—
Discharged before labour hours, . . .	1	—
Total, ...	30	10

Amount received for produce of Prisoners' Labour disposed of outside the Gaol for the last three years.

1872, . £5 6s. 6d. | 1873, . £4 7s. 10d. | 1874, . £4 8s. 3d.

Net average daily cost of ordinary diet for each prisoner in the three preceding years.

1872, . 4d. | 1873, . 4d. | 1874, . 4d.

Net cost of gaol, including diet and salaries, for the three preceding years.

1872, £1,695 2s. 7d. | 1873, £1,816 15s. 6d. | 1874, £1,800 7s. 2d.

Total cost of officers, including clothing, value of rations, &c.

1872, . £1,154 4s. 3d. | 1873, . £1,251 0s. 6d. | 1874, . £1,272 16s. 3d.

Average cost of each prisoner per annum in each of the last three years.

1872, . . £33 11s. 6d. | 1873, . £36 8s. 3d. | 1874, . . £38 6s. 1d.

Amounts repaid by the Inland Revenue Department for excise prisoners for the last three years.

1872, . £14 6s. 3d. | 1873, . £7 16s. 9d. | 1874, . £4 17s. 1·5d.

Amounts repaid from the Consolidated Fund for the maintenance, &c., of prisoners during the years

1872, . £181 14s. 8d. | 1873, . £161 0s. 6d. | 1874, . £163 1s. 11d.

Labour.

The hard labour is enforced by means of a tread-wheel, at which men so sentenced work for two hours a day—being about fifteen minutes absolutely on the mill and the same time off. The mill is a very heavy one, and requires more men to turn it than can conveniently stand upon it without touching one another. In fact, I witnessed the greatest possible confusion on the day of my visit amongst the prisoners who were thus employed; so much so that discipline and regularity could not be and were not observed. If the tread-wheel is to be continued here, I submit that it should be put into proper repair, so that it can be worked with advantage to those prisoners who are sentenced to hard labour, and without being a detriment to discipline and order, as it is at present. In my report of 1873 I fully laid down my views on the subject of labour in this gaol, and am still of opinion that a sufficient quantity is not carried on, either of hard labour or industrial labour. Prisoners are allowed too much leisure and idleness; and I submit that the time spent by men absolutely at hard labour is insufficient, for two hours on the mill, with fifteen minutes rest out of every half-hour, cannot be considered a due amount of hard labour for prisoners so sentenced. The principal other occupation at which men are employed is that of stone-breaking; but no specified quantity is required of any of the men, and very little of this labour is performed throughout the year. Too many prisoners are told off in the gaol as wardsmen, which in many cases is only an excuse for idleness. The consequence of this want of industry is that the amount received for the produce of prisoners' labour is extremely small, being for the whole of the year 1874 only £4 8s. 3d. This, I submit, is but a wretched return for the labour of the daily average number of prisoners committed here during that year, namely, 46; yet the cost of the prison for that year amounted to the large sum of £1,800 7s. 2d.; but the cost of officers from that sum was £1,272 6s. 2d.; so that it is not to be wondered that the average cost of a prisoner here per annum amounts to £38 6s. 1d.

Officers and Salaries.

	£	s.	d.		£	s.	d.
Non-Resident.				Thomas Armstrong, Clerk			
Francis O'Donel, esq., Local				and Warder, . .	42	0	0
Inspector, . . .	100	0	0	Michael Bourke, .	35	0	0
Rev. W. C. Townsend, Protest-				Isaac Fair, . .	35	0	0
ant Episcopal Chaplain, .	46	3	0	Edward Acton, .	35	0	0
Rev. Patk. Waldron, Roman				Rbt. M'Quuigue, *Carpenter*,	35	0	0
Catholic Chaplain, .	46	3	0	James Devine, *Tailor*, .	35	0	0
M. J. Jordan, Physician, .	50	0	0	Patrick Lyons, . .	35	0	0
A. T. Sullivan, Apothecary,	30	0	0	Thomas Rogers, Gate Warder,	45	0	0
				Rebecca Layng, Matron, .	45	0	0
Resident.				Anne Bourke, Assist. do.,	35	0	0
Davis R. Young, esq., Governor,	300	0	0	Mary Cunniff, Hosptl. Nurse,	25	0	0
Harry M'Clung, Deputy-				Julia Rogers, Female Searcher,	7	10	0
Governor, . . .	60	0	0				

(Turnkeys.)

K 2

NORTH
DISTRICT.

*Mayo
County
Gaol.*

<table>
<tr><td colspan="3" align="center">*Officers' Visits.*</td></tr>
<tr><td></td><td>From 1st Jan. to
31st Dec., 1874.</td><td>From 1st Jan., 1875, to
day of Inspection.</td></tr>
<tr><td>Number of times the Board of Superintendence met and discharged business,</td><td>12</td><td>8</td></tr>
<tr><td>Local Inspector to Gaol,</td><td>152</td><td>99</td></tr>
<tr><td>Do.   each Bridewell,</td><td>4</td><td>3</td></tr>
<tr><td>Chaplain, Protestant Episcop. Church,</td><td>227</td><td>149</td></tr>
<tr><td>Chaplain, Roman Catholic,</td><td>205</td><td>114</td></tr>
<tr><td>Physician,</td><td>298</td><td>226</td></tr>
<tr><td>Apothecary,</td><td>385</td><td>249</td></tr>
</table>

Officers.

In my last report on this prison I pointed out that the staff was much in excess of its requirements. Having regard to the daily average number in custody at the time of my inspection this year, I again laid my views on this subject before the Board, and recommended the abolition of the office of Deputy Governor, which is by no means required in this gaol, as his duties, such as they are, can very easily be performed by the clerk. An officer is employed during the day as a watchman or guard; but inasmuch as all prisoners should be under the eye of an officer, I do not see the necessity of a day watchman; and as the daily average number of females during the year is so small, I am of opinion that two female officers are quite sufficient to maintain discipline and regularity in that prison. In the neighbouring prison of Roscommon there is only one female officer, and her department is well kept, and reflects much credit upon her. If prisoners were more concentrated, and not scattered so much over the building as they are at present, fewer officers would be required, and supervision would be more easy; and even under these circumstances, a greater amount of supervision than exists at present could be maintained. All the subordinate officers have rooms and sleep in the prison, except those who are allowed occasionally to sleep out. Their quarters very much required to be painted, and would be improved if the floors were boarded, as at present they look untidy, and are not so well kept as they should be. The whole of the prison building seemed to be in good repair; but some painting was required throughout.

Contracts.

Bread, white, per 4-lb. loaf, 6d.; ditto, brown, per 4-lb. loaf, 5½d.; oatmeal, per cwt., 12s.; Indian meal, per cwt., 9s.; potatoes, per cwt., 2s. 10d.; new milk, per gallon, 6½d.; buttermilk, per gallon, 4d.; salt, per cwt., 2s. 6d.; turf, per box, 1s.; straw, per cwt., 2s. 2d.; candles, per lb., 5½d.; soap, per cwt., £1 8s.; linen, per yard, 7¼d.; lime, per barrel, 1s. 8d.

Provisions.

The contracts are taken yearly, and are all sanctioned by the Board. The provisions appeared to be excellent, and are usually reported on favourably by the Chaplains, who inspect them by alternate weeks, but frequently by substitute.

Hospital.

<table>
<tr><td></td><td colspan="2" align="center">1872.</td><td colspan="2" align="center">1873.</td><td colspan="2" align="center">1874.</td><td colspan="2" align="center">1875
(To day of
Inspection).</td></tr>
<tr><td></td><td>M.</td><td>F.</td><td>M.</td><td>F.</td><td>M.</td><td>F.</td><td>M.</td><td>F.</td></tr>
<tr><td>No. of prisoners in hospital,</td><td>49</td><td>16</td><td>62</td><td>23</td><td>22</td><td>18</td><td>—</td><td>—</td></tr>
<tr><td>Average daily number in hospital,</td><td>1·6</td><td>·6</td><td>1·3</td><td>·5</td><td>1</td><td>1</td><td>—</td><td>—</td></tr>
<tr><td>No. of prisoners prescribed for and treated out of hospital,</td><td>197</td><td>71</td><td>172</td><td>87</td><td>179</td><td>106</td><td>—</td><td>—</td></tr>
<tr><td>No. of deaths in the Gaol,</td><td>—</td><td>2</td><td>—</td><td>—</td><td>—</td><td>—</td><td>—</td><td>—</td></tr>
<tr><td>Cost of medicine,</td><td colspan="2">£0 2s. 7d.</td><td colspan="2">£7 19s. 9d.</td><td colspan="2">£4 17s. 5d.</td><td colspan="2">—</td></tr>
<tr><td>Cost of diet for prisoners in hospital,</td><td colspan="2">£1 11s. 1d.</td><td colspan="2">£19 8s. 0d.</td><td colspan="2">£16 15s. 0d.</td><td colspan="2">—</td></tr>
<tr><td>Cost of extra diet ordered by Medical Officer for prisoners not in hospital,</td><td colspan="2">£14 2s. 3d.</td><td colspan="2">£1 2s. 6d.</td><td colspan="2">£5 5s. 0d.</td><td colspan="2">—</td></tr>
</table>

NORTH
DISTRICT.

*Mayo
County
Gaol.*
Hospital.

No alteration has been made in the hospital since my last visit. It is principally occupied by the matron and her husband, who is still there, bedridden. At the time of my visit one male was in hospital who was suffering from heart disease, and was exempted consequently from labour by the Doctor. As no books are provided in this gaol for prisoners except what may be given to them by the Chaplains, this man was compelled to remain brooding over his cares and disease all the day long. In all well regulated gaols a certain number of books are kept, and I would strongly recommend that a selection be made by the Board for the use of the prisoners. During the year 1874 22 males, and 18 females were treated in hospital here. The medicines are procured from the Apothecaries' Hall, Dublin, and are all compounded by the apothecary in the gaol, and cost in 1874 £4 17s. 5d.

Books and Journals.

The Clerk keeps the books of registry and finance with much care and precision. They are also regularly and attentively overlooked by the Governor; and the Local Inspector also devotes considerable time to this portion of his duty. This officer also keeps an excellent journal, as does the Governor, who, on this occasion, as on previous inspections, I found most attentive to duty, and anxious to carry out, as far as lies in his power, the directions of his superiors. He adopts the very useful system of entering all matters of importance in his journal in red ink. I have again to draw attention to the non-compliance by the Chaplains with the statute relating to their duties. This is a matter that I have referred to in former reports, but hitherto with no avail; so that I fear it is little use in my again drawing attention to this subject. The Medical Officer keeps an excellent journal, and devotes much of his time and attention to his prison duties; and the hospital books are carefully kept by him. Most of the prescribed prison books are in use, with the exception of the Morning State Book, which should be procured and regularly written up. I would also recommend that the registries be more amalgamated, as an unnecessary number are now kept. One of the prisoners complained to me of the irregularity in the hours for meals, and I made inquiry into this subject, and I found that there was some truth in his statement. I therefore trust that the hours for breakfast, dinner, and supper will be more regularly laid down and strictly attended to. I would also submit that an hour for breakfast and an hour for dinner are too long periods to allow for those meals, during which time prisoners are altogether unoccupied; and as the officers take their meals in the gaol, I am of opinion that half an hour for breakfast and the same for dinner is quite sufficient time to allow for that purpose. I am glad to learn that since two people have been prosecuted for introducing tobacco into the prison, that this breach of prison rule has been put a stop to; but if persons are carefully searched, as they should be before being admitted, I cannot understand how any prohibited article can be introduced.

Board of Superintendence.

The meetings of the Board take place once a month, at which time the subordinate officers' salaries are paid, and small accounts are settled. The superior officers receive their salaries twice a year at assizes.

NORTH
DISTRICT.

STATE OF BRIDEWELLS.

*Mayo
County.*

Bridewells.

	Ballinrobe.		Westport.*		Swinford.	
	M.	F.	M.	F.	M.	F.
No. of Committals in past year, .	20	2	15	10	27	9
Of whom were Drunkards,	8	–	3	2	2	–
Committals in quarter preceding inspection, . .	6	1	3	2	9	2
Of whom were Drunkards,	–	–	–	–	1	–
Petty Sessions and Transmittals, how often?	Petty Sessions on every Monday; transmittals sometimes immediate. Criminal Quarter Sessions twice here, and twice at Claremorris.		Weekly, on Thursdays; transmittals direct and regular.		Petty Sessions fortnightly; Criminal Quarter Sessions four times a year; transmittals generally on the following day.	
Committals, . .	Regular.		Regular.		Regular.	
Registry, . .	Regular.		Correctly kept.		Regular.	
Repairs and Order,	Good.		In good repair and order, but the woodwork has not been painted for many years, and it should be done.		Improved since last inspection, and roof now about to be stanched.	
Security, . .	Fair, with care.		No change since last inspection.		Fair, with care.	
Accommodation, .	Two cells for males, one for females; two day-rooms.		Two day-rooms and six cells, each with one bed.		Six cells, and two day-rooms.	
Furniture, Bedding, and Utensils.	Good; but some sheets very dirty.		Good and sufficient.		A good supply, but some of the sheets were torn, and very dirty.	
Water, how supplied?	By pump, now in repair.		None on premises; but about 500 yards distant.		None on premises.	
Sewerage, . .	Cesspools, lately cleaned.		Sufficient.		Cesspools, which can only be cleaned out through the house.	
Cleanliness, Dryness, and Ventilation.	Dry, and fairly ventilated.		Clean, dry, and well ventilated.		Pretty clean, and well ventilated.	
Cost of Dietary, .	5d. per head per day.		2½d. each meal.		5d. per head per day.	
Salary of Keeper, and whether he follows any other employment.	£15; £6 a year for fuel and straw.		£15 per annum; Keeper is Petty Sessions Clerk and Court-keeper.		£15; £6 for fuel, light, and straw. Is Court-keeper, at £8; is a carpenter, but does not now do much at his trade, owing to illness.	
Date of Inspection,	25th August, 1875.		16th Sept., 1875.		28th August, 1875.	
Remarks, . .	No prisoner in custody, and only 2 this quarter.		No prisoner in charge.		No prisoner in custody. The yards are covered with mud, and should be kept cleaner.	

* Inspected by my colleague for me.

STATE OF BRIDEWELLS—*continued.*

—	Ballina.*	
	M.	F.
No. of Committals in past year,	28	9
Of whom were Drunkards,	1	1
Committals in quarter preceding inspection,	14	7
Of whom were Drunkards,	2	4
Petty Sessions and Transmittals, how often?	Weekly, on Tuesdays; transmittals direct and regular.	
Committals,	Regular.	
Registry,	Correctly drawn.	
Repairs and Order,	Building in good repair; walls lately whitewashed.	
Security,	Yards insecure; a down-pipe from roof, in each yard. The long forms in the day-room would facilitate an escape.	
Accommodation,	Seven cells and two day-rooms; but one of the latter is used by Keeper as a kitchen, as his apartment is confined to one room, which must serve as office and sleeping apartment for himself and family.	
Furniture, Bedding, and Utensils,	Good and sufficient.	
Water, how supplied?	None; no water within a quarter of a mile distance.	
Sewerage,	A deep cesspool lies behind each privy, which I found on former occasions full of stinking water; on this occasion the cesspools were almost dry, and I learn that they do not communicate with the privies, and are merely intended to drain the yards of surface water. I would suggest that, if such is the case, they be filled up, and a small pipe drain to carry off the surface water be made in each yard.	
Cleanliness, Dryness, and Ventilation,	Clean, dry, and well ventilated.	
Cost of Dietary,	2½d. for each meal.	
Salary of Keeper, and whether he follows any other employment.	£18 a year. His wife has no salary, yet she has to attend the female prisoners, wash the bedding, and keep the place in order. She complains that she was compelled to hire a woman for two days, and expend 2s. on soap to clean some blankets, and she has not been repaid the expense she was at.	
Date of Inspection,	15th September, 1875.	
Remarks,	I found no prisoner in charge when I visited.	

CHARLES F. BOURKE, *Inspector-General.*

* Inspected by my colleague for me.

MEATH COUNTY GAOL, AT TRIM.—STATUTABLE INSPECTION, 29TH
DECEMBER, 1875.

Number in
custody.

The total number of prisoners committed here at the above date was 33 males and 3 females. Seven of these were untried ; 8 were cases disposed of at quarter sessions or assizes, and the remainder were summary convictions. Up to the above date 5 juveniles were committed during this year, and two of these were sent to reformatories. One of them, a male, had been twice in gaol since his first commitment.

Number of Prisoners of all classes in Gaol on the day of Inspection, and on the corresponding date in the three preceding years.

	M.	F.		M.	F.
1872, ...	28	3	1874, ...	19	6
1873, ...	25	1	1875 (day of Inspection),	33	3

Number of Vagrants in Gaol on the day of Inspection, and on the corresponding date in the three preceding years.

	M.	F.		M.	F.
1872, ...	5	—	1874, ...	6	—
1873, ...	7	—	1875 (day of Inspection),	3	—

Commitments.

					From 1st January to 31st Dec., 1874.		From 1st Jan., 1875, to day of Inspection.	
					M.	F.	M.	F.
Debtors,	.	.	.	.	3	—	1	—
Criminals,	.	.	.	.	160	22	215	29
Vagrants,	.	.	.	.	92	—	142	7
Drunkards,	.	.	.	.	59	8	108	15
Total,	.	.	.	.	314	30	466	51

Commit-
ments.

As compared with previous years, the number of male prisoners in custody on the day of my visit here this year was very large, and the commitments to this prison during 1875 were in excess of the previous year, being up to the time of my visit this year of males 466 and of females 51, against 314 and 30 respectively for the whole of the year 1874. The foregoing table will show that there is an increment in nearly all the classes of commitments here with the exception of those of debtors during 1875 ; but I would specially draw attention to the large increase this year in the commitments of vagrants and drunkards, and I also observe that there is an increase in the criminal commitments both of males and females. Indeed, the management of this prison is little calculated to deter people in this county from crime, or to discourage professional vagrants from frequenting the district.

[TABLE.

Number of Individual Prisoners (exclusive of Debtors), and Number of times each had been committed during the following periods, distinguishing Adults from Juveniles.

NUMBER OF TIMES COMMITTED.	1874.				1875, to day of Inspection.			
	Juveniles.		Adults.		Juveniles.		Adults.	
	M.	F.	M.	F.	M.	F.	M.	F.
Once within the year.	9	1	248	23	4	–	330	37
Twice "	–	–	20	3	–	–	43	5
Thrice "	–	–	2	–	–	–	7	–
4 times "	–	–	2	–	–	–	2	1
5 times "	–	–	–	–	–	–	2	–
6 times "	–	–	–	–	–	–	1	–
Total,	9	1	272	26	4	–	385	43
No. of above who had not been in Gaol previous to 1st Jan. in	9	1	200	18	3	–	295	30

Number of Individual Prisoners, exclusive of Debtors, committed in the year 1874, and to the day of Inspection in 1875, who had been once and oftener in custody from their first Commitment in any year, so far as can be ascertained, distinguishing Adults from Juveniles.

NUMBER OF TIMES COMMITTED.	1874.				1875, to day of Inspection.			
	Juveniles.		Adults.		Juveniles.		Adults.	
	M.	F.	M.	F.	M.	F.	M.	F.
Once only,	9	1	191	16	3	–	287	30
Twice,	–	–	27	4	1	–	40	7
Thrice,	–	–	18	1	–	–	24	2
4 times,	–	–	17	2	–	–	15	1
5 "	–	–	2	–	–	–	3	–
6 "	–	–	5	–	–	–	6	1
7 to 11 "	–	–	10	1	–	–	5	1
12 to 16 "	–	–	1	–	–	–	2	–
17 to 20 "	–	–	–	–	–	–	1	1
21 to 30 "	–	–	1	1	–	–	2	–
31 to 40 "	–	–	–	1	–	–	–	–
Total No. of Individuals committed,	9	1	272	26	4	–	385	43
No. of Commitments represented in foregoing,	9	1	523	107	5	–	809	85

Averages, and Highest and Lowest Numbers (exclusive of Debtors).

—	From 1st January to 31st December, 1874.			From 1st January, 1875, to day of Inspection.		
	M.	F.	Date.	M.	F.	Date.
Average daily number of prisoners in custody.	20	2	—	35	3	—
Highest number of prisoners at any one time,	39		9th May.	71		3rd Nov.
Lowest ditto,	12		13th Aug.	22		3rd Jan.
Highest number of males at any one time,	36		9th May.	65		3rd Nov.
Ditto, of females,	6		16th May.	7		16th Feb.
Lowest number of males at any one time,	11		16th Sept.	20		3rd Jan.
Ditto, of females,	–		1st Jan.	–		16th March.

NORTH DISTRICT.

Meath County Gaol.

Highest Number of Prisoners (exclusive of Debtors), in Gaol during each of the previous seven years, and up to day of Inspection in 1875.

31st January, 1868,	. . 31	22nd April, 1872, . . . 40
5th February, 1869,	. . 45	23rd February, 1873, . . 40
16th February, 1870,	. . 55	9th May, 1874, . . . 89
20th May, 1871,	. . 46	3rd November, 1875, . . 71

Recommitments.

During the year 1874 twice was the greatest number of times that any female and four that any male was committed here, but up to the time of my visit this year one female had been committed as often as four times, and a male six times within the year, and in both years males were imprisoned here who had over 21 convictions recorded against them. In most prisons the recommitments are far more numerous amongst the females than amongst males, but here it is the contrary, which I attribute very much to the large number of vagrants and drunkards of the latter sex who appear to wander through this county. The total number of adult individuals committed here in 1874 was 272 males and 26 females. Two hundred of the former and 18 of the latter had not, however, been before in gaol. But, nevertheless, the recommitments numbered 523 of males, and 107 of females. In the expired portion of this year the individuals committed were 385 males and 43 females; of these 295 and 30 respectively had not been in gaol previously. However, the recommitments of old offenders

Want of discipline.

numbered respectively 809 and 85. I am of opinion that if more discipline and a greater amount of separation and labour were carried out here that the number of these recommitments would very soon diminish, as I had abundant proof during my inspection of the little attention there is given here to these important matters. I found an incorrigible female here in association with a woman who was in gaol for her first offence, and who was probably being every moment corrupted by this infamous woman. There was no reason, whatsoever, for this irregularity, as there was ample room for those prisoners to be employed in separation. I also found a male prisoner in custody, committed for vagrancy, who was allowed to walk about in his class as he was suffering from a slight whitlow. This man should certainly have been confined to one of the large cells, which, although they are not heated, he could have been left in during most of the day, and permitted to warm himself from time to time at the fire in the day-room. I also found two men in the hospital who were not considered by the doctor, nor were they, proper subjects to be sent to hospital. One was an old offender sentenced to 13 months' imprisonment, and the other to one month with hard labour. These men should have been employed either at oakum picking or some other such industry, for with the commonest arrangement suitable cells could have been provided for them. As long as sentences of the law are carried out here in this manner, I fear old offenders will continue to frequent this county and be a constant source of expense to the rate-payers, both in and out of gaol. Another prisoner in custody complained to me of having been punished harshly for fighting with a fellow prisoner. On investigating this case I found that, in my opinion, both prisoners were to blame, but that if discipline and order were observed and that proper supervision was maintained such an occurrence could never have taken place. It also appears that this prisoner, since this dispute, was kept altogether idle in his class, provided with a good fire, by which he was allowed to remain unemployed the whole day, inasmuch as the Governor was afraid of a second *rencontre* taking place between him and the other prisoner. This is not, I submit, a method calculated either to preserve order or discipline, or to have any deterrent effect upon hardened offenders, and is, in my opinion, a serious error of judgment on the part of the superior officers. Owing to the considerable increase of vagrancy in this county some of the magistrates have communicated with me on the subject of the treatment of such prisoners in gaol, but I fear that unless their sojourn here is made much more irksome than it is at present, this class of wanderer will continue to frequent the county. The average daily number of males in custody this year was 15 in excess of last, but that of females was only one in excess of the daily average of 1874, and at one period in both years there was no prisoner of that sex in custody, while at no period in either years did their numbers exceed 7. But, notwithstanding this, two officers are considered necessary for management of these few prisoners. The only person in custody this year classed as a debtor was a male, committed for contempt of court, but who did not remain long in prison. As it is not likely that prisoners of this class will in future be committed here, their quarters can be appropriated for other purposes.

NORTH DISTRICT.

Meath County Gaol.

Vagrants.

Debtor.

Accommodation.

	M.	F.		M.	F.
Yards,	11	5	Laundry,	–	1
Day Rooms,	5	2	Drying Room,	–	1
Solitary Cells,	3	1	Lavatories,	1	1
Single Cells of *less* than 432 cubic feet,	50	30	Baths, with Hot and Cold Water laid on,	1	1
Cells to contain three persons,	10	5	Privies,	10	4
Sleeping Rooms,	6	–	Water-closets,	2	2
No. of Beds in such Rooms,	6	–	Fumigating Apparatus,	1	1
Hospital Rooms,	2	2	Reception Rooms, or Cells,	1	1
Chapel,	1	–	Pumps,	2	–
Workshops,	3	–	Wells,	2	–
Workshed,	1	–	Tread-wheels,	2	–
Kitchen,	1	–	Tell-tale Clocks,	2	–
Store Rooms,	3	1			

The structural condition of this gaol has not undergone any alteration since my last visit. No proper arrangement exists in the female prison as to the reception class, and at the time of my visit the matron being absent the female prisoners were in charge of the assistant-matron, who is a very inexperienced officer, and who has evidently not been taught her duties by her superiors; and I regret to find that the classification of prisoners of this sex, as I have already pointed out, was not sufficiently attended to by the Governor. Some of the cells in this section could easily be appropriated to a reception class, in which prisoners should be kept until passed by the doctor into their proper wards, in compliance with the 109th section of the Prisons Act. One good bath, with hot and cold water, is provided in the female prison, in which, I was informed, all females are cleansed as they come in; but no period is subsequently fixed for the repetition of this operation, which should certainly take place weekly. There is a suitable reception class in the male prison, and a good bath is provided there, in which all are cleansed as they come in, and subsequently once in three weeks during imprisonment. I submit that men as well as women should certainly be washed weekly. Prisoners after being washed are, I am informed, allowed to put on their dirty clothes again until inspected by the doctor, instead of being at once dressed in prison clothes. It is obvious that in order to prevent dirt and infection being carried into the prison, such a system as this should not be permitted. I therefore submit that all prison clothes be at once purified, and that while this operation is being performed prisoners whose sentence is less than a month, or those who are committed for trial should be provided with a suit of prison clothes, and those sentenced to a

Reception.

Baths.

month or more should be at once dressed in the county clothing. Two basins are fitted as a lavatory in the male reception, and in addition there is one in each class, in which prisoners are required to wash their hands and face every morning. No alteration has taken place in the supply of water-closets and privies since my last inspection, nor has the sewerage undergone any alteration; but it is said to be effective. The water is provided in the same manner as on my last visit, and there is an abundance on the premises. None of the cells are heated, nor are they fitted with gas or bells, but both are provided in the day-rooms, and the corridors are also lighted with gas. A fumigating apparatus is provided to each prison, so that there is no excuse for the clothing not being properly purified immediately on the admission of a prisoner. No alteration has been made in the chapel since my last visit. It is only used for Roman Catholic worship, as the Protestant service is performed in the vestry, there being seldom more than one or two prisoners of that religion in custody. The laundry arrangements have not either undergone any alterations, and are quite sufficient for the ordinary purposes of this prison, as so few female prisoners are committed here. One male prisoner is still employed in the kitchen, but I am informed that he now goes to other labour, and, in case of the cook being a hard labour man, he takes his turn at the mill with the remainder of the prisoners so sentenced daily. Photography is now carried on by the tailor-warder, who appears to perform this duty very efficiently, and who is allowed 6d. for each prisoner photographed. A copy of all photographs is kept in a book, attached to which is a description, the counterpart being sent to the Habitual Criminals Office; but at the time of my visit these photographs were not properly arranged in the book, and I drew the attention of the photographer to this subject. I do not, however, consider that sufficient care is taken here to trace out old offenders, as I found a woman in custody whom I recognised as having met lately in another gaol; yet, this was not known to the Governor, nor was there, as far as I could learn, any attempt made to ascertain her previous convictions. Two telltale clocks are provided, one of which is at the gate and the other in the male class, the keys of which are kept by the Governor. One is marked every quarter of an hour, and the other every half hour from 6 P.M. to 6 A.M. during the year, and the markings are taken either by the Governor or Deputy Governor every morning, and are entered in the Lockings Book, and all omissions are noted in the Conduct Book; but I am glad to find that this duty is, as a rule, very carefully performed by the night watchman. Lock-up takes place at 6 P.M., and unlock at 7 A.M. both in summer and winter. I submit that unlock should certainly take place an hour earlier in summer, as work should be commenced not later than seven o'clock during that season. The Governor, or in his absence, the Deputy Governor is present at the final lock-up, and then takes possession of all the keys of the prison, which are taken by him to his bed-room at night. The rules as to visitors to prisoners, and the arrangements for the admission of visitors here, are the same as at my last inspection. Convicted prisoners are allowed a visit once a month, but the Governor has the discretion of refusing this privilege to those who are not of good character. This fact should, however, be always noted by him in his journal. I am still of opinion that no prisoner should be allowed a visit or should be permitted to write a letter, except in very exceptional cases, until the first three months of the sentence has expired, for where such rules exist imprisonment has a much greater effect upon ordinary offenders. All the cells in the prison, except two in each class, are too small for the maintenance of the separate system, but they were generally clean and tidily kept.

Stock at the time of Inspection.

	In Use.	In Store.	Male Clothing.		In Use.	In Store.	Female Clothing.		In Use.	In Store.
Blankets, pairs of, . . .	109	12	Shirts, .	.	130	–	Shifts, .	.	3	71
Sheets, pairs of,	171	–	Jackets, .	.	27	49	Jackets, .	.	3	24
Rugs, .	110	12	Vests, .	.	27	89	Petticoats,	.	3	105
Bedticks, .	119	–	Trowsers, .	.	27	109	Aprons, .	.	3	55
Bedsteads, .	122	–	Caps, .	.	27	143	Neckerchiefs, .		3	34
			Stockings or Socks, pairs of,		–	5	Caps, .	.	3	46
							Stockings, prs.of,		3	31
			Shoes, Slippers, & Clogs, pairs of,		27	142	Shoes, Slippers, & Clogs, pairs of,		3	40

The store of male clothing is kept by the Deputy Governor, and that *Stores.* of the females by the matron. This department was better arranged than at my last visit, but the system followed is still very faulty, and open to great abuse. The cutting out of the materials is managed altogether by subordinate officers, and there appears to be no proper checks to regulate these matters. The prisoners' own clothing is now labelled, but as the labels are not properly signed they are of little use. I find that of late a large number of shoes have been mended here, but so little care is taken of them that they are not ever cleaned. I have in former reports drawn attention to the want of arrangement of this department, and fear that so long as it is in charge of the present store-keeper little improvement will be effected, unless the Governor and Local Inspector devote more time to the stores than they have hitherto done. The bedding throughout the prison was generally clean and in good order, the sheets being changed once in three weeks, and I am informed that all prisoners get a pair as they come in.

Number of Punishments for Prison Offences.

	From 1st January to 31st Dec, 1874.		From 1st Jan., 1875, to day of Inspection.	
	M.	F.	M.	F.
By Magisterial authority, . . .	1	–	1	–
By Governor—				
Dark or refractory cells, . .	16	–	40	2
Stoppage of diet, . . .	16	–	38	–
Other punishments, . . .	1	–	5	–
Total, . . .	34	–	84	2

Up to the time of my visit 84 males and 2 females had been punished *Punishments.* this year for breach of prison rule, for one of whom (a male) it was found necessary to have recourse to magisterial authority. This man was such an obstreperous character that, on the application of the Governor, he was removed from this gaol to the County Dublin Prison, as he threatened the Governor's life ; and as the officers of this prison seemed to be incapable of managing him, my colleague and I recommended his removal to a prison where the separate system is maintained, and where strict discipline can be carried out. The two solitary cells that are used here are heated and provided with spiral bells, but at the time of my visit these bells were much too stiff and should have been oiled. Prisoners are allowed their bedding at night while in solitary ; an indulgence which I do not think at all called for or necessary. In such a prison as this, where so much association is permitted, there is always a greater amount of punishment than where prisoners are kept in separation ; and I regret to state that I attribute the great number of punishments for breach of prison rule imposed here to the want of discipline and proper supervision of prisoners.

Summary of Labour.

						M.	Y.
Industrial Labour,	.	.	.	.	.	28	3
Sick,	.	.	.	.	.	4	-
Discharged (before labour hours),	.	.	.	.	.	1	-
Total in custody,				.	.	33	3

Amount received for produce of Prisoners' Labour disposed of outside the Gaol for the last three years.

1872, . £11 11s. 0d. | 1873, . £5 11s. 0d | 1874, . £10 7s. 11d.

Net average daily cost of ordinary diet for each Prisoner in the three preceding years.

1872, . 4·5d. | 1873, . 5·6d | 1874, . 6d.

Net cost of Gaol, including Diet and Salaries for the three preceding years.

1872, . £2,106 15s. 4d. | 1873, . £2,189 19s. 6d. | 1874, . £1,970 2s. 9d.

Total cost of Officers, including Clothing, Value of Rations, Washing, Gas, &c.

1872, . £1,164 0s. 10d. | 1873, . £1,217 10s. 6d. | 1874, . £1,215 18s. 6d.

Average cost of each Prisoner per annum in each of the last three years.

1872, .. £81 0s. 11d. | 1873, . £81 18s. 8d. | 1874, . £85 18s. 2d.

Amounts repaid by the War Department for Military Prisoners in each of the last three years.

1872, . £5 13s. 9d. | 1873, . £1 3s. 0d. | 1874, . £2 8s. 0d.

Amounts repaid from the Consolidated Fund for the maintenance, &c., of Prisoners during the years

1872, . £74 13s. 2d. | 1873, . £72 19s. 9d. | 1874, . £35 18s. 7d.

Labour.

The amount of labour carried on in this gaol is, as I have before stated, most unsatisfactory. At the time of my visit, and sometime previous to it, there was absolutely no hard labour exacted from prisoners so sentenced, as I was informed that there were not sufficient men in custody sentenced to hard labour to work the tread-wheel, and that it was stiff, having been affected by the late frost. I, however, subsequently ascertained that there were as many as 17 men in custody so sentenced, and that it only required 9 to work the mill, and although the machinery was somewhat stiff its action would have been much improved if the commonest precautions had been taken to oil it and keep it in order. It is obvious that unless the Local Inspector and the Governor (for it is the duty of both to see that the sentence of the law is carried out) attend to such ordinary matters, the subordinate officers will certainly not attend to their duties. If at any time the mill cannot be worked, prisoners sentenced to hard labour here, in the absence of any other such labour, should be put to shot-drill for a certain number of hours each day. The only labour for males pursued at the time of my visit was that of stone-breaking, at which men were employed in association in a very irregular and slovenly way; there were also some few prisoners employed at shoemaking. An excellent loom is provided by the Board for mat-making, but since the appointment of the present bridewell-keeper to Navan no other officer has been taught this simple handicraft, consequently, no mat-making has been carried on here for some time. If a warder were either sent to Navan to the bridewell-keeper there, or that the latter officer were to come to Trim for a day, he could with very little trouble be taught the art of mat-making, which is very simple, and which could be learned in a very short time. The stone-sheds should also be better adapted to the carrying out of labour in separation; and I would suggest that such labour as oakum-picking and fibre-teasing should be introduced, in which case the men sentenced to hard labour should be required to pick a certain amount of oakum daily, and those not so sentenced should be also employed in their cells. If such labour were required to be performed by prisoners confined here the two men referred to as being in the hospital in a state of total idleness from day's end to day's end could have been so employed, their time in the prison would not have been entirely thrown away, and the sentence of the law would have been more closely carried out. The shoemakers that I saw employed here were allowed to sit together, so that conversation could be maintained. Such matters of discipline as these should be more closely attended to, and the Governor should take care to carry out a more effective system of separation than is at present maintained here. The consequence of so little labour being exacted from prisoners is that the amounts received as the produce of their labour disposed of outside the gaol are very small, being in 1874 only £10 7s. 11d., whereas the average annual cost of a prisoner for that year came to £85 13s. 2d. In that year the net cost of the gaol amounted to £1,970 2s. 9d., of which sum the cost of officers came to £1,215 18s. 6d. When one knows that in some countries gaols are self-supporting, and even in Ireland that prisoners can be maintained in gaols at the rate of about £16 per head per annum, the foregoing figures would certainly appear alarming, and strongly call for the re-organization of the whole of this establishment. I trust, however, that the coming session of Parliament will not pass without legislation taking place in regard to the prison system of this country, and in no county is reform in this direction more needed than in the County Meath. The employment of women is chiefly in washing for the prison and sewing; and I must remonstrate with the system in existence here of giving extra diet to women employed in the laundry. This is altogether contrary to prison rule, as the ordinary dietary scale is laid down by law, and should not be departed from except in cases of sickness or exhaustion, and then only under the orders of the medical officer. In many prisons women are employed in the laundry the whole day long, and on every day throughout the week, and do not receive extra diet, but such labour is not required here; nevertheless, this class of prisoner is indulged by extra diet. I am also informed that extra diet is given to other prisoners during the year without the consent of the medical officer, for which there is no authority, and therefore submit that these irregularities should be at once discontinued.

Margin notes: NORTH DISTRICT. Meath County Gaol. Expenditure.

Schools.

	From 1st Jan. to 31st Dec., 1874.		From 1st Jan., 1875, to day of Inspection.	
	M.	F.	M.	F.
Number of individual prisoners who attended school,	249	27	378	41
Average daily number of pupils,	15	2	30	2
Number of days on which school was held,	302	131	303	230

School-hours.—Males—7½ to 8½ A.M.; 4 to 5 P.M. Females—7½ to 8½ A.M.; 4 to 5 P.M.

The male school is carried on for two hours a day, and the female for an hour, but neither are stalled, so that prisoners are in association there as elsewhere. I fear that very little good results from the instruction imparted here, and would suggest that one hour is quite sufficient to allow for the secular instruction of prisoners, and further, that the schoolroom be partitioned, in order that separation may be maintained there, and as gas is provided in the schoolroom instruction should

Margin note: School.

.NORTH DISTRICT.

Meath County Gaol.

be conducted after dark in winter, so as not to interfere with the labour hours of the day. The males are taught by one of the warders who was brought up at the National School at Bective, but is not a trained teacher. The females are taught by the Assistant Matron, who has been accustomed to teach in the workhouse. The School has not yet been placed in connexion with the National Board of Education as I submit it should be.

Contracts.

Bread, white, per 4-lb. loaf, 5¼d.; ditto, brown, per 4-lb. loaf, 5¼d.; oatmeal, per cwt., 14s.; Indian meal, per cwt., 9s. 9d.; potatoes, per cwt., 6s.; meat, per lb. 9d.; newmilk, per gallon, 10d.; buttermilk, per gallon, 2d.; salt, per cwt., 2s. 6d.; coal, per ton, £1 5s. 3d.; turf, per gauge, 2s.; straw, per cwt., 2s. 9d.; gas, per 1,000 cubic feet, 8s. 4d.; candles, per lb., 6d.; soap, per cwt., £1 6s. Other contracts—keeping waterworks in repair, £10 per annum; keeping clocks in repair, £2 per annum; conveyance of prisoners, per Irish mile, 1s.

Provisions.

The provisions are obtained by contract sanctioned by the Board of Superintendence, and the materials are got in as required by tenders, which are also approved of by the Board. The samples of diet that I saw appeared to be excellent, and none of the prisoners complained to me of its quality; I observe, however, by the Inspection of Provisions Book, that the chaplains occasionally during the year have considered the milk poor.

Officers and Salaries.

Non-Resident.	£	s.	d.			£	s.	d.
Rev. C. Burton, Local Inspector,	50	0	0	James Corry,		45	0	0
				Francis Griffith,		40	0	0
Archdeacon C. P. Reichel, Protestant Chaplain,	50	0	0	William Lowe, *Tailor*,		37	10	0
				Thomas Montgomery,		37	10	0
Rev. John Duncan, Roman Catholic Chaplain,	50	0	0	John Aikins, *Schoolmaster*,		42	10	0
				Michael Brady, Junior Watchman,		30	5	0
Edmund C. Nicholson, esq., Surgeon,	74	0	0	Edward Montgomery, Junior Watchman,		30	5	0
Geo. M'Manus, esq., Apothecary,	20	0	0	Geo. Marshall, Gate Porter,		50	0	0
				Thomas G. Perry, Hospital Turnkey,		25	0	0
Resident.				Miss M. A. Allen, Matron,		40	0	0
Capt. A. C. Knox, Governor,	206	0	0	Mrs. Mary Cusack, Assist.				
Adam Boyd, Deputy Governor,	99	15	0	Matron and Hospital Nurse,		35	0	0

[All the turnkeys, except James Corry, assist the schoolmaster in teaching.]

Vacancies in the staff since last inspection, how caused, and how filled up, viz.

Thomas G. Perry appointed Hospital Turnkey, vice Patrick Maguire resigned; George M'Manus, esq., appointed Apothecary, vice E. C. Nicholson, esq., resigned; Archdeacon C. P. Reichel, D.D., appointed Protestant Chaplain, vice Archdeacon E. F. Berry, deceased; Miss M. A. Allen appointed Matron, vice Mrs. Jane Gordon, superannuated; Mrs. Mary Cusack appointed Assistant Matron and Hospital Nurse, vice M. A. Allen, promoted; E. Montgomery, Assistant Junior Watchman, vice H. Lawlor, resigned.

Officers on Gaol Allowance.

The intern officers are provided with fuel and gaslight in their apartments. The male turnkeys and watchmen are provided with uniform. No other allowances are given, except to the Governor and Deputy Governor, who receive gaol rations.

Visits paid by Officers.

	From 1st Jan. to 31st Dec., 1874.	From 1st Jan., 1875, to day of Inspection.
Number of times the Board of Superintendence met and discharged business,	12	13
Local Inspector, to Gaol,	112	120
„ to each Bridewell, { Navan,	23	20
{ Kells,	9	10
Chaplain, Protestant Episcopal Church,	—	110
Roman Catholic Chaplain,	126	139
Surgeon,	347	326
Apothecary,	—	77

The subordinate officers have apartments in the gaol, and their rooms on the day of my visit were all, with the exception of two, clean and in good order. I am sorry to observe by the Officers' Conduct-Book that a good deal of irregularity has from time to time taken place amongst the subordinate officers. Unless discipline is maintained amongst prison officers it is quite impossible to expect it to be carried out by them amongst prisoners. I have already in former reports pointed out the necessity for giving the Governor more assistance here in the form of an efficient deputy. The present Governor is doubtless anxious to discharge his duties faithfully, but his health has lately been impaired, and owing to the want of an efficient head turnkey or deputy governor to take his place in his absence several matters, as I have already pointed out, have been sadly neglected in this gaol. Thirteen discipline officers, independent of extern officers are still maintained here at a very large expense to the county, which is about the rate of one officer for every three prisoners of the daily average number in custody in 1874. Making every allowance for the faulty condition of this prison, I am, nevertheless of opinion that the staff is in excess of the requirements of the gaol.

Hospital.

	1872.		1873.		1874.		1875 (to day of Inspection).	
	M.	F.	M	F.	M.	F.	M.	F.
No. of prisoners in hospital,	43	2	45	1	75	1	–	–
Average daily number in hospital,	2·2	·1	2·7	·1	4	–	–	–
Number of prisoners prescribed for and treated out of hospital,	213	29	113	9	105	8	–	–
Cost of medicine,	£45 0s. 7d.		£16 9s. 11d.		£22 5s. 6d.		—	
Cost of diet for prisoners in hospital,	£44 11s. 8d.		£39 12s. 10d.		£41 15s. 11d.		—	
Cost of all extra diet ordered by medical officer for prisoners not in hospital,	£14 2s. 7d.		£6 17s. 6d.		£3 16s. 10d.		—	

The hospital arrangements have undergone no alteration since my last inspection. A suitable place is fitted up in the female prison for the treatment of sick prisoners of that sex, so that the hospital is only used, as a rule, for male prisoners. A wardsman is still employed in the hospital, and at the time of my inspection this man was a prisoner sentenced to six months' hard labour, whose only duties were to clean up about the hospital, and to attend to one man who was laid up with itch. The hospital warder has nothing to do but look after this department. I therefore submit that it is quite unnecessary to devote the whole time of an officer and a prisoner to hospital duties, and that a prisoner should only be made use of here in the event of any washing or scrubbing being required, except in extraordinary cases. I am also of opinion that prisoners should not be sent to hospital unless they are really ill, for slight cases of indisposition can be much better treated in the cells, where the prisoners can be kept in separation. A store of medicine is kept in the prison, which is obtained from the Apothecaries' Hall, Dublin. The cost under this head amounted in 1874 to £22 5s., and that for extra diet to prisoners in hospital £41 15s. 11d., and to prisoners not in hospital £3 16s. 10d. As compared with other gaols of its size these charges here appear to be extremely large, which may be seen on reference to the tables contained in the annual reports of the Inspectors-General of Prisons. In small gaols such as this is the medical officer frequently compounds the medicines, by which means the services of an apothecary

NORTH DISTRICT. are dispensed with, and consequently economy is effected. But I find here that both a surgeon and apothecary are employed, which is in my Meath County Gaol. opinion unnecessary.

Books. Some of the books of finance and the registries are kept by the Deputy-Governor, some by the Schoolmaster Warder, some by the Head Turnkey, and some by the Gatekeeper. The Cook Wardor keeps the Dietary Book, and has also charge of all the provisions. This, for obvious reasons, is a very objectionable system, and one that is open to much abuse. I regret to state that I found several errors in some of the books, to which I drew the attention of the Governor, and more especially in the Dietary Book. As a great portion of the expenditure of the gaol is recorded in this book, I submit that it should be more regularly and carefully supervised by both the Local Inspector and the Governor, and not left entirely, as it is now, to the keeping of a subordinate officer ; and I am of opinion that the dietary account should be checked daily by the Governor, and should be kept by the Deputy Governor ; in fact all the books require more careful supervision by the superior officers. The journal of the Local Inspector is carefully written, and is a useful book of reference, from which I learnt the particulars relating to many matters in the prison. At the time of my visit the Protestant Chaplain had lately been appointed, and had not yet entered upon his duties, but I find that the Roman Catholic Chaplain has two substitutes not legally appointed, and who, therefore, have no legal status in this gaol). As I have pointed out in my previous report, the 11th section of the 19th and 20th Vic., chapter 68 can alone regulate the appointments of chaplains' substitutes. The medical officer's journal is carefully and well written up, and both from it and that of the Local Inspector I perceive that a great deal of insubordination has existed from time to time in the gaol during this year. The Governor also carefully notes in his journal all the principal events occurring in the gaol throughout the day, together with the regular record of his routine duty. Prisoners here are allowed to exercise themselves in the yard in Too much association. association, and in a very irregular manner. I am of opinion that when it is necessary to allow prisoners walking exercise that they should be required to walk round and round in a ring at five paces apart, as is done in well-regulated gaols ; but when prisoners are employed for a certain number of hours in the open air it is not necessary to waste time in this manner.

Board of Superintendence.

Right Hon. Lord Dunsany.	William Thompson, esq.	G. A. Rotheram, esq.
Thomas FitzHerbert, esq.	Abraham Collas, esq.	Richard Odlum, esq.
Robert Fowler, esq.	William Tisdall, esq.	Alex. S. Montgomery, esq.
James S. Winter, esq.	George W. Cuppage, esq.	Edward M'Evoy, esq.

Board. The second Saturday of each month is the day appointed for the meeting of the Board of Superintendence, on which occasion the salaries of the intern officers are paid, and the Local Inspector receives a cheque for the payment of small current accounts. The salaries of extern officers are paid half-yearly at Assizes. I annex my report upon the bridewells of the county.

[BRIDEWELLS.

State of Bridewells.

	Navan.		Kells.	
	M.	F.	M.	F.
No. of Committals in past year,	19	3	24	9
Of whom were Drunkards,	4	3	6	1
No. of Committals in the quarter preceding Inspection,	23	2	14	—
Of whom were Drunkards,	9	—	5	—
Petty Sessions and transmittals, how often?	Petty Sessions fortnightly; transmittals direct.		Petty Sessions on first and third Monday of each month; transmittals regular.	
Committals,	Well kept, and regular.		Regular; but remands not on a fresh stamp.	
Registry,	Well kept.		Regular.	
Repairs and Order,	Good.		Good.	
Security,	Very good.		Good.	
Accommodation,	Ample, but only the upper cells are now used.		Eight cells and one day-room for each sex.	
Furniture, Bedding, and Utensils,	Clean and sufficient.		Sufficient and good, but some sheets torn.	
Water, how supplied,	By a pump in each yard.		By pump, not yet painted.	
Sewerage,	Said to be good.		Said to be effective.	
Cleanliness, Dryness, and Ventilation.	Clean and well ventilated, but cells damp.		Clean, but ventilation of cells not sufficient.	
Cost of Dietary,	Males, 6½d.; females, 5d. per day.		5½d. per day.	
Salary of Keeper, and whether he follows any other employment.	£40 a year, a suit of clothes, fire, and light.		£40 a year, and £6 10s. for fuel, light, and straw, a suit of clothes yearly, and a great coat every two years.	
Date of Statutable Inspection.	31st December, 1875.		5th April, 1875.	
Remarks,	No prisoner in custody.		One male in custody. A man who was whitewashing was allowed to be with him without an officer being present.	

Charles F. Bourke, *Inspector-General.*

Monaghan County Gaol, at Monaghan.—Statutable Inspection, 13th August, 1875.

Twenty males and 6 females formed the total number of prisoners in custody at the above date. Nine of them were cases disposed of at assizes or quarter sessions, and 21 were disposed of summarily, while 13 were untried, and 1 was a military offender. Eleven juveniles in all were in charge during this year up to the period of my visit, 5 of whom were sent to reformatories; and 1 of the latter, a male, was in charge when I inspected. He was sentenced to four years in a reformatory, and although the Governor had in his charge five suits of good clothing for

NORTH
DISTRICT.

Monaghan
County
Gaol. juveniles, this boy was absolutely in rags. This negligence on the part of the Governor is all the more unpardonable, inasmuch as I had occasion at my previous inspection of this prison to call attention to this subject, as there was a youth in charge at that time who was also most improperly and imperfectly dressed.

Number of Prisoners of all classes in Gaol on the day of Inspection, and on the corresponding date in the three preceding years.

	M.	F.		M.	F.
1872,	33	3	1874,	19	6
1873,	22	7	1875 (day of Inspection),	20	6

Number of Returned Convicts in Gaol on the day of Inspection, and during each of the three preceding years.

	M.	F.		M.	F.
1872,	2	–	1875 (up to and including day		
1873,	2	1	of Inspection),	3	–
1874,	3	2	Day of Inspection,	3	–

Commitments.

CLASSES.	From 1st January to 31st December, 1874.		From 1st January, 1875, to day of Inspection.	
	M.	F.	M.	F.
Debtors,	–	–	1	–
Criminals,	88	32	73	15
Vagrants,	11	1	6	–
Drunkards,	52	45	34	17
Total,	151	78	114	32

Commit-
ments. The total number of commitments this year was, up to the time of my inspection, 114 of males and 32 females, against 151 males and 78 females during the whole of the year 1874. Only one of these was committed as a debtor; so that as imprisonment for debt in Ireland is almost extinct, I should recommend the quarters allotted to this class of prisoners here to be turned into officers' quarters, for at present the arrangements in regard to the officers here are very objectionable. The commitments of females during this year, especially of the criminal and drunken class, are proportionally less than during 1874; but I am afraid that the same remark will not apply to males when the numbers at the end of the year are computed.

Number of Individual Prisoners (exclusive of Debtors), and Number of Times each had been committed during the following periods.

NUMBER OF TIMES.	1874.				1875, to day of Inspection.			
	Juveniles.		Adults.		Juveniles.		Adults.	
	M.	F.	M.	F.	M.	F.	M.	F.
Once within the year,	4	1	125	33	10	–	93	26
Twice "	–	–	8	4	–	–	5	–
Thrice "	–	–	2	4	–	–	–	2
Six times "	–	–	–	3	–	–	–	–
Total,	4	1	135	50	10	–	98	28
No. of above who had not been in Gaol previous to 1st Jan. in	4	1	115	33	10	–	79	16

Number of Individual Prisoners (exclusive of Debtors) committed in the year 1874, and to the day of Inspection in 1875, who had been once and oftener committed from their first Commitment in any year, so far as can be ascertained.

NORTH DISTRICT.

Monaghan County Gaol.

NUMBER OF TIMES.	1874. Juveniles.		1874. Adults.		1875, to day of Inspection. Juveniles.		1875, to day of Inspection. Adults.	
	M.	F.	M.	F.	M.	F.	M.	F.
Once only,	4	1	115	30	10	—	79	16
Twice,	—	—	7	5	—	—	5	1
Thrice,	—	—	5	2	—	—	5	3
Four times,	—	—	4	—	—	—	3	—
Five ,,	—	—	—	1	—	—	1	—
Six ,,	—	—	1	3	—	—	—	—
7 to 11 ,,	—	—	1	6	—	—	1	3
12 to 16 ,,	—	—	1	—	—	—	2	3
17 to 20 ,,	—	—	—	1	—	—	—	1
21 to 30 ,,	—	—	1	2	—	—	2	2
Total No. of Individuals committed,	4	1	135	50	10	—	98	28
No. of commitments represented in foregoing,	4	1	208	191	10	—	199	145

Averages, and Highest and Lowest Numbers (exclusive of Debtors).

—	From 1st January to 31st December, 1874. M.	F.	Date.	From 1st January, 1875, to day of Inspection. M.	F.	Date.
Average daily number of prisoners in custody,	23	8	—	21	6	—
Highest number of prisoners at any one time,	49		1st Dec.	32		2nd July.
Lowest ditto,	20		23rd Aug.	19		29th April.
Highest number of males at any one time,	38		1st Dec.	30		2nd July.
Ditto, of females,	13		2nd July.	10		25th May.
Lowest number of males at any one time,	16		2nd Oct.	13		16th April.
Ditto, of females,	4		6th Jan.	2		2nd July.

Highest Number of Prisoners (exclusive of Debtors) in Gaol during each of the previous seven years, and up to day of Inspection in 1875.

16th June, 1868, . . . 46   3rd July, 1872, . . . 56
5th April, 1869, . . . 58   7th February, 1873, . . . 51
13th April, 1870, . . . 111   1st December, 1874, . . . 49
4th August, 1871, . . . 47   2nd July, 1875, . . . 32

Up to the time of my visit no prisoner had been committed this year more than three times, but during 1874 three females had been committed as often as six times, and the greatest number of times that any individuals were committed from their first offence was from 21 to 30 in both 1874 and 1875. The total number of adults committed in 1874 was 135 males and 50 females, whose commitments from their first offence numbered respectively 208 and 191. In 1875, 98 adult males and 28 females were committed, whose previous convictions numbered respectively 199 and 145. As compared with other districts these figures speak very well for the conduct of the inhabitants of this county,

Recommitments.

NORTH
DISTRICT.

*Monaghan
County
Gaol.*

for, comparatively speaking, few habitual offenders frequent it; and I have no doubt, by an improved management of this prison, that even the existing number of this class would in a very short time be considerably reduced. At no time during this year did the prisoners in custody exceed 32, which is fewer than the highest number in the gaol in any time for the last eight years.

Accommodation.

	M.	F.		M.	F.
Wards, ...	3	3	Kitchen, ...	1	–
Yards, ...	2	2	Store Rooms, . . .	3	1
Solitary Cells, . . .	1	1	Laundry, ...	–	1
Single Cells, not less in size			Drying Room, . . .	–	1
than 9 ft. long, 6 ft. wide,			Lavatories, . . .	3	3
and 8 ft. high=432 cubic ft.,	59	40	Baths, with hot and cold		
Do., heated and furnished			water laid on, . .	1	1
with bells, . . .	59	40	Privies, ...	3	1
Sleeping Rooms, . . .	3	2	Water-closets, . .	7	5
No. of Beds in such Rooms,	3	–	Fumigating Apparatus, .	1	1
Hospital Rooms, . . .	3	2	Reception Rooms or Cells,	4	3
Chapel, ...	1	–	Pumps, ...	1	1
School Rooms, . . .	1	1	Crank-pump, . . .	1	–
Workshops, . . .	2	–	Well, ...	1	–
Worksheds, . . .	24	–	Tell-tale clock, . .	1	–

Reception.

The accommodation of this prison has not undergone any alteration since my last inspection. Four reception cells for males and three for females are reserved in each prison in which prisoners are kept until they are passed by the Doctor into their proper ward. The cells were all clean and tidy, but are badly ventilated, as the windows cannot be opened without the assistance of a ladder. This is a matter which Lavatories should be rectified. There is a sufficient quantity of lavatories and and Baths. water-closets in both prisons, which were in good order at the time of my visit. Only one bath is provided for each prison; and I was informed that prisoners are not washed immediately after coming in, but wait until the Doctor sees them. This is quite unnecessary, as in the generality of cases the officers are quite competent to judge, whether a prisoner should or should not be bathed on admission, and in the event of any prisoner objecting to it on the score of ill health, the Doctor should be at once called in; but one of the warders informed me, that in the male prison the prisoners are washed immediately on admission. This statement was not, however, supported by the Governor, so that I was at a loss to know who to credit. I submit, however, that all prisoners be in future washed Water. on admission, and subsequently weekly. No improvement has been made since my last report as regards the supply of water, which is still occasionally defective, and at the time of my visit was scarce, and was only turned on in the morning for a short time. This is a matter Sewerage. which I drew attention to in my last report. The sewerage is reported to me to be good and effective; and all the cells are artificially heated and Chapel. provided with gas. Protestant, Presbyterian, and Roman Catholic worship are performed in the chapel on Sundays, and the arrangements in Laundry. this respect are the same as on the occasion of my last inspection. The laundry is fitted with eight open stalls, and is provided with a good soft water pump; but I remarked that both the sheets and sheeting throughout the prison were disgracefully washed, for which the matron is much to blame. A fumigating box is provided in each prison, and all clothing Photo- is now purified before it is put away. The photography is still done by graphy. an artist in the town, who receives 3s. for four copies. More care should be taken to arrange these photographs properly, as suggested in my last Kitchen. report. The arrangements with regard to the kitchen are the same as at my visit in 1873, and the suggestions I then made in regard to it have not been carried out. I found on the occasion of my last visit, a male prisoner sentenced to hard labour, who, in consequence of being employed in the kitchen, was exempt therefrom. In a small prison, as this is, there cannot be sufficient work to occupy the time of a man all day long in the kitchen. He should therefore be required not only to perform a due amount of hard labour, but also on the days on which potatoes are not used his time should be occupied in other than kitchen duties. There is one tell-tale clock provided, which is said to be marked half-hourly, from 9 P.M. to 6 A.M., by the night watch; but at the time of my visit the clock was not properly protected from being tampered with, as the Chubb lock was broken, the key of which the Governor informed me he usually kept The record of the markings are entered in the Lockings Book.

Stock at the time of Inspection.

	In Use.	In Store.	Male Clothing.	In Use.	In Store.	Female Clothing.	In Use.	In Store.
Blankets, pairs of,	93	8	Shirts,	40	19	Shifts,	12	6
Sheets, pairs of,	77	5	Jackets,	16	58	Jackets,	6	20
Rugs,	75	15	Vests,	16	44	Petticoats,	12	24
Hammocks or Cots,	100	—	Trowsers,	16	33	Aprons,	6	6
Bed-ticks,	94	35	Caps,	16	15	Neckerchiefs,	6	12
Bedsteads	18	—	Stockings or socks, pairs of,	16	34	Caps,	6	6
						Stockings, pairs of,	6	6
			Shoes, Slippers, & Clogs, pairs of,	16	20	Shoes, Slippers, & Clogs, pairs of,	6	14

All the female clothing is made up within the prison, and is kept by the matron; but no proper account or books of any sort are kept between her and the Governor relating to the prison property in her charge, so that no proper checks are observed, and the greatest irregularities are possible. The same defect exists in the male prison, as the Governor keeps no account of the clothing issued to warders. Some of the sheets and sheeting were very bad and torn. I am informed that no new male clothing has been made since 1867. The Governor's store was most irregularly and carelessly kept, and some of the articles therein were, owing to his negligence, moth eaten. I was informed that the Governor takes stock of the clothes occasionally; but I was unable to ascertain that this duty is performed regularly either by him or by the Local Inspector. As the latter officer is by law empowered to order a sufficient quantity of clothing for all prisoners, I consider that it is his duty— more especially as he is the principal officer of the gaol—to look carefully into this department of the prison; and I regret to state that this duty has been lamentably neglected by the Local Inspector. Proper advantage has not been taken of tradesmen coming into the goal to mend and make up male clothing; and it has, I am informed, been the custom here to purchase jackets and trowsers for males by contract, whereas, if advantage were taken of tailors, and that there was a good tailor warder in the prison, a considerable saving could be effected in this item. Some of the sheets and shirts were very dirty, and, as I have before remarked, badly washed. I was informed that they are changed once a week; but this statement, together with many others made to me by the Governor, I regret to state was not reliable. No proper system exists by which matters of this sort are attended to. The consequence is, that they are left entirely to the management and control of the subordinate officers. Some of the blankets at the prison were thin and worn—a matter to which I drew the attention of the Governor.

NORTH
DISTRICT.

———

*Monaghan
County
Gaol.*

Number of Punishments for Prison Offences.

	From 1st January to 31st December, 1874.		From 1st January, 1875, to day of Inspection.	
	M.	F.	M.	F.
By Governor—				
Dark or Refractory Cells,	5	19	2	-

Punish-
ments.

Up to the time of my inspection this year only 2 males, and no female prisoners were punished for the breach of prison rule. Both solitary cells are heated and provided with bells, but the bell in the female solitary cell was broken. Prisoners are left in solitary all night during their periods of punishment, but as a rule are given their bedding, an indulgence which I submit should not be permitted.

School.

	From 1st Jan. to 31st Dec., 1874.		From 1st Jan., 1875, to day of Inspection.	
	M.	F.	M.	F.
Number of individual prisoners who attended school,	22	-	17	-
Average daily number of pupils,	8	-	6	-
Number of days on which school was held,	287	-	185	-

School-hours—Males, 12 to 2.

School.

The males are taught for two hours a day, and all of that sex who are capable of learning are permitted to go to school. They are instructed by one of the warders, who has been educated under the Church Education Society, but is not a certified teacher. More discretion, I submit, should be exercised as to the selecting of prisoners for school, for at the time of my visit I found a man attending school who was quite as well informed as the teacher, and knew arithmetic as far as fractions. He was, I am told, a returned convict and pickpocket, but as he was untried he was not compelled to work. I submit that all prisoners, who are supported at the public expense, should work in gaol, though of course it is not lawful for them to be required to do hard labour. There has been no school for females in this prison for some years. Considering that prison schools are meant chiefly for the instruction of the illiterate, I submit that (especially during the short days in winter), one hour would be quite sufficient to devote to the literary instruction of prisoners.

Employment on day of Inspection.

	M.	F.
Crank-wheel and stone-breaking,	15	-
Shoemaking,	1	-
Painting,	1	-
Prison duties,	1	1
Chipping bogwood,	1	-
Flowering, sewing, and knitting,	-	5
Sick,	1	-
Total,	20	6

Amount received for produce of Prisoners' labour disposed of outside the Gaol.

1872, . £7 3s. 4d. | 1873, . £8 4s. 9d. | 1874, . £8 3s. 1d.

Labour.

The hard labour is carried out here by means of a crank-pump, at which men only work for about an hour and a half daily, but during which time they are absolutely on the pump only eighteen minutes at a time. They are occupied for the remainder of the day chiefly at stone-breaking, and in wet weather they pick oakum. In winter time also they are required to pick oakum from 6. P.M. till 8 P.M., during which time I was informed that they each pick about a pound of oakum, but this is evidently not regularly measured. I could learn no reason why prisoners in summer do not do the same amount of oakum-picking from 6 to 8 P.M., as in winter. Lock-up takes place at this time all the year round. It is the custom here to allow men who are employed in the open air to have an hour's walking exercise which is quite unnecessary, as it is evident the statute only requires those who are engaged in sedentary pursuits, and not employed in the open air, to have a certain quantity of walking exercise daily. The consequence of the want of industrial employment in this gaol, and the idleness permitted, is that the amount received from the produce of prisoners' labour is extremely small indeed, being in 1874 only £8 3s. 1d., or less than one-fourth of the average annual cost of each prisoner. This cannot be considered a creditable or satisfactory state of things when one contemplates that the daily average number of prisoners for that year was 23 males and 8 females.

North District.
Monaghan County Gaol.

Net average daily cost of ordinary diet for each Prisoner.

1872, . 5d. | 1873, . 5d. | 1874, . 4d.

Net cost of gaol, including diet and salaries.

1872, . £1,938 3s. 10d. | 1873, . £1,229 13s. 4d. | 1874, . £1,257 11s. 7d.

Total cost of officers, including clothing, value of rations, &c.

1872, . £768 5s. 2d. | 1873, . £804 10s. 2d. | 1874, . £837 18s. 2d.

Average cost of each Prisoner per annum.

1872, . £30 19s. 1d. | 1873, . £40 16s. 1d. | 1874, . £40 11s. 4d.

Amounts repaid by the War Department for Military Prisoners.

1872, . £3 17s. 0d. | 1873, . £4 1s. 0d. | 1874, . £5 10s. 0d.

Amount repaid by the Inland Revenue Department for Excise Prisoners.

1872, — | 1873, — | 1874, . £3 5s. 0d.

Amounts repaid from the Consolidated Fund for the maintenance, &c.,
of Prisoners.

1872, . £176 5s. 3d. | 1873, £37 1s. 3d. | 1874, . £145 16s. 8d.

From the net cost of the gaol in 1874, £1,257 11s. 7d., the cost of officers came to £837 18s. 2d., so that it is no wonder that the average cost of each prisoner per annum came to the large sum of £40 11s. 4d. In a small gaol, as this is, and with the easy facilities for supervision, the number of officers under an efficient governor could be very much reduced; but, as I am in hopes that another session of Parliament will not pass without legislation on our prison system, I do not here propose such a reduction as otherwise I should be compelled to recommend.

Expenditure.

Officers and Salaries.

Non-resident.	£	s.	d.	Resident.	£	s.	d.
Thos. A. Young, esq., Local Inspector, . . .	110	0	0	John Temple, Governor, .	150	0	0
A. K. Young, esq., Medical attendant, . . .	74	0	0	Robert Brown, 1st Turnkey,	50	0	0
The Ven. C. M. Stack, Protestant Chaplain, .	30	0	0	Wm. Somervill, 2nd do.	41	10	0
Rev. J. A. Allisson, Presbyterian Chaplain, . . .	30	0	0	Robert Farley, 3rd do.	35	0	0
Rev. Richard Owens, Roman Catholic Chaplain, . .	30	0	0	Alex. Linton, 4th do.	35	0	0
				John Adams, 5th do.	35	0	0
				William Boyd, 6th do.	35	0	0
				James Cassiday, Night watchman, ...	31	0	0
				Mary Anne Somers, Matron, .	35	0	0
				Eleanor Nicholl, Assistant, .	25	0	0

NORTH
DISTRICT.

___

*Monaghan
County
Gaol.*

Visits paid by Officers.

Number of times the Board of Superin-	From 1st Jan. to 31st Dec., 1874.	From 1st Jan., 1875, to day of Inspection.
tendence met and discharged business,	14	8
Local Inspector to Gaol, . . .	174	107
Do. to each Bridewell, .	4	2
Chaplain, Protestant Episcopal Church,	157	98
,, Presbyterian, . . .	165	104
,, Roman Catholic, . . .	175	109
Surgeon, ...	149	75

Officers.

At the time of my visit I had so many and such serious faults to find with the management of this prison, and with the incapacity of the Governor, that I was reluctantly compelled to recommend the Board to ask for his resignation, and this matter I am informed will be arranged at the coming spring assizes, until which time his superannuation papers cannot be completed. Having said this much, it is unnecessary for me to point out still further any of this officer's various defaults. He has been a long time in the service, and is now no longer young, so that his conduct of late may be attributed to declining years. Considering the want of super-vision by the Governor, the subordinate officers appear to be efficient and attentive to duty ; but a new Governor will, I fear, have a great deal to do in order to establish a due amount of discipline and order amongst a staff that has been so long subject to so little authority, and left so much to its own guidance. At the time of my visit I discovered amongst other things a matter which showed gross neglect of duty on the part of several of the officers. Perceiving one of the prisoner's pockets rather fuller than it should be, I had him searched, and found that he had on him 2s. 6d., some tobacco, and other articles. On investigation of this matter, the prisoner informed me that he brought in the money, and that his wife had during his imprisonment brought him the tobacco, but notwithstanding that he had been committed in July, these breaches of prison discipline were not discovered until I pointed them out. This was the prisoner that I have already referred to as employed in the kitchen, and sentenced to twelve months' imprisonment with hard labour. Had the gatekeeper, the class officer, or the Governor been ordinarily careful about the searching and inspection of prisoners, such irregularities could not have occurred except through bribery. Since my visit, owing to irregularities between the matron and the gatekeeper, they have both been required by the Board to resign, and cannot, of course, be employed again in the prison service.

Hospital.

	1872.		1873.		1874.		1875 (to day of Inspection).	
	M.	F.	M.	F.	M.	F.	M.	F.
No. of prisoners prescribed for and treated out of hospital, . . .	64	12	44	12	37	7	—	—
Cost of medicine, . .	£3 7s. 6d.		£4 14s. 11d.		£6 7s. 7d.		—	

Hospital.

Neither hospitals have been used for several years, as the health of the gaol is most satisfactory. The bedding, therefore, which is in these buildings should be returned to store, as it could be easily taken out again if required. The Medical Officer carefully attends to the wants of the sick, and treats all trivial cases in their cells. The medicines are procured as required from an apothecary in the town, the cost of which came in the year 1874 to £6 7s. 7d., which, as compared with some other gaols, is a large charge, having regard to the few people prescribed for and medically treated here. The apothecary's bill is paid half-yearly at assizes, but is not certified for by the doctor, as it should be, before being NORTH DISTRICT. paid.

Monaghan County Gaol.

Books and Journals.

Books. The registries and books of finance are kept by the clerk, who devotes much care and attention to them, but they are not supervised by the Governor or, as far as I can ascertain, by any superior officer. The cases for further examination are not entered in the General Registry, and no proper reference is kept of them. This is an omission that should be corrected, as it is important for the due administration of justice that a record or registry should be kept of all such cases, and be handed to the presiding justice or judge. The Local Inspector's Journal contains very little information regarding the management of the prison, and does not throw any light upon the different subjects relating to his duty. The Chaplains' Journals record their regular attendance, but no details of their duty are noted therein. The Surgeon's Journal is full and explicit, and shows that this officer is most painstaking and attentive. The Journal of the Governor is meagre, and his remarks are almost identical from day to day. The General Visitors' Book is not properly kept, as I myself discovered omissions in its entries; but inasmuch as no superior officer takes any trouble in the supervision of the books of this prison, I consider their keeping as a whole reflected much credit on the clerk and the other subordinate officers who are engaged in this work. The only complaint any Complaints of prisoners. prisoner made to me during my inspection was that one male had lost his eye from a splinter of a stone in the stone-sheds. I inquired into this matter, and am informed by the Medical Officer that the eye is not permanently injured. However, to avoid such accidents, wire goggles should be provided for all stone-breakers, who should be compelled to use them.

Contracts.

Bread, brown, per stone, 1s. 6d.; oatmeal, per cwt., 14s. 4d.; potatoes, per cwt., 4s.; new milk, per gallon, 10d.; buttermilk, per gallon, 3d.; salt, per cwt., 3s.; coal, per ton, £1 0s. 10d.; gas, per 1,000 cubic feet, 8s. 9d.; candles, per lb., 0d.; soap, per cwt., £1 1s.

Provisions. The contracts for provisions are all sanctioned by the Board. That for bread is taken every six months, for potatoes, meal, milk, and coal every twelve months. The samples of the diet that I saw appeared to me to be excellent, and are reported on favourably as a rule by the Chaplains, who inspect them regularly three days in each week; and I was informed that each prisoner's portion is now weighed or measured. I was, however, surprised to find that potatoes were not yet supplied to prisoners, as required by the legally prescribed dietary scale, for which I consider both the Local Inspector and Governor to blame, as there was an abundance of good potatoes to be procured at the market at the time of my visit.

Board of Superintendence.

R. B. Evatt, esq.	Wm. Fra. D. V. Kane, esq.	H. G. Brook, esq.
James Hamilton, esq.	Captain Thomas Coote.	John T. Holland, esq.
Colonel Jesse Lloyd.	Edward Richardson, esq.	John Jackson, esq.
A. A. Murray Ker, esq.	William Murray, esq.	John Brady, esq.

Board. On the first Monday in the month the Board meets for the discharge of business, when the salaries of the intern officers, and small accounts are paid; and extern officers receive their salaries at the assizes.

Annexed is my tabular report upon the bridewells of the county.

NORTH DISTRICT.

Monaghan County.

Bridewells.

STATE OF BRIDEWELLS.

	Carrickmacross.		Clones.		Castleblayney.	
	M.	F.	M.	F.	M.	F.
No. of committals in past year,	27	12	35	13	50	23
Of whom were Drunkards,	15	3	19	8	16	7
No. of committals in the quarter preceding Inspection,	13	5	14	4	19	3
Of whom were Drunkards,	7	5	3	–	5	1
Petty Sessions and Transmittals, how often,	Petty Sessions fortnightly; transmittals direct.		Fortnightly; transmittals on following day.		Petty Sessions every second Thursday; Criminal Quarter Sessions four times a year; transmittals immediate.	
Committals, whether regular.	Regular.		Regular; but one woman committed hereon May 1st, to be tried on the 14th inst., was kept here and remanded during that time. She should have been sent direct to the county prison.		Regular.	
Registry,	Carefully kept.		Correctly kept.		Carefully kept.	
Repairs and Order,	Good.		Good.		Good; dampness on back wall corrected.	
Security,	Fair, but yards still insecure.		Walls still very low, and shed on the outside not yet removed from it.		Fair, except in yard.	
Accommodation,	Three cells for males, two for females, two day-rooms.		Four cells and a day-room for males; three for females, and a day-room.		Four cells for males, three for females, two day-rooms.	
Furniture, Bedding, and Utensils.	Good and clean, but some untidily kept.		Good, clean, and in good order.		Good, clean, and sufficient.	
Water, how supplied,	By pump on premises.		By pump on premises.		By good pump.	
Sewerage,	Good.		Effective.		Effective.	
Cleanliness, Dryness, and Ventilation.	Clean, and well ventilated.		Clean, and well ventilated.		Clean, but damp.	
Cost of Dietary per head per day.	6d. for females; 7d. for males.		6d. per day for three meals, and 4d. for two.		6d. per head per day.	
Salary of Keeper, and whether he follows any other employment.	£40, and £9 a year for fuel, light, and straw. Has no other employment.		£40, and £9 for fuel and light Is Court-keeper, at £10.		£40; £9 for fuel, light, and straw. No other employment.	
Statutable Inspection,	30th April, 1875.		13th August, 1875.		2nd Sept., 1875.	
Remarks,	Two prisoners in custody, but at the Petty Sessions, so I did not see them.		No prisoner in custody. The house in excellent order, reflecting much credit on Keeper.		No prisoner in custody.	

CHARLES F. BOURKE, *Inspector-General.*

ROSCOMMON COUNTY GAOL, AT ROSCOMMON.—STATUTABLE INSPECTION,

24TH AUGUST, 1875.

NORTH DISTRICT.

Roscommon County Gaol.

At the above date 17 males and 7 females were the total number of prisoners in custody. Two were untried, 7 were cases disposed of at quarter sessions and assizes, 1 was a debtor, 1 was a military offender, and the remainder were summary convictions. No prisoner who was classed as a juvenile was in custody at the time of my visit, although there was a youth here (in for a workhouse offence) who informed me that he was only 15 years of age, notwithstanding that he was registered as 18. I submit that more care should be taken by the local authorities to ascertain the age of youths of this sort, and in this case it would not have been difficult to learn from the workhouse registry the age of this boy, for it is important that the committing justice or judge should always be made aware of the exact age of juvenile offenders, so that they may, if they consider it expedient, commit them to reformatory schools. Five was the total number of juveniles committed here in 1875, two of whom were subsequently sent to reformatories.

Number in custody.

Juveniles.

Number of Prisoners of all Classes in Gaol on the day of Inspection, and on the corresponding date in the three preceding years.

	M.	F.		M.	F.
1872,	25	4	1874,	25	8
1873,	30	5	1875 (day of Inspection),	17	7

Number of Returned Convicts in Gaol on the day of Inspection, and during each of the three preceding years, and the expired portion of 1875.

	M.	F.		M.	F.
1872,	—	1	1875 (up to and including day		
1873,	1	1	of Inspection),	—	—
1874,	2	3	Day of Inspection,	—	—

Commitments.

CLASSES.	From 1st January to 31st December, 1874.		From 1st January, 1875, to day of Inspection.	
	M.	F.	M.	F.
Debtors,	11	—		
Criminals,	155	39	92	17
Vagrants,	13	—	18	—
Drunkards,	49	21	26	10
Total,	218	60	136	27

The commitments this year up to the time of my visit numbered 126 of males and 27 of females, against 218 of the former and 60 of the latter during the whole of 1874. I regret to state that the pauper debtor (T. D.) committed here in June, 1873, under an attachment of the Court of Probate,

Commitments.

NORTH DISTRICT.

Roscommon County Gaol.

was still in custody. His case was referred to in the reports of Inspectors-General in 1873 and 1874, and was also brought before the House of Commons, by the member for the county, this year. Subsequent to my visit here I made a special report to the Government, in compliance with directions from the Chief Secretary, as to the probability of this man's release. The Executive then called the attention of the judge of the Court of Probate to the case, and after a lengthened correspondence the man was discharged on the 28th of September last, by order of the Court of Bankruptcy. No alteration has taken place since my last inspection in the quarters for debtors, but now that this man has been released, I am in hopes that no prisoner of that class will in future be committed here, so that these quarters may now be converted to other purposes.

Number of Individual Prisoners (exclusive of Debtors), and Number of Times each had been committed during the following periods, distinguishing Adults from Juveniles.

NUMBER OF TIMES COMMITTED.	1874.				1875, to day of Inspection			
	Juveniles.		Adults.		Juveniles.		Adults.	
	M.	F.	M.	F.	M.	F.	M.	F.
Once within the year,	3	3	185	34	4	–	118	17
Twice ,,	–	–	10	3	–	–	7	2
Thrice ,,	–	–	3	1	–	–	–	2
Four times within the year,	–	–	–	2	–	–	–	–
Six ,, ,,	–	–	–	1	–	–	–	–
Total,	3	3	198	41	4	–	125	21
No. of above who had not been in Gaol previous to 1st January in	2	3	151	24	3	–	108	21

Number of Individual Prisoners (exclusive of Debtors), committed in the year 1874, and to the day of Inspection in 1875, who had been Once, Twice, Thrice, Four Times, Five Times, &c., &c., from their first Commitment in any year, so far as can be ascertained, distinguishing Adults from Juveniles.

NUMBER OF TIMES COMMITTED.	1874.				1875, to day of Inspection.			
	Juveniles.		Adults.		Juveniles.		Adults.	
	M.	F.	M.	F.	M.	F.	M.	F.
Once only,	2	3	145	24	3	–	100	11
Twice,	–	–	24	4	1	–	14	5
Thrice,	–	–	7	3	–	–	1	1
Four times,	–	–	5	2	–	–	2	1
Five ,,	–	–	4	–	–	–	–	–
Six ,,	–	–	3	2	–	–	4	–
7 to 11 ,,	–	–	7	4	–	–	1	2
12 to 16 ,,	–	–	2	–	–	–	2	–
17 to 20 ,,	–	–	1	–	–	–	1	–
31 to 40 ,,	–	–	–	2	–	–	–	1
Total No. of Individuals committed,	2	3	198	41	4	–	125	21
No. of commitments represented in foregoing,	4	3	377	155	5	–	216	69

Averages, and Highest and Lowest Numbers (exclusive of Debtors).

—	From 1st January to 31st December, 1874.			From 1st January, 1875, to day of Inspection.		
	M.	F.	Date.	M.	F.	Date.
Average daily number of prisoners in custody,	23	5	—	21	4	—
Highest number of prisoners at any one time,	44		16th Dec.	44		31st Jan.
Lowest ditto, .	18		24th Sept.	17		12th Aug.
Highest number of males at any one time, .	38		16th Dec.	41		31st Jan.
Ditto of females,	9		30th May.	7		20th Aug.
Lowest number of males at any one time, .	15		24th Sept.	15		12th Aug.
Ditto of females,	1		15th Nov.	1		7th July.

Highest Number of Prisoners (exclusive of Debtors), in Gaol during each of the previous seven years, and up to day of Inspection in 1875.

12th October, 1868,	. . 32		19th November, 1872,	. . 41
9th February, 1869,	. . 32		23rd January, 1873,	. . 41
6th April, 1870, .	. . 47		16th December, 1874,	. . 44
31st March, 1871, .	. . 47		31st January, 1875,	. . 44

The recommitments to this gaol are, I am glad to observe, not so numerous as in a great many other districts in Ireland. During 1874 the total number of adult individuals committed was 198 of males and 41 of females ; up to the time of my inspection this year they numbered respectively 125 and 21. The recommitments of those committed in 1874 numbered 377 and 155 respectively, and of those committed in 1875 their recommitments from first offence numbered 216 and 69 respectively. In the former year, however, 151 of the males and 24 of the females committed had not previously been in gaol, and in the latter year those who had not previously been committed numbered 103 males and 12 females, so that it will be seen repetition of crime is confined here to very few individuals. In both years females were committed here who had been from between 30 and 40 times in gaol, and males who had been from 17 to 20 times in prison. The females committed here are very few in number, so much so that at different periods in 1874 and 1875 there was only one female in custody.

Recommitments.

Accommodation.

	M.	F.		M.	F.
Wards, ...	7	1	Kitchen, . . .	1	—
Yards, ...	7	1	Store Rooms, . .	2	1
Day Rooms, . . .	7	1	Laundry, . . .	—	1
Solitary Cells, . . .	3	1	Drying Room, .	—	1
Single Cells, 9 ft. long, 6 ft. wide, and 8 ft. high=432 cubic feet, . . .	36	—	Lavatories, . .	—	2
			Baths, . . .	1	2
			Privies, . . .	6	—
Do. heated and furnished with bells, . . .	—	16	Water-closets, .	1	1
			Fumigating Apparatus,	—	1
Cells to contain three persons,	4	—	Reception Cells, .	10	—
Sleeping Rooms, . .	4	3	Pumps, . . .	2	—
No. of Beds in such rooms,	2	2	Wells, . . .	2	—
Hospital Rooms, . .	4	3	Tread-wheel, . .	1	—
Chapel, . . .	One.		Other machines for hard labour		
School Rooms, . .	—	—	—shot drill.		
Workshop, . . .	1	—	Tell-tale Clock, . .	One.	

NORTH DISTRICT.

Roscommon County Gaol.

Baths.

Water.

Sewerage.

Heating.

Gas.

Kitchen.

Photography.

Chapel.

Cells.

Nightwatch.

The structural condition of this prison has undergone no material alteration since my last visit, so that the defects so frequently enumerated still exist. A good bath is provided in the male reception class, in which all prisoners of that sex are washed as they come in, and subsequently weekly. The same rule is followed in the female prison in this respect, and all prisoners remain in that class until inspected by the doctor and passed into their proper wards. No lavatories have yet been provided in the male prison, so that prisoners of that sex can only wash in the yards in the morning. There are good wells on the premises, from one of which water is raised by means of the tread-wheel, the same as at my last visit. There is no sewerage yet made from the privies, but eave-gutters have been put up, and the down pipes now run to the cesspools. However, these are doubtful improvements, as the cesspools are not connected with any sewer. I am informed that there is an excellent sewer running through the yards of the gaol into two large ponds about 800 yards off, so that the sewerage from the privies could easily be connected with this large drain. There is one water-closet in the female prison, but none for the males. The gaol has not been artificially heated since my last visit, and the only fires that are provided are those in the day rooms, and in small stoves in the female prison. Prisoners are therefore left very much in association in the day rooms during the cold weather. Although gas is introduced into the prison in some places, it is not yet provided in the cells. Prisoners, therefore, still remain in idleness during the long winter evenings and mornings. The arrangements in the kitchen were the same as at my last visit, as this department has not yet been removed to the female prison, as already suggested. At the time of my inspection the debtor before mentioned acted as cook. The laundry too has undergone no change, so that the suggestions I made respecting both of these departments in my report of 1873 have not yet been adopted. The photography is still carried on by an artist in the town who receives 5s. for each set of four copies. In my last report I suggested that this duty should be performed, for obvious reasons, by an officer of the prison, but I regret that this suggestion is still disregarded; and I am bound to remark that some of the copies shown to me were very imperfect and badly executed. One good fumigating apparatus is now provided, in which all prisoners' clothing is now fumigated before being put away. The chapel is suitably arranged for prison purposes, and both Protestant and Roman Catholic worship are performed in it. The cells are all of the required size for separate confinement, but those for males are not furnished with bells, nor were there any labels descriptive of prisoners over the doors. Each cell should have a shelf in it; and, as I was informed there was a prisoner in custody at the time of my visit who was capable of making these requirements, I trust by this time they have been put up. The duty of the night-watch is performed by the warders by rotation, and the vigilance of the night-watch is tested by means of one tell-tale clock, which is marked hourly from 9 P.M. to 6 A.M. in summer, and from 5 P.M. to 7 A.M. in winter. The markings are taken by the Governor, and are entered by him in the Lockings Book; but my suggestions in regard to his entering all omissions of this duty in the Officers' Conduct Book have not yet been adopted. As I observe that some of the officers occasionally neglect this duty, I again submit that the omissions be recorded against them, and that the attention of the Board be directed to them on each occasion of such neglect. Unlock takes place in summer at 6 A.M., and in winter at 7 o'clock. In the former season lock-up takes place at 6 P.M., and in the latter at 5 P.M., after which time prisoners are not required to do any work. The Governor takes charge of the keys of the cells and day-rooms at lock-up, of the outside gate at 10.30 P.M., and, I am informed that all the keys are kept by him in his bedroom at night. No improvement has been made here since my last visit in respect to the arrangements for visitors for prisoners. They still see their friends through a hole in the door—convicted prisoners at any time during their imprisonment, by order of a member of the Board or by the Local Inspector, and the untried twice a week. I am informed that all visitors to prisoners are searched before being admitted. As these arrangements are very defective, and are open to great abuse, I would again submit that the rules with regard to visitors to prisoners existing in Londonderry and Naas gaols be adopted here. When I was making my visit the roof of the prison, which was very much out of order, was being repaired.

Stock at the time of Inspection.

	In Use.	In Store.	Male Clothing.	In Use.	In Store.	Female Clothing.	In Use.	In Store.
Blankets, pairs of,	96	29	Shirts, . .	98	–	Shifts, . .	14	8
Sheets, pairs of, .	162	–	Jackets, .	12	29	Jackets, . .	7	15
Rugs, . .	113	25	Vests, . .	12	28	Gowns, . .	7	5
Bedticks, .	87	–	Trowsers, .	12	22	Petticoats, .	7	5
Bedsteads, . .	121	–	Caps, . .	12	30	Aprons, . .	16	–
			Shoes, Slippers, &			Neckerchiefs, .	11	–
			Clogs, pairs of,	12	53	Caps, . . .	24	–
						Stockings, pairs of,	16	–
						Shoes, Slippers, &		
						Clogs, pairs of,	7	15

The general store of new clothing is kept by the Governor, who issues the articles to the Clerk and Matron as they are required for use, those officers being responsible for all clothing in use. Females are now required to wear caps; but I regretted to find that stockings and socks are not yet supplied to them, as frequently suggested by Inspectors-General. Prisoners' own clothing is put away and properly labelled, after being fumigated; but the labels attached to the male clothing were not signed according to the rules laid down on this subject. The sheets are said to be changed once a fortnight, and the bedding was all clean and in good order; but I find that all prisoners do not receive clean sheets as they come in. I submit that no prisoner should be required to sleep in sheets that have already been used by another prisoner. Stock is taken by the Governor about twice a year; and as the Local Inspector is the principal officer of the gaol, and should be responsible for all prison property, I would recommend that he also perform this duty periodically.

Punishments for Prison Offences.

	From 1st January to 31st December, 1874.		From 1st January, 1875, to day of Inspection.	
	M.	F.	M.	F.
By Governor—				
Dark or Refractory Cells, . .	37	5	14	1

The solitary cells provided for both sexes have recently been boarded, but are not yet artificially heated, nor are they provided with bells. These requirements should, I submit, be supplied to those cells, as it is not lawful to confine any person in solitary without giving him or her, as the case may be, the means of communicating with the officer on duty. Up to the period of my visit this year only 14 males and 1 female were punished for breach of prison rule, against 37 of the former and 5 of the latter during the whole of the previous year.

M

Summary of Employment on day of Inspection.

	M.	F.
Hard Labour,	8	–
Industrial Labour,	9	7
Total,	17	7

*Received for produce of prisoners' labour disposed of outside the gaol
for the last three years.*

1872, . £5 13s. 6d. | 1873, . £5 5s. 0d. | 1874, . £6 14s. 6d.

*Net average daily cost of ordinary diet for each prisoner in the three
preceding years.*

1872, . . 5½d. | 1873, . . 5d. | 1874, . . 5d.

Net cost of gaol, including diet and salaries for the three preceding years.

1872, . £1,364 4s. 8d. | 1873, . £1,701 3s. 0d. | 1874, . £1,735 8s. 4d.

Total cost of officers, including clothing, value of rations, washing, gas, &c.

1872, . £849 13s. 0d. | 1873, . £898 14s. 0d. | 1874, . £890 18s. 0d.

Average cost of each prisoner per annum in each of the last three years.

1872, . £52 9s. 0d. | 1873, . £53 17s. 2d. | 1874, . £61 19s. 7d.

*Amounts repaid by the War Department for military prisoners in each
of the last three years.*

1872, . £1 5s. 0d. | 1873, . £16 16s. 0d. | 1874, . £16 18s. 0d.

*Amounts repaid from the Consolidated Fund for the maintenance, &c., of
prisoners during the years*

1872, . £72 7s. 4d. | 1873, . £120 12s. 5d. | 1874, . £94 10s. 5d.

Labour. Since my last visit I am happy to find that hard labour is more strictly
enforced than heretofore amongst the male prisoners. Those so sentenced
are now required to work on the tread-wheel for about two hours and forty
minutes of each day, and are absolutely on the wheel about thirty-five
minutes at a time, with intervals of rest of five minutes. Shot drill is
also performed by the hard labour prisoners for an hour daily. During the
remainder of the day male prisoners are employed at stone-breaking, with
the exception of those who are engaged at their trades; but I regret
that no labour is carried on in the cells after lock-up or during the
hours allotted for breakfast or dinner. I would therefore strongly
recommend that a certain amount of oakum-picking be required from
each prisoner daily, and that this or some such other industry be
performed in the cells during that part of the day while there is light.
Prisoners sentenced to hard labour should of course be required to pick a
Want of separation. greater amount of oakum than those not so sentenced. Although this
prison is not yet adapted to the separate system, I am of opinion that much
more separation than is now the practice should be carried out; and by this
means a greater amount of labour would be produced during the year;
for it is lamentable to perceive how small is the result of the labour of
the prisoners confined in this gaol, amounting in 1874 to only £6 14s. 6d.
This is, I submit, a very paltry return from the labour of a daily average
Expenditure. of 28 prisoners. The net cost of the gaol in that year amounted to
£1,735 8s. 4d.; but the cost of officers came to more than half of that
sum, namely, £890 18s.; and I fear, as long as the present defects both
in the construction and in the system of conducting this gaol remain
unaltered, there can be very little hope of reducing the present staff of
officers, which is quite out of proportion as compared with the daily
average number of prisoners in custody.

Officers and Salaries.

Roscommon County Gaol.

Non-Resident.	£	s.	d.
Joseph Plunkett Taaffe, esq., J.P., Local Inspector,	92	6	2
John Harrison, esq., Medical Officer,	74	0	0
Rev. Mathew N. Thompson, Protestant Chaplain,	46	3	1
Very Rev. Thos. M. Phillips, Roman Catholic Chaplain,	46	3	1
Henry T. Doud, Clerk and Schoolmaster,	60	0	0

	£	s.	d.
Thomas Paden, Reception Warder,	45	0	0
Resident.			
George Speer, Governor,	200	0	0
Joseph Minchin,	40	0	0
Daniel Hutchinson,	38	0	0
James Hanley,	38	0	0
Mathew Morrison,	38	0	0
Peter Murray,	30	0	0
Anne Brennan, Assistant-Matron and Schoolmistress,	35	0	0

(Warders)

Vacancies in the staff since last inspection, how caused, and how filled up.

Maria Corry, Matron, superannuated; Anne Brennan, Assistant-Matron, promoted. Grier Hughes, Warder, resigned; Peter Murray, Warder, appointed.

Visits paid by Officers.

	From 1st Jan. to 31st Dec., 1874.	From 1st Jan., 1875, to day of Inspection.
Meetings of Board of Superintendence,	12	10
Local Inspector, to Gaol,	177	154
„ to each Bridewell,	3	2
Chaplain, Protestant Episcopal Church,	267	121
„ Roman Catholic,	202	97
Physician,	170	170

As the female hospital is not used three male officers occupy it as their Officers. quarters, and two other subordinate officers sleep at the gate. Their apartments at the time of my visit were fairly clean; and all these officers take their meals in the prison. Under these circumstances I consider that the hours allowed for meals are too long, and submit that half an hour would be quite sufficient to allow for breakfast and the same for dinner, by which means so much time would not be wasted as at present. The Matron does the whole work of the female prison, which was clean and in good order, reflecting much credit upon her. As this officer is seldom relieved from duty, I would recommend that some arrangement be made with one of the warders' wives, in order that the Matron might always be able to call her to her assistance if necessary, and that she might be relieved from her duty occasionally. The Clerk having been ill for some time previous to my visit, the whole duty of keeping the books and accounts was thrown upon the Governor.

Schools.

	From 1st Jan. to 31st Dec., 1874.		From 1st Jan., 1875, to day of Inspection.	
	M.	F.	M.	F.
Number of individual prisoners who attended school,	177	45	–	21
Average daily number of pupils,	17	4	–	3·47
Number of days on which school was held,	246	293	–	192
School-hours.—Males—10 to 12. Females—10 to 12.				

For some time previous to my visit no male school had been carried on, School. inasmuch as the Clerk and Schoolmaster was, as I have already stated, away on sick leave. The female school is conducted by the Matron, and prisoners of that sex are taught one hour a day in their cells, as there is no regular schoolroom in the female prison. In my report of 1873 I drew

NORTH
DISTRICT.
—
Roscommon
County
Gaol.

attention to the non-compliance by the Chaplains with the by-laws with regard to the inspection of the schools, and regret to state that I have now again to remark unfavourably upon the same subject, as I find no entry in the female school registry this year of the Chaplains, and only one in the male registry, namely, that of the Protestant Chaplain. The school not being connected with any educational board makes it more important that it should be visited constantly by the Chaplains, who, I trust, will in future be more attentive to this portion of their duty.

Contracts.

Bread, white, per 4-lb. loaf, 5½d.; ditto, brown, per 4-lb. loaf, 4½d.; oatmeal, per cwt., 14s. 6d.; Indian meal, per cwt., 9s. 11d.; rice, per cwt., £1 3s. 4d.; potatoes, per cwt., 4s.; new milk, per gallon, 8d.; salt, per cwt., 2s. 4d.; coal, per ton, £1 9s. 10d.; gas, per 1,000 cubic feet, 9s. 2d.; candles, per lb., 5d.; soap, per cwt., £1 0s. 6d.

Provisions.

The contracts for provisions are taken either yearly or half-yearly, and are sanctioned by the Board. The samples that I saw appeared to be good, and are generally reported on favourably by the Chaplains; but occasionally they note their dissatisfaction in the Inspection Provisions Book as to the quality of some of the provisions. None of the prisoners, however, complained to me of the quality of the provisions. It is the duty of the Clerk to keep the store of provisions, and to see that each portion is of proper weight and measure.

Hospital.

	1872.		1873.		1874.		1875 (To day of Inspection).	
	M.	F.	M.	F.	M.	F.	M.	F.
Prisoners in hospital, .	5	–	5	2	–	–	5	–
Average daily number in hospital, . . .	0·18	–	0·1	0·6	–	–	0·44	–
Prisoners treated out of hospital, . . .	70	22	64	24	79	20	–	–
Cost of medicine, . .	£24		£24		£24		—	
Cost of diet for prisoners in hospital, . . .	£1 0s. 0d.		£0 14s. 6d.		—		—	
Cost of extra diet for prisoners not in hospital, .	£4 0s. 0d.		—		—		—	

Hospital.

A room in the female prison is fitted up as an hospital for prisoners of that sex, and there is also ample provision made for the male hospital here in a separate building. Bells and water-closets are attached to each ward, but the former were out of repair at the time of my visit, and the roof also of this building was letting in rain. The medicines are procured from an apothecary in the town, at a cost of £24 a year, which I consider, as compared with some other gaols, an extravagant price, especially as there are seldom any prisoners in hospital. Having made suggestions on this subject in former reports, I do not consider it necessary to repeat them here.

Books.

Books and Journals.

The Governor deserves every credit for the careful manner in which he, singlehanded, has lately kept the books of registry and finance. Indeed, this officer is most attentive to his duties, for which every praise is due to him. The journal of the Local Inspector is full and well written up, as also is that of the Governor. The Surgeon does not, I regret to find, write up his journal regularly, in compliance with the 72nd section of the Prisons Act; but I am aware that he is most attentive to his duties, and visits the gaol regularly. I have explained to the Governor how some of the hospital books should be kept, and requested him to point these matters out to the Medical Officer. The journals of the Chaplains were very meagre, and contained little or no information in regard to their duties; and I regret to find that the Roman Catholic Chaplain still disregards the requirements of the 11th section of the 19th and 20th Vic., chap. 68, in reference to the appointment of a substitute; but the substitutes of the Protestant Chaplain are now, I am glad to find, properly appointed. The prescribed Work Ledger, Check Ticket Book, and the General Visitors Book are not kept. As these books are all important, and are directed to be kept in all prisons, I submit that they should be procured and as carefully written up as the other books.

Board of Superintendence.

Right Hon. Lord Crofton, D.L. | Capt. P. H. O'Conor, J.P., D.L. | Capt. Patrick Balfe, J.P.
Major-Gen. J. W. Mitchell, J.P. | Thomas A. P. Mapother, esq., J.P. | Colonel C. R. Chichester, J.P., D.L.
Joseph A. Holmes, esq., J.P., D.L. | Henry Smyth, esq., J.P. | Thomas Y. L. Kirkwood, esq., J.P.
B. W. Bagot, esq., J.P. | Major H. Taaffe Ferrall, J.P., D.L. | Captain E. R. King-Harman, J.P.

The Board meets on the second Saturday of the month, when cheques are handed to the Local Inspector for the payment of the different accounts, and the intern officers also receive their salaries. The Chaplains' salaries are paid half-yearly, and those of the Medical Officer and Local Inspector quarterly. Annexed are my reports upon the bridewells of the county.

STATE OF BRIDEWELLS.

	Strokestown.	
	M.	F.
No. of Committals in past year,	49	7
Of whom were Drunkards,	12	2
No. of Committals in quarter preceding Inspection,	19	2
Of whom were Drunkards,	3	—
Petty Sessions and Transmittals, how often?	Fortnightly, on Thursdays; transmittals on following day.	
Committals,	Several irregular; and justices sign remands for 8 days without having the prisoner brought before them. The Petty Sessions Clerk is also careless in drawing out the committals, as I find several dates wrong.	
Registry,	Regular.	
Repairs and Order,	Repairs good, except that the house should be painted inside; order indifferent.	
Security,	Fair, except in yard; only one yard for both sexes.	
Accommodation,	Two cells up, and one down stairs, containing five beds, and only one day-room.	
Furniture, Bedding, and Utensils,	Sufficient and good.	
Water, how supplied,	By pump, which wants to be repaired.	
Sewerage,	Said to be effective.	
Cleanliness, Dryness, and Ventilation,	Fairly ventilated, but cells damp, and not as clean as they should be.	
Cost of Dietary,	6½d. a day for untried, and 5d. for drunkards.	
Salary of Keeper, and whether he follows any other employment.	£20 a year, and £6 for fuel and light; a suit of clothes yearly. Is Courthouse-keeper at £9 4s. 6d. a year.	
Date of Inspection,	8th May, 1875.	
Remarks,	No prisoner in custody.	

State of Bridewells—*continued.*

NORTH DISTRICT.		Athlone.		Boyle.		Castlerea.	
Roscommon County.							
Bridewells.	No. of Committals in past year, .	M. 28	F. 1	M. 32	F. 5	M. 44	F. 36
	Of whom were Drunkards, .	–	–	5	1	18	18
	No. of Committals in quarter preceding inspection, . .	12	1	10	1	9	6
	Of whom were Drunkards, .	–	–	1	–	4	6
	Petty Sessions and Transmittals, how often?	Petty Sessions fortnightly; transmittals same day.		Petty Sessions fortnightly; transmittals on same evening.		Petty Sessions weekly; transmittals sometimes not for two days, the Petty Sessions being on Saturday. Quarter Sessions in April and Oct.	
	Committals, whether regular.	Regular.		Regular, except two, which were informal.		Some quite illegal; and remands without a stamp.	
	Registry, . . .	Carefully kept.		Correctly kept.		Regular.	
	Repairs and Order, .	Fair; two locks required on keeper's doors.		Good.		No improvement; painting wanted, and yard out of order.	
	Security, . .	Very insecure; but walls of yard lately raised.		Good.		Fair, but yard still very insecure.	
	Accommodation,	Two cells for each sex; 2 day-rooms.		Three cells for each sex up stairs, and two down; two day-rooms. The cells down stairs need not be used, as they are damp, and are not required.		One cell for each sex; only one day-room and 1 yard.	
	Furniture, Bedding, and Utensils.	Good, but 2 sheets wanting in repair; also a bed-stead and three new ticks wanted.		Clean; but the blankets and ticks were defective at my last visit, and have not yet been replaced by new ones.		Clean and sufficient, except one pair of sheets, which were not clean.	
	Water, how supplied,	By pump.		By good pump on premises.		None on premises except rain, and very scarce sometimes in summer.	
	Sewerage, . .	Good.		Effective.			
	Cleanliness, Dryness, and Ventilation.	Clean, and well ventilated.		Clean, and fairly ventilated.		Clean, and well ventilated.	
	Cost of Dietary, .	6½d. per head per day.		5d. per head per day.		7½d. for all, which is too much.	
	Salary of Keeper, and whether he follows any other employment.	£15; £6 for fire and light. Court-keeper at £7 7s. Is a military pensioner.		£15 a year. Is Court-keeper at £7; £6 a year for fuel, light, and straw. Is a pensioner of the R. I. C.		£20; £6 for fuel and light. Court-keeper at £7 7s. 7d. a year. Is a pensioner of the R. I. C. at £22 a year.	
	Date of Inspection, .	28th August, 1875.		6th May, 1875.		25th August, 1875.	
	Remarks, . . .	No prisoner in custody.		No prisoner in custody.		Two males in custody. This Bridewell should be closed, as a good police look-up would answer all the requirements of this district.	

CHARLES F. BOURKE, *Inspector-General.*

SLIGO COUNTY GAOL, AT SLIGO.—STATUTABLE INSPECTION,
7TH AND 8TH MAY, 1875.

At the above date 24 males and 5 females formed the total number of
prisoners in custody here. Two were untried, 7 were cases disposed of **Number in custody.**
at quarter sessions or assizes, and the remainder were summary convictions. At the time of my visit no male juvenile was in custody, though
there was one girl who was committed as a juvenile, but who appeared **Juveniles.**
to be beyond that age, namely, 16. Six of this class were in custody
here during the year up to the time of my visit, 1 of whom had been
twice in prison. None, however, were sent to reformatories from this
jurisdiction during the year.

*Number of Prisoners of all classes in Gaol on the day of Inspection, and on
the corresponding date in the three preceding years.*

	M.	F.		M.	F.
1872,	18	6	1874,	18	10
1873,	18	6	1875 (day of Inspection),	24	5

*Number of returned Convicts in Gaol on the day of Inspection, and during
each of the three preceding years, and the expired portion of 1875.*

	M.	F.		M.	F.
1872,	2	1	1875 (up to and including	1	—
1873,	—	1	day of Inspection),		
1874,	2	—	Day of Inspection,	1	—

Commitments.

CLASSES.	From 1st January to 31st December, 1874.		From 1st January, 1875, to day of Inspection.	
	M.	F.	M.	F.
Criminals,	166	42	102	13
Vagrants,	7	9	7	4
Drunkards,	77	27	32	8
Total,	250	78	141	25

More prisoners were in charge at the time of my visit this year than **Commitments.**
was the case on the corresponding date during the three preceding years,
but considering the size and population of this county serious crime
cannot be said to exist in any great degree. The greater part of the
offences for which prisoners are committed here are common assaults and
drunkenness. Up to the time of my visit this year the commitments
numbered of males 141, and of females 25, against 250 of the former, and
78 of the latter during the whole of the previous year. It is pleasing to
remark that no debtors have been confined here for the last two years, so
that their quarters are now occupied by the warders.

NORTH
DISTRICT.

Sligo
County
Gaol.

Number of Individual Prisoners (exclusive of Debtors), and Number of Times each had been committed during the following periods, distinguishing Adults from Juveniles.

NUMBER OF TIMES COMMITTED.	1874.				1875, to day of Inspection.			
	Juveniles.		Adults.		Juveniles.		Adults.	
	M.	F.	M.	F.	M.	F.	M.	F.
Once within the year, . .	10	–	151	29	3	–	101	9
Twice ,, . .	–	–	19	7	–	1	12	2
Thrice ,, . .	–	–	7	2	–	–	3	–
4 times ,, . .	–	–	4	1	–	–	1	1
5 ,, ,, . .	–	–	1	1	–	–	–	–
6 ,, ,, . .	–	–	–	–	–	–	–	1
9 ,, ,, . .	–	–	1	–	–	–	–	–
10 ,, ,, . .	–	–	–	2	–	–	–	–
Total, . .	10	–	183	42	3	1	117	13
No. of above who had not been in Gaol previous to 1st Jan. in .	9	–	128	25	3	1	69	6

Number of Individual Prisoners (exclusive of Debtors) committed in the year 1874, and to the day of Inspection in 1875, who had been Once, Twice Thrice, Four Times, Five Times, &c., &c., from their first Commitment in any year, so far as can be ascertained, distinguishing Adults from Juveniles.

NUMBER OF TIMES COMMITTED.	1874.				1875, to day of Inspection			
	Juveniles.		Adults.		Juveniles.		Adults.	
	M.	F.	M.	F.	M.	F.	M.	F.
Once only, ...	9	–	110	21	3	–	54	7
Twice, ...	1	–	32	7	–	1	26	2
Thrice, ...	–	–	11	1	–	–	8	–
4 times, . .	–	–	5	–	–	–	6	–
5 ,, . .	–	–	3	1	–	–	3	–
6 ,, . .	–	–	1	–	–	–	2	–
7 to 11 ,, . .	–	–	10	4	–	–	2	1
12 to 16 ,, . .	–	–	3	1	–	·	4	–
17 to 20 ,, . .	–	–	2	1	–	–	1	–
21 to 30 ,, . .	–	–	5	5	–	–	1	3
51 to 60 ,, . .	–	–	1	1	–	–	–	–
Total No. of Individuals committed,	10	–	183	42	3	1	117	13
No. of commitments represented in foregoing, . . .	11	–	585	296	3	2	301	103

Highest number of Prisoners (exclusive of Debtors) in Gaol during each of the previous seven years, and up to day of Inspection in 1875.

28th December, 1868, . .	48	27th February, 1872, . .	39
1st January, 1869, . .	44	17th February, 1873, . .	46
13th June, 1870, . .	46	11th August, 1874, . .	37
12th April, 1871, . .	41	24th February, 1875, . .	46

Averages, and Highest and Lowest Numbers (exclusive of Debtors).

—	From 1st January to 31st December, 1874.			From 1st January, 1875, to day of Inspection.		
	M.	F.	Date.	M.	F.	Date.
Average daily number of prisoners in custody,	19	6	—	24·4	5	—
Highest number of prisoners at any one time,	37		11th Aug.	46		24th Feb.
Lowest ditto, .	15		10th Nov.	15		8th April.
Highest number of males at any one time, .	31		11th Aug.	37		24th Feb.
Ditto, of females,	11		13th May.	9		24th Feb.
Lowest number of males at any one time, .	9		10th Nov.	12		9th April.
Ditto, of females,	2		20th Aug.	3		8th April.

The number of adult male individuals committed here in 1874 was 183, Recommitments. and of females 42, against 117 of the former and 13 of the latter previous
to my inspection in 1875. Of those committed in 1874 their recommitments since their first offence numbered of males 585 and of females 296.
The recommitments of those in custody here up to the time of my inspection in 1875 numbered 301 of males and 103 of females ; but 128 of
males and 125 females committed in 1874, and 69 males and 6 females
committed in 1875, had not previously been in gaol; so that it will be
seen that the few individuals who are constantly committed to this prison
are the principal cause of the necessity of maintaining a gaol in this district.
For it will be observed by one of the foregoing tables that some individuals
have been committed here who have been over fifty times in prison. Up
to the above date the daily average number of males committed here was
5 in excess of that of last year ; but the daily average number of females
was 1 less in 1875 than in 1874.

Accommodation.

	M.	F.		M.	F.
Wards, . . .	9	2	Kitchen, . . .	One	
Yards, . . .	12	4	Store Rooms, . .	2	1
Day Rooms, . .	12	2	Laundry, . . .	—	1
Solitary Cells, . .	5	1	Drying Room, . .	—	1
Single Cells, 9 feet long, 6 feet wide, and 8 feet high, or which contain 432 cubic feet,	69	6	Baths, with hot and cold water laid on, . . .	2	2
			Privies, . . .	20	3
Sleeping Rooms, . .	9	8	Water-closets, . .	2	—
No. of Beds in such Rooms, .	6	13	Fumigating Apparatus, .	1	—
Hospital Rooms, . .	2	2	Reception Rooms or Cells, .	6	1
Chapel, . . .	One		Pumps, . . .	2	—
School Rooms, . .	1	1	Well, . . .	1	—
Workshops, . . .	5	—	Tread-wheel, . .	1	—
Worksheds, . .	56	—	Tell-tale Clocks, . .	2	—

I am happy to be able to report that since my last inspection of this Improvements
effected. gaol many suggestions of my colleague and myself have been carried out,
and I consequently observe an improvement in the order, discipline, and
regularity of the whole establishment. I was consulted by the Local
Inspector as to the reorganization of the female prison, and I then pointed
out what I considered would be necessary to adapt this section to the
separate system. Since then plans have been submitted for the approval
of the Lord Lieutenant, and I have every hope before long that the female
prison here will be entirely remodelled. Suitable arrangements exist for
the reception of prisoners, by which means they are not now permitted Reception.
to have access to those who have been in gaol previously until they are

NORTH DISTRICT.
~ Sligo County Gaol.

Bath.

duly inspected by the Doctor. All prisoners are washed and cleansed as they come in, but no time is fixed subsequently for bathing them, as suggested in my last report. I submit that this operation should take place at least once a week. At present hot water is obliged to be carried to the bath, which is an inconvenient arrangement. I would therefore suggest that a boiler be put up in the apartment next to that in which the bath is situate in the male prison, so that hot and cold water may be obtained at any moment of the day. As suggested in my last report basins are now provided in the cells, and prisoners are required to wash themselves in the mornings before they go out. None of the cells here have

Heating.

yet been artificially heated, or provided with bells or gas, so that it is impossible to carry on the separate system in this prison. The water supply is abundant, for in addition to two excellent pumps on the premises it is also brought into the gaol by pipes from an excellent well outside,

Water.

and, in addition, river-water is pumped into a cistern by means of

Sewerage.

the tread-wheel. The sewerage is effective, and is carried away into

Chapel.

cesspools outside the walls. The chapel has not been altered since my last inspection, and is suitably arranged. The recommendations of Inspectors-General with regard to the stalling of the laundry are not yet adopted, but I trust that this will be done when the improvements of

Fumigator.

the female prison have been undertaken. One fumigating apparatus is provided, in which all prison clothing is, I am informed, fumigated as soon as prisoners enter the gaol, so that both infection and vermin are thereby removed.

Kitchen.

As the ordinary kitchen is unnecessarily large for the requirements of the prison the cooking is performed in one of the day-rooms. This department should certainly be removed into the female prison, so that the labour of a male prisoner may be turned to greater advantage.

Photography.

I have again to draw attention to the photography being performed by an artist who lives seven miles from the town, whose service at times it is impossible to procure so as to photograph prisoners before they leave. As it is now made imperative by law that certain classes of prisoners should be photographed, I again submit that this art should be taught to one of the officers, and should be carried on by him. The photographer at present receives five shillings for four copies, which expense would be diminished if this duty were performed by a prison officer; and as crime is now-a-days frequently traced by means of this art it is all the more important that every attention should be paid to it by the gaol authorities.

Night-watch.

The vigilance of the night-watch is tested by two tell-tale clocks, which are marked hourly—from 7 P.M. to 6 A.M. Two warders patrol within the prison from lock-up until 10 o'clock, after which hour the watch is kept by one officer until 6 A.M. The keys of the tell-tale clocks are kept by the Governor, the markings are taken by him every morning, and the omissions are entered in the Lockings Book, and are also noted in the Officers' Conduct Book. I however observe that there are a great many omissions in the marking of the clocks, and I find that the officers are not punished sufficiently for neglect of this duty. I would therefore suggest that a scale of fines such as exists in other gaols be established here for any neglect of duty on the part of an officer, and that the markings of the tell-tale clocks be more carefully performed. Lock-up takes place at 6.30 P.M. all the year round, and unlock in summer at 6.15 A.M., and at daylight in the winter. All the locks of the prison are reported to be in good repair, and the keys are taken by the Governor to his room at night.

Visitors.

No improvement has taken place in the arrangements for visitors to prisoners. The visits take place at the gate, a turnkey being on each side during visits; but I am informed by the Governor that the new rule in regard to the number of visits permitted to convicted prisoners has had

a good effect upon the habitual offenders of this district. The convicted North District.
prisoners now receive a visit every two months, the untried once a week,
or oftener if necessary for the purposes of their trial; and all visitors to *Sligo County Gaol.*
prisoners are, I am informed, searched at the gate before being admitted.

Stock at the time of Inspection.

	In Use.	In Store.	Male Clothing.		In Use.	In Store.	Female Clothing.		In Use.	In Store.
Blankets, pairs of,	125	8	Shirts, .	.	77	–	Shifts, .	.	13	30
Sheets, pairs of,	277	–	Jackets, .	.	34	46	Jackets, .	.	16	21
Rugs,	121	16	Vests, .	.	22	33	Petticoats,	.	18	8
Bedticks, .	122	–	Trowsers,	.	27	23	Aprons, .	.	20	48
Bedsteads,	116	–	Caps, .	.	23	17	Caps, .	.	30	–
			Socks, pairs of,		–	10	Shoes, Slippers,			
			Shoes, Slippers,				and Clogs,			
			and Clogs,				pairs of, .		10	4
			pairs of, .		33	26				

The Clerk has charge of the general store of male clothing, and the Store.
Matron that of females; and I am glad to report that they are all
neatly arranged and tidily kept. The Governor takes stock of all prison
clothing monthly, and no articles are issued from the store either by
the Matron or Clerk into the store of things in use without the order
of the Governor. Prisoners' own clothing are now properly labelled and
tidily put away. All the clothing is made up in the gaol, the Governor
superintending the cutting out of the male clothing, and the Matron that
of females. Indeed the former officer's knowledge of trades is most
useful as he is able to instruct prisoners in them, by which means a considerable amount of industry is carried on. Both bedding and clothing at
the time of my visit were abundant, and all were clean and orderly.
Sheets are said to be changed once a month, and oftener if necessary, but
I submit that they should be changed once a fortnight, and if prisoners
were washed once a week the bedding and clothing would easily be kept
clean.

Punishments for Prison Offences.

				From 1st January to 31st December, 1874.		From 1st January, 1875, to day of Inspection.	
				M.	F.	M.	F.
By Governor—							
Dark or Refractory Cells,	.	.	.	9	5	10	3
Stoppage of Diet,	.	.	.	2	–	1	–
Total.	.	.	.	11	5	11	3

Three solitary cells are provided for males, which are heated; there Punish-
is also one for females, but no bells are attached to any. I would certainly ments.
recommend that a properly fitted up solitary cell be provided in each
prison, and with spiral bells, as it is illegal to confine prisoners to any
cell without the means of communication with the officer on duty. Were
this suggestion carried out a prisoner might be left in a solitary cell
during the night, and I have no doubt, under these circumstances, it
would be found necessary much less frequently to administer punishment for breach of prison rule, for when prisoners are removed to their
ordinary cells at night punishment has very little effect upon them.

Summary of Employment.

							M.	F.
Hard labour,	.	.	.	.	.	.	22	1
Industrial Labour,	.	.	.	.	.	.	1	3
Sick,	.	.	.	.	.	.	1	1
			Total,	.	.	.	24	5

NORTH
DISTRICT.

Sligo
County
Gaol.

Amount received for produce of prisoners' labour disposed of outside the gaol during the last three years.

1872, . £9 11s. 1d. | 1873, . £10 13s. 7d. | 1874. . £12 9s. 3d.

Net average daily cost of ordinary diet for each prisoner in the three preceding years.

1872, . 4·8d. | 1873, . 5d. | 1874, . 6d.

Net cost of Gaol, including Diet and Salaries, for the three preceding years.

1872, . £1,634 6s. 1d. | 1873, £1.775 7s. 5d. | 1874, . £1,754 7s. 1d.

Total cost of Officers, including Clothing, Value of Rations, &c.

1872, . £959 11s. 6d. | 1873, . £980 6s. 7d. | 1874, . £977 9s. 9d.

Average cost of each Prisoner per annum in each of the last three years.

1872, . £65 11s. 8d. | 1873, . £59 3s. 7d. | 1874, . £67 9s. 6d.

Amounts repaid by the Inland Revenue Department for Excise Prisoners for the last three years.

1872, . £4 1s. 8d. | 1873, . £1 10s. 4d. | 1874, . £1 1s. 9d.

Amounts repaid from the Consolidated Fund for the maintenance, &c., of Prisoners during the years

1872, . £35 0s. 3d. | 1873. . £27 18s. 5d. | 1874, . £71 11s. 10d.

Labour.

Hard labour is carried on here three days a week by means of the tread-mill, and the other three days by means of shot-drill; prisoners so sentenced also pick oakum. Since my last visit the mill has been repaired, but has not been partitioned. Men are, I am informed, absolutely employed on it for 20 minutes at a time and have 10 minutes intervals of rest, during which latter period they are required to pick oakum. A certain amount of stone-breaking is also performed here now, and I am glad to find that the arrangements as regards hard labour have been improved since my last visit. Yet I do not consider that a sufficient quantity of reproductive labour is yet carried out. I would therefore recommend that mat-making be adopted, and that a greater amount of oakum be required to be picked by the prisoners in custody. There is ample room in the day-rooms to establish workshops for the purpose of carrying on trades, so that, I submit, advantage should be taken of them, in order, if possible, to diminish the large expenditure of the gaol, which in 1874 amounted to £1,754 7s. 1d.; but from that sum the cost of officers came to £977 9s. 9d., and so small was the return received from the produce of prisoners' labour, namely, £12 9s. 3d., that the average annual cost of a prisoner here for that year was larger than it had been for sometime, namely, £67 9s. 6d. Making every allowance for the ill-construction of this gaol, as well as for the large staff which it is necessary to employ, I am certainly of opinion that a greater amount of reproductive labour should be pursued, in order that the charge on the rate-payers for gaol purposes may be diminished.

Expenditure.

School.

	From 1st Jan. to 31st Dec., 1874.		From 1st Jan., 1875, to day of Inspection.	
	M.	F.	M.	F.
Number of individual prisoners who attended school,	116	50	95	21
Average daily number of pupils,	14	4	13	4
Number of days on which school was held,	244	244	90	90

School-hours.—Males, 7 to 8 o'clock, A.M.; Females, 7 to 8 o'clock, A.M.

North
District.

Sligo
County
Gaol.

School.

The school is held for one hour daily, the males being taught by the Clerk and the females by the Matron, who, although not trained teachers, are quite competent to instruct here. In former reports I had to call attention to the neglect of the Chaplains in not inspecting the school, and regret to have again to state that this duty this year has been altogether neglected by these gentlemen, for up to the time of my visit the school had only once been inspected, namely, by the Roman Catholic Chaplain on one occasion. Inasmuch as the school is not connected with any educational body it is all the more important that the by-laws with regard to the inspection of schools by the Chaplains should be carried out; and I trust that the Board will insist upon this duty being performed.

Contracts.

White bread, per 4-lb. loaf, 7*d.*; brown bread, per 4-lb. loaf, 6½*d.*; oatmeal, per cwt., 16*s.* 6*d.*; Indian meal, per cwt., 10*s.* 0*d.*; potatoes, per cwt., 6*s.*; new milk, per gallon, 11*d.*; coal, per ton, £1 5*s.* 6*d.*; straw, per cwt., 3*s.*; candles, per lb., 5½*d.*; soap, per cwt., £1 5*s.*

The provisions are all obtained by contract, sanctioned by the Board, once in twelve months, but the materials for clothing, &c., are got by the Local Inspector with the sanction of that body. A yearly contract is also obtained for the supply of blankets. The storekeeper, who is also the cook-warder has charge of the provisions. Every portion is weighed or measured before being issued. None of the prisoners made any complaint to me regarding the provisions, samples of which I saw, and appeared excellent. They are always reported on favourably by the Chaplains, who inspect them regularly.

Officers and Salaries.

Non-Resident.	£	s.	d.			£	s.	d.
Thomas M. Wood, esq., Local Inspector,	100	0	0		Alexr. Crawford, Shoemaker,	30	0	0
Rev. A. M. Kearney, Protestant Chaplain,	30	0	0		James Buchanan,	28	0	0
Rev. John Sloane, Roman Catholic Chaplain,	30	0	0	Turnkeys. {	Robert Kerr,	35	0	0
Thos. S. Murray, Physician,	50	0	0		William Duncan,	26	0	0
Resident.					Patrick Coleman,	26	0	0
					William Shaw,	25	0	0
Edwd. Walsh, esq. Governor,	300	0	0		Catherine Ryan, Matron,	40	0	0
Richard Browne, Clerk and Schoolmaster,	50	0	0		Elizabeth Griffith, Assistant Matron and Hospital Nurse,	15	0	0

[All the turnkeys, except Alexander Crawford, assist the schoolmaster in teaching.]

Vacancies in the staff since last inspection, how caused, and how filled up.

John Black, Turnkey, resigned; William Shaw, appointed in his stead. Edward Powell, M.D., Apothecary, resigned; vacancy not yet filled up.

Officers on Gaol Allowance.

Turnkeys, clerk and schoolmaster, matron, and assistant matron and hospital nurse.

Visits paid by Officers.

	From 1st Jan. to 31st Dec., 1874.	From 1st Jan., 1875, to day of Inspection.
Number of times the Board of Superintendance met and discharged business,	12	5
Local Inspector, to Gaol,	188	82
" to Bridewell,	4	3
Chaplain, Protestant Episcopal Church,	153	50
" Roman Catholic,	145	60
Physician,	181	68
Apothecary,	138	23

NORTH
DISTRICT.
―――
*Sligo
County
Gaol.*

Officers.

As I have already stated, some of the debtors' quarters have been given over to the subordinate officers, but I was sorry to find that some of their rooms were very untidy and badly kept. I would recommend that some presses and shelves be hut up in these rooms for the use of the officers, and that they be required to keep them in better order than they are in the habit of doing now. Their quarters should be regularly inspected by the Governor and Local Inspector, who should bring any officer before the Board in the event of his not keeping his room tidy. I was glad to learn from the Governor that there had been somewhat of an improvement in the discipline of the subordinate officers; but unless the Board establish a scale of fines, as suggested, for small omissions of duty, it cannot be expected that proper discipline and regular hours will be observed amongst the staff. I have now, as on former occasions, to hear my testimony to the zeal and devotion to duty on the part of the Governor, and trust that the Board will give him increased powers to enable him to maintain a due amount of discipline and regularity amongst the subordinate staff; for unless the Governor is so empowered it is impossible that he can be responsible for the good management of the prison, upon which regularity, order, and discipline so much depends.

Hospital.

	1872.		1873.		1874.		1875 (to day of Inspection)	
	M.	F.	M.	F.	M.	F.	M.	F.
No. of prisoners in hospital,	9	1	7	2	9	5	—	
Average daily number in hospital, . . .	·55	·25	·4	·2	·6	·2	—	
No. of prisoners prescribed for and treated out of hospital, . . .	82	13	77	25	110	55	56	11
Number of deaths in the gaol, ...	—	—	—	—	—	—	1	—
Cost of medicine, . .	£5 2s. 6d.		£8 3s. 7d.		£7 4s. 6d.		£5 0s. 0d.	
Cost of extra diet for prisoners in hospital, .	£6 4s. 7d.		£6 0s. 9d.		£10 16s. 10d.		£1 5s. 7d.	
Cost of all extra diet ordered by Medical Officer for prisoners not in hospital, . . .	—		3s. 3d.		6s. 11d.		£3 11s. 8d.	

Hospital.

At the time of my visit there was a very bad case of typhoid fever in the hospital, which was the cause of great alarm in the prison. I therefore obtained by telegraph the sanction of the Lord Lieutenant for the release of the prisoner, who was immediately removed to the fever hospital. The hospital arrangements were the same as at my last visit, and the suggestions with regard to the erection of water-closets here have not been adopted. The medicines are compounded by the Medical Officer, who is, I am informed, willing to perform this duty, so that I do not consider the appointment of an apothecary necessary, the late apothecary having resigned. The medicines are procured from the Apothecaries' Hall, the cost of which came in 1875 to £5.

Books.

Most of the books of finance and registries are carefully kept by the Clerk, and are regularly supervised by the Governor, and both of these officers devote much time and attention to them. I would, however, suggest that fewer registries be kept, and that the existing ones be condensed, as so many are quite unnecessary. The journal of the Local Inspector not having been written up since last February contained little or no information regarding the performance of his duty. The Surgeon keeps an excellent journal, and he also takes care that the other hospital books are regularly and carefully written up. I regret, however, to find that he orders tobacco to be smoked occasionally by prisoners, which is an indulgence not usually permitted in gaol, and is absolutely forbidden by the 12th rule of the 109th section of the Prisons Act. I learned from one of the other journals that even before prisoners are tried the Doctor orders tobacco without any specific reason being stated. In the event of tobacco ever being used in prison I submit that full reasons should be stated in the Doctor's journal for such an exceptional course. The Governor keeps an excellent journal, and records therein all matters of importance relating to his duty. The Punishments Book is laid before the Board of Superintendence, and regularly initialled by the Chairman at each meeting.

Board of Superintendence.

Capt. Richd. Gethin, J.P.	Major Jas. Jones, D.L., J.P.	Peter O'Connor, esq., J.F.
Sir R. Gore Booth, bt., M.P.	Commander Jas. W. Arm-	Capt. W.G Wood Martin.
Jemmett Duke, esq., J.P.	strong.	Capt. O. Wynne, D.L., J.P.
C. W. O'Hara, esq., D.L., J.P.	Col. Edward H. Cooper,	Robert Crawford esq., J.P.,
Col. John Ffolliott, D.L, J.P.	D.L., J.P.	Mayor of Sligo.

On the first Saturday of the month the Board meets for the purpose of business, when the Governor receives a cheque for the payment of the subordinate officers' salaries, and when small accounts are paid. The salaries of the superior officers are paid half-yearly at assizes. Annexed is my tabular report on the bridewell of Ballymoate.

STATE OF BALLYMOTE BRIDEWELL.

	M.	F.
No. of Committals in past year,	7	1
Of whom were Drunkards, .	–	1
No. in quarter preceding inspection, ...	7	2
Of whom were Drunkards, .	1	2

Petty Sessions and Transmittals, how often?	Petty Sessions fortnightly; transmittals generally on the following day.
Committals, ...	Regular.
Registry, ...	Carefully kept.
Repairs and Order, . .	Very good.
Security, ...	Good, except in exercise yards.
Accommodation, . .	Two cells for males, and 4 beds; one cell for females, with 3 beds.
Furniture, Bedding, and Utensils	Good, clean, and well kept.
Water, how supplied? .	By pump on premises.
Sewerage, ...	Effective.
Cleanliness, Dryness, and Ventilation	Very clean, and well ventilated.
Cost of Dietary, . . .	5d. per head, per day.
Salary of Keeper, and whether he follows any other employment?	£40; £6 a year for fuel, light, and straw. Has no other employment; is a pensioner of the R.I.C.
Date of Inspection, . .	8th May, 1875.
Remarks, ...	No prisoner in custody. The condition of this establishment reflects much credit on the keeper and his wife.

CHARLES F. BOURKE, *Inspector-General.*

NORTH DISTRICT.

Tyrone County Gaol.

TYRONE COUNTY GAOL, AT OMAGH.—STATUTABLE INSPECTION, 16TH AUGUST, 1875.

Number in Custody.

Juveniles.

At the above date forty-nine formed the total number of prisoners in custody. Of these, twenty-four cases were disposed of at assizes or quarter sessions, four were untried, three were as prisoners classed as debtors, and the remainder were disposed of by summary jurisdiction. No juveniles were in charge at the time of my visit, but four were committed here during this year, one of whom only were sent to a reformatory. During the year 1874 a male juvenile was committed here who had been already in custody five times, and one this year who had been in charge twice. I was informed that care was taken to keep juveniles altogether apart from adult prisoners.

Number of Prisoners of all classes in gaol on the day of Inspection, and on the corresponding date in the three preceding years.

	M.	F.		M.	F.
1872,	27	19	1874,	43	13
1873,	40	21	1875 (day of Inspection),	38	11

Number of Vagrants in Gaol on the day of Inspection, and on the corresponding date in the three preceding years.

	M.	F.		M.	F.
1872,	1	10	1874,	–	1
1873,	–	3	1875 (day of Inspection),	1	3

Number of Returned Convicts in gaol on the day of inspection, and during each of the three preceding years, and the expired portion of 1875.

	M.	F.		M.	F.
1872,	–	2	1875 (up to and including		
1873,	–	2	day of inspection),	3	2
1874,	1	2	1875, day of inspection,	1	–

Commitments.

CLASSES.	From 1st January to 31st December, 1874.		From 1st January, 1875, to day of Inspection.	
	M.	F.	M.	F.
Debtors,	6	–	3	1
Criminals,	263	56	133	36
Vagrants,	1	11	1	8
Drunkards,	94	60	53	33
Total,	364	127	190	78

Commitments.

Debtors.

Up to the time of my visit this year there were 190 commitments of males and seventy-eight of females in this prison against 364 of the former and 127 of the latter during the whole of 1874. I regret to state that three prisoners were in custody for debt. One (J. G.), an old man of seventy-two years of age, was in for a civil bill decree; and the other (J. A.), was committed under a writ of attachment from the Landed Estates Court. The master debtor was a gentleman already referred to in reports of Inspectors-General, as he has been in custody here for some time. Subsequent to my inspection, I brought his case under the notice of the Lord Chancellor, who kindly investigated it, but could not interfere, as the matter had already been referred to the Vice-Chancellor, on whose order the prisoner was detained. I then communicated with the Vice-Chancellor, who also was good enough to take the case into his consideration, and informed me that under the circumstances he had no power to order the discharge of the prisoner, except on an application or notice to the other parties concerned, and further, that the course was open to the prisoner of applying for his discharge to the Bankruptcy Court. I subsequently communicated this information to the master debtor. I also drew the attention of the Executive to the case of one of the pauper debtors (J. A.), who was in a very precarious state of health. He was confined under an attachment of the Landed Estates Court. Judge Flanagan was at once communicated with, and he very considerately directed that an order should be made out for this prisoner's immediate release, which was consequently effected in a few days. During this year four males had been committed for conspiring against life, and two for manslaughter, but no person had been in custody since the year 1873 charged with murder. Assaults, larceny, and drunkenness are the offences for which people in this district are chiefly sent to prison.

Number of Individual Prisoners (exclusive of Debtors), and Number of Times each had been committed during the following periods, distinguishing adults from juveniles.

NUMBER OF TIMES COMMITTED.	1874.				1875, to day of Inspection.			
	Juveniles.		Adults.		Juveniles.		Adults.	
	M.	F.	M.	F.	M.	F.	M.	F.
Once within the year,	9	–	268	64	2	–	148	47
Twice ,,	–	–	15	5	1	–	13	10
Thrice ,,	–	–	8	5	–	–	3	2
Four times ,,	–	–	–	4	–	–	–	1
Five times ,,	–	–	3	2	–	–	–	–
Six times ,,	–	–	2	2	–	–	–	–
Total,	9	–	296	62	3	–	164	60
No. of above who had not been in Gaol previous to 1st Jan. in .	7	–	256	58	3	–	136	41

Number of Individual Prisoners (exclusive of Debtors), committed in the year 1874, and to the day of Inspection in 1875, who had been once and oftener committed from their first Commitment in any year, so far as can be ascertained.

NUMBER OF TIMES COMMITTED.	1874.				1875, to day of Inspection.			
	Juveniles.		Adults.		Juveniles.		Adults.	
	M.	F.	M.	F.	M.	F.	M.	F.
Once only, .	7	–	248	55	2	–	129	38
Twice, .	1	–	13	3	1	–	13	8
Thrice, .	–	–	3	1	–	–	4	2
Four times within the year,	–	–	8	4	–	–	5	1
Five times ,,	1	–	8	–	–	–	2	2
Six times ,,	–	–	4	1	–	–	2	–
7 to 11 times, ,,	–	–	7	6	–	.	7	3
12 to 16 ,, ,,	–	–	3	4	–	–	1	1
17 to 20 ,, ,,	–	–	–	–	–	–	1	1
21 to 30 ,, ,,	–	–	1	3	–	–	–	2
31 to 40 ,, ,,	–	–	1	2	–	–	–	1
41 to 50 ,, ,,	–	–	–	2	–	–	–	–
51 to 60 ,, ,,	–	–	–	1	–	–	–	1
Total No. of Individuals committed,	9	–	296	62	3	–	164	60
No. of commitments represented in foregoing, .	14	–	554	539	4	–	301	262

NORTH DISTRICT.

Tyrone County Gaol.

Re-commitments.

During the year 1874 two males and two females were committed here six times, but only one female was committed up to the time of my inspection this year four times. However, in each of these years one female had been in custody who had over fifty-one commitments recorded against her. The total number of adult individuals committed in 1874 was 296 males and eighty-two females. Their previous commitments respectively numbered 554 and 539, but of these individuals 256 males and fifty-eight females had not previously been in gaol. In the expired portion of the year 1875 164 adult males and sixty adult females had been committed here whose previous commitments since their first offence numbered respectively 301 and 262, but of these individuals 136 males and forty-one females had not, as far as was known, been in gaol previously. These figures demonstrate clearly how important it is to endeavour, as far as possible, to make the strong arm of the law felt by habitual offenders, for it is evident that this gaol is chiefly frequented by a few individuals, who form the disorderly population of the county.

Averages, and Highest and Lowest Numbers (exclusive of Debtors).

—	From 1st January to 31st December, 1874.			From 1st January, 1875, to day of Inspection.		
	M.	F.	Date.	M.	F.	Date.
Average daily number of prisoners in custody,	35	16	—	25	15	—
Highest number of prisoners at any one time,	82		4th Nov.	36		9th Jan.
Lowest ditto, .	33		25th May.	28		12th April.
Highest number of males at any one time,	64		4th Nov.	38		14th August.
Ditto, of females,	22		30th Oct.	20		21st July.
Lowest number of males at any one time, .	18		4th May.	19		7th April.
Ditto, of females,	9		5th Aug.	10		4th April.

Highest number of prisoners (exclusive of debtors), in gaol during each of the previous seven years, and up to day of Inspection in 1875.

4th January, 1868, . . . 73   22nd June, 1872, . . . 63
1st January, 1869, . . . 67   22nd July, 1873, . . . 76
10th August, 1870, . . . 64   15th January, 1874, . . . 75
29th April, 1871, . . . 55   9th January, 1875, . . . 56

The daily average number of male prisoners in custody this year was, I am happy to observe, ten less than in the year 1874, and the daily average number of females was one less than in that year; and at one period in 1875, namely, in April, the numbers both of male and female prisoners were lower than they had been for several years.

Accommodation.

	M.	F.		M.	F.
Wards, ...	5	3	Single Cells of smaller size, .	51	—
Yards, ...	5	2	Sleeping Rooms, .	5	—
Day Rooms, . . .	3	1	Hospital Rooms, .	6	—
Solitary Cells, . .	2	2	Chapel, . .		One.
Single Cells, 9 feet long, 6 feet wide, and 8 feet high, or which contain 432 cubic feet, heated and furnished with bells, ...	19	37	Schoolroom, . .	1	—
			Workshops, . .	4	—
			Worksheds, . .	29	—
			Kitchen, . .		One.
			Store Rooms, . .	2	2

Accommodation—continued.

	M.	F.			M.	F.	
Laundry,	–	1	Fumigating Apparatus,	.	1	1	*Tyrone*
Drying Room,	–	1	Reception Cells,	.	5	3	*County*
Lavatories,	4	3	Pumps,	.	3	–	*Gaol.*
Baths, with hot and cold water			Wells,	.	2	–	
laid on,	3	2	Tread-wheel,	.	1	–	
Privies,	4	–	Watchman's Watch,	.	1	–	
Water-closets,	10	4	Tell-tale Clock,	.	1	–	

The structural condition of this gaol has undergone little or no altera- *Repairs.* tion since my last visit. Some of the walls have lately been painted, but others, including the boundary wall, require attention and repair. A suf- *Reception.* ficient number of cells are reserved in each prison for reception, and care is taken to bathe all the prisoners as they come in. The females are at once washed and cleansed, but the males still wait to be inspected by the Doctor before they are bathed. This is, I consider, quite unnecessary, and would recommend that the same rule be followed in this respect in the male prison as in the female, for it is impossible that the bedding and clothing can be kept in a thorough state of cleanliness unless these pre-cautions are adopted. The supply of baths, water-closets, and lavatories *Baths.* throughout the prison is abundant, and they appeared all to be clean and in good order at the time of my visit. The water supplied to the prison *Water.* is procured from the same source as at my last inspection, and is provided in abundance throughout the gaol. I was also informed sewerage is *Sewerage.* effective, and has lately been thoroughly overhauled, and in some respects improved. Gas is, I regret to say, not yet introduced into the cells, *Gas.* although it is provided in the corridors of both prisons and in other places throughout the gaol. In order that a full amount of labour be carried on in the cells, I again submit that gas should be introduced into a certain number of them. One fumigating apparatus is provided, in which all *Fumigator.* clothing is at once purified before it is put away, and I am glad to find that this operation is carefully and regularly performed. The arrange- *Chapel.* ments at the chapel are the same as at my last visit, and are suitable for prison purposes. The only alteration that has taken place in the laundry *Laundry.* since my last inspection was by placing two doors to the washing stalls, by which means the prisoners employed here are now kept more in sepa-ration than formerly. The photography is carried on by the Deputy *Photo-* Governor, at a cost to the Board of about 2*d*. for each copy, the materials *graphy.* being found by the Board. A copy of all prisoners photographed is kept, and carefully registered; and I am informed that prisoners are often discovered by means of photography to be old offenders, their former convictions being traced by this means. I am glad to find that since my *Kitchen.* last visit the kitchen has been removed into the female prison, and placed under the Matron. This officer also has charge of the meal, and issues it daily to the Deputy Matron, and all prisoners' portions are weighed and measured before being issued. The cleanliness and order of this depart-ment reflected as much credit on the Matron as did the regularity and discipline of the whole of her part of the gaol. The place for visitors to *Visitors.* prisoners, and the rules by which they are admitted, are the same as at my last visit, every necessary precaution being taken to prevent the introduc-tion to the gaol of prohibited articles. One tell-tale clock is provided, also *Night-* a watchman's watch, by which means the vigilance of the night watch is *watch.* carefully tested. This officer goes on duty at 9.45, up to which time one of the turnkeys is on patrol in the male prison. The tell-tale clock is marked hourly, and the watch three times during the night up to 6 A.M. All the markings are taken by the Deputy Governor every morning, and are entered in the Lockings Book. All omissions of duty on the part of the night watchman are reported to the Governor, and are entered in the

NORTH DISTRICT.

Tyrone County Gaol.

Cells.

Officers' Conduct Book. Unlock takes place in summer at 6 A.M., and in winter at sunrise, the prisoners are locked up in the former season at 6 P.M., and in the latter at sunset. All the keys are kept at night in a safe in the Governor's bedroom, and are taken up by him at ten o'clock, P.M. The male cells are very properly provided with tables, but there are none in the female cells; with this exception, all the cells are conveniently fitted; those on the upper tier in the male prison are considerably smaller than the lower ones; these, however, are only used for summary convictions and short-timed prisoners. All the floors of the cells in the female prison are boarded, and are consequently warm and comfortable, the cells being all artificially heated.

Stock at the time of Inspection.

	Male Clothing.					Female Clothing.		
	In Use.	In Store.		In Use.	In Store.		In Use.	In Store.
Blankets, pairs of,	144	–	Shirts,	90	38	Shifts,	50	24
Sheets, pairs			Jackets,	136	40	Jackets,	55	9
of,	140	12	Vests,	54	28	Gowns, }	130	50
Rugs,	98	44	Trowsers,	56	56	Petticoats, }		
Bedticks,	112	–	Caps,	32	26	Aprons,	60	18
Bedsteads,	109	–	Stockings or			Neckerchiefs,	50	25
			Socks, pairs of,	60	47	Caps,	54	49
			Shoes, Slippers, &			Stockings, pairs of,	34	45
			Clogs, pairs of,	58	20	Shoes, Slippers, &		
						Clogs, pairs of,	40	10

Stores.

The general store of male clothing is kept by the master tailor, who issues nothing from it to the store of clothing in use, except by the written order of the Governor. The Matron keeps both the store of prison clothing in use and the store of new clothing for females, but nothing is issued from the latter without the Governor's direction in writing. The Governor, with the Local Inspector, takes stock of all prison property quarterly, at which time old clothing is condemned. The clothing is all made up within the gaol by prison labour. The jackets of the men, I submit, are made of too thin a material for winter use. I would therefore suggest that some heavier material be obtained to be worn in cold weather. The bedding was all clean and in good order at the time of my visit, the sheeting being changed once a week. I especially remarked the cleanliness of the sheeting in the female prison, which I attribute to the excellent rule adopted by the Matron, of bathing all healthy prisoners immediately as they come in. The prisoners' own clothing is properly labelled and carefully put away, and altogether the stores here are kept with great precision and neatness.

Number of Prisoners sentenced to Solitary Confinement and Whipping by order of Court.

		From 1st January to 31st December, 1874.		From 1st January, 1875, to day of Inspection.	
		M.	F.	M.	F.
Solitary Confinement,		25*	–	31*	–

* All sentenced by Commanding Officer.

Number of Punishments for Prison Offences.

		From 1st January to 31st December, 1874.		From 1st January, 1875, to day of Inspection.	
		M.	F.	M.	F.
By Magisterial authority,		–	2	–	–
By Governor—					
Dark or Refractory Cells,		31	12	20	10
Stoppage of Diet,		104	7	20	1
Other Punishments,		–	1	–	–
Total,		135	22	40	11

The thirty-one prisoners sentenced to solitary confinement here were all military offenders, sentenced by court-martial. On no occasion this year was it found necessary to have recourse to magisterial authority for the punishment of a prisoner for the breach of prison rule, but two females were sentenced in 1874 to refractory cells by magisterial authority for violently assaulting the two Matrons. The solitary cells for both sexes are heated and provided with bells, and I am glad to find that the pipe which runs overhead in these cells is now boarded up, so as to prevent prisoners so inclined from hanging themselves by this means. Prisoners in solitary are, however, allowed bedding at night, an indulgence which I do not consider necessary to extend to prisoners so sentenced, and which, if disallowed, would, I have no doubt, considerably lessen the necessity for punishing prisoners for breach of prison rule.

Employment on day of Inspection.

Summary.					M.	F.
Hard labour,	.	.	.	.	24	–
Industrial labour,	.	.	.	.	12	10
Sick,	.	.	.	.	1	1
Debtors (unemployed),	.	.	.	.	1	–
Total in custody,		.	.		38	11

Amount received for produce of Prisoners' Labour, disposed of outside the Gaol for the last three years.

1872, . £81 15s. 5d. | 1873, . £72 19s. 0d. | 1874, . £90 4s. 10d.

Net average daily cost of ordinary diet for each Prisoner in the three preceding years.

1872, . . 4d. | 1873, . . 5d. | 1874, . . 5d.

Net cost of Gaol, including Diet and Salaries for the three preceding years.

1872, . £1,949 19s. 0d. | 1873, . £2,676 9s. 5d. | 1874, . £2,432 17s. 9d.

Total cost of Officers, including Clothing, Value of Rations, Washing, Gas, &c.

1872, . £1,066 15s. 0d. | 1873, . £1,022 0s. 10d. | 1874, . £1,039 1s. 8d.

Average cost of each Prisoner per annum in each of the last three years.

1872, . £42 6s. 11d. | 1873, . £51 5s. 10d. | 1874, . £45 18s. 0d.

Amounts repaid by the War Department for Military Prisoners in each of the last three years.

1872, . £0 19s. 0d. | 1873, . £2 11s. 0d. | 1874, . £6 8s. 0d.

Amounts repaid from the Consolidated Fund for the maintenance, &c., of Prisoners during the years

1872, . £102 19s. 9d. | 1873, . £167 11s. 10d. | 1874, . £213 4s. 8d.

Hard labour is carried on here by means both of the crank-pump and tread-wheel. The water from the river is pumped by the former apparatus, at which two men work for twenty minutes at a time, being then relieved by two others. The tread-wheel is worked for about two hours and a half a day. Men sentenced to hard labour are also required to pick about four pounds of prepared oakum a day, and those not so sentenced three pounds; but I submit that the oakum given to hard-labour prisoners is too much prepared, and consequently the labour is made too easy

NORTH DISTRICT.

Tyrone County Gaol.

for them. I consider that hard-labour prisoners should be required to pick a less prepared description of oakum than those not so sentenced. No work is carried on in the cells, except some matmaking. I would strongly recommend that gas be introduced into some of the cells, and that labour be carried on in them up to 8 P.M. during the winter months, and I see nothing to prevent this rule being carried out even now during the summer. Prisoners should be thoroughly employed during the entire day, except the time allowed for their meals, and if this rule were enforced here I feel sure that a greater amount of industrial labour would be obtained, and consequently the sum received from the produce of prisoners' labour disposed of outside the gaol would be much larger than at present. I am glad, however, to find that there is somewhat of an improvement in this respect in the year 1874 as compared with the two previous years, for the sum received under that head during that year was £90 4s. 10d., or somewhat less than the average annual cost of two prisoners in this

Expenditure.

gaol. The average cost of a prisoner here in 1874 amounted to £45 18s. In the same year the net cost of the gaol came to £2,432 17s. 9d., and the cost of officers £1,039 1s. 8d. Although the staff is very large compared with the daily average number in custody, having regard to the difficulties of supervision in this prison, and to the duties which the subordinate officers are called upon to perform, I cannot now recommend any further reduction of the staff, especially as I am in hopes that in the next session of Parliament our prison system in Ireland will be brought under the consideration of the Legislature, but at the same time it must be evident that so large and expensive a staff as is maintained here would not under improved arrangements be necessary for the safe keeping of the small number of prisoners usually committed to this gaol. At the time of my visit a prisoner (W. H.), complained to me of not being allowed a proper amount of exercise in the open air. This is a matter which I have brought before the Board in my report left in the gaol, and which I have no doubt has since been corrected. This prisoner also made some complaints to me about his not having received proper attention from the Medical Officer, but I was unable to verify this statement. Means, I submit, should be devised for giving prisoners exercise in the open air, and at the same time profitable employment, for all prisoners are entitled by statute to two hours' open exercise during the day, but it does not, therefore, follow that the time should not be profitably employed.

Schools.

	From 1st Jan. to 31st Dec. 1874.		From 1st Jan., 1875, to day of Inspection.	
	M.	F.	M.	F.
Number of individual prisoners who attended school,	229	70	85	64
Average daily number of pupils,	32	14	18	13
Number of days on which school was held,	218	153	79	109

School-hours.—Males, 11 A.M. to 1 P.M.   Females, 4 P.M. to 5 P.M.

Schools.

A good school-room has now been arranged for male prisoners, consisting of sixteen stalls, and I am informed that instruction is now much more easily imparted to prisoners than heretofore. Females are still taught in their cells for an hour a day by the Matron. I trust that before long a good stalled school-room will also be fitted up in the female prison. I submit that one hour a day is quite sufficient to allow for the secular instruction of prisoners, and that gas be introduced into the school-room, in order that it may be carried on in winter after dark, so as not to interfere with the short hours of labour during that season. Up to the time of my inspection the school had been only inspected three times by the Presbyterian, twice by the Episcopalian, and not at all this year by the

Roman Catholic Chaplain, and as the schools are not in connexion with any board of education, I again submit that it is all the more important that the bye-laws in respect to the inspection of the schools by the Chaplains should be more carefully attended to. All prisoners are permitted to go to school except the aged and those who are already well educated.

Contracts.

Bread, white, per 4-lb. loaf, 6*d.*; oatmeal, per cwt., 15*s.*; Indian meal, per cwt., 10*s.*; rice, per lb., 3*d.*; potatoes, per cwt., 3*s.* 8*d.*; meat, per lb., 10*d.*; new milk, per gallon, 9½*d.*; buttermilk, per gallon, 6*d.*; salt, per cwt., 2*s.* 6*d.*; coal, per ton, £1 1*s.* 9*d.*; turf, per box of 80 cubic feet, 3*s.* 10½*d.*; straw, per cwt., 2*s.* 6*d.*; gas, per 1,000 cubic feet, 7*s.* 6*d.*; candles, per lb., 5¾*d.*; soap, per cwt., £1 8*s.* 6*d.*; calico, per yard, 7*d.*; flannel, per yard, 1*s.* 8*d.*; leather, per lb., 2*s.* 4*d.*

The contracts are taken once a year, and are sanctioned by the Board of Superintendence. The diet, samples of which I saw on the day of my visit, appeared excellent, but some of the prisoners in custody complained to me about the quality of the milk, which I observe is somewhat unfavourably criticised by the Chaplains in their reports on this subject. This is a matter which I trust the Board will pay strict attention to, for as milk is the only animal food given in our dietary formula to prisoners in our county and borough gaols, it should always be of the best quality. I had also at the time of my visit occasion to call attention to a departure from the prescribed dietary scale in reference to the vegetable soup, which I find was not given as a substitute for potatoes, in compliance with the directions of the Lord Lieutenant on that subject. This is a matter that should have been more carefully attended to by the Local Inspector, as it is his duty to see that the legally prescribed dietary scale is properly carried out, and is required to report thereon to the Inspectors-General of Prisons in every quarter.

Officers and Salaries.

Non-Resident.	£	s.	d.	Resident.	£	s.	d.
George A. Rogers, esq., Local Inspector,	150	0	0	Geo. E. Mason, esq.,Governor,	200	0	0
Rev. William Chartres,	40	0	0	John Bleakly, Gate,	33	0	0
Rev. John Arnold, } Each alternate year.				William Ellis, Tailor,	28	0	0
Rev. Josias Mitchell, }	40	0	0	James Donnell, Schoolmaster,	30	0	0
				John J. Fulton, Superintendent of Trades,	25	0	0
Rev. Bernard M'Namee,	40	0	0	Marshall Robinson,	20	0	0
E. C. Thompson, esq., M.D.,	—			William Wright, Night Guard,	22	0	0
Francis Trenar, esq.,	20	0	0	Mrs. A. Black, Matron,	35	0	0
H. Patterson, Deputy Governor,	67	10	0	Miss Jane Delap, assistant do.,	22	0	0
				Miss Magt. Hamilton, do.,	13	0	0

Vacancies in the staff since last Inspection, how caused, and how filled up.

Mrs. J. Patterson resigned; Miss M. Hamilton appointed in her stead. H. Thompson, esq., Surgeon, deceased; E. C. Thompson, esq., appointed Surgeon in his stead. Joseph M'Farland, Turnkey, resigned; John J. Fulton, appointed in his stead.

Officers on Gaol Allowance.

The Deputy Governor receives £18 per annum; each of the intern officers receives £16 per annum in lieu of rations.

Visits paid by Officers.

	From 1st Jan. to 31st Dec., 1874.	From 1st Jan., 1875, to day of Inspection.
Number of times the Board of Superintendence met and discharged business,	14	9
Local Inspector, to Gaol,	163	103
" to each Bridewell,	4	3
Chaplain, Protestant Episcopal Church,	151	95
" Presbyterian,	158	91
" Roman Catholic,	149	85
Physician and Surgeon,	137	82

Now that the debtors' quarters are comparatively speaking empty, I would strongly urge that the subordinate officers be provided with apartments in this portion of the prison, for, as I have already observed in former reports, it is highly objectionable that the officers off duty should have any access to prisoners. The rooms of the subordinate officers are well and tidily kept, and are evidently carefully supervised by the Governor, whom I had not the pleasure of seeing, as he was on leave of absence at the time of my visit. In his absence his place appears to be very capably and well filled by the Deputy Governor, who is attentive to his duty, and anxious to carry out discipline and order in the prison. In justice to the Governor, I think it right here to remark that since his appointment to this prison I have observed a steady improvement in its management, and also in the discipline and order maintained amongst the subordinate staff. Since the appointment of Mrs. Black as Matron to this prison, the female department has also undergone considerable improvement both in cleanliness, order, and discipline, for which she deserves a full acknowledgment.

NORTH DISTRICT.

Tyrone County Gaol.

Officers.

Hospital.

	1872.		1873.		1874.		1875 (to day of Inspection.)	
	M.	F.	M.	F.	M.	F.	M	F.
No. of prisoners in hospital,	4	4	17	8	7	3	—	—
Average daily No. in hospital,	·04	·2	·5	·3	·3	·1	—	—
No. of prisoners prescribed for and treated out of hospital,	37	51	97	104	68	79	—	—
Number of deaths in the gaol,	—	—	1	—	—	1	—	—
Cost of medicine,	£4 14s. 0d.		£22 8s. 1d.		£2 16s. 0d.		—	
Cost of diet, &c., for prisoners in hospital,	£2 11s. 8d.		£3 15s. 8d.		£2 14s. 3d.		—	
Cost of all extra diet ordered by Medical Officer for prisoners not in hospital,	—		—		£0 7s. 6d.		—	

Hospital.

The defects pointed out in my last report as to the hospital arrangements have not yet been remedied, but a slipper bath is provided here, and a certain number of cells are set apart in each prison for slight cases of illness, so that the hospital proper is only used in cases of infection, which, I am happy to learn, seldom occur. The supply of medicines is procured from the county infirmary, which is always an economical system. The consequence is that the charge for them in 1874 only came to £2 16s., whereas in other gaols of this size, where the medicines are procured from an apothecary in the town, a large bill is generally run up.

Books and Journals.

Books.

The registries and books of finance are carefully kept by the Deputy Governor, but I submit that they should be more closely supervised both by the Local Inspector and the Governor; as I had occasion to point out some omissions in some of these books at the time of my visit, which should not have been passed over unnoticed. The prescribed Work Ledger and Daily Employment Book, which has not hitherto been kept, should be procured and regularly written up, for without such books the statutes relating to the employment of prisoners cannot be properly carried out. I pointed out these matters to the Local Inspector, who has promised in future to be more exact in the supervision of these books, which is a very important part of his duty. The Punishment Book and Officers Conduct Book are, I am informed, kept by the Governor, but the latter was not at the time of my visit fully written up. From the journals of the Protestant and Presbyterian Chaplains I find that their duties are duly performed by

them in person ; but I must again call attention to the omissions of duty
on the part of the Roman Catholic Chaplain, who does not comply with
the 11th section of the 19th and 20th Vic., chap. 68. This is a matter
that I have already referred to in former reports on this gaol. I have
also again to draw attention to the defects in the journal of the Surgeon,
which should be written up on every occasion of his visit, in compliance
with the 72nd section of the Prisons Act. Owing to the defects of this
journal I was unable fully to ascertain how the duties of this officer are
performed throughout the year. The portion of the Local Inspector's
journal that I saw, namely, from the month of May to the time of my
visit, was very full and regularly kept. In consequence of the absence
of the Governor I did not see his journal.

I would here draw attention to the very objectionable practice prevailing throughout Ireland, of keeping deserters for lengthened periods in
gaols and bridewells awaiting the escort warrant, although they may be
within a few miles of their regiments, and acknowledge themselves to be
deserters from them. The result is that men are constantly detained, in
either gaols or bridewells, for weeks together, awaiting the War Office warrant, and occasionally under circumstances of great hardship. At the time
of my visit to this gaol a deserter had been in prison here nine days, and
before the bench of magistrates acknowledged that he had deserted from
the 108th Regiment, the depot of which was at Enniskillen, so that he could
have been identified and returned to his regiment certainly within two
days. There was also a soldier of the 27th Regiment in custody charged
with desertion from his regiment, also quartered at Enniskillen. He had
overstayed his pass twenty-four hours, and was arrested on the railway
platform when returning to his regiment, by the Constabulary, who I am
informed are allowed £1 for the arrest of every deserter. This man was
therefore detained by them and sent to prison. On my inspection of
Clogher bridewell I found that a deserter whose regiment was also at
Enniskillen, close by, had been kept there awaiting the War Office warrant
from the 20th of July to the 7th of August. I cannot but think that some
more prompt arrangements should be made by which deserters could be
more expeditiously sent back to their regiments, especially when the
regiment is quartered within easy distance of the place where they are
arrested, as was the case in these three instances.

Board of Superintendence.

Sir John M. Stewart, bart.	T. W. D. Humphreys, esq., J.P.	Captain Thos. Auchinleck, J.P., D.L.
Fras. J. Gervais, esq., J.P.	Wm. F. Black, esq., J.P.	James Greer, esq., J.P.
Colonel Fras Ellis, J.P.	Alex. M. Lyle, esq., J.P.	Captain M. Gledstanes, J.P.
Saml Vesey, esq., J.P., D.L.	Courtney Newton, esq., J.P.	
Maj.A.W.C.Hamilton, J.P., D.L.		

The Board meets once every month for the discharge of business, on
which occasions the salaries of all officers and other current accounts are
paid, and the Local Inspector produces vouchers at the following meeting
of the Board. Subjoined will be found my tabular reports upon the
bridewells of the county.

NORTH DISTRICT.

Tyrone County

Bridewells.

	Dungannon (certified) Bridewell.		Clogher (certified) Bridewell.	
	M.	F.	M.	F.
No. of Committals in past year, . .	96	36	38	11
Of whom were Drunkards, .	45	18	21	2
No. of Committals in the quarter preceding Inspection, .	33	3	14	1
Of whom were Drunkards, .	19	–	6	–

	Dungannon (certified) Bridewell.	Clogher (certified) Bridewell.
Petty Sessions and Transmittals, how often?	Petty Sessions fortnightly; transmittals on same day; Criminal Quarter Sessions 4 times a-year.	Petty Sessions on second Tuesday of each month; Criminal Quarter Sessions 4 times a year; transmittals on the following day.
Committals, whether regular?	Regular, with one exception; but I find that prisoners on remand are not always brought before a justice to be remanded, as they should be.	Regular, but some remands not stamped.
Registry, . . .	Regular, and well kept.	Regularly kept.
Repairs and Order, .	Good.	Good.
Security, . . .	Good.	Good.
Accommodation, . .	8 cells and two day-rooms for males; one sleeping cell for females, but another can be fitted down stairs; one day-room.	2 cells and a day-room for each sex.
Furniture, Bedding, and Utensils.	Good, clean, and sufficient.	Good, and sufficient.
Water, how supplied?	By good pump.	To each yard from a cistern.
Sewerage, . . .	Effective.	Good.
Cleanliness, Dryness, and Ventilation.	Clean and well ventilated.	Clean and dry.
Cost of Dietary per head, per day.	4d. per head per day.	4¼d.
Salary of Keeper, and whether he follows any other employment?	£60, and wife £25, and £10 each for rations; a suit of clothing for keeper. Is also Court-keeper, at £50 a-year.	£40; matron £20; £15 in lieu of rations, also fuel and light and uniform.
Date of Statutable Inspection.	October 1st, 1875.	August 12th, 1875.
Remarks, . . .	One male in custody. Since my last visit several of my colleague's and my own suggestions have been adopted, which have improved the condition of the prison very much.	A deserter here from the 20th July to the 7th of August, though his regiment is in Enniskillen. A male and a female in custody, yet the Keeper is obliged to go to Omagh to-day with a prisoner, leaving his wife in charge here; and police do not take the prisoners without the Keeper.

CHARLES F. BOURKE, *Inspector-General.*

WESTMEATH COUNTY GAOL, AT MULLINGAR.—STATUTABLE INSPECTION, 30TH AUGUST, 1875.

Twenty-seven formed the total number of prisoners in custody at the above date, 3 of whom were untried, 6 were military offenders, 3 cases were disposed of at quarter sessions or assizes, and the remainder summarily. There were no juveniles in charge at the time of my visit, but 11 had been committed here this year up to that period. Two of them (males) had been twice in gaol, and the same number were sent to reformatories. I was glad to learn that care is now taken to separate the juveniles altogether from the adults, both during work-hours and at other times, in accordance with the suggestions of Inspectors-General. Two prisoners were in custody during the year who were known to have been previously in reformatories.

Prisoners of all classes in Gaol on the day of Inspection, and on the corresponding date in the three preceding years.

	M.	F.		M.	F.
1872,	30	9	1874,	31	7
1873,	26	7	1875 (day of Inspection),	21	6

Number of Returned Convicts in Gaol on the day of Inspection, and during each of the three preceding years, and the expired portion of 1875.

	M.	F.		M.	F.
1872,	—	2	1875 (up to and including		
1873,	3	2	day of Inspection),	—	—
1874,	—	4	Day of Inspection,	—	1

Commitments.

CLASSES.					From 1st January to 31st Dec., 1874.		From 1st Jan., 1875, to day of Inspection.	
					M.	F.	M.	F.
Debtors,					—	—	—	—
Criminals,					268	36	133	31
Vagrants,					1	10	21	12
Drunkards,					129	41	58	29
Total,					398	87	212	72

During the eight months previous to my inspection this year there were 212 commitments of males and 72 of females to this prison, against 398 of the former and 87 of the latter in the whole of the previous year. Four males were in charge this year who were accused of murder, or conspiring to take life; with these exceptions, the remaining cases were chiefly assaults, larceny, and drunkenness, for which latter offence there were this year 58 male and 29 female commitments. The military offences also formed a considerable proportion of the commitments to this gaol, and should not properly be included amongst the criminal class of the county. They numbered up to the time of my inspection this year 21. There were no persons committed here this year for debt, nor has there been for some years, so that having regard to recent legislation it is to be hoped that there will be no more of such commitments to this prison.

Number of Individual Prisoners (exclusive of Debtors), and number of times each had been Committed during the following periods, distinguishing Adults from Juveniles.

NUMBER OF TIMES COMMITTED.	1874.				1875, to day of Inspection.			
	Juveniles.		Adults.		Juveniles.		Adults.	
	M.	F.	M.	F.	M.	F.	M.	F.
Once within the year,	5	1	296	41	10	–	169	31
Twice „	1	–	13	8	–	–	11	3
Thrice „	–	–	6	5	–	–	5	2
4 times „	–	–	4	2	–	–	–	2
5 „ „	–	–	3	–	–	–	–	–
6 „ „	–	–	1	1	–	–	1	–
12 „ „	–	–	1	–	–	–	–	–
15 „ „	–	–	–	–	–	–	–	1
Total,	6	1	326	57	10	–	186	40
No. of above who had not been in Gaol previous to 1st January in .	4	1	289	36	8	–	151	26

Number of Individual Prisoners (exclusive of Debtors) committed in the year 1874, and to the day of Inspection in 1875, who had been Once, Twice, Thrice, Four Times, Five Times, &c., &c., from their first Commitment in any year, so far as can be ascertained, distinguishing Adults from Juveniles.

NUMBER OF TIMES COMMITTED.	1874.				1875, to day of Inspection.			
	Juveniles.		Adults.		Juveniles.		Adults.	
	M.	F.	M.	F.	M.	F.	M.	F.
Once only,	4	1	278	33	8	–	145	25
Twice,	1	–	20	6	2	–	8	3
Thrice,	–	–	7	2	–	–	6	1
4 times,	–	–	2	2	–	–	3	2
5 „	–	–	1	1	–	–	7	–
6 „	–	–	4	1	–	–	2	1
7 to 11 „	–	–	7	5	–	–	9	2
12 to 16 „	–	–	2	2	–	–	3	3
17 to 20 „	–	–	4	–	–	–	2	–
21 to 30 „	–	–	–	–	–	–	–	–
41 to 50 „	–	–	–	2	–	–	–	–
61 to 70 „	–	–	–	1	–	–	–	–
81 to 90 „	–	–	1	–	–	–	1	–
91 to 100 „	–	–	–	1	–	–	–	1
251 to 328 „	–	–	–	1	–	–	–	–
Total No. of Individuals committed,	6	1	326	57	10	–	196	40
No. of Commitments represented in foregoing,	9	1	623	688	12	–	510	327

The foregoing tables show a very lamentable repetition in crime amongst a certain number of individuals in this district, for even up to the time of my inspection in 1875 one female was committed as often as

15 times, and a male and a female as often as 6 times in that year, while in 1874, 12 was the greatest number of times that any individual was committed here; but in that year one female was committed here who had been in gaol from her first offence 328 times, and in both years a female who was in custody had been in gaol over 90 times, and a male over 80 times. It will thus be seen that there is a certain class here who would almost appear to spend their lives in gaol, and upon whom imprisonment seems to have little effect for good, but so long as justices continue to commit these delinquents for short periods I fear that imprisonment will effect no permanent improvement in their conduct. Two women in custody at the time of my visit complained to me of the nature of their sentences, and the manner in which they had been dealt with by the committing justice. Their case appeared to me to be so exceptional that I submitted it to the Executive, who I understand have communicated with the local authorities on the subject. The total number of adult individuals committed here in 1874 was 326 males and 57 females, whose recommitments numbered respectively 623 and 688. In the expired portion of 1875 the total number of adult individuals committed was 186 males and 40 females, but the previous commitments of these few individuals numbered respectively 510 and 327, showing clearly that this gaol is mainly frequented by a comparatively small number of individuals, as compared with the number of commitments.

Averages, and Highest and Lowest Numbers (exclusive of Debtors).

—	From 1st January to 31st December, 1874.			From 1st January, 1875, to day of Inspection.		
	M.	F.	Date.	M.	F.	Date.
Average daily number of prisoners in custody,	29	9	—	29	9	—
Highest number of prisoners at any one time,	48		12th Feb.	54		8th June.
Lowest ditto,	20		17th July.	24		24th Aug.
Highest number of males at any one time,	39		12th Feb.	42		8th June.
Ditto, of females,	13		7th May.	16		26th July.
Lowest number of males at any one time,	13		17th July.	17		24th Aug.
Ditto, of females,	3		17th Sept.	5		13th Jan.

Highest Number of Prisoners (exclusive of Debtors) in Gaol during each of the previous seven years, and up to day of Inspection in 1875.

4th January, 1868,	. . 43		2nd February, 1872,	. . . 47
26th May, 1869,	. . 36		7th June, 1873,	. . 45
9th June, 1870,	. . 53		12th February, 1874,	. . 48
1st September, 1871,	. . 56		8th June, 1875,	. . . 54

The average daily number of prisoners in custody in 1875 was very nearly the same as in the previous year—namely, 28 males and 9 females in 1875, and 29 males and the same number of females in 1874. But there was a larger number of prisoners in custody at one time in 1875 than at any period since September, 1871.

NORTH DISTRICT.

Westmeath County Gaol.

Accommodation.

	M.	F.		M.	F.
Yards,	10	7	Bakery,	1	-
Day Rooms,	5	2	Store Rooms,	2	1
Solitary Cells,	5	1	Laundry,	-	1
Single Cells 9 feet long, 6 feet wide, and 8 feet high = 432 cubic feet,	93	14	Drying Room,	-	1
			Lavatories,	4	-
Ditto, heated and furnished with bells,	43	13	Baths, with Hot and Cold Water laid on,	3	1
Cells to contain three persons,	6	-	Privies,	15	2
Sleeping Rooms,	4	-	Water-closets,	7	6
Hospital Rooms,	3	2	Fumigating Apparatus,	1	1
Chapel,	1	-	Reception Rooms or Cells,	7	2
School Rooms,	1	1	Pumps,	4	3
Workshops,	5	1	Wells,	2	1
Worksheds,	16	-	Crank-mills,	2	-
Kitchen,	1	-	Shot Drill,	1	-
			Tell-tale Clocks,	2	-

Improvements. Since my last visit several improvements have been carried out in this prison, and others are contemplated. The new cells arranged for the reception class and hospital in the female prison are very good, but I would recommend that these be kept for prisoners after being passed into their proper wards, and that some of the old cells be apportioned for the reception class. A door should be broken out in the passage of the middle tier, in order to pass prisoners from one section to another, and to facili-

Reception. tate supervision. I am informed that all prisoners are immediately bathed on coming in, and are then kept in the reception class until inspected by the Medical Officer. In the event of the foregoing suggestions being carried out, some of the cells in the upper tier of the uninhabited portion of the female prison could be converted into an excellent hospital for prisoners of that sex; and I would also recommend a few cells in the male prison to be adapted for hospital purposes for cases that are not considered infectious, as by this means the service of an hospital warder may be

Cells. altogether dispensed with. The cells throughout the prison were all clean and tidily kept, but some of the window sashes were very bad and wanting in repair, and I would recommend that they be glazed with a non-transparent glass, as it is not right that prisoners should be able to have such a view of the surrounding country as is now possible from

Water. Sewerage, &c. Heating. the female prison. Both prisons are fully supplied with lavatories, water-closets, and baths, and the sewerage is reported to be good and effective. Forty-three male and 13 female cells are heated, and furnished with bells, and are of the required size. There is an abundant supply of water throughout the gaol, the arrangements in this respect being the same

Chapel. as at my last inspection. The defects in the chapel have not been remedied, and the Protestant worship is not performed in it, but is carried on in the school-room. However, very few prisoners of that per-

Laundry. suasion are ever in custody here. The arrangements of the laundry and drying-room are the same as when I last visited, and are suitable for the requirements of the prison, but I regret to find that as yet no profit is derived from the laundry, as no washing contracts are yet procured. In this large garrison town I have no doubt that if washing was properly

Gas. done in the gaol much profit would be derived therefrom. There is gas supplied throughout the corridors and school, but is only introduced into 11 of the male cells, and it is of not much avail here, as no work is carried on in the cells after 6 o'clock in the evening, a matter which I

Photography. shall refer to further on. I am glad to find that a warder now performs the photography. He is supplied with chemicals at the expense of the Board, and in addition receives £3 per year for this addition to his other

Kitchen. duties. At the time of my visit it was contemplated to remove the kitchen,

Noरण
District.

*Westmeath
County
Gaol.*

Fumigator.

Night-
watch.

Visitors.

Stores.

as suggested, into the female department of the gaol, thereby diverting the time of a male prisoner throughout the year to more profitable purposes. The cook at the time of my visit was a man who was sentenced to hard labour, but was exempt therefrom, and in addition to his culinary duties he was employed at making tins. I pointed out to the Governor at the time of my visit how very suitable arrangements could be made for the new kitchen, so that I trust by this time they have been carried out. A good fumigating apparatus is now provided in each prison in which all clothing of the prisoners is disinfected and purified. Two tell-tale clocks are provided, and are each marked hourly from 6, P.M., to 6, A.M., at different half hours. The markings are taken by the Deputy Governor every morning, and entered by him in the Lockings Book, and the omissions are also noted in the Officers' Conduct Book. The duty of night-watch is performed by the warders in rotation, and the clocks are well protected from being tampered with. Lock-up takes place at 6, P.M., all the year round, and unlock at 6.30, A.M., in summer, and at daybreak in the winter. I am of opinion that unlock should take place an hour earlier in summer, and that as gas is provided in the prison unlock should not take place later than 6.30, A.M., in winter, so that prisoners may be able to commence labour at daybreak, as I see no reason why criminals should not be required to work as hard as free and industrious labourers. All the keys of the prison are kept in an iron box in the Governor's bedroom during the night, and I am informed that a superior officer frequently visits the gaol at night at unexpected hours. No alteration has been made in the rules for visitors to prisoners or the place they are visited in since my last inspection. All orders for visits to prisoners go through the Local Inspector. The untried are allowed a visit upon every Saturday, or oftener if necessary for their defence, and the convicted prisoners once a month, but not until they have been in custody for a month.

Stock at the time of Inspection.

	In Use.	In Store.	Male Clothing.	In Use.	In Store.	Female Clothing.	In Use.	In Store.
Blankets, pairs of,	107	26	Shirts,	42	21	Shifts,	8	9
Sheets, pairs of,	130	30	Jackets,	16	20	Jackets,	8	10
Rugs,	96	38	Vests,	16	17	Petticoats,	14	14
Bed-ticks,	93	26	Trowsers,	16	40	Aprons,	8	4
Bedsteads,	136	–	Caps,	16	20	Neckerchiefs,	6	4
			Stockings or socks, pairs of,	42	18	Caps,	9	6
						Stockings, pairs of,	8	13
			Shoes, Slippers, & Clogs, pairs of,	18	30	Shoes, Slippers, & Clogs, pairs of,	4	11

The general store of male clothing is kept by the Deputy Governor, and the Matron keeps that of the females. Each of these officers superintends the dressing of the prisoners of the different sexes as they come in, and are responsible to the Governor for all the clothing in their charge. The class warders are responsible for the clothing served out to prisoners by the Deputy Governor as they come in, and as soon as the clothing is made up either by the female prisoners or by the tailor, it is marked and duly entered in the Stock Book. This department is now managed in a satisfactory manner, and the stores are carefully and well kept. The bedding and clothing was all clean and in good repair at the time of my visit, and there was an abundant stock in store. I made some suggestions to the Governor in regard to improving the female clothing store, which I have no doubt he will carry out. The Governor takes stock of all prison property twice a year, and, I am informed, sometimes oftener. This duty should also be performed by the Local Inspector, who is the officer responsible for the proper supply of bedding and clothing to the prison.

NORTH
DISTRICT.

Westmeath.
County
Gaol.

Number of Punishments for Prison Offences.

	From 1st January to 31st December, 1874.		From 1st January, 1875, to day of Inspection.	
	M.	F.	M.	F.
By Magisterial authority,	3	-	3	-
By Governor—				
Dark or Refractory Cells,	33	4	35	4
Total,	36	4	38	4

Punish-
ments.

On three occasions during this year it was found necessary to have recourse to magisterial authority for the punishment of a prisoner. Five punishment cells for males and one for females have been provided. Two of the former have been properly fitted up with bells, and can be heated, so that prisoners may now be left in them during the night time ; and though up to this punishments were very numerous, yet since these cells have been improved, the Governor informed me that he had not had occasion to use them for the punishment of prisoners, showing how important it is that every gaol should be supplied with proper punishment cells, as required by the 6th section of the Prisons Act. During my inspection a male prisoner complained to me of having been attacked and beaten by another prisoner. I laid this matter before the Board, and since my inspection I am informed that one of these prisoners received a sentence of seven days' solitary from the Board for his conduct in this matter.

Schools.

	From 1st Jan. to 31st Dec., 1874.		From 1st Jan., 1875, to day of Inspection.	
	M.	F.	M.	F.
Number of individual prisoners who attended school,	76	44	55	16
Average daily number of pupils,	13·48	5·47	11·19	5·6
Number of days on which school was held,	305	263	202	187

School hours.—Males, 7 to 9, A.M.; Females, 3 to 4, P.M.

School.

There is now a good school-room in each section of the prison, in which gas has been introduced, so that the short labour hours in the winter should not be interfered with, as the school should be carried on after dark. The male school has been taught for some years by an old master of the National Board, who is not a prison officer, but who, I am informed, takes great pains in the instruction of the prisoners. The Matron teaches the female prisoners, and is fully capable of doing so efficiently. The school is in connexion with the National Board of Education. I have again to call attention to the irregularities on the part of the Chaplains in not inspecting the schools, as required by the by-laws. I have referred to this subject so often that it is painful to have to return to it here again.

Employment on the day of Inspection.

	M.	F.
Hard Labour,	13	2
Industrial Labour,	5	3
Unemployed (blind),	1	-
Discharged before labour hours,	-	1
Prison Duties,	2	-
Total in Custody,	21	6

Amount received for produce of Prisoners' labour disposed of outside the Gaol for the last three years.

1872, . £63 19s. 0d. | 1873, . £84 15s. 9d. | 1874, . £84 13s. 5d.

Net average daily cost of Ordinary Diet for each Prisoner in the three preceding years.

1872, . 5d. | 1873, . 5d. | 1874, . 4d.

Net cost of Gaol, including Diet and Salaries, for the three preceding years.
1872, . £1,603 11s. 9d. | 1873, . £1,746.18s. 10d. | 1874, . £1,881 4s. 11d.

Total cost of Officers, including Clothing, Value of Rations, Washing, Gas, &c.
1872, . £993 1s. 11d. | 1873, . £1,037 3s. 11d. | 1874, . £1,085 12s. 7d.

Average cost of each Prisoner per annum in each of the last three years.
1872, . £43 17s. 3d. | 1873, . £50 6s. 11d. | 1874, . £49 10s. 2d.

Amounts repaid by the War Department for Military Prisoners in each of the last three years.
1872, . £17 15s. 6d. | 1873, . £50 3s. 9d. | 1874, . £93 7s. 6d.

Amounts repaid from the Consolidated Fund for the maintenance, &c., of Prisoners during the years
1872, . £96 0s. 0d. | 1873, . £87 1s. 3d. | 1874, . £81 0s. 10d.

Hard labour here is carried on chiefly by the crank-mill and stone- Labour. breaking. When there is sufficient corn to grind, the mill is used for about four hours a day, but otherwise the hard labour men are compelled to break from 7 to 10 cwt. of stones a day. The only employment pursued in the cells is that followed by tradesmen, as there is no oakum-picking or matmaking done. During the many hours that prisoners are now allowed to remain in idleness in their cells much profitable labour could be performed, especially in those 11 cells in which gas is provided. I would therefore strongly recommend that oakum-picking or some such industrial pursuit be at once established, and that a greater amount of such labour be carried on, for at present the amount received for the produce of prisoners' labour is very small as compared with the daily average number of prisoners here throughout the year. That sum amounted in 1874 only to £84 13s. 5d., whereas the average annual cost of a prisoner came for the same year to £49 10s. 2d. It is evident that unless every Expendi-effort is made to turn prison labour to profitable account that the burden ture. on the ratepayers must be very large. The net cost of the gaol in the same year came to £1,881 4s. 11d., but in this sum the cost of officers is included, namely, £1,085 12s. 7d. In a badly constructed gaol, as this is, the number of officers must always be large in proportion to the number of prisoners; but, taking all things into consideration, I am of opinion that the gaol could be efficiently worked with fewer officers than at present; but I trust that legislation will this year take place upon our prison system, and that such abuses as these will be rectified.

Contracts.

Bread, white, per 4lb. loaf, 6d.; brown, per 4lb. loaf, 6d.; oatmeal, per cwt., 15s.; Indian meal, per cwt., 11s. 6d.; potatoes, per cwt., 4s.; meat, per lb., 8d.; new milk, per gallon, 9d.; salt, per cwt., 4s. 3d.; coal, per ton, £1 5s. 2d.; turf, per 100 boxes, £5 15s.; straw, per cwt., 2s. 4d.; gas, per 1,000 cubic feet, 8s. 4d.; candles, per lb., 5d.; soap, per cwt., £1 4s.

All contracts are sanctioned by the Board yearly, but the materials for Provisions. clothing, &c., are bought by the Governor half-yearly, who produces a sample, and informs the Board of the price. In other gaols materials are advertised for, and are procured by tender, which, I submit, is a more business like manner of procedure. The samples of the diet that I saw were excellent, and are generally reported on favourably by the Chaplains, and by their substitutes, but as the latter gentlemen are not legally appointed I submit that they have no power to perform this or any other duty in the gaol. This is a matter that I have called the attention of the Board to in previous reports.

Q

NORTH
DISTRICT.

*Westmeath
County
Gaol.*

Officars.

Hospital.

Officers and Salaries.

Non-Resident.	£	s.	d.
F. B. Fetherstonhaugh, esq., Local Inspector,	75	0	0
Rev. C. P. Reichel, Protestant Chaplain,	40	0	0
Rev. John Martin, Roman Catholic Chaplain,	40	0	0
W. H. Middleton, esq., M.D., Surgeon,	75	0	0
William Middleton, esq., M.D., Apothecary,	35	0	0
Thos. Brady, Schoolmaster,	20	0	0

Resident.	£	s.	d.
Jas. Tyrrell, esq., Governor,	220	0	0
George Hayes, Deputy Governor and Clerk,	90	0	0
Wm. Cain, 1st, and Tailor, Photographer, &c.,	49	0	0
Benjamin Power, Carpenter,	43	0	0
Samuel Bollard, Gate,	40	0	0
Patrick Oulahan,	37	10	0
James Carey, Miller,	37	10	0
Hannah Thomas, Matron,	35	0	0
Margaret Russell, Assistant Matron,	25	0	0

(Turnkeys bracket for Wm. Cain through James Carey)

Vacancies in staff since last Inspection, how caused, and how filled up.

William Trydell, First Class Warder, superannuated.

Officers' Visits.

	From 1st Jan. to 31st Dec., 1874.	From 1st Jan. 1875, to day of Inspection.
Number of times the Board of Superintendence met and discharged business,	19	11
Local Inspector to Gaol,	41	78
Do. each Bridewell,	3	3
Chaplain, Protestant Episcopal Church,	140	76
„ Roman Catholic,	158	109
Surgeon,	186	144
Apothecary,	191	81

All the officers sleep within the prison, and on the day of my inspection their rooms were tidy and well kept. The married men take their meals outside, and an hour is allowed for breakfast and an hour for dinner, which I submit is too long a time for prisoners to be idle, especially as they are not given any employment in their cells. At the time of my visit I drew the attention of the Board to one of the warders who has been some time ill, and quite unfit to take charge of prisoners, and should be superannuated. The Deputy Governor's house at the gate was at this time being repaired, and a new roof being put upon it, so that this officer and his family were then living in the female hospital.

Hospitals.

	1872.		1873.		1874.		1875 (to day of Inspection).	
	M.	F.	M.	F.	M.	F.	M.	F.
No. of prisoners in hospital,	30	7	13	4	10	11	–	–
Average daily number in hospital,	1·0	0·18	0·6	0·1	0·3	0·6	–	–
Prescribed for and treated out of hospital,	131	26	208	23	160	46	–	–
Cost of medicine,	£6 11s. 4d.		£10 6s. 8d.		£10 13s. 10d.		—	
Cost of diet for prisoners in hospital,	£10 0s. 0d.		£11 1s. 2d.		£6 11s. 6d.		—	
Cost of all extra diet ordered by Medical Officer for prisoners not in hospital,	£4 2s. 9d.		£3 1s. 6d.		£2 1s. 3d.		—	

Since my last visit the hospital arrangements have been altogether altered, as already explained, so that this building is now seldom or never used, but is in charge of the deputy matron; however, in the event of a number of serious infectious cases occurring a nurse could be procured from the town. The hospital is sufficiently provided with baths and water-closets, and the medicines are procured from Dublin, and are compounded by the apothecary here. Considering that there were only 10 male prisoners and 11 female prisoners treated in hospital during the year 1874,

NORTH
DISTRICT.

*Westmeath
County
Gaol.*

Books.

I am of opinion that the charge for medicines during that year was excessive as compared with that in some other gaols, namely, £10 13s. 10d.

The books of registry and finance are kept by the Deputy Governor, who devotes much care and attention to this portion of his duties, and are supervised by the Governor daily. The journal of this officer is carefully and well kept, and I have much pleasure in recording my approval of the cleanliness and order of the establishment, for which he deserves every credit. The Matron too is most diligent, and performs her duties with much care and credit to herself. Owing to a domestic affliction I regret that the Local Inspector was not able to be present, but I saw his journal, which I submit does not contain sufficient information regarding the discipline and management of the prison, though it is evident that his visits have lately been frequent. I therefore trust that in future his journal will contain more information. The Surgeon's Journal is good and full, and the hospital books are carefully and well kept by him, from which it is evident that he pays every attention to his prison duties. As remarked in my former reports the Chaplains do not perform their duties in conformity with the requirements of either the by-laws, or the statute relating to those duties. The Protestant Chaplain has a substitute illegally appointed, and previous to my visit he had not attended the gaol for a week. The Roman Catholic Chaplain had four substitutes not legally appointed. These gentlemen, therefore, having no status in the gaol, should not be permitted to have access to the prisoners.

Board of Superintendence.

Robert Smyth, esq.	Richd. W. Reynell, esq.	John D. Lemon, esq.
Henry Murray, esq.	Sir Walter Nugent, bart.	Lieut.-Col. Nugent.
Capt. T. J. Smyth.	John Swift, esq.	Colonel Cooper
Wm. Fetherstonhaugh, esq.	Edward Maxton, esq.	(Vacant).

The first Tuesday of each month is the day appointed for the Board to meet, when the salaries of subordinate officers are paid. Those of the superior officers are settled half-yearly at assizes, as well as the bills of the different contractors.

STATE OF MOATE BRIDEWELL.

	M.	F.
No. of committals in past year, .	43	10
Of whom were drunkards,	–	–
No. of committals in the quarter preceding inspection, . .	10	4
Of whom were drunkards, .	–	–

Petty Sessions and transmittals, how often.	Fortnightly.
Committals, ...	Now regular.
Registry, ...	Correctly kept.
Repairs and order, . .	In good order and repair.
Security, ...	Sufficient.
Accommodation, . . .	Two day-rooms, two exercising yards, and one cell with two beds, below; six cells with one bed each, above.
Furniture, Bedding, and Utensils,	Sufficient, and of a fair description.
Water, how supplied, . .	A pump, in order, in male yard; a pipe conveys water into female yard.
Sewerage, ...	Efficient.
Cleanliness, Dryness, and Ventilation.	Clean, dry, and well ventilated.
Cost of Dietary, . . .	4d. for two meals; 5½d. for three meals.
Salary of Keeper, and whether he follows any other employment.	£46.
Date of Inspection, . .	26th April, 1875.
Remarks, ...	One male prisoner in charge for threatening to assault.

CHARLES F. BOURKE, *Inspector-General.*

SOUTH DISTRICT.

CARLOW COUNTY GAOL, AT CARLOW.—STATUTABLE INSPECTION, 9TH
NOVEMBER, 1875.

State.

Denomination of Class.	No. in each Class.			No. of whom were Sick in Hospital.		
	M.	F.	Total.	M.	F.	Total.
UNTRIED.						
For Larceny,	1	-	1	-	-	-
,, further Examination,	2	-	2	-	-	-
TRIED.						
Cases disposed of at Assizes and Quarter Sessions.						
Of Larceny—						
To Imprisonment,	4	-	4	-	-	-
Of Misdemeanors, &c.,	3	-	3	-	-	-
Disposed of Summarily.						
In default of Bail,	1	-	1	-	-	-
Misdemeanors,	1	-	1	-	-	-
Drunkards,	2	1	3	-	-	-
Total in Custody,	14	1	15	-	-	-

*Number of Prisoners of all classes in Gaol on the day of Inspection, and
on the corresponding date in the three preceding years.*

	M.	F.		M.	F.
1872,	15	8	1874,	17	5
1873,	12	7	1875 (day of Inspection),	14	1

Juveniles.

CLASSES, &C., OF OFFENDERS.	In custody on the day of Inspection.				From 1st January to day of Inspection.			
	12 years old and under.		Above 12 and not exceeding 16 years.		12 years old and under.		Above 12 and not exceeding 16 years.	
	M.	F.	M.	F.	M.	F.	M.	F.
Convicted at Quarter Sessions,	-	-	1	-	-	-	1	-
,, summarily,	-	-	-	-	-	-	4	-
Committed for Trial,	-	-	-	-	-	-	1	-
Total,	-	-	1	-	-	-	6	-
Number sent to Reformatories,	-	-	-	-	-	-	1	-
Included in the preceding— Workhouse offenders,	-	-	-	-	-	-	1	-

At the time of my visit one young offender, 15 years of age, a country lad, was in custody. He had been convicted at Quarter Sessions of sheep stealing, and had been sentenced to an imprisonment of nine months with hard labour. I found him in association with two adult criminals. He had, no doubt, committed a grave offence, which required exemplary punishment, but it was, I understand, his first, and there are many other crimes of deep depravity which he probably will learn in association day after day with grave criminals during the nine months of his sentence of imprisonment in this gaol. No better proof can he given of the imperfect prison system which prevails in this kingdom than that such a case should he kept in association here when the adjoining prisons of Kilkenny and Kildare, in which the separate system is strictly enforced, have abundant unoccupied cellular accommodation.

The management of this associated prison is more expensive than the improved system in the other gaols. The cost of each prisoner in the Carlow prison averaged during the past year £69 8s., while in the well-managed cellular prison of Kildare, which adjoins, it was £30 15s. 10d. I trust, however, that the Legislature will, during the next session of Parliament, make arrangements to prevent this anomaly in future.

Altogether five juveniles (males), were committed to this prison in 1875. No female juvenile was committed. One male was sent to a reformatory, and one received a sentence of imprisonment of two months, both for larceny. Two others were sentenced to an imprisonment of seven days for assault, and one workhouse offender was not sentenced and discharged.

In 1874 one young offender was sentenced to be whipped by order of court. No such sentence was inflicted in 1875.

Thirteen adult offenders (males), were inmates of this gaol on the day of inspection. Of these, three were on remand or for trial, and ten under sentences—one of two years for an indecent assault, one of nine, two of six, and two of one month, for common assaults. Two others were under sentences for offences against property—one sentenced for six months for highway robbery, the other for two months for obtaining goods under false pretences.

Two males and the only female prisoner in custody at the time of my visit had been sentenced for periods varying from one month to seven days for drunkenness. The female, a prostitute, thirty-three years of age, has already been forty times committed to this prison. She is one of a class who are constantly re-committed. Although only nineteen individual females were inmates of this prison during the ten months which preceded my inspection, the number of their committals within that period was twenty-nine ; and these nineteen females have sixty-three previous committals recorded on the prison books against them.

Only five individual females were committed to this prison between May and November in 1875 ; and from the 19th September to the 31st October no female was in custody. I am informed that the Board of Superintendence during that time hired a woman from outside to wash the linen of the prison, yet three female officers are on the staff of the gaol, and, I may add, that the cost of officers in 1874 amounted to £846 9s. 4d. The average cost of each prisoner in 1874 was £69 8s., and the average in 1875 was £90 18s. 6d., the average daily number of prisoners in custody being thirteen males and two females in 1875. In June previous to my visit only seven prisoners of all classes were in charge, the permanent resident staff consisting of ten individuals, besides four extern officers ; yet in order to economize the management, there is no school in the prison, and no watch held at night.

Debtors.

No debtor was lodged in this gaol in 1875.

Commitments.

CLASSES.	From 1st January to 31st December, 1874.		From 1st January, 1875, to day of Inspection.	
	M.	F.	M.	F.
Debtors,	2	–	–	–
Criminals,	136	24	111	11
Vagrants,	31	4	12	3
Drunkards,	73	14	55	15
Total,	242	42	178	29

Number of Individual Prisoners (exclusive of Debtors), and Number of times each had been Committed.

NUMBER OF TIMES COMMITTED.	1874.				1875, to day of Inspection.			
	Juveniles.		Adults.		Juveniles.		Adults.	
	M.	F.	M.	F.	M.	F.	M.	F.
Once within the year,	9	1	167	39	6	–	151	14
Twice „	1	–	16	1	–	–	9	3
Thrice „	–	–	2	–	–	–	1	1
Four and six times „	–	–	1	–	–	–	–	1
Total,	10	1	206	40	6	–	161	19
No. of above who had not been in Gaol previous to 1st January in .	10	1	148	35	6	–	143	14

Individual Prisoners (exclusive of Debtors) committed in 1874, and to the day of Inspection in 1875, and number of their Commitments, from their first Commitment in any year, so far as can be ascertained.

NUMBER OF TIMES COMMITTED.	1874.				1875, to day of Inspection.			
	Juveniles.		Adults.		Juveniles.		Adults.	
	M.	F.	M.	F.	M.	F.	M.	F.
Once only,	9	1	148	35	6	–	143	14
Twice,	1	–	29	2	–	–	7	3
Thrice,	–	–	18	2	–	–	3	1
4 times,	–	–	6	–	–	–	5	–
5 „	–	–	2	–	–	–	1	–
6 to 11 „	–	–	3	1	–	–	2	–
31 to 40 „	–	–	–	–	–	–	–	1
Total No. of Individuals committed,	10	1	206	40	6	–	161	19
No. of commitments represented in foregoing,	11	1	215	52	6	–	203	63

Highest Number of Prisoners (exclusive of Debtors) in gaol during each of the previous seven years, and up to day of Inspection in 1875.

28th February, 1868,	35	19th May, 1872,	27
1st December, 1869,	23	24th December, 1873,	28
29th March, 1870,	20	26th August, 1874,	30
15th September, 1871,	23	3rd April, 1875,	23

Averages, and Highest and Lowest Numbers (exclusive of Debtors).

—	From 1st January to 31st December, 1874.			From 1st January, 1875, to day of Inspection.		
	M.	F.	Date.	M.	F.	Date.
Average daily number of prisoners in custody,	16	6	—	13	2	—
Highest number of prisoners at any one time,	30		28th Aug.	23		3rd April.
Lowest ditto,	14		14th Jan.	7		20th June.
Highest number of males at any one time,	26		28th Aug.	20		3rd April.
Ditto of females,	10		11th March.	5		8th Jan.
Lowest number of males at any one time.	9		28th Dec.	7		20th June.
Ditto of females,	2		20th Aug.	—		20th June.

Accommodation.

	M.	F.			M.	F.
Wards,	4	1	Workshops,		3	—
Yards,	9	6	Kitchen,		1	—
Day Rooms,	10	2	Store Rooms,		3	1
Solitary Cells,	3	1	Laundry,		—	1
Single Cells, 9 feet long, 6 feet wide, and 8 feet high = 432 cubic feet,	—	22	Drying Room,		—	1
			Lavatories,		8	4
Ditto, heated and furnished with bells,	—	16	Privies,		8	4
			Water-closets,		1	2
Ditto, not so furnished,	47	19	Fumigating Apparatus,		1	1
Sleeping Rooms,	13	—	Pump,		1	—
No. of Beds in such rooms,	6	—	Wells,		2	—
Hospital Rooms,	2	2	Tread-wheel,		1	—
Chapel,	1	—	Tell-tale Clocks.		2	—

I found this gaol very much in the same state as when I inspected it in 1873. The same structural defects pointed out in former reports by my colleague and myself still continue, but it would be a waste of public money to incur expense in the alteration of the prison buildings, when so few prisoners exist in this county, more especially as large, well-appointed prisons, with abundant accommodation, are in part unoccupied in the adjoining counties of Kildare and Kilkenny. In them the few offenders belonging to the county Carlow could be treated under an improved prison system at half the cost now expended on prisoners here.

Should long-sentenced prisoners be removed from this jurisdiction to some other prison (where they would be treated under a strict penal system in separation), one small block of the buildings of this gaol might be isolated from the rest. It would be sufficient to accommodate prisoners for trial and those under short sentences. The staff might then be diminished to very few officers, and the greater part of the present gaol might be added to the adjoining military barracks. This station is admirably suited for a military centre, from its healthful position, the abundance of forage in the neighbourhood, and the excellence of the water. By this arrangement the buildings would be turned to profitable use.

The gaol buildings were when I made my inspection very clean and orderly, in good repair, and well kept, fires were in the different day-rooms, the store, and the chapel. The female prison is imperfectly heated by a stove in the central hall, but the cells in the male prison are not heated. Gas is introduced into the officers' quarters and externally, but is not used in either prison. Lavatories and water-closets are in the female prison, but only stone troughs and privies in that for males.

No bath, with hot and cold water laid on, is in either gaol. There is however a tin bath in each prison, in it prisoners on reception are bathed, but not afterwards. The bath for females is in the hospital.

The laundry is now divided into four compartments, and a stove is in the drying-closet.

A suitable photographic room is provided, in which the photographs of prisoners are taken by the Governor, for which duty he receives a gratuity of £5 yearly.

Although there are two tell-tale clocks on the premises, they are only marked between 6 P.M. and 10 P.M., when the gas outside the buildings is extinguished, and no watch is kept after that hour.

Stock at the time of Inspection.

	In Use.	In Store.	Male Clothing.	In Use.	In Store.	Female Clothing.	In Use.	In Store.
Blankets, pairs of,	90	100	Shirts,	12	45	Shifts,	1	27
Sheets, pairs of,	40	90	Jackets,	12	36	Jackets,	1	27
Hammocks or Cots,	16	–	Vests,	12	60	Petticoats,	2	25
Bedticks,	40	36	Trowsers,	12	70	Aprons,	1	22
Bedsteads,	96	–	Caps,	12	23	Neckerchiefs,	1	36
			Shoes, Slippers, & Clogs, pairs of,	12	24	Caps,	1	39
						Shoes, Slippers, & Clogs, pairs of,	1	11

I found the bedding and prison clothing clean and sufficient; it was in good repair, but no stockings or socks are given to prisoners of either sex.

The stores are well kept and orderly; a fire was at the time of my visit in the store for females to air the clothing; the private clothing of prisoners are properly labelled; an excellent fumigating closet, to cleanse and disinfect the clothes of prisoners, is in the female prison (a disused privy altered for the purpose), and a fumigating box in the male prison is applied to a like use.

Stock is now taken half-yearly by the Local Inspector and Governor. They then condemn worn-out clothing and bedding, and sign the Stock Book.

Lock-up is held in this prison at 6 P.M. in summer, and at dusk in winter. The prisoners are unlocked at 6 A.M. in summer, and at daylight in winter.

No visits to convicted prisoners are permitted. The untried see their friends at the prison gate, a prison officer being present, master debtors, when in custody, are the only prisoners who are permitted to see visitors inside the gaol.

Number of Punishments for Prison Offences.

	From 1st January to 31st Dec., 1874.		From 1st Jan., 1875, to day of Inspection.	
	M.	F.	M.	F.
By Magisterial authority,	1	–	–	–
By Governor—				
Dark or Refractory Cells,	35	1	21	–

All the punishments during 1875 were inflicted on the sole authority of the Governor, the book in which they are recorded is duly laid before the Board at its meeting.

The punishment cells are quite unfit for occupation by prisoners at night.

Employment on day of Inspection.

						M.	F.
Tread-wheel,						6	–
Mat Making,						1	–
Tailoring,						1	–
Prison duties,						4	–
Washing,						–	1
Unemployed,						2	–
Total in custody,						14	1

One tailor and one matmaker were employed at reproductive labour on the day of my visit, and the solitary female in custody was at work in the laundry.

No profits accrue from the work of the prisoners in this gaol, whose time is occupied in prison duties and on the tread-wheel, which pumps water for the use of the establishment.

One man, not previously a tradesman, was instructed in tailoring during his confinement in the prison during 1875.

South District.
Carlow County Gaol.

School.

No scholastic instruction is given to the inmates of this gaol. School.

Diet and Contracts.

Bread, white, per 4 lb. loaf, 7d.; brown, per 4 lb. loaf, 5½d.; oatmeal, per cwt., 15s. 6d.; Indian meal, per cwt., 9s. 10d.; potatoes, per cwt., 4s.; new milk, per gallon, 1s.: salt, per cwt., 3s.; coal, per ton, £1 6s. 8d.; turf, per 20 cubic feet, 2s. 6d.; straw, per cwt., 2s. 6d.; gas, per 1,000 cubic feet, 8s. 9d.; soap, per cwt., £1 12s. 0d.

Net average Daily Cost of Ordinary Diet for each Prisoner in the three preceding years.

1872, . 4·6d. | 1873, . 4·8d. | 1874, . 4·5d.

I questioned all the prisoners in custody on the day of my visit; no complaint was made to me by any. The food, which I tasted, was of a fair description, but I observe that the Chaplains frequently note complaints of the quality of the samples of food submitted for their inspection. In fact, in no prison in Ireland have I found such frequent complaints recorded in the Inspection of Provisions Book as in this gaol, especially against the milk; and I find that the Contractor has been fined up to the time of my visit in 1875 £2 3s. 8d. My colleague called attention to his former delinquencies in his report for 1874, and I regret to find the same complaints reiterated. Provisions.

Officers and Salaries.

Non-resident.	£	s.	d.		£	s.	d.
Thos. J. Rawson, esq., Surgeon,	—			John Earl, Head Warder and Clerk,	54	0	0
A. Fitzmaurice, esq., Local Inspector,	60	0	0	Richard Walsh, Turnkey,	36	0	0
				John Tyndell, Gate,	36	0	0
Rev. A. B. Perry, Protestant Chaplain,	30	0	0	George Strickland, Turnkey,	36	0	0
				Robert Byrne, ,,	36	0	0
Rev. A. Wall, Roman Catholic Chaplain,	30	0	0	John Daly, ,,	36	0	0
				Mrs. C. Gavan, Matron,	59	0	0
Resident.				Mrs. C. Croghan, Deputy Matron,	15	0	0
Edward Croghan, esq., Governor,	180	0	0	Harriett Cope, Hospital Nurse & Female Turnkey,	15	0	0

Vacancies in the Staff since last Inspection, how caused, and how filled up.

Richard Walsh, invalided. William Halpin, resigned; Robert Byrne, appointed probationary. John Daly, appointed probationary.

Officers on Gaol Allowance.

All the intern officers.

Visits paid by Officers.

Number of times the Board of Superintendence met and discharged business,	From 1st Jan. to 31st Dec., 1874.	From 1st Jan., 1875, to day of Inspection.
	11	9
Local Inspector to Gaol,	108	92
Chaplain, Prot. Episcopal Church,	149	133
Chaplain, Roman Catholic,	169	139
Surgeon,	92	89

SOUTH DISTRICT. The officers' quarters were tidy when I visited. There is no mess-room for officers in the gaol.

Carlow County Gaol

Hospital

Hospital.

	1872.		1873.		1874.		1875. (to day of Inspection)	
	M.	F.	M.	F.	M.	F.	M.	F.
No. of prisoners in hospital,	2	2	–	5	–	6	–	–
Average daily number in hospital, . . .	·1	·1	–	·2	–	·1	–	–
No. of prisoners prescribed for and treated out of hospital, . . .	33	13	47	8	34	22	–	–
No. of deaths in the gaol, .	–	–	–	–	–	–	–	–
Cost of medicine. . .	£16 13s. 5d.		£8 11s. 3d.		£5 16s. 4d.		—	

The hospital in this prison is seldom used, yet a nurse is paid a salary to attend it. Four males were treated in hospital during 1875, but no female.

Books and Accounts.

Net cost of Gaol, including Diet and Salaries.

1872, . £1,465 3s. 9d. | 1873, . £1,432 1s. 3d. | 1874, . £1,526 16s. 7d.

Total cost of Officers, including Clothing, value of Rations, Washing, Gas, &c.

1872, . £764 7s. 4d. | 1873, . £810 2s. 10d. | 1874, . £846 9s. 4d.

Average cost of each Prisoner per annum.

1872, . £74 9s. 0d. | 1873, . £79 11s. 2d. | 1874, . £69 8s. 0d.

Amounts Repaid by the War Department for Military Prisoners.

1872, . £6 15s. 0d. | 1873, . £1 12s. 0d. | 1874, . £5 12s. 0d.

Amounts Repaid from the Consolidated Fund for the Maintenance, &c., of Prisoners.

1872, . £70 7s. 9d. | 1873, . £48 16s. 3d. | 1874, . £87 18s. 10d.

The various registries of discipline and finance in this prison are kept with much care, and in a business-like manner. All accounts and records of expenditure are initialled by the Local Inspector and Governor in red ink. The Local Inspector reports in writing to the Board, and checks the dietary monthly, the Governor daily. The Governors' journal is well kept. The extern officers record in their journals the duties they perform in the gaol. I have already remarked on the frequent defaults of the milk contractor, who has been fined ten per cent. on his monthly contract for supplying an inferior article.

Board of Superintendence.

Henry Bruen, esq., M.P. | R. C. Browne, esq., D.L. | D. H. Cooper, esq., J.P.
Sir C. W. C. Burton, bart. | P. J. Newton, esq., D.L. | J. Alexander, esq., J.P.
Sir Thos. P. Butler, bart. | William Duckett, esq., J.P. | William Elliott, esq., J.P.
Horace Rochfort, esq., D.L. | Hardy Eustace, esq., J.P. | J. F. Leckey, esq., J.P.

Board.

The Board meets on the first Monday of each month for the discharge of business, when small accounts are liquidated, and the salaries of the intern officers are paid by cheque to the Governor, who produces vouchers at the next meeting of the Board. The extern officers receive their salaries on presentment half-yearly at assize.

There are no bridewells in this county.

JOHN LENTAIGNE, *Inspector-General.*

CLARE COUNTY GAOL, AT ENNIS.—STATUTABLE INSPECTION, 25TH
SEPTEMBER, 1875.

Prisoners of all classes in Gaol on the day of Inspection, and on the corresponding date in preceding years.

	M.	F.		M.	F.
1872,	21	12	1874,	22	10
1873,	30	9	1875 (day of Inspection),	24	10

Returned Convicts in Gaol on the day of Inspection, and during each of the three preceding years.

	M.	F.		M.	F.
1872,	1	1	1875 (up to and including		
1873,	3	1	day of Inspection),	1	—
1874,	2	1	Day of Inspection,	—	—

Number of Prisoners in custody during the year known to have been in Reformatories.

	M.	F.		M.	F.
1872,	—	1	1875 (up to and including		
1873,	—	1	day of Inspection),	—	—
1874,	—	—	Day of Inspection,	—	—

Juveniles.

No young offender was in custody at the period of my inspection ; but 9 males, none of whose ages exceeded sixteen years, had previously been in custody, 1 was sent to a reformatory for larceny, 1 was under twelve years of age, 1 was a workhouse offender, 1 had been sentenced for stealing rabbits, another for stealing wood, the rest for assaults.

Commitments.

CLASSES.	From 1st January to 31st December, 1874.		From 1st January, 1875, to day of Inspection.	
	M.	F.	M.	F.
Criminals,	168	64	149	55
Vagrants,	14	3	8	4
Drunkards,	77	30	77	16
Total,	279	97	234	75

Number of Individual Prisoners (exclusive of Debtors), and Number of Times each had been committed during the following periods, distinguishing Adults from Juveniles.

NUMBER OF TIMES COMMITTED.	1874.				1875, to day of Inspection.			
	Juveniles.		Adults.		Juveniles.		Adults.	
	M.	F.	M.	F.	M.	F.	M.	F.
Once within the year,	22	1	155	32	8	—	132	31
Twice " "	3	—	30	7	1	—	31	14
Three and four times,	1	—	7	5	—	—	7	3
Five and six times,	—	—	2	5	—	—	1	—
Seven times,	—	—	—	1	—	—	—	1
Total,	26	1	194	50	9	—	171	49
No. of above who had not been in Gaol previous to 1st Jan. in	25	1	142	26	8	—	105	27

SOUTH
DISTRICT.

Clare
County
Gaol.

Number of Individual Prisoners (exclusive of Debtors), committed in the year 1874, and to the day of Inspection in 1875, who had been Once, Twice, Thrice, Four Times, Five Times, &c., &c., from their first Commitment in any year, so far as can be ascertained, distinguishing Adults from Juveniles.

NUMBER OF TIMES COMMITTED.	1874.				1875, to day of Inspection.			
	Juveniles.		Adults.		Juveniles.		Adults.	
	M.	F.	M.	F.	M.	F.	M.	F.
Once only, .	22	1	133	24	5	–	103	24
Twice,	3	–	30	4	4	–	33	10
Thrice,	1	–	11	6	–	–	13	3
4 times,	–	–	5	4	–	–	6	3
5 „	–	–	5	–	–	–	3	2
6 „	–	–	3	–	–	–	3	–
7 to 16 „	–	–	5	9	–	–	8	3
17 to 20 „	–	–	–	–	–	–	–	–
21 to 40 „	–	–	2	3	–	–	1	2
41 to 50 „	–	–	–	–	–	–	–	2
51 to 60 „	–	–	–	–	–	–	1	–
Total No. of Individuals committed,	26	1	194	50	9	–	171	49
No. of commitments represented in foregoing, . . .	31	1	389	246	13	–	408	214

Averages, and Highest and Lowest Numbers (exclusive of Debtors).

—	From 1st January to 31st December, 1874.			From 1st January, 1875, to day of Inspection.		
	M.	F.	Date.	M.	F.	Date.
Average daily number of prisoners in custody,	31	8	—	22	7	—
Highest number of prisoners at any one time,	44		23rd Feb.	41		19th Sept.
Lowest ditto, .	17		10th July.	19		24th July.
Highest number of males at any one time,	33		23rd Feb.	29		17th Sept.
Ditto of females,	14		25th Nov.	13		24th Jan.
Lowest number of males at any one time, .	11		9th July.	10		20th Jan.
Ditto of females,	3		25th March.	–		23rd July.

Highest Number of Prisoners (exclusive of Debtors) in Gaol during each of the previous seven years, and up to day of Inspection in 1875.

1st January, 1868, ... 56 | 25th June, 1872, ... 40
4th May, 1869, ... 33 | 16th June, 1873, ... 51
2nd September, 1870, ... 39 | 23rd February, 1874, ... 44
3rd April, 1871, ... 45 | 19th September, 1875, ... 41

Commit-
ments.

At the time of my visit 24 males and 10 females of all classes were inmates of this gaol. Two males were for trial, 1 committed for a rape the other for larceny. Five others convicted by jury at assizes and quarter sessions were under sentences of imprisonment, 1 for two years for rape, 3 for one year each for sheep stealing, arson, and robbery, and 1 for six months for an assault. Seventeen had been summarily convicted before justices sitting at petty sessions and sentenced ; 2 to be imprisoned for three months, 1 for perjury, the other for an assault ; 4 had been sentenced for two months, 1 for leaving service, and 3 for drunkenness and assaults. The other male prisoners in custody convicted of drunkenness, larceny, vagrancy, and assaults, had been sentenced for periods of from one month to fourteen days.

One female was for trial charged with larceny, all the other females in custody had been convicted before justices at petty sessions of drunkenness, disorderly conduct, and larceny, and had been sentenced for terms of from fourteen days to two months.

In 1874, 220 individual male and 51 female prisoners were committed to this gaol, of whom 26 males and 1 female were under sixteen years of age. Up to the time of my visit in September, 1875, 180 males and 49 females were committed, of these 9 (males) were under sixteen years of age, 3 of these 9 juveniles had previously been inmates of this prison; no female under 16 years of age was committed to this prison in 1875.

Of the 180 individual male and 49 female prisoners who were committed to this gaol in 1875, 69 males and 22 females had previously been in custody, 1 male had been upwards of fifty times committed, and 2 females upwards of forty times. The total committals represented by the 180 males numbered 420, and those of the 49 females 214.

One returned convict (male) was in custody in 1875, and 1 male and 1 female (also returned convicts) in 1874.

Accommodation.

	M.	F.		M.	F.
Wards,	8	2	Kitchen,	1	–
Yards,	8	2	Bakery,	1	–
Day Rooms,	7	2	Store Rooms,	4	1
Solitary Cells,	4	2	Laundry,	–	1
Single Cells, of size stated			Drying Room,	–	1
below,	65	12	Baths, with hot and cold		
Do., heated and furnished with bells, of the			water laid on,	1	1
			Water-closets,	20	6
size stated below,	19	19	Fumigating Apparatus,	1	–
Sleeping Rooms,	9	–	Reception Room or Cell,	1	–
Hospital Rooms,	2	2	Pump,	1	–
Chapel,	1	–	Crank do. .	1	–
School Rooms,	1	1	Well,	1	–
Workshops,	3	–	Tread-wheel,	1	–
Worksheds,	4	–	Tell-tale Clocks,	2	–

This gaol was, when I made my inspection, very clean and orderly. The buildings generally in sound repair and the place well kept. Since last inspection by my colleague in September, 1874, a second tell-tale clock had been procured, and five separate stalls had been put up in the laundry. The clothes when washed are dried in a room overhead fitted with lines.

At the time of my visit the females were usefully employed whitewashing the walls, and scrubbing the floors of the female prison under the charge of Miss Palmer, the matron, who is a useful officer, and utilizes the labour of the few female prisoners committed to her charge to the best advantage.

The great defect of this gaol is, that large unnecessary buildings incumber the grounds, the keeping of which in repair entails a constant expense, and occupies the prisoners who might otherwise be usefully employed. The Board have now removed the prisoners from the central building, and they occupy small cellular prisons apart in which they are now as far as possible concentrated. These prisons have each nineteen cells which are artificially heated, and are fitted up with bells to meet the requirements of the separate system.

The bath for males is in the No. 5 central building, that for females in the laundry. Both have hot and cold water laid on. The exterior of the prison, the entrance gate, and the corridors of both separate prisons are lighted by gas; but only the Governor's house and office, the day rooms, and four cells in the female prison are so lighted.

Sewerage.

The sewerage is effective and twelve effluvium traps were in October, 1874, placed at the openings of the sewers which discharge into the river. The supply of water is abundant from a well adjoining the tread-wheel, by the power of which it is driven into the tank which supplies the establishment. All the water taps of the prison and the closets are now in order, and are kept in repair by contract. The tread-wheel is not partitioned. The water of a second well on the premises to which I referred in my report for 1873, as having been polluted by sewage matter is not used.

The Inspectors-General have frequently suggested, that the cooking for prisoners should be carried on in the female prison. My colleague in his report for 1874, pointed out the advantage of uniting the laundry and kitchen, by which arrangement one fire would be made to heat water for both purposes, as well as the heating of a drying-room. To carry out this object the entrance to the kitchen should be changed, and a closet cut off for the delivery of the food for the use of prisoners in the male prison.

Occasionally only very few females are in custody, and in July last, not a single female prisoner was in the gaol; yet there are three female officers on the prison staff, and when there are no prisoners under their charge, they should be employed to prepare the food for the use of the few males who may be inmates of the prison.

Stock at the time of Inspection.

	In Use.	In Store.	Male Clothing.	In Use.	In Store.	Female Clothing.	In Use.	In Store.
Blankets, pairs of,	46	5	Shirts, .	47	16	Shifts, .	9	11
Sheets, pairs of,	60	6	Jackets,	25	33	Jackets, .	9	12
Rugs, .	51	23	Vests, .	23	17	Petticoats,	9	8
Hammocks or			Trowsers,	24	15	Aprons, .	9	11
Cots,	46	–	Caps, .	20	13	Neckerchiefs, .	9	13
Bedticks,	10	8	Stockings or			Caps. .	9	17
			Socks, pairs of,	31	37	Stockings, pairs of,	9	12
			Shoes, Slippers, &			Shoes, Slippers, &		
			Clogs, pairs of,	31	2	Clogs, pairs of,	9	4

Stores and clothing.

The prison clothing is now sufficient, and socks or stockings are given to all prisoners. Some new jackets and trowsers were in store when I visited, but very few shoes. I found the bedding sufficient for the requirements of the establishment; the cots, however, were much worn; new ones should be provided. Some of the pillows also in use were not clean. The sheets are changed fortnightly, or oftener if necessary, and fresh sheets are stated to be given to all new comers.

Since my last visit a good fumigating closet has been fitted up in the male prison, and in it the clothes of all prisoners male and female are cleansed and disinfected.

The private clothing of the prisoners are duly tied up in bundles and labelled.

The prison stores are now properly kept. The suggestion of my colleague that the provisions be weighed by the storekeeper has not been adopted, but the tins for the provisions are marked to measure the supply. When an artisan tailor or shoemaker is in custody he repairs or makes prison clothing, but as a rule the male clothing is supplied by contract. But few articles are made in the gaol. I do not think that sufficient care is taken to utilize the labour of the male prisoners.

Long sentenced prisoners are frequently in custody; I found 1 sentenced for two years, and 3 for one year, yet not a single male prisoner received instruction in any trade during 1875—hence the heavy expenditure for work which should be executed by prison labour. Formerly much work was done in the factory of this prison, which is not now utilized as it should be.

All the female clothing is made in the prison under the instruction of Miss Palmer, the matron.

The photographing of prisoners is executed by an artist of the town of Ennis, who receives 4s. for four copies of each photograph taken, which is a very high cost for the work.

No change has been made in the seats of the chapel which is set apart for Roman Catholic service. Protestant prisoners when in custody attend divine worship in the Board-room.

Lock-up is held at 6, P.M., at all seasons of the year, the prisoners are unlocked at 6, A.M., in summer, and 7, A.M., in winter. One watchman patrols at night from 7, P.M., to 6, A.M. A superior officer goes his rounds finally at 10, P.M., and two tell-tale clocks, placed in the rear of the prison, record the vigilance of the watch.

No change has been made in the arrangements for visitors to prisoners since last inspection.

No escape was attempted from this prison in 1875, but one male charged with sheep stealing made his escape from the bridewell at Killaloe. He was retaken.

Number of Punishments for Prison Offences.

			From 1st Jan. to 31st Dec., 1874.		From 1st Jan., 1875, to day of Inspection.	
			M.	F.	M.	F.
By Magisterial authority,	.	.	1	–	3	–
By Governor—						
Dark or Refractory Cells,	.	.	46	21	28	16
Stoppage of Diet,	.	.	166	12	74	12
Other Punishments,	.	.	1	–	1	–
Total,	.	.	214	33	106	28

The punishment cells in the female prison are furnished with bells which have spiral springs, one is darkened, the other has light. Four cells for punishment of male prisoners are in Nos. 7 and 5 of the old central building, they are not heated, but prisoners do not remain in them at night. One prisoner (P. C.) complained to me that he had been kept six days under punishment in a solitary cell by order of the Governor, contrary to the rule of the 109th sec. of the "Prisons Act." I inquired into the matter, and ascertained from the Governor and head turnkey, that the man was first kept three days in the solitary cell, not on punishment diet, waiting for a magistrate to visit the prison; but afterwards a magistrate not having been found, the Governor gave the man punishment diet for three days more in the cell. In future when a prisoner is reserved for such punishment, the Governor should at once apply to some magistrate to attend. Another prisoner (R.) complained that when ill he was shut up in a solitary cell and punished; I learn, however, from the Local Inspector, that the man was first examined by the

SOUTH
DISTRICT.
―――
*Clare
County
Gaol.*

Medical Officer and pronounced to be a malingerer. These men made some other complaints which had already been investigated by the Board, and found to be groundless.

Schools.

	From 1st Jan. to 31st Dec., 1874.		From 1st Jan., 1875, to day of Inspection.	
	M.	F.	M.	F.
Number of individual prisoners who attended school, ...	27	18	42	16
Average daily number of pupils, . .	7	3	9	4
Number of days on which school was held, .	41	190	65	112

School-hours.—Males, no fixed hour observed ; Females, 12 o'clock to 1 o'clock, P.M.

School.

The school for females is held from 12 to 1 o'clock, P.M., that for males is not at fixed hours. Such an arrangement is very irregular. Only sixty-five days schooling were given to the males, the number of pupils who attended averaging but 9. None but prisoners under sentence for periods exceeding three months are given secular instruction. I regret that this branch of the prison service is not better attended to, more especially as the teacher who is chief-warder is very well qualified ; the Governor should see that the duty is performed.

The school-room is not stalled, and the prisoners are in association during the time school is held.

The school is in connexion with the Board of National Education.

Their Inspector reports :— " From 1st July, 1874, till 30th June, 1875, this school was open on only fifty-seven days, and the pupils therefore received but fifty-seven hours' instruction in the year. This accounts for one pupil, whom I found in first class last year, being still in same class, and having made no apparent progress."

Employment on day of Inspection.

						M.	F.
Tread-wheel,	.	.	.	.	.	14	–
Stone-breaking,	.	.	.	.	.	8	–
Cooking,	.	.	.	.	.	1	–
Shoemaking,	.	.	.	.	.	1	–
Unemployed,	.	.	.	.	.	–	1
Washing,	.	.	.	.	.	–	6
Knitting, Sewing, Quilting,	.	.	.	.	.	–	3
Total in custody,		.	.	.		24	10

Amount received for produce of Prisoners' labour disposed of outside the Gaol.

1872, . £8 5s. 6d. | 1873, . £15 7s. 3d. | 1874, . £29 6s. 10d.

One male artisan, a shoemaker, was at work in the factory when I visited, 8 males were stone breaking, 1 was cook and the rest were at work on the tread-wheel which pumps water. One female was usefully occupied at quilting, which is a profitable employment, and should be more generally carried on in prisons, the other females were washing, knitting, and sewing. There are twenty-one sheds for stone-breaking in this prison. Oakum-picking is not carried on in this gaol, the Governor states that the insurance company objects to its use.

An improvement is recorded in the amount of work by prisoners sold outside the gaol, but still the amount is insufficient having regard to the number of prisoners in charge.

Contracts.

Bread, white, per 4-lb. loaf, 6d.; ditto, brown, per 4-lb. loaf, 5½d.; oatmeal, per cwt., 16s.; Indian meal, per cwt., 10s.; potatoes, per cwt 6s.; meat, per lb., 9d.; new milk, per gallon, 10d.; salt, per cwt., 4s.; coal, per ton, £1 3s. 6d; straw, per cwt. 2s.; gas, per 1,000 cubic feet, 9s. 2d.; candles, per lb, 5d.; soap, per cwt., £1. Other Contracts —Conveyance of prisoners to petty sessions towns, per mile going, 6d.; do. returning, 3d.; horsing prison van, 13s.

Net average daily cost of Ordinary Diet for each Prisoner.

1872,	. 5d.	1873,	. 5d.	1874,	. 3d.

I questioned all the prisoners in charge at the time of my visit, and 2 male prisoners lodged complaints to which I have already referred. The food for prison use which I tasted was of a good description, and the Chaplains report favourably of the samples of provisions submitted for their inspection.

Officers and Salaries.

Non-Resident.	£	s.	d.	Resident.	£	s.	d.
Captain C. M. Parkinson, J.P., Local Inspector,	100	0	0	Capt. J. H. Healey, Governor,	300	0	0
Rev. P. Dwyer, Protestant Chaplain,	46	3	0	Patk. Slattery, 1st Turnkey, and Schoolmaster,	70	0	0
Rev. R. Fitzgerald, Roman Catholic Chaplain,	46	3	0	Thos Leydon, 2nd Turnkey, and Gate Porter,	48	0	0
P. M. Cullinan, esq., Surgeon,	54	0	0	Jas M'Mahon, 3rd Turnkey,	36	0	0
Ml. Greene, esq., Apothecary,	20	0	0	Patk. Daly, Acting Turnkey,	36	0	0
Michl. Considine, Clerk &c.	60	0	0	Mary Palmer, Matron,	65	0	0
Patrick Halpin, Acting Night Watchman,	28	0	0	Mary Kenny, Assist. Matron,	20	17	0
				Eliza M'Donnell, Nursetender,	24	0	0

Vacancies in the staff since last Inspection, how caused, and how filled up.

Two Night Watchmen appointed in room of two others resigned. One Turnkey dismissed; one Turnkey appointed; and one Turnkey resigned. Sixmile-bridge Bridewell-keeper (P. Deviney) died, and vacancy not filled up.

Visits paid by Officers.

	From 1st Jan. to 31st December, 1874.	From 1st Jan., 1875, to day of Inspection.
Number of times the Board of Super-intendence met and discharged business,	13	10
Local Inspector to Gaol,	132	95
„ to each Bridewell,	4	3
Chaplain, Protestant Episcopal Church,	89	52
Chaplain, Roman Catholic,	147	102
Surgeon,	144	109
Apothecary,	104	78

I found the officers' quarters tidy and well kept when I visited.

Net cost of Gaol, including Diet and Salaries.

1872,	. £1,597 9s. 2d.	1873,	. £1,770 0s. 1d.	1874,	. £1,695 10s. 9d.

Total cost of Officers, including Clothing, Value of Rations, Washing, Gas, &c.

1872,	. £950 16s. 2d.	1873,	. £1,019 18s. 3d.	1874,	. £1,067 17s. 3d.

Average cost of each Prisoner per annum.

1872,	. £53 1s. 1d.	1873,	. £48 7s. 3d.	1874,	. £57 19s. 3·86d.

P

Amounts repaid by the War Department for Military Prisoners.

1872, . . £2 14s. | 1873, . £1 19s. | 1874, . £1 8s.

*Amounts repaid from the Consolidated Fund for the maintenance, &c., of
Prisoners.*

1872, £106 14s. 3d. | 1873, . £95 18s. 7d. | 1874, . £94 13s. 0d.

Books and Accounts.

The various registries of discipline and finance are kept with much
care and attention by the office clerk. The Governor's journal is well
kept, in it all matters of importance as well as punishments are marked in
red ink. The Local Inspector who is a most attentive officer keeps his
journal with praiseworthy care, and from it I learned some matters to
which it was my duty to call the attention of the Board for inquiry.
The Medical Officer has his books satisfactory, and the Chaplains record
the duties they perform. The Local Inspector checks and initials the
pass books monthly before being submitted to the Board, the dockets are
signed by the Local Inspector and the Governor.

Hospital.

	1872.		1873.		1874.		1875 (to day of Inspection).	
	M.	F.	M.	F.	M.	F.	M.	F.
No. of prisoners in hospital,	16	14	24	11	31	14	21	3
Averagedaily No. in hospital,	·8	·3	1·4	·3	1·2	·5	·9	·3
No. of prisoners prescribed for and treated out of hospital, . . .	145	80	94	82	94	70	70	51
Cost of medicine, . .	£5 4s. 5d.		£8 12s. 0d.		£14 15s. 6d.		—	
Cost of diet for prisoners in hospital, . . .	£3 0s. 3d.		£11 2s. 1d.		£10 0s. 0d.		—:	
Cost of all extra diet ordered by Medical Officer for prisoners not in hospital, . .	—		£3 0s. 0d.		£4 0s. 4d.		—	

No change has been made in the hospital arrangements since last inspection. The health of the prisoners is very good. The only prisoners in
hospital at the time of my visit were two of unsound mind (male and
female), who gave much trouble.

The hospital books are well kept, and the Medical officer carefully discharges his duties in the gaol.

Board of Superintendence.

The Right Hon. Lord Inchiquin.
Lt.-Col. W. E. A. MacDonnell, D.L.
Lt.-Colonel Augustine Butler, D.L.
Lt.-Colonel Marcus Paterson, J.P.
Major W. M. Molony, D.L.
Richard Stacpoole, esq., J.P.

J. F. V. Fitzgerald, esq., D.L.
Joseph Hall, esq., J.P.
George Sampson, esq., J.P.
Nicholas Butler, esq., J.P.
Major C. W. Studdert, J.P.
Andrew Enright, esq.

The Board meets on the first Saturday of each month for the discharge
of business, when liabilities are discharged by separate cheques in favour
of each creditor unless the amounts are small, in which case they are
included in one cheque payable to the Local Inspector, who passes the
vouchers at the next meeting of the Board.

STATE OF BRIDEWELLS.

	Kilrush.		Ennistimon.	
	M.	F.	M.	F.
No. of Committals in past year, . . .	26	6	36	11
Of whom were Drunkards, . . .	14	3	13	3
No. of Committals in the quarter preceding Inspection, . . .	12	3	7	–
Of whom were Drunkards, . . .	8	1	2	–

	Kilrush.	Ennistimon.
Petty Sessions and Transmittals.	Weekly at Kilrush; fortnightly at Knock, Carrigaholt, and Kilkee.	Fortnightly.
Committals, . . .	Regular.	Some illegal prisoners sentenced to imprisonment in this Bridewell for fighting and for begging.
Registry, . . .	Correctly kept.	Correctly kept.
Repairs and Order, .	In good repair and order; walls should be dashed.	In fair repair.
Security, . . .	Sufficient, with care.	Yard for females insecure.
Accommodation, . .	Males—day-room and six cells, including one for drunkards, but without bedding; females—day-room and two cells.	Males—day-room and two cells, with large yard; same accommodation for females.
Furniture, Bedding, and Utensils.	Sufficient and good.	Sufficient.
Water, ...	By pump; in order.	Abundant, by pump in yard for females, and well in yard for males.
Sewerage, . . .	Effective.	Stated to be good.
Cleanliness, Dryness, and Ventilation.	Clean and well kept; ventilation good.	Clean and well kept; ventilation good, but flags damp.
Cost of Dietary per head per day.	6d. per day for prisoners of both sexes.	6d. per day for both sexes.
Salary of Keeper, . .	£35.	£25.
Whether Keeper follows any other employment.	Court-keeper; salary, £8.	Court-keeper; salary, £8.
Statutable Inspection, .	7th October, 1875.	27th September, 1875.
Remarks, . . .	No prisoner in charge.	No prisoner in charge.

STATE OF BRIDEWELLS—*continued.*

SOUTH DISTRICT. Clare County. Bridewells.	—	Tulla.		Killaloe.	
		M.	F.	M.	F.
No. of Committals in past year, . .		16	7	73	7
Of whom were Drunkards, .		5	4	30	2
No. of Committals in the quarter preceding Inspection		8	1	11	2
Of whom were Drunkards, .		1	—	4	—
Petty Sessions and Transmittals.		Fortnightly at Tulla, Feakle, and Tomgraney.		At Killaloe fortnightly, on Tuesdays.	
Committals, . .		Regular.		Apparently regular, but prisoners are sometimes not brought before the committing Justice when remanded.	
Registry, . . .		Correctly kept.		Correctly kept.	
Repairs and Order, .		In fair repair and order.		In good repair and order; walls lately whitewashed.	
Security, . . .		Improved. The lower part of the down pipe into yard has been removed, but the removal of it makes the wall very damp. The pipe should be removed to the front of the building.		Yards very insecure; iron spikes put up at gutter on roof, but insufficient.	
Accommodation, .		Badly arranged; males—day-room and four cells; females—day-room and two cells.		Males—day-room and three cells; females — day-room and two cells. Small yards, with low walls.	
Furniture, Bedding, and Utensils.		Bedding required—one pair of blankets, and one rug much worn.		Bed-ticks and sheets much worn, and no sheets to replace those in the wash; one rug much worn. Some ticks, sheets, and rugs should be supplied.	
Water, how supplied,		A pump in yard.		None on premises.	
Sewerage, . .		Stated to be sufficient.		None; earth-closets should be procured.	
Cleanliness, Dryness, and Ventilation.		Clean and orderly, but very damp.		Very clean and well kept; ventilation sufficient.	
Cost of Dietary per head per day.		6d. for all prisoners.		6d. for both sexes.	
Salary of Keeper, .		£20.		£20.	
Whether Keeper has other employment.		Court-keeper; salary, £8.		Court-keeper; salary £8.	
Statutable Inspection,		25th September, 1875.		4th July, 1875.	
Remarks, . .		No prisoner in charge.		No prisoner in charge. In February, 1875, an old man charged with sheep-stealing escaped from this Bridewell; he was afterwards retaken. I investigated the case, and consider the keeper to blame. The door of the privy can be taken off its hinges, and with the long forms in the day-rooms, can be used to facilitate the crossing of the low walls of the exercising yards.	

JOHN LENTAIGNE, *Inspector-General.*

CORK COUNTY GAOL, AT CORK.—STATUTABLE INSPECTION, 17TH AND 20TH NOVEMBER, 1875.

Prisoners of all classes in Gaol on the day of Inspection, and on the corresponding date in preceding years.

		M.	F.		M.	F.
1872,	. . . .	157	53	1874, ...	140	32
1873,	. . . .	148	35	1875 (day of Inspection),	182	26

Workhouse Offenders in Gaol on the day of Inspection, and on the corresponding date in preceding years.

		M.	F.		M.	F.
1872,	. . . .	1	2	1874, ...	1	—
1873,	. . . .	—	3	1875 (day of Inspection),	—	1

Vagrants in Gaol on the day of Inspection, and on corresponding date in preceding years.

		M.	F.		M.	F.
1872,	. . . .	1	—	1874, ...	4	1
1873,	. . . .	—	1	1875 (day of Inspection),	3	—

Returned Convicts in Gaol on the day of Inspection, and during each of the preceding years.

		M.	F.		M.	F.
1872,	. . . .	2	1	1875 (up to and including		
1873,	. . . .	8	4	day of Inspection), .	2	3
1874,	. . . .	8	4	Day of Inspection, .	1	—

Juveniles.

I found when I made my inspection 2 young offenders in custody; the age of 1 was under twelve years. Both had been summarily convicted—1 of larceny, the other of a workhouse offence.

Two adult offenders, who at one period had been inmates of reformatories, were also in custody, and 3 others had previously been committed during the year.

Fifteen young offenders who had escaped from reformatories were committed to this gaol during 1875.

Forty-seven male and 2 female juveniles (under sixteen years of age) were in custody in 1875. One (male) was twice committed during the year.

Fourteen males (11 under twelve years of age) were sent to reformatories, after the period of their imprisonment as a punishment in this gaol, and one young offender was whipped by order of court in 1875.

Commitments.

CLASSES.				1874.		1875, to day of Inspection.	
				M.	F.	M.	F.
Debtors,	.		.	7	1	4	—
Criminals,			.	717	205	703	183
Vagrants,	.	.		25	3	14	4
Drunkards,	.	.		184	122	172	116
		Total,	.	**933**	**331**	***893**	***303**

* Including 11 males and 2 females, received from Tralee Gaol, by order of Lord Lieutenant.

*Individual Prisoners (exclusive of Debtors), and Number of Times each
had been committed during 1874 and 1875.*

Cork
County
Gaol.

NUMBER OF TIMES COMMITTED.	1874.				1875, to day of Inspection.			
	Juveniles.		Adults.		Juveniles.		Adults.	
	M.	F.	M.	F.	M.	F.	M.	F.
Once within the year,	35	2	737	192	46	2	710	197
Twice ,,	1	–	56	29	1	–	47	22
Thrice ,,	–	–	9	7	–	–	8	9
4 times ,,	–	–	1	7	–	–	2	3
5, 6, and 7 times within the year,	–	–	1	5	–	–	1	4
Total,	36	2	806	240	47	2	768	235
No. of above who had not been in Gaol previous to 1st January in	36	2	541	119	47	2	552	128

*Individual Prisoners (exclusive of Debtors) committed in the year 1874,
and to the day of Inspection in 1875, who had been Once, and oftener
committed in any year, so far as can be ascertained.*

NUMBER OF TIMES COMMITTED.	1874.				1875, to day of Inspection.			
	Juveniles		Adults.		Juveniles.		Adults.	
	M.	F.	M.	F.	M.	F.	M.	F.
Once only,	35	2	511	115	46	2	531	119
Twice,	1	–	122	28	1	–	108	24
Thrice,	–	–	97	16	–	–	49	22
4 times,	–	–	21	9	–	–	30	7
5 ,,	–	–	14	6	–	–	10	10
6 ,,	–	–	6	13	–	–	10	8
7 to 11 times,	–	–	26	25	–	–	21	26
12 to 16 ,,	–	–	5	15	–	–	6	6
17 to 20 ,,	–	–	3	5	–	–	1	3
21 to 30 ,,	–	–	1	4	–	–	1	3
31 to 50 ,,	–	–	–	4	–	–	1	6
61 to 70 ,,	–	–	–	–	–	–	–	1
Total No. of Individuals committed,	36	2	806	240	47	2	768	235
No. of commitments represented in foregoing,	37	2	1,603	1,134	48	2	1,460	1109

Averages, and Highest and Lowest Numbers (exclusive of Debtors).

—	From 1st January to 31st December, 1874.			From 1st January, 1875, to day of Inspection.		
	M.	F.	Date.	M.	F.	Date.
Average daily number of prisoners in custody,	129	31	—	160	32	—
Highest number of prisoners at any one time,	229		2nd Sept.	228		27th Oct.
Lowest ditto,	117		11th May.	136		4th Jan.
Highest number of males at any one time,	185		2nd Sept.	199		27th Oct.
Ditto of females,	46		5th Aug.	50		11th Sept.
Lowest number of males at any one time,	94		17th May.	117		4th Jan.
Ditto of females,	15		1st May.	19		4th Jan.

Highest Number of Prisoners (exclusive of Debtors) in Gaol during each of the previous seven years, and up to day of Inspection in 1875.

Souru
District.

Cork
County
Gaol.

13th June, 1868, .	. 152	15th November, 1872, .	. 202
11th September, 1869, .	. 170	7th June, 1873, .	. 229
27th September, 1870,	. 173	2nd September, 1874,	. 229
20th September, 1871, .	. 171	27th October, 1875, .	. 228

Number of Prisoners sentenced to Solitary Confinement by order of Court.

	From 1st January to 31st December, 1874.		From 1st January, 1875, to day of Inspection.	
	M.	F.	M.	F.
Solitary Confinement, . . .	5	5	7	2

One hundred and eighty-two male prisoners and 26 females were inmates of this prison at the time of my inspection; of these, 13 males and 4 females were for trial.

Forty-seven naval and military offenders, tried by courts-martial, were under sentence, besides 14 sailors and 11 soldiers tried by civil tribunals. They numbered altogether 72 offenders belonging to the military and naval service, and therefore cannot be counted amongst the ordinary offenders of the county Cork district. Four other offenders had been transferred to this prison from the gaol of the county Kerry at Tralee, and 1 from the city of Cork prison.

The sentences on the male offenders in custody were—1 military offender sentenced to an imprisonment of 1,008 days by court-martial; 17 others had been sentenced for terms of two years and above one year; 41 for terms of ten, eleven, and twelve months, and 20 for six, eight, and nine months. Thirty were for shorter periods.

Five female offenders were under sentences of imprisonment for six months, 2 for five, 2 for four, and 2 for three months each.

Eight females were in custody for larceny, 1 for a workhouse offence, the remainder had been convicted of drunkenness, disorderly conduct, soliciting for prostitution, and assaults.

By reference to the preceding tables it will be seen that the 842 males committed to this prison in 1874 have been 1,639 times in custody, and the 242 females 1,136 times. The males committed in 1875 numbered 815; they have 1,508 committals recorded against them on the prison books; and the 237 females committed during the year have been 1,111 times in custody. One female has been between 60 and 70 times an inmate of the prison, and six others between 30 and 50 times. One male, although only 45 years of age, had already undergone four terms of penal servitude.

Accommodation.

	M.	F.		M.	F.
Wards, ...	9	5	Chapel, ...	One	
Yards, ...	8	7	School-room, . . .	1	–
Day Rooms, . . .	8	6	Kitchen, . . .	–	1
Solitary Cells, . .	2	2	Laundry, . . .	–	1
Single Cells, not less than 9 feet			Drying Room, . .	–	1
long, 6 feet wide, and 8 feet			Lavatories, . . .	24	13
high=432 cubic feet, . .	34	–	Baths, with Hot and Cold		
Do. heated and furnished			Water laid on, . .	1	1
with bells, . . .	120	40	Privies, . . .	1	–
Do. of smaller size, not so fur-			Water-closets, . .	17	9
nished, . . .	36	51	Fumigating Apparatus, .	1	1
Cells to contain three persons,	2	2	Treadwheels, . . .	2	–
Sleeping Rooms, . . .	4	4	Recording Watches, .	2	–
Hospital Rooms, . . .	4	2			

In consequence of floods in the river when I made my inspection sand and gravel had found their way into the pipes which convey water from the river, driven by the power of the tread-wheel into the tank for flushing the sewerage of the prison; consequently, the pipes being choked the tread-wheel could not be used for pumping water from the river. Water is, however, supplied to the gaol from the city main, to meet the necessary requirements of the establishment.

I found, also, that the pipes which are intended to convey hot water from the lime-kiln, "Cahen's Patent Heating Apparatus," had burst. The heating apparatus was therefore not in order, and was under repair ; but as the old furnace which formerly heated the prison had not been removed no inconvenience was experienced by the accident which caused the bursting of the pipes. As, however, such an accident may again occur, I would suggest that the old heating apparatus be permitted to remain until the new process is thoroughly tested.

The heating of the old wing for males opposite the female prison is insufficient. The apparatus but imperfectly heats the cells, which are flagged, hence the cells are too cold in winter. Neither are the cells of this prison, nor those in the end block of the old prison, artificially lighted, and the inmates remain in darkness during the long nights of winter. The cells in the end prison are far too small for separation ; but in consequence of the crowded state of the gaol a number of prisoners occupied them at the time of my visit.

The heating apparatus in the female prison works satisfactorily. The cells in that block are roomy and well ventilated. When at some future time the wall of the central hall has been thrown back, so as to give the hall sufficient breadth, this block will be in every respect suitable for carrying out the separate system with advantage. The block contains forty cells, besides rooms ; and as only 27 female prisoners were inmates of the gaol on inspection the accommodation for females was fully equal to the requirements.

The new reception-ward, with baths for females adjoining the kitchen, answers the object in view, and the food for the inmates of both prisons is economically cooked by females under the present arrangement.

The unusually large number of males in custody when I visited was principally caused by a number of naval and military offenders, and some prisoners transferred from the Kerry and city of Cork prisons who were then inmates of this prison.

Stock at the time of Inspection.

	In Use.	In Store.	Male Clothing.	In Use.	In Store.	Female Clothing.	In Use.	In Store.
Blankets, pairs of,	287½	8	Shirts,	374	8	Shifts,	83	9
Sheets, pairs of,	300½	31	Jackets,	325	12	Jackets,	69	17
Rugs,	250	9	Vests,	193	1	Petticoats,	121	-
Hammocks or			Trowsers,	209	-	Aprons,	75	29
Cots,	28	34	Caps,	203	53	Neckerchiefs,	90	20
Bed-ticks,	215	16	Stockings or			Caps,	148	80
Bedsteads,	385	-	Socks, pairs of,	384	-	Stockings, pairs of,	96	123
			Shoes, Slippers, &			Shoes, Slippers, &		
			Clogs, pairs of,	206	14	Clogs, pairs of,	47	-

All parts of the gaol were, at the time of my inspection, in sound repair, the cells very clean and orderly, but some bedding, blankets, and sheets were much worn, and a supply should be provided. The locks and fittings in the cells of the different prisons were, when I visited, in good order, and the lighting by gas of the new prison is very satisfactory. The arrangement for lighting the cell from a chamber in the wall, separated by glass from the interior, was first carried out in this prison and the Inspectors-General have recommended that the model should be adopted elsewhere. It has been now tested and is found perfectly to answer the object in view. The Boards of Superintendence of the Tralee and the Cork city gaols have adopted it, and I trust to see the system carried out in every cellular prison.

Both the male and the female prisons have a sufficient supply of water-closets and lavatories. Seventeen water-closets and twenty-four lavatories are in the male prisons, and nine water-closets and thirteen lavatories in that for females.

One hundred and twenty cells in the male and forty in the female prison are artificially lighted, warmed, ventilated, and furnished with means for prisoners to communicate with a prison officer. Sixty-five other cells for males and four for females are capable of being furnished with these appliances; of these thirty-eight are already heated, but have not other necessary requirements. Some cells in the old male prison are too small for separation.

Photographs of habitual criminals are taken by the clerk and schoolmaster, for which a charge of 6d. per copy is made to the Board.

Three prison officers have charge of the night-patrol—two in the interior of the prison, who divide the watch between them, and one on the outside patrols the insulating area. Their vigilance is tested by Dent's Recording Watch, which is the most perfect method for testing the regularity of the patrol in a prison.

The apartments of the chief warder are so arranged that he can always during the night ascertain the watchfulness of the night patrol within the prison.

The prison is unlocked at 6 A.M. in summer and 7 A.M. in winter, and the lock-up is held at 6 P.M. during all seasons of the year.

Convicted prisoners may receive visits on orders by a member of the Board, monthly; untried prisoners fortnightly, or oftener if necessary. The visiting-room has two divisions (by wire-work), a warder is stationed between them, and the arrangements are such that the visiters cannot possibly convey prohibited articles to the prisoners.

No escape was attempted from this prison in 1874 or 1875, but 3 prisoners escaped from the bridewells of the county during the period—1 (male) from Queenstown Bridewell in October, 1874, and 2 (male and female) from the Dunmanway Bridewell, 1 in October, 1874, the other in August, 1875. They were retaken.

The sewerage, which discharges itself into the river below the gaol, is effective.

Number of Punishments for Prison Offences.

	From 1st January to 31st December, 1874.		From 1st January, 1875, to day of Inspection.	
	M.	F.	M.	F.
By Magisterial authority,	4	1	–	2
By Governor—				
Dark or Refractory Cells,	200	26	221	33
Stoppage of Diet,	243	20	836	84
Total,	447	47	1,057	119

It is seen from the preceding table that the punishments of prisoners during the year were very numerous, which was mainly due to the fact that the prisoners are given a certain amount of task-work, to pick oakum, which if not accomplished they are punished. I found 1 male under punishment from that cause. The punishment cells in the male prison are under the central hall, and are properly fitted up.

Schools.

	From 1st Jan. to 31st Dec., 1874.		From 1st Jan., 1875, to day of Inspection.	
	M.	F.	M.	F.
Number of Individual prisoners who attended school,	14	–	11	–
Average daily number of pupils,	7	–	5·5	–
Number of days on which school was held,	86	–	94	–

School Hours.—Males, 12 to 2 o'clock; Females, not in operation.

No improvement has been made in the schoolroom of the male prison : it is still undivided, and insufficiently lighted, the suggestions which I made in 1873 to make it answer the purpose of a schoolroom not having been adopted.

The prisoners when at school sit in association together. The room is lighted by a single window. It is too dark ; and unless the Board of Superintendence will open a second window in the blank wall of the schoolroom it will never be suitable.

School for males was not regularly held during the last two years, and no school was held in the female prison.

During the period (four months) in which school was held in the male prison in 1875, the Protestant Chaplain recorded his observations in the School Registry seven times and the Roman Catholic Chaplain twice ; but I am informed that they visited the school on other occasions without making entries.

Employment on day of Inspection.

	M.	F.
Treadwheel and shot drill, . . .	27	–
Picking oakum, ...	104	5
Shoemaking, weaving, and tailoring, . .	5	–
Mat-making, ...	8	–
Masons, carpentering, and tinmen, . .	4	–
Washing and ironing, ...	–	5
Sewing, knitting, and spinning, . .	–	8
Cooking, ...	–	3
Cleaning prison and labourers . . .	22	3
Sick, ...	1	1
Unemployed.	4	–
Discharged (before labour hours), . .	7	1
Total in custody, . .	182	26

Amount received for produce of Prisoners' Labour disposed of outside the Gaol.

1872, . £105 19s. 6d. | 1873, . £143 16s. 2d. | 1874, . £135 6s. 8d.

Prisoners sentenced to hard labour work on the tread-wheel, and at shot-drill for two hours daily. They work on the mill for six minutes between each relief, and then have rest for three minutes. Twelve separate stalls are provided for those waiting for their turn on the mill. The tread-wheel is partitioned.

All prisoners sentenced to hard labour are named in the Morning State, and those exempt by the Doctor are deducted from the total. Industrial labour consists in mat-making, weaving, shoemaking, tailoring, carpentry, tinwork, and such other employments as can be turned to advantage for the benefit of the establishment. Prisoners of both sexes pick oakum, and the women are likewise employed in washing, spinning, knitting, and needlework.

During 1875 186 artisans were inmates of this gaol, of whom 20 were in custody at the time of my visit.

Two of the staff are shoemakers by trade.

Dietary and Contracts.

Bread, white, per 4-lb. loaf, 5½d. ; bread, brown, per 12-lb. loaf, 1s. 1½d. ; oatmeal, per cwt., 13s. 2½d. ; Indian meal, per cwt., 7s. 11½d. ; potatoes, per cwt., 3s. 8d. ; meat, per lb. 9d. ; skim-milk, per gallon, 3½d. ; salt, per cwt., 2s. 11½d. ; coal, per ton, £1 3s. ; gas, per 1,000 cubic feet, 4s. 6d. ; candles, per lb., 9d. ; soap, per cwt., 19s. 9d.

Net average Daily Cost of Ordinary Diet for each Prisoner.

1872, . . 4d. | 1873, . . 4d. | 1874, . . 4d.

The food prepared for the use of the prisoners on the day of my visit was of a good description ; but I observe that the Chaplains occasionally

SOUTH DISTRICT. — Cork County Gaol.

report unfavourably of the milk supplied by the contractor. I learn from the Governor that on all such occasions good milk is purchased in the city, at the expense of the contractor, and substituted for the inferior article, which is returned.

I questioned all the inmates of the prison on the day of my visit. No grave complaint was made to me by any. One man informed me that his officer did not let him to the closet when required, and he also stated that the gruel supplied was sometimes thin and cold.

Officers and Salaries.

	£	s.	d.			£	s.	d.
Non-Resident.				Warders.	George Glascott, . .	44	4	0
William Penrose, Local Inspector, ...	250	0	0		George Hayes, Shoemaker,	41	12	0
Rev. J. Q. Connolly, Protestant Chaplain, . . .	46	3	0		Peter Carey, . . .	36	8	0
Rev. J. O'Keeffe, Roman Catholic Chaplain, . .	46	3	0		Jeffrey Smith, . .	36	8	0
William Beamish, Surgeon, . Do. Compounding Medicine, . .	74	0	0		John Murphy, . .	36	8	0
Resident.					Edward Cooper, . .	36	8	0
John Joyce, Governor, .	350	0	0		Charles Oxford, . .	36	8	0
Timothy Byrne, Chief Warder,	85	0	0		James Browne, . .	36	8	0
James Wilson, Clerk and Schoolmaster, . . .	65	0	0		Michael O'Sullivan, .	36	8	0
William Bibby, Gatekeeper,	57	8	0		Patrick O'Connor, .	36	8	0
					John P. Clifford, Shoemaker,	36	8	0
					William Sweeny, Messenger,	26	0	0
					Elizabeth Delmage, Matron,	56	0	0
					Maria Perrody, Sub-Matron,	32	10	0
					Margaret Sweeny, do., .	26	0	0
					Anne M'Guire, do., .	26	0	0

Vacancies in Staff since last inspection, how caused, and how filled up.

All changes in Staff have been duly reported to Inspectors-General.

Officers on Gaol Allowance.

The Chief Warder, Matron, and all subordinate officers, receive "plain rations" of bread and milk, and, (Matron excepted) are supplied annually with uniform clothing.

Visits Paid by Officers.

	From 1st Jan. to 31st Dec., 1874.	From 1st Jan., 1875, to day of Inspection.
Number of times the Board of Superintendence met and discharged business, .	12	10
Local Inspector to Gaol, ...	107	88
Do. to each Bridewell, . . .	4	3
Chaplain, Protestant Episcopal Church, .	266	229
,, Roman Catholic, . . .	236	229
Surgeon, and Compounder of Medicine, .	375	325

The officers' quarters in this prison were, at the time of my visit, very clean and tidy. They are regularly inspected by the Governor, and occasionally by the Local Inspector. Some warders mess within the gaol, but those who are married and who reside in the neighbourhood are permitted to take their meals with their families.

Books and Accounts.

Net cost of Gaol, including Diet and Salaries.

1872, . £3,885 2s. 3d. | 1873, . £4,367 3s. 7d. | 1874, . £4,047 6s. 0d.

Total cost of Officers, including Clothing, Value of Rations, Washing, Gas, &c.

1872, . £1,786 6s. 10d. | 1873, . £1,961 8s. 1d. | 1874, . £1,904 19s. 4d.

Average cost of each Prisoner per annum.

1872, . £23 10s. 9d. | 1873, . £22 6s. 0d. | 1874, . £25 0s. 3½d.

Amounts repaid by the War Department for Military Prisoners.

1872, . £287 14s. 0d. | 1873, . £279 18s. 0d. | 1874, . £460 4s. 0d.

SOUTH
DISTRICT.
———
Cork
County
Gaol.

Amounts repaid by the Admiralty Department for Naval Prisoners.
1872, . £31 10s. 0d. | 1873, . £27 7s. 0d. | 1874, . £45 16s. 0d.

Amounts repaid out of the Consolidated Fund for the maintenance, &c., of Prisoners.
1872, . £492 8s. 6d. | 1873, . £493 17s. 2d | 1874, . £355 1s. 7d.

The various registries of discipline and finance in this prison are well and carefully kept by the clerk, who is also schoolmaster and photographer. He is assisted by the head warder in the office duty. The books are checked daily by the Governor, who marks with his initials the principal books. The Local Inspector also occasionally examines the books; his journal is carefully kept. The journal of the Governor is likewise a valuable record of the various occurrences in the prison. And I desire here to repeat the expression of the high appreciation which I entertain of the services of the Governor, who is, in my opinion, a zealous and very efficient prison officer.* The journal of the Medical Officer is well and regularly kept, and the Chaplains in their journals state the duties they perform. Some of the forms in use are on an improved plan, and proper checks are established in the storekeeper's department.

Hospitals.

	1872.		1873.		1874.		1875 (to day of Inspection).	
	M.	F.	M.	F.	M.	F.	M.	F.
Number of prisoners in hospital,	38	18	46	1	43	13	37	16
Average daily number in hospital,	·7	·5	1·	·1	2·4	·6	1¼	1⅘
Number of prisoners prescribed for and treated out of hospital,	1,429	311	855	162	890	210	687	304
Number of deaths in the gaol, .	1	1	–	–	–	–	1†	–
Cost of medicine, . . .	£12 2s. 9d.		£9 1s. 5d.		£7 11s. 10d.		£6 3s. 1d.	
Cost of diet for prisoners in hospital, . . .	£20 1s. 4d.		£14 15s. 6d.		£9 12s. 6d.		£7 13s. 9d	
Cost of all extra diet ordered by Medical Officer for prisoners not in hospital, . . .	£2 18s. 0d.		£6 10s. 2d.		£1 6s. 11d.		£0 6s. 4d.	

† Execution.

No change has been made in the hospital arrangements since last inspection. Separate hospitals are in each prison. They have water-closets and movable baths, and the accommodation in them is ample. The sanitary condition of the prison is satisfactory. On the day of my visit only 2 prisoners, male and female, were in hospital—the male suffering from a bad leg; yet at that time 203 prisoners were in custody. The Medical Officer gives much time to the careful discharge of his duties in the gaol. I observe in his carefully written up journal the case of a prisoner (C.) who in April, 1875, when discharged from this prison left Cork by train for Bandon, where he fainted at the railway station, and died on his arrival at the workhouse. But the verdict of the Coroner's jury fully acquitted the prison officers. The great mistake in this case was that the man was put bolt upright when sent to the workhouse; he should have been in a horizontal position.

Board of Superintendence.

Lord Viscount Bernard.
Sampson T. W. French, esq.
Daniel Conner, esq.
William R. Meade, esq.
Robert Nettles, esq.
Nicholas Dunscombe, esq.

Thomas J. Leahy, esq.
Richard Longfield, esq.
Daniel F. Leahy, esq.
Abraham J. Forster, esq.
Thomas Garde, esq.
Sir George C. Colthurst, bart.

The Board meets on the last Friday of each month, when a cheque is drawn in favour of the Local Inspector, which includes all small accounts and the salaries of subordinate officers, who are paid weekly. Large accounts are discharged by cheque in favour of each individual creditor.

* I regret that as this report was passing through press, Mr. Joyce, the Governor of prison, was compelled to resign his office of Governor through bad health.

State of Bridewells.

	Bantry.		Clonakilty.		Macroom.	
	M.	F.	M.	F.	M.	F.
No. of committals in past year, . .	40	80	47	14	31	3
Of whom were Drunkards, .	14	1	29	5	6	—
No. of Committals in the Quarter preceding Inspection, .	9	7	22	4	7	2
Of whom were Drunkards, .	1	—	11	3	—	—
Petty Sessions and Transmittals, how often.	Bantry, fortnightly, on Thursdays; Castletown and Carrigbue on alternate Fridays; Blenineen on alternate Tuesdays.		Clonakilty, weekly; Roscarbery and Timolcague, fortnightly.		Fortnightly at Macroom, Millstreet, and Ballyvourney.	
Committals, whether regular.	Regular.		Regular.		Some illegal, not brought before justice who commits.	
Registry, . . .	Correctly kept.		Correctly kept.		Correctly kept.	
Repairs and Order, .	Some repairs required.		In good repair and order.		In very good repair and order; lately painted.	
Security, . . .	Not sufficient.		Sufficient, with care.		No change.	
Accommodation, .	Males — day-room and four cells, including one with a guard bed; females — day-room and two cells.		Males — day-room and four cells; females — day-room and two cells.		Day-room and 4 cells for males; day-room and 2 cells for females.	
Furniture, Bedding, and Utensils.	Good and sufficient.		Good and sufficient.		Good and sufficient.	
Water, how supplied,	A pump of good water outside gate.		None, except water collected from roof.		None, except from roof.	
Sewerage, . .	A sewer flushed by a small river.		Earth-closets put up.		Earth-closets.	
Cleanliness, Dryness, and Ventilation.	Very clean, and well kept.		Clean, and well kept; ventilation sufficient.		Very clean, dry, and ventilation sufficient.	
Cost of Dietary, per head per day.	4½d. and 2½d.		2½d. and 3½d.		5d. and 3d.	
Salary of Keeper, .	£35 a year.		£32 12s.		£31 12s., and £11 8s. contingent allowance.	
Whether Keeper follows any other employment.	Court-keeper.		Court-keeper; salary, £5.		Court-keeper; salary £5.	
Date of Statutable Inspection.	24th May, 1875.		26th May, 1875.		23rd May, 1875	
Remarks, . . .	No prisoner in charge.		No prisoner in custody.		No prisoner in charge.	

SOUTH DISTRICT.

Cork County.

Bridewells.

STATE OF BRIDEWELLS—*continued.*

—	Kanturk.		Fermoy.		Kinsale.	
	M.	F.	M.	F.	M.	F.
No. of Committals in past year, . .	46	4	161	72	37	12
Of whom were Drunkards, .	4	1	55	24	7	7
No. of Committals in the quarter preceding inspection,	4	2	33	15	4	1
Of whom were Drunkards, .	–	1	7	5	–	–
Petty Sessions and Transmittals, how often.	Fortnightly at Kanturk. Cecilstown, and Newmarket; at Knocknagree monthly.		Fortnightly at Fermoy, Conna, and Rathcormack.		Kinsale. weekly, on Saturday ; Ballymartle and Tracton on alternate Fridays.	
Committals, whether regular.	Regular.		Some illegally remanded without being brought before the committing justice.		Regular.	
Registry, . . .	Correctly kept.		Correctly kept.		Correctly kept.	
Repairs and Order, .	In good repair ; woodwork lately painted.		In very good repair; lately painted.		In very good repair.	
Security, . . .	Sufficient, with care.		Sufficient, with care.		Sufficient, with care, but outer wall low.	
Accommodation, .	Males — day-room and four cells, one used as a store ; females — day-room and two cells ; guard beds, with space for two beds on each.		Two large day-rooms, six cells on ground floor, and six cells above ; one used as a store.		Males—day - room and four cells ; females—day-room and three cells.	
Furniture, Bedding, and Utensils.	Good and sufficient.		Sufficient and good.		Sufficient.	
Water, how supplied,	None except rain-water from roof.		Pump in order, but difficult to pump.		None, except from roof.	
Sewerage, . .	Effective to river ; earth-boxes are in use.		Sewerage improved; earth-closets used.		Sufficient ; earth-boxes used.	
Cleanliness, Dryness, and Ventilation.	Ventilation fair ; very clean, orderly, and neatly kept.		Very clean and well kept ; ventilation good.		Clean, dry, and well kept ; ventilation good.	
Cost of Dietary per head per day.	5¼d. for both sexes.		2¼d. for both sexes.		3¼d. for both sexes.	
Salary of Keeper, .	£32 10s.		£37 12s.		£27 12s.	
Whether Keeper follows any other employment.	Court-keeper, salary £5.		None.		None, but has a military pension.	
Date of Statutable Inspection, .	25th July, 1875.		21st May, 1875.		25th May, 1875.	
Remarks, . .	No prisoner in custody.		Two soldiers in charge.		No prisoner in charge.	

STATE OF BRIDEWELLS—*continued.*

—	Charleville.		Mitchelstown.		Skibbereen.	
	M.	F.	M.	F.	M.	F.
No. of Committals in past year, . .	57	5	117	15	72	11
Of whom were Drunkards, .	23	1	32	4	13	–
No. of Committals in the quarter preceding Inspection	6	–	15	2	13	5
Of whom were Drunkards, . .	2	–	7	1	4	–

—	Charleville.	Mitchelstown.	Skibbereen.
Petty Sessions and Transmittals, how often.	Charleville, fortnightly, on Mondays; Liscarroll, on second Wednesday; and Buttevant on second Saturday.	Fortnightly, on Fridays.	Weekly at Skibbereen; fortnightly at Ballydehob, Skull, Union Hall, and Goleen.
Committals, whether regular.	Regular.	Regular.	Committals regular; lunatic in charge of the police.
Registry, . .	Correctly kept.	Correctly kept.	Correctly kept.
Repairs and Order, .	In good repair.	Orderly, and lately whitewashed, but damp, and leakage from roof.	In good repair and order.
Security, . . .	Sufficient, with care.	Building too close to street.	Sufficient.
Accommodation, .	Day-room and two cells for each sex.	Two cells above and two below, one day-room, two small yards.	Males—day-room and four cells, one with guard bed; females—day-room and two cells.
Furniture, Bedding, and Utensils.	Good and sufficient.	Sheets required.	Good and sufficient.
Water, how supplied.	None on premises, except from roof; a pump is in street near, but out of order.	None, except from roof.	A well of good water on premises.
Sewerage, . .	Earth-boxes used, but not emptied sufficiently often.	Earth closets are used.	Earth-closets used.
Cleanliness, Dryness, and Ventilation.	Clean and well kept; ventilation good.	Clean and orderly; ventilation sufficient.	Clean and well kept, but damp.
Cost of Dietary per head per day.	3½d. and 4d.	4d. for both sexes.	4½d.
Salary of Keeper, .	£27 12s.	£36.	£32 12s.
Whether Keeper follows any other employment.	None; has a pension from Constabulary of £36.	None.	Court-keeper, salary £5.
Date of Inspection, .	26th July, 1875.	21st May, 1875.	25th May, 1875.
Remarks, . .	Two males in charge.	Five prisoners in custody — three males and two females—for drunkenness.	No prisoner in custody.

STATE OF BRIDEWELLS—*continued.*

SOUTH DISTRICT.

Cork County.

Bridewells.

	Dunmanway.		Midleton.		Queenstown.	
	M.	**F.**	**M.**	**F.**	**M.**	**F.**
No. of Committals in past year, . .	40	5	31	13	121	24
Of whom were Drunkards, .	12	–	1	3	10	10
No. of Committals in the quarter preceding Inspection,	13	8	11	1	4	–
Of whom were Drunkards, .	3	–	–	–	–	–
Petty Sessions and Transmittals, how often.	Dunmanway, Ballyneen, and Drimoleague, fortnightly.		Fortnightly. Midleton, Thursdays; Castlemartyr, Fridays; Cloyne, Tuesdays.		At Queenstown on Mondays, Wednesdays, and Fridays in each week; at Passage West on Tuesdays.	
Committals, whether regular.	Regular.		Regular.		Regular.	
Registry, . . .	Correctly kept.		Correctly kept.		Correctly kept.	
Repairs and Order, .	In fair repair and order.		In good repair and order.		In good repair.	
Security, ...	Yards insecure.		Sufficient; a double door at entrance to yard of bridewell.		Sufficient with care, but one prisoner escaped in Oct., 1874; he was retaken.	
Accommodation, .	Two cells, one for each sex; the cell for females off bedroom of keeper, that for males off his sitting-room.		Males—day-room and four cells; one of these has a guard bed; females—day-room and two cells.		Males — day-room and three cells, with bedding, a dark cell not used, another which opens from outside with guard bed, but no bedding; a cell used as a store. Females — three cells, one with two beds; day-room, but exercising yard very small.	
Furniture, Bedding, and Utensils.	Sufficient for accommodation.		Sufficient, but some blankets thin; an extra blanket given in cold weather.		Sufficient.	
Water, how supplied,	None on premises.		A well of good water on premises. water collected from the roof.		Supplied from town reservoir.	
Sewerage, . .	None; earth-closets used.		Earth-closets are used.		Effective.	
Cleanliness, Dryness, and Ventilation.	Clean and well kept		Clean and well kept, but damp in winter.		Clean, orderly, and well kept.	
Cost of Dietary, per head per day.	2½d.		3d.		3½d. for both sexes.	
Salary of Keeper, .	£28 12s.		£37 12s.		£30.	
Whether Keeper follows any other employment.	None.		Court-keeper, salary £5; keeps a tailoring establishment.		None.	
Date of Statutable Inspection.	24th May, 1875.		17th Nov., 1875.		21st Nov., 1875.	
Remarks, . . .	One male in charge. One male escaped from this bridewell in August, 1875, a female having previously escaped in October, 1874.		No prisoner in custody.		No prisoner in custody.	

STATE OF BRIDEWELLS—*continued.*

—	Mallow.		Youghal.		Bandon.	
	M.	F.	M.	F.	M.	F.
No. of Committals in past year, . .	40	24	63	11	42	16
Of whom were Drunkards,	20	7	17	4	15	9
No. of Committals in the quarter preceding Inspection,	13	2	6	6	58	11
Of whom were Drunkards, .	–	–	1	3	14	4

—	Mallow.	Youghal.	Bandon.
Petty Sessions and Transmittals, how often.	Mallow weekly, on Thursdays; Doneraile on alternate Mondays; Castletownroche on alternate Thursdays.	Youghal, weekly, on Thursdays.	Bandon, weekly, on Mondays.
Committals, whether regular.	The magistrates remand prisoners without seeing them, which is illegal. Lunatics are sometimes committed to this bridewell.	Regular.	Regular.
Registry, . . .	Correctly kept.	Correctly kept.	Correctly kept.
Repairs and Order, .	In good repair and order.	In good repair and order.	In good repair and order ; lately painted.
Security, . . .	Now sufficient with care; double doors provided.	Sufficient.	Very secure.
Accommodation, .	Males—day-room and four cells ; females—day-room and three cells ; guard beds in cells with two beds in each ; drunkards' cell has no bedding.	Males—day-room and four cells ; females, day-room and two cells.	Males—day-room and four cells; same for females, but one used as a store. No beds in two cells. Gas in entrance hall and keeper's apartments, but not in prison.
Furniture, Bedding, and Utensils.	Sufficient and good.	Good and sufficient.	Sufficient and good.
Water, how supplied,	Tanks of slate with pipes into each yard ; the tank filled by water cart.	Pump useless; water collected from roof of bridewell.	Rain water only from roof; water in pump impregnated with iron.
Sewerage, . .	Earth boxes are used.	None; earth-boxes are used.	None; earth-boxes are used.
Cleanliness, Dryness, and Ventilation.	Ventilation good ; very clean and orderly.	Very clean and orderly ; ventilation good.	Very clean and well kept.
Cost of Dietary, per head per day.	3½d. for both sexes.	2¾d. for both sexes.	3d. for both sexes.
Salary of Keeper,	£35.	£25.	£42 12s.
Whether Keeper follows any other employment.	Is court-keeper, salary £5.	Has charge of the Court-house without salary.	Court-keeper ; salary £5.
Date of Statutable Inspection.	21st May, 1875.	19th Nov., 1875.	22nd May, 1875.
Remarks, . . .	No prisoner in custody.	No prisoner in charge.	No prisoner in custody.

JOHN LENTAIGNE, *Inspector-General.*

CORK CITY GAOL, AT CORK.—STATUTABLE INSPECTION, 18TH AND 20TH NOVEMBER, 1875.

Number of Prisoners of all classes in Gaol on the day of Inspection, and on the corresponding date in the three preceding years.

	M.	F.		M.	F.
1872,	77	89	1874,	83	66
1873,	49	58	1875 (day of Inspection),	68	80

Number of Returned Convicts in Gaol on day of Inspection, and during each of the three preceding years.

	M.	F.		M.	F.
1872,	1	2	1875 (up to and including		
1873,	3	2	day of Inspection),	4	4
1874,	4	8	Day of Inspection,	-	2

Number of Prisoners in Custody during the year known to have been in Reformatories.

	M.	F.		M.	F.
1872,	4	1	1875 (up to and including		
1873,	6	1	day of Inspection),	2	2
1874,	4	2	Day of Inspection,	-	1

Juveniles.

Three young offenders (males) under sixteen years of age were in custody at the time of my visit; 1, although only fifteen years of age, had two previous convictions recorded against him—he had been sentenced at quarter sessions for larceny to an imprisonment with hard labour for four months in this associated prison, in which, from its overcrowded state, many prisoners sleep 3 in one cell. He was also sentenced to receive twelve strokes of a birch rod at the end of the third month of his imprisonment; but the sentence will scarcely arrest the career of crime into which this young thief, who already belongs to the criminal class, has plunged. His mother is, I am informed, an old offender; and in association with other criminals for four months, he probably will leave the prison thoroughly corrupt; and when next in custody, having passed the age for being birched, the twelve strokes which he will now receive cannot act as a deterrent.

Another boy in custody at the time of my visit, likewise fifteen years of age, was under a sentence to be sent to a reformatory for absconding from the Greenmount Industrial School.

The third boy (aged thirteen years) was on remand for larceny.

Thirty-eight males and 9 females under sixteen years of age were committed to this prison in 1875; 2 of the latter were under twelve years; 1 of the females and 6 males were sentenced to reformatories. Four males and 2 females were twice committed during the year.

It was with regret I found in this gaol a young girl (C. L.) sixteen years of age, who had been discharged from the reformatory at Limerick by order of the Chief Secretary on memorial. She is now under sentence of four months' imprisonment for obtaining money under false pretences. Her sentence is that she is to spend three days in each month in solitary, but she is permitted to associate with the other rogues, her companions in the gaol, during the remaining period of her imprisonment. Cases such as this are not of unfrequent occurrence. A child neglected by her parents falls into crime, and is sent by the court, before whom she has been judged, to a reformatory ; but the parent when sued to contribute towards her maintenance in the institution, finding his means of enjoyment in the public-house curtailed, obtains the signature of magistrates, clergymen, and others, to a memorial for her discharge, which, when granted on the faith of the respectable names attached to the memorial, the young person returns to a life of crime.

SOUTH DISTRICT.

Cork City Gaol.

Commitments.

	From 1st January to 31st Dec., 1874.		From 1st Jan , 1875, to day of Inspection.	
	M.	F.	M.	F.
Debtors,	1	1	3	–
Criminals,	744	723	653	528
Vagrants,	22	22	10	8
Drunkards,	608	825	665	702
Total,	1,375	1,571	1,331	1,238

Averages, and Highest and Lowest Numbers (exclusive of Debtors).

—	From 1st January to 31st December, 1874.			From 1st January, 1875, to day of Inspection.		
	M.	F.	Date.	M.	F.	Date.
Average daily number of prisoners in custody,	79	63	—	89	62	—
Highest number of prisoners at any one time,	197		25th Sept.	213		20th Aug.
Lowest ditto.	112		10th Jan.	119		11th Jan.
Highest number of males at any one time,	112		23rd Sept.	123		20th Aug.
Ditto, of females,	90		2nd Sept.	95		25th Aug.
Lowest number of males at any one time,	63		4th April.	65		19th Nov.
Ditto, of females,	39		19th Jan.	35		11th Jan.

Individual Prisoners (exclusive of Debtors) and Number of Times each had been committed.

NUMBER OF TIMES COMMITTED.	1874.				1875, to day of Inspection.			
	Juveniles.		Adults.		Juveniles.		Adults.	
	M.	F.	M.	F.	M.	F.	M.	F.
Once within the year,	61	19	827	513	29	9	743	426
Twice "	4	2	112	106	3	–	129	95
Thrice "	–	–	41	50	1	–	43	31
4 times "	–	–	15	32	–	–	16	26
5 " "	–	–	7	16	–	–	8	25
6 " "	–	–	–	11	–	–	2	15
7 " "	–	–	1	9	–	–	4	9
8 " "	–	–	2	9	–	–	2	8
9 " "	–	–	–	9	–	–	–	2
10 to 11 times "	–	–	1	16	–	–	–	5
Total,	65	21	1006	771	33	9	947	642
No. of above who had not been in Gaol previous to 1st January in	57	19	553	346	27	8	478	263

SOUTH
DISTRICT.

Cork City
Gaol.

Individual Prisoners (exclusive of Debtors) committed in 1874, and to Inspection in 1875, who had been Once and oftener recommitted from their first Commitment in any year, so far as can be ascertained.

NUMBER OF TIMES COMMITTED.	1874.				1875, to day of Inspection.			
	Juveniles.		Adults.		Juveniles.		Adults.	
	M.	F.	M.	F.	M.	F.	M.	F.
Once only, .	57	19	497	292	24	8	427	227
Twice, .	8	2	188	119	7	1	195	109
Thrice, .	–	–	106	84	1	–	101	49
4 times, .	–	–	68	50	1	–	50	30
5 ,, .	–	–	49	39	–	–	34	26
6 ,, .	–	–	26	24	–	–	33	28
7 to 11 ,, .	–	–	37	61	–	–	63	59
12 to 16 ,, .	–	–	22	25	–	–	25	20
17 to 20 ,, .	–	–	5	12	–	–	7	21
21 to 30 ,, .	–	–	5	21	–	–	9	21
31 to 40 ,, .	–	–	2	13	–	–	3	16
41 to 50 ,, .	–	–	–	13	–	–	–	14
51 to 60 ,, .	–	–	1	8	–	–	–	7
61 to 70 ,, .	–	–	–	2	–	–	–	3
71 to 80 ,, .	–	–	–	3	–	–	–	6
81 to 90 ,, .	–	–	–	2	–	–	–	2
91 to 100 ,, .	–	–	–	1	–	–	–	1
101 to 120 ,, .	–	–	–	2	–	–	–	2
121 to 140 ,, .	–	–	–	–	–	–	–	1
Total No. of Individuals committed,	65	21	1006	771	33	9	947	642
No. of Commitments represented in foregoing, .	73	23	2801	5251	45	10	3019	5514

Highest Number of Prisoners (exclusive of Debtors) in Gaol during each of the previous seven years, and up to day of Inspection in 1875.

22nd September, 1868,	. 145	30th April, 1872,	. 164
5th November, 1869, .	. 138	1st August, 1873,	. 182
23rd September, 1870, .	. 202	25th September, 1874, .	. 197
29th March, 1871, .	. 160	20th August, 1875, .	. 213

Number of Prisoners sentenced to Solitary Confinement and Whipping, by order of Court.

	From 1st January to 31st December, 1874.		From 1st January, 1875, to day of Inspection.	
	M.	F.	M.	F.
Solitary Confinement, .	5	7	5	4
Young offenders to be Whipped, .	–	–	2	–

Inspection.

I found when I made my inspection 68 males and 80 females for trial, or under sentences of imprisonment, in this gaol, which contains but thirty-eight separate cells for males, and fifty-six for females. Associated together the prisoners mutually contaminate each other, and, as may be expected, they are constantly recurrent to the prison, the women especially, for the most part utterly depraved. One woman, committed during 1875, has between 120 and 140 convictions recorded against her on the prison books; others have upwards of 100, and 36 have more than 40.

Commitments.

Nine hundred and eighty individual males, and 651 females were committed during 1875. They have been—including previous recommittals—the males 3,064, the females 5,524 times inmates of this prison.

At present one wing of the male prison is being remodelled, but the entire structure should be altered to render the building adequate for the requirements of the jurisdiction.

The males were—5 for trial or on remand, 61 convicted, and 2 deserters waiting for escort; 2 military offenders were under sentences of 336 and 168 days respectively; 19 had been sentenced by civil tribunals for larceny, embezzlement, or robbery; 2 for malicious injuries; and 33 for drunkenness, disorderly conduct, or attempt to violate. One man had been convicted of bigamy; 6 others of various offences, including fraudulent enlistment and being absent from militia training. One juvenile in custody had absconded from an industrial school.

Nineteen females had been convicted of larceny, or obtaining goods under false pretences; 2 of assaults and robbery. Others, who numbered 56, were under sentences for drunkenness, disorderly conduct, and assaults. A large number of young women of this class, who never have had the slightest training, are constantly inmates of this gaol. They have evidently been totally neglected through life; and many are subject to fits, showing defective nurture during the first years of their existence.

The sentences on the convicted prisoners in charge on the day of my visit were—the males—1 sentenced for eighteen, and 2 for twelve months, 1 for eight, and 13 for six months, 9 had been sentenced for terms of four and five months respectively, 12 for two and three months; the remainder for short periods. The sentences on the female prisoners in custody were— 2 to be imprisoned for twelve, and 1 for eight months, 10 for six, and 11 for three and four months; 10 had been sentenced for two, and the remainder for short periods not exceeding one month. With only four or five exceptions, all the female prisoners in the gaol when I visited had previous convictions. One had been 126 times a prisoner here; another, only thirty years of age, 109 times; and others from 50 to 93 times.

The 80 females in the prison on my inspection had 1,390 convictions recorded on the books of this prison. Bred to no industry by which they could earn a livelihood, they have not means to support life except by prostitution: they will not remain in the workhouse, and this associated prison is not deterrent for them. To introduce a proper system of industrial training for the children of the poor Industrial Schools were established, and the large sum subscribed by the city of Cork for their erection shows how much the advantages of such institutions are appreciated by the people of Cork.

Accommodation.

	M.	P.		M.	F.
Wards, . . .	–	3	Workshops, . .	3	1
Yards, . . .	4	4	Worksheds, . .	1	2
Solitary Cells (separate), .	–	8	Kitchen, . .	1	–
Single Cells, 9 feet long, 6 feet wide, and 8 feet high, or which contain 432 cubic feet, heated and furnished, . .	26	48	Store Room, . .	2	2
			Laundry, . .	–	1
			Drying Room, . .	–	1
Ditto, heated and furnished with bells, . . all above			Lavatories, . .	6	9
			Baths, with hot and cold water laid on, . .	2	2
Single cells of smaller size, heated and furnished with bells, .	2	–	Privies, . .	2	2
Cells to contain three persons, heated and furnished, .	10	–	Watercloseets, . .	7	10
Sleeping Rooms, . .	9	1	Fumigating apparatus, .	2	1
No. of Beds in such Rooms, .	32	3	Reception Rooms or Cells,	1	6
Hospital Rooms, . .	3	3	Crank Pump, . .	1	–
Chapels, . .	1	1	Well, . .	1	–
			Tread-wheel, . .	1	–
			Tell-tale Clocks, . .	2	–

When I visited the prison in November, 1875, the new wing had just been completed, with the exception of the heating apparatus, which was then being set by the contractor. So soon, therefore, as the walls are sufficiently dry for habitation, the cells will be certified by the Inspectors-

General, under the Acts 3 and 4 Vic., cap. 44, as the bells and appliances required under that statute are in order and sufficient. The prison will then have forty-eight new cells, well suited for an improved prison system. It is most desirable that another wing of the prison should be altered on the same model, and the other suggestions of the Inspectors-General carried out, by which arrangement ninety-six cells, well suited for an improved prison system, would be provided to meet the requirements of the district.

The new cells have various improvements, recently introduced into prison construction, including the lighting of the cells by gas in a chamber separated from the cell by glass.

One great defect in this prison is the want of a suitable chapel or chapels, to meet the requirements of the 17th section of the Prisons Act, which directs that —"One or more chapel or chapels shall be provided in every prison, in such a convenient situation as to be easy of access to all the prisoners." The Act further directs that—"It shall be fitted up with separate divisions for males and females, and also for the different classes, and shall be strictly set apart for religious worship, or for the occasional religious and moral instruction of the prisoners, and shall never be appropriated to, or employed for, any other purpose whatsoever." Divine service is at present held in the common hall of the prison; but now that the hall has been opened out in the recent alterations it is even more unsuited for the purpose than hitherto. My colleague in his report for 1874 called attention to the fact that the chapel is used for prisoners to pick oakum, and for other purposes, contrary to the provisions of the statute, and is a mere passage-room, without separation; now it has been thrown completely open by the removal of walls, and has become from drafts in every direction, dangerous to health.

I regret that in consequence of the thickness of the walls in the new prison it has been found necessary to place a jet of gas to light each cell. It was intended that two cells should be lighted by each jet, thereby causing a saving in the consumption of gas. This arrangement has been carried out in the Tralee prison with success; and should another wing be altered it will be of importance that the construction have the improvement suggested.

No change has been made in the old wings of the prison since last inspection. The heating apparatus in them, especially in the female prison, is very defective. The stone troughs at the end of each corridor, used as lavatories, are faulty, and the closets offensive; but should at any time the entire prison be remodelled on the plan of the block now completed, the prison could be made well suited for the purposes of separation of prisoners. I am informed that the alteration of each wing would cost about £3,800.

The prison is well situated for health on a rising ground over the river, the only defect being that it is far from the centre of the city, and that the cartage of stones and other materials for the employment of male prisoners is, in consequence of the hill, expensive; but should at any future period the two prison jurisdictions in Cork be amalgamated (as can be done under the Prisons Act) this would make an excellent prison for females when altered, and the present Cork County Gaol might be used for males only.

Since last inspection some yard walls have lately been removed, and the yards have been levelled, drained, and otherwise improved by prison labour. Earth closets have been put to some of the privies on the male side, and a water-closet (Macfarlane's Patent) fixed in the female prison.

I found, on my visit to this prison on the 20th November, the male prisoners picking oakum in one of the day-rooms of the prison without a

Marginal notes:
SOUTH DISTRICT.
Cork City Gaol.
Cells.
Defects.

fire, and they complained to me of the cold. On a former inspection of this prison in 1873 a like complaint was made to me, and I now desire to call the attention of the Board to the 7th rule of the 109th section of the 7 George IV., cap. 74, which requires that—"A fire shall be lighted in the day-rooms of the prison for ten hours in each day, from the first day of October to the first day of April in every year." I trust, therefore, that in future the prescriptions of this section of the statute will be strictly carried out.

SOUTH DISTRICT.

Cork City Gaol.

Stock at the time of Inspection.

	In Use.	In Store.	Male Clothing.	In Use.	In Store.	Female Clothing.	In Use.	In Store.
Blankets, pairs of . . .	227	31	Shirts, . . .	133	–	Shifts, . . .	159	6
Sheets, pairs of,	232	5	Jackets, . .	78	54	Jackets, . .	163	–
Rugs, . .	212	87	Vests, . .	73	14	Petticoats, .	131	–
Hammocks or Cots, . .	112	56	Trowsers, . .	71	8	Aprons, . .	162	–
			Caps, . .	76	63	Neckerchiefs, .	102	–
Bed-ticks, . .	187	50	Stockings, or Socks, pairs of,	47	31	Caps, . .	124	–
Bedsteads, . .	8	–	Shoes, Slippers, & Clogs, pairs of,	100	4	Stockings, pairs of, . .	60	–
						Shoes, Slippers & Clogs, pairs of,	60	–

I found the cells of the general prison very clean and orderly, the bedding of a good description; but the majority of the prisoners, including all the females, were still wearing clogs with canvass uppers. These clogs are not economical, and are dangerous. They destroy the stockings which the prisoners wear, and I have known prisoners in other gaols to have had their ankles dislocated from their use. The Board has directed that shoes of leather be now substituted for the clogs, and many of the male prisoners have them, but they should likewise be supplied to the females with as little delay as possible. The general clothing of the prisoners has been improved in other respects, and the females are given stockings, caps, aprons, and neckerchiefs.

The prison stores were, when I visited, tidy and in good order, and proper checks have been established by the Governor and Local Inspector in the issue of the articles from the general store of the prison. The private clothes of prisoners are now cleansed and disinfected on admission, and are properly put up in store. The bedding is abundant and clean. Store.

Gas has been introduced into the officers' quarters, the halls, the hospital, the guard-room, and at the entrance-gate. The cells of the new wing will be likewise lighted by it.

Unlock is held at 6 A.M. in summer and at 7 in winter. The prison is locked for the night at 6 during all seasons of the year. The night-watch comes on duty at 9 P.M., and the prison is patrolled by two warders alternately during the night. Dent's Recording Watch is in use in this prison. Three dials are placed—one in the hall of the male prison, one in the circular walk near the hospital, and the third in the marshalsea, where, during the alterations, a number of prisoners are placed.

The sewerage of the prison has been improved during the year, but still, occasionally, the smell from the sewers is offensive. Sewerage.

Habitual criminals are photographed in this prison by one of the staff, for which he receives 6d. for each copy, and all chemicals are provided by the Board.

Thirty-seven cells for males and sixty-two for females are in use in this prison; they are heated and have bells.

In the new prison forty-eight cells have been fitted up, artificially heated and lighted, and have every requirement for separation.

SOUTH
DISTRICT.

*Cork City
Gaol.*

During the alterations the marshalsea has been occupied by criminal prisoners.

No change has been made in the kitchen arrangements, but in the plan of the new buildings it is proposed to fit up a kitchen in the female prison.

The laundry, the reception wards, and other parts of the prison, are as on last inspection by my colleague in September, 1874.

Visitors to prisoners see their friends as formerly at the prison gate.

Number of Punishments for Prison Offences.

	From 1st January to 31st December, 1874.		From 1st January, 1875, to day of Inspection.	
	M.	F.	M.	F.
By Magisterial authority, . .	—	1	1	—
By Governor—				
Dark or Refractory Cells, .	468	215	389	152
Stoppage of Diet, . . .	—	—	63	36
Total, . . .	468	215	452	188

Punish-
ments.

The large number of punishments in this prison is, I am informed, due to the facility with which prisoners can obtain prohibited articles from their friends, principally pipes and tobacco. It has for many years been found that prohibited articles are frequently thrown into the prison over the boundary wall from a field at the back of the gaol, where the ground rises to within a few feet of the top of the boundary wall. I find, in the journal of the Local Inspector, it stated that tobacco and money have been found at that place inside the boundary wall, where they have been thrown over. In former reports the Inspectors-General have called attention to the subject, and have suggested that arrangements be made to have the field at once properly fenced in, so that this cause of breach of prison discipline and punishment should cease. I trust, therefore, the Board will now take the necessary steps for the removal of this cause of breaches of discipline.

Four of the ordinary cells which can be darkened, are used as punishment cells in the prison.

School.

School.

No scholastic teaching is provided in this prison, but Sisters of Mercy attend to give religious and moral instruction to the females of their own faith, and to Roman Catholic patients of both sexes in hospital. I am informed that a Protestant lady visitor gives instruction to those of her own religious persuasion when in custody.

Employment on day of Inspection.

	M.	F.
Tread-wheel and levelling yard, . . .	32	—
Carpenter, ...	1	—
Weaving, winding, brush and mat making, .	7	—
Tailoring and shoemaking, . . .	4	—
Sick and unemployed, ...	4	—
Picking oakum, ...	13	—
Picking wool, ...	—	45
Knitting and sewing, ...	—	14
Cleaning prison, ...	6	12
Washing, ...	—	6
Discharged (before labour hours), . .	1	3
Total in custody, . .	68	80

Amount received for produce of Prisoners' Labour disposed of outside the Gaol.

1872, . £49 5s. 9d. | 1873, . £56 19s. 3d. | 1874, . £222 2s. 6d.

Profits.

The very great increase in the amount of profits realized from the labour of prisoners during the past year shows the result of the endeavours of the present superior officers of the prison to render the labour of the inmates of the gaol as profitable as possible.

Prisoners sentenced to hard labour work on the tread-wheel and at stone breaking. They are so employed for three hours in winter and four in summer, working half the time stated on the tread-wheel. Industrial labour is enforced for seven hours in winter and eight in summer. Carpentry, weaving, mat-making, tailoring, and recently shoemaking, have been carried on in the prison. Inmates of both sexes are for the most part employed picking oakum. All the materials for the clothing of the prisoners are manufactured and made up in the gaol.

Dietary and Contracts.

Bread, white 4lb loaf, 5¼d.; ditto, brown, per 12lb loaf, 1s. 2½d.; oatmeal, per cwt., 16s.; Indian meal, per cwt., 9s. 6d.; potatoes, per cwt., 4s.; new milk, per gallon, 1s.; salt, per cwt., 2s. 10d.; coal per ton, £1 2s. 3d.; straw, per cwt.,—no contract; gas, per 1,000 cubic feet, 5s. 3d.; candles, per   (mould), 5s. 9d.; do. (dipt), 5s. 4½d.; soap, per cwt., £1 7s.; horsing prison van, per trip, 3s. 9d.

Net average daily cost of Ordinary Diet for each Prisoner.

1872, . . 4¼d. | 1873, . . 4½d. | 1874, . . 4d.

The food served to prisoners on the day of my visit, which I tasted, was of a fair description, but well-founded complaints have from time to time been made of the provisions supplied by contractors. I learn, however, that in all such cases care has been taken by the prison officials that the default be remedied; and the milk contractor has been fined, and milk purchased by him instead. The bread, potatoes, and stirabout have likewise, on some occasions, been faulty, and when I visited a few of the female prisoners complained to me of the stirabout; but on that occasion, as far as I could learn, they had not reason. When potatoes are bad, bread is substituted.

Officers and Salaries.

Non-resident.	£	s.	d.		£	s.	d.
Patrick Kennedy, Local Inspector, . . .	100	0	0	John Radford, Warder and Storekeeper, . .	46	16	0
Rev. Wm. C. Neligan, Protestant Chaplain, .	46	3	0	John Barry, Weaver, Warder of Works, . .	46	16	0
Rev. John Fahy, Roman Catholic Chaplain, .	46	3	0	David Lyons, Warder at Gate,	46	16	0
Wm. Beamish, M.D., Surgeon,	55	0	0	Daniel M'Cormick, Warder,	41	12	0
Henry M. Jones, M.D., Apothecary, . . .	10	0	0	Thomas Connolly, do.,	41	12	0
James N. O'Brien, Assistant Clerk, . . .	52	0	0	John Enright, do., .	41	12	0
				Edward Mulcahy, do., .	41	12	0
Resident.				Thomas Havonhill, do., & Shoemaker,	41	12	0
Wm. Minhear, Governor, .	250	0	0	Denis Sheahan, do., .	41	12	0
Wm. Plant, Chief Warder and Clerk, . .	80	0	0	Thomas Mahony, do., .	41	12	0
				A. M. Cosgrave, Matron, .	52	0	0
				Sarah E. Kemp, Assist. do., .	28	12	0
				Mary Stanley, do., .	28	12	0
				Sarah O'Brien, do., .	31	4	0
				Elizabeth Radford, do., Nurse,	27	6	0

Vacancies on Staff since last Inspection, how caused, and how filled up.

One Assistant Matron dismissed; one Warder superannuated; three Warders resigned. The vacancies filled by new appointments.

No officer on gaol allowance.

Visits paid by Officers.

	From 1st January to 31st December, 1874.	From 1st January, 1875, to day of Inspection.
Number of times the Board of Superintendence met and discharged business,	30	14
Local Inspector to Gaol, . .	134	121
Chaplain, Protestant Episcopal Church,	156	141
Roman Catholic Chaplain, . .	171	155
Physician and Surgeon, . .	365	326
Apothecary, ...	116	149

SOUTH
DISTRICT.

Cork City
Gaol.

I have reason to be satisfied with the attention of the superior officers —the Local Inspector, Governor, and Medical Officer; but I observe by the journals of the Local Inspector and Governor that some of the subordinate staff have on several occasions been negligent in the discharge of their duties.

Hospitals.

	1872.		1873.		1874.		1875 (to day of Inspection).	
	M.	F.	M.	F.	M.	F.	M.	F.
No. of prisoners in hospital, . . .	51	57	24	44	21	76	–	–
Average daily number in hospital, . . .	2	·6	·6	·6	1	2	–	–
Number of prisoners prescribed for and treated out of hospital,	716	557	617	549	480	760	–	–
No. of deaths in the gaol,	–	–	2	1	1	–	1	–
Cost of medicine,	£23 17s. 2d.		£17 4s. 4d.		£17 10s. 4d.		—	
Cost of diet for prisoners in hospital,	£30 2s. 10d.		£20 6s. 4d.		£29 19s. 5d.		—	
Cost of all extra diet ordered by Medical Officer for prisoners not in hospital, .	£2 6s. 7d.		—		£3 10s. 2d.		—	

Hospital.

No alteration has been made in the hospital arrangements since last inspection. The hospitals for both sexes are in the same building. The wards are spacious and well ventilated, with separate yards for each sex for exercise. Water-closets are off the lower wards. A bath, with hot and cold water laid on, is placed between the wards, and a slipper bath is in the hospital for females.

In April, 1875, a military prisoner died in hospital of fever and inflammation of the lungs; and I learn from the report of the Local Inspector that since my visit a prisoner in a dying state was committed, and died soon after.

Books and Accounts.

Net cost of Gaol, including Diet and Salaries.

1872, . £3,302 16s. 10d. | 1873, . £3,382 17s. 10d. | 1874, . £3,260 8s. 1d.

Total cost of Officers, including Clothing, Value of Rations, Washing, Gas, &c.

1872, . £1,519 12s. 0d. | 1873, . £1,564 3s. 6d. | 1874, . £1,521 18s. 0d.

Average cost of each Prisoner per annum.

1872, . £21 3s. 5d. | 1873, . £23 19s. 10d. | 1874, . £22 16s. 0d.

Amounts repaid by the War Department for Military Prisoners.

1872, . £59 2s. 3d. | 1873, . £22 12s. 0d. | 1874, . £52 18s. 0d.

Amounts Repaid from the Consolidated Fund for the Maintenance, &c., of Prisoners.

1872, . £400 14s. 8d. | 1873, . £318 4s. 8d. | 1874, . £334 10s. 7d.

Books.

The various records of discipline and finance in this prison are kept with much precision by the Deputy Governor—the prescribed forms are in use—and are carefully checked by the Governor, who marks them with his initials. The Local Inspector also occasionally checks the books. The Governor enters in the Morning State the markings on the dials of the detection watch during the night. The very full reports in the journals of the Local Inspector and Governor show the great attention

which both officers bestow in the discharge of their duties in the prison. SOUTH DISTRICT.
The Medical Officer also notes in his journal the various matters which
come within the sphere of his duties, and all his books are well kept. Cork City Gaol.
The Chaplains state the duties they discharge.

Board of Superintendence.

J. Daly, esq., J.P. Alderman	John Waters, esq., J.P.	D. Finn, esq., Alderman.
John W. Clery, esq., J.P.	Henry Unkles, esq., J.P.	W. Hogarty, esq., Alderman.
William H. Lyons, esq., J.P.	C. Keller, esq., Alderman.	Isaac Julian, esq.
Robert Scott, esq., J.P.	T. Burrowes, esq. Alderman.	Jos. E. Tracey, esq., T.C.

The Board meets for the discharge of business on the last Monday of *Board.*
each month, when the salaries of the intern officers and other liabilities
are paid by cheque to Local Inspector, vouchers being produced by him
at the next meeting of the Board. The turnkeys are paid weekly, the
superior officers monthly.

JOHN LENTAIGNE, *Inspector-General.*

DUBLIN COUNTY GAOL, AT KILMAINHAM.—STATUTABLE INSPECTION, *Dublin County Gaol.*
10TH AND 28TH DECEMBER, 1875.

---

*Number of Prisoners of all Classes in Gaol on the day of Inspection, and
on the corresponding date in the three preceding years.*

	M.	F.		M.	F.
1872,	51	15	1874,	74	22
1873,	96	32	1875 (day of Inspection),	42	24

*Number of Returned Convicts in Gaol on the day of Inspection, and during
each of the three preceding years.*

	M.	F.		M.	F.
1872,	7	1	1875 (up to and including		
1873,	5	6	day of Inspection),	1	5
1874,	2	4	Day of Inspection,	—	2

Juveniles.

No young offender was in custody at the time of my inspection of this *Juveniles.*
prison; but 39 males and 4 females, whose ages did not exceed sixteen
years had previously been in custody. Of these, 13 (males) were under
twelve years of age. One (male) was twice committed during the year.
Eleven (males, 3 under twelve years of age) were sent to reformatories
during the year after the period of their gaol punishment.

Ten prisoners (9 males and 1 female), of ages varying from eighteen
to thirty, who had previously been in reformatories, were committed to
this prison in 1875. One (male) was acquitted; 1 was seven times committed, 1 four times, and 1 twice during the year. One was sentenced to
seven years' penal servitude; 1 to an imprisonment of three months;
4 for one month; the others for short periods. One was in custody when
I made my inspection.

Two lads in the prison when I inspected, were under sentences of imprisonment with hard labour, 1 for one, the other for two months. They
were registered in the prison books as being each seventeen years of

SOUTH
DISTRICT.

Dublin
County
Gaol.

age—beyond the age when they might be legally sent to a reformatory; but they did not appear to be so old. One especially was apparently not more than fourteen years old. He was under sentence for stealing lead, and had several previous convictions recorded against him. It is to be regretted that the convicting Justice did not exercise the discretion which the Reformatory Schools Act gives, and sentence him to a reformatory, as " being apparently under sixteen years of age."

Debtors.

Debtors.

One male and 3 female debtors were inmates of this prison at the time of my visit. They had been transferred from the Four Courts Marshalsea on the abolition of that prison. The male prisoner and 1 of the females have since been discharged, through the instrumentality of the fund left for the discharge of pauper debtors, by Messrs. Higgins and Powell. A scheme has been laid before the Law Adviser of the Crown, drawn up by the Commissioners of Charitable Bequests, to render this fund more useful under the altered state of the law as regards debtors.

Two of the female pauper debtors in custody when I visited made various complaints to me against the Local Inspector and Matron of the gaol, which complaints I inquired into, and ascertained that they were quite unfounded. These women were for many years inmates of the Four Courts Marshalsea, now abolished, and since their transfer to this prison they have given much trouble by lodging complaints against the superior officers of the prison in order to obtain privileges which the rules do not permit. Broken down in constitution they are ordered by the medical officer, meat, tea, and other diet not generally given to pauper prisoners; hence they prefer to remain in the prison living at the cost of the rates, rather than take their discharge. As the law at present stands there is no means to compel their discharge, and they may continue a burden on the prison funds, until imprisonment for debt shall cease.

Tramps.

Tramps.

Forty-five tramps were committed to this gaol as vagrants in 1875. The Governor reports that the greater number of these had evidently been soldiers, and I find on my inspections throughout the country many such in custody; discharged after short service, without pension, and ignorant of a trade as well as of agricultural work, they wander about the country, and are committed to gaol for being drunk and disorderly, or else for seeking admission into the workhouse, or for larceny. Seven of this class of military prisoners were inmates of this gaol on the day of my visit; 3 committed for larceny, 3 for being drunk and disorderly and for assaults, amongst them was one who had been transferred, for destroying prison property, from Trim gaol, where his conduct was very outrageous; it is, however, remarkable that since his transfer to this prison he has been most orderly and industrious, showing the good results of a well managed separate prison, even when the offender is most violent.

Commitments.

CLASSES.				1874.		1875, to day of Inspection.	
				M.	F.	M.	F.
Debtors,	.	.	.	4	–	20	1
Criminals,	.	.	.	719	230	661	261
Vagrants, .	.	.	.	3	6	19	11
Drunkards,	.	.	.	370	273	328	276
Total,	.	.	.	1,096	509	1,028	549

Individual Prisoners (exclusive of Debtors) and Number of Times each had been committed during 1874 and 1875.

SOUTH DISTRICT.

Dublin County Gaol.

NUMBER OF TIMES COMMITTED.	1874.				1875, to day of Inspection.			
	Juveniles.		Adults.		Juveniles.		Adults.	
	M.	F.	M.	F.	M.	F.	M.	F.
Once within the year,	52	6	683	211	38	4	652	213
Twice ,,	6	—	81	32	1	—	77	46
Thrice ,,	—	—	30	14	—	—	16	18
4 times ,,	—	—	10	5	—	—	11	6
5 ,, ,,	—	—	4	3	—	—	5	6
6 ,, ,,	—	—	3	4	—	—	3	3
7 ,, ,,	—	—	1	3	—	—	3	2
8 ,, ,,	—	—	1	2	—	—	2	1
10 ,, ,,	—	—	—	1	—	—	—	3
11 ,, ,,	—	—	—	—	—	—	—	1
12 ,, ,,	—	—	—	3	—	—	—	2
13 ,, ,,	—	—	—	2	—	—	—	2
18 ,, ,,	—	—	—	1	—	—	—	—
Total,	58	6	813	281	39	4	767	305
No. of above who had not been in Gaol previous to 1st January in	56	6	613	162	34	4	588	184

Individual Prisoners (exclusive of Debtors) committed in the year 1874, and to the day of Inspection in 1875, who had been Once and oftener in Custody, from their first Commitment in any year, so far as can be ascertained.

NUMBER OF TIMES COMMITTED.	1874.				1875, to day of Inspection.			
	Juveniles.		Adults.		Juveniles.		Adults.	
	M.	F.	M.	F.	M.	F.	M.	F.
Once only,	49	6	560	171	36	4	532	167
Twice,	7	—	100	91	2	—	65	42
Thrice,	1	—	55	10	1	—	40	21
4 times,	1	—	25	9	—	—	25	11
5 ,,	—	—	15	4	—	—	27	11
6 ,,	—	—	13	6	—	—	10	3
7 to 11 ,,	—	—	24	12	—	—	21	16
12 to 16 ,,	—	—	10	10	—	—	12	7
17 to 20 ,,	—	—	4	1	—	—	5	1
21 to 30 ,,	—	—	3	7	—	—	6	4
31 to 40 ,,	—	—	4	5	—	—	4	5
41 to 50 ,,	—	—	—	2	—	—	—	2
51 to 60 ,,	—	—	—	2	—	—	—	5
61 to 80 ,,	—	—	—	3	—	—	—	1
91 to 100 ,,	—	—	—	1	—	—	—	—
101 to 120 ,,	—	—	—	2	—	—	—	3
121 to 140 ,,	—	—	—	3	—	—	—	—
141 to 160 ,,	—	—	—	—	—	—	—	2
161 to 180 ,,	—	—	—	2	—	—	—	1
181 to 200 ,,	—	—	—	—	—	—	—	1
Total No. of Individuals committed,	58	6	813	281	39	4	767	303
No. of Commitments represented in foregoing,	70	6	1,811	2,370	43	4	1,846	2,402

SOUTH
DISTRICT.

Averages, and Highest and Lowest Numbers (exclusive of Debtors).

Dublin
County
Gaol.

—	From 1st January to 31st December, 1874.			From 1st January, 1875, to day of Inspection.		
	M.	F.	Date	M.	F.	Date.
Average daily number of prisoners in custody,	83	22	—	72	25	—
Highest number of prisoners at any one time,	143		4th Aug.	130		19th May.
Lowest ditto,	64		20th Feb.	51		27th Dec.
Highest number of males at any one time, .	115		4th Aug.	102		19th May.
Ditto of females,	36		28th Aug.	36		16th Sept.
Lowest number of males at any one time, .	53		2nd Mar.	32		27th Dec.
Ditto of females,	11		23rd Mar.	15		14th Jan.

Highest Number of Prisoners (exclusive of Debtors) in Gaol during each of the previous seven years, and up to the day of Inspection in 1875.

20th June, 1868,	.	.	.	93	19th September, 1872,	.	.	.	101
20th July, 1869,	.	.	.	114	1st August, 1873,	.	.	.	146
6th August, 1870,	.	.	.	140	4th August, 1874,	.	.	.	143
29th July, 1871,	.	.	.	95	19th May, 1875,	.	.	.	130

Inspection.

When I made my inspection of this gaol, on the 10th December, 41 males and 24 females of all classes were in charge, including the 4 debtors already mentioned, transferred from the Four Courts Marshalsea, and also 2 grave offenders (males) transferred from the Meath Gaol, at Trim.

One woman under sentence of penal servitude was waiting for removal to the convict depot, at Mountjoy, and 1 male and 1 female were on remand for larceny.

One of the male prisoners under sentence appeared to me quite idiotic, incapable of understanding right from wrong, and most unfit for penal treatment in a gaol. I found him crouched in a corner of his cell, and when I spoke to him he would not answer. The stench from his person was most sickening, and it is impossible to keep his cell clean. He destroys the bedding and clothes given to him, and the prison officers report that he constantly howls like a wild beast. The man had been sentenced to an imprisonment with hard labour for two months, for stealing an iron pot, but he is incapable of labour of any description, and merely remains in his cell attended by an officer to keep it clean. I am informed that he is a frequent inmate of the Loughlinstown Union Workhouse, and it is to be regretted that he cannot be compelled to remain in it or some other asylum, as the criminal prosecution of a person in his state is not attended with advantage.*

Solitary
cells.

I found 1 female under punishment in a solitary cell. She belongs to a class most difficult to manage, who cannot be subdued by any amount of punishment, and, who in paroxysms of wild excitement will destroy all property within reach, and reckless of their own lives as those of others, they assault the officers of the prison when within their reach, or if an opportunity offers they will commit suicide. When in a punishment cell I have remarked that persons, especially women, of this class, are as a rule, strongly tainted with scrofula, and in some cases medical treatment has been found far more effective than severe punishment, which only exasperates and aggravates the paroxysms of wild excitement to which they are subject.

I have to observe that bells have lately been put up in the punish-

* This man soon after his discharge was recommitted for another offence, but he has since been removed to the district lunatic asylum.

ment cells of the female prison here with handles shaped like the letter **T**. Within the last few years a male prisoner under punishment in the Richmond Bridewell, committed suicide by hanging himself from a bell-handle in his cell, which was exactly formed as this is. I therefore urge the Board to lose no time in making an alteration, either by substituting a spiral spring, or by altering the handle of the bell so that a halter cannot hang on it.

When I spoke to this woman she told me that she was tired of life, and was sometimes tempted to put an end to her existence. A grave responsibility will therefore rest with the Board unless they make the alteration which I suggest.*

For prisoners of this class long sentences under the convict penal system are the most effectual treatment. Sentences of imprisonment in a county gaol without hope of ultimate improvement in their condition after discharge, are alike injurious to the prisoner and destructive to the discipline of the gaol. The reckless conduct of these prisoners is the result of a total abandonment of hope.

Eight hundred and six individual male and 307 female prisoners were committed to this prison in 1875; but the same prisoners, especially females, were very frequently recommitted during the year. By reference to the prison records I learn that the 806 males have been 1,887 times in custody, and the 307 females 2,406 times. Four women have been between 140 and 200 times each inmates of the prison, 3 upwards of 100 times, and 6 upwards of 50 times.

(margin note: Commit-ments.)

Of the 806 males committed during 1875, 238 represent 1,319 committals, and 171 females 2,335. On my second inspection of the prison, on the 28th December, only 51 criminal prisoners were in charge—being the lowest number at any one time in the gaol for many years; one of the warders having misconducted himself has since been dismissed; his place has not been filled up, and it is hoped that the staff can be still further reduced without interfering with the discipline of the gaol.

Accommodation.

	M.	F.		M.	F.
Wards,	5	5	Workshed,	1	—
Yards,	5	5	Kitchen,	1	—
Day Rooms,	1	—	Store Rooms,	7	3
Solitary Cells,	5	3	Laundry,	—	1
Single Cells not less than 9 feet long, 6 feet wide, and 8 feet high=432 cubic feet, heated and furnished with bells,	92	31	Drying Rooms,	—	2
			Lavatories,	4	3
			Baths, with Hot and Cold Water laid on,	4	2
Single Cells of smaller size not so furnished	19	—	Water-closets,	16	9
Sleeping Rooms,	7	3	Fumigating Apparatus,	1	1
No. of Beds in such Rooms,	4	3	Pump,	1	—
Hospital Rooms,	1	1	Crank do.,	1	—
Chapel,	1	—	Well,	1	—
School Rooms,	1	1	Crank Pump,	1	—
Workshop,	1	—	Mat Tables,	10	—
			Mangle,	—	1
			Tell-tale Clocks,	2	1

Since my last inspection new boilers have been erected, to replace those in both male and female prisons. The new boiler in the male prison has, I understand, cost £40, that in the female prison £35. The heating apparatus in both prisons now work satisfactorily; baths, however, are still required in the ranges in the male prison. There are two in the basement, but they are not sufficient. My colleague called attention to this matter in his report for 1874, but there is some difficulty in carrying out the suggestion without incurring considerable expense.

(margin note: Improve-ments.)

* The alterations have now been made.

SOUTH
DISTRICT.

Dublin
County
Gaol.

The cells, which number 92 for males, and 31 for females, are suitably fitted up. All the appliances for separation are on the most approved principle, with the exception of the bell-handles already mentioned. The bells, locks, and cell fastenings are in the best order, and there are abundant water-closets and lavatories in both the male and female prisons. The cells in both prisons (with the exception of six in the male prison) are artifically heated, and are lighted by gas, which remains burning in the cells until 7 p.m. in winter, and in early morning they are lighted after unlock.

Stock at the time of Inspection.

	In Use.	In Store.	Male Clothing.	In Use.	In Store.	Female Clothing.	In Use.	In Store.
Blankets, pairs of,	171	20	Shirts, . .	144	39	Shifts, . .	58	–
Sheets, pairs of,	195	67	Jackets, .	126	35	Jackets, . .	55	57
Rugs, . .	174	–	Vests, . .	136	28	Petticoats, .	103	36
Hammocks or			Trowsers, .	128	32	Aprons, . .	71	–
Cots, . .	191	15	Caps, . .	112	21	Neckerchiefs, .	41	6
Bed-ticks, . .	165	16	Shoes, Slippers, &			Caps, . .	67	–
Bedsteads, . .	16	–	Clogs, pairs of,	151	60	Stockings, pairs of,	48	–
						Shoes, Slippers, &		
						Clogs, pairs of,	39	22

Bedding.

The general bedding in the cells of both prisons was, when I inspected, clean and well cared. The sheets in the cells are now changed fortnightly, that is, the sheets of each side of the prison alternately each week. All the pillow covers are changed weekly. All prisoners are given clean under-clothing weekly, and the cooks have change of linen three times in the week. All prisoners are bathed on reception, and fortnightly afterwards in summer, but only once a month in winter. The matron reports that the linen is now in a good state when sent to the wash, and consequently the great wear and tear which formerly was complained of is prevented. I found some of the blankets rather thin and worn, but not sufficiently so to be cast.

I found the prison clothing of a good description, clean, and in good repair, but hitherto socks have not been supplied to male prisoners.* An abundance of both bedding and prison clothing was, when I made my inspection, in use and in store.

Stores.

The stores are tidily kept and well arranged. The private clothing of prisoners and that which is prison property in use are in separate stores. All new clothing is in a general store, from which it is given out on requisition from the Governor.

All prison clothing, including shoes, ie made up in the prison, and other articles whenever artificers are in custody. On every Thursday prisoners are shaved, and their hair closely cut, when necessary, by order of the medical officer.

An effective fumigating closet, in which the clothes of prisoners are cleansed from vermin, and disinfected, is in each prison. The Governor is making arrangements to remake and upholster the prison beds, as the cocoa fibre with which they are stuffed has got into hard lumps from constant use. This would be prevented if some curled hair were put in the centre of each bed at the place where the prisoner lies in bed.

The storekeeper has charge of the clothing and bedding for male prisoners, the matron those belonging to her prison. The Local Inspector and Governor take stock twice in the year.

Since my last official inspection an alteration has been made in the seats of the chapel by the throwing back of the separation between the sexes,

---

* As this report was passing through press I was informed that the Board has lately ordered socks to be supplied to male prisoners.

by which arrangement the part allotted for the male prisoners has been enlarged. Boards of separation have been put up between the seats to prevent prisoners from communicating during Divine Service. Another improvement, much required, could be effected almost without expense whenever a stone mason is in custody, at the entrance to the gaol, between the front and the back hatch, where two steps at the inner gate are very dangerous. The place is quite dark, and a stranger is liable to fall, not expecting to meet a step there. I would suggest that the steps be removed, and the passage reflagged on an incline. The incline might commence outside the inner gate, and it would not be then too abrupt. The present flags would answer again, and would merely require to be reset.*

Water for prison use is abundant—it is taken from three sources : from the River Liffey as hitherto, whence it is distributed over the gaol by the power of the crank pump.† There is likewise a well on the premises. The Vartry water has also been conveyed to the prison, and is used for drinking and cooking purposes.

The laundry in this gaol is divided into 13 separate compartments for washing, and has suitable ironing-room and drying-closet.

The Deputy Governor takes photographs of habitual criminals, for which he is paid 2s. for three copies ; the work is well done.

The present Governor has attached an apparatus to the gas metre of the prison, which equalizes the gas supply and prevents waste, by which a considerable saving has already been effected. The saving on the item gas during the quarter ending December, 1875, was £16 as compared with the corresponding quarter in 1874.

Unlock is held at 6.50 A.M., and lock-up at 5.30 P.M. at all periods of the year. One warder on watch in rotation patrols the interior of the prison during the night. Bells from the male hospital and pauper debtors' apartment ring into the central hall.

Two tell-tale clocks in the male and 1 in the female prison mark the vigilance of the night patrol; they are well secured by Chubb's patent locks. Tell-tale clocks.

No change has been made since last inspection in the arrangements for visitors to prisoners, which are satisfactory. Visitors.

Visits to convicted criminal prisoners are permitted monthly on orders signed by a member of the Board of Superintendence ; untried prisoners receive visits weekly, and master debtors daily between the hours of 10 and 5. The arrangements for visitors to criminal prisoners are very satisfactory. Untried prisoners see their professional advisers daily at reasonable hours.

All prisoners exercise for two hours daily ; if the weather is wet the males take their exercise in the central hall, the females in the corridor of the prison.

No escape was attempted in 1874 or 1875 from this prison, which is perhaps the most secure gaol in the kingdom, being protected in all points by iron check gates.

The sewerage is stated to be effective, but complaints have been made of an offensive effluvium from the closets, and I would recommend that the improved system of ventilating the sewers be introduced which is done by conveying a pipe to the top of the building from the sewers, so that noxious gases can escape on a higher level than the openings into the buildings.

---

* Since my visit this work has been done by the employment of a stone mason, a prisoner in the gaol.
† The crank pump is divided into 12 separate compartments, with an equal number of boxes for persons who are waiting for their turn on the mill.

R

SOUTH DISTRICT.

Dublin County Gaol.

Since last inspection a new drain has been constructed in the passage under the central hall on the basement of the male prison which opened into the scullery hitherto imperfectly drained. The basement is now quite dry, and the offensive water which formerly accumulated there no longer exists.

A ventilating shaft has been put up in the crank shed which renders the atmosphere of the place pure in hot weather.

Number of Punishments for Prison Offences.

	From 1st Jan. to 31st Dec., 1874.		From 1st Jan., 1875, to day of Inspection.	
	M.	F.	M.	F.
By Magisterial authority, .	–	–	–	1
By Governor—				
Dark or Refractory Cells, .	72	4	128	10
Stoppage of Diet, . .	240	2	311	7
Other Punishments, . .	8	–	–	–
Total, . . .	320	6	439	18

Nature of the Punishments included under "Other Punishments," viz. :--Extra hours at crank pump.

Since last inspection a sewer under the punishment cell in the female prison has been covered over and cemented.

In one instance it was found necessary to call in magisterial interference in the punishment of a female prisoner already referred to in this report.

Employment on day of Inspection.

	M.	F.
Hard labour prisoners, {Crank pump,	9	–
{Washing, .	–	6
Tailoring and shoemaking, .	2	–
Picking oakum, . . .	21	7
Needlework and sewing machine, .	–	3
Wardsmen and women, .	6	2
In solitary, .	–	1
Unemployed (female nursing), .	1	2
Debtors, .	1	3
Discharged before labour hours, .	1	–
Total in custody, . .	41	24

Amount received for produce of prisoners' labour disposed of outside the Gaol.
1873, . £46 16s. 5d. | 1874, . £65 17s. 0d. | 1875, . £73 12s. 4d.

Labour.

I quite agree in the opinion expressed by my colleague in his report for 1874, that the periods allowed to labour in this gaol are insufficient, and that they should be extended. The profits on prison labour have increased from £23 0s. 6d. in 1872 to £46 16s. 6d. in 1873, to £65 17s. in 1874, and to £73 12s. 4d. in 1875; but still a larger sum should be realized, having regard to the large number of inmates in custody. I have, however, to observe that all the clothing of the prisoners, including shoes, are made up by prison labour in the gaol.

Prisoners sentenced to hard labour work at the crank pump for three hours, and pick 2½ lbs. of junk daily. Industrial labour consists in stone-breaking, carpentry, tailoring, shoemaking, painting, tinwork, and other trade industries for the benefit of the institution. Eleven sheds for stone-breakers have now been provided, and it is proposed to add to the number.

The females pick oakum, wash, knit, and do the needlework of the establishment. The laundry is suitably fitted up, and is efficiently carried on.

Schools.

SOUTH DISTRICT.

Dublin County Gaol.

	From 1st Jan. to 31st Dec., 1874.		From 1st Jan., 1875, to day of Inspection.	
	M.	F.	M.	F.
Number of individual prisoners who attended school,	46	17	60	40
Average daily number of pupils,	8	3	7·2	4
Number of days on which school was held,	174	100	163	122

School-hours—Males, 4 to 5.15 o'clock; Females, 12 to 2 o'clock.

The school is managed in connexion with the Board of National Education, and is inspected by their officer, who states male teacher classed 2nd of third class, female teacher not classed. He considers the method of conducting the school tolerable. On his late inspection, 15th March, 1876, nine males were in attendance—one only of whom was learning arithmetic, and two writing on slates; three of the nine could not read. No attendance in female school. Average on roll in 1875, 13·4 males, 3·8 females. Average attendance 6·9 males, 3·8 females. The female school was only open 122 days in 1875. The school-rooms in both prisons are stalled.

The Protestant Chaplain visited the school nine times, the Presbyterian Chaplain eight times, and the Roman Catholic Chaplain once during 1875.

Dietary and Contracts.

Bread, white, per 1 lb., 1½d.; brown do., per 1 lb., 1⅓d.; oatmeal, per cwt., 16s. 0d.; potatoes, per cwt., 5s. 4d.; meat, per lb., 9½d.; new milk, per gallon, 1s.; salt, per cwt., 2s.; coal, per ton, £1 4s.; gas, per 1,000 cubic feet, 5s. 4d.; soap, per cwt., £1 2s.

Net average daily cost of ordinary diet for each prisoner.

1872, . . 6d. | 1873, . . 7d. | 1874, . . 6d.

The food prepared on the day of my visit, for the use of the inmates of the prison, and which I tasted, was good. The chaplains generally report favourably of the samples submitted for their inspection; but I learn from the journal of the Governor that he first examines the provisions when delivered by the contractor, and at once returns them when not equal to sample. On two occasions the milk contractor was fined by him according to agreement.

The kitchen is nicely kept, and the cooking apparatus works well.

I questioned individually, all the prisoners in custody on the day of my visit. With the exception of the unfounded complaints by the female debtors, the only other complaint lodged was by a male prisoner, who complained that the blankets supplied to him were thin. I found them so, and directed that an additional blanket should be given him during the winter.

Officers and Salaries.

Non-Resident.	£	s.	d.		£	s.	d.
Capt. Langrishe, Local Insp.,	150	0	0	James Reynolds, Chief Warder, Tailor, and Storekeeper,	65	0	0
Rev. Robert Flemyng, Protestant Chaplain,	65	0	0	Samuel Wallace, Gate Warder,	45	0	0
				James Kenny, Warder,	40	0	0
Rev. S. G. Morrison, Presbyterian Chaplain,	65	0	0	Andrew Armstrong, do.,	40	0	0
				John Peacock, do.,	40	0	0
Rev. Edwd. Kennedy, Roman Catholic Chaplain,	65	0	0	George Bartley, do.,	40	0	0
J. R. Kirkpatrick, esq., Surgeon,	100	0	0	John Wallace, Warder and Schoolmaster,	45	0	0
				Samuel Graham, Warder,	35	0	0
				John Tomkins, do.,	35	0	0
Resident.				Hamilton Davison, do.,	35	0	0
Captain St. George Gray, Governor,	300	0	0	Mary Jane Dyer, Matron,	50	0	0
				Ellen Nevin, Assistant Matron,	30	0	0
Thomas Flewett, Deputy Governor and Clerk,	130	0	0	Mary Byrne, Laundry Superintendent,	25	0	0

R 2

South
District.
___
*Dublin
County
Gaol.*

Vacancies in the staff since last inspection, how caused, and how filled up.

Captain Hugh M'Neill Dyer, died; Captain St. George Gray, appointed. Dr. Thornhill, died; Dr. J. R. Kirkpatrick, appointed. James Gordon, superannuated; Hamilton Davison, appointed. Warder George W. Ifill, resigned; John Tomkins, appointed. Warder James Kerr, dismissed; vacancy not filled up.

Officers on Gaol Allowance.

The Governor, Deputy Governor, Chief Warder, 9 Warders, 3 Matrons.

Visits paid by Officers.

	From 1st Jan. to 31st Dec., 1874.	From 1st Jan., 1875, to day of Inspection.
Number of times the Board of Superintendence met and discharged business,	19	15
Local Inspector to Gaol,	104	103
Chaplain, Prot. Episcopalian Church,	175	180
Presbyterian Chaplain,	174	179
Roman Catholic Chaplain,	168	172
Surgeon,	162	153

I regret to have to record the loss by death of two efficient superior officers of this prison, during 1875. Scarcely a year had elapsed since Captain Hugh Dyer, R.N., after a brilliant career in the Naval Service, was appointed Governor, to succeed the late Mr. Price, and he likewise has now passed away. During the short period of his official connexion with this gaol, he showed that he possessed all the qualities of a good prison officer.

Doctor William Thornhill also died suddenly in 1875, and by his death the Board have been deprived of a skilful, painstaking, and humane public servant.

The staff has been reduced during 1875, by one warder, who was dismissed, his place has not been filled up; and should the number of inmates continue to diminish, it is hoped that a further reduction can be made.

Five warders sleep in the central hall of the male prison, and the female officers have apartments in the female prison, but not in proximity with the cells of the prisoners. These apartments have been nicely fitted up, papered, and painted during the year. Prisoners, with the sanction of the Board, clean the apartments of the officers.

Hospital.

	1872.		1873.		1874.		1875 (to day of inspection).	
	M.	F.	M.	F.	M.	F.	M.	F.
No. of prisoners in hospital,	27	21	35	14	39	22	25	17
Average daily number in hospital,	2·1	2·1	1·3	1·4	·2	0·8	2·8	2·4
Number of prisoners prescribed for and treated out of hospital,	221	72	344	76	366	110	191	72
Number of deaths,	–	–	1	–	2	–	1	2
Cost of medicine,	£29 17s. 2d.		£30 2s. 0d.		£39 3s. 8d.		£26 16s. 2d.	
Cost of diet, &c., for prisoners in hospital,	£51 9s. 8d.		£36 10s. 7d.		£56 12s. 7d.		—	
Cost of all "extra diet" ordered by Medical Officer for prisoners *not* in hospital,	£54 6s. 10d.		£67 14s. 6d.		£14 10s. 7d.		—	

The hospitals were unoccupied at the time of my visit. One female debtor was under the care of the Medical Officer in her own apartment. On the transfer of the debtors from the Four Courts Marshalsea to this prison, the former hospital for male prisoners was appropriated for their use, and an apartment adjoining the female hospital, but with a separate entrance, has been used as an hospital for males. It has a water-closet, but no bath. When imprisonment for debt shall cease, the former hospital can be resumed. A bell has been put up, by which prisoners in hospital can communicate at night with the watchman in the central hall. No change has been made in the hospital for females during the year.

South District.

Dublin County Gaol.

Hospitals.

Books and Accounts.

Net cost of gaol, including diet and salaries.

1872, . £3,707 19s. 3d. | 1873, . £3,859 12s. 9d. | 1874, . £4,056 11s. 5d.

Total cost of officers, including clothing, value of rations, washing, gas, &c.

1872, . £1,674 14s. 4d. | 1873, . £1,824 9s. 1d. | 1874, . £1,802 18s. 0d.

Average cost of each prisoner per annum.

1872, . £46 18s. 9d. | 1873, . £36 1s. 4d. | 1874, . £37 13s. 4d.

Amounts repaid by the War Department for military prisoners.

1872, . £44 16s. 0d. | 1873, . £1 9s. 0d. | 1874, . £3 10s. 0d.

Amounts repaid from the Consolidated Fund for the maintenance, &c., of prisoners.

1872, . £194 1s. 2d. | 1873, . £301 3s. 7d. | 1874, . £346 19s. 10d.

I found the various registries of discipline and finance in the prison kept with much care and attention. They are in charge of Mr. Flewett, who is Deputy Governor and clerk, and is a very efficient prison officer. Some books not formerly in use have now been adopted, and the General Visitors' Book contains the names of all persons who visit the gaol. Suggestions with reference to the books, made by my colleague in his report on this gaol for 1874, have been adopted; and I observe a desire both by the Board and its officers to carry out the suggestions of the Inspectors-General as far as possible. The journal of the present Governor, as that of his predecessor, is full and well kept; it records all matters worthy of note which occur in the prison. The Local Inspector and Chaplains likewise have journals, and the Medical Officer, enters in the Hospital Book the diseases and treatment of the patients under his care.

Books.

Board of Superintendence.

Edward H. Kinahan, esq.	Colonel C. C. Vesey, D.L.
Phineas Riall, esq.	Sir Roger W. Palmer, bart.
Jon Trant Hamilton, esq., M.P.	Thomas H. Guinness, esq.
Thomas Drury, esq.	Major Hartley.
Richard Manders, esq.	Malachi S. Hussey, esq.
Henry J. M'Farlane, esq.	Edmund P. Brenan, esq.

The Board meets very regularly for the discharge of business on the first Thursday of each month, when petty expenses and the salaries of subordinate officers are paid in the aggregate, by cheque drawn in favour of the Local Inspector, who produces receipts at next meeting of the Board. The salaries of superior officers are paid quarterly, and all large sums by separate cheque to order of each creditor.

Board.

There are no bridewells in this county.

JOHN LENTAIGNE, *Inspector-General.*

SOUTH
DISTRICT.

*Galway
County and
Town
Gaol.*

GALWAY COUNTY AND TOWN GAOL, AT GALWAY.

STATUTABLE INSPECTION, 20TH SEPTEMBER, 1875.

*Number of Prisoners of all Classes in Gaol on the Day of Inspection, and
on the corresponding date in the three preceding years.*

		M.	F.		M.	F.
1872,	. . . .	44	13	1874, ...	45	17
1873,	. . . .	32	24	1875 (day of Inspection), 46	46	20

*Number of Returned Convicts in Gaol on the Day of Inspection, and during
each of the three preceding years.*

		M.	F.		M.	F.
1872,	. . . .	2	3	1875 (up to and including		
1873,	. . . .	3	–	day of Inspection), .	2	2
1874,	. . . .	3	2	Day of Inspection, .	–	–

Juveniles.

Javeniles. One young offender was in custody when I made my inspection, but
26 males and 5 females whose ages did not exceed sixteen years were
inmates of this gaol in 1875.

Three (males) were twice convicted, and 1 four times during the year.
Seven males and 2 females were under twelve years of age.

The 26 young offenders (males) committed during the year had already
thirty-six committals recorded against them on the prison books.

One was sentenced at quarter sessions to an imprisonment of six months
for larceny, the others for terms not exceeding fourteen days, and the
great majority for periods of seven days and under.

One male, who absconded from an industrial school, was sent to a
reformatory after the period of his sentence in the prison, and 2 females
for larceny.

With two exceptions all the young offenders convicted during 1875
had been summarily tried by justices at petty sessions—5 for larceny,
but of a trifling nature, stealing grass, apples, &c. The rest had been
convicted of assaults, trespass, illegal fishing, killing rabbits, being drunk,
and of police offences. It is of such that adult criminals are formed.

In June, 1875, a young offender (J. H.) was sentenced from this jurisdiction to an imprisonment of fifteen days and three years in a reformatory; but the boy was suffering, according to the report of the Medical
Officer of the gaol, from scrofulous disease of the bones of both legs, which
would render him quite unfit for industrial labour, and was stated to be
likewise subject to epilepsy. The boy was therefore refused admittance
into the institution, and rightly so.

Another young offender (female, E. K.) was in November following, at the
Clifden Petty Sessions, sentenced to an imprisonment of fourteen days in
this prison and two years in a reformatory, for absconding from the
industrial school of that town, and otherwise misconducting herself; but
the committing justice having neglected to name the reformatory to which

SOUTH
DISTRICT.

*Galway
County and
Town
Gaol.*

the child should be sent, and the Governor of the prison not having informed the Inspector of Reformatory Schools of the mistake, no steps were taken in the matter, the period for naming the reformatory was permitted to expire, and the girl was discharged at the expiration of her gaol sentence. The Governor states that immediately on receipt of the warrant he communicated with the committing justice, asking him to send the order naming the reformatory, but he is reprehensible for not having informed the authorities in Dublin of the failure of justice in this case. The girl, on her return to Clifden, was afterwards placed on licence by the managers, but again escaped, and when brought before the justices at petty sessions they dismissed the case, although it was (as I am informed) a repetition of the offence of which she had been previously convicted by them.

—*Debtors.*

One male and 1 female debtor were in custody at the time of my visit. The female had been an inmate of this prison since August, 1864. She has, however, been discharged since the period of my visit.

Commitments.

CLASSES.	From 1st January to 31st December, 1874.		From 1st January, 1875, to day of Inspection.	
	M.	F.	M.	F.
Debtors,	2	–	2	–
Criminals,	446	168	352	156
Vagrants,	3	15	27	17
Drunkards,	155	144	97	77
Total,	606	327	478	250

Highest Number of Prisoners (exclusive of Debtors) in gaol during each of the previous seven years, and up to day of Inspection in 1875.

1868,	54	1872,		89
1869,	64	1873,		79
1870,	77	1874,		84
1871,	78	1875,		93

Number of Individual Prisoners (exclusive of Debtors), and Number of Times each had been committed during 1874 and 1875.

NUMBER OF TIMES COMMITTED	1874.				1875, to day of Inspection.			
	Juveniles.		Adults.		Juveniles.		Adults.	
	M.	F.	M.	F.	M.	F.	M.	F.
Once within the year,	33	6	361	103	22	8	319	27
Twice „	1	–	47	21	3	–	28	17
Thrice „	–	–	13	7	–	–	14	8
Four times, „	–	–	7	5	1	–	1	3
5 „ „	–	–	2	4	–	–	2	1
6 „ „	–	–	1	6	–	–	1	3
7 „ „	–	–	2	2	–	–	1	1
8 „ „	–	–	1	4	–	–	–	3
9 „ „	–	–	1	1	–	–	–	9
10 „ „	–	–	–	1	–	–	–	1
Above 12 times within the year,	–	–	–	1	–	–	–	–
Total,	34	6	435	155	26	8	366	73
No. of above who had not been in Gaol previous to 1st January in	33	6	378	98	24	8	284	49

SOUTH
DISTRICT.

Galway
County and
Town
Gaol.

Number of Individual Prisoners (exclusive of Debtors), committed in the year 1874, and to the day of Inspection in 1875, who had been Once and oftener re-committed from their first Commitment in any year, so far as can be ascertained.

NUMBER OF TIMES COMMITTED.	1874.				1875, to day of Inspection.			
	Juveniles.		Adults.		Juveniles.		Adults.	
	M.	F.	M.	F.	M.	F.	M.	F.
Once only, . . .	32	6	290	75	20	8	268	18
Twice, ...	2	—	66	18	5	—	49	24
Thrice, ...	—	—	21	14	—	—	12	7
4 times, . . .	—	—	13	9	—	—	8	2
5 „ . . .	—	—	12	3	1	—	2	2
6 „ . . .	—	—	5	4	—	—	3	1
7 to 11 „ . . .	—	—	18	8	—	—	5	7
12 to 20 „ . . .	—	—	7	8	—	—	6	4
21 to 30 „ . . .	—	—	1	6	—	—	—	3
31 to 50 „ . . .	—	—	2	7	—	—	1	4
51 to 80 „ . . .	—	—	—	2	—	—	2	—
121 to 140 „ . . .	—	—	—	1	—	—	—	1
Total No. of Individuals committed,	34	6	435	155	26	8	356	73
No. of commitments represented in foregoing, . . .	36	6	979	1,098	35	8	750	581

Averages, and Highest and Lowest Numbers (exclusive of Debtors).

—	From 1st January to 31st December, 1874.			From 1st January, 1875, to day of Inspection.		
	M.	F.	Date.	M.	F.	Date.
Average daily number of prisoners in custody,	48	17	—	52	17	—.
Highest number of prisoners at any one time,	84		17th March	93		27th June.
Lowest ditto,	52		7th Jan.	51		6th Mar.
Highest number of males at any one time, .	66		17th May.	67		22nd April.
Ditto, of females,	29		12th July.	27		27th June.
Lowest number of males at any one time, .	32		6th July.	35		6th Mar.
Ditto, of females,	7		4th May.	9		19th April.

I found, when I made my inspection of this prison, 46 male and 20 female prisoners in custody. Seven males and 7 females were for trial, 20 males and 6 females had been convicted by juries at quarter sessions ; and 19 males and 7 females summarily by justices at petty sessions within the district. One male and 3 females were drunkards ; 2 males were revenue offenders, and 2 males and 1 female had been convicted under the Poor Law Acts. No military or naval offender or deserter was committed to the prison in 1875.

The sentences on the convicted prisoners in custody were—the males, 1 sentenced to an imprisonment of two years, 5 for twelve and 3 for eighteen months, 10 for terms of six months and under twelve months, 14 for two and three months, the remainder for one month and under.

Two females had been sentenced to an imprisonment of one year each, ·

Soute
District.

Galway
County and
Town
Gaol.

2 others for six months, and 1 for three months. The remaining prisoners in custody were for terms varying from one month to forty-eight hours.

By reference to the preceding tables it will be seen that 392 individual males and 81 females were committed to this prison in 1875. One female was committed ten times, and 9 others nine times during the year. One has been upwards of 120 times an inmate of this prison since her first committal, and 2 males have been upwards of seventy times. The constant recommittals of these habitual offenders have swelled the number of their committals, so that the 81 females have 589 committals and the 392 males 785 recorded against them on the books of the prison.

Accommodation.

	M.	F.			M.	F.
Wards,	4	3	Workshop,		1	—
Yards,	4	3	Worksheds,		—	13
Day Rooms,	4	3	Kitchen,		—	1
Solitary Cells,	1	1	Bakery,		—	1
Single Cells, not less in size than			Store Rooms,		7	—
9 ft. long, 6 ft. wide, 8 ft.			Laundry,		—	1
high = 432 cubic ft.,	81	15	Drying Room,		—	1
Ditto, heated and furnished with			Lavatories,		4	—
bells,	53	—	Baths, with hot and cold water			
Single Cells of smaller size not			laid on,		2	1
heated or furnished with bells,	26	—	Privies,		2	2
Cells to contain three persons,	7	5	Water-closets,		13	2
Sleeping Rooms,	2	1	Fumigating apparatus,		1	—
Number of beds in such rooms,	6	6	Pump,		1	—
Hospital Rooms,	2	2	Treadwheels,		2	—
Chapel,		One	Tell-tale Clock,			One

No change has been made in the gaol since last inspection by my colleague in October, 1874, and the alterations in the female prison, which were commenced, have been left incomplete. The architect of the Board of Works asked for some explanation on some matters which he did not deem satisfactory, and the works have in consequence remained for a long time unfinished. At the period of my visit the County Surveyor for the west district was absent on leave, but I hoped to have seen the Surveyor of the eastern portion of the county but missed doing so, and I learn that up to the present date nothing has been done.

In December, 1875, the Board of Superintendence made a communication to the Board of Works stating their intention to borrow £2,000 for the contemplated alteration in the prison; but, pending legislation, no steps will now be taken until the wishes of Parliament are known.

Stock at the time of Inspection.

Male Clothing.	In Use.	In Store.		In Use.	In Store.	Female Clothing.	In Use.	In Store.
Blankets, pairs of,	198½	14½	Shirts,	39	79	Shifts,	15	22
Sheets, pairs of,	201½	24	Jackets,	39	51	Jackets,	15	7
Rugs,	124	4	Vests,	39	62	Petticoats,	13	22
Hammocks or Cots,	153	5	Trowsers,	39	47	Aprons,	15	6
Bedticks,	149	65	Caps,	39	15	Neckerchiefs,	15	20
			Shoes, Slippers, &			Stockings, pairs of,	30	—
			Clogs, pairs of,	39	41	Shoes, Slippers, &		
						Clogs, pairs of,	15	8

When I made my inspection the prison buildings (with the exception of the female prison, which was in the same state as when I had previously visited) were in sound repair, very clean, and well kept, the prisoners suitably dressed, except that the males are not given stockings, nor the females caps, which, although not specified in the Prisons Act, are now supplied to prisoners in every well-regulated prison. The blankets and other bedding in use were of a good description, but the cots, were much

SOUTH
DISTRICT.

Galway
County and
Town
Gaol.

Fumigation.

Heating
and gas.

Night-
watch.

worn. I directed that some should be provided, and I am informed that twenty-five new cots have been ordered for the male separate prison.

A good iron fumigating box has been placed adjoining the bath and clothes store; and at the time of my visit a room over the Governor's office was being fitted up as an office for the Clerk and a Board-room; it was also proposed to place a water-closet at the foot of the stairs. Some improvements have likewise lately been made in the apartments of the Governor, and the work has been done by prison labour. A store is required in the separate prison in which the milk could remain under lock and key, and the tin vessels used by the prisoners be kept, instead of as at present, in a press on the range. I suggested that one of the cells be fitted up for the purpose, and I understand that it will be done. Since last inspection a suitable place—a wooden sentry box with wire netting—has been provided in which prisoners can see their friends without the danger of prohibited articles being introduced into the prison.

The fittings in the cells of the male separate prison, and other appliances for separation in it, were, when I visited, in good order. A bath where prisoners are washed when admitted, and afterwards weekly, is in the basement story of that prison, and four lavatories are also provided in it; but although there is a bath with hot and cold water laid on in the laundry of the prison for females, there is no lavatory and only one water-closet in it. The boiler and drying closet are now in order, and the stores are sufficient, but the many defects of the female prison already pointed out in former reports of the Inspectors-General still exist, and until the prison is remodelled the gaol cannot be considered in a satisfactory state.

Fifty-three cells in the male prison are provided with the necessary appliances for separation and are artificially heated, but gas has not been introduced into any of the cells of either prison, it is solely in use at the gate, in the halls, corridors, round the boundary wall, and in the house of the Governor.

All male prisoners criminally committed are subject to partial separation—they take their meals and sleep in their cells and work under supervision, but the females are in perfect association, and there is no gaol in Ireland more defective in this respect.

The supply of water to the prison from the town main is abundant, and the sewerage is good.

Unlock is held at 6 A.M. in summer and at daylight in winter. The prison is locked for the night at 8 P.M. in summer and at dark in winter. One tell-tale clock only marks the rounds of the night-watch, which is held by four turnkeys, who relieve each other, but there is no patrol in the interior of the prison after 10 P.M.

The photographs of habitual criminals are taken by a photographer from the town of Galway, who is paid 9d. for each copy taken.

In April, 1875, a male prisoner escaped from the bridewell at Tuam, and in September following another male prisoner from this gaol. Both were retaken.

Number of Punishments for Prison Offences.

	From 1st January to 31st December, 1874.		From 1st January, 1875, to day of Inspection.	
	M.	F.	M.	F.
By Magisterial authority,	—	—	2	—
By Governor—				
Dark or Refractory Cells,	30	—	27	—
Stoppage of Diet,	46	5	38	—
Total,	76	5	67	1

No improvement has been made in the punishment cells since last inspection; they are not artificially heated, and have no means for the inmates to communicate with an officer of the prison.

School.

No secular teaching is given to prisoners, but Sisters of Mercy twice in the week afford moral and religious instruction to the Roman Catholics, who constitute almost the entire criminal population of the gaol.

Employment on day of Inspection.

	M.	F.
Tread-wheel,	19	—
Carpentering,	1	—
Bone Mill,	2	—
Mat making,	6	—
Store,	1	—
Cooking,	—	3
Oakum picking,	10	—
Flag washing,	1	1
Sewing,	—	11
Sick,	3	—
Unemployed,	—	1
Discharged (before labour hours),	2	3
Debtors,	1	1
Total,	46	20

Amount received for produce of Prisoners' Labour disposed of outside the Gaol.

1872, . £44 10s. 9d. | 1873, . £50 9s. 4d. | 1874, . £48 0s. 5d.

Punitive labour is enforced in this gaol by work on the tread-wheel, the power of which is applied to the pumping of water and the crushing of bones for manure. The prisoners work on the mill for 6¾ hours in summer and 4¾ in winter. A turnkey gives instructions in matmaking and another is a shoemaker. Artificers when in custody are employed at their trades for the benefit of the institution. The prisoners of both sexes pick oakum, and the females wash, sew, knit, and cook the food for prison use.

Two and a half tons of crushed bones, value £15; four tons of oakum, value £84; and one and a half tons of coir yarn, value £56, were on hands at the close of the year.

Contracts.

Bread, white, per 4-lb. loaf, 6½d.; ditto, brown, per 4-lb. loaf, 6d.; oatmeal, per cwt., 13s.; potatoes, per stone, 5½d.; meat, per lb., 5d.; new milk, per gal., ¼d.; salt, per cwt., 2s. 3d.; turf, per box, 1s. 6d.; straw, per cwt., 2s. 3d.; gas, per 1,000 cubic feet, 8s. 6d.; candles, per lb., 6d.; soap, per stone, 3s. 4d.

Net average daily cost of Ordinary Diet for each Prisoner.

1872, . 4d | 1873, . 4d. | 1874, . 5d.

The food for prison use on the day of my visit, which I tasted, was of a good description, and the Chaplains report favourably of the samples submitted to their inspection during the year.

I questioned all the prisoners individually—1 female (M. N.) lodged a complaint against the Governor of the gaol, which complaint I investigated, and was assisted in doing so by the Local Inspector. We examined different officers of the gaol and the prisoners named by her. I find that the woman had formerly been a house servant of the Governor, but had been convicted of robbing her master, and was, at the time of my visit, under sentence for that offence. She stated that prisoners had been employed to alter and paint the house of the Governor, to scrub the floors, shake carpets, and repair some chairs, the property of the Governor, and that some towels belonging to him had been washed in the prison laundry.

South
District.
—
Galway
County and
Town
Gaol.

I learned that in the absence of the Governor in England some towels and rubbers had been washed in the prison laundry, and that a press had been made and two chairs repaired by a carpenter, a prisoner in the gaol. All the other work done was in the service of the Board. I pointed out to the Governor and reported to the Board that it was highly improper that work should be done by a prisoner for any officer of the gaol.

Officers and Salaries.

Non-Resident.	£	s.	d.		£	s.	d.
				Martin M'Cormack, .	44	0	0
Captain T. C. Lambert, Local				Wm. Humphreys, Hosp.			
Inspector, ...	130	0	0	Assistant, . .	55	0	0
Rev. John Greaven, Roman				Thomas Hession, . .	48	0	0
Catholic Chaplain, . .	46	3	0	Patrick Coen, *Mat-maker*,	44	0	0
Jas. V. Browne, esq., Surgeon,	74	0	0	John Madden, . .	44	0	0
J. M. O'Connor, Clerk, .	60	0	0	Thomas Kelly, . .	44	0	0
				Michael Forde, . .	44	0	0
				John Martin, . .	44	0	0
				Margaret Foy, Matron, .	33	0	0
Resident.				Mary Hogan, Assistant Ma-			
				tron, ...	27	10	0
W. J. Joyce, esq., Governor,	300	0	0	Catherine Hogan, Hospital			
Charles Ford, Head Turnkey,	70	10	0	Nurse, ...	15	0	0

Vacancies in Staff since last Inspection, how caused and how filled up.

Rev. John D'Arcy, Protestant Chaplain, died; unfilled. Thomas Hogan, resigned; succeeded by Michael Forde. Patrick Smith, transferred to Tuam Bridewell; succeeded by John Martin.

Officers on Gaol Allowance.

Margaret Foy, Matron; Catherine Hogan, Hospital Nurse.

Visits paid by Officers.

	From 1st Jan. to 31st Dec., 1874.	From 1st Jan., 1875, to day of Inspection.
Number of times the Board of Superintendence met for the discharge of business,	14	8
Local Inspector, to Gaol, . .	159	127
Ditto, to each Bridewell, .	4	3
Chaplain, Prot. Episcopalian Church,	168	97
Roman Catholic Chaplain,	249	174
Surgeon, ...	146	136

The Local Inspector informs me that it is proposed to alter the uniform of the prison warders, and I consider that the alterations which he suggests would be an improvement, and make the uniform more suited to the office the men hold.

Hospitals.

	1872.		1873.		1874.		1875, (to day of Inspection).	
	M.	F.	M.	F.	M.	F.	M.	F.
No. of prisoners in hospital, . .	27	26	37	31	46	27	42	22
Average daily No. in hospital, .	1·1	1·1	2·1	1·1	·7	2·	4·2	2·24
No. of prisoners prescribed for and treated out of hospital, . .	47	55	48	86	68	72	27	21
Cost of medicine, .	£10 8s. 2d.		£11 6s. 8d.		£11 4s. 2d.		—	
Cost of diet for prisoners in hospital,	£73 2s. 8d.		£92 10s. 0d.		£103 3s. 9d.		—	
Cost of all extra diet ordered by Medical Officer for prisoners not in hospital, .	£5 17s. 3d.		£0 13s. 7d.		£4 5s. 0d.		—	

The hospitals for prisoners of both sexes are under one roof, and no change has been made in them for many years. My colleague in his report for 1874 pointed to the irregularity of having a healthy female prisoner, sentenced to hard labour, employed in the hospital, receiving extra diet, when no patient of her sex is in it. I quite agree in the opinion which he expresses, and I would urge that the arrangement be discontinued. I also consider that the door between the two hospitals, which is now only locked, be permanently closed up.

South District.

Galway County and Town Gaol.

Hospitals.

Since my last visit a water-closet has been put up in the hospital.

Books and Accounts.

Net cost of Gaol, including Diet and Salaries.
1872, . £2,446 5s. 3d. | 1873, . £2,438 9s. 7d. | 1874, . £2,552 17s. 8d.

Total cost of Officers, including Clothing, Value of Rations, &c.
1872, . £1,236 12s. 6d. | 1873, . £1,248 14s. 7d. | 1874, . £1,326 13s. 7d.

Average cost of each Prisoner per annum.
1872, . £40 3s. 9d. | 1873, . £41 5s. 2d. | 1874, . £38 6s. 3d.

Amounts repaid by the Inland Revenue Department for Excise Prisoners.
1872, . £18 14s. 11d. | 1873, . — | 1874, . —

Amounts repaid from the Consolidated Fund for the Maintenance, &c., of Prisoners.
1872, . £151 2s. 4d. | 1873, . £143 6s. 11d. | 1874, . £206 15s. 9d.

The registries of discipline and finance of this gaol are well and carefully kept by the Clerk, with the assistance of the Hospital Warder, and are frequently checked by the Governor, the more important books at the close of each week. The Local Inspector also occasionally checks the various prison books. Many of the forms might be improved, and I am glad to learn that some new books have now been ordered on the plan of those in use in Waterford Gaol, by which the keeping of the books will be much simplified.

Books.

The journals of the Local Inspector and Governor are well and carefully kept, and in them are noticed all matters of importance which occur in the prison. I learn from the journal of the Governor that in April, 1875, a female prisoner, a lunatic, gave much trouble; she attempted to throw herself from the gallery of the prison and made other attempts to commit suicide, in doing which she received serious injuries.

The journal of the Medical Officer contains observations on cases under his care. The Chaplains in their journals state the duties they perform.

Board of Superintendence.

Sir Thomas J. Burke, bart.	Capt. J. O'Hara, D.L.	C. T. Redington, esq., D.L.
Robert Bodkin, esq., D.L.	Major John A. Daly, D.L.	John W. H. Lambert, esq.
Pierce Joyce, esq., D.L.	Walter P. Lambert, esq.	Walter Shaw Taylor, esq.
Major J. W. Lynch, D.L.	George Morris, esq., M.P.	Thomas R. Roche, esq.

The Board meets on the last Saturday of each month, when the journals and books are examined, subordinate officers paid, and other liabilities discharged. The salaries of the superior officers and accounts of contractors are settled quarterly, by cheques signed by three members of the Board, and countersigned by the Governor. The accounts are audited half-yearly at assizes by a committee of the Grand Jury.

Board.

STATE OF BRIDEWELLS.

SOUTH DISTRICT.

Galway County.

Bridewells.

		Tuam.		Loughrea.		Ballinasloe.	
		M.	F.	M.	F.	M.	F.
No. of Committals in past year, . .		119	30	83	17	47	9
Of whom were Drunkards, .		25	10	31	8	15	4
No. of Committals in the quarter preceding Inspection, .		21	19	16	11	16	16
Of whom were Drunkards, .		5	5	4	4	3	3
Petty Sessions and Transmittals, how often.		Fortnightly.		Weekly.		Weekly at Ballinasloe; at Ballygar fortnightly.	
Committals, . .		Now regular.		Regular.		Regular.	
Registry, . .		Carefully kept.		Correctly kept.		Carefully kept.	
Repairs and Order, .		Fair, but painting required.		In fair repair, except leakage from roof; old boiler should be removed, and woodwork painted.		In good repair and order.	
Security, . . .		Fair, with care.		Sufficient, with care.		Sufficient.	
Accommodation, .		Four cells for males and three for females; two day-rooms.		Two day-rooms and six cells occupied by prisoners.		Nine cells and two day-rooms.	
Furniture, Bedding, and Utensils.		Good and sufficient.		Good and sufficient.		Sufficient and good.	
Water, how supplied,		None; pump out of order.		Pump in order; water good.		Water in both yards; a forcing pump.	
Sewerage, . .		Cesspool.		None; earth-closets required.		Effective; water from roof passes through privies.	
Cleanliness, Dryness, and Ventilation.		Clean and orderly, but damp.		Clean, dry; ventilation imperfect from small windows in cells.		Clean, dry, and well ventilated.	
Cost of Dietary, . .		5½d. per head per day.		6d. per day.		5d. per head per day.	
Salary of Keeper, and whether he follows any other employment,		£24 12s.; is court-keeper at £6; contingencies, £5.		£33 12s.		£24 12s.	
Date of Inspection,		27th April, 1875.		24th April, 1875.		26th April, 1875.	
Remarks, . .		Three males in charge. One male escaped from this Bridewell in 1875.		No prisoner in charge. A new book should be provided.		No prisoner in custody.	

STATE OF BRIDEWELLS—*continued.*

—	Oughterard.		Portumna.		Eyrecourt.	
	M.	F.	M.	F.	M.	F.
No. of Committals in past year, . .	78	24	26	5	13	2
Of whom were Drunkards, .	2	–	13	1	2	1
No. of Committals in the quarter preceding inspection, .	20	6	20	1	6	3
Of whom were Drunkards, .	–	–	4	1	1	–
Petty Sessions and Transmittals, how often.	Fortnightly.		Fortnightly, on Mondays.		Eyrecourt on every second Tuesday.	
Committals, . .	Regular.		Regular.		Regular, with one exception.	
Registry, . . .	Correctly kept.		Correctly kept.		Correctly kept.	
Repairs and Order, .	In good repair and order.		In good repair; but dashing has fallen off yard walls.		In fair repair and order.	
Security, . .	Sufficient with care.		A down-pipe in each yard impairs the security.		Very insecure.	
Accommodation, .	Males—day-room and 2 cells; females—day-room used as a kitchen by keeper by permission, and 1 cell with two beds.		Males—day-room and four cells. Females — day-room and three cells.		Two day-rooms and one cell below; and two cells, one with two beds, upstairs.	
Furniture, Bedding, and Utensils.	Sufficient and good.		Bedding ample.		Sufficient for the few prisoners committed.	
Water, how supplied,	None.		By pump, from which both yards are supplied by pipe.		No water on premises.	
Sewerage, . .	Cesspool outside, supplied with turf mould.		Privies have cesspool behind them.		None; a cesspool under privy.	
Cleanliness, Dryness, and Ventilation.	Clean, dry, and well ventilated.		Clean and orderly, but damp in winter.		Clean and dry; ventilation sufficient.	
Cost of Dietary, .	4½d. per day.		5½d.		5d. per day.	
Salary of Keeper, and whether he follows any other employment.	£24 12s.; and Court-keeper, salary £8. Interpreter at Quarter Sessions.		£24 12s. Court-keeper, salary £8.		£34 12s. 4d. Is Clerk of the Church.	
Date of Inspection, —	19th Sept., 1875.		24th April, 1875.		24th April, 1875.	
Remarks, . .	No prisoner in custody.		No prisoner in custody.		No prisoner in custody.	

SOUTH DISTRICT.

STATE OF BRIDEWELLS—*continued.*

Galway County.

Bridewells.

	Clifden.		Gort.	
No. of Committals in past year, ...	M. 58	F. 8	M. 19	F. 10
Of whom were Drunk-ards, . . .	35	2	1	—
No. of Committals in the quarter preceding In-spection, . . .	10	5	10	5
Of whom were Drunk-ards, . . .	5	—	3	—
Petty Sessions and Trans-mittals, how often.	At Cliffen and Carna fort-nightly ; at Roundstone and Letterfrack monthly.		Fortnightly. Transmittals on the following day.	
Committals, . . .	Now regular.		Regular.	
Registry, . . .	Correctly kept.		Correctly kept.	
Repairs and Order, .	In good repair, except leak-age in one spot from roof.		In good repair.	
Security, . . .	One yard insecure from privy against outer wall.		Sufficient, with care.	
Accommodation, .	Males—day-room and four cells ; females—day-room and three cells with one bed, and one with four beds.		Three sleeping-cells for each sex, and two day-rooms.	
Furniture, Bedding, and Utensils.	Good and sufficient.		Good and sufficient, except sheets, which should be provided.	
Water, how supplied, .	No water except from roof ; river and spring well near.		By a pump.	
Sewerage, . . .	Effective.		Effective.	
Cleanliness, Dryness, and Ventilation.	Very clean and well kept.		Clean and well ventilated.	
Cost of Dietary, per head, per day.	$6\frac{1}{4}d.$ per day.		6d. for males, and 5d. for females.	
Salary of Keeper, and whether he follows any other employment.	£33 12s. None.		£32 12s., also fuel. Is court-keeper at £8.	
Date of Inspection, .	17th September, 1875.		26th September, 1875.	
Remarks, . . .	No prisoner in custody.		No prisoner in custody.	

JOHN LENTAIGNE, *Inspector-General.*

KERRY COUNTY GAOL, AT TRALEE.—STATUTABLE INSPECTION, 23RD AND 25TH AUGUST, 1875.

Prisoners of all classes in Gaol on the day of Inspection, and on the corresponding date in the three preceding years.

	M.	F.		M.	F.
1872,	60	7	1874,	29	14
1873,	46	12	1875 (day of Inspection),	24	11

Returned Convicts in Gaol on the day of Inspection, and during each of the three preceding years.

	M.	F.		M.	F.
1872,	7	2	1875 (up to and including		
1873,	5	1	day of Inspection),	4	3
1874,	3	3	Day of Inspection,	—	—

Juveniles.

No young offender under 16 years of age was in custody when I visited, but 22 males and 5 females of that class had previously been committed to this prison during the year 1875. Of these, 8 (males) were under twelve years of age ; 1 (female) had been convicted at quarter sessions ; the other young offenders summarily by magistrates sitting in petty sessions. Two males and 1 female were sent to reformatories after the period of their sentences of imprisonment as a punishment in the gaol.

Juveniles.

Commitments.

CLASSES.	From 1st January to 31st December, 1874.		From 1st January, 1875, to day of Inspection.	
	M.	F.	M.	F.
Debtors,	5	—	1	—
Criminals,	383	108	234	60
Vagrants,	5	4	10	3
Drunkards,	187	81	75	40
Total,	580	193	320	103

Individual Prisoners (exclusive of Debtors), and Number of Times each had been committed during 1874–1875.

NUMBER OF TIMES COMMITTED.	1874.				1875, to day of Inspection.			
	Juveniles.		Adults.		Juveniles.		Adults.	
	M.	F.	M.	F.	M.	F.	M.	F.
Once within the year,	18	4	315	72	20	5	217	53
Twice ,,	2	—	57	13	1	—	23	6
Thrice ,,	1	—	15	9	—	—	4	2
4 times ,,	—	—	9	2	—	—	3	3
5 and 6 times ,,	—	—	3	1	—	—	2	1
7 times ,,	—	—	1	1	—	—	—	—
8 ,, ,,	—	—	1	3	—	—	—	—
9 ,, ,,	—	—	1	1	—	—	—	—
10 and 11 times ,,	—	—	—	1	—	—	—	1
Total,	21	4	402	103	21	5	249	66
No. of above who had not been in Gaol previous to 1st January in	20	4	249	57	17	5	152	39

SOUTH
DISTRICT.
───
Kerry
County
Gaol.

Individual Prisoners (exclusive of Debtors), committed in 1874, and to day of Inspection in 1875, who had been Once and oftener recommitted, from their first commitment in any year, so far as can be ascertained.

NUMBER OF TIMES COMMITTED.	1874.				1875, to day of Inspection.			
	Juveniles.		Adults.		Juveniles.		Adults.	
	M.	F.	M.	F.	M.	F.	M.	F.
Once only,	18	4	212	49	17	5	138	37
Twice,	1	–	90	13	4	–	43	7
Thrice,	2	–	26	9	–	–	21	6
4 times,	–	–	22	7	–	–	11	3
5 ,,	–	–	12	3	–	–	9	1
6 ,,	–	–	10	2	–	–	4	1
7 to 11 times,	–	–	16	8	–	–	14	3
12 to 16 ,,	–	–	4	2	–	–	13	1
17 to 20 ,,	–	–	4	3	–	–	1	2
21 to 30 ,,	–	–	4	2	–	–	2	2
31 to 50 ,,	–	–	1	1	–	–	2	1
51 to 60 ,,	–	–	1	1	–	–	1	1
61 to 80 ,,	–	–	–	1	–	–	–	1
101 to 120 ,,	–	–	–	1	–	–	–	–
Total No. of Individuals committed,	21	4	402	103	21	5	249	66
No. of Commitments represented in the foregoing,	26	4	1,127	692	25	5	667	369

Averages, and Highest and Lowest Numbers (exclusive of Debtors).

—	From 1st January to 31st December, 1874.			From 1st January, 1875, to day of Inspection.		
	M.	F.	Date.	M.	F.	Date.
Aggregate number of prisoners in custody,	12,556	4,028	—	8,073	1,778	—
Average daily number of prisoners in custody,	34	11	—	34·3	7·5	—
Highest number of prisoners at any one time,	63		14th June.	59		20th Jan.
Lowest ditto,	25		11th Aug.	29		23rd April.
Highest number of males at any one time,	48		23rd May.	48		28th Feb.
Ditto, of females,	22		1st Oct.	16		19th Jan.
Lowest number of males at any one time,	13		11th Aug.	23		6th Aug.
Ditto, of females,	4		10th July.	2		14th April.

Highest Number of Prisoners (exclusive of Debtors) in Gaol during each of the previous seven years, and up to the day of Inspection in 1875.

15th January, 1868,	.	. 73	10th November, 1872,	. . 77
10th September, 1869,	.	. 62	8th April, 1873,	. . 61
9th September, 1870,	.	. 71	14th June, 1874,	. . 63
9th November, 1871,	.	. 73	20th June, 1875,	. . 59

Commitments.

Twenty-four males and 11 females were inmates of this gaol when I made my inspection, of whom 20 males and 10 females were under sentences—3 (males) having been tried at the summer assizes, two for manslaughter and one for rape, and sentenced to an imprisonment of twelve months each ; eight males convicted by jurors at quarter sessions —four of larceny and four of assaults and obstructing the police—had been sentenced, 1 to an imprisonment for twelve, 1 for nine, 1 for six, and 5 for two and three months each ; eight summarily convicted at petty sessions had been sentenced for periods varying from seven days to three months, all for assaults, disorderly conduct and drunkenness.

Two females tried at quarter sessions had been sentenced for larceny for terms of six and twelve months respectively, and 8 others summarily convicted of larceny, assaults, drunkenness, and one poor law offender, were under sentence for terms of one, two, and three months each.

Two hundred and seventy individual male prisoners and 71 females were committed to this prison previously to my inspection in 1875. Many were old offenders frequently reconvicted, one female having upwards of sixty reconvictions recorded against her on the prison books ; two others upwards of fifty. The 71 females have been 374 times inmates of this gaol, and the 270 males 692 times.

I regret to have observed on my late visits to Tralee a spirit of drunkenness and disorderly conduct amongst young lads of the town, which appears to be on the increase and requires to be put down by the strong hand of the law.

Accommodation.

As the gaol premises are now being remodelled, the accommodation in the gaol will in future be quite different from that hitherto provided, but as yet the works are not sufficiently advanced for me to give accurate details.

Notwithstanding that the prison buildings were occupied by workmen who were making extensive alterations to suit them to the separate system, under the Act 3 and 4 Victoria, cap. 44, I found the order and discipline in the establishment at the time of my inspection satisfactory. The Local Inspector and Governor deserve great credit for their vigilance under difficult circumstances in preventing the abuses which so frequently arise when externs are permitted within a prison as here.

I found various defects in the new buildings which I pointed out to the Local Inspector and Governor, who undertook to explain my views to the Board, and have them remedied.

I was disappointed on my visit to observe the little progress made in the works, as I hoped when I made my inspection that the cells would be in a position to be certified by me under the 4th section of the statute.

Rules framed under the Act 19 and 20 Victoria, cap. 68, have been for some time ready to be submitted for approval to his Grace the Lord Lieutenant, but it has been deemed better to wait until the cells are ready for the reception of prisoners under the separate system, in order that new rules might be drawn up when the prison is certified under the Act 3 and 4 Victoria, cap. 44.

On the day of my visit prisoners were put to work for the first time at the newly erected crank-pump. I found a defect in the handles of the crank which however can be remedied, and in other respects the crank worked satisfactorily.

An alteration which I pointed out is likewise required in the seats in the chapel, and the arrangement of the sittings in the school for males is very faulty. These and various other matters the Local Inspector has undertaken to have altered.

The Local Inspector expressed to me the desire of the Board of Superintendence to alter the present officers' quarters, part of which they wish to have converted into a board-room. The alteration would be a great improvement, but would be attended with considerable expense. I therefore suggested that the matter be postponed until after the spring assizes, when the wishes of Parliament respecting the future of prisons are known.

SOUTH DISTRICT.

Kerry County Gaol.

Stock at the time of Inspection.

	In Use.	In Store.	Male Clothing.	In Use.	In Store.	Female Clothing.	In Use.	In Store.
Blankets, pairs of,	125	64	Shirts,	40	20	Shifts,	9	26
Sheets, pairs of,	76	46	Jackets,	13	60	Jackets,	7	19
Bed-ticks,	89	67	Vests,	12	54	Petticoats,	12	12
Bedsteads,	54	96	Trowsers,	12	109	Aprons,	3	3
			Caps,	13	48	Neckerchiefs,	3	3
			Stockings or socks, pairs of,	25	66	Caps,	9	41
			Shoes, Slippers, & Clogs, pairs of,	15	10	Stockings, pairs of,	9	16
						Shoes, Slippers, & Clogs, pairs of,	12	12

Bedding.   I found an abundant supply of bedding in the gaol. It was of a fair description.

Stores, &c.   The prison clothing for males was good, but the stock of female clothing insufficient. Pending the alterations, and the fitting up of the new stores, it was considered desirable to postpone the purchase of additional clothing until the buildings are completed.

Gas   In the new building the cells will be artificially heated and lighted, with all necessary appliances for separation ; the gas-jet which lights the cell will be in a chamber of the wall and separated by glass from the interior, so that in case of an escape of gas no mischief to the inmate can happen, and the prisoner cannot tamper with the burner.

Water.   Water will be abundantly supplied to every part of the building by the power of the crank-pump.

Baths, &c.   All necessary lavatories and baths, with hot and cold water laid on, will be put up ; the laundry and cook-house will be in the female prison ; all the appliances for an effective prison system will be provided ; and I have no doubt that under the care of the present Local Inspector and Governor the gaol will be well managed.

Under the new arrangement an efficient steam chamber for cleansing and disinfecting the private clothing of prisoners will be used, superseding the present steam presses which are inefficient and useless.

Night-watch.   Two tell-tale clocks are on the premises ; they are secured by Hobbs' patent locks, and are put up at the extreme ends of the boundary wall. They are pegged half hourly during the night.

Unlock.   Unlock is at 6.30 A.M. in summer and at 7 A.M. in winter. Lock-up is at 6 P.M. in summer and at 4 P.M. in winter, but when the new building is completed the early locking of the prison will be no longer necessary, and I trust to see an alteration in the arrangement.

Photography.   Photographs of habitual criminals are taken by the Governor, for which work 9d. per copy is allowed by the Board of Superintendence.

One prisoner (male) effected his escape from this gaol on the 6th of May, 1874. He was retaken on the same day. No escape was attempted in 1875.

Number of Punishments for Prison Offences.

	From 1st Jan. to 31st Dec., 1874.		From 1st Jan., 1875, to day of Inspection.	
	M.	F.	M.	F.
By Magisterial authority,	—	—	2	—
By Governor—				
Dark or Refractory Cells,	42	6	66	
Stoppage of Diet,	49	10	49	2
Other punishments,	1	—	—	—
Total,	92	16	117	8

Punishments.   The new punishment cells will be heated, and have every appliance for carrying out the solitary system satisfactorily.

Two prisoners were punished by magisterial authority for outrageous Sourn
conduct during 1875, one of whom (a discharged soldier) was sentenced Disstrict.
to fourteen days' imprisonment on bread and water.

Kerry
County
Gaol.

Schools.

	From 1st Jan. to 31st Dec., 1874.		From 1st Jan., 1875, to day of Inspection.	
	M.	F.	M.	F.
Number of individual prisoners who attended school, ...	37	15	–	–
Average daily number of pupils, . .	9	2	–	–
Number of days on which school was held, .	95	274	–	–

School-hours.—Males—10 to 12 noon; Females—10 to 11½, A.M.

No school for males has been held in this prison since June, 1874, and School.
no school for females since December in that year. Sisters of Mercy,
however, visit prisoners of their own persuasion, to whom they give moral
and religious instruction.

The new school-room is well planned, and when the sittings are re-
arranged will fully meet the requirements of a good prison school.

Employment on day of Inspection.

	M.	F.
Stone-breaking and pumping water, . .	13	–
Labouring for contractor altering gaol, per contract,	6	–
Shoemaking, ...	1	–
Prison duties, ...	2	–
Needlework and knitting, . . .	–	10
Unemployed—nursery.	–	1
Discharged (before labour hours), . .	2	–
	—	—
Total in custody, . . .	24	11

Amount received for produce of Prisoners' Labour disposed of outside the Gaol.

1872, £41 15s. 11d. | 1873, £49 9s. 6d. | 1874, £15 4s. 5d.

Although the amount received for the sale of work outside the prison Labour.
in 1874 was only £15 4s. 5d., and £28 2s. during the expired portion of
1875, a large sum amounting to £149 8s. was put to the credit of the
Board by the contractor, in payment for the labour of the prisoners
furnished to him, as per agreement.

Punitive labour has been maintained by pumping water and by stone-
breaking. Prisoners not sentenced to hard labour also break stones, and
artisans work at their trades.

Prisoners are reported to work for from seven to eight hours daily.

Dietary and Contracts.

Bread, white, per 4lb. loaf, 5d.; brown, per 4lb. loaf, 5d.; potatoes, per cwt.,
3s. 5d.; new milk, boiling skimmed milk, per gallon, 4½d.; coal, per ton, £1 3s. 3d.
gas, per 1,000 cubic feet, 6s. 8d; candles, per lb., 8d., soap, per cwt. £1 4s.

Net average daily cost of Ordinary Diet for each Prisoner.

1872, . 3·66d. | 1873, . 4·24d. | 1874, . 3·9d.

The food for the use of the prisoners which I tasted on the day of my Food.
visit was of a good description, and the Chaplains generally report
favourably of the samples submitted for their inspection.

I questioned all the prisoners in custody. No complaint was made to
me by any.

SOUTH DISTRICT.

Kerry County Gaol.

Officers and Salaries.

Non-Resident.

	£	s.	d.
F. M'G. Denny, esq., Local Inspector,	140	0	0
Rev. R. D. A. Orpen, Protestant Chaplain,	50	0	0
Very Rev. John Mawe, Roman Catholic Chaplain,	50	0	0
Wm. H. Lawlor, esq, Physician,	—		
Michael Lawlor, esq., Apothecary,	30	0	0

Resident.

	£	s.	d.
Robt. Harris, esq., Governor,	200	0	0
Sylvester Murphy, C. W. and Clerk,	50	0	0

Turnkeys.

	£	s.	d.
Robert Farmer,*	40	0	0
Edwd. Meara, *Shoemaker*,*	40	0	0
Patrick Lenihan, *Tailor*,*	40	0	0
Patk. Kane, *Gatekeeper*,*	40	0	0
Michl. O'Sullivan, *Schoolmaster*,*	40	0	0
John Duggan,*	35	0	0
Thomas West,	35	0	0
Jeremiah Howe, *Porter*,*	15	0	0
James Dunning, Night Watchman,*	20	0	0
Ellen Riordan, Matron,	45	0	0
Anne Murphy, Assist. Matron,*	20	0	0
Mary Quinnell, Nursetender,*	20	0	0

* Receiving 2s. per week extra.

Vacancies in the Staff since last Inspection, how caused, and how filled up.

Warder Garrett Cotter dismissed; John Duggan appointed to his place. Warder Thomas O'Brien superannuated; William Sims appointed to his place. Warder Thomas Walsh resigned; his place has not been filled up, being deemed unnecessary. Warder William Sims resigned; Thomas West appointed to his place.

Officers on Gaol Allowance.

Jeremiah Howe, Porter.

Governor's salary.

I am happy to learn that a recommendation of the Board of Superintendence for an increase to the Governor's salary was laid before the Presentment Sessions in November last, and was agreed to, a large majority of the ratepayers having voted for it.

Mr. Harris has been a long time in the service of the Board, he is an efficient prison officer; and I have no hesitation in stating that his case is well worthy of the consideration of the Grand Jury. I therefore approve of the recommendation of the Board that the presentment do pass at the ensuing assizes.

Visits paid by Extern Officers.

	From 1st Jan. to 31st Dec., 1874.	From 1st Jan., 1875, to day of Inspection.
Number of times the Board of Superintendence met and discharged business,	17	11
Local Inspector to Gaol,	106	73
Do. each Bridewell,	4	2
Chaplain, Prot. Episcopal Church,	115	70
,, Roman Catholic,	185	117
Physician and Surgeon,	369	239
Apothecary,	350	230

Hospital.

	1872.		1873.		1874.		1875 (to day of Inspection).	
	M.	F.	M.	F.	M.	F.	M.	F.
No. of Prisoners in hospital,	40	11	63	42	52	17	47	7
Average daily number in hospital,	1·8	0·63	1·82	1·02	2	·23	2·5	·15
No. of prisoners prescribed for and treated out of hospital,	91	16	145	10	85	9	43	11
No. of deaths in the gaol,	1	–	2	–	1	–	–	–
Cost of medicine,	£22 19s. 10d.		£3 16s. 1d.		£5 12s. 8½d.		—	
Cost of diet for prisoners in hospital,	£22 10s. 7d.		£23 11s. 4d.		£27 18s. 11½d.		—	
Cost of all extra diet ordered by medical officer for prisoners not in hospital,	£2 6s. 8d.		£1 1s. 10d.		£16 0s. 4d.		—	

The present hospital building will in future be appropriated for male prisoners only, and an hospital for females will be fitted up in the prison for inmates of that sex. This arrangement will have many advantages.

Books and Accounts.

Net cost of gaol, including diet and salaries.

1872, . £2,203 7s. 8d. | 1873, . £2,245 8s. 9d. | 1874, . £2,315 8s. 6d.

Total cost of officers, including clothing, value of rations, Washing, Gas, &c.

1872, . £1,194 1s. 11d. | 1873, . £1,276 12s. 10d. | 1874, . £1,238 0s. 7d.

Average cost of each prisoner per annum.

1872, . £35 19s. 11d. | 1873, . £40 19s. 7d. | 1874, . £49 5s. 6d.

Repaid by the War Department for military prisoners.

1872, . — | 1873, . £3 5s. 0d. | 1874, . £0 11s. 0d.

Repaid by the Inland Revenue Department for excise prisoners.

1872, — | 1873, . £0 10s. 6d. | 1874, —

Repaid out of the Consolidated Fund for the maintenance, &c., of prisoners.

1872, . £206 1s. 9d. | 1873, . £149 2s. 4d. | 1874, . £96 6s. 5d.

The registers, books, journals, and accounts in this prison are well and Books, &c. carefully kept by the clerk, and checked by the Governor. He marks with his initials the State of Prison at Lockings Book and the Consumption Book daily, and the Local Inspector again checks them weekly. The journal of the Governor is very full and satisfactory. In it he notes all matters deserving of observation which occur in the prison. He is an officer, who, as my colleague in his report for 1874 observes, has conducted himself during the many years he has held office in the prison in such a manner as to merit the confidence of the Board and the public. The journal of the Local Inspector is well kept. He also is an efficient officer; and I have no doubt that under the supervision of these officers the new system of separation will be satisfactorily administered. Both the Chaplains have journals in which they record the duties they perform. The journal of the Medical Officer is well and carefully kept, as are all the books of his department; and his constant attendance in the gaol shows the attention he pays to his duties in it.

Board of Superintendence.

Wilson Gun, esq., D.L.	Maurice F. Sandes, esq.	Henry Herbert, esq.
D. D'C. M'Gillicuddy, esq.	Samuel M. Hussey, esq.	Daniel Jas. O'Connell, esq.
Nicholas Donovan, esq., n.L.	Col. B. Blennerhassett.	Gerard O'Connor, esq.
Francis B. Chute, esq.	Major Crosbie, n.L.	Thomas W. Sandes, esq.

The Board meets for the discharge of business on the last Thursday of Board. each month, when accounts are paid by cheque in favour of the Local Inspector, who produces vouchers at the next meeting of the Board. Salaries of subordinate officers are paid weekly; those of the superior officers and the large contractors half-yearly at assizes.

Bridewells.

Since my inspection the bridewell at Milltown has been closed as useless, Bridewells. and now that a railway runs between Castleisland and Tralee the Castle-island bridewell should also be abolished.

SOUTH DISTRICT.

Kerry County.

Bridewells.

STATE OF BRIDEWELLS.

—	Killarney.		Dingle.		Milltown.	
	M.	F.	M.	F.	M.	F.
No. of Committals in past year, . .	143	29	17	1	14	2
Of whom were Drunkards, .	38	10	13	–	–	1
No. of Committals in the quarter preceding inspection, .	37	8	4	1	–	–
Of whom were Drunkards, .	6	3	1	–	–	–

—	Killarney.	Dingle.	Milltown.
Petty Sessions and Transmittals, how often?	Weekly, on Wednesdays.	Fortnightly ; on Fridays at Dingle; on every third Thursday at Augherick.	Monthly.
Committals, whether regular?	Regular.	Regular.	Some illegal.
Registry, . . .	Correctly kept.	Correctly kept.	Correctly kept.
Repairs and Order, .	In sound repair, except some flagging in kitchen which should be mended.	In fair repair, except roof, which should be pointed; painting required, and front door to be repaired.	In fair repair.
Security, . .	Sufficient, with care.	Still insecure.	Sufficient, with ca[...]
Accommodation, .	Males—one day-room and four sleeping cells. Females—one day-room and two cells.	Males — day-room and two cells below. Females— day - room and two cells below.	Two day - roo[m] and six cells.
Furniture, Bedding, and Utensils.	Sufficient, but one pair of blankets much worn.	Good and sufficient.	Sufficient for t[...] few prisoners co[m]mitted, but or[...] blanket in hole[...]
Water, how supplied?	A good pump in front yard.	None on premises, but a stream on opposite side of road.	None on premise[s]
Sewerage, . .	Sufficient ; earth boxes would be an improvement.	Sufficient.	A cesspool.
Cleanliness, Dryness, and Ventilation.	Very clean and well kept ; ventilation sufficient, but damp.	Clean and orderly, ventilation sufficient.	Very clean ; ven[...] lation sufficie[...] but damp.
Cost of Dietary per head per day.	Males, 6d.; females, 5d.	Males, 6d. ; females, 5d.	Males, 6d.; femal[...] 5d.
Salary of Keeper, .	£20.	£10.	£15 a year.
Whether Keeper follows any other employment.	Weighmaster, salary £31 ; court-keeper, salary £8.	Is a carpenter, by which trade he supports himself.	None.
Official Inspection, .	19th August, 1875.	21st August, 1875.	22nd August, 18[...]
Remarks, . .	One female prisoner in custody, on remand for larceny. I regret that the Board refused to increase the salary of the Keeper, who is a deserving public servant insufficiently paid.	One male in custody for drunkenness.	No prisoner in c[...] tody when I visited. Since my visit [...] Bridewell has b[...] closed.

STATE OF BRIDEWELLS—*continued.*

—	Cahersiveen.		Listowel.	
	M.	F.	M.	F.
No. of Committals in past year, .	68	16	75	11
Of whom were Drunkards, .	39	5	45	7
No. of Committals in the quarter preceding inspection,	10	3	24	2
Of whom were Drunkards,	4	—	3	1
Petty Sessions and Transmittals, how often?	Fortnightly; on Saturdays. In other parts of the district monthly.		Weekly; on Saturdays.	
Committals, whether regular.	—		Some illegal; for more than three days signed by one justice.	
Registry, . .	Correctly kept.		Correctly kept.	
Repairs and Order,	Building in fair repair, except roof, which admits the wet.		In good repair and order.	
Security, .	Sufficient with care.		Sufficient, with care.	
Accommodation, .	Males—one day-room and two cells below, two above. Females—one day-room and two cells below.		Males — day-room and two cells off it on ground floor. Females—same accommodation.	
Furniture, Bedding, and Utensils.	Sufficient.		Sufficient and good.	
Water, how supplied	None on premises, or near.		None on premises; it should be introduced from town main.	
Sewerage, . .	Stated to be sufficient.		Stated to be sufficient.	
Cleanliness, Dryness, and Ventilation.	Clean, but very damp; ventilation sufficient.		Clean and dry; ventilation sufficient.	
Cost of Dietary, per head, per day.	Males, 6d.; females, 5d.		Males, 6d.; females, 5d.	
Salary of Keeper, .	£10.		£30.	
Whether Keeper follows any other employment.	Has a pension of £27 a year.		None.	
Official Inspection,	21st August, 1875.		24th August, 1875.	
Remarks, . .	No prisoner in custody.		No prisoner in custody.	

STATE OF BRIDEWELLS—*continued.*

Kerry County.

	—	Castleisland.		Kenmare.	
Bridewells.	No. of Committals in past year,	**M.** 74	**F.** 9	**M.** 58	**F.** 6
	Of whom were Drunkards,	21	2	9	5
	No. of Committals in the quarter preceding inspection,	20	1	10	4
	Of whom were Drunkards,	3	—	1	1
	Petty Sessions and Transmittals, how often?	Fortnightly; on Thursdays.		Fortnightly; on Mondays.	
	Committals, whether regular.	Regular.		Regular.	
	Registry,	Correctly kept.		Correctly kept.	
	Repairs and Order,	In good repair, except two outside doors, which should be repaired.		In good repair and order.	
	Security,	Sufficient.		Fair.	
	Accommodation,	Males — day-room and four cells two below and two above, off Keeper's room. Females—day-room and two cells.		Males—day-room and three cells. Females—day-room and three cells.	
	Furniture, Bedding, and Utensils.	Good and sufficient.		Good, and sufficient.	
	Water, how supplied,	None on premises, but near.		None on premises; distant.	
	Sewerage,	Sufficient.		Stated to be sufficient.	
	Cleanliness, Dryness, and Ventilation.	Clean, dry, and orderly; ventilation sufficient.		Clean, dry, and orderly; ventilation sufficient.	
	Cost of Dietary, per head per day.	Males, 6d.; females, 5d.		Males, 6d.; females, 5d.	
	Salary of Keeper,	£10.		£10.	
	Whether Keeper follows any other employment.	Is Petty Sessions Clerk, salary £100 a year.		Holds some land; is process-server.	
	Official inspection,	25th August, 1875.		20th August, 1875.	
	Remarks,	No prisoner in custody.		No prisoner in custody.	

JOHN LENTAIGNE, *Inspector-General.*

KILDARE COUNTY GAOL, AT NAAS.—STATUTABLE INSPECTION, 3RD DECEMBER, 1875.

Number of Prisoners of all Classes in Gaol on the day of Inspection, and on the corresponding date in the three preceding years.

	M.	**F.**		**M.**	**F.**
1872,	39	23	1874,	73	17
1873,	62	16	1875 (day of Inspection),	43	16

Number of Returned Convicts in Gaol on the day of Inspection, and during each of the three preceding years.

	M.	**F.**		**M.**	**F.**
1872,	7	2	1875 (up to and including		
1873,	1	3	day of Inspection),	3	1
1874,	2	1	Day of Inspection,	2	—

Juveniles.

Commitments of young offenders under 16 years of age during 1875.

	M.	F.
12 years old and under,	3	1
Above 12 and not exceeding 16 years,	7	1
Total,	10	2
Sent to reformatories during 1875,	3	1
Workhouse offenders,	2	1

One juvenile (J. H.), fourteen years of age, was, when I visited, in Juveniles. custody, sentenced to an imprisonment of one month for leaving service, having been apprenticed from the workhouse to a farmer at wages of 10s. a quarter.

Five males under 16 years of age had been committed in 1875 for periods of from seven days to twenty-four hours for drunkenness and disorderly conduct, and 7 for larceny, three of whom were sentenced to be whipped by order of the court before which they were tried.

Commitments.

CLASSES.	From 1st January to 31st December, 1874.		From 1st January, 1875, to day of Inspection.	
	M.	F.	M.	F.
Debtors,	1	—	—	—
Criminals,	475	189	369	178
Vagrants,	2	2	12	2
Drunkards,	147	105	194	116
Total,	625	296	575	296

Number of Individual Prisoners (exclusive of Debtors), and Number of Times each had been committed during 1874 and 1875.

NUMBER OF TIMES COMMITTED.	1874.				1875, to day of Inspection.			
	Juveniles.		Adults.		Juveniles.		Adults.	
	M.	F.	M.	F.	M.	F.	M.	F.
Once within the year,	24	3	336	92	8	2	375	46
Twice ,,	—	—	39	18	1	—	40	24
Thrice ,,	—	—	11	12	—	—	12	5
4 times ,,	1	—	5	7	—	—	6	11
5 ,, ,,	—	—	—	4	—	—	2	3
6 ,, ,,	—	—	1	1	—	—	—	2
7 ,, ,,	—	—	2	2	—	—	1	2
8 ,, ,,	—	—	—	3	—	—	—	4
9 ,, ,,	—	—	4	1	—	—	1	3
10 ,, ,,	—	—	6	—	—	—	—	3
11 ,, ,,	—	—	1	—	—	—	1	1
12 ,, ,,	—	—	—	—	—	—	—	—
13 ,, ,,	—	—	—	1	—	—	1	—
14 ,, ,,	—	—	—	—	—	—	—	—
15 ,, ,,	—	—	—	1	—	—	—	—
Total,	25	3	407	142	9	2	439	104
No. of above who had not been in Gaol previous to 1st January in	24	3	300	68	8	2	304	44

South District
Kildare County Gaol.

Number of Individual Prisoners (exclusive of Debtors) committed in the year 1874, and to the day of Inspection in 1875, who had been Once, Twice, Thrice, Four Times, Five Times, &c., &c., from their first Committment in any year.

NUMBER OF TIMES COMMITTED.	1874.				1875, to day of Inspection.			
	Juveniles		Adults.		Juveniles.		Adults.	
	M.	F.	M.	F.	M.	F.	M.	F
Once only,	23	3	260	64	7	2	250	2
Twice,	1	–	49	9	1	–	82	17
Thrice,	–	–	33	6	–	–	30	–
4 ,,	1	–	13	4	–	–	24	7
5 ,,	–	–	9	9	1	–	6	5
6 ,,	–	–	14	4	–	–	6	5
7 to 11 times,	–	–	16	13	–	–	28	11
12 to 16 ,,	–	–	6	2	–	–	7	5
17 to 20 ,,	–	–	3	6	–	–	2	4
21 to 30 ,,	–	–	4	8	–	–	1	10
31 to 40 ,,	–	–	–	6	–	–	3	2
41 to 60 ,,	–	–	–	–	–	–	–	4
61 to 70 ,,	–	–	–	4	–	–	–	1
71 to 80 ,,	–	–	–	2	–	–	–	4
81 to 120 ,,	–	–	–	4	–	–	–	4
161 to 180 ,,	–	–	–	1	–	–	–	–
Total No. of Individuals committed,	25	3	407	142	9	2	439	104
No. of Commitments represented in foregoing,	29	3	1,015	1,791	14	2	1,164	1617

Averages, and Highest and Lowest Numbers (exclusive of Debtors).

—	From 1st January to 31st December, 1874.			From 1st January, 1875, to day of Inspection.		
	M.	F.	Date.	M.	F.	Date.
Average daily number of prisoners in custody,	66	20	—	57	15	—
Highest number of prisoners at any one time,	124		9th Sept.	98		18th Feb.
Lowest ditto,	46		25th March.	46		14th May.
Highest number of males at any one time,	102		12th Nov.	80		17th April.
Ditto, of females,	34		25th March.	25		8th July.
Lowest number of males at any one time,	34		19th May.	38		14th May.
Ditto, of females,	9		25th Dec.	4		26th March.

Highest number of Prisoners (exclusive of Debtors) in Gaol during each of the previous seven years, and up to day of Inspection in 1875.

1st March, 1868, . . . 104	9th February, 1872, . . 87
3rd October, 1869, . . 101	4th October, 1873, . . 101
6th May, 1870, . . 110	9th September, 1874, . . 124
6th October, 1871, . . 94	18th February, 1875, . . 98

Solitary.

During 1875 two adult males were sentenced to solitary confinement, by order of the court before which they were tried.

Commitments.

Forty-three males and 16 females of all classes were inmates of this gaol, under criminal commitments, on the day of my visit. Of these, 7 males and 3 females were on remand or for trial; 19 males and 2 females had been convicted by juries, having been tried at assizes or quarter sessions; 3 were military offenders tried by courts-martial. The remaining prisoners in custody had been convicted by justices at petty sessions of vagrancy, drunkenness, and petty larcenies. I found in the gaol one man, under observation, who is without doubt a lunatic.

Eight males were under sentences for periods exceeding six months—1 being for two years; 2 for one year; 1 for eighteen; and 4 for nine months.

Four had been sentenced for six months each, and 19 for three months and under six months. The remaining male prisoners under sentences in custody were for periods varying from three weeks to two months.

The females, with one exception, were prostitutes, sentenced for terms varying from seven days to six months, convicted of larceny from the person, drunkenness, disorderly conduct, trespass on the Curragh Camp, and one for misconduct in the Lock Hospital at the Camp.

Twenty-two male prisoners in custody had been committed for crimes against property; 6 for assaults, and other offences against the person; 7 for false attestation or desertion; 1 for attempted suicide; and 6 for drunkenness, threatening, trespass, leaving service, and begging.

One prisoner, evidently of unsound mind, had been committed on remand for observation.

Seven females were under charges of larceny; one had been convicted of an assault; 1 of insubordination in the Lock Hospital; the remainder had been convicted of drunkenness, disorderly conduct, and trespass on the Curragh Camp.

I found amongst the inmates of the gaol many discharged so'diers, two of whom were returned convicts, both sentenced for terms of three months—one an old man, seventy-five years of age, for attempting suicide; the other for assaulting the police.

The prisoner under observation was in hospital, in charge of two prisoners. They were the only inmates of the hospital on the day of my visit. Another man was in bed in his cell suffering from cold, but not sufficiently ill to be removed to the hospital.

The inspection which I made of this gaol at the close of the year 1875 was very satisfactory, so far as the discipline of the gaol and its general management was concerned. The arrangements of the male prison and the appliances in that prison are well suited for discipline; but the circumstances of the female prison and its structural defects render the building quite unfit for the purposes of separation, under the Act 3 and 4 Vic., cap. 44. The cells in that prison are not artificially heated. They are flagged; and at the time of my visit in December the weather was extremely cold. During such weather prisoners should not be kept during the day in flagged, unheated cells. There were doubtless fires in two day-rooms, and one woman at a time was permitted to be at each; but the arrangement is insufficient, and does not meet the requirements of the statute. I found in one of the cells a woman who had been committed on the previous day. The woman was without shoes; and I learned that her shoes had been taken from her by the police to identify foot-tracks on soft ground, where potatoes had been stolen; but it was the duty of the Matron of the prison, under such circumstances, to have at once supplied her with prison shoes. An extra supply of bedding is issued to prisoners in the cells, but during the day they have no protection from the cold. I directed that in future during severe weather the women be employed in the laundry, where there are separate stalls; and the matter is of special importance here, as syphilitic patients are sometimes committed to this prison for insubordination in the Lock Hospital attached to the Curragh Camp. One female, an inmate of the prison at the time of my visit, had been so committed.

SOUTH DISTRICT.

Kildare County Gaol.

I found the prison for males, as it always has been since the appointment of the present Governor, very clean and well kept; all the appliances for separation in a satisfactory condition; the heating apparatus effective; and the hulls in order. A list of tools entrusted to the prisoner for his trade hangs on the outside of each cell—an arrangement which should be generally adopted elsewhere. The list is duly checked, and at night the warder on duty receives the articles from the prisoner, and is responsible that they are locked up.

Baths, &c.

There is a sufficient supply of good baths in the prison. A bath-room with hot and cold water laid on, has been fitted up in the basement of the male prison, and another in the laundry, for females. Prisoners are bathed on reception.

Stock at time of Inspection.

	In Use.	In Store.	Male Clothing.		In Use.	In Store.	Female Clothing.		In Use.	In Store.
Blankets, pairs of,	193½	54½	Shirts, .	.	201	39	Shifts, .	.	34	40
Sheets, pairs of,	230	27	Jackets, .	.	130	18	Jackets,	.	48	44
Rugs, .	. 183	10	Vests, .	.	115	19	Petticoats,	.	66	24
Hammocks or			Trowsers,	.	68	63	Aprons,	.	39	7
Cots,	. 87	11	Caps, .	.	99	11	Neckerchiefs, .		33	28
Bedticks, .	. 76	16	Socks, pairs of,	202	16		Caps, .	.	60	16
Bedsteads, .	. 36	—	Shoes,Slippers,&				Stockings,pairs of,	65	70½
			Clogs, pairs of,	90	24		Shoes,Slippers,&			
							Clogs, pairs of,	33	3

Bedding.

I found an ample supply of good bedding and prison clothing in use and in store. The bed-clothes in the cells are so arranged that they are kept always aired, and can be inspected at once.

Prisoners of both sexes are supplied with stockings; and caps, neckerchiefs, and aprons are given to the females.

Fumigator.

A fumigating apparatus has been provided for disinfecting and cleansing the clothes of prisoners in both prisons.

Stores.

The prison stores are well kept and suitably arranged. A new store has been fitted up since my last visit, in which the private clothing of prisoners is kept made up in bundles, and lists are appended stating the different articles, the property of each prisoner.

Water.

An abundant supply of water for prison use is obtained from the canal which adjoins the prison. It is driven into the cistern placed over the male prison by the power of the crank pump.

Lavatory.

The lavatories and water-closets are sufficient. Thirteen water-closets are in the male prison, and eight in the female prison.

Sewerage.

The sewerage is at present effective. It discharges itself by a pipe under the canal into a field adjoining. The pipe was not staunch, and contaminated the water of the well adjoining the hospital; but it has now been reset, and glazed pipes used.

Laundry.

The laundry in the female prison is well arranged. There are eight washing troughs, with hot and cold water laid on, and they are properly stalled for separation, and have lattice doors. There is a good drying-closet, and every appliance for separation of prisoners when employed in the laundry.

A laundry is likewise provided for males, in which coarse washing is done. It also has a drying-room attached; but the laundry is too small.

Gas.

Gas is supplied to the male prison, and to one day-room of the female prison; to both laundries, and to other parts of the gaol premises. It is supplied on working days to the cells in the male prison until 8 P.M.

Lock-up.

The prison cells are unlocked in summer at 6.30 A.M., at all periods of the year, and are locked for the night at 6 P.M., in summer, and at dark in winter.

At 10 P.M. the night watch comes on duty. One warder in rotation patrols the interior of the prison. There is no patrol of the exterior hounds at night. The vigilance of. the night watch is tested by two tell-tale clocks in the male prison, and one in that for females. They are protected from being tampered with by locks of Chubbs' make. The Governor visited the prison at late and unexpected hours fifty-two times during 1875, to test the vigilance of the night watch.

SOUTH DISTRICT.

Kildare County Gaol.

Night-watch.

The photographing of habitual prisoners is executed by the Head Warder, for which duty he receives 8½d. for each copy.

Photo-graphy.

Visits to prisoners are permitted as hitherto. The place where visits are held is well arranged, and has since my last inspection been caged off by prison labour so that it would be impossible for a prohibited article to be handed to a prisoner without the knowledge of the officer in charge ; but a seat should be provided for the prisoner, especially as untried prisoners may be occasionally detained with their law adviser for some time.

Visitors.

Number of Punishments for Prison Offences.

	From 1st January to 31st December, 1874.		From 1st January, 1875, to day of Inspection.	
	M.	F.	M.	F.
By Magisterial authority,	–	–	2	–
By Governor—				
Dark or Refractory Cells,	96	9	62	2
Other Punishments,	3	–	2	–
Total,	99	9	66	2

Five punishment cells are fitted up in the basement of the male prison ; they are heated, and have bells which ring in the central hall. Two are for females, in the basement next the laundry. No change has been made as recommended in the position of the pipes which convey heat to the cells.

Punish-ments.

Schools.

	From 1st Jan. to 31st Dec., 1874.		From 1st Jan., 1875, to day of Inspection.	
	M.	F.	M.	F.
Number of individual prisoners who attended school,	31	–	39	–
Average daily number of pupils,	9·5	–	9·3	–
Number of days on which School was held,	269	–	258	–

School-hours.—Males—12 to 1.30, P.M.

The school is in connexion with the National Board of Education, and was inspected by their District Inspector on the 15th January, 1876. He reports :—"The teacher appears to be attentive, but has not had much experience as a teacher, and he declined to become a candidate for classification. He is employed as work superintendent of shoemaking. Number of roll—11 present, and examined 7. Class 1, up to programme ; class 2, in advance of programme in all subjects. No senior class."

School.

The school-room for males is stalled, being divided into eleven compartments. No school for females was held during the year 1875 ; but Roman Catholic females and the males, under certain restrictions, receive moral and religious instruction from Sisters of Mercy who visit the gaol. The Chaplains frequently visit the school. I find that the Protestant Chaplain visited the school thirty-seven times during the year, and he records very fully his observations on the progress the prisoners make. The Roman Catholic visited thirteen times.

SOUTH
DISTRICT.

*Kildare
County
Gaol.*

Employment on day of Inspection.

					M.	F.
Picking Oakum and Pumping,	.	.	.	.	25*	7
Mat-making, .	.	.	.	.	4	–
Shoemaking, .	.	.	.	.	2	–
Tailoring, .	.	.	.	.	1	–
Cleaning prison,	.	.	.	.	3	–
Cooking, .	.	.	.	.	1	–
Sewing and Washing,	.	.	.	.	–	14
Unemployed one, sick one, a lunatic,	.	.	.	3	–
Discharged (before labour hours), .	.	.	.	1	2
		Total in custody,	.	.	43	16

* Twenty-one males under sentences of hard labour included in the above are employed at shot drill.

Amount received for produce of Prisoners' Labour disposed of outside the Gaol.

1872, . £83 0s. 6d. | 1873, . £53 13s. 6d. | 1874, . £90 6s. 7d.

Hard
labour.

Punitive labour is enforced in this prison by shot drill, for four hours in summer and three in winter, and by work on the crank pump from three to five hours per day, varying according to the number of prisoners in custody sentenced to hard labour. Relief stalls are provided in which prisoners pick oakum when waiting for their turn on the mill.

Artisans when in custody work at their trades. All the clothes worn in the establishment are made up in the prison. Barrack washing is done by the males ; the females also wash, sew, knit, and repair the clothing of the prisoners. The inmates of both sexes pick oakum.

There are good workshops in the basement of the male prison, in which the men can work in separation.

Contracts.

Bread, white, per 4-lb. loaf, 7¼d.; ditto, brown, per 4-lb. loaf, 6¼d.; oatmeal, per cwt., 16s. 3¼d.; potatoes, per cwt., 4s. 4d.; new milk, per gallon, 10d.; coal (Scotch), per ton, 19s. 9d; ditto (Whitehaven), £1 4s. 9d.; straw, per cwt., 3s. 7d.; gas, per 1,000 cubic feet, 7s. 6d.; soap, brown, per cwt., £1 3s. 0d; ditto, white, per cwt., £1 6s. Other Contracts—Black tea, per lb., 2s. 3d.; soft sugar, per lb., 3d.; starch, per stone, 4s.; blue, per lb., 10d.; washing soda, per cwt., 9s.; heavy butt leather, per lb., 1s. 8d.; slitter leather, per lb., 1s. 8d.; kip leather, per lb., 2s. 8d.; hemp, per lb., 2s. 2d.; closing yarn, per doz., 10d.; needles, per 100, sewing, 9½d.; ditto, knitting, 2s.; thimbles, per doz.. 4½d.; grey frieze, per yard, 4s. 10d.; tweed, for petticoats, per yard, 1s. 3d.; linsey woolsey, per yard, 1s. 3½d.; woollen kerchiefs, 2s ; black and blay thread, per lb., 2s. 5½d; white spools, per doz., 6d.; white tape, per piece, 2½d.; blankets, each according to weight, 12s. 6d.; rugs, each according to pattern to be seen at the prison, 6s.; blay calico (yard wide), per yard, 5d.; check, linen (yard wide), per yard, 10½d.; bleached calico (yard wide), per yard, 5½d.; blay linen (yard wide), per yard, 7¼d.; bed ticken (yard wide), per yard, 9½d.; twilled calico, for sheeting (2 yards wide), per yard, 1s. 1d.; lime brushes, 2s. 9d.; sweeping brushes, 1s. 10d.; floor scrubbers, 1s. 8d.; best oaten straw, for beds, per ton, 72s.; also 10 pair of summer trowsers, at 17s. 9d. each, for officers, as may be selected, and 3 shawls for matrons—one at 15s., and two at 10s. 3d. each.

Net Average daily cost of Ordinary Diet for each Prisoner.

1872, . . 4·5d. | 1873, . . . 5d. | 1874, . . . 5d.

Food.

The food prepared for the use of the inmates on the day of my visit was of a good description ; and I found from the reports of the Chaplains that it has been invariably so during the year. The meal used is of a superior description, and being kept in a dry, heated cell, it improves, and consequently the stirabout is excellent.

I questioned individually all the prisoners in custody on the day of my inspection. No complaints were made to me by any.

Officers and Salaries.

Non-resident.	£	s.	d.
Augustus Warburton, esq., Local Inspector. . .	80	0	0
Rev. M. T. De Burgh, Protestant Chaplain, . .	45	0	0
Rev. James Hughes, R. C. Chaplain, . . .	45	0	0
Fred. Falkiner, esq., Surgeon,	65	0	0
Resident.			
Edw. J. Gildea, esq., Governor,	300	0	0
Jeremiah M'Kenna, Head Warder, . . .	75	0	0
William Shaw, Clerk, .	60	0	0
Wm. Manders, *Carpenter* and Warder, . .	45	0	0

	£	s.	d.
John Seaborne, *Schoolmaster* and Warder, . . .	40	0	0
Peter Molloy, temporary Gate-warder, . .	30	0	0
William Glen, Warder, .	30	0	0
Joseph Connell, do., .	30	0	0
John Fox, do., .	30	0	0
Daniel Ball, do., .	30	0	0
Michael Hopkins, temporary Warder, . . .	30	0	0
Miss Esther Tormey, Matron,	45	0	0
Mrs. Mary Molloy, Assist. Matron, . . .	25	0	0
Mrs. Margt. Lyons, Hospital Matron, . . .	25	0	0

Vacancies in staff since last Inspection, how caused and how filled up.

Myles Synnott, Warder, resigned; Thomas M'Guire appointed in his stead. William Phayer, Gate Warder, superannuated; John Fox appointed. Thomas M'Guire, Warder, called upon to resign; Daniel Ball appointed in his stead. Thomas O'Grady, Warder, resigned; vacancy not yet filled up.

Officers on Gaol Allowance.
All the intern.

Visits paid by Officers.

	From 1st Jan. to 31st Dec., 1874.	From 1st Jan., 1875, to day of Inspection.
Number of times the Board of Superintendence met and discharged business,	14	13
Local Inspector to Gaol, . .	213	165
Chaplain, Protestant Episcopal Church,	176	148
Roman Catholic Chaplain, f. .	217	183
Surgeon, ...	182	170

The Governor reports to me that he is well satisfied with the care and attention which the Head Warder bestows on his duties in the prison, and I have always found him an efficient prison officer.

Books and Accounts.

Net cost of Gaol, including Diet and Salaries.
1872, . £2,371 6s. 8d. | 1873, . £2,868 16s. 11d. | 1874, . £2,676 17s. 8d.

Total cost of Officers, including Clothing, value of Rations, &c.
1872, . £1,261 17s. 1d. | 1873, . £1,420 9s. 3d. | 1874, . £1,404 18s. 5d.

Average cost of each Prisoner per annum.
1872, . £32 17s. 9d. | 1873, . £30 9s. 9d. | 1874, . £30 15s. 10d.

Amount repaid by the War Department for Military Prisoners.
1872, . £207 17s. 0d. | 1873, . £12 10s. 0d. | 1874, . £19 15s. 2d.

Amounts repaid from the Consolidated Fund for the Maintenance, &c., of Prisoners.
1872, . £165 19s. 10d. | 1873, . £352 2s. 1d. | 1874, . £347 11s. 10d.

I was much pleased on my inspection with the great care bestowed in Books. the keeping of the various registries of discipline and finance in this prison. They are for the most part kept by the clerk, but are supervised by the Governor who marks them with his initials. He checks daily the

T

SOUTH
DISTRICT.
———
*Kildare
County
Gaol.*

issues of food, and all matters of consumption in the gaol. He selects all the prisoners employed in the different duties—in the cook-house, in the wards, and on special service of every description. He marks in red ink the names of the men he selects. He has adopted all the best forms for the checking of the accounts, and, being constantly on the spot, he sees that the work is properly done. His journal is a useful record of the various occurrences in the prison. The Local Inspector also devotes much time and attention to the discharge of his duties in the prison. His journal is kept with much care and attention ; and I have to congratulate the Board in having found a worthy successor in him to fill the place left vacant by the lamented death of the late Mr. Cannon. The journals of the Medical Officer and of the Chaplains are well and fully kept.

Hospital.

	1872.		1873.		1874.		1875 (to day of Inspection).	
	M.	F.	M.	F.	M.	F.	M.	F.
No. of prisoners in hospital,	4	1	4	5	2	6	4	1
Average daily number in hospital, . . .	·2	·1	·5	·2	·1	·2	·328	·222
No. of prisoners prescribed for and treated out of hospital, . . .	97	61	156	49	158	34	62	19
Number of deaths, . .	–	–	–	–	–	–	1	–
Cost of medicine, . .	£14 11s. 10d.		£14 16s. 8d.		£12 9s. 0d.		—	
Cost of diet for prisoners in hospital, . . .	£2 0s. 0d.		£7 1s. 0d.		£3 0s. 5d.		—	
Cost of all extra diet ordered by Medical Officer for prisoners not in hospital,	£14 7s. 4d.		£16 3s. 4d.		£3 12s. 8d.		—	

Hospital.

The hospitals, although under the same roof, are separate. They have every appliance for the treatment of the sick—baths, water-closets, and exercising grounds. The Medical Officer is attentive in the discharge of his duties ; but the hospitals are seldom occupied. One male only was in hospital on the day of inspection.

Board of Superintendence.

John La Touche, esq., D.L. | Richard Moore, esq., J.P. | The Baron De Robeck, J.P.
Major H. L. Barton, D.L. | G. P. L. Mansfield, esq., | Saml. G. Ireland, esq., J.P.
Major R. H. Burrowes, J.P. | D.L., J.P. | G. L. O'Kelly, esq., J.P.
Patrick Nolan, esq. | Thos. Cooke Trench, esq., | Thos. Hendrick, esq., J.P.
W. R. Bulwer, esq., J.P. | J.P. |

Board.

The Board meets for the discharge of business on the first Wednesday of each month, when the salaries of intern officers and liabilities under £2 are discharged by cheques drawn in favour of the Local Inspector, who produces receipts at the next meeting of the Board.

Large amounts are paid by cheque to the creditor.

The salaries of the extern officers are paid by presentment half-yearly at assizes.

A committee of the grand jury visit the prison at assizes, and enter their report in the Visitors' Book, and I observe that their reports are always favourable.

There are no bridewells in this county.

JOHN LENTAIGNE, *Inspector-General.*

KILKENNY COUNTY AND CITY GAOL.—STATUTABLE INSPECTION, 10TH
NOVEMBER, 1875.

*Number of Prisoners of all classes in Gaol on the day of Inspection, and
on the corresponding date in the three preceding years.*

	M.	F.		M.	F.
1872,	41	6	1874,	21	6
1873,	55	9	1875 (day of Inspection),	54	15

Number of Vagrants in Gaol on the day of Inspection.

	M.	F.		M.	F.
1874,	2	—	1875,	3	—

*Number of Returned Convicts in Gaol on the day of Inspection, and during
each of the three preceding years.*

	M.	F.		M.	F.
1872,	—	2	1875 (up to and including		
1873,	2	—	day of Inspection), .	2	1
1874,	1	—	Day of Inspection, .	—	1

*Number of Prisoners in Custody during the year known to have been in
Reformatories.*

	M.	F.		M.	F.
1872,	—	2	1875 (up to and including		
1873,	1	—	day of Inspection), .	1	—
1874,	1	—	Day of Inspection, .	—	—

Juveniles.

No young offender was in custody on the day of my inspection, but 15
males, and 3 females were inmates of the gaol during the year; of
these 6 males belonged to the county jurisdiction, the others to the city.
Three males and 1 female committed were under twelve years of age.
Three males and 1 female were sent to reformatories during 1875.

Commitments.

CLASSES.	From 1st January to 31st December, 1874.		From 1st January, 1875, to day of Inspection.	
	M.	F.	M.	F.
Debtors,	1	—	—	—
Criminals,	205	63	237	66
Vagrants,	6	2	34	3
Drunkards,	77	27	108	43
Total,	289	92	379	112

*Individual Prisoners (exclusive of Debtors), and Number of Times each
had been committed during the following periods.*

NUMBER OF TIMES COMMITTED.	1874.				1875, to day of Inspection.			
	Juveniles.		Adults.		Juveniles.		Adults.	
	M.	F.	M.	F.	M.	F.	M.	F.
Once within the year,	18	4	206	49	13	3	279	60
Twice " "	1	—	19	9	1	—	25	3
Thrice " "	—	—	2	2	—	—	5	1
4 times " "	—	—	2	—	—	—	2	4
5 and 6 " "	—	—	2	1	—	—	1	2
7 " "	—	—	—	—	—	—	1	2
10 " "	—	—	—	1	—	—	—	—
Total,	19	4	231	62	14	3	313	72
No. of above who had not been in Gaol previous to 1st January in .	14	3	154	38	12	2	196	47

SOUTH DISTRICT.

Kilkenny County and City Gaol.

Individual Prisoners (exclusive of Debtors) committed in the year 1874, and to the day of Inspection in 1875, who had been Once and oftener Re-committed, from their first Commitment in any year, so far as can be ascertained.

NUMBER OF TIMES COMMITTED.	1874.				1875, to day of Inspection.			
	Juveniles.		Adults.		Juveniles.		Adults.	
	M.	F.	M.	F.	M.	F.	M.	F.
Once only, ...	14	3	138	25	13	3	192	42
Twice, ...	3	1	39	12	1	—	54	8
Thrice, ...	1	—	15	2	—	—	14	6
4 times, ...	1	—	8	6	—	—	20	2
5 „	—	—	5	4	—	—	11	—
6 „	—	—	9	2	—	—	2	4
7 to 11 „	—	—	12	5	—	—	12	5
12 to 16 „	—	—	2	2	—	—	5	2
17 to 20 „	—	—	—	2	—	—	1	2
21 to 30 „	—	—	3	1	—	—	2	—
31 to 40 „	—	—	—	1	—	—	—	1
Total No. of Individuals committed,	19	4	231	62	14	3	313	72
No. of Commitments represented in foregoing, . . .	27	5	571	284	15	3	739	263

Highest Number of Prisoners (exclusive of Debtors) in Gaol during each of the previous seven years, and up to day of Inspection in 1875.

14th October, 1868,   .   49   13th November, 1872,   .   .   44
7th June, 1869,   .   .   39   18th November, 1873,   .   .   70
16th August, 1870, .   .   40   17th May, 1874,   .   .   64
6th June, 1871,   .   .   40   16th October, 1875,   .   .   81

Averages, and Highest and Lowest Numbers (exclusive of Debtors).

—	From 1st January to 31st December, 1874.			From 1st January, 1875, to day of Inspection.		
	M.	F.	Date.	M.	F.	Date.
Average daily number of prisoners in custody,	30	8	—	35	9½	—
Highest number of prisoners at any one time,	64		17th May.	81		16th Oct.
Lowest ditto,	27		31st Dec.	24		4th Jan.
Highest number of males at any one time, .	51		19th May.	71		17th Oct.
Ditto of females,	14		14th May.	18		26th Feb.
Lowest number of males at any one time, .	18		30th Dec.	14		5th Jan.
Ditto of females,	4		24th Aug.	3		30th July.

Number of Prisoners sentenced to Solitary Confinement and Whipping by order of Court.

	From 1st January to 31st December, 1874.		From 1st January, 1875, to day of Inspection.	
	M.	F.	M.	F.
Solitary Confinement, . . .	—	—	1	—
Whipping, ...	—	—	1	—
Total, ...	—	—	2	—

I found 54 males and 15 females in custody on my inspection of this prison, but 18 males and 3 females being on remand or for trial swelled the number of inmates far beyond the ordinary daily averages. Six were military prisoners. One of these had been sentenced for a term of 840 days. He is very violent; constantly committing offences; and the Governor showed me a mark on the wall of the central hall made by a stone which this prisoner had thrown from the stone-yard, through the window, at one of the prison officers.* On reference to the journal of the Medical Officer, I observe that he has noted in September and October last that he considers that a padded cell should be specially prepared for this prisoner, and others who threaten suicide. This man having already attempted his own life as well as that of others, every precaution should be taken to prevent another attempt.

The 5 other military prisoners in custody had been sentenced—1 for 672 days, and 4 for 336 days each.

Thirty prisoners were under sentence, tried by civil tribunals. Of these 12 males had been convicted of offences against property, and sentenced to imprisonments—1 for two years, 2 for one year, 1 for nine, and 5 for six months; the others for periods of two and three months each.

Eighteen had been sentenced for assaults, vagrancy, and drunkenness —4 to be imprisoned for one year each, 1 for nine months, 2 for four, 1 for three, 3 for two, and 7 for short terms of from seven days to one month.

Amongst the latter an old soldier (J. R.), committed as a vagrant, for seeking relief in the Kilkenny Union Workhouse, was a melancholy object—one mass of rags, and afflicted with softening of the brain and paralysis. Born at Newport, county Tipperary, his parents emigrated with him to England when he was three months old, where he was educated, and served for three years at Hong Kong; but, having received a sunstroke, he became paralysed and was treated in Netley Hospital, from which he was sent to the Nenagh Union Workhouse. £4 of his money were given to the guardians, and on his leaving the union they deducted the cost of his keep, and gave him the balance. This money is now all expended, and he besought to be sent back to Nenagh that he might be again admitted into the workhouse there, and not be permitted to die in the streets after his discharge from the gaol.

Two females were under sentences of imprisonment for twelve months —one for larceny, with six previous convictions against her; the other, a young girl, for arson. She is an orphan, without friends. It was her first offence, and it is exactly a case which would be benefited by a prisoners' aid society.

The other females under sentence were for periods varying from two months to seven days, for drunkenness, assaults, and larceny.

Three hundred and twenty-seven individual males and 75 females were committed to this prison in 1875. The males have 754 and the females 366 convictions recorded against them in the prison books. Two females and one male had been each seven times committed to this prison previously to my inspection in 1875.

Commitments.

Accommodation.

	M.	F.		M.	F.
Wards,	14	8	Kitchens,	1	1
Yards,	4	3	Store Rooms,	3	4
Day Rooms,	3	2	Laundry,	–	1
Solitary Cells,	5	5	Drying Room,	–	1
Single Cells, not less than 9 feet long, 6 feet wide, and 8 feet high—432 cubic feet,	44	–	Lavatories,	4	4
Do. heated and furnished with bells,	†91	7†	Baths, with hot and cold water laid on,	1	1
Sleeping Rooms,	6	1	Privy,	1	–
No. of Beds in such Rooms,	5	–	Water-closets,	4	4
Hospital Rooms,	3	3	Fumigating Apparatus,	1	–
Chapel, partitioned for both sexes,	One.		Pumps,	2	–
School Room—14 stalls in inspection hall			Wells,	2	–
Workshops,	3	–	Tread-wheel,	1	–
Worksheds,	13	–	Other machines for hard labour —shot drill,	1	–
			Tell-tale clock,	1	–

* In May, 1876, this prisoner with others violently assaulted some of the officers of the prison, and ultimately it became necessary to transfer them to the Naas prison where more strict discipline is maintained.

† Out of this number of cells there are used 6 for males, and 4 for females, for reception.

SOUTH
DISTRICT.
———
*Kilkenny
County and
City Gaol.*
———

Since last inspection fifteen panels have been placed on hinges against the wall in the central hall of the male prison, which, when opened out, form fourteen separate compartments in which prisoners sit at school, and afterwards are closed up and do not obstruct the view.

The entire of the sewerage of the prison has lately been opened up and cleansed, and it is now in perfect working order.

No other improvement has been made in the prison buildings during the year. The left side only of the prison is artificially heated, and in consequence of the number of male prisoners for trial, some of necessity were located in cells not heated.

Stock at the time of Inspection.

	In Use.	In Store.	Male Clothing.	In Use.	In Store.	Female Clothing.	In Use.	In Store.
Blankets,pairs of,	89	6	Shirts, . .	49	–	Shifts, . .	15	20
Sheets, pairs of,	192	14	Jackets, .	61	51	Jackets, . .	6	2
Rugs, . .	92	5	Vests, .	46	46	Petticoats, .	6	24
Hammocks or			Trowsers, .	40	70	Aprons, . .	4	2
Cots, . .	50	47	Caps, . .	35	53	Neckerchiefs, .	12	14
Bedticks, .	40	63	Stockings or			Stockings, pairs		
Bedsteads,	30	64	Socks, pairs of,	30	34	of, . .	6	-
			Shoes,Slippers,&			Shoes,Slippers,&		
			Clogs,pairs of,	27	-	Clogs,pairs of,	3	2

I found the prison clean and orderly, the bells and appliances of the cells in good order, but much of the bedding—both blankets and sheets—very bad; the sheets more especially—many were in rags. I instructed the Local Inspector, under the 87th section of the Prisons Act, to order a quantity of sheeting, and sufficient blankets, besides prison clothing, especially shoes, which were quite insufficient, I am informed they have since been supplied.

The females also ought to wear caps, as in a penitentiary. They should be part of the costume of a prison, and insisted on. Women of the abandoned class object to wear them, but they should be compelled to do so. Stockings are not supplied to prisoners sentenced for terms under one month. I cannot approve of this arrangement.

Stores.

I found, on my inspection, the prison stores well kept and orderly.

A cell in the old part of the male prison is properly fitted up as a disinfecting closet, and in it the private clothes of prisoners of both sexes are cleansed and disinfected before being placed in store.

Water for the use of the prison is obtained in sufficient quantity from a well hole on the premises, whence it is driven by the power of the crank-pump to a large cistern which supplies the building; but the crank-pump is still unchanged. In former reports I called attention to the danger to life from having a continuous crank worked by prisoners in stalls who do not see each other, and the necessity to have ratchet wheels between each crank-handle, to prevent the loss of life which has happened in other gaols. The arrangement here has been improved, but it is still unsafe. It has four cranks, two on each side of the wheel.

The laundry is well arranged; prisoners work in it in separation. A tank for soft water has been put up, and a good drying-room adjoins. Food for prison use is now cooked by females, except potatoes, which are still cooked in the old kitchen, in which water is heated for the baths in the male prison.

A good bath has been put up in the female prison, and the lavatories and water-closets in both prisons were fully sufficient and in good order when I visited.

Forty-seven cells for males, which are on one side of the prison, and thirty-two cells for females are artificially heated. All in the male prison are lighted by gas, and have appliances for separation; but only seventeen in the female prison are lighted by gas. Gas is supplied to the closets, lavatories, cook-house, main hall, and externally.

An artist belonging to Kilkenny takes photographs of habitual criminals, and receives 5s. remuneration for each prisoner whose photograph he takes —four copies being provided.

Unlock is held at 6 A.M. in summer, and at 6.45 A.M. in winter. The prison is locked for the night at 6 P.M. in summer, and 5 P.M. in winter.

The night-watch remains on duty from 10 P.M. to 6 A.M. His vigilance is tested by one tell-tale clock in the central hall of the male prison, which is pegged each half hour during the night. The markings of the clock are entered in a book kept for the purpose.

A superior officer is stated to visit the prison at unexpected hours during the night, three times in the week.

Individual cellular separation is enforced in this prison with prisoners of both sexes. The prisoners do not work in the cells in which they sleep.

One hundred and four cells are in the male prison and 88 in that for females. Of these, 16 have been converted into lavatories and 8 into water-closets, 2 are used for punishments, and 91 for males and 73 for females are available for sleeping cells and for work.

Convicted prisoners receive visits from their friends monthly; the untried weekly. The apartment in which they receive visits is divided by partition.

Number of Punishments for Prison Offences.

	From 1st Jan. to 31st Dec., 1874.		From 1st Jan., 1875, to day of Inspection.	
By Governor—	M.	F.	M.	F.
Dark or Refractory Cells, . .	10	2	10	8

The punishment cells now used are heated and have bells. The male prisoner under punishment when I visited complained to me that he has not sufficient food, but states that he gets the full allowance which the rules direct. I directed the Medical Officer to examine his state.

Two punishment books are kept in this gaol, one for county, the other for city prisoners. This is unnecessary; one book is sufficient for all.

Employment on day of Inspection.

					M.	F.
Pumping water and breaking stones,		.		.	29	—
Tailoring, washing, and knitting,	.	.		.	1	8
Unemployed,	.	.	.	.	18	2
Prison duties,	.	.	.	.	6	3
Nursing children,	.	.	.	.	—	2
	Total in custody, .		.	.	54	15

There is no reproductive labour in this gaol, notwithstanding the large number of prisoners in custody, and no profit is derived thereby. The prisoners do not work in their cells after lock-up. Punitive labour is enforced by the tread-wheel, the crank pump, and stone-breaking. The prisoners work in summer for seven and in winter for five hours. My colleague and I have in former reports called attention to the insufficiency of the labour extracted from the prisoners, but without effect.

Schools.

	From 1st Jan., to 31st Dec., 1874.		From 1st Jan., 1875, to day of Inspection.	
	M.	F.	M.	F.
Number of individual prisoners who attended school, ...	87	10	80	12
Average daily number of pupils, .	7	4	6	3
Number of days on which School was held, .	259	259	224	224

School-hours.— Males, 12 to 2, P.M.; females, 12 to 2, P.M.

The arrangement for school in the male prison is found to work satisfactorily, but the prisoners are taught by ordinary turnkeys who were

SOUTH DISTRICT.

Kilkenny County and City Gaol.

never trained and cannot be competent to give instruction, more especially as the school is not inspected by or in connexion with any public educational board. I observe, however, that the chaplains very frequently report that it is satisfactory. In the female prison the women are instructed in their cells, there being no school-room.

Contracts.

Bread, white, per 4-lb. loaf, 4½d.; ditto, brown, per 4-lb. loaf, 4½d; oatmeal, per cwt., 15s. 6d.; Indian meal, per cwt., 9s. 3d.; potatoes, per cwt., 4s. 0d.; meat, per lb., 8½d.; new milk, per gallon, 8d.; buttermilk, per gallon, 4d.; salt, per cwt., 3s.; coal, per ton, £1 5s. 5d; turf, per box of 20 stone, 2s. 10d.; straw, per cwt., 2s. 6d.; gas, per 1,000 cubic feet, 7s. 6d.; candles, per lb., 5d.; soap, per cwt., £1 6s. Other contracts—Plumbing, £8.

Net average daily cost of ordinary Diet for each Prisoner.

1872, . 4d | 1873, . 4d. | 1874, . 6d

Provisions.

The food prepared for the use of the prisoners on the day of my visit, which I tasted, was of a good description, and the chaplains usually report favourably on the samples of provisions submitted for their inspection. Stirabout is boiled for prison use in a pot in the female prison; potatoes twice in the week in the kitchen in the male prison. I learn, however, that the man employed as cook also breaks stones.

I questioned all the prisoners in custody. The only complaint made was by the military prisoner already mentioned.

Hospitals.

	1872.		1873.		1874.		1875 (to day of Inspection).	
	M.	F.	M.	F.	M.	F.	M.	F.
No. of prisoners in hospital,	29	5	19	2	14	–	–	–
Average daily number in hospital, . . .	2·9	1·4	·2	·3	1	–	–	–
No. of prisoners prescribed for and treated out of hospital, . . .	86	39	129	45	195	60	–	–
No. of deaths in the gaol, .	–	1	–	–	..	1	–	–
Cost of medicine, .	£26 16s. 10d.		£45 2s. 4d.		£37 16s. 1d.		—	
Cost of diet for prisoners in hospital, .	£27 4s. 5d.		£47 16s. 10d.		£21 12s. 3d.		—	
Cost of all extra diet ordered by Medical Officer for prisoners not in hospital,	£2 0s 2d.		£22 4s. 11d.		£12 19s. 0d.		—	

Both hospitals were unoccupied at the time of my visit, and the sanitary condition of the prison was satisfactory.

One female died of brain disease in the prison in 1874, but no death occurred in 1875.

The improvement made in the hospital since my last inspection fully answers the purpose intended.

A good bath and water-closet have been provided for each hospital.

Officers and Salaries.

Non-resident.

	£	s.	d.
William Hayden, esq., jun., Local Inspector,	170	0	0
Rev. Y. R. Heatly, Protestant Chaplain,	46	3	0
Rev. Martin Howley, Roman Catholic Chaplain,	46	3	0
Zachariah Johnston, esq., Physician and Surgeon,	65	0	0

Resident.

	£	s.	d.
E. H. Robbins, esq., Governor,	300	0	0

	£	s.	d.
Thos. M'Cullagh, sen. Turnkey, *can instruct in mat and brush making,*	70	0	0
James Leonard, *Clerk and Storekeeper,*	58	0	0
Thos. Molloy, *Shoemaker,*	45	0	0
William Cole, *Gate Porter,*	45	0	0
John Butler,	45	0	0
Joseph Phelan,	45	0	0
Thomas Tobin, *Carpenter,*	45	0	0
Martin Walsh,	36	0	0
Mrs. M. A. M'Cullagh, Matron,	55	0	0
Mrs. Bridget Butler, Assistant Matron,	35	0	0

Each Turnkey instructs in schooling; Matron and Assistant Matron for females.

Vacancies in Staff since last Inspection, how caused, and how filled up.
Michael Leonard, senior Turnkey, superannuated; Thomas M'Cullagh got his place. Martin Walsh appointed Turnkey.

SOUTH DISTRICT.
Kilkenny County and City Gaol.

Visits paid by Officers.

	From 1st Jan., to 31st Dec., 1874.	From 1st Jan., 1875, to day of Inspection.
Number of times the Board of Superintendence met and discharged business,	11	8
Local Inspector to Gaol,	161	104
Do. to each Bridewell,	–	–
Chaplain, Protestant Episcopal Church,	168	150
Chaplain, Roman Catholic,	237	202
Physician and Surgeon,	157	115

The officers' quarters were clean and tidy when I visited.

Books and Accounts.
Net cost of Gaol, including Diet and Salaries.
1872, . £2,049 14s. 7d. | 1873, . £2,147 0s. 5d. | 1874, . £2,091 4s. 0d.

Total cost of Officers, including Clothing, Value of Rations, &c.
1872, . £1,102 14s. 0d. | 1873, . £1,212 10s. 5d. | 1874, . £1,213 17s. 10d.

Average cost of each Prisoner per annum.
1872, . £69 18s. 8d. | 1873, . £55 6s. 5d. | 1874, . £56 3s. 7d.

Amounts Repaid by the War Department for Military Prisoners.
1872, . £10 11s. 0d. | 1873, . £44 4s. 0d. | 1874, . £32 1s. 0d.

Amounts repaid by the Inland Revenue Department for Excise Prisoners.
1872, . — | 1873, . £1 2s. 10½d. | 1874, . —

Amounts Repaid from the Consolidated Fund for the maintenance, &c., of Prisoners.
1872, . £101 18s. 10d. | 1873, . £142 7s. 4d. | 1874, . £159 18s. 2d.

The various registries of discipline and finance in this prison are carefully kept by the clerk, and are very frequently checked by the Governor, as well as occasionally by the Local Inspector. The journals of the Local Inspector and Governor are full and contain all noteworthy occurrences in the gaol. The Medical Officer and the Chaplains record in their journals the duties they perform. *Books.*

Board of Superintendence.

Lieut.-Col. H. St. George, D.L., J.P.	Harvey De Montmorency, esq., J.P.	Mathew R. Weld, esq.
Maj. Sir James Langriche, bart., D.L., J.P.	F. R. M. Reade, esq., J.P.	Alex. Hamilton, esq., J.P.
Capt. Thos. P. T. Bookey, J.P.	John Waring, esq., J.P.	John P. Hyland, esq.
	R. L. Warren, esq., D.L., J.P.	Thomas Power, esq., J.P.
		Joseph Empson, esq.

The meetings of the Board are held monthly on the second Wednesday of each month, when the salaries of subordinate officers are paid and petty disbursements are made. The salaries of the superior officers and large accounts are paid half-yearly at the assizes. *Board.*

NOTE.—The Local Inspector of this gaol having met with a severe accident he has been for some time quite incapacitated by illness from discharging his duties in the prison, and the Governor also having lately quite broken down in health the discipline of the prison became very lax, and it became necessary for me to visit Kilkenny, and have a special meeting of the Board of Superintendence called. They gave the Governor leave of absence until the Summer Assizes, in order that he might be then superannuated; and on the recommendation of the Inspectors-General, Mr. Flewett, an efficient prison officer, was appointed *locum tenens* in his place.

STATE OF BRIDEWELLS.

SOUTH DISTRICT.

Kilkenny County.

Bridewells.

—	Thomastown.	Callan.	Urlingford.
	M. F.	M. F.	M. F.
No. of Committals in past year, .	11 2	42 3	6 2
Of whom were Drunkards, .	7 –	29 2	– –
No. of Committals in the quarter preceding inspection,	3 1	4 3	3 –
Of whom were Drunkards, .	– –	2 –	– –
Petty Sessions and Transmittals, how often?	Petty Sessions weekly; transmittals direct.	Monthly on Thursdays; transmittals direct.	No Petty Sessions nearer than Johnstown.
Committals, . .	Apparently regular; but magistrates do not always see prisoners whom they remand.	Regular.	Regular.
Registry, . .	Correctly kept.	Correctly kept.	Correctly kept.
Repairs and Order,	In bad repair; wood-work requires to be painted; water-closets repaired; place to be tidied.	In fair repair; painting required.	In fair repair; but woodwork should be painted.
Security, . .	Sufficient.	Yard very insecure, only one for both sexes.	Very insecure.
Accommodation, .	Ample.	Two small cells for each sex, and two small day-rooms.	Two cells and a small day-room for each sex.
Furniture, Bedding, and Utensils.	Sufficient for the few prisoners committed.	Sufficient.	Good and sufficient.
Water, how supplied,	By pump.	None, except from roofs.	Pump out of order.
Sewerage, . .	Effective.	A cesspool.	None; an open cesspool in yard, cleaned through house.
Cleanliness, Dryness, and Ventilation.	Clean, but damp.	Very clean, but damp.	Very clean and dry.
Cost of Dietary, .	6d. per day.	6d. per head.	6d. per day.
Salary of Keeper, and whether he follows any other employment.	£30; is court-keeper.	£15, with fuel and light; is court-keeper at £8 a year.	£15; £6 for fuel; court-keeper at £8 a year, is a constabulary pensioner.
Official Inspection,	13th June, 1875.	12th June, 1875.	12th June, 1875.
Remarks, . .	No prisoner in custody.	No prisoner in custody.	No prisoner in custody.

JOHN LENTAIGNE, *Inspector-General.*

KING'S COUNTY GAOL, AT TULLAMORE.—STATUTABLE INSPECTION, 13TH OCTOBER, 1875.

Number of Prisoners of all classes in Gaol on the day of Inspection, and on the corresponding date in the three preceding years.

				M.	F.					M.	F.
1872,	.	.	.	45	5	1874,	.	.	.	42	3
1873,	.	.	.	54	2	1875 (day of Inspection),			46	6

Juveniles.

One juvenile only, under 16 years of age (a male), was committed to this prison previously to the period of my inspection in October, 1875. He was sentenced to an imprisonment of one month for drunkenness. No young offender was sent to a reformatory from this jurisdiction during the year, and no person known to have been trained in a reformatory or industrial school was an inmate of the prison during the period.

Juveniles.

Individual Prisoners, and Number of Times each had been committed.

NUMBER OF TIMES COMMITTED.	1874.				1875, to day of Inspection.			
	Juveniles.		Adults.		Juveniles.		Adults.	
	M.	F.	M.	F.	M.	F.	M.	F.
Once within the year, .	3	1	144	19	1	–	119	21
Twice ,,	–	–	13	4	–	–	5	2
3 and 4 times ,,	–	–	6	–	–	–	7	–
5 ,, ,,	–	–	2	–	–	–	–	–
Total, . .	3	1	165	23	1	–	131	23
No. of above who had not been in Gaol previous to 1st Jan. in .	3	1	158	20	1	–	110	18

Individual Prisoners committed in 1874, and to the day of Inspection in 1875, who had been Once and oftener Committed in any year, so far as can be ascertained

NUMBER OF TIMES COMMITTED.	1874.				1875, to day of Inspection.			
	Juveniles.		Adults.		Juveniles.		Adults.	
	M.	F.	M.	F.	M.	F.	M.	F.
Once only, .	3	1	120	17	1	–	105	16
Twice, .	–	–	10	2	–	–	7	5
Thrice, .	–	–	10	1	–	–	4	–
4 times,	–	–	9	–	–	–	3	1
5 ,,	–	–	6	1	–	–	2	–
6 ,,	–	–	3	–	–	–	2	1
7 to 11 ,,	–	–	5	1	–	–	7	–
12 to 16 ,,	–	–	1	1	–	–	–	–
21 to 30 ,,	–	–	1	–	–	–	1	–
Total No. of Individuals committed,	3	1	165	23	1	–	131	23
No. of Commitments represented in foregoing. .	31	1	330	50	1	–	250	50

Averages, and Highest and Lowest Numbers (exclusive of Debtors).

—	From 1st January to 31st December, 1874.			From 1st January, 1875, to day of Inspection (9¼ months).		
	M.	**F.**	**Date.**	**M.**	**F.**	**Date.**
Average daily number of prisoners in custody,	41	3	—	37	4	—
Highest number of prisoners at any one time,	57		21st Sept.	62		15th Sept.
Lowest ditto, .	26		30th Dec.	26		9th Jan.
Highest number of males at any one time, .	53		21st Sept.	53		15th Sept.
Ditto of females,	8		5th June.	9		15th Sept.
Lowest number of males at any one time, .	23		3rd Dec.	23		9th Jan.
Ditto of females,	—		4th March.	3		9th Jan.

Highest Number of Prisoners (exclusive of Debtors) in gaol during each of the previous seven years, and up to day of Inspection in 1875.

17th January, 1868, . . 35	23rd July, 1872, . . . 59
24th October, 1869, . . . 37	18th August, 1873, . . 77
23rd September, 1870, . . 33	21st September, 1874, . . 57
24th January, 1871, . . 35	15th September, 1875, . . 62

When I made my inspection I found 46 males and 6 females in charge.

Five males were for trial—4 charged with murder and 1 with larceny.

Thirteen were under sentences of civil tribunals—5 convicted by juries at assize or quarter sessions, and 8 summarily by justices at petty sessions. Of these, 3 had been convicted of larceny, and 11 of assaults, poor law offences, vagrancy, or drunkenness.

The military offenders tried by courts-martial, inmates of the gaol at the time of my visit, numbered 28. They were under sentences for the most part for long periods.

The 6 females in custody were, 3 under sentences convicted by juries at assizes or quarter sessions—2 of larceny and 1 of concealing a birth—and 3 (prostitutes) summarily committed by justices at petty sessions for assaults and drunkenness.

The sentences on the convicted prisoners were :—The males tried before civil tribunals—2 sentenced for twelve months each, 2 for six months, 2 for four, and 7 for terms of one and two months.

The military prisoners were—1 sentenced for two and a-half years, 7 for two years, 5 for one year, and 15 for periods varying from five and a-half to two months each.

Two females in custody were old offenders, sentenced each to an imprisonment of twelve months for larceny. One of these, a returned convict, has spent the greater part of her life in crime, or under punishment for her offences. She has twice suffered penal servitude.

The sentences on the other female offenders in custody were—1 to be imprisoned for four months, 2 for one, and 1 for three weeks.

Debtors.

No person was imprisoned for debt in this prison in 1874, or up to my inspection in October, 1875.

During 1874 165 individual male and 23 female prisoners were committed to this gaol. In 1875, up to the period of my visit, 131 males and 23 females were in custody, but the same individuals, especially females, were in charge in both years, for the most part constantly re-committed.

The female returned convict who was in custody at the time of my visit was the only prisoner committed to this gaol in 1875 who had suffered penal servitude.

Accommodation.

	M.	F.			M.	F.
Wards,	4	2	Kitchen,		1	–
Yards,	3	1	Bakery,		1	–
Day Rooms,	4	1	Store Rooms,		3	2
Solitary Cells,	1	–	Laundry and Drying Room,		–	1
Single Cells not less than 9 feet long, 6 feet wide, and 8 feet high=432 cubic feet,	91	40	Lavatories,		7	2
			Baths, with Hot and Cold Water laid on,		6	1
Do. heated and furnished with bells,	71	10	Privies,		1	1
Hospital Rooms,	5	5	Water-closets,		11	3
Chapel,	1	–	Fumigating Apparatus,		1	1
School-room,	1	–	Reception Rooms or Cells,		6	2
Workshop,	1	–	Crank Pumps,		2	–
Worksheds,	16	–	Crank Mill,		1	–
			Tell-tale Clocks,		2	–

I found this gaol when I made my inspection in a most creditable condition of cleanliness and order—the buildings all in sound repair, the different apartments well kept, the cell fittings and other appliances in good order and on the most approved principle; the bells ring by spiral springs, hydrants are placed on the landings in case of fire; a lavatory, water-closet, and bath are on every corridor of the male prison.

A new boiler has been put up since last inspection in connexion with the heating apparatus of the male prison, and it works satisfactorily. The warders' quarters are clean and orderly.

Discipline appears to be well maintained in the prison.

The suggestions of the Inspectors-General have been in many points carried out satisfactorily. Twelve stalls have been fitted up in the central hall for a school for males. The work is well and tastefully done; the woodwork, being stained and varnished, has a good effect.

There are two good pumps on the premises. One of which has been fitted up with new machinery, and is worked by a crank divided into six compartments, at which prisoners can work in perfect safety in separation, and twelve stalls with lattice-work doors have been provided for the relays of prisoners who are waiting for their turn on the pump. A cut-stone building has been erected over the pump by prison labour, the masonwork of which is most creditable.

The second pump is worked by a wheel with two handles.

The Protestant Chaplain, who accompanied me on my inspection, suggests an alteration in the arrangement of the seats in the chapel, of which I quite approve, and when a carpenter prisoner is in custody the suggestion should be carried out.

Stock at the time of Inspection.

	In Use.	In Store.	Male Clothing.	In Use.	In Store.	Female Clothing.	In Use.	In Store.
Blankets, pairs of,	97	–	Shirts,	103	–	Shifts,	5	22
Sheets, pairs of,	121	–	Jackets,	36	67	Jackets,	5	25
Rugs,	47	–	Vests,	36	49	Gowns,	5	19
Hammocks or Cots,	63	–	Trowsers,	36	47	Petticoats,	5	8
Bedticks,	50	120	Caps,	36	96	Aprons,	5	13
Bedsteads,	76	–	Socks, pairs of,	72	–	Neckerchiefs,	5	7
			Shoes, Slippers,&			Caps,	5	7
			Clogs, pairs of,	63	32	Stockings,pairs of,	5	21
						Shoes, Slippers, & Clogs, pairs of,	5	5

SOUTH
DISTRICT.

*King's
County
Gaol.*

The bedding and prison clothing in this gaol, in use and in store, are of a good description and suitable. Stockings and socks are given to all prisoners. The shoes are of leather, and in winter worsted stockings are supplied. The females have also neckerchiefs, caps, and aprons. Every arrangement is made to keep the prisoners in good health, at the same time that discipline is strictly enforced, a system of prison management which should be generally adopted.

The stores are properly fitted up, and are frequently inspected by the Local Inspector and Governor. They were tidy and orderly when I visited.

A fumigating apparatus is in use in each prison to cleanse and disinfect the private clothing of prisoners, which is effected by fumes from a mixture of sulphuric acid and salt.

Photo-
graphy.

The photographs of habitual criminals are taken by the Deputy Governor, who supplies all materials, and charges 9d. for each copy, the negatives becoming the property of the Board. The photographic room is very effective and well arranged.

The laundry is suitably fitted up for separation. The troughs have hot and cold water laid on. The drying-room has eight horses, and a washing and wringing-machine has been provided.

Chapel.

The chapel is properly fitted up.

Lock-up is held at 6 P.M. in summer and 5 P.M. in winter. The prison is unlocked at 6.30 A.M. at all seasons of the year. A night-watch patrols the interior of the prison, and two tell-tale clocks mark the vigilance of the watch.

Gas has been introduced into the interior of both male and female prisons. It is kept lighting in the cells until 8 P.M., and in the morning while cleaning up the cells and washing.

Visitors.

Visitors to convicted prisoners are only admitted once in three months, and then always subject to the approval of the Governor, who refuses admission in case of misconduct of the prisoner. No change has been made in the place where the visits are made.

The sewerage of the prison is very effective.

Punishments for Prison Offences.

| | From 1st January to 31st December, 1874. | | From 1st January, 1875, to day of Inspection. | |
	M.	F.	M.	F.
By Governor—				
Dark or Refractory Cells, . .	23	–	29	2
Stoppage of Diet, . . .	47	–	20	–
Total, . .	70	–	49	2

These punishments were all inflicted on the sole authority of the Governor, and it was not necessary in any case to call for magisterial interference. The same prisoners were frequently under punishment during the year. One male was nine times punished in 1875; others were two, three, four, and five times. Altogether, the 51 punishments inflicted were on 22 individuals.

The punishment cell in the female prison is artificially heated, but not those in the male prison. My colleague, in his report for 1874 on this prison, calls attention to the want of a properly heated punishment cell in the male prison, and I would suggest that it be provided.

Schools.

| | From 1st Jan. to 31st Dec., 1874. | | From 1st Jan., 1875, to day of Inspection. | |
	M.	F.	M.	F.
Number of individual prisoners who attended school, ...	43	–	58	–
Average daily number of pupils, . .	18	–	26	–
Number of days on which school was held, .	300	–	240	–

School-hours.—Males, from 4 to 6 o'clock, P.M.; females, from 4 to 6 o'clock, P.M.

As already observed, well arranged school seats and desks have been fixed since last inspection by my colleague in October, 1874, in the central hall of the prison for males, but no suitable school exists in that for females. The teachers are not trained, but are stated to be efficient. Scholastic instruction is given to the males by the Deputy Governor, assisted by one of the turnkeys—to the females by the Matron, who teaches from cell to cell. The school is not in connexion with any educational body.

The Protestant Chaplain visited the school four times during 1875, and I found three reports in the School Registry of his visits. I found no entry by the Roman Catholic Chaplain ; but as now a suitable school-room has been fitted up in the male prison, I understand that he will attend.

Employment on day of Inspection.

						M.	F.
Tailoring,	.	.	.	.	.	1	–
Mason Work,	.	.	.	.	.	1	–
Shoemaking,	.	.	.	.	.	1	–
Painting,	.	.	.	.	.	1	–
Sackmaking,	.	.	.	.	.	39	–
Cleaning, Cooking, Washing, &c.,	.	.	.			3	4
Sewing,	.	.	.	.	.	–	2
	Total,	.	.	.		46	6

Amount received for produce of Prisoners' labour disposed of outside the gaol.

1872, . £84 7s. 0d. | 1873, . £244 8s. 6d. | 1874. . £215 2s. 0d.

The principal employment of the male prisoners in this gaol is sack-making, which is found remunerative, and well suited for prisoners working in separation. Thirty-nine male prisoners were so employed on the day of my visit ; 4 others, artisans, were engaged in tailoring, shoemaking, mason-work, and painting ; 1 man only is now employed in the kitchen. Artisans when in custody are employed at their trades for the benefit of the prison. Four males, previously ignorant of trades, received instruction—3 in shoemaking and 1 as a smith—in the gaol during the year.

By authority of the Board occasionally a prisoner is employed to dig in the garden of the Governor.

The profits realized by prison labour in 1875, £134 8s., was duly lodged to the credit of the county by the Board of Superintendence.

Contracts.

Bread, white, per 100 lbs., 13s. 9d.; brown, per 100 lbs., 11s. 6d.; oatmeal, per cwt., 15s. 6d.; potatoes, per cwt., 3s. 4d. ; meat, per lb., 8½d.; newmilk, per gallon, 8½d. ; buttermilk, per gallon, 4d.; salt, per cwt., 3s. 4d. ; coal, per ton, £1 6s. 0d.; turf, per 100 boxes, £5 5s.; gas, per 1,000 cubic feet, 9s. 2d. ; candles, per lb., 6½d. ; soap, per cwt., £1 10s.

Net average daily cost of Ordinary Diet for each Prisoner.

1872, . 4d. | 1873, . 5d. | 1874, . 6d.

The food for prison use on the day of my visit was of a good description, except that the brown bread was not sufficiently baked. The Chaplains occasionally report unfavourably of the samples of milk submitted for their inspection, and that the bread is not always sufficiently baked and of light weight, but the Governor in all such cases has it returned, and orders other food of a better description.

I questioned all the prisoners in custody ; the only complaint made was by a returned convict, who informed me that she had been employed to wash some linen belonging to the families of the Governor and Deputy Governor. I inquired into the matter, and ascertained that the work was done under the authority of the Board of Superintendence.

Officers and Salaries.

Non-Resident.

	£	s.	d.
Robert Gunning, esq., Local Inspector,	90	0	0
Rev. Graham Craig, Church of Ireland Chaplain,	40	0	0
Rev. M. M'Alroy, Roman Catholic Chaplain,	40	0	0
James Ridley, esq., Medical Officer and Apothecary,	20	0	0
Edward Drumm, Messenger and Watchman,	31	17	0

Resident.

	£	s.	d.
Captain H. Fetherstonhaugh, Governor,	230	0	0

	£	s.	d.
W. E. Haines, Deputy Governor, Clerk, &c.,	80	0	0
Patk. Cooke, 1st Turnkey, Weaver,	40	0	0
Thos. Johnson, 2nd Turnkey, Shoemaker,	35	0	0
Joseph Bagnal, 3rd Turnkey,	35	0	0
Benj. Kenahan, 4th Turnkey, Smith,	35	0	0
Thos. Haines, 5th Turnkey, Assists in Teaching School,	30	0	0
George Bagnal, 6th Turnkey,	30	0	0
Maria Armstrong, Matron,	35	0	0
Catherine Toomey, Deputy Matron,	30	0	0

Vacancies in the staff since last Inspection, how caused, and how filled up.

John Ridley, esq., the Medical Officer, died on the 3rd May, 1875; James Ridley, esq., was appointed Medical Officer, on the 7th June, 1875.

Officers on Gaol Allowance.

The Deputy Governor and Turnkeys are allowed £10 yearly in lieu of rations. The Matron is allowed £8, and the Deputy Matron £5 yearly in lieu of rations.

Visits paid by Officers.

	From 1st Jan. to 31st Dec., 1874.	From 1st Jan., 1875, to day of Inspection.
Number of times the Board of Superintendence met and discharged business,	13	11
Local Inspector to Gaol,	149	125
Do. do. to Bridewell,	4	4
Chaplain, Protestant Episcopal Church,	168	146
Roman Catholic Chaplain,	187	144
Physician, Surgeon, and Apothecary,	77	147

The quarters of the officers were clean and tidy when I visited.

Hospital.

	1872.		1873.		1874.	
	M.	F.	M.	F.	M.	F.
No. of prisoners in hospital,	–	1	–	–	–	–
Average daily No. in hospital,	–	1	–	–	–	–
No. of prisoners prescribed for and treated out of hospital,	38	17	40	20	125	11
Cost of Medicine,	—		—		£13 7s. 5d.	
Cost of all extra diet ordered by Medical Officer for prisoners not in hospital,	£42 7s. 6d.		£29 2s. 11d.		£39 10s. 5d.	

The hospitals in this prison are unnecessarily large. They are separate, and have water-closets, lavatories, and other appliances, but have not been occupied since 1873. There has been no death in the prison since 1870.

Books and Accounts.

Net cost of Gaol, including Diet and Salaries.

1872, . £1,701 17s. 4d. | 1873, . £1,874 2s. 1d. | 1874, . £1,861 18s. 4d.

Total cost of Officers, including Clothing, Value of Rations, &c.

1872, . £923 1s. 0d. | 1873, . £934 0s. 2d. | 1874, . £989 18s. 4d.

Average cost of each Prisoner per annum.

1872, . £45 11s. 6d. | 1873, . £37 15s. 1d. | 1874, . £42 16s. 1d.

Amounts repaid by the War Department for Military Prisoners.

1872, . £231 18s. 0d. | 1873, . £356 8s. 0d. | 1874, . £375 11s. 0d.

Amounts Repaid from the Consolidated Fund for the Maintenance, &c., of Prisoners.

1872, . £77 1s. 6d. | 1873, . £118 13s. 9d. | 1874, . £79 15s. 0d.

The registries connected with the discipline of the prison are kept by the Deputy Governor; those belonging to finance by the Local Inspector; most of the prescribed forms are in use; the various books are daily checked by the Governor; and this department of the prison is well managed.

Books.

The journals of the Local Inspector and Governor are well and carefully kept, and both these officers discharge their duties in the prison in a very satisfactory manner. They were present when I made my inspection, and it gives me pleasure to repeat the observations of my colleague in his report for 1874, in which he refers to the vigilance and zeal of the Governor in the execution of his prison duties. The journal of the Medical Officer is full and well kept. The Chaplains also have journals.

Board of Superintendence.

The Earl of Rosse, J.P.	Capt. A. W. C. Cox, J.P.	George Ridley, esq., J.P.
Colonel Bernard, L.L., J.P.	Captain M. Fox, J P.	Reginald Digby, esq., J.P.
Dawson French, esq., J.P.	Marcus Goodbody, esq., J.P.	T. N. Ridgeway, esq., J.P.
Capt. T. A. Pierce, J.P.	Edward J. Briscoe, esq.	[Vacant].

Board.

The Board meets for the discharge of business on the first Thursday of each month, when the salaries of the intern officers are paid, and small liabilities discharged by cheque in favour of Local Inspector, who accounts at next meeting of the Board. The extern officers are paid their salaries half-yearly by presentment at assizes.

STATE OF PARSONSTOWN BRIDEWELL.

Bridewell.

	M.	F
No. of Committals in past year,	54	21
Of whom were Drunkards,	20	7
No. of Committals in the quarter preceding inspection,	28	12
Of whom were Drunkards,	5	2

Petty Sessions and Transmittals, how often?	Weekly, on Saturdays; transmittals direct.
Committals,	Regular.
Registry,	Correctly and carefully kept.
Repairs and Order,	In good repair and order; the bed-room of keeper very damp. I would suggest that a door be opened between sitting-room and bed-room of keeper.
Security,	Very secure. High walls round yards.
Accommodation,	For males—On ground floor, a large day-room and three large cells, two with four beds, the third used as a store for straw; one small cell also used as a store; a large exercising yard, with privy in centre. For females—On upper story, large day-room and three cells with three beds in each; a small cell now used as store; a good exercising yard.
Furniture, Bedding, and Utensils,	Good, but some sheets and prison dresses required.
Water how supplied?	By pump in yard for females; a lavatory has been fixed in day-room for males; another should be put in that for females.
Sewerage,	Good sewerage for surface drainage. Earth-closets are provided for the privies.
Cleanliness, Dryness, and Ventilation,	Very clean and well kept. Ventilation sufficient; cells sufficiently dry, but not keeper's apartment.
Cost of Dietary,	5d. for both sexes.
Salary of Keeper, and whether he follows any other employment.	£55; wife as matron, £10; has no other employment.
Date of Inspection,	24th April, 1875.
Remarks,	Two male prisoners, deserters, were in custody at the time of my visit.

JOHN LENTAIGNE, *Inspector-General.*

SOUTH DISTRICT.

LIMERICK COUNTY GAOL, AT LIMERICK.—STATUTABLE INSPECTION, 6TH AND 8TH OCTOBER, 1875.

Limerick County Gaol.

Number of Prisoners of all classes in Gaol on the day of Inspection, and on the corresponding date in the three preceding years.

	M.	F.		M.	F.
1872,	36	4	1874,	71	8
1873,	42	9	1875 (day of Inspection),	69	24

Number of Returned Convicts in Gaol on the day of Inspection, and during each of the three preceding years.

	M.	F.		M.	F.
1872,	1	3	1875, up to and including		
1873,	3	3	day of Inspection,	3	3
1874,	2	1	Day of Inspection,	1	1

Juveniles.

Juveniles. One female and 26 male young offenders, sixteen years of age and under, were committed to this prison previously to my inspection in 1875. Of these, 7 males were twelve years of age and under; 7 had previous convictions recorded against them; 16 males and the female were work-house offenders.

Two young offenders (males) were in custody at the time of my inspection—one convicted by jury at assizes of obtaining money under false pretence; the other on remand for an assault.

Seven (males) were sent to reformatories from this district up to the day of inspection in 1875; one was twelve years of age; six were above that age.

No person, known to have been in a reformatory or industrial school, was committed to this prison in 1875.

*Commitments.**

CLASSES.	From 1st January to 31st December, 1874. M.	F.	From 1st January, 1875, to day of Inspection. M.	F.
Debtors,	2	–	–	–
Criminals,	367	43	290	65
Vagrants,	32	–	19	4
Drunkards,	115	22	105	25
Total,	516	65	414	94

†*Individual Prisoners (exclusive of Debtors), and Number of Times each had been committed during 1874 and 1875.*

NUMBER OF TIMES COMMITTED.	1874. Juveniles. M.	F.	Adults. M.	F.	1875, to day of Inspection. Juveniles. M.	F.	Adults. M.	F.
Once within the year,	34	1	336	50	24	1	282	63
Twice ,,	3	–	38	3	1	–	24	6
Thrice ,,	–	–	5	1	–	–	9	2
4 times ,,	1	–	2	-	–	–	4	-
5 and 6 ,, ,,	–	–	5	1	–	–	1	1
7 and 8 ,, ,,	–	–	2	-	–	–	–	1
9 ,, ,,	–	–	–	-	–	–	1	-
Total,	38	1	388	55	25	1	321	73
No. of above who had not been in Gaol previous to 1st Jan. in	32	1	246	36	19	1	179	39

* Table F, Commitments, 1874, includes 35 males and 11 females from County Kerry Gaol, and in 1875, 6 males; and 16 males and 13 females from Limerick City Gaol.

† Table G I contains the same prisoners from County Kerry Gaol, and from Limerick City Gaol, for 1874 and 1875, as are detailed in note to Table F.

Individual Prisoners (exclusive of Debtors), committed in the year 1874, and to the day of Inspection in 1875, who had been Once and oftener in custody from their first Commitment in any year.

SOUTH DISTRICT.

Limerick County Gaol.

NUMBER OF TIMES COMMITTED.	1874.				1875, to day of Inspection.			
	Juveniles.		Adults.		Juveniles.		Adults.	
	M.	F.	M.	F.	M.	F.	M.	F.
Once only, ...	28	1	217	34	18	1	169	38
Twice, ...	9	–	72	5	5	–	63	10
Thrice, ...	–	–	33	3	2	–	31	5
4 times, ...	–	–	21	4	–	–	22	9
5 „	1	–	14	3	–	–	12	2
6 „	–	–	8	1	–	–	7	1
7 to 11 „	–	–	16	3	–	–	11	6
12 to 16 „	–	–	2	–	–	–	3	1
17 to 20 „	–	–	3	1	–	–	–	–
21 to 30 „	–	–	–	–	–	–	1	–
31 to 50 „	–	–	2	–	–	–	2	–
51 to 70 „	–	–	–	1	–	–	–	–
71 to 80 „	–	–	–	..	–	–	–	1
Total No. of Individuals committed,	38	1	386	55	25	1	321	73
No. of commitments represented in foregoing, . . .	51	1	945	205	34	1	816	258

Averages, and Highest and Lowest Numbers (exclusive of Debtors).

	From 1st January to 31st December, 1874.			From 1st January, 1875, to day of Inspection.		
	M.	F.	Date.	M.	F.	Date.
Average daily number of prisoners in custody,	63	10	—	55	11	—
Highest number of prisoners at any one time,	99		7th Dec.	97		2nd Oct.
Lowest ditto,	51		18th April.	47		24th March.
Highest number of males at any one time, .	88		7th Dec.	73		2nd Oct.
Ditto of females,	18		3rd Jan.	25		22nd Sept.
Lowest number of males at any one time, .	42		21st March.	41		24th March.
Ditto of females,	4		24th Nov.	6		5th March.

Highest Number of Prisoners (exclusive of Debtors) in Gaol during each of the previous seven years, and up to day of Inspection in 1874.

22nd February, 1868, .	. 101		6th September, 1872, .	.	69
5th December, 1869, .	. 84		15th November, 1873, .	.	95
12th January, 1870, .	. 88		6th August, 1874, .	.	93
19th April, 1871, .	. 77		2nd October, 1875, .	.	97

Prisoners sentenced to Solitary Confinement by order of Court.

	From 1st January to 31st Dec., 1874.		From 1st Jan., 1875, to day of Inspection.	
	M.	F.	M.	F.
Solitary confinement, . . .	17	–	14	–

I found in custody when I made my inspection 69 males and 24 female prisoners. Of these, 16 males and 13 females belonged to the

* They include 16 males and 13 females from Limerick City Gaol, and 4 males and 2 females from County Kerry Gaol,

U 2

city of Limerick jurisdiction, and 4 males and 2 females transferred from the county Kerry prison, in consequence of alterations being made in that gaol to suit it to the separate system of prison discipline ; 9 were military offenders.

It thus appears that, deducting military offenders and prisoners transferred from other gaol districts, 40 males and 9 female inmates of the gaol at the time of my visit were offenders committed from the jurisdiction of the county Limerick.

The sentences on the convicted prisoners (males) were—24 for periods of twelve months and upwards, including 8 for two years, and 6 for fifteen and eighteen months ; 10 were for terms of six and nine months ; 6 for four and five months, and 19 for from one to three months. Seven males and 2 females were for trial.

The sentences passed on the female convicted prisoners in custody were—3 for twelve ; 2 for eighteen ; 2 for nine ; 11 for six, and 1 for five months. Three were for one, two, and three months respectively.

Five males and 3 females (returned convicts) were committed to this prison in 1875.

The offences for which the prisoners in custody had been committed were—10 (males) for military offences ; 23 males and 5 females for offences against property ; 1 male for perjury ; and a female for an attempt at suicide. Five males and 14 females for drunkenness, vagrancy, and disorderly conduct ; and 28 males and 5 females for offences against the person. Of the 24 females in custody on the day of inspection, 13 were prisoners transferred from the City of Limerick Gaol, nine of whom had been convicted for drunkenness and disorderly conduct.

The individual prisoners committed to this prison up to the day of my inspection in 1875 numbered 346 males and 74 females. They have—the males 850, and the females 259—re-committals recorded against them. As however prisoners from other jurisdictions were in custody, the above is not a correct record of the criminal statistics of the county.

Accommodation.

	M.	F.		M.	F.
Yards, ...	4	3	Worksheds, . . .	27	–
Day Rooms, . . .	2	–	Kitchen, . . .	1	–
Solitary Cell, . . .	1	–	Store Rooms, . . .	4	1
Single Cells, not less than 9 feet long, 6 feet wide, and 8 feet high = 432 cubic feet, .	6	–	Laundry, . . .	–	1
			Drying Room, . .	–	1
			Lavatories, . . .	9	4
Do., heated and furnished with bells, . . .	62	36	Baths, with Hot and Cold Water laid on, . .	5	1
Cells to contain three persons,	3	1	Water-closets, . . .	20	9
Sleeping Rooms, . . .	7	1	Fumigating Apparatus, .	1	–
No. of beds in such rooms, .	7	1	Pumps, . . .	2	–
Hospital Rooms, . . .	2	2	Crank do., . . .	1	–
Chapel, ...	One.		Tread-wheel, . . .	1	–
School Rooms, . . .	1	1	Tell-tale Clocks, . .	2	–

I found the gaol buildings on my inspection in sound repair, remarkably clean, and well kept. The appliances for the carrying on of the separate system of prison discipline, under the Act 3 and 4 Vic., cap. 44, all in good working order. The ventilation in the cells sufficient, the walls of the interior lately limewashed, and the iron and woodwork painted. The heating apparatus in both prisons works satisfactorily.

The sewerage is effective, and a considerable sum has been expended thereon ; yet the prison with all these advantages is not healthy; and on my inspection I found a young man (T. T.) who (I was informed) was in rude health on committal to prison, now stricken down in typhoid fever. On my previous statutable inspection in May, 1873, typhoid fever prevailed, and one man died of it four days afterwards. My colleague, in his report for 1874, mentions the case of a juvenile who died in the gaol of blood poisoning, which was then attributed to the effluvium which emanated from a sewer on the road outside the prison, and which likewise affected the health of some of the officers.

Whatever may be the cause of the frequent inroads of zymotic disease amongst the inmates of this prison, the matter is one into which, on public grounds, and in mercy to the offenders confined in this prison, it is the duty of the authorities carefully to inquire. Persons under the depressing influences of strict cellular confinement are particularly liable to catch the spores of contagion which may float in the atmosphere; and it is above all incumbent on all connected with the management of the prison to satisfy themselves that the air the prisoners breathe and the water they drink is pure, and free from the contamination of sewerage or decomposing animal or vegetable matter.

Neglect of this precaution caused the fearful gaol fevers of former times, which not only destroyed such multitudes of prisoners, but even the judges and juries before whom they were tried were stricken down and died from inhaling the atmosphere of the courthouse, contaminated by the breath of the sufferers.

In former reports I referred to this subject, and I now again urge the Board to have a careful scientific examination of the cause of the frequent zymotic diseases in this prison.

Nothing tends so much to health as pure water, and it should be obtained at any cost. I learn that the supply of water from the old quarry at the rere of the prison is sometimes very limited. The Governor reports that the well at the rere is only 50 feet deep. It might be deepened. But why not procure water from the city main, and so introduce pure water into the prison, of which, I understand, an unlimited supply can be procured. The front well is, I am informed, 90 feet deep, sunk to the rock, with 30 feet jumper holes through it, yet the water to the gaol is sometimes insufficient, and my colleague reports that it was so at the time of his inspection in 1874.

Stock at the time of Inspection.

	In Use.	In Store.	Male Clothing.	In Use.	In Store.	Female Clothing.	In Use.	In Store.
Blankets, pairs of,	104	3	Shirts,	54	92	Shifts,	33	35
Sheets, pairs of,	127	6½	Jackets,	54	63	Wrappers,	35	3
Rugs,	100	3	Vests,	54	100	Petticoats,	53	55
Bed-ticks,	107	38	Trowsers,	54	30	Aprons,	27	–
Bedsteads,	107	28	Caps,	54	129	Caps,	8	8
			Socks, pairs of,	54	149	Stockings, pairs of,	30	39
			Shoes, pairs of,	54	102½	Shoes, pairs of,	25	5

I found in use and in store an abundant supply of bedding and prison clothing of a good description. Socks for males, and stockings and caps are provided for females. I would recommend that neckerchiefs be likewise given to the females; they are inexpensive and prevent bronchial attacks, especially when at exercise in the open air. The stores are well arranged, properly kept, and tidy. The arrangement to dye and make up the thin and worn blankets for petticoats for females and for jackets for male prisoners works economically. The dye consists of logwood and copperas by which a useful cloth is made.

Stock is taken quarterly by the Local Inspector and Governor, when articles unfit for use are condemned and removed. A proper system of checks is in use.

There is only one fumigating apparatus in the gaol; a second should be provided. It can be made by prison labour.

SOUTH
DISTRICT.
___
Limerick
County
Gaol.

I found the women usefully employed in the laundry when I visited. The laundry is fitted up with six stalls, having latticed doors. Rain-water is conveyed from the roof to a tank, for laundry purposes. The drying closet has five horses. Water for the laundry, the bath in the female prison, and the drying closet, is heated from one fire. It might be likewise used to generate steam for cooking purposes. If the kitchen were removed to that part of the old tread-wheel building which adjoins the laundry, a door from the laundry might be opened into it, and the cooking placed under the charge of the matron, the female prisoners might thus be employed to cook for the whole establishment. As, however, the alteration would be attended with expense, I do not suggest that it be carried out, pending legislation, at present.

Since last inspection pipes have been put to water-closets to carry off sewerage gas—a precaution which should be adopted in every institution.

Gas has been introduced into every part of this prison, except the reception cells and debtors' sleeping rooms, which latter are now seldom used. It is supplied to the separate cells up to 9 P.M. in winter. The burners in the cells have been improved, to prevent the danger of suicide.

At 9 P.M. the inside guard of one warder, and at 9.30 P.M. the outside night watchman, come on duty.

Two tell-tale clocks—one in central hall of male prison, the other at back of female prison—test the vigilance of the night watch.

The clocks are well protected, and cannot be tampered with.

Visitors.
Visitors to prisoners are prevented from contact with the prisoners by wire lattice, an officer being present; and a record is kept whenever their being searched is dispensed with. Visitors now see their friends at entrance to male prison.

Sixty cells in the male prison and 38 in the female prison are artificially lighted by gas, heated, and furnished with means to enable the prisoner to communicate with an officer of the prison.

Twelve cells in the male prison are not supplied with the necessary requirements for separation.

Photo-
graphy.
The photographing of habitual prisoners is performed by an artist belonging to Limerick, who receives 3s. 4d. for four copies, one of which is kept in the prison.

Divine Worship for Protestant prisoners on Sundays is held in the board-room, and a screen has been provided for the separation of the sexes; that for Roman Catholics is in the chapel.

Number of Punishments for Prison Offences.

	From 1st January to 31st December, 1874.		From 1st January, 1875, to day of Inspection.	
	M.	F.	M.	F.
By Magisterial authority,	-	-	3	-
By Governor—				
Dark or Refractory Cells,	59	3	64	5
Total,	59	3	67	5

Punish-
ments.
A darkened cell in the side block in which the hospital is situated is used for punishment for male prisoners. The record of punishments is duly submitted to the Board at its meetings.

Schools.

	From 1st Jan. to 31st Dec., 1874.		From 1st Jan., 1875, to day of Inspection.	
	M.	F.	M.	F.
Number of individual prisoners who attended school,	259	37	182	43
Average daily number of pupils,	21	6	23	8
Number of days on which school was held,	222	165	170	181

School-hours.—Males, 12 to 2 o'clock; Females, 10 to 11 o'clock.

Sovth
District.

Limerick
County
Gaol.

School.

No alteration has been made in the school-room, which is too small and not stalled ; hence the prisoners are in association at school, a discipline officer being present. The teacher of the male school has been trained under the Board of National Education, and holds a certificate of the first class. The females are taught by the matron. I regret that the school is not in connexion with the Board of National Education, but the Chaplains devote much time to the supervision of the school ; the Protestant Chaplain more especially, who, up to the period of my inspection, had visited the school 23 times. The Roman Catholic Chaplain, nine times ; and they regularly record their observations in the books of the prison.

Employment on day of Inspection.

		M.	F.
Stone-breaking and crank pump,	. . .	43	–
Picking oakum,	. . . . . .	14	7
Mat-making,	. . . . . .	1	–
Carpentry,	. . . . . .	1	–
Coopery,	. . . . . .	1	–
Tailoring,	. . . . . .	1	–
Cooking,	. . . . . .	1	–
Prison duties,	. . . . . .	4	–
Washing,	. . . . . .	–	7
Knitting,	. . . . . .	–	8
Needlework,	. . . . . .	–	2
Sick,	. . . . . .	1	–
Discharged before labour hours,	. . .	2	–
Total in custody,	. . .	**69**	**24**

Amount received for produce of Prisoners' Labour disposed of outside the Gaol.

1872, . £78 1s. 2d. | 1873, . £96 13s. 8d. | 1874, . £166 4s. 5d.

The large amount of profits received for the produce of prison labour shows that remunerative labour is effectively carried on. I found the males employed breaking stones, and those that were artisans working at their trades ; the females washing, knitting, sewing, and some of both sexes picking oakum. Prisoners sentenced to hard labour work at the crank pump and stone-breaking.

Shoemaking, tailoring, carpentry, coopering, painting, glazing, tin work, mat-making, and basket-making have been done by prisoners during the year.

The head warder superintends carpentry, another warder shoemaking and tailoring, and a third the other industrial work carried on in this prison.

Contracts.

Bread, brown, per 4 lb. loaf, 6¼d. ; oatmeal, per cwt., 16s. ; Indian meal, per cwt., 9s. 6d. ; potatoes, per cwt., 4s. ; meat, per lb., 7¼d. ; new milk, per gallon, 9d. ; salt, per cwt., 3s. ; coal, per ton, £1 4s. 8d. ; straw, per cwt., market price ; gas, per 1,000 cubic feet, 4s. 9d. ; candles, per lb., 5d. ; soap, per cwt. £1 10s.

Net average daily cost of Ordinary diet for each Prisoner.

1872, . 4·9d. | 1873, . 4·76d. | 1874, . 5d.

The food for prison use which I tasted at the time of my visit was of a good description, and the Chaplains have invariably reported favourably of the samples submitted for their inspection during the year.

I questioned all the prisoners in custody. One man only lodged a complaint. I fully inquired into his statements, and found them totally without foundation. The Medical Officer states in his journal that the man is feigning insanity, and I believe that he is right in the opinion he expresses.

SOUTH DISTRICT.

Limerick County Gaol.

Books and Accounts.

Net cost of Gaol, including Diet and Salaries.

1872, . £2,373 4s. 4d. | 1873, . £2,661 4s. 4d. | 1874, . £2,779 11s. 3d.

Total cost of Officers, including Clothing, Value of Rations, &c.

1872, . £1,911 17s. 5d. | 1873, . £1,252 15s. 4d. | 1874, . £1,368 3s. 9d.

Average cost of each Prisoner per annum.

1872, . £34 13s. 6d. | 1873, . £46 2s. 3d. | 1874, . £38 1s. 6d.

Amounts repaid by the War Department for Military Prisoners.

1872, . £77 15s. 7d. | 1873, . £3 2s. 0d. | 1874, . £31 18s. 0d.

Amounts repaid by the Admiralty Department for Naval Prisoners.

1872, . £17 16s. 0d. | 1873, . £23 9s. 0d. | 1874, . £50 12s. 0d.

Amounts repaid from the Consolidated Fund for the Maintenance, &c., of Prisoners.

1872, . £107 7s. 11d. | 1873, . £217 10s. 10d. | 1874, . £346 19s. 10d.

Books.

The prison books and registries are well and carefully kept, and I have every reason to be satisfied with the arrangements in this department. The journals of the principal officers show the great care and attention they bestow in the discharge of the duties attached to their respective offices in the gaol. I was with the Medical Officer when he visited the patient suffering from fever, and his care and attention to the poor man is deserving of praise. The journals of the Chaplains are more full than those in many other prisons, and they give much time to the efficient performance of their duties. The Local Inspector examines the various books, and places his initials thereon. The Governor checks the books of discipline and finance, the provision books, and the custody and discharge of prisoners ; his journal is a careful record of the occurrences in the prison. The Local Inspector takes much care to have the bridewells well appointed and managed.

Officers and Salaries.

Non-resident.	£	s.		£	s.
Capt. Wm. Vanderkiste, Local Inspector, ...	100	0	Bernard O'Loughlin, Head Warder (*Cabinetmaker, superintends Carpentry*), .	75	0
Rev. James F. Gregg, Protestant Chaplain, .	50	0	John Sharpley, Warder (*Storekeeper*), . . .	50	0
Rev. Jas. M'Coy, Adm., Roman Catholic Chaplain, .	50	0	Thomas Weekes, Warder (*Gatekeeper*), . . .	48	0
Thomas Jas. Gelston, esq., M.D., Medical Attendant, . .	44	0	Rich. Halloran, Warder (*Cooper, instructs in and superintends trades,*	48	0
Samuel Hunt, esq., Apothecary,	30	0	Patrick Fay, Warder, . .	40	0
			Thomas Keating, Warder, .	40	0
Resident.			Edward Huddy, Warder, . .	36	10
			Daniel Madigan, . .	36	10
Fras. M·G. Eagar, esq., Governor,	350	0	John Farrell, Night Watch, .	39	0
James W. Hogan, Clerk and Schoolmaster, . . .	70	0	Aphra Griffin, Matron, . .	50	0
			Margaret Gabbett, Assist. Matron,	36	0

Vacancies in Staff since last Inspection, how caused, and how filled up, viz.

Thomas Harwood, Warder, superannuated ; Robert Chamberlain, Warder, left the prison. Edward Huddy and Daniel Madigan appointed Warders.

Visits paid by Officers.

	From 1st January to 31st December, 1874.	From 1st January, 1875, to day of Inspection.
Number of times the Board of Superintendence met and discharged business,	13	10
Local Inspector, to Gaol,	115	95
" to each Bridewell,	4	3
Chaplain, Protestant Epis. Church,	167	130
" Roman Catholic,	174	132
Physician and Surgeon,	226	196
Apothecary,	319	265

The officers' quarters which I visited were clean and tidy. All the subordinate officers reside with their families within the gaol, but the apartments of the warders are not in that part of the prison in which the cells of the prisoners are situate. By the permission of the Board of Superintendence the garden of the Governor is tilled and his carpets shaken by prisoners. His washing and that of his family, as likewise that of the prison officers, is done in the laundry; and coal is carried to the officers' quarters by prisoners.

Hospitals.

	1872.		1873.		1874.		1875 (to day of Inspection).	
	M.	F.	M.	F.	M.	F.	M.	F.
No. of prisoners in hospital,	6	2	5	—	4	4	—	—
Average daily number in hospital,	·2	·29	·23	—	·2	·2	—	—
No. of prisoners prescribed for and treated out of hospital,	136	26	157	36	149	28	153	29
No. of deaths in the gaol,	—	—	1	—	1	—	1	—
Cost of medicine,	£13 14s. 1d.		£26 6s. 6d.		£32 1s. 9d.		—	
Cost of diet for prisoners in hospital,	£18 7s. 3d.		£17 15s. 3d.		£28 17s. 1d.		—	
Cost of all extra diet ordered by Medical Officer for prisoners not in hospital,	£25 16s. 9d.		£16 19s. 3d.		£16 12s. 4d.		—	

No change has been made in the hospital during 1875. The hospital arrangements are sufficient and effective; water-closets and baths are attached to both hospitals. *Hospital.*

The frequent visits of the Medical Officer to this gaol shows his zeal and attention.

Board of Superintendence.

Henry Maunsell, esq., J.P.
Eyre Lloyd, esq., D.L., J.P.
Right Hon. Lord Massy, D.L., J.P.
John White, esq., D.L., J.P.
Edward Croker, esq., D.L., J.P.
Sir D. V. Roche, bart., D.L., J.P.

Edwd. W. O'Brien, esq., D.L., J.P.
Henry Lyons, esq., D.L., J.P.
James C. Cooper, esq., J.P.
Right Hon. Lord Clarina, D.L., J.P.
S. E. De Vere, esq., J.P.
John Bolton Massy, esq.

The Board meets for the discharge of business on the second Saturday *Board.*
of each month, when the salaries of the intern officers and small amounts of disbursements by the Governor since the previous Board are paid by cheque in the aggregate, in his favour; cheques are also signed in the name of other parties, the proper vouchers in each case being produced. The extern officers receive their salaries half-yearly at assizes.

STATE OF BRIDEWELLS.

—	Rathkeale.		Bruff.	
	M.	F.	M	F.
No. of Committals in past year, ...	26	8	123	12
Of whom were Drunkards, ...	–	–	21	4
No. of Committals in the quarter preceding Inspection, . . .	11	4	20	6
Of whom were Drunkards, . . .	–	–	–	–

—	Rathkeale.	Bruff.
Petty Sessions and Transmittals, how often ?	Fortnightly, on Thursdays.	Fortnightly at Bruff, Hospital, Bruree, and New Pallas.
Committals, whether regular ?	Now regular, and prisoners are brought before the committing justices when remanded.	Regular.
Registry, . . .	Correctly kept.	Irregularly kept.
Repairs and Order, . .	In good repair and order; lately painted, and walls limewashed.	In sound repair, and well kept.
Security, . . .	Sufficient, with care.	The down-pipe which endangered the security of this prison has been removed.
Accommodation, . .	This Bridewell, which is under Court-house, is damp and inconvenient. It has two day-rooms and nine cells.	Males—day-room and two cells; females—day-room and two cells.
Furniture, Bedding, and Utensils.	The bedding, blankets, and furniture very good and sufficient.	Sufficient and good.
Water, how supplied ? .	No water on premises, but rain-water saved.	None on premises.
Sewerage, . . .	Earth-closets are provided.	Cesspool cleanable through building. Earth-closets are provided.
Cleanliness, Dryness, and Ventilation.	Very clean, and well kept.	Clean and orderly, but damp in winter.
Cost of Dietary per head per day.	6d.; three meals are given.	6¼d.; three meals.
Salary of Keeper, and whether Keeper follows any other employment.	£35 a year, and firing; matron £5. Is paid £14 a year for Court-house; has a pension.	£30; wife, £5. None.
Official Inspection, . .	8th October, 1875.	25th July, 1875.
Remarks, . . .	No prisoner in charge. The flag roofs of the privies have been repaired since my visit. One lunatic was committed to this prison in 1875; he was 10 nights in the bridewell.	Two males in charge; one a small boy.

JOHN LENTAIGNE, *Inspector-General.*

LIMERICK COUNTY OF CITY GAOL, AT LIMERICK.—STATUTABLE
INSPECTION, 8TH AND 9TH OCTOBER, 1875.

*Number of Prisoners of all classes in Gaol on the day of Inspection, and
on the corresponding date in the preceding years.*

	M.	F.		M.	F.
1872,	43	16	1874,	47	26
1873,	50	19	1875 (day of Inspection),	48	25

Juveniles.

One young offender (male), 15 years of age, was in custody at the Juveniles.
time of my visit; he had been summarily convicted of the larceny of a
watch, and sentenced to an imprisonment of one-month.

During 1875 18 young offenders—12 males and 7 females—were committed; of these 5 males and 1 female were for larceny, the remainder
for assaults, drunkenness, disorderly conduct, gambling, and ball-playing
in the streets of Limerick. They had been sentenced to various terms of
imprisonment, varying from one month to 24 hours. Two males and one
female were sent to Reformatories during the year.

Commitments.

CLASSES.	From 1st January to 31st Dec., 1874.		From 1st January, 1875, to day of Inspection.	
	M.	F.	M.	F.
Debtors,	2	–	2	–
Criminals,	519	170	462	156
Vagrants,	4	19	9	5
Drunkards,	496	164	380	118
Total,	1,021	353	853	279

*Individual Prisoners (exclusive of Debtors), and Number of Times each
had been committed during* 1874 *and* 1875.

NUMBER OF TIMES COMMITTED.	1874.				1875, to day of Inspection.			
	Juveniles.		Adults.		Juveniles.		Adults.	
	M.	F.	M.	F.	M.	F.	M.	F.
Once within the year,	15	4	694	181	12	4	615	150
Twice ,, ,,	–	–	56	26	–	–	64	27
Thrice ,, ,,	–	–	25	11	–	–	18	10
4 times ,, ,,	–	–	12	6	–	–	5	6
5 ,, ,,	–	–	6	4	–	–	3	2
6 ,, ,,	–	–	4	3	–	–	–	–
7 ,, ,,	–	–	3	3	–	–	1	1
Total,	15	4	800	234	12	4	706	196
No. of above who had not been in Gaol previous to 1st Jan. in	15	4	661	159	12	4	558	132

SOUTH
DISTRICT.

Limerick
City
Gaol.

Individual Prisoners (exclusive of Debtors), committed in 1874, and to the day of Inspection in 1875, who had been Once and oftener recommitted, from their first Commitment in any year, so far as can be ascertained.

NUMBER OF TIMES COMMITTED.	1874.				1875, to day of Inspection.			
	Juveniles.		Adults.		Juveniles.		Adults.	
	M.	F.	M.	F.	M.	F.	M	F.
Once only,	15	4	604	139	12	4	504	108
Twice,	~	–	52	24	–	–	86	24
Thrice,	–	–	32	15	–	–	39	16
4 times,	–	–	21	9	–	–	10	12
5 „	–	–	15	9	–	–	14	9
6 „	–	–	13	8	–	–	11	7
7 to 11 „	–	–	44	18	–	–	18	5
12 to 16 „	–	–	10	5	–	–	6	4
17 to 20 „	–	–	2	1	–	–	3	3
21 to 30 „	–	–	3	2	–	–	4	3
31 to 40 „	–	–	2	1	–	–	2	–
41 to 50 „	–	–	1	1	–	–	–	2
51 to 60 „	–	–	–	1	–	–	–	1
61 to 70 „	–	–	1	–	–	–	–	1
71 to 80 „	–	–	–	1	–	–	–	1
Total No. of Individuals committed,	15	4	800	234	12	4	706	196
No. of commitments represented in foregoing,	15	4	1,820	851	12	4	1,481	827

Averages, and Highest and Lowest Numbers (exclusive of Debtors).

—	From 1st January to 31st December, 1874.			From 1st January, 1875, to day of Inspection.		
	M.	F.	Date.	M.	F.	Date.
Average daily number of prisoners in custody,	50	25	—	65	32	—
Highest number of Prisoners at any one time,	98		4th June.	124		28th Aug. 29th Aug.
Lowest ditto,	54		12th March.	62		30th Sept.
Highest number of males at any one time,	70		25th June.	83		11th June. 12th June.
Ditto of females,	41		17th Oct. 18th Oct.	50		28th Aug.
Lowest number of males at any one time,	36		6th April.	42		27th Sept. 30th Sept.
Ditto of females,	16		27th March. 28th March. 15th July.	17		8th March. 9th March. 11th March. 26th Sept.

Highest Number of Prisoners (exclusive of Debtors) in Gaol during each of the previous seven years, and up to day of Inspection in 1875.

7th May, 1868, . . . 56   22nd September, 1872, . 88
15th October, 1869, . . 67   25th September, 1873, . . 89
10th August, 1870, . . 57   4th June, 1874, . . 98
30th October, 1871, . . 63   28th & 29th August, 1875, . 124

At the time of my visit some prisoners belonging to this jurisdiction had been transferred to the gaol of the county, in consequence of this prison having become overcrowded. I found in custody here 48 males and

25 females of all classes. Two males were master debtors, 6 males and 4 females were on remand or for trial, 2 males were deserters, and 2 were military prisoners under sentences of Courts Martial. Of the convicted prisoners 3 males were under sentence, charged with crimes against property; 1, the young offender already mentioned, convicted of stealing a watch, and 2 sentenced to imprisonment, 1 for four and 1 for six months also, for larceny; all the other tried male offenders, inmates of the gaol at the time of my inspection, had been convicted of assaults, wounding, vagrancy, drunkenness, or fraudulent enlistment; 1 had been sentenced to an imprisonment of two years, 1 for one year, 1 for eight, 1 for six, and 1 for nine months for assaults. Seven tramps had been sentenced to an imprisonment of three months as vagrants. The remainder, with the exception of 2 for fraudulent enlistment, had been convicted of drunkenness, assaults, and disorderly conduct in the streets of Limerick, and sentenced for periods varying from four months to seven days. Fourteen were for drunkenness.

Two female offenders were on remand, and two had been committed for trial.

Two convicted of larceny had been sentenced to an imprisonment, 1 for twelve and 1 for three months.

Two others convicted of assaults had been sentenced for nine and two months respectively. All the other female inmates of the gaol had been convicted of drunkenness and disorderly conduct in the streets of Limerick, and sentenced to imprisonments—8 for six months, 4 for three months, 1 for two, and 5 for one month; 1 was for seven days. Some of the sentences on these women were for the longest periods the law will permit, but to persons of their class I fear they will not have a deterrent effect. They have no means to earn a livelihood unless by prostitution, they will not remain in the workhouse, and for many the only chance of reformation is committal to a Government prison, where, removed from the opportunities to obtain spirituous liquor, for a long period under the strict system there carried out, and afterwards placed in refuges, they gradually acquire the power of self-control, and may become useful members of society. One woman in the gaol had been upwards of 70 times in custody, another upwards of 60 times, and by reference to the preceding tables it will be seen that the 196 females lodged in this gaol during 1875 have 827 convictions recorded against them on the prison books.

Seven hundred and six males were in custody during 1875. They have been 1,481 times inmates of this prison.

Accommodation.

	M.	F.		M.	F.
Wards,	3	3	Store Rooms,	3	1
Yards,	6	3	Laundry,	–	1
Solitary Cells,	3	2	Drying Room,	–	1
Single Cells, not less in size than 9 ft. long, 6 ft. wide, 8 ft. high, containing 432 cubic ft.	68	30	Lavatories,	15	6
			Baths, with hot and cold water laid on,	2	2
Ditto, heated and furnished with bells,	68	30	Privies,	3	2
			Water-closets,	13	3
Sleeping rooms,	9	3	Fumigating Apparatus,	1	1
Hospital Rooms,	4	1	Pumps,	3	–
Chapels,	2	2	Crank-pump,	1	–
Workshops,	2	–	Treadwheel,	1	–
Kitchen,	1	–	Tell-tale Clocks,	2	–

This prison has many advantages, and should the jurisdiction of the county and city be amalgamated it would make an excellent prison for females for both jurisdictions.

SOUTH DISTRICT.

[Limerick City Gaol.

When I made my inspection of this prison on the 8th and 9th October the prison buildings were in sound repair, very orderly, and well kept ; the cells were clean and properly cared ; the hells and other appliances for separation, the water-closets, baths, and lavatories in order, and the heating apparatus working satisfactorily.

Since my last visit check gates have been put up at the entrance to the central hall of the male prison, which improve the ventilation in warm weather and render the prison more secure. Additional stone-sheds have been erected, of which there are now 31 in the gaol.

Water.

The supply of water is abundant from the river and the city main, and I found the water-closets and lavatories had a sufficient supply of water, which is pumped into a large tank from the river by the power of the tread-wheel. There is a good bath in each prison with hot and cold water laid on ; and I am informed that prisoners are bathed on admission, and afterwards weekly.

Sewerage.

The sewerage is good ; it is flushed by the tide twice in the twenty-four hours.

Gas.

Gas has been introduced into all the cells, and into the various departments of the gaol. It is kept lighting in the cells until 7 P.M.

The laundry has six separate compartments for washing, with hot and cold water laid on, and has ironing and drying rooms. The washing in this prison is well and carefully done. Three prisoners were at work in the laundry at the time of my inspection.

Stock at the time of Inspection.

	In Use.	In Store.	Male Clothing.	In Use.	In Store.	Female Clothing.	In Use.	In Store.
Blankets, pairs of,	109	20	Shirts,	38	117	Shifts,	22	78
Sheets, pairs of,	146	44	Jackets,	38	32	Jackets,	22	47
Rugs,	101	38	Vests,	38	47	Petticoats,	44	60
Hammocks or Cots,	3	–	Trowsers,	38	55	Aprons,	22	73
Bedticks,	102	18	Caps,	38	44	Neckerchiefs,	22	9
Rollers,	11	23	Shoes, Slippers, & Clogs, pairs of,	38	39	Caps,	22	90
						Stockings, pairs of,	12	–
						Shoes, Slippers, & Clogs, pairs of,	22	28

Bedding.

I examined the bedding in both prisons, which I found clean and of a good description. The clothing of the prisoners was also sufficient, but I regret to find that stockings or socks are not generally supplied to prisoners, a few of the females had them but none of the males. Stockings are not enumerated in the Prisons Act as obligatory, but there are now few gaols in which they are not given, and I trust that this requirement will not be withheld in future. The sheets in the female prison are changed weekly, and those in the male prison fortnightly. The clothes of male prisoners are fumigated in a small closet prepared for the purpose, those of females in a wooden box in laundry-yard.

The prison stores are suitably fitted up. The general store in the male prison is in charge of the Chief Warder. The stores belonging to the female prison are in charge of the Matron. The stores are tidy and well kept. The private clothes of prisoners are put up in bundles, and are now labelled. Stock is taken monthly by the Governor, and quarterly by the Local Inspector.

The prison is unlocked at 6 A.M. in summer and 7 A.M. in winter ; it is locked for the night at 6 P.M. at all seasons of the year.

Two tell-tale clocks are on the premises ; they are marked one hourly

the other half-hourly.   The night-watch remains in the interior of the
prison during the night.

Photographs of habitual prisoners are taken by the Governor, for which
duty he receives remuneration of 10d. for each copy.

The arrangements for visitors to prisoners are satisfactory.

Number of Punishments for Prison Offences.

	From 1st January to 31st Dec., 1874.		From 1st Jan., 1875, to day of Inspection.	
	M.	F.	M.	F.
By Magisterial authority, . . .	1	–	1	–
By Governor—				
Dark or Refractory Cells, . . .	125	27	124	32
Stoppage of Diet, ...	57	19	18	9
Other Punishments, . . .	1	1	–	–
Total, . . .	184	47	143	41

Three cells in the male prison, and two in that for females, are set
apart for punishment; they are furnished with the statutable appliances
for separation, and are heated.

In no instance was it necessary to call in magisterial interference in
the treatment of refractory prisoners during 1875, the powers granted by
the Prisons Act to the Governor having been found sufficient.

The Punishment Book is duly laid before the Board at its meetings,
and checked by the Chairman.

Employment on day of Inspection.

	M.	F.
Stone-breaking, ...	26	–
Matmaking, ...	2	–
Shoemaking, ...	1	–
Do. Binding, ...	1	2
Tailor, ...	1	–
Sewing, ...	–	6
Quilting, ...	–	8
Knitting, ...	–	1
Mattress-making, ...	–	1
Washing, cooking, cleaning, . .	2	3
Oakum-picking, ...	10	2
Unemployed, ...	3	2
Debtors, ...	2	–
Total, ...	48	25

*Amount received for produce of Prisoners' Labour disposed of outside the
Gaol.*

1872, . £118 6s. 9d. | 1873, . £136 16s. 6d. | 1874, . £155 3s. 0d.

It is satisfactory to observe the progressive increase in the amount
derived from the industrial labour of the prisoners sold outside the prison,
which amounted to £136 16s. 6d. in 1873, £155 5s. in 1874, and
£237 1s. in 1875.

I found the prisoners usefully employed.   All the females were engaged
at reproductive work, some quilting and others sewing and knitting.   Three
were in the laundry.   There are now 31 stone-breakers' sheds in the prison,
in which prisoners were occupied at the time of my visit.   Males sentenced
to hard labour work on the tread-wheel for two hours daily, at intervals
of eight minutes on and four off.   Prisoners not so sentenced pick oakum;
artisans work at their trades.

The females make mattresses, quilt, sew, and knit; they pick fibre, and work in the laundry. The matron of this prison is indefatigable in her endeavours to usefully employ the very disorderly class of females placed in her charge, and she is very successful in doing so.

School.

No scholastic teaching is given to the prisoners in this gaol, but Sisters of Mercy give moral and religious instruction to Roman Catholic females on one day in the week, and to prisoners of both sexes who belong to that creed in hospital.

Dietary and Contracts.

Bread, brown, per 4-lb. loaf, 5¾d.; oatmeal, per cwt., 1s. 3d.; Indian meal, per cwt., 9s. 3d.; Potatoes bought in public market; new milk, per gallon, 8d. to 1st November, 1875, and 10d. to 1st May, 1876; salt, per cwt., 4s.; coal, per ton, 18s. 3d.; gas, per 1,000 cubic feet, 5s.; candles, per lb., 6d.; soap, per cwt., £1 12s. Other contracts:—Raw oil, per gallon, 3s. 2d.; boiled oil, per gal., 3s. 4d.; turpentine, per gal., 3s. 6d.; starch, per lb., 4d.; washing soda, per lb., 1d.; blue, per lb., 1s. 2d.; limestone, per ton, 1s. 4d.

Net average daily cost of Ordinary Diet for each Prisoner.

1872, . 4d. | 1873, . 4·5d. | 1874, . 5d.

I tasted the food for prison use on the day of my inspection. It was of a good description, and the chaplains report favourably of the samples submitted for their inspection.

I questioned all the prisoners in charge. One female stated to me that she had been cut and bruised by one of the city watchmen when she was arrested. I had an inquiry instituted into the matter, and the evidence showed that she had fallen when drunk and that she had hurt herself, and had not been assaulted as she stated.

Books and Accounts.
Net cost of Gaol, including Diet and Salaries.

1872, . £1,458 3s. 7d. | 1873, . £1,620 19s. 8d. | 1874, . £1,657 13s. 0d.

Total cost of Officers, including Clothing, Value of Rations, Washing, Gas, &c.

1872, . £811 7s. 8d. | 1873, . £791 7s. 1d. | 1874, . £653 2s. 6d.

Average cost of each Prisoner per annum.

1872, . £27 10s. 7d. | 1873, . £25 3s. 1d. | 1874, . £22 2s. 0d.

Amounts repaid by the War Department for Military Prisoners.

1872, . £20 5s. 0d. | 1873, . £100 17s. 6d. | 1874, . £114 1s. 0d.

Amounts repaid from the Consolidated Fund for the Maintenance, &c., of Prisoners.

1872, . £139 17s. 8d. | 1873, . £94 3s. 5d. | 1874, . £139 2s. 6d.

The prison books are kept by the Governor with most praiseworthy care and attention; he is assisted by the store-keeper in keeping some of them. His journal is a minute record of the occurrences in the gaol, and he marks in red ink all matters deserving special attention.

The Local Inspector also and the Medical Officer keep journals, in which they note all matters connected with the discharge of their duties within the prison. The Chaplains have journals, in which they state the duties they perform.

One of the prison registries is now exhausted. I have recommended that a registry on a more approved form be adopted, and in future only one registry will be kept instead of two as hitherto.

Officers and Salaries.

Non-Resident.	£	s.	d.		£	s.	d.
Wm. M'Donnell, esq., Local Inspector,	60	0	0	Michael O'Meara, Supernumerary Warder,	39	0	0
R. R. Gelston, M.D.,	40	0	0	Thos. Maxwell, Night Warder,	45	10	0
Rev. F. Meredyth, Protestant Chaplain,	40	0	0	*Resident.*			
Very Rev. Dr. Casey, P.P., Roman Catholic Chaplain,	40	0	0	Thomas Kelly, Governor,	155	0	0
				Jas. M'Guire, Chief Warder,	55	0	0
Thos. Kilbridge, Warder,	45	10	0	Miss Brice, Matron,	50	0	0
George Sadlier, Warder,	45	10	0	Miss Shealian, Assistant do.,	35	0	0
William Daly, Warder,	45	10	0	Wm. M'Carty, Gate Porter,	49	12	4

Vacancies in Staff since last Inspection, how caused, and how filled up, viz.

Mrs. B. Carey died 8th July, 1875, and Miss Shenhan was appointed on probation at Board meeting, 27th August, 1875. Thomas Maxwell, Night Guard Warder, Jan. 8, 1875.

Officers on Gaol Allowance.

Thomas Kelly, Miss Brice, and Miss Shealian, get coal, gas, and washing done; James M'Guire gets coal and gas.

Visits paid by Officers.

	From 1st Jan. to 31st Dec., 1874.	From 1st Jan., 1875, to day of Inspection.
Number of times the Board of Superintendence met and discharged business,	25	19
Local Inspector to Gaol,	165	135
Chaplain, Protestant Episcop. Church,	220	198
Roman Catholic Chaplain,	310	239
Physician,	145	161

Hospital.

	1872.		1873.		1874.		1875 (To day of Inspection)	
	M.	F.	M.	F.	M.	F.	M.	F.
No. of prisoners in hospital,	5	11	3	1	1	2	—	—
Number of prisoners prescribed for and treated out of hospital,	115	11	86	14	74	12	79	27
Cost of medicine,	£11 10s. 6d.		£5 16s. 3d.		£3 5s. 2d.		£3 6s. 0d.	
Cost of diet for prisoners in hospital,	£3 5s. 0d.		£2 11s. 0d.		£1 0s. 6d.		—	
Cost of all extra diet ordered by Medical Officer for prisoners not in hospital,	£7 5s. 10d.		£7 0s. 3d.		£5 1s. 6d.		—	

The hospitals are little used; both were unoccupied when I visited. No change has been made in the hospital arrangements since my last inspection. The Medical Officer carefully discharges his duties, and there has been no death in the prison for many years.

The hospital for males is separate, and unnecessarily large. That for females consists of a room at the top of the female prison, and, opening into it, can be attended by the assistant matron.

Board of Superintendence.

Alderman Myles.	Alderman Carte.	Maurice Lenehan, esq., T.C.
John F. Walker, esq. T.C.	John F. Moloney, esq., R.C.	Alderman Synan
Wm. Player, esq., T.C.	John J. Cleary, esq., T.C.	Alderman O'Callaghan.
Laurence Kelly, esq., R.C.	Alderman Quaulivau.	Alderman Tinsley.

The Board meets for the transaction of business in the courthouse adjoining the prison, fortnightly, on every second Friday in each month,

X

SOUTH
DISTRICT.

*Limerick
City
Gaol.*

when the liabilities are discharged by cheques payable to each creditor, if of sufficient amount. A sum of £50 remains in the hands of the Local Inspector, out of which he pays small accounts, and produces vouchers at the next meeting of the Board.

The salaries of the Governor and chief warder are paid monthly ; those of the inferior staff weekly.

JOHN LENTAIGNE, *Inspector-General.*

---

*Queen's
County
Gaol.*

QUEEN'S COUNTY GAOL, AT MARYBOROUGH.—STATUTABLE INSPECTION,
22ND OCTOBER, 1875.

---

*Number of Prisoners of all classes in Gaol on the day of Inspection, and
on the corresponding date in the three preceding years.*

	M.	F.		M.	F.
1872,	15	4	1874,	31	5
1873,	17	6	1875 (day of Inspection),	24	3

Juveniles.

Juveniles.

One young offender (male), aged 15 years, was an inmate of the prison at the time of my visit ; he had been convicted before the chairman at quarter sessions, of larceny, and sentenced to an imprisonment of six months with hard labour. Eleven (males) were committed during the year. No females. Four were committed for larceny, of whom 2, aged 12 and 15 years, were sent to reformatories ; and 2, aged 14 and 15, were sentenced to imprisonments—1 for two and the other for six months with hard labour. Six other young offenders were committed during the year, of whom 2 were for assaults, 1 for sending a threatening letter, 1 for being drunk, and 1 for playing ball in the streets. One charged with perjury was not tried, and was discharged.

Commitments.

CLASSES.				From 1st Jan. to 31st Dec., 1874.		From 1st Jan., 1875, to day of Inspection.	
				M.	F.	M.	F.
Debtors,	.	.	.	—	—	1	—
Criminals,	.	.	.	179	32	146	35
Vagrants,	.	.	.	2	2	32	3
Drunkards,	.	.	.	53	11	61	7
Total,	.	.	.	234	45	240	45

*Individual Prisoners (exclusive of Debtors) and Number of Times each
had been committed.*

NUMBER OF TIMES COMMITTED	1874.				1875, to day of Inspection.			
	Juveniles.		Adults.		Juveniles.		Adults.	
	M.	F.	M.	F.	M.	F.	M.	F.
Once within the year,	10	3	198	32	9	—	206	45
Twice „	..	—	9	5	1	—	8	—
Thrice „	—	—	—	—	—	—	2	—
Four times „	—	—	2	—	—	—	—	—
Total, .	10	3	209	37	10	—	216	45
No. of above who had not been in Gaol previous to 1st Jan. in .	10	3	172	22	8	..	184	45

Individual Prisoners (exclusive of Debtors) committed in the year 1874, and to the day of Inspection in 1875, who had been Once and oftener re-committed from their first Commitment in any year, so far as can be ascertained.

NUMBER OF TIMES COMMITTED.	1874.				1875, to day of Inspection.			
	Juveniles.		Adults.		Juveniles.		Adults.	
	M.	F.	M.	F.	M.	F.	M.	F.
Once only,	10	3	172	22	8	–	175	33
Twice,	–	–	20	8	1	–	27	8
Thrice,	–	–	4	1	1	–	6	–
Four times,	–	–	3	1	–	–	3	–
Five „	–	–	5	1	–	–	1	1
Six „	–	–	–	1	–	–	1	1
7 to 11 times,	–	–	–	2	–	–	1	–
12 to 16 „	–	–	4	2	–	–	1	1
21 to 40 „	–	–	2	–	–	–	1	–
41 to 50 „	–	–	–	–	–	–	–	1
Total No. of Individuals committed,	10	3	209	37	10	–	216	45
No. of Commitments represented in foregoing,	10	3	367	96	13	–	310	113

Averages, and Highest and Lowest Numbers (exclusive of Debtors).

—	From 1st January to 31st December, 1874.			From 1st January, 1875, to day of Inspection.		
	M.	F.	Date.	M.	F.	Date.
Average daily number of prisoners in custody,	27	4	—	27	5	—
Highest number of prisoners at any one time,	36		11th May.	46		4th March.
Lowest ditto,	25		18th Aug.	22		14th Oct.
Highest number of males at any one time,	38		11th May.	40		4th March.
Ditto of females,	9		24th Oct.	8		25th June.
Lowest number of males at any one time,	18		11th Jan.	19		20th July.
Ditto of females,	–		21st April.	1		13th Oct.

Highest Number of Prisoners (exclusive of Debtors) in Gaol during each of the previous Seven Years, and up to day of Inspection in 1875.

8th January, 1868, . . 33
20th January, 1869, . . 32
3rd April, 1870, . . 33
4th March, 1871, . . 46

30th June, 1872, . . 27
25th June, 1873, . . 39
11th May, 1874, . . 38
4th March, 1875, . . 46

Prisoners sentenced to Solitary Confinement by order of Court.

	From 1st January to 31st December, 1874.		From 1st January, 1875, to day of Inspection.	
	M.	F.	M.	F.
Solitary Confinement,	41	1	48	–

Twenty-seven prisoners of all classes were in custody at the time of my inspection, viz., 24 males, and 3 females. One of the latter was for trial at the assizes, charged with perjury; the other 2 females in custody were

SOUTH DISTRICT.

—1 sentenced for fourteen days for being drunk, the other for six months for larceny of money. Both are habitual offenders.

Queen's County Gaol.

The male prisoners were—1 for trial for stabbing; 6 for larceny, and sentenced—1 for twelve, 1 for five, 1 for nine, and 3 for six months each—one of the latter was the boy of fifteen years of age already mentioned.

The remaining prisoners in custody were under sentences for assaults, drunkenness, vagrancy, being absent from militia training, and 1 for rescue. They had been sentenced to imprisonments—1 for two years, 2 for one year; 2 for six, 2 for four, 1 for three, and 4 for one month each. Three others had been sentenced for terms of from seven to fourteen days.

My colleague and I in our annual reports for many years have recommended that all long sentenced prisoners be transferred to a central depot, and only prisoners for trial, and those under short sentences, remain in county gaols. Should this suggestion be carried out, the inmates of this gaol will be very few indeed, and a small building with a much diminished staff will be sufficient to meet the requirements of the district.

Commitments.

The total number of individuals committed to this prison in 1875 was 226 males and 45 females. Many, however, were old offenders, and they represent 323 committals of males, and 113 of females, on the books of the gaol in the present and former years.

Debtors.

One debtor was in custody in 1875; none in 1874.

Accommodation.

	M.	F.		M.	F.
Wards,	6	2	Worksheds,	12	—
Yards,	13	5	Kitchens,	2	—
Day Rooms,	8	4	Bakery,	1	—
Solitary Cells,	4	4	Store Rooms,	2	2
Single Cells, not less than 9 feet long, 6 feet wide, and 8 feet high = 432 cubic feet,	91	20	Laundry,	—	1
			Drying Room,	—	1
			Lavatories,	12	10
Ditto, heated and furnished with bells,	30	20	Baths, with hot and cold water laid on,	3	1
Single Cells of smaller size, heated and furnished with bells,	18	—	Privies,	4	4
Ditto, not so furnished,	36	—	Water-closets,	4	4
Cells to contain three persons,	7	—	Fumigating Apparatus,	1	—
Sleeping Rooms,	7	—	Reception Rooms or Cells,	1	1
Hospital Rooms,	2	2	Pump,	1	—
Chapel,	One		Crank-pump,	1	—
School Rooms,	1	1	Wells,	2	—
Workshops,	10	4	Tread-wheel,	1	—
			Tell-tale Clocks,	2	—

Since last inspection the walls of No. 8 block, the hospital building, and the passage to the matron's quarters have been pointed with Portland cement, the coping of the walls has been re-set, the yards have been paved, and some woodwork which was decayed has been repaired. The work was done by the labour of the prisoners. A new saddle boiler has been put up, and a heating apparatus has been fixed in Nos. 7 and 8 blocks, and it is proposed to extend the pipes for heating into blocks 5 and 6—the female prison.

Repair.

I found the buildings in sound repair, very clean and tidy. Some improvements have been made, and the working of the establishment is satisfactory; but the Board of Superintendence hesitate to expend money on the buildings, pending legislation. And, having regard to the small amount of crime in the district, this large prison is quite unnecessary. If long sentenced prisoners were removed to a central depot, as is contemplated, the officers on the staff would sometimes outnumber the prisoners. On the day of my visit only 3 females were in custody, and in the previous week (on the 13th of the month) only 1.

At present forty-eight cells in the male prison and twenty cells in that for females have bells and are artificially heated and lighted by gas. The Board of Superintendence express a desire to introduce gas into the remaining cells of the prison ; but I cannot recommend that expense be incurred in doing so until the wishes of the Legislature are known as to the future prison system to be adopted in this Kingdom. The extern parts of the prison, the officers' quarters, and the work-rooms of two classes of males, are lighted by gas.

Stock at the time of Inspection.

	In Use.	In Store.	Male Clothing.	In Use.	In Store.	Female Clothing.	In Use.	In Store.
Blankets, pairs of,	90	55	Shirts, . .	69	32	Shifts, . .	6	30
Sheets, pairs of, .	95½	20½	Jackets, . . .	24	44	Jackets, . .	6	32
Rugs, . .	96	47	Vests, . . .	24	46	Petticoats,	6	63
Hammocks or			Trowsers, . .	24	39	Aprons, . .	6	20
Cots, . .	–	23	Caps, . . .	24	40	Neckerchiefs, .	6	23
Bed-ticks, . .	96	57	Socks, pairs of,	60	50	Caps, . .	6	30
Bedsteads, . .	136	–	Shoes, Slippers, &			Stockings, pairs of,	6	37
			Clogs, pairs of,	24	51	Shoes, Slippers, &		
			Braces, . .	24	24	Clogs, pairs of,	3	15

I found an abundant supply of good prison clothing in use and in store. Prisoners of both sexes are given stockings or socks, and the females caps, aprons, and neckerchiefs. There is also a sufficient supply of bedding. Some of the blankets in use were thin when I examined them, but not sufficiently so to be cast. I suggested that an extra blanket be supplied during cold weather so long as they are in use. The clothing of prisoners is properly cleansed and disinfected before being put into store. The fumigating apparatus is in the prison for males. The stores are properly kept. I found them clean, tidy, and well arranged. The private clothes of prisoners are properly tied up and labelled when in store. The Governor takes stock monthly.

Water for the use of the establishment is supplied from a river which passes through the prison grounds, and it is raised by the power of the tread-wheel into a large cistern capable of containing 12,500 gallons, whence it is distributed to the different sections of the prison. I observe, however, by the journal of the Local Inspector, that the occupiers of the adjoining lands sometimes divert the stream for agricultural purposes, by which the supply to the gaol becomes insufficient. This trespass should not be permitted. Water for drinking purposes is obtained from a well on the premises.

The laundry has hot and cold water laid on, with drying-room and other appliances.

Three baths in the male prison, and one in the female prison have likewise hot and cold water laid on. There are water-closets and lavatories in both prisons.

The female prison is supplied with water by a force pump from a well on that part of the prison grounds.

The sewerage is stated to be effective ; but the privies are open without effluvium traps, and the pipes from the sewers do not connect with those to the top of the building, by which foul air might be got rid of—an important improvement now generally adopted.

The suggestions of the Inspectors-General as regards the laundry and cook-house, have not been carried out by the Board, in order to avoid expense, under the impression that a new prison system will be introduced during next session of Parliament.

No change has been made in the arrangements for the photographing of habitual criminals. The present system is expensive and not satisfactory.

[margin notes: Sooth District. | Queen's County Gaol. | Stock. | Water. | Sewerage.]

SOUTH
DISTRICT.

Queen's
County
Gaol.

In summer the prisoners are unlocked at 6 A.M., and they are locked for the night at 6 P.M.

The winter unlock is held at daybreak, and the prison is locked at dark, but gas is kept lighting in the cells where prisoners work until 8 P.M.

Two warders patrol during the night—one from 9.45 P.M. to 1 A.M.; the other from that hour until morning.

Two tell-tale clocks test the vigilance of the night watch, and are protected by Chubbs' locks.

Visitors.

Visitors see prisoners at the watch-house near the entrance to the gaol which has been fitted up for the purpose.

No escape was attempted from this gaol in 1874 or 1875.

Number of Punishments for Prison Offences.

	From 1st Jan. to 31st Dec., 1874.		From 1st Jan., 1875, to day of Inspection.	
	M.	F.	M.	F.
By Governor—				
Dark or refractory cells,	41	1	48	–
Stoppage of diet,	14	–	12	–
Total,	55	1	60	–

Punish-
ments.

Two punishment cells are provided for females, which are now properly heated and have bells. There are four in the male prison, but they are not heated, and have not means for the inmates to communicate with a prison officer.

The record of punishments is regularly submitted to the Board at its meetings, and signed by the chairman.

One male was under punishment at the time of my inspection.

Employment on day of Inspection.

	M.	F.
Sack-making,	18	–
Mat-making,	1	–
Shoemaking,	1	–
Cleaning Prison,	2	–
Undergoing punishment,	1	–
Sewing and Knitting,	–	3
Discharged before labour hours,	1	–
Total,	24	3

Amount received for produce of Prisoners' labour disposed of outside the Gaol.

1872, . £15 10s. 8d. | 1873, . £27 6s. 0d. | 1874, . £21 8s. 3d.

Labour.

Prisoners sentenced to hard labour work on the tread-wheel for three hours daily. The tread-wheel is divided into ten compartments, with five reliefs, so that prisoners can work on the tread-wheel in gangs of fifteen.

Sack-making has lately been introduced into the prison, but as the materials are supplied by Mr. Goodbody, at Clara, and the work when finished must be returned to him, the cost of transit reduces the profits on the prisoners' work very considerably.

Shoe-making, tailoring, and mat-making are likewise carried on ; and sewing, knitting, and washing by the females.

School.

	From 1st Jan., to 31st Dec., 1874.		From 1st Jan., 1875, to day of Inspection.	
	M.	F.	M.	F.
Number of individual prisoners who attended school,	118	24	76	16
Average daily number of pupils,	9·01	2	7·3	2
Number of days on which school was held,	139	235	183	173

School-hours.—Males, 3 to 4.   Females, 3 to 4½.

No school was held for some time previously to my visit in the female prison, the assistant-matron not being well. The teacher in the male prison was never trained; he had been a policeman. The male school-room is not stalled, and is wanting in appliances. The prisoners sit at a table in association together, which is very objectionable. The school-room in the female prison has maps, but none are in that for males.

Contracts.

Bread, white, per 4 lb. loaf, 5d.; oatmeal, per cwt., 15s.; Indian meal, per cwt., Contracts. 8s.; potatoes, per cwt., 2s. 8d.; meat, per lb., 8d.; new milk, per gallon, 8d.; butter-milk, per gallon, 1½d.; salt, per cwt., 3s.; coal, per ton, £1 5s. 9d.; straw, per cwt., 2s. 2d.; gas, per 1,000 cubic feet, 8s. 4d.; candles, per lb., 8d.; soap, per cwt., £1 4s. Other contracts—linen, per yard, 11½d.; sheeting, per yard, 1s. 8d.; chambey, per yard, 10d.; check, per yard, 10d.; shoes, per pair, 8s. 6d.

Net average daily cost of ordinary Diet for each Prisoner.

1872,	. 4d.	1873,	. 4·5d.	1874,	. 4d.

The food for prison use, which I tasted on the day of my visit, was of Food. a good description, and the Chaplains almost uniformly report favourably of the samples of provisions submitted for their inspection. In a few cases the quality of the milk and stirabout was objected to by them.

I questioned, individually, all the prisoners in custody on my inspection. One male only lodged a complaint. He was under punishment at the time of my visit, and stated that the warder had wrongfully accused him of the offence for which he was punished. I investigated the case and satisfied myself that he deserved his punishment.

Officers and Salaries.

Non-Resident.	£	s.	d.	Resident.	£	s.	d.
				A. Cashel Bulkeley, esq., Governor, . . .	200	0	0
Charles Moore, esq., Local Inspector, . . .	90	0	0	William Sythes, 1st Assistant,	60	0	0
Rev. E. L. Eves, Protestant				Thomas Cobbe, Gate Porter,	40	0	0
Episcopal Chaplain, .	40	0	0	Wm. Sturkey, Turnkey and Schoolmaster, . . .	35	0	0
Rev. Thomas Morrin, Roman Catholic Chaplain, .	40	0	0	James Monaghey, Warder, .	32	10	0
D. B. Jacob, esq., M.D., Physician and Surgeon, . .	—			George Rickaby, Watchman,	32	10	0
Joseph M'Namara, Apothecary,	—			Thos. Robinson, Watchman, .	30	0	0
				Mary Anne Sythes, Matron,	25	0	0
				Mary Anne Nicholl, Matron and Schoolmistress, . .	25	0	0

Vacancies in the staff since last inspection, how caused, and how filled up.

A. Case, superannuated; vacancy not filled up. Thomas Cobbe resigned; J. Monaghey appointed. Francis Johnson resigned; Thomas Robinson appointed.

Visits paid by Officers.

	From 1st Jan., to 31st Dec., 1874.	From 1st Jan., 1875, to day of Inspection.
Number of times the Board of Superintendence met and discharged business,	12	10
Local Inspector to Gaol, . . .	132	117
Chaplain, Protestant Episcopal Church, .	199	166
,, Roman Catholic, . .	177	182
Physician and Surgeon, . . .	130	97

The officers' quarters were tidy when I inspected them. The warders Officers' have no mess-room in the gaol, and the majority take their meals outside quarters. in their homes. When they leave the prison they have passes signed by the Governor.

Books and Accounts.

Net cost of Gaol, including Diet and Salaries.

1872, . £1,401 6s. 7d. | 1873, . £1,606 19s. 2d. | 1874, . £1,421 5s. 1d.

Total cost of Officers, including Clothing, Value of Rations, &c.

1872, . £834 3s. 1d. | 1873, . £884 1s. 0d. | 1874, . £846 3s. 3d.

Average cost of each Prisoner per annum.

1872, . £66 5s. 2d. | 1873, . £72 2s. 2d. | 1874, £46 9s. 1d.

Amounts repaid by the War Department for Military Prisoners.

1872, . £3 3s. 0d. | 1873, . £1 17s. 0d. | 1874, . £0 2s. 0d.

Amounts repaid from the Consolidated Fund for the maintenance, &c., of Prisoners.

1872, . £93 19s. 9d. | 1873, . £83 15s. 4d. | 1874, . £152 5s. 5d.

Books.

The different prison books and registries in this prison are kept with much care and attention by the Governor with the assistance of the chief warder, who has charge of the statistical registries. Those which refer to finance are specially kept by the Governor. The Local Inspector occasionally checks the different books. His journal, as likewise that of the Governor, is a full record of the various occurrences in the gaol. Matters deserving of special observation are marked in red ink.

The Medical Officer records in his journal all cases under his treatment worthy of note. The Chaplains state in their journals the duties they perform.

Hospital.

	1872.		1873.		1874.		1875 (to day of Inspection).	
	M.	F.	M.	F.	M.	F.	M.	F.
No. of prisoners in hospital,	15	2	11	2	11	2	3	1
Average daily number in hospital, . . .	·9	·1	·11	·10	·2	·1	·4	·1
No. of prisoners prescribed for and treated out of hospital, . . .	164	9	143	15	88	7	69	6
Cost of medicine, . .	£10 9s. 0d.		£15 5s. 2d.		£20 18s. 6d.		—	
Cost of diet for prisoners in hospital, . .	£2 16s. 9d.		£3 12s. 0d.		£6 16s. 4d.		—	
Cost of all extra diet ordered for prisoners not in hospital,	£2 9s. 4d.		£2 8s. 0d.		£0 11s. 5d.		—	

Hospital.

There is abundant hospital accommodation in this prison. It is for both sexes in the same building, with a common staircase ; communication is, however, cut off by an iron gate. Two wards are for each sex, with water-closets and a bath.

The sanitary condition of the prison is satisfactory, no death having occurred in it since 1869.

Board of Superintendence.

Viscount De Vesci. | Capt. R. G. Cosby. | M. Dunne, esq.
Earl of Portarlington. | Robert Staples, esq. | E. S. R. Smyth, esq.
Sir Allen Walsh, bart. | R. S. Hawkesworth, esq. | R. F. Stubber, esq.
Colonel H. D. Carden. | Thomas Kemmis, esq. | M. H. Franks, esq.

Board.

The Board meets on the second Wednesday of each month for the transaction of business, when liabilities are discharged ; large accounts are settled by cheques to each creditor. The salaries of inferior officers are paid by cheques to Local Inspector, and small accounts under £2 to the Governor, vouchers being produced at next meeting of the Board.

The salaries of the superior officers are paid by presentment at assizes. There are no bridewells in this county.

I cannot conclude this report without reiterating the expression of opinion of my colleague, in his report on this gaol for 1874, where he states that the Local Inspector and Governor of the prison are both valuable public servants, and deserve great praise for their attention to duty, and for the regularity and order which they maintain in the prison. I further desire to add that the defects in the prison arise not from the fault of these officers but from circumstances over which they have no control.

Soutu Distaict.

Queen's County Gaol.

JOHN LENTAIGNE, *Inspector-General.*

TIPPERARY COUNTY (NORTH RIDING) GAOL, AT NENAGH.—STATUTABLE INSPECTION, 14TH OCTOBER, 1875.

Tipperary County (North Riding) Gaol.

Number of Prisoners of all classes in Gaol on the day of Inspection, and on the corresponding date in the three preceding years.

	M.	F.		M.	F.
1872,	32	5	1874,	41	4
1873,	44	6	1875 (day of Inspection),	35	3

Number of Returned Convicts in Gaol on the day of Inspection, and during each of the three preceding years.

	M.	F.		M.	F.
1872,	2	1	1875 (up to and including	—	—
1873,	1	–	day of Inspection),	—	—
1874,	1	2	Day of Inspection,	—	—

No prisoner in custody during 1875 was known to have been in a reformatory or industrial school.

Juveniles.

One young offender under 12 years of age was in custody for trial at the time of my visit; 20 males and 2 females had previously been in charge in 1875; 1 girl and 6 of the boys were under 12 years of age. The little girl and 1 boy were sent to reformatories. One boy was twice and 1 four times committed to this gaol during the year.

Juveniles.

Commitments.

CLASSES.	From 1st January to 31st December, 1874.		From 1st January, 187 , to day of Inspection.	
	M.	F.	M.	F.
Debtors,	–	–	–	–
Criminals,	198	45	153	38
Vagrants,	14	–	29	5
Drunkards,	210	35	141	34
Contempt of Court,	1	–	–	–
Total,	423	80	323	77

Number of Individual Prisoners (exclusive of Debtors) and Number of Times each had been committed during the following periods, distinguishing Adults from Juveniles.

NUMBER OF TIMES COMMITTED.	1874.				1875, to day of Inspection.			
	Juveniles.		Adults.		Juveniles.		Adults.	
	M.	F.	M.	F.	M.	F.	M.	F.
Once within the year,	6	2	267	40	14	2	233	41
Twice, ,,	-	-	30	3	1	-	21	5
Thrice, ,,	1	-	13	-	-	-	5	3
4 times ,,	-	-	5	1	1	-	2	1
5 & 6 times ,,	-	-	4	1	-	-	1	2
7 ,, ,,	-	-	1	2	-	-	-	-
9 ,, ,,	-	-	-	1	-	-	-	-
Total,	7	2	320	48	16	2	262	52
No. of above who had not been in Gaol previous to 1st January in .	6	2	250	36	16	2	183	37

Number of Individual Prisoners (exclusive of Debtors) committed in the year 1874, and to the day of Inspection in 1875, who had been Once, Twice, Thrice, Four Times, Five Times, &c., &c., from their first Commitment in any year, so far as can be ascertained, distinguishing Adults from Juveniles.

NUMBER OF TIMES COMMITTED.	1874.				1875, to day of Inspection.			
	Juveniles.		Adults.		Juveniles.		Adults.	
	M.	F.	M.	F.	M.	F.	M.	F.
Once only, .	6	2	282	34	14	2	174	31
Twice,	-	-	37	3	1	-	42	7
Thrice,	-	-	17	1	-	-	11	3
4 times,	1	-	7	2	1	-	10	-
5 ,,	-	-	4	1	-	-	3	3
6 ,,	-	-	3	1	-	-	2	1
7 to 11 ,,	-	-	8	3	-	-	9	2
12 to 20 ,,	-	-	8	1	-	-	7	2
21 to 40 ,,	-	-	2	1	-	-	2	1
41 to 50 ,,	-	-	1	-	-	-	1	-
71 to 80 ,,	-	-	-	1	-	-	-	-
181 to 200 ,,	-	-	1	-	-	-	1	-
Total No. of individuals committed,	7	2	320	48	16	2	262	50
No. of commitments represented in foregoing.	10	2	905	209	20	2	639	163

Highest Number of Prisoners (exclusive of Debtors) in Gaol during each of the previous seven years, and up to day of Inspection in 1875.

23rd January, 1868,	. 37	21st June, 1872, .	. 59
20th June, 1869,	. 51	27th November, 1873, .	. 65
1st September, 1870,	. 56	25th January, 1874, .	. 56
20th June, 1871,	. 56	28th February, 1875, .	. 58

Averages, and Highest and Lowest Numbers (exclusive of Debtors).

—	From 1st January to 31st December, 1874.			From 1st January, 1875, to day of Inspection.		
	M.	F.	Date.	M.	F.	Date.
Average daily number of prisoners in custody,	38	5	—	35	8	—
Highest number of prisoners at any one time,	58		25th Jan.	58		28th Feb.
Lowest ditto.	33		17th June.	22		17th Sept.
Highest number of males at any one time,	54		25th Jan.	48		21st Jan.
Ditto of females,	13		21st Aug.	14		5th Feb.
Lowest number of males at any one time,	26		16th June.	19		17th Sept.
Ditto of females,	2		1st Feb.	2		10th Oct.

Thirty-five male and 3 female prisoners were in custody on the day of my inspection.

The females were 3 prostitutes committed for drunkenness and loitering for prostitution ; the males were—2 for trial ; 1 military offender tried by court-martial, and sentenced to an imprisonment of 504 days ; 3 convicted of larceny, two tried by juries at assize and quarter sessions, and sentenced for terms of 6 and 12 months ; the third had been summarily convicted by magistrates at petty sessions, and sentenced for one month. All the other offenders in custody were under sentences for drunkenness, vagrancy, and assaults, some of the latter of a serious character. Two had been sentenced for periods of 2 years each, two for 1 year, and one for nine months ; one other had been sentenced for 3, and two for 2 months each. The remainder for short terms, in no case exceeding 1 month.

Two hundred and seventy-eight individual males and 52 females were committed to this prison in 1875, but the same individuals were frequently recommitted during the year. One young offender was committed 4 times in 1875, and some adults 5 and 6 times in the course of that year ; one male, also committed in 1875, has nearly 200 convictions recorded against him on the journals of this prison ; another between 40 and 50. The 278 males committed in 1875 have been 859 times in custody, and the 52 females 165 times, showing that crime in this district is confined to comparatively few individuals ; and the small number of offences against property is evidence that the paramount crimes in the jurisdiction are the results of the lawless violence and drunkenness which prevail in this county.

Commit-ments.

Accommodation.

	M.	F.		M.	F.
Wards,	8	4	Lavatories,	8	4
Yards,	10	6	Baths, with Hot and Cold		
Day Rooms,	6	4	Water laid on,	3	3
Solitary Cells,	2	2	Privies,	19	9
Single Cells not heated or furnished with bells,	64	16	Water-closets,	3	—
Hospital Rooms,	4	4	Fumigating Apparatus,	1	1
Chapels,	1	1	Reception Rooms or Cells,	1	—
School Rooms,	1	1	Tread-wheel,	1	—
Workshops,	2	—	Crank Mill,	1	—
Worksheds, Stalls,	26	—	Cells heated and furnished with gas—		
Kitchens,	2	—	Male, 800 cubic feet,	60	—
Store Rooms,	7	2	Female, 700 „	—	14
Laundry,	—	1	Tell-tale Clocks,	2	—
Drying Room,	—	1			

Since the inspection of this gaol by my colleague in September, 1874, section No. 2 of the male prison has been remodelled, heated, and artifi-

Improve-ments.

SOUTH DISTRICT.

Tipperary County (*North*) Riding Gaol.

cially lighted by gas; section No. 4 has likewise been artificially heated. I find also that since I last visited, the cells have been enlarged, two having been thrown into one, two water-closets have been put up in No. 5 block, two earth-closets have been placed in the hospitals, one in that for each sex; and twenty-six sheds for stone-breakers have been erected by prison labour in No. 6 exercising yard; but as yet no improvement has been made in the lavatories, which are very faulty.

The Local Inspector and Governor accompanied me over the establishment, and I found it remarkably clean and well kept, the buildings in sound repair, the prisoners suitably clothed, properly cared, and apparently well subject to discipline. They are regularly bathed on admission, and afterwards on Saturdays, hot and cold water baths being provided for prisoners of both sexes.

Cells.

Fifty-six cells in the male prison are artificially heated and lighted by gas; sixteen have bells; twenty-four cells for females are likewise heated, but only seven are furnished with gas and bells. The lavatories could be improved at a trifling cost by being furnished with delf basins which could be filled in the evening by a man from a can, who in the morning might empty them. Gas is supplied to the apartments of the Governor and other intern officers, the school-room, and central hall. The exterior of the prison is likewise lighted by gas at night.

Stock at the time of Inspection.

	In Use.	In Store.	Male Clothing.	In Use.	In Store.	Female Clothing.	In Use	In Store.
Blankets, pairs of,	127	187	Shirts, .	117	42	Shifts, .	38	22
Sheets, pairs of,	130	7	Jackets,	50	25	Jackets,	18	–
Rugs,	147	77	Vests, .	54	14	Petticoats,	36	–
Hammocks or Cots,	–	8	Trowsers,	54	80	Aprons, .	23	36
Bed-ticks,	153	–	Caps, .	56	34	Neckerchiefs,	12	2
Bedsteads,	161	–	Stockings or Socks, pairs of,	80	109	Caps, .	46	–
			Shoes, Slippers, & Clogs, pairs of,	62	34	Stockings, pairs of,	46	14
						Shoes, Slippers, & Clogs, pairs of, 21	–	

Stock.

There was at the time of my visit an abundant supply of bedding and prison clothing in use and in store; the clothing of a good description, and socks or stockings are provided for prisoners of both sexes; and neckerchiefs, aprons, and caps for the females. Some of the bed-ticks in use were much worn when I visited, and new ones should be supplied. The stores are properly fitted up; and there is a fumigating box in each prison, by which the private clothing of prisoners is cleansed. The sewerage, which discharges into the town drainage, is effective, and the supply of water abundant. The laundry is divided into ten stalls, where prisoners can work in separation; it has a large drying loft overhead, with wooden louvres, where clothes are quickly dried, unless in very moist weather.

Photography.

Photographs of habitual criminals are taken by the head warder, for which work he receives £10 yearly as remuneration. Lock-up is held at 6 P.M. in summer and 5 P.M. in winter. The prisoners are unlocked at 6 A.M. in summer and 7 A.M. in winter.

The night-watch comes on duty at 9 P.M., and his circuits are tested by two tell-tale clocks—one in the Governor's house, the other at the rere of the building.

Visitors.

No change has been made since last inspection in the arrangements for visitors to prisoners, who see their friends at the gate—the untried on Thursdays, and convicted prisoners monthly.

No escape was attempted from this gaol, or from any of the bridewells of the county during 1875.

Number of Punishments for Prison Offences.

	From 1st January to 31st Dec., 1874.		From 1st Jan., 1875, to day of Inspection.	
	M.	F.	M.	F.
By Magisterial authority, . . .	1	–	–	–
By Governor—				
Dark or refractory cells, . .	16	–	17	1
Stoppage of diet, . . .	33	–	25	–
Total, . . .	50	–	43	1

Notwithstanding the lawless class of inmates of this prison, punishments are unfrequent, a firm and strict discipline rendering an appeal to magisterial authority seldom necessary. The punishment cells are artificially heated, and boarded; two are for each sex.

Punishments.

Schools.

	From 1st Jan. to 31st Dec., 1874.		From 1st Jan., 1875, to day of Inspection.	
	M.	F.	M.	F.
Number of individual prisoners who attended school, ...	77	–	20	–
Average daily number of pupils, . . .	12	–	12	–
Number of days on which school was held. .	240	–	111	–

School-hours.—Males, 4 to 5.

The school for males is in connexion with the Board of National Education. The teacher is reported to be competent, but has not been trained under any educational public body. No school is held for females.

The school-room is not stalled, and the pupils sit in association together, which is very objectionable. The school was visited by the Protestant Chaplain nine times in 1875, but there is no record that the Roman Catholic Chaplain visited the school during the year.

School.

Employment on day of Inspection.

	M.	F.
Stone-breaking, ...	24	–
Mat-making, ...	1	–
Carpenter and Smith, ...	2	–
Picking oakum, ...	1	–
Cleansing cells, Washing, . . .	2	3
Sick and unemployed, . . .	3	–
Discharged (before labour hours), . .	2	–
Total, . .	35	3

Amount received for produce of Prisoners' labour disposed of outside the Gaol for the last three years.

1872, . £72 16s. 5d. | 1873, . £124 14s. 10d. | 1874, . £100 10s. 4d.

Punitive labour consists of two hours' work on the tread-wheel, at intervals of five minutes off and five minutes on. The tread-wheel is partitioned.

Stone-breaking is the principal employment of the male inmates, who also pick oakum in their cells at night; artisans, when in custody, work at their trades for the use of the prison.

The women knit, sew, and wash.

Labour.

Contracts.

Bread, white, per 4-lb. loaf, 5½d.; brown, per 4-lb. loaf, 5d.; oatmeal, per cwt., 16s.; potatoes, per cwt., market price; meat, per lb., 10d.; new milk, per gallon, 8½d.; salt, per cwt., 2s. 10d.; coal, per ton, £1 1s., straw, per cwt., market price; gas, per 1,000 cubic feet, 8s. 9d.; candles, per lb., moulds, 5½d., dips, 5d.; soap, per cwt., white, £1 9s., yellow, £1 1s. 9d.

SOUTH DISTRICT.

Tipperary County (North Riding) Gaol.

Net average daily cost of Ordinary Diet for each Prisoner.

1872, . ⁊. . 4·8d. | 1873, . 5·23d. | 1874, . 5d.

The food for prison use, which I tasted when I made my inspection, was of a good description, and the Chaplains generally report favourably of the samples submitted for their examination, except that the milk has on several occasions been so faulty, that the Board were compelled, on the report of the Governor, to levy fines on the Contractor for furnishing an inferior article.

I questioned all the prisoners in custody. One man only lodged complaints. He stated that he had been assaulted by the chief warders, but on inquiry I ascertained that the charge was false; he also stated that he had been given an unclean bed, but that statement also was disproved by the Local Inspector.

Books and Accounts.

Net cost of Gaol, including Diet and Salaries.

1872, . £2,186 4s. 8d. | 1873, . £2,125 15s. 4d. | 1874, . £2,322 8s. 6d.

Total cost of Officers, including Clothing, Value of Rations, Washing, Gas, &c.

1872, : £1,163 15s. 11d. | 1873, . £1,157 10s. 3d. | 1874, . £1,192 3s. 6d.

Average cost of each Prisoner per annum.

1872, . £49 13s. 8d. | 1873, . £45 18s. 0d. | 1874, . £52 15s. 8d.

Amounts repaid by the War Department for Military Prisoners.

1872, : £32 2s. 1d. | 1873, . £91 9s. 0d. | 1874, . £67 11s. 0d.

Amounts repaid from the Consolidated Fund for the maintenance, &c., of Prisoners.

1872, . £171 2s. 6d. | 1873, . £130 16s. 4d. | 1874, . £137 6s. 6d.

Books.

The head warder, who is also clerk, keeps the various registries of discipline and finance, which are very creditable to that officer. They are daily checked by the Governor, and monthly by the Local Inspector. The Governor likewise checks and initials the other books of the prison; he is always at his post, and to his care and attention is due the satisfactory working of the prison; he regularly inspects the tell-tale clocks, and enters in his journal any default which he may observe; his journal is a valuable record of the occurrences in the prison; and he marks in red ink matters requiring special attention. The journal of the Local Inspector is likewise kept with much care, and he makes a special report to the Board at its meetings. The journal and books of the Medical Officer are carefully kept. The Chaplains state in their journals the duty they perform.

Officers and Salaries.

Non-Resident.	£	s.	d.		£	s.	d.
Michael Head, esq., Local Inspector,	100	0	0	Thos. Morrow, Head Warder and Clerk,	90	0	0
Rev. W. B. Chester, Protestant Chaplain,	50	0	0	Samuel Lett, Gate,	40	0	0
Rev P. O'Mailly, D.D., Roman Catholic Chaplain,	50	0	0	John Duffy, *Tailor*,	40	0	0
Edward J. Nickson, esq., M.D., Physician,	53	0	0	Fras. Sheppard, *Schoolmaster*,	40	0	0
Thos. Spain, esq., Apothecary,	21	0	0	John Gleeson,	40	0	0
John Boyd, Night Watch,	40	0	0	Chrstr Jones, *Carpenter*,	40	0	0
Resident.				Eva Duggan, Matron,	48	0	0
W. S. Minchin, esq., Governor,	250	0	0	Eliza Field, Laundress,	24	0	0
				Catherine Alcock, Hospital Nurse,	24	0	0

Vacancies in the Staff since last Inspection, how caused and how filled up, viz.—

Warder James Buggle dismissed; Christopher Jones appointed.

Officers on Gaol Allowance.

All the intern officers and the night watchman receive gaol allowance.

Visits paid by Officers.

	From 1st Jan., to 31st Dec., 1874.	From 1st Jan., 1875, to day of Inspection.
Number of times the Board of Superintendence met and discharged business,	12	10
Local Inspector to gaol,	119	151
Do. to each bridewell,	4	3
Chaplain, Protestant Episcopal Church,	195	169
Roman Catholic Chaplain,	119	127
Physician,	300	216
Apothecary,	147	71

Hospital.

	1872.		1873.		1874.		1875 (to day of Inspection).	
	M.	F.	M.	F.	M.	F.	M.	F.
No. of prisoners in hospital,	–	–	–	2	3	1	–	–
Average daily number in hospital,	–	–	–	0·1	·1	·2	–	–
Number of prisoners prescribed for and treated out of hospital,	157	29	97	21	282	27	121	
No. of deaths in the Gaol,	–	–	–	–	–	–	–	
Cost of medicine,	£3 5s. 2d.		£3 19s. 8d.		£11 2s. 7d.		£8 0s. 4d.	
Cost of diet for prisoners in hospital,	—		£0 16s. 0d.		£7 17s. 4d.		£5 11s. 4d.	
Cost of all extra diet ordered by Medical Officer for prisoners not in hospital,	£3 4s. 4d.		£4 18s. 10d.		£4 16s. 4d.		£4 7s. 4d.	

The hospital buildings are separate—one for each sex. They are roomy, but are little used. Since last inspection an earth-closet has been provided for each hospital. No other change has been made. Two sick prisoners were in custody on the day of my visit—one, a man labouring under hip disease, the other with a broken leg, caused by an accident at the pump.

Hospital.

Board of Superintendence.

Anthony Parker, esq., J.P., Chairman.
Bassett W. Holmes, esq., J.P., D.L.
Joshua R. Minnett, esq., J.P.

Capt. W. H. Carroll, J.P.
John Bayly, esq., J.P., D.L.
John Going, esq., J.P.
William Ryan, esq., J.P.
R. H. Falkiner, esq, J.P.

Count D'Alton, J.P., D.L.
Major W. C. Gason, J.P.
Caleb Going, esq., J.P.
James J. Poe, esq.

The meetings of the Board of Superintendence are held on the first Saturday of each month, when the salaries of subordinate officers and other liabilities are paid.

Board.

Separate cheques are drawn in favour of each creditor, unless when the amounts are small.

The superior officers are paid their salaries by presentment half-yearly at assizes.

[BRIDEWELLS.

STATE OF BRIDEWELLS.

		Thurles.		Templemore.	
Tipperary County (North Riding). Bridewells.		**M.**	**F.**	**M.**	**F.**
No. of Committals in past year,		118	24	99	38
Of whom were Drunkards,		45	7	37	18
No. of Committals in the quarter preceding Inspection,		20	5	22	8
Of whom were Drunkards,		6	2	4	3
Petty Sessions and Transmittals, how often.		Petty Sessions are held weekly, on Saturdays; the Town Commissioners hold Court on Wednesdays.		Petty Sessions are held weekly, on Wednesdays, at Templemore; and fortnightly at Borrisoleigh.	
Committals, whether regular,		Regular.		Regular.	
Registry,		Correctly kept.		Correctly kept.	
Repairs and Order,		In good repair and order.		In fair order and repair, but painting required, and door into female yard unsound.	
Security,		Security sufficient.		—	
Accommodation,		Two day-rooms and twenty cells, ten on each story of the building; two large exercising yards. Two cells on the ground floor, without bedding or sash to windows, are now used.		Two day-rooms, one for each sex, below; four small rooms upstairs, two for each sex; one with two beds.	
Furniture, Bedding, and Utensils.		Sufficient, only bedding in lower cells; some blankets are thin and worn.		Sufficient, except sheets required for change.	
Water, how supplied,		Abundant, from two pumps, one a forcing pump.		Pump requires repair.	
Sewerage,		Stated to be sufficient and flushable.		An open cesspool outside wall; no doors to privies.	
Cleanliness, Dryness, and Ventilation.		Clean, dry, and very well kept.		Clean and orderly; ventilation imperfect; dark and damp.	
Cost of dietary per head per day.		5½d. for both sexes; two meals per day.		6⅜d. for both sexes.	
Salary of Keeper,		£55 per annum.		£35 per annum.	
Wife as Matron,		—		£5.	
Whether Keeper follows any other employment.		None.		None.	
Statutable Inspection,		9th April, 1875.		11th June, 1875.	
Remarks,		Two male prisoners in custody; one, a discharged soldier, committed for asking relief from the union; the other, a young offender, for robbery.		One male prisoner in custody for assault.	

STATE OF BRIDEWELLS—*continued.*

	Roscrea.		Newport.	
	M.	F.	M.	F.
No. of Committals in past year, ...	23	3	12	–
Of whom were drunkards,	6	–	1	–
No. of Committals in the quarter preceding Inspection, . . .	2	4	3	1
Of whom were drunkards,	–	2	–	–
Petty Sessions and transmittals, how often.	On Mondays; transmittals regular.		On Fridays; transmittals regular.	
Committals, whether regular.	Apparently regular.		Regular.	
Registry, ...	Correctly kept.		Correctly kept.	
Repairs and Order, . .	In fair repair.		In good repair; woodwork lately painted, and walls lime-washed.	
Security, ...	Yards not secure, from turf-house against wall, and down pipe from roof.		Sufficient; down pipe from roof now protected.	
Accommodation, . .	There are dangerous winding stone stairs to the cells and day-rooms of this bridewell; two day-rooms and six cells are for prisoners.		Males, day-room and four cells; females, day-room and three cells.	
Furniture, Bedding, and Utensils.	Sufficient.		Sufficient and good.	
Water, how supplied, .	None, except from roof.		Pump in order, in front yard of bridewell.	
Sewerage, ...	None; a cesspool behind each privy.		Sufficient.	
Cleanliness, Dryness, and Ventilation.	Clean; ventilation sufficient.		Clean and orderly; ventilation sufficient.	
Cost of dietary per head per day.	6d. males; 5½d. females.		7½d. per day.	
Salary of Keeper, . .	£35.		£35.	
Wife Matron, . . .	£5.		£5.	
Whether Keeper follows any other employment.	None.		Court - keeper; salary £2 2s.	
Statutable Inspection, .	23rd April, 1875.		July 4th, 1875.	
Remarks, ...	Two male prisoners, deserters, in custody.		No prisoner in custody.	

JOHN LENTAIGNE, *Inspector-General.*

SOUTH
DISTRICT.

Tipperary
County
(South
Riding)
Gaol.

TIPPERARY COUNTY GAOL, SOUTH RIDING, AT CLONMEL.—STATUTABLE
INSPECTION, 5TH OCTOBER, 1875.

*Number of Prisoners of all classes in Gaol on the day of Inspection, and
on the corresponding date in the three preceding years.*

	M.	F.		M.	F.
1872,	58	12	1874,	42	26
1873,	66	25	1875 (day of Inspection),	58	22

*Number of returned Convicts in Gaol on the day of Inspection, and during
each of the three preceding years.*

	M.	F.		M.	F.
1872,	4	5	1875 (up to and including		
1873,	4	3	day of Inspection),	–	4
1874,	3	4	Day of Inspection,	–	1

Juveniles.

Juveniles.   I found amongst the inmates of this gaol, when I made my inspection, a young female offender for trial, not more than fifteen years of age, in hospital labouring under syphilis; she has already been previously convicted of drunkenness and disorderly conduct. Her father is dead, and her mother has no means to support her. The girl is perfectly ignorant of any employment by which she could earn a livelihood. She is now charged with a larceny committed in company with two other prostitutes, and unless sent to a reformatory, if convicted, she will continue a burden on the rates until she ends her miserable life, or is sentenced to penal servitude.

One other female and 6 males under sixteen years of age were committed to this prison previously to my inspection in October, 1875; 2 (males) were sent to reformatories from the workhouse.

Commit-   On the day of my inspection of this prison 58 males and 22 females of
ments.   all classes were in custody; 1 male and 4 females (prostitutes) committed for trial; 2 military offenders; 19 males and 4 females convicted by juries at assizes or quarter sessions; and 36 males and 14 females under summary convictions by justices at petty sessions.

The offences were—the males, 38, for assaults, drunkenness, riot and disorderly conduct, including one case of murder and one of manslaughter; 11 for larceny, embezzlement, forgery, and passing base coin; 4 military and militia offenders; 3 sentenced for Poor Law offences and vagrancy; 1 for injury to a horse; 1 for illegal distillation; and 1 for an offence against the Fishery Laws.

The females were—11 charged with larceny; and 11 with assaults, drunkenness, disorderly conduct, and soliciting for prostitution.

The sentences on the convicted prisoners were—2 (military) sentenced for terms each of 336 days; 6 sentenced for two, and 8 for one year each; 8 for six months and less than twelve; 11 for periods under six and above one month; 12 for one month; and 11 for shorter periods.

The sentences on the convicted females were—1 had been sentenced to an imprisonment of two years; 3 of one year; 4 for terms of two and three months; 5 for one month; and 5 for short periods.

SOUTH
DISTRICT.

Tipperary
County
(South
Riding)
Gaol.

Debtors.

Debtors.

No debtor was an inmate of this gaol in 1875. One male was in custody in 1874, and 4 males and 1 female in 1873.

Commitments.

CLASSES.	From 1st January to 31st December, 1874.		From 1st January, 1875, to day of Inspection.	
	M.	F.	M.	F.
Debtors,	1	—	—	—
Criminals,	421	204	281	133
Vagrants,	4	2	26	4
Drunkards,	318	123	219	67
Total,	744	329	526	224

Averages, and Highest and Lowest Numbers (exclusive of Debtors).

—	From 1st January to 31st December, 1874.			From 1st January, 1875, to day of Inspection.		
	M.	F.	Date.	M.	F.	Date.
Average daily number of prisoners in custody,	57	23	—	52	20	—
Highest number of prisoners at any one time,	112		31st March.	92		10th Sept.
Lowest ditto,	51		17th Oct.	46		6th April.
Highest number of males at any one time,	84		19th March.	65		2nd Sept.
Ditto, of females,	31		17th June.	32		7th Sept.
Lowest number of males at any one time,	33		17th Oct.	36		6th April.
Ditto, of females,	15		27th Oct.	10		6th April.

Number of Individual Prisoners (exclusive of Debtors), and Number of Times each had been committed.

NUMBER OF TIMES COMMITTED.	1874.				1875, to day of Inspection.			
	Juveniles.		Adults.		Juveniles.		Adults.	
	M.	F.	M.	F.	M.	F.	M.	F.
Once within the year,	22	3	490	122	6	—	378	102
Twice "	1	—	62	17	—	1	29	15
Thrice "	—	—	15	6	—	—	15	8
4 times "	—	—	6	3	—	—	4	4
5 " "	—	—	1	5	—	—	3	4
6 " "	—	—	—	2	—	—	—	2
7 " "	—	—	2	3	—	—	—	1
8 " "	—	—	7	3	—	—	1	—
9 " "	—	—	—	3	—	—	—	—
10 " "	—	—	—	2	—	—	—	—
11 " "	—	—	—	1	—	—	—	1
17 " "	—	—	1	—	—	—	—	—
Total,	23	3	577	167	6	1	430	137
No. of above who had not been in Gaol previous to 1st January in.	21	3	256	32	6	1	175	37

Number of Individual Prisoners (exclusive of Debtors), committed in the year 1874, and to the day of Inspection in 1875, who had been Once and oftener re-committed from their first Commitment in any year, so far as can be ascertained.

NUMBER OF TIMES COMMITTED.	1873.				1874, to day of Inspection.			
	Juveniles.		Adults.		Juveniles.		Adults.	
	M.	F.	M.	F.	M.	F.	M.	F.
Once only,	20	3	250	30	6	–	171	32
Twice,	2	–	86	25	–	1	60	18
Thrice,	1	–	38	16	–	–	38	12
4 times,	–	–	26	10	–	–	25	10
5 ,,	–	–	29	12	–	–	26	13
6 ,,	–	–	22	13	–	–	24	8
7 to 11 ,,	–	–	86	32	–	–	22	7
12 to 16 ,,	–	–	14	9	–	–	30	3
17 to 20 ,,	–	–	8	7	–	–	14	9
21 to 30 ,,	–	–	14	6	–	–	12	8
31 to 40 ,,	–	–	1	4	–	–	5	3
41 to 50 ,,	–	–	2	1	–	–	1	6
51 to 70 ,,	–	–	1	1	–	–	2	5
71 to 80 ,,	–	–	–	1	–	–	–	2
81 to 90 ,,	–	–	–	–	–	–	–	1
Total No. of Individuals committed,	23	3	577	167	6	1	430	137
No. of Commitments represented in foregoing,	27	3	2,549	1,335	6	2	2,153	1522

Highest Number of Prisoners (exclusive of Debtors) in gaol during each of the previous seven years, and up to day of Inspection in 1875.

19th March, 1868,	.	102	14th November, 1872, .	. 91
20th November, 1869,	.	97	6th November, 1873, .	. 110
6th May, 1870,	.	102	31st March, 1874,	. 112
18th March, 1871,	.	91	10th September, 1875,	. 92

Accommodation.

	M.	F.		M.	F.
Wards,	4	2	Kitchen,	1	–
Yards,	7	2	Store Rooms,	3	2
Day Rooms,	2	–	Laundries,	1	1
Solitary Cells,	2	2	Drying Rooms,	1	2
Single Cells, 9 feet long, 6 feet wide, and 8 feet high, or which contain 432 cubic feet,	120	59	Lavatories, Bath, with Hot and Cold	12	6
Ditto, heated and furnished with bells,	120	59	Water laid on,	1	–
			Privies,	6	2
Cells to contain three persons,	12	–	Water-closets,	25	13
Hospital Rooms,	6	4	Fumigating Apparatus,	1	–
Chapels,	2	–	Pumps,	1	1
School Room,	1	–	Tread-wheel,	1	–
			Tell-tale Clocks,	4	–

Cleanliness.   I found the prison when I made my inspection in a very creditable state of order and cleanliness. The Governor was on leave, but the Local Inspector accompanied me over the gaol.

The marshalsea has not been occupied for the last twelve months, and the woodwork is beginning to show signs of decay. It is a large isolated building, and I consider that it might be advantageously dispensed with. Should a debtor be committed during the period that it will be legal to commit to prison for debt, some other part of the premises might be arranged for debtors under the circumstances.

If also the Roman Catholic chapel, the water cistern, and the pumps were removed within the premises of the new prison, I am satisfied that the arrangement would enable much more profitable industrial work to be carried on, as the prisoners would then be constantly under supervision; besides, the cost of keeping in repair unnecessarily large and seldom occupied old buildings would by this arrangement be saved. Pending legislation, however, this and other useful changes in the management of the establishment must be postponed until the wishes of Parliament as regards the proposed new prison system has been ascertained.

All the occupied portion of the prison was, when I visited, in sound repair and nicely kept, the walls lately whitewashed, and the wood-work painted.

The various appliances for the separate confinement of prisoners were in good order, and the heating apparatus in both prisons working in a satisfactory manner. The boiler of the apparatus for heating the male prison had been recently re-set.

Since my last inspection of this prison a cistern has been placed behind the laundry in which the females work. It collects soft water for washing, from the roof, and answers well the object intended.

Both laundries are now in good working order; and the privy adjoining the laundry, for males, faulted on last inspection by my colleague, has been improved. The gas burners in the punishment cells, which are very dangerous, as suggesting suicide to prisoners in an excited state, have not been altered, notwithstanding that my colleague called attention to the subject in his report on the prison for 1874. In the Limerick County Prison the gas burners are set at an angle downwards, which renders them safe; and the arrangement is found to be economical, as it prevents a waste of gas which is more fully consumed thereby.

The Protestant chapel in the prison is still damp and ill ventilated; it requires improvement.

The apartments of the warders were clean and tidily kept when I visited.

Stock at the time of Inspection.

	In use.	In store.	Male Clothing.	In use.	In store.	Female Clothing.	In use.	In store.
Blankets, pairs of,	142	56	Shirts,	50	76	Shifts,	72	45
Sheets, pairs of,	143	104	Jackets,	50	74	Jackets,	44	50
Rugs,	137	51	Vests,	50	71	Petticoats,	69	39
Hammocks or Cots,	95	21	Trowsers,	50	94	Aprons,	44	42
Bed-ticks,	133	77	Caps,	50	60	Neckerchiefs,	40	35
Bedsteads,	9	—	Stockings or socks, pairs of,	50	60	Caps,	60	59
			Shoes, Slippers, & Clogs, pairs of,	60	20	Stockings, pairs of,	41	9
						Shoes, Slippers, & Clogs, pairs of,	22	11

I found an ample supply of bedding in use and in store; but some of the sheets and blankets were much worn, and should be cast. There was an abundant supply of prison clothing of a good description. Stockings or socks are given to all prisoners, and caps and neckerchiefs to the females.

The stores are ample, well fitted up, and tidily kept.

The suggestion of my colleague to have a second fumigating box provided, in which the private clothing of female prisoners would be cleansed and disinfected, has not been adopted. The box could be made at a trifling cost by a carpenter prisoner when in custody, and should be provided.

A small apartment has been fitted up since last inspection for prisoners to receive visits. It is well arranged, and answers the object intended.

SOUTH DISTRICT.

Tipperary County (South Riding) Gaol.

It would be very desirable if the Medical Officer would visit the gaol daily, and pass the prisoners lately committed into their wards after having been given a bath. The heating apparatus of the bath room is now in order, and connected with the kitchen. There is therefore every facility for the cleansing of prisoners at once, and they should not be detained in the reception ward unnecessarily.

By placing prisoners newly committed in the reception wards the Medical Officer could see them at once, and pass them in a very short time. They would then be bathed, clothed, and removed to their respective classes.

Lock-up.

Lock-up is held at 6 P.M. in summer, and 5.45 P.M. in winter. The gaol is unlocked at 6 A.M. in summer, and 7 A.M. in winter.

Night watch.

The vigilance of the night patrol is tested by four tell-tale clocks, and their markings are regularly entered in the Lockings Book ; all defaults by the night-watch in the pegging of the clocks are marked against the officer in the Officers' Conduct Book.

Photography.

The photographs of habitual criminals in this prison are taken by an artist who is not a prison officer. He receives 6d. per copy as remuneration for his services.

No escape was attempted from this prison in either 1874 or 1875.

Number of Punishments for Prison Offences.

	From 1st January to 31st December, 1874.		From 1st January, 1875, to day of Inspection.	
	M.	F.	M.	F.
By Governor—Dark or Refractory Cells, Stoppage of Diet, . .	} 223	18	159	16

Two punishment cells for males and one for females are provided ; they are artificially heated, and properly fitted up. As I have already observed, the gas burners have not been altered as suggested by my colleague.

School.

No school is held in this gaol.

Employment on day of Inspection.

	M.	F.
Tread-wheel, . . .'	31	—
Tailoring and Shoemaking, .: . . .	3	—
Tin man and Painting, ...	2	—
Washing and Scouring for War Department, . .	10	8
Sewing.	—.	8
Prison Duties, ...	6	—
Sick, ...	2	2
Unemployed, ...	3	3
Discharged before labour hours, ...	1	1
Total in custody, . . .	58	22

Amount received for produce of Prisoners' labour disposed of outside the Gaol.

1872, . £235 1s. 2d. | 1873, . £229 5s. 8d. | 1874, £213 3s. 11d.

Labour.

Male prisoners sentenced to hard labour work on the tread-wheel during three hours daily in alternate gangs, each prisoner working for half the period, viz., one hour and a half.

Industrial labour for males consists in shoemaking, tailoring, carpentry, tinwork, painting, barrack washing and scouring for the War Department. A sufficiently qualified warder superintends the shoemaking department. The females wash for private families, and the work is well done. They also knit and sew.

Contracts.

Bread, white, per 4 lb. loaf, 6d.; brown, per 4 lb. loaf, 5d.; oatmeal, per cwt., 17s. 10d.; Indian meal, per cwt. 8s. 2d.; potatoes, per cwt., 5s. 4d.; meat, per lb., 7½d.; new milk, per gallon, 8d.; salt, per cwt., 2s. 6d.; coal, per ton, £1 4s. 0d.; gas, per 1,000 cubic feet, 6s. 8d.; candles, per lb., 5½d.; soap, per cwt., £1 2s. 6d.

Net average daily cost of Ordinary Diet for each Prisoner.

1872, . 4d. | 1873, . 4·27d. | 1874, . 4·5d.

The food prepared for the prisoners on the day of my visit, which I tasted, was of a good description; and I observe that the Chaplains report very favourably of the samples submitted for their inspection. I questioned all the prisoners in custody. No complaint was made to me by any.

Food.

Officers and Salaries.

Non-Resident.	£	s.	d.		£	s.	d.
Percy Gough, esq., Local Inspector,	150	0	0	H. Colborne, Warder,	50	0	0
W. D. Hemphill, esq., Surgeon,	74	0	0	R. Lanigan, do.	50	0	0
				E. Fennessy, do.	50	0	0
				M. Byrne, do.	50	0	0
Rev. Roger Power, Roman Catholic Chaplain,	50	0	0	R. Geoghegan, do.	50	0	0
				M. Egan, do. *Shoemaker*,	47	0	0
Rev. Wm. Sandford, Prot. Chaplain,	50	0	0	M. Fennessy, do.	47	0	0
				J. Lee, Hospital Warder,*	47	0	0
Resident.				Miss S. Woods, Matron,	52	0	0
George Massy Robbins, esq., Governor,	250	0	0	Mrs. M. Conway, Assistant Matron,	32	0	0
J. M'Caffery, Head Warder,	110	0	0	Miss M. J. Garvan, Assistant Matron,	32	0	0
E. Power, Clerk, &c.,	77	0	0	Miss A. M'Carthy, Nurse,	34	0	0
J. Quinn, Gate Warder,	67	0	0	Mrs. J. Atkins, Laundress,	42	0	0

* John Lee resigned on last Board day; Michael Culliton appointed in his stead, not yet entered office.

Vacancies in the Staff since last Inspection, how caused, and how filled up.

Thomas Summers and Joseph Ardagh were superannuated; filled by John Lee and Michael Fennessy. Stephen Burke, Warder, and Mrs. Coughlan, Laundress, resigned; filled up by Patrick Hyland and Johanna Atkins. Patrick Hyland, dismissed; filled up by Mitchel Egan.

Visits paid by Officers.

	From 1st Jan. to 31st Dec., 1874.	From 1st Jan. 1875, to day of Inspection.
Number of times the Board of Superintendence met and discharged business	12	10
Local Inspector to Gaol,	115	105
Do. to each Bridewell,	4	3
Chaplain, Protestant Episcopal Church,	154	125
,, Roman Catholic,	172	147
Surgeon,	247	243

The officers' quarters were very tidy, clean, and well kept when I visited them.

Officers' quarters.

Books and Accounts.

Net cost of Gaol, including Diet and Salaries.

1872, . £2,781 11s. 6d. | 1873, . £2,901 3s. 9d. | 1874, . £2,995 16s. 1d.

Total cost of Officers, including Clothing, Value of Rations, &c.

1872, . £1,531 7s. 10d. | 1873, . £1,558 0s. 10d. | 1874, . £1,592 13s. 9d.

Average cost of each Prisoner per annum.

1872, . £40 17s. 8d. | 1873, . £34 9s. 1d. | 1874, . £37 8s. 11d.

SOUTH DISTRICT.

Amounts repaid by the War Department for Military Prisoners.

1872, . £15 10s. 0d. | 1873, . £74 0s. 0d. | 1874, . £56 3s. 0d.

Tipperary County (South Riding) Gaol.

Amounts repaid from the Consolidated Fund for the maintenance, &c., of Prisoners.

1872, . £267 12s. 10d. | 1873, . £314 15s. 2d. | 1874, . £349 19s. 9d.

Books.

The prison books of this gaol are very carefully kept by the gaol clerk, whom I have always found attentive in the discharge of his duties. Each warder has a journal, which is regularly submitted to the Governor, and examined by him. The journals of the Local Inspector, the Governor, and the Medical Officer are fully written up, and in them are detailed the various occurrences in the gaol which come within the sphere of the duties of these officers. The Local Inspector notes the inspections of the bridewells which he makes; and I remark on my inspections of these institutions, the care he takes to have them efficiently managed. The Chaplains state in their journals the duties which they perform.

Hospital.

	1872.		1873.		1874.		1875 (to day of Inspection).	
	M.	F.	M.	F.	M.	F.	M.	F
No. of prisoners in hospital,	55	10	74	32	85	35	79	27
Average daily No. in hospital,	1·9	0·6	3·1	0·9	2	3	3·55	1·78
No. of prisoners prescribed for and treated out of hospital, . . .	441	192	551	226	540	260	734	191
No. of deaths in the Gaol, .	–	–	1	1	1	–	1	–
Cost of medicine, . .	£11 0s. 8d.		£13 0s. 7d.		£12 12s. 11d.		—	
Cost of diet for prisoners in hospital, . . .	£43 19s. 1d.		£77 4s. 11d.		£84 13s. 5d.		—	

Hospital.

The hospitals in this prison are separate—one for each sex. No change has been made in them since last inspection. The wards are roomy and well ventilated.

The frequent attacks of zymotic disease in this gaol would show defective sanitary arrangements.

One death of a male occurred from typhoid fever in 1874, the result it would appear of the polluted water of the well which supplies the cistern filled by the tread-wheel. This class of diseases can always be traced to bad water or defective sewerage; and it behoves the Board to take steps to prevent its recurrence.

Board of Superintendence.

John Bagwell, esq.
S. H. Gerald Adams, esq.
R. U. Bayley, esq.
Joseph Kenny, esq.
Colonel E. B. Purefoy.
Thomas Lalor, esq.

John Riall, esq.
Captain Sankey, R.N.
F. Wise Lowe, esq.
Thomas Butler, esq.
Captain S. Moore, M.P.
Samuel Cooper, esq.

Board.

The Board meets on the first Saturday of each month, when subordinate officers are paid and liabilities discharged. The Governor is paid quarterly, and the extern officers half-yearly at assizes.

[BRIDEWELLS.

STATE OF BRIDEWELLS.

—	Cashel.		Clogheen.		Caher.	
	M.	F.	M.	F.	M.	F.
No. of Committals in past year.	44	12	41	8	36	13
Of whom were Drunkards.	35	2	16	–	21	5
No. of Committals in the quarter preceding inspection.	14	4	17	–	12	5
Of whom were Drunkards.	6	–	5	–	1	3
Petty Sessions and Transmittals, how often ?	Weekly; Cashel on Wednesdays; fortnightly in Dundrum and Golden.		Fortnightly at Clogheen and Ballyporeen.		Fortnightly, except at New Inn, where monthly.	
Committals, . .	Regular.		Now regular.		Regular.	
Registry, . . .	Correctly kept.		Correctly kept.		Correctly kept.	
Repairs and Order, .	In good repair, but very damp.		In good repair.		In sound repair, and well kept.	
Security, . . .	Sufficient.		Sufficient, with care.		Sufficient.	
Accommodation, .	No change since last inspection.		Two cells and one day-room for each sex.		Two day-rooms, with stove between them; six cells for all prisoners.	
Furniture, Bedding, and Utensils.	Sufficient for requirements; but some bedding worn.		Good and sufficient.		Sufficient.	
Water, how supplied ?	From city reservoir.		None on premises; supplied by contract.		None on premises; taken from river.	
Sewerage, . .	Cesspools; earth-closets.		Cesspools.		Sufficient.	
Cleanliness, Dryness, and Ventilation.	Clean and well ventilated, but very damp.		Clean and well ventilated.		Clean and well ventilated.	
Cost of Dietary, .	5d. per day.		6d. per day.		6d. per day.	
Salary of Keeper, and whether he follows any other employment.	£45; matron £5.		£45 a year; £5 as court-keeper; a suit of clothes each year, with fuel and light.		£40. None.	
Date of Inspection, .	8th April, 1875.		18th August, 1875.		18th August, 1875.	
Remarks, . .	No prisoner in charge.		Two deserters in custody.		No prisoner in charge when I visited.	

SOUTH
DISTRICT.

*Tipperary
County
(South
Riding).*

Bridewells.

	Carrick-on-Suir.		Tipperary (certified bridewell).	
	M.	F.	M.	F.
No. of Committals in past year.	153	33	198	44
Of whom were Drunkards,	76	12	130	26
No. of Committals in the quarter preceding Inspection.	44	22	68	10
Of whom were Drunkards,	19	8	29	3
Petty Sessions and Transmittals, how often?	Fortnightly; at Carrick on Thursdays, at Borough on Mondays.		Weekly in Tipperary; fortnightly at Cappawhite, Bansha, and Galbally.	
Committals,	Apparently regular; but prisoners on remand are not always brought before committing justice.		Regular; but vouchers should remain with keeper.	
Registry,	Correctly kept.		Correctly kept.	
Repairs and Order,	In good repair and order; lately painted.		In good repair; and woodwork lately painted.	
Security,	Sufficient; walls high.		Very secure; has outside boundary wall.	
Accommodation,	Day-room and two cells for males; females, day-room and three cells.		Day-room and eight cells for each sex, besides cell for drunkards.	
Furniture, Bedding, and Utensils.	An ample supply of good bedding.		Sufficient and good bedding, except one bed-tick.	
Water, how supplied?	Pump in each yard, in order.		A good pump on premises.	
Sewerage,	Sufficient; discharges into main sewer of street.		Cesspools behind the privies, without sewerage.	
Cleanliness, Dryness, and Ventilation.	Clean and dry; ventilation sufficient.		Clean and orderly; ventilation sufficient, but yards very damp from want of drainage.	
Cost of Dietary,	6½d. for both sexes.		6d. per day for all prisoners.	
Salary of Keeper, & whether he follows any other employment.	£45. None.		£45; matron £15. Court-keeper; salary, £8.	
Date of Inspection,	5th October, 1875.		8th April, 1875.	
Remarks,	Three male prisoners in charge.		Four males in charge; three for grave assaults.	

JOHN LENTAIGNE, *Inspector-General.*

WATERFORD COUNTY AND CITY GAOL, AT WATERFORD.—STATUTABLE
INSPECTION, 10TH SEPTEMBER, 1875.

*Number of Prisoners of all classes in Gaol on the day of Inspection, and
on the corresponding date in the three preceding years.*

	M.	F.		M.	F.
1872, ...	47	30	1874, ...	50	21
1873, ...	39	37	1875 (day of Inspection),	44	18

Juveniles.

One young offender (male), under sixteen years of age, was in custody Juveniles.
when I visited. He was for trial, charged with obtaining money under
false pretences. His case appeared to me to be suitable for a sentence to a
reformatory.

Two other young offenders, both eighteen years of age, were in custody, one
F. O. H., under a sentence of one month for assault. He is a very bad boy,
having already been seven times convicted. When only eleven years of
age, in 1868, he was punished by an imprisonment in this gaol for
drunkenness; and after three other convictions for larceny and the robbery of a letter from a pillar-box, was sent to Upton Reformatory, from
which he was discharged unreformed in July, 1875; since which time he
has been three times an inmate of this prison for drunkenness, assault on
the police and on a prison officer. For him the only chance of reformation is a long sentence to penal servitude.

The other young offender, J. S., likewise eighteen years of age, who has
also been an inmate of this gaol, constantly re-committed, since he was
eleven years of age, was for trial at the Lismore Quarter Sessions,
charged with larceny, when I visited. He likewise had been an inmate
of the Upton Reformatory, and discharged unreformed. He has since my
visit been sentenced to penal servitude for seven years.

Thirteen males and 3 females under sixteen years of age were committed to this prison in 1875. The age of 1 male did not exceed
twelve years.

Three males and 1 female were sent to reformatories during the year. Commitments.
I found when I made my inspection 44 males and 18 females in
custody. Five males and 2 females were for trial; 14 males and 2
females had been convicted at assizes and quarter sessions; and 25 males
and 14 females summarily by justices at petty sessions. Many were
habitual offenders, constantly recurrent to prison. One woman, although
only thirty-nine years of age, has 104 convictions recorded against her;
another aged twenty-four, 53 convictions; and a third, aged thirty-six,
has been 38 times convicted. One male, aged fifty-seven, has been 85
times committed; another, aged thirty-seven, 69 times; and a third, aged
thirty nine, 61 times.

The convicted prisoners in custody were — 19 for assaults, manslaughter, rape, and other offences against the person; 1 for sending an
unseaworthy ship to sea; 9 for robbery, larceny, cattle stealing, fraud, and
obtaining goods under false pretences; 3 for malicious injury and forcible

possession, and one for a Poor Law offence ; 9 were for drunkenness and disorderly conduct.

The females had been convicted—4 of offences against property ; 3 of assaults ; the remainder of drunkenness and disorderly conduct.

The sentences on the convicted prisoners in custody were—1 male was under a sentence of two years ; 1 for eighteen ; 3 for twelve ; 2 for nine ; and 6 for six months each. Eight were for periods of above one and under six months each ; 11 were for one month ; the remainder for short periods.

Two females were under sentences of imprisonment of twelve months each, for larceny and robbery ; all the other females had been sentenced for terms not exceeding one month, for drunkenness, disorderly conduct, assaults, and larceny.

The 44 male prisoners, inmates of the gaol when I visited, had 385 convictions entered in the books of this prison against them ; and the 18 females, 252.

Commitments.

CLASSES.				From 1st January to 31st December, 1874.		From 1st January, 1875, to day of Inspection.	
				M.	F.	M.	F.
Debtors,	.	.	.	—	—	1	1
Criminals,	.	.	.	370	140	254	114
Vagrants,	.	.	.	13	6	6	4
Drunkards,	.	.	.	414	247	211	128
Total,	.	.	.	797	393	472	247

Highest Number of Prisoners (exclusive of Debtors) in Gaol during each of the previous seven years, and up to day of Inspection in 1875.

15th September, 1868,	. . 88	21st February, 1872,	. . 86
25th September, 1869,	. . 96	4th September, 1873,	. . 85
1st September, 1870,	. . 94	24th November, 1874,	. . 87
5th September, 1871,	. . 92	6th August, 1875,	. . 74

Number of Individual Prisoners (exclusive of Debtors), and Number of Times each had been committed during the following periods, distinguishing Adults from Juveniles.

NUMBER OF TIMES COMMITTED.			1874.				1875, to day of Inspection.			
			Juveniles.		Adults.		Juveniles.		Adults.	
			M.	F.	M.	F.	M.	F.	M.	F.
Once within the year,	.	.	30	—	427	120	13	3	293	98
Twice ,,	.	.	—	—	73	22	—	—	35	19
Thrice ,,	.	.	—	—	26	14	—	—	15	8
4 times ,,	.	.	—	—	8	8	—	—	5	4
5 ,, ,,	.	.	—	—	5	3	—	—	2	3
6 ,, ,,	.	.	—	—	1	3	—	—	1	2
7 ,, ,,	.	.	—	—	1	1	—	—	2	2
8 ,, ,,	.	.	—	—	3	5	—	—	—	2
9 ,, ,,	.	.	—	—	—	4	—	—	—	—
10 ,, ,,	.	.	—	—	1	—	—	—	—	1
11 ,, ,,	.	.	—	—	—	1	—	—	—	—
12 ,, ,,	.	.	—	—	1	—	—	—	—	—
13 ,, ,,	.	.	—	—	—	1	—	—	—	—
15 ,, ,,	.	.	—	—	—	1	—	—	—	—
Total,	.	.	30	—	546	183	13	3	353	139
No. of above who had not been in Gaol previous to 1st January in			25	—	318	73	12	3	196	64

Individual Prisoners (exclusive of Debtors) committed in the year 1874, and to the day of Inspection in 1875, who had been Once, and oftener remanded from their first Commitment in any year, so far as can be ascertained.

NUMBER OF TIMES COMMITTED.	1874.				1875, to day of Inspection.			
	Juveniles.		Adults.		Juveniles.		Adults.	
	M.	F.	M.	F.	M.	F.	M.	F.
Once only,	25	—	288	62	12	3	192	60
Twice,	3	—	85	34	1	—	35	18
Thrice,	2	—	42	16	—	—	20	12
4 times,	—	—	35	10	—	—	19	—
5 ,,	—	—	17	7	—	—	16	6
6 ,,	—	—	13	5	—	—	11	3
7 to 11 ,,	—	—	35	16	—	—	30	15
12 to 16 ,,	—	—	12	9	—	—	15	10
17 to 20 ,,	—	—	7	2	—	—	2	3
21 to 30 ,,	—	—	4	7	—	—	5	2
31 to 40 ,,	—	—	3	5	—	—	2	4
41 to 50 ,,	—	—	1	4	—	—	3	1
51 to 60 ,,	—	—	1	2	—	—	—	1
61 to 70 ,,	—	—	1	2	—	—	2	1
71 to 80 ,,	—	—	1	1	—	—	—	1
81 to 90 ,,	—	—	1	—	—	—	1	1
91 to 120 ,,	—	—	—	1	—	—	—	1
Total No. of Individuals committed,	30	—	546	183	13	3	353	139
No. of Commitments represented in foregoing,	37	—	2,030	1,512	14	3	1,590	1115

Averages, and Highest and Lowest Numbers (exclusive of Debtors).

—	From 1st January to 31st December, 1874.			From 1st January, 1875, to day of Inspection.		
	M.	F.	Date.	M.	F.	Date.
Average daily number of prisoners in custody,	42	20	—	37	16	—
Highest number of prisoners at any one time,	87		24th Nov.	74		6th Aug.
Lowest do.,	42		3rd July.	38		5th April.
Highest number of males at any one time,	67		25th Nov.	51		1st Aug.
Ditto of females,	27		18th Oct.	29		4th July.
Lowest number of males at any one time,	23		3rd July.	24		5th April.
Ditto of females,	7		27th Dec.	8		4th Jan.

Accommodation.

	M.	F.		M.	F.
Wards,	2	2	Kitchen,	1	—
Yards,	6	3	Store Rooms	2	1
Solitary Cells,	1	1	Laundries,	1	1
Single Cells, not less than 9 feet long, 6 feet wide, and 8 feet high = 432 cubic feet,	73	30	Drying Rooms,	1	1
			Lavatories,	3	3
Ditto, heated and furnished with bells,	69	30	Baths, with hot and cold water laid on,	1	1
			Water-closets,	9	9
Hospital Rooms,	2	2	Fumigating Apparatus,	1	1
Chapel,	One.		Pumps,	4	1
Workshops,	2	2	Tread-wheel,	1	—
Worksheds,	6	—	Tell-tale Clock,	1	—

SOUTH
DISTRICT.

Waterford County and City Gaol.

I found this prison on my inspection in a most creditable state of order and cleanliness. The buildings in sound repair and well kept, a large sum (£200) having lately been expended on lead, which has been placed on the flat portion of the roof. The entire woodwork has lately been painted, and the walls limewashed.

Sixty-nine cells for males and thirty for females are fitted up with bells, lighted by gas, and artificially heated; having water-closets and lavatories on each corridor, with an abundant supply of water for the establishment.

The appliances for separation are all in good order, and the heating apparatus works satisfactorily.

Baths.

There is on the basement story of each prison a good bath, with hot and cold water laid on, in which all prisoners are bathed on reception, and afterwards weekly on Saturdays.

Water is raised to the tank which supplies the prison by the force of a wheel pump, worked by four male prisoners in association, while the power of the tread-wheel which is stalled is wasted, and the time of the men employed on it who might be engaged in reproductive labour is turned to no account. Another waste of labour is in the laundry, where two females are employed to work an old-fashioned mangle; when, with a proper patent mangle one female could do the work; by which arrangement association of prisoners would be prevented.

In my report for 1873 I pointed out the necessity to place a small shed over the heating stove in the female laundry; but it has not been done. The Inspectors-General have also suggested that one cook only be employed in the kitchen who could both cook the provisions and wash the cooking utensils, tins, &c.

My colleague also in his reports for 1872 and 1874 called attention to the fact that a young man committed suicide in this gaol in June, 1872, by hanging himself from the gas burner in his cell; yet the Grand Jury have hitherto refused to alter the burners, which could be done at a very trifling cost by merely bending the gas pipes downward, so that the halter could not have a hold on them. I again urge the Grand Jury to alter the decision to which they have come, as a suicide may again happen from this cause.

Laundry.

There are two good laundries in the prison. In that for males coarse washing is carried on. In the laundry for females washing for respectable families in the town is well done; and the prisoners are taught a useful trade by which they can earn a livelihood after discharge; but there is too much association of prisoners in the laundries. This is a matter to which my colleague called attention in his report for 1874.

Stock at the time of Inspection.

	In Use.	In Store.	Male Clothing.	In Use.	In Store.	Female Clothing.	In Use.	In Store.
Blankets, pairs of,		150	Shirts, . .	68	80	Shifts, . .	36	45
		59	Jackets, .	34	19	Gowns, .	34	85
Sheets, pairs of,	150	57	Vests, .	34	46	Petticoats,	36	91
Rugs, . .	130	26	Trowsers, .	34	14	Aprons, .	36	68
Hammocks or Cots, . .		107	Caps, .	34	6	Caps, .	18	55
Bed-ticks, .	130	17	Stockings or Socks, pairs of,	34	71	Stocking, pairs of,	18	46
Bedsteads, .	14	46	Shoes, Slippers, & Clogs, pairs of,	34	52	Shoes, Slippers, & Clogs, pairs of,	18	8

Clothing.

The prison clothing is of a good description and suitable, except that the females are not provided with neckerchiefs. They are, however, now given stockings; and socks are supplied to the males. The socks and

stockings for prison use are knitted by the females, and some not required Sourn
Distaicr.
are sold. The bedding is good and sufficient.

A new store has been fitted up for the private clothes of female *Waterford*
prisoners, and a serviceable fumigating apparatus (an iron box) has been put *County and*
up adjoining, by which arrangement all danger of infection is prevented, *City Gaol.*
and the clothes are properly cleansed from vermin.

A photographic chamber has been erected in the gaol, where Mr. Photo-
Andrews, the chief warder, takes photographs of prisoners ; and the work graphy.
is well done. He receives 6d. for each copy as remuneration for the
performance of this duty. The Board supply the materials.

Unlock is held at 6 A.M. in summer, and at 6.30 in winter. Gas is Lock-up.
supplied to every part of the prison. The prisoners are locked for the
night at 6 P.M. at all seasons of the year.

One watchman goes round the entire prison every half hour during the
night. His vigilance is tested by one tell-tale clock placed at the hospital.
It is marked every half hour during the night.

Visitors are admitted to see prisoners in an apartment which is Visitors.
separated into three compartments, a warder being in the centre, so that
no prohibited article can be conveyed to a prisoner during the interview.

No escape was attempted from this prison for many years ; but a
military deserter escaped from the Dungarvan Bridewell in May, 1874 ;
and in August, 1873, another prisoner also escaped from the bridewell.

Number of Punishments for Prison Offences.

	From 1st January to 31st December, 1874.		From 1st January, 1875, to day of Inspection.	
	M.	F.	M.	F.
By Governor—				
Dark or Refractory Cells,	8	4	13	4
Stoppage of Diet,	83	2	93	8
Total,	91	6	106	12

It was not necessary during 1874 or 1875 to call for magisterial inter- Punish-
ference in awarding punishment for a prison offence in this gaol, the ments.
powers of the Governor being sufficient to deal with all breaches of rules
which occurred. One punishment cell is provided in each prison, and is
duly fitted up with the necessary requirements for dealing with offenders.
The solitary cell in the male prison is flagged.

Schools.

	From 1st Jan. to 31st Dec, 1874		From 1st Jan., 1875, to day of Inspection.	
	M.	F.	M.	F.
Number of individual prisoners who attended school,	32	38	19	33
Average daily number of pupils,	7	5	8	4
Number of days on which school was held,	235	209	138	140

School-hours.—Males, 4 to 5.30. Females, 4 to 5.30.

The schools are in connexion with the Board of National Education, Schools.
and inspected by their officers. The males are instructed by one of the
turnkeys, and the females by the assistant matron ; but the teachers are
not trained.

The school-rooms are not stalled, and the prisoners are in association
together during school hours ; a defect which has been pointed out by
the Inspectors-General for many years, but has not been remedied.

Employment on day of Inspection.

	M.	F.
Smith,	1	–
Washing,	3	3
Cookhouse,	2	–
Shoemaking,	3	–
Weaving and Winding,	3	–
Tailoring,	3	–
Matmaking,	3	–
Picking oakum,	7	–
Prison duties, Pumping Water, Whitewashing,	8	2
Cleaning grounds,	4	2
Mangling, Smoothing, Knitting,	–	11
Sick and Unemployed,	4	–
Discharged (before labour hours),	3	–
Total in custody,	**44**	**18**

Male prisoners sentenced to hard labour also break stones and work on the treadwheel.

Amount received for produce of Prisoners' labour disposed of outside the Gaol.

1872, . £68 11s. 0d. | 1873, . £66 10s. 1d. | 1874, . £90 5s. 10d.

Labour.

Prisoners sentenced to hard labour work on the tread-wheel and break stones. The prisoners are likewise employed at other industrial works; but I do not consider that the labour of the prisoners is sufficiently utilised in this gaol. There has, however, been a considerable improvement in this respect during the last year, the profits from prison labour having increased from £66 10s. 1d., in 1873, to £90 5s. 10d. in 1874.

There is too much association of trades in this gaol. Shoemakers and other artisans should not work in association; and I would suggest that in future they be employed each in a cell, as is done in other well managed prisons.

Contracts.

Bread, brown, per 4-lb. loaf, 4½d.; oatmeal, per cwt., 17s. 3d.; Indian meal per cwt., 9s. 5d.; new milk, per gallon, 8½d.; salt, per cwt., 3s.; coal, per ton, £1 3s. 9d.; gas, per 1,000 cubic feet, 6s.; soap, per cwt., £1 11s. 6d.

Net average daily cost of Ordinary Diet for each Prisoner.

1872, . 4d. | 1873, . 4d. | 1874, . 4d.

Food.

The food prepared for the use of the prisoners on the day of my visit, which I tasted, was excellent; and I observe that the Chaplains have, in no instance during the year, recorded a complaint against the quality of the provisions furnished to this gaol for the inmates.

I questioned all the prisoners in custody. No complaint was made to me by any. They are well cared and kindly treated, yet strictly under discipline.

Officers and Salaries.

Non-Resident.	£	s.	d.
Charles Newport Bolton, esq., B.A., Local Inspector,	100	0	0
William Carroll, esq., M.D.,	80	0	0
Very Rev. E. N. Hoare, Protestant Chaplain,	50	0	0
Rev. P. Nolan, Roman Catholic Chaplain,	50	0	0
T. W. Evans, esq., M.B., Apothecary,	—		
William Nicholson, Watchman,	30	0	0

Resident.			
Joseph Lapham, esq. Governor	250	0	0

	£	s.	d.
Mr. Thomas Andrews, Chief Warder, Accountant, and Photographer,	115	0	0
Andrew Kelter,	45	0	0
Michael Murphy, *Tailor*,	40	0	0
James Kirby, *Shoemaker*,	40	0	0
Henry Mansfield,	40	0	0
T. Furlong, *Schoolmaster*,	35	0	0
Patrick Mara,	35	0	0
Laurence Power,	35	0	0
Alice M'Donald, Matron,	45	0	0
Ellen Hill, Assistant Matron and Schoolmistress,	25	0	0
Mary Fitzgerald, Nurse,	25	0	0
Margaret Farrell, Laundress,	23	0	0

(Turnkeys: Andrew Kelter, Michael Murphy, James Kirby, Henry Mansfield, T. Furlong, Patrick Mara, Laurence Power.)

Vacancies in the Staff since last Inspection, how caused, and how filled up.

Thomas Walsh, Schoolmaster, appointed Bridewell Keeper at Lismore ; Laurence Keily appointed in his stead. Walter Foley Turnkey, superannuated ; Patrick Mara appointed in his stead.   Laurence Keily, Schoolmaster, probationary appointment not confirmed ; Thomas Furlong appointed in his stead.   James Flynn, Turnkey, dismissed ; Laurence Power appointed in his stead.

Officers on Gaol Allowance.
All resident officers get £1 per month in lieu of rations.

Visits paid by Officers.

	From 1st Jan. to 31st Dec., 1874.	From 1st Jan., 1875, to day of Inspection.
Number of times the Board of Superintendence met and discharged business,	14	9
Local Inspector to Gaol,	189	137
Do. each Bridewell,	4	2
Chaplain, Protestant Episcopal Church,	163	123
,, Roman Catholic,	207	134
Physician,	183	113

Books and Accounts.

Net cost of Gaol, including Diet and Salaries.
1872, . £2,376 9s. 5d. | 1873, . £2,377 9s. 6d. | 1874, . £2,844 12s. 10d.

Total cost of Officers, including Clothing, value of Rations, Washing, Gas, &c.
1872, . £1,319 0s. 4d. | 1873, . £1,321 17s. 9d. | 1874, . £1,374 19s. 3d.

Average cost of each Prisoner per annum.
1872, . £33 9s. 5d. | 1873, . £36 17s. 2·4d. | 1872, . £42 13s. 1d.

Amounts repaid by the War Department for Military Prisoners.
1872, . £19 14s. 0d. | 1873, . £34 12s. 0d. | 1874, . £49 16s. 0d.

Amounts repaid by the Inland Revenue Department for Excise Prisoners.
1872, . £2 7s. 3d. | 1873, . £1 19s. 9d. | 1874, . £0 11s. 3d.

Amounts repaid from the Consolidated Fund for the Maintenance, &c., of Prisoners.
1872, . £219 0s. 1d. | 1873, . £160 16s. 5d. | 1874, . £143 17s. 11d.

The various registries of discipline and finance in this gaol are kept by the Chief Warder and Clerk, with much care and attention. The most approved forms are in use. The Morning State is on an improved plan ; and proper checks are established. The books are checked by the Local Inspector and Governor, whose initials are appended after each examination. The journals of both these officers are very full, and contain a record of all noteworthy occurrences in the prison. Those specially deserving of attention are marked in red ink. The Local Inspector makes a special report to the Board at each meeting. The journal of the Medical Officer is likewise fully kept, and cases which require observation are recorded. The Chaplains also have journals, which are regularly entered up, and state the routine of their duties.

Hospital.

	1872.		1873.		1874.		1875 (to day of Inspection).	
	M.	F.	M.	F.	M.	F.	M.	F.
No. of prisoners in hospital,	50	38	49	13	58	18	—	—
Average daily number in hospital,	1	2	1·84	0·75	2	0·3	—	—
No. of prisoners prescribed for and treated out of hospital,	76	69	67	51	62	24	—	—
No. of deaths,	1	—	—	—	—	—	—	—
Cost of medicine,	£17 5s. 1d.		£22 8s. 2d.		£27 3s. 7d.		—	
Cost of extra diet for prisoners in hospital,	£20 7s. 10d.		£20 13s. 0d.		£18 10s. 6d.		—	
Cost of all extra diet ordered by Medical Officer for prisoners not in hospital,	£14 9s. 3d.		£17 19s. 9d.		£14 7s. 9d.		—	

SOUTH DISTRICT.

Waterford County and City Gaol.

The hospitals belonging to this prison, although under one roof, are sufficiently separate and fitted up with all necessary appliances for the treatment of the sick, including water-closets and baths. The accommodation is much greater than is required to meet the wants of the establishment. The Medical Officer devotes much care and attention to the discharge of his duties in the prison.

Board of Superintendence.

Sir Robert J. Paul, bart., J.P.	Fitzmaurice G. Bloomfield, J.P.	Wray Bury Palliser, J.P.
Edward Roberts, J.P.	Pierse M. Barron, J.P., D.L.	William Armstrong, J.P.
Robert Thos. Carew, J.P., D.L.	Edmond Power, J.P.	Thomas W. Jacob, J.P.
	Matthew Slaney, J.P.	William Johnson, J.P.
		John Slattery, J.P.

Board.

The Board meets for the discharge of business on the first Saturday of each month, when the salaries of subordinate officers are paid, with other small accounts, by cheque to Local Inspector, who produces vouchers at the next meeting of the Board. The salaries of superior officers are paid by presentment half-yearly at the assizes.

Bridewells.

STATE OF BRIDEWELLS.

	Dungarvan District Bridewell		Lismore.	
	M.	F.	M.	F.
No. of Committals in past year,	110	33	23	4
Of whom were Drunkards,	33	19	10	-
No. of Committals in the quarter preceding Inspection,	38	15	6	1
Of whom were Drunkards,	6	1	3	-
Petty Sessions and Transmittals, how often?	Dungarvan, weekly; fortnightly at Ballymore, Ardmore, Clashmore, Kilmacthomas, & Stradbally.		Fortnightly at Lismore, but Town Commissioners sit on alternate weeks; fortnightly at Cappoquin and Tallow.	
Committals, whether regular,	Legal.		Regular.	
Registry,	Correctly kept.		Correctly kept.	
Repairs and Order,	In good order and repair.		Orderly and in sound repair.	
Security,	Sufficient, with care, yet two escapes occurred within the last three years.		Sufficient, with care.	
Accommodation,	Males—eleven cells and two day-rooms; females—seven cells and one day-room.		No change. Two day-rooms and two cells, one with three and one with two beds;—a third cell not furnished.	
Bedding, Furniture, and Utensils.	Sufficient for requirements. Some blankets rather thin.		Sufficient, and of a fair description.	
Water, how supplied?	None on premises, and half a mile distant; pump-water brackish.		Supplied from town main.	
Sewerage,	A sewer to the sea, but not effective.		Sufficient.	
Cleanliness, Dryness, and Ventilation.	Very clean, orderly, now dry, and sufficiently ventilated.		Very clean and orderly; ventilation sufficient.	
Cost of Dietary, per head per day.	3½d for all prisoners per day.		Males, 4d., females, 3½d per day.	
Salary of Keeper,	£40; matron £15.		£20; wife as matron, £5.	
Whether Keeper follows any other employment.	Court-house keeper, salary £8; also collector of borough rates.		Court-keeper, salary £8; weighmaster.	
Statutable Inspection,	26th August, 1875.		26th July, 1875.	
Remarks,	No prisoner in custody.		No prisoner in custody.	

JOHN LENTAIGNE, *Inspector-General.*

WEXFORD COUNTY GAOL, AT WEXFORD.—STATUTABLE INSPECTION, 8TH SEPTEMBER, 1875.

Prisoners of all classes in Gaol on the day of Inspection, and on the corresponding date in the three preceding years.

	M.	F.		M.	F.
1872, ...	32	9	1874, ...	44	11
1873, ...	26	8	1875 (day of Inspection),	39	17

Returned Convicts in Gaol on the day of Inspection, and during each of the three preceding years, and the expired portion of 1875.

	M.	F.		M.	F.
1872, ...	1	1	1875 (up to and including		
1873, ...	1	–	day of Inspection), .	3	1
1874, ...	2	1	Day of Inspection, .	1	–

Prisoners in Custody known to have been in Reformatories.

	M.	F.		M.	F.
1872, ...	1	–	1875 (up to and including		
1873, ...	–	–	day of Inspection), .	1	–
1874, ...	1	1	Day of Inspection, .	–	–

Juveniles.

I found 3 young offenders in custody; one a boy of fifteen years of age, **Juveniles.** sentenced at assizes to an imprisonment of two years with hard labour, for an attempt at rape. If this is an incorrigible young ruffian, as I suppose must be the case from the length of his sentence, and from the fact that it was not thought advisable to send him to a reformatory, I regret that he was not sentenced to penal servitude. He will now be let loose on the world at an age when his worst passions are most rife (seventeen years); and already accustomed to a prison life for so long a period, the deterrent influence of a prison will, I fear, be weakened on him.

The two other young offenders, whose ages did not exceed sixteen years, were females—one sentenced to an imprisonment of twelve months for larceny. It was her first offence. The other a young girl of fifteen, on remand, charged with stealing a pair of boots. This juvenile has one previous conviction recorded against her, and if now sentenced to a long period of imprisonment in this gaol will very possibly follow in the career of vice into which she has entered, and will end her days in the prison, if a worse fate does not befal her. Her mother is with her in this prison under a sentence of imprisonment here for two years for the same offence; and it is to be regretted that this young woman was not sent to a reformatory, to be removed from the pernicious influence of her parent. After her twelve months' imprisonment, thrown on the world without friends, and a blighted character, it is more than probable that she will return to crime and continue a burden on the rates of the county.

Fourteen male and 5 female young offenders, under sixteen years of age, were committed to this prison previously to my visit in 1875. One of these, a female, and 3 males were under twelve years of age.

Three males were sentenced to reformatories during the year. Two were workhouse offenders.

One male known to have been in a reformatory was in custody in this prison in 1875, and one male and one female in 1874. The female was, on re-conviction, sentenced to penal servitude at the Wexford Quarter Sessions, June, 1874, which I believe to be the only chance for the reformation of young offenders over whom the influences of a reformatory are of no avail.

Commitments.

SOUTH
DISTRICT.

Wexford
County
Gaol.

		From 1st Jan. to 31st Dec., 1874.		From 1st Jan., 1875, to day of Inspection.	
		M.	F.	M.	F.
Criminals,	. . . .	169	71	119	49
Vagrants,	.	26	4	35	5
Drunkards,	. . . .	125	15	76	8
	Total, . .	320	90	230	62

Individual Prisoners (exclusive of Debtors), and Number of times each had been committed during 1874 and 1875.

	1874.				1875, to day of Inspection.			
NUMBER OF TIMES COMMITTED.	Juveniles.		Adults.		Juveniles.		Adults.	
	M.	F.	M.	F.	M.	F.	M.	F.
Once within the year, . .	23	3	215	76	14	5	154	45
Twice　,, . .	6	–	12	4	–	–	15	3
Thrice　,, . .	–	–	7	1	–	–	7	2
4 & 5 times ,, . .	–	–	6	–	–	–	1	–
7　,,　,, . .	–	–	–	–	–	–	1	–
Total, . .	29	3	240	81	14	5	178	50
No. of above who had not been in Gaol previous to 1st January in	28	3	161	53	13	5	109	35

Individual Prisoners (exclusive of Debtors) committed in the year 1874, and to the day of Inspection in 1875, who had been Once, and oftener recommitted from their first Commitment in any year, so far as can be ascertained.

	1874.				1875, to day of Inspection.			
NUMBER OF TIMES COMMITTED.	Juveniles.		Adults.		Juveniles.		Adults.	
	M.	F.	M.	F.	M.	F.	M.	F.
Once only, ...	23	3	159	53	13	5	104	33
Twice, ...	5	–	26	12	1	–	25	5
Thrice, ...	1	–	14	6	–	–	15	6
4　times, ...	–	–	10	3	–	–	6	2
5 to 6 ,, ...	–	–	9	2	–	–	7	1
7 to 11 ,, ...	–	–	10	5	–	–	11	2
12 to 16 ,, ...	–	–	5	–	–	–	3	1
17 to 20 ,, ...	–	–	4	–	–	–	4	–
21 to 30 ,, ...	–	–	2	–	–	–	1	–
31 to 40 ,, ...	–	–	1	–	–	–	2	–
Total No. of Individuals committed,	29	3	240	81	14	5	178	50
No. of commitments represented in foregoing, . . .	36	3	640	164	15	5	550	107

Highest number of Prisoners (exclusive of Debtors) in Gaol during each of the previous seven years, and up to day of Inspection in 1875.

January 8th, 1868,	. .	93	January 7th, 1872, . .	53
January 5th, 1869,	. .	46	February 28th, 1873, . .	46
October 25th, 1870,	. .	50	December 9th, 1874, . .	62
February 26th, 1871,	. .	63	July 15th, 1875, . . .	58

Averages, &c. (exclusive of Debtors).

—	From 1st January to 31st December, 1874.			From 1st January, 1875, to day of Inspection.		
	M.	F.	Date.	M.	F.	Date.
Average daily number of prisoners in custody,	30	12	—	28	11	—
Highest number of prisoners at any one time,	62		9th Dec.	58		15th July.
Lowest ditto, .	33		19th May.	26		3rd May.
Highest number of males at any one time, .	50		8th Dec.	46		15th July.
Ditto of females,	16		10th Feb.	17		8th Sept.
Lowest number of males at any one time, .	18		20th May.	15		3rd May.
Ditto of females,	7		12th Aug.	6		17th Aug.

I found in custody when I made my inspection 39 males and 17 females, of all classes, criminally committed as under:—The males—4 on remand or for trial; 6 tried prisoners, sentenced for terms of two years each; 1 for eighteen, 2 for twelve, and 2 for three months each; 4 for two months; and 20 for one month and under.

The females—One for trial, 1 for two years; 4 for twelve, 2 for six, 1 for three, and 8 for one month and under.

Nine male prisoners had been convicted of larceny and other offences against property; 9 of assaults; 7 were tramps—principally discharged soldiers, committed for asking relief at the union workhouse; and 6 were drunkards and disorderly.

Five females in custody had been found guilty of larceny; another had been convicted of abandoning her child; and one of selling spirits without a licence; the remainder were under sentence for drunkenness, disorderly conduct, and vagrancy.

One hundred and ninety-two individual males and 55 females were committed to this prison previously to my inspection in 1875. They had—the males 565, the females 112 commitments recorded against them on the books of the prison. Two males had been between 30 and 40 times in custody, and another between 20 and 30 times.

No debtor was an inmate of this prison when I made my inspection; an old man, upwards of eighty years of age, who had been for several years in custody having been discharged a short time previously.

Accommodation.

	M.	F.		M.	F.
Yards, ...	17	5	Store Rooms, . . .	8	3
Solitary Cells, . . .	3	1	Laundry, ...	—	1
Single Cells, not less in size than 9 ft. long, 6 ft. wide, and 8 ft. high = 432 cubic ft.,	23	14	Drying Room, . . .	—	1
			Lavatories, . . .	8	4
Do., heated and furnished with bells, . . .	64	44	Baths, with Hot and Cold Water laid on, . .	2	1
Cells to contain three persons,	2	–	Privies, ...	14	3
Sleeping Rooms, . . .	8	–	Waterclosets, . . .	8	4
No. of Beds in such Rooms,	10	–	Fumigating Apparatus, . .	1	1
Hospital Rooms, . .	3	2	Reception Rooms or Cells, .	6	5
Chapels, ...	Two		Pumps, ...	8	2
School Rooms, . . .	1	1	Other Machines for Hard Labour :—		
Workshops, . . .	5	–	Washing Machine, . .	—	1
Workshed, . . .	1	–	Mangling Machine, . .	—	1
Kitchen, . . .	One		Tell-tale Clocks, . . .	3	–

Early in the year of 1875 the Board of Superintendence had denuded the old prison building, long unoccupied, of the metal and ironwork which it contained, consisting chiefly of doors, windows, shutters, bedsteads, railings, and

SOUTH DISTRICT.

Wexford County Gaol.

other articles which, together with a carding and weaving machine, had been sold by auction. The Board had further under consideration to remove the building from which these articles were taken, but it is very solidly built, and to take it down would be attended with considerable expense. It has, besides, a good roof ; and, under the circumstances, it was decided to permit it to remain, pending legislation on the subject of prisons.

Heating.

An estimate for heating the male and female prisons, the laundry, and kitchen from one fire, was also under consideration which, if carried out, would effect a very considerable saving of fuel, and the heating of the prisons would be more effectual ; but it also has been postponed.

The present heating apparatus of the male prison is most wasteful of coals. It is computed to consume upwards of forty-seven tons yearly. The heating apparatus of the female prison consumes upwards of twenty-four tons.

By the proposed arrangement, the heating of the two prisons, the boiling of water for the laundry and baths, and the generating of steam for the cooking apparatus, could (it is computed) be accomplished from one fire, consuming about eighteen tons of coals ; thus effecting a saving of fifty-three tons in the year. The alterations would, according to the estimate, cost £183 ; but the saving in fuel would very soon reimburse the Board for the expenditure. Should legislation on prisons next session not alter the circumstances of the gaol, it is an alteration which, in my opinion, should be carried out.

Another advantage would be that the cooking which is now done in the male prison would be transferred to that for females, and placed in charge of the matron of the gaol, an officer peculiarly well suited for the purpose, as she is a person in whom every confidence might be placed. She has two assistants, who could see that the cooking is cleanly and well done. She might also have charge of the provision store, and the male officers and prisoners who now discharge the duties of storekeeper and cooks might then be employed at other works with advantage and profit to the institution.

I found when I made my inspection the gaol premises in a most creditable condition of order and cleanliness, the occupied buildings all in sound repair, the various appliances for separation, the lavatories, water-closets, and bells in order, and the prison in every part artificially lighted by gas made on the premises.

The grounds are tastefully planted with shrubs, and the order in which I found the establishment indicates care and attention. Some of the suggestions of my colleague in his report for 1874 have been carried out.

All prisoners are now bathed on reception, and weekly afterwards. I found them suitably dressed, usefully employed, and orderly ; but the profits from the labour of the prisoners are still very trifling. It was £26 18s. 6d. in 1874 and in 1875 ; the average cost of each prisoner being £56 2s. 6d. in 1874, and £58 4s. 1½d. up to the date of inspection in 1875.

Gas.

Excellent gas is made on the premises, under the charge of a warder assisted by a prisoner, by which arrangement it is stated a considerable saving is effected.

Individual separation is strictly enforced with regard to all classes of prisoners, except the sick and those employed in prison duties.

Photography.

The photographs of habitual criminals are now taken by one of the turnkeys, who receives a gratuity of £3 for his trouble, the chemicals being paid for by the Board.

Clothing.

The clothing of the prisoners in this gaol is good and sufficient. The male are clothed in warm frieze, and the dress of the females is suitable. All are supplied with socks or stockings. The bedding also was of a good description when I inspected ; and at present all the prison clothes are made up in the gaol.

Stores.

The stores are roomy, and properly fitted up. There is now a fumigating apparatus in each prison, and the clothes of all prisoners are cleansed and disinfected when necessary. The private clothes of prisoners are tied up in bundles, and labelled when put in store.

Stock at the time of Inspection.

Male Clothing.	In Use.	In Store.		In Use.	In Store.	Female Clothing.	In Use.	In Store.
Blankets, pairs of,	179	77	Shirts,	82	196	Shifts,	27	89
Sheets, pairs of,	122	140½	Jackets,	40	83	Jackets,	27	95
Rugs,	—	15	Vests,	40	114	Petticoats,	34	71
Hammocks or Cots,	40	4	Trowsers,	40	92	Aprons,	17	87
Bed-ticks,	119	101	Caps,	40	48	Neckerchiefs,	30	85
Bedsteads,	90	—	Stockings or Socks, pairs of,	70	102	Bonnets,	20	43
			Shoes, Slippers, & Clogs, pairs of,	39	86	Stockings, pairs of,	35	49
						Shoes, Slippers, & Clogs, pairs of,	29	18

The laundry is stalled (four troughs), and is fitted up with mangle, washing and wringing machines. The drying-room, which is overhead, has nine horses.

Stock is taken half-yearly, and articles no longer fit for use are then condemned, by the Governor and Local Inspector.

Water is supplied to the different sections of the prison by means of a wheel pump worked by prisoners. I called attention on my last inspection of this prison to the unwholesome water of one of the wells, which has since been found to be tainted from a privy close by. That privy was then used by the inmates of the debtors' prison. It is not now used; but the privy is still in existence, and should be pulled down as useless; the cesspool should also be filled up to prevent the possible contamination of the water of the well which adjoins.

Unlock is held in this prison at 6.30 A.M., at all seasons of the year. The prisoners are locked for the night at 6 P.M., in summer, and 4.30 P.M. in winter. Gas is supplied to the cells for three hours after locking up.

Six of the warders are appointed to patrol, in rotation, the prison during the night. Their vigilance is tested by three tell-tale clocks—two are in the hall of the prison, and marked, one every half-hour, the other at 12 o'clock, and at 2, 4, and 6 A.M. The third clock, which is fixed on the boundary wall, is marked at 1 and 5 A.M. during the watch.

No escape was attempted from this gaol, or from any of the bridewells of the county, during 1875.

Number of Punishments for Prison Offences.

	From 1st January to 31st December, 1874.		From 1st January, 1875, to day of Inspection.	
	M.	F.	M.	F.
By Magisterial authority,	3	—	1	—
By Governor—				
Dark or Refractory Cells,	39	6	47	5
Stoppage of Diet,	51	—	46	—
Other punishments—Hand-cuffs and Leg-bolts,	5	—	—	—
Total,	98	6	94	5

Three cells in the male prison and one in that for females are darkened, and used for prisoners under punishment. They are heated and furnished with bells.

The record of punishments is laid before the Board of Superintendence, and signed by the chairman, at its meetings.

School.

	From 1st Jan. to 31st Dec., 1874.		From 1st Jan., 1875, to day of Inspection.	
	M.	F.	M.	F.
Number of individual prisoners who attended school,	24	9	22	12
Average daily number of pupils,	6	3	5	4
Number of days on which school was held,	157	227	117	158

School-hours.—Males, 3 to 4.30, P.M.; Females, 12 to 1.30 P.M.

SOUTH
DISTRICT.

Wexford
County
Gaol.

School is held in the central hall of the male prison, and in one of the day-rooms of the female prison.

Both schools are stalled; the school for males has twelve stalls; that for females, eight. The teacher is not trained, and the schools are not in connexion with any educational body. The females are taught by the male teacher, the assistant matron being present.

Employment on day of Inspection.

							M.	F.
Carpenter work,	.	.	.	.	.	.	2	–
Mason work,	.	.	.	.	.	.	1	–
Shoemaking,	.	.	.	.	.	.	2	–
Painting,	.	.	.	.	.	.	2	–
Tailoring,	.	.	.	.	.	.	1	–
Cooking,	.	.	.	.	.	.	1	–
Gasmaking,	.	.	.	.	.	.	1	–
Matmaking,	.	.	.	.	.	.	1	–
Cleaning,	.	.	.	.	.	.	3	–
Picking oakum,	.	.	.	.	.	.	25	3
Washing, Knitting, and Sewing,	.	.	.	.	.	–	14
							—	—
Total in custody,	.	.	.	.	.	39	17

Amount received for produce of Prisoners' Labour disposed of outside the Gaol.

1872, . £10 17s. 10d. | 1873, . £14 8s. 6d. | 1874, . £26 19s. 4d.

Labour.

Prisoners sentenced to hard labour now break a greater quantity of stones than those not so sentenced; they also pick oakum.

Twelve separate compartments are fitted up for stone-breakers. Artisans when in custody work at their trades. The women wash, sew, knit, and pick oakum.

The cells are artificially lighted by gas, and prisoners work in them up to 8 P.M.

Dietary and Contracts.

Bread, white, per 4 lb. loaf, 7d.; brown, per 4 lb. loaf, 6¼d.; oatmeal, per cwt., 18s. 9d.; Indian meal, per cwt., 10s.; potatoes, per cwt., 4s.; meat, per lb., 9d.; new milk, per gallon, 10½d.; salt, per cwt, 2s. 4d.; coal, per ton, £1 0s. 9d.; straw, per cwt., 1s. 10d.; candles, per lb., 6d.; soap, per cwt., £1 16s.

Net average daily cost of Ordinary Diet for each Prisoner.

1872, . 5d. | 1873, . 5d. | 1874, . 5d.

Food.

The food prepared for the use of the prisoners in custody when I made my inspection was of a good description; and I observe that the Chaplains, for the most part, report favourably of the qualities of the provisions submitted for their inspection.

I questioned all the inmates of the gaol on the day of my visit. No complaint was made to me by any. The prisoners are treated with kindness; yet discipline appears to me to be strictly maintained.

Books and Accounts.

Net cost of Gaol, including Diet and Salaries.

1872, . £1,838 6s. 11d. | 1873, . £2,053 9s. 2d. | 1874, . £2,413 5s. 5d.

Total cost of Officers, including Clothing, Value of Rations, Washing, Gas, &c.

1872, . £1,045 16s. 11d. | 1873, . £1,094 0s. 4d. | 1874, . £1,075 18s. 6d.

Average cost of each Prisoner per annum.

1872, . £45 9s. 10d. | 1873, . £54 1s. 3d. | 1874, . £56 2s. 6d.

Amounts repaid by the War Department for Military Prisoners.

1872, . £0 18s. | 1873, . £0 16s. | 1874, . £3 15s.

Amounts repaid from the Consolidated Fund for the maintenance, &c., of Prisoners.

1872, . £169 18s. 0d. | 1873, . £148 6s. 11d. | 1874, . £212 7s. 4d.

The Deputy Governor and Head Warder have charge of the books and registries of the gaol, which are well kept. The books are daily checked by the Governor, who then marks them with his initials. The journals of the Local Inspector and Governor are kept with much care and attention. The quarterly reports of the Local Inspector to the Prisons Office note all matters of an exceptional character which occur in the prison; he likewise reports very fully on the state of the bridewells, and he occasionally adds extracts from his journal on matters of which the Inspectors-General should be informed. The Deputy Governor has a journal which is regularly checked by the Governor. The Medical Officer and Chaplains also keep journals, in which the Chaplains state the duty they perform, and the Medical Officer records such observations as he considers necessary to report respecting the cases which he treats. The markings of the telltale clocks are entered in the State of Prison at Lockings Book.

Officers and Salaries.

Non-Resident.	£		£	s.
Samuel Johnson, esq., J.P., Local Inspector,	100	Mr. Nicholas E. Walsh, Assistant Clerk and Schoolmaster	40	0
Rev. James Peed, Prot. Chaplain,	50	Edward Cox, *Tailor*,	40	0
Rev. Edward Aylward, Roman Catholic Chaplain,	50	Patrick Keegan,	40	0
		Samuel Tackaberry,	40	0
Henry H. Boxwell, esq., Surgeon,	—	James Clancy,	40	0
J. H. Hadden, esq., Apothecary,	30	Peter Pender,	30	0
		Wm. Murphy, *Shoemaker*,	30	0
Resident.		Mrs. Gladwin, Matron,	45	0
John R. Gildea, esq., Governor,	200	Mrs. Murphy, 1st Assist. Matron,	17	10
Mr. Jas. Kelly, Deputy-Governor,	80	Miss M. Meyler, 2nd Assist. Matron,	15	0

(Edward Cox through Wm. Murphy bracketed as Turnkeys.*)*

Vacancies in the staff since last inspection, how caused, and how filled up.

Mr. Philip Duggan, Deputy-Governor, resigned; Mr. James Kelly, Schoolmaster and Storekeeper, appointed in his stead; Mr. N. E. Walsh appointed Assistant Clerk and Schoolmaster in his stead. Edward Hanlon, Warder, resigned; Peter Pender, Warder, appointed in his stead. Edmond Underwood, Warder, dismissed; William Murphy, Warder, appointed in his stead. Anne E. Gill, Second Assistant Matron, dismissed; Margaret Meyler appointed in her stead. Rev. James Keating, Roman Catholic Chaplain, resigned; Rev. Edward Aylward appointed in his stead.

Officers on Gaol Allowance.
All intern officers receive an allowance of bread and milk.

Visits paid by Officers.

	From 1st Jan. to 31st Dec., 1874.	From 1st Jan., 1875, to day of Inspection.
Number of times the Board of Superintendence met and discharged business,	17	8
Local Inspector, to Gaol,	181	102
,, to each Bridewell,	4	3
Protestant Episcopalian Chaplain,	162	103
Roman Catholic ,,	171	115
Surgeon,	211	106
Apothecary,	332	260

Hospitals.

	1872.		1873.		1874.		1875 (to day of Inspection).	
	M.	F.	M.	F.	M.	F.	M.	F.
No. of prisoners prescribed for and treated out of hospital,	65	5	55	5	116	29	86	20
Cost of medicine,	£0 12s. 2d.		£5 1s. 4d.		£2 0s. 0d.		£2 10s. 0d.	
Cost of Diet, &c., for Prisoners in Hospital,	—		—		—		£0 11s. 2d.	
Cost of all extra diet ordered by Medical Officer for prisoners not in hospital,	£5 15s. 10d.		£5 17s. 8d.		£9 19s. 0d.		£1 11s. 10d.	

SOUTH DISTRICT.

Wexford County Gaol.

The hospitals for both sexes are in the same building, with a common staircase. The wards are well ventilated. They have water-closets and bath, but they are seldom used.

In March, 1875, a case of scarlatina occurred in an infant who was committed with its mother ; but the mother and child were discharged, by the order of the judge at the assizes then being held.

Board of Superintendence.

George Le Hunte, esq., J.P.
Major John Harvey, D.L.
Colonel Alcock, D.L.
Patrick Breen, esq., J.P.
John Greene, esq., J.P.

Major Huson, J.P.
W. A. Redmond, esq., M.P.
Captain T. J. Walker, J.P.
The Right Hon. the Earl of Granard.

E. S. Flood, esq., J.P.
Chas. H. Peacock, esq., J.P.
Capt. P. L. Harvey, J.P.

Board.

The Board meets on the second Saturday of each month, when salaries of subordinate officers and small accounts are paid by cheque, drawn in the aggregate in favour of the Local Inspector, who produces vouchers at the next meeting of the Board. The superior officers and creditors for large sums are paid quarterly.

Bridewells.

STATE OF BRIDEWELLS.

	New Ross.	
	M.	F.
No. of Committals in past year, .	60	20
Of whom were Drunkards, .	12	1
No. of Committals in the quarter preceding inspection, . . .	15	9
Of whom were Drunkards, .	8	1

Petty Sessions and Transmittals, how often ?	New Ross fortnightly ; Arthurstown monthly.
Committals, ...	Apparently regular, but prisoners when remanded not brought before committing justice, which is illegal.
Registry, ...	Correctly kept.
Repairs and Order, . . .	In good repair, except a crack in the ceiling of the large cell in the female prison.
Security, ...	Exercising yards perfectly insecure ; and the prison building 100 feet from Keeper's residence, so that he could not hear the noise if an attempt were made at prison breach.
Accommodation, ...	Males—day-room and six cells, and drunkard's cell, with guard bed; females—day-room and two cells.
Furniture, Bedding, and Utensils, .	Bedding and furniture sufficient.
Water, how supplied ? . . .	Pump in yard for males out of order; but forcing pump at court-house.
Sewerage, ...	None, a cesspool; earth-closets should be provided.
Cleanliness, Dryness, and Ventilation.	Clean and orderly ; now quite dry.
Cost of Dietary per head per day, .	Males, $6\frac{3}{4}d$.; females, $5\frac{1}{2}d$.
Salary of Keeper, and whether he follows any other employment.	£30; matron, £5. Court-keeper, salary, £8.
Date of Inspection, . . .	9th September, 1875.
Remarks, ...	One male in charge, committed on remand, by one magistrate on 28th August, for drunkenness and assault, and not brought before committing justice when remanded.

STATE OF BRIDEWELLS—*continued.*

—	Gorey.		Enniscorthy.	
	M.	F.	M.	F.
No. of Committals in past year,	17	5	28	9
Of whom were Drunkards,	5	1	4	—
No. of Committals in the quarter preceding Inspection,	4	3	5	—
Of whom were Drunkards,	2	1	—	—
Petty Sessions and Transmittals, how often.	Fortnightly; transmittals following day.		Petty Sessions on Monday in each week.	
Committals, . . .	Regular.		Correct, except one remand illegal, signed by one justice for more than three days.	
Registry, ...	Correctly kept.		Correctly kept.	
Repairs and Order, . .	In fair repair; lately done up, and wood-work painted.		In good repair and order lately painted.	
Security, ...	Yards very insecure, walls too low, and ceiling of day-room lath and plaster.		Sufficient with care, but construction faulty.	
Accommodation, . .	Three cells for males, and seven beds; two for females, and six beds; two day-rooms.		Males—day-room and six cells; females—day-room and two cells (one large, with four beds); exercising yard for females too small.	
Furniture, Bedding, and Utensils. . . .	Ample, good, and clean.		Sufficient for requirements; some blankets thin; additional blankets have been ordered.	
Water, how supplied, . .	Good pump on premises; also pipe water from town.		From town reservoir; fountain in street outside Bridewell.	
Sewerage, ...	The only privy has no seat; an earth box should be provided.		New sewer lately made.	
Cleanliness, Dryness, and Ventilation.	Clean, and well kept, but damp.		Clean, dry, and ventilation sufficient.	
Cost of dietary, . . .	7d. for males; 6d. for females.		7d.; drunkards 6d.	
Salary of Keeper, & whether he follows any other employment.	£35; sister £5 as matron; court-house keeper at £8 a year.		£30; matron £5; court keeper, salary £8; also is paid for assisting Staff Officer of Pensioners at intervals.	
Date of Inspection, . .	7th September, 1875.		8th September, 1875.	
Remarks, ...	No prisoner in custody.		No prisoner in charge.	

JOHN LENTAIGNE, *Inspector-General.*

SOUTH
DISTRICT.
—
*Wicklow
County
Gaol.*

WICKLOW COUNTY GAOL, AT WICKLOW.—STATUTABLE INSPECTION, 1ST DECEMBER, 1875.

Number of Prisoners of all classes in Gaol on the day of Inspection, and on the corresponding date in the three preceding years.

	M.	F.		M.	F.
1872,	39	6	1874,	32	7
1873,	35	7	1875 (day of Inspection),	34	4

Workhouse offenders in Gaol on the day of Inspection.

Six males, and one female.

Juveniles.

Juveniles.

One young offender under sixteen years of age was an inmate of this gaol at the time of my visit, under a sentence of imprisonment for one month as a tramp. He appeared to me to be remarkably intelligent, but grossly ignorant—an orphan, of no settled place of abode, who had lately wandered into the county Wicklow from the Curragh Camp. The Governor of the gaol tells me that the boy is anxious to earn his bread if he knew how, but he never was taught any means of doing so. The Governor will, however, now endeavour to put him in a way to earn a livelihood. But it is to be regretted that this friendless orphan was not sent to a reformatory instead of being sent to prison, afterwards to be discharged without having a home but the workhouse, or a human being to give him advice except the humane Governor of this prison, who will, I know, do his best to save him from a life of crime. Another young offender (T. W.), who had already advanced another step in the career of crime, was convicted at Wicklow Quarter Sessions, in June, 1875, of housebreaking and robbery, and was by order of court sent, on the expiration of his gaol sentence, to the Glencree Reformatory, from which he soon afterwards escaped, and having been arrested in the county Meath was sentenced at the Dunshaughlin Petty Sessions, in the November following, to an imprisonment of three months in the county Meath Gaol at Trim. This young offender, the illegitimate child of a tramp woman (J. K.) whose residence is unknown, and who supports herself by begging through the country or by crime, although he does not belong to the county Wicklow, has been mercifully taken by the Wicklow magistrates from a career of crime, and it is hoped he may be taught to be a useful and self-supporting member of the community.

Altogether, 10 males and 1 female whose ages did not exceed sixteen years were committed to this gaol previously to December in 1875, of whom 7 males and the female were sent to reformatories after the period of their imprisonment as a punishment.

Commitments.

At the time of my inspection 31 males and 4 females of all classes were inmates of this gaol, 2 of whom (male and female) were evidently of unsound mind, and were in a condition which rendered them quite unsuited for treatment in a criminal prison. I called the attention of the Medical Officer to their state. He is of opinion that they should be placed in a lunatic asylum, and he has promised to take steps for their removal to the asylum. The man has taken an antipathy to one particular lamp in the town of Bray, he has already suffered two imprisonments for breaking it, and states that he will do so again when discharged. The woman was, at the time of my visit, very violent; she had been sentenced to an imprisonment of one month for destroying her clothes in the union workhouse.

I found also in custody 6 tramps (males), committed for tearing clothes belonging to the union in the workhouse.

Situate on the road between the metropolis and the south-east of Ireland, a large number of tramps, both boys and men, constantly infest the district, and contribute to fill this gaol, and the reformatory at Glencree in the county.

Two of the tramps in this prison when I visited had been soldiers, discharged at the end of short service; and I observe in different gaols throughout the country a large number of discharged soldiers, committed for wandering from workhouse to workhouse, asking for food, or else committed for breaches of the peace in order to get lodged in prison.

Commitments.

CLASSES.	From 1st January to 31st December, 1874.		From 1st January, 1875, to day of Inspection.	
	M.	F.	M.	F.
Criminals,	283	52	208	47
Vagrants,	7	1	12	.-
Drunkards,	118	12	123	18
Total,	408	65	343	65

Averages, and Highest and Lowest Numbers (exclusive of Debtors).

—	From 1st January to 31st December, 1874.			From 1st January, 1875, to day of Inspection.		
	M.	F.	Date.	M.	F.	Date.
Average daily number of prisoners in custody,	36	7	—	33	5	. —.
Highest number of prisoners at any one time,	58		31st Dec.	59		2nd Jan.
Lowest ditto,	28		25th June.	26		31st July.
Highest number of males at any one time,	55		31st Dec.	56		2nd Jan.
Ditto of females,	11		8th Sept.	9		24th Oct.
Lowest number of males at any one time,	23		25th June.	23		31st July.
Ditto of females,	3		31st Dec.	2		7th Aug.

Number of Individual Prisoners (exclusive of Debtors), committed in the year 1874, and to the day of Inspection in 1875, who had been Once, Twice, Thrice, Four Times, Five Times, &c., &c., from their first Commitment in any year, so far as can be ascertained, distinguishing Adults from Juveniles.

NUMBER OF TIMES COMMITTED.	1874.				1875, to day of Inspection.			
	Juveniles.		Adults.		Juveniles.		Adults.	
	M.	F.	M.	F.	M.	F.	M.	F.
Once only,	11	2	260	43	10	1	203	28
Twice,	—	—	32	4	-	-.	26	8
Thrice,	—	—	13	1	—.	—	12	9
4 times,	—	—	7	1	—	—	8	1
5 „	—	—.	4	1	—	—	7	1
6 „	—	—	3	—	—	—	6	1
7 to 11 „	—	—	12	2	—	—	7	1
12 to 16 „	—	—	6	1	-.	—	5	2
17 to 20 „	—	—	.—	1	—	—	3	—
21 to 30 „	—	—	3	—	—	—	4	—
Total No. of Individuals committed,	11	2	340	54	10	1	281	51
No. of commitments represented in foregoing,	11	2	694	195	10	1	680	118

SOUTH DISTRICT.

Wicklow County Gaol.

Number of Individual Prisoners (exclusive of Debtors), and number of times each had been committed during the following periods distinguishing Adults from Juveniles.

NUMBER OF TIMES COMMITTED.	1874.				1875, to day of Inspection.			
	Juveniles.		Adults.		Juveniles.		Adults.	
	M.	F.	M.	F.	M.	F.	M.	F.
Once within the year, . .	11	2	302	47	10	1	246	41
Twice „ . .	–	–	24	5	–	–	24	7
Thrice „ . .	–	–	10	2	–	–	6	3
4 times „ . .	–	–	3	–	–	–	4	–
5 „ „ . .	–	–	1	–	–	–	1	–
Total, . . .	11	2	340	54	10	1	281	51
No. of above who had not been in Gaol previous to 1st January in .	11	2	280	46	10	1	218	33

Highest number of Prisoners (exclusive of Debtors) in Gaol during each of the previous seven years, and up to day of Inspection in 1875.

29th May, 1868,	. . . 45		28th November, 1872,	. . 46
23rd May, 1869,	. . . 39		29th August, 1873, .	. . 52
30th July, 1870,	. . . 41		31st December, 1874,.	. . 58
13th February, 1871,	. . . 46		2nd January, 1875, .	. . 59

The Local Inspector, Governor, and Medical Officer accompanied me over the establishment, which I found very clean and orderly; and the general condition of the institution evinces the care and attention which the Governor bestows in the discharge of his duties in the prison.

Heating.

The heating apparatus of both the male and the female prison were in good order when I visited, but the defective structure of the female prison renders the heating of the cells very expensive, when few inmates are in custody. I found only 4 females in custody, yet the entire prison was of necessity heated for them. There are twenty-three cells in the female prison, heated and furnished with bells. The average number of females in custody during 1875 was 5, and at one period only 2 females were in charge.

The cells in the separate prison for males are properly heated, but only four are artificially lighted by gas; they are used as workshops for artificers (tailors or shoemakers) when in custody. The cells in the untried class have not bells or means of communication with an officer, as required by the Act 3 and 4 Vic., cap. 44, and I would prefer that a part of the separate prison which has these appliances were used for prisoners belonging to the untried class.

Since my last visit to this gaol a good bath has been fitted up for females in the laundry, but no change in the bathing arrangements has been made on the male side of the prison, and male prisoners are only bathed on admission.

Stock at the time of Inspection.

Male Clothing.   *Female Clothing.*

	In Use.	In Store.		In Use.	In Store.		In Use.	In Store.
Blankets, pairs of,	86	18	Shirts, . .	52	66	Shifts, . .	8	44
Sheets, pairs of,	86	15	Jackets, . .	30	70	Jackets, .	4	26
Rugs, . .	86	25	Vests, . .	30	65	Petticoats, .	8	44
Bed-ticks, .	86	25	Trowsers, .	60	95	Aprons, . .	8	44
Bedsteads, .	89	–	Caps, . .	30	70	Neckerchiefs, .	8	44
			Stockings or Socks, pairs of,	28	30	Caps, . .	8	44
						Stockings, prs.of,	8	22
			Shoes, pairs of,	28	90	Shoes, pairs of,	4	25

The blankets, sheets, and other bedding in this gaol when I visited
were clean, sufficient, and in fair condition. There was a sufficient
supply in store both of bedding and of prison clothing, but the trowsers
given to male prisoners are made of Russia duck, and are too cold
for wear during the winter season ; some woollen material should be procured for their use ; it might be woven in the gaol by prisoners. In
other respects the clothing of the prisoners was suitable ; they have good
leather shoes, and stockings or socks, and the women aprons, neckerchiefs, and caps. All prison clothing is now made in the gaol by prison
labour.

The stores in both prisons are properly fitted up and well arranged.
A separate store is provided for the private clothing of prisoners, which
is tidily made up in bundles and labelled. A stove in the store of the
male prison was lighting at the time of my visit, to keep the clothes dry
and well aired.

There is in each prison a fumigating apparatus, by which all private
clothing of prisoners is cleansed and disinfected before being put into
store.

Three lavatories are in each prison ; eight water-closets are in the
male and six in the female prison. Some of the old privies have since
my last visit been fitted up as water-closets.

The laundry has a good drying-closet, with five horses and five washing troughs, which are stalled, and have hot and cold water laid on.
A mangle and washing-machine (Taylor's) are in the laundry. The
new bath for females is also in the laundry.

A good bath is in the reception ward for males. All prisoners are
bathed on admission, but the males not afterwards during the winter
season. There is an abundance of water on the premises.

The power of the tread-wheel is applied to no useful purpose and is
wasted. It is partitioned, and has stalls for relays.

Gas has been introduced into the lavatories, the halls, and schoolrooms,
but only into the cells which are occupied by tradesmen.

The sewers are effective.

One of the outer walls is not in a good state, and should be repaired.
Some dashing of the walls is also required.

Since last inspection the chapel has been painted, and is heated by a
stove. The schoolrooms have been stalled, and are well arranged.

Unlock is held in this prison at 6 A.M. in summer and at daylight in
winter, and prisoners are locked for the night at 6 P.M. at all seasons of
the year.

One warder patrols at night the interior of the prison. His circuits
are tested by two tell-tale clocks—one placed in the gallery of the interior
of the prison, the other in the passage in front of the class of untried
prisoners (males). The clocks are marked half-hourly during the night.

Photographs of habitual criminals are taken by a prison officer, for
which a charge of one shilling is made for the first, and threepence for
each subsequent copy.

Visitors to prisoners are separated from the prisoners by two gates
seven feet apart, a warder being placed between the gates, so that no prohibited article can be conveyed to the prisoners.

Fifty-six cells are in the male prison and twenty-three in that for
females ; all those in the female prison, and forty in the male prison have
bells, but only four are artificially lighted. The cells in the class for
untried prisoners are heated, but have neither bells nor artificial light.

No escape was attempted from the prison, or either of the bridewells
of the county, in either 1874 or 1875.

Side notes:

SOUTH DISTRICT.

Wicklow County Gaol.

Stores.

Gas.

Photography.

Visitors.

Number of Punishments for Prison Offences.

	From 1st January to 31st December, 1874.		From 1st January to 31st December, 1875.	
	M.	F.	M.	F.
By Governor,				
Dark or Refractory Cells, . . .	13	1	9	–
Stoppage of Diet, . . .	3	–	–	–
Total, . . .	16	1	9	–

The above table shows that punishments are few in this prison, as is generally the case when prisoners are treated with consideration, but, at the same time, with firmness.

In no instance was it necessary, in either 1874 or 1875, to call in magisterial interference, to order a more severe punishment than the rules empower the Governor to inflict.

The punishment cells in this prison are heated, but have not bells.

The record of punishments is duly submitted to the Board at its meetings, and signed by the Chairman.

Employment on day of Inspection.

	M.	F.
Shot-drill and Tread-wheel, ...	7	–
Carpenter, Shoemakers, and Tailors, . . .	5	–
Mat-making, . . .	2	–
Prison duty and Cooking, ...	6	1
Painting and White-washing, ...	4	–
Pumping Water, ...	5	–
Knitting and Sewing, ...	–	2
Sick, ...	1	–
Unemployed, ...	3	1
Discharged (before labour hours), . . .	1	–
Total in custody, . . .	34	4

Punitive labour is maintained in this prison by work on the tread-wheel and shot-drill; but, as I have already remarked, the labour of prisoners so employed is perfectly unremunerative; and the management of this prison cannot be considered satisfactory so long as no profit is derived from the labour of the inmates, who averaged 36 daily in 1874, and 33 in 1875; hence, the average cost of each prisoner was £43 4s. 9d. in 1874, and £41 3s. 4d. in 1875.

Artisans are, however, employed for the service of the prison when in custody, and I saw some good shoes and other clothing in store done by them.

Tailors not sentenced to hard labour are allowed 3d. for making a suit of prison clothing, shoemakers 2d. for each pair of shoes they make, and 1d. for those repaired, carpenters and masons 4d. and 6d. per day, and tinmen 8d. per dozen quart tins; the females, 1d. for making a shirt, and 1d. per day for washing.

Schools.

	From 1st Jan. to 31st Dec., 1874.		From 1st Jan., 1875, to day of Inspection.	
	M.	F.	M.	F.
Number of individual prisoners who attended school, . . .	162	44	142	40
Average daily number of pupils, . . .	25	5	21	4
Number of days on which school was held, .	312	140	285	135

School-hours.—Males, from 1 to 3 o'clock; females, from 12½ to 2½ o'clock.

The schoolrooms are properly stalled and are lighted by gas. Both chaplains visit the school, and make remarks in the School Register. I find twelve entries by the Protestant, but only one by the Roman Catholic Chaplain in the School Registry.

Contracts.

Bread, white, per 4-lb. loaf, ¼d. under Dublin price; brown, per 4-lb. loaf, ¼d. under price of white; oatmeal, per cwt., £1; Indian meal, per cwt., 10s.; new milk, per gallon, 10d.; buttermilk, per gallon, 3d.; coal, per ton, £1 2s.; gas, per 1,000 cubic feet, 7s. 6d.; candles, per lb., 7½d.; soap, per cwt., £1 9s.

Net average daily cost of Ordinary Diet for each Prisoner.

| 1872, | . | 5d. | 1873, | . | 5d. | 1874, | . | 5d. |

The food for prison use, which I tasted on my inspection, was very good, and I observe that the chaplains report favourably of the samples submitted for their inspection.

Food.

I questioned all the prisoners in charge; no complaint was made to me by any. They appear kindly treated, at the same time that discipline is maintained.

Officers and Salaries.

Non-Resident.	£	s.	d.			£	s.	d.
John W. Fetherston H., esq., Local Inspector,	99	4	0		John Manley, *Painter*,	40	0	0
Rev. Henry Rooke, Protestant Chaplain,	46	18	5½		William Roberts, Storekeeper,	40	0	0
				Turnkeys.	Michael Doyle, *Tailor*,	40	0	0
Rev. Patrick O'Doherty, Roman Catholic Chaplain,	46	18	5½		Samuel Thorpe, *Shoemaker*,	35	0	0
Hugh B. Brew, esq., Surgeon,	100	0	0		James Ost,	35	0	0
					Mrs. Mary Storey, Matron,	40	0	0
Resident.					Miss Susan Morris, Assistant Matron,	30	0	0
Mr. Edwd. Storey, Governor,	200	0	0					
Robt. Graham, Gatekeeper, and School Teacher,	45	0	0					

Vacancies in Staff since last Inspection, how caused and how filled up.

Richard Skerrett, Turnkey, retired on superannuation; Edward Broderick appointed in his stead. Edward Broderick resigned, and James Ost appointed to fill the vacancy so created.

Officers on Gaol Allowance.

The Governor and Matrons are allowed coals and candles throughout the year. The warders are allowed coals during the winter months, a suit of uniform annually, and a great coat every third year.

Visits paid by Officers.

	From 1st Jan. to 31st Dec., 1874.	From 1st Jan., 1875, to day of Inspection.
Number of times the Board of Superintendence met and discharged business,	12	11
Local Inspector to Gaol,	152	146
„ to each Bridewell,	4	4
Protestant Episcopalian Chaplain,	278	224
Roman Catholic Chaplain,	222	169
Surgeon,	358	326

Hospitals.

	1872.		1873.		1874.		1875.	
	M.	F.	M.	F.	M.	F.	M.	F.
No. of prisoners in hospital,	2	2	3	–	7	–	7	–
Average daily number in hospital,	·36	·23	·15	–	·5	–	·5	–
No. of prisoners prescribed for and treated out of hospital,	175	25	170	15	354	25	340	28
No. of deaths in the gaol,	–	–	1	–	–	–	–	–
Cost of medicine,	£7 2s. 1d.		£7 8s. 11d.		£8 2s. 1d.		£6 17s. 4d.	
Cost of diet for prisoners in hospital,	£2 15s. 8d.		£3 18s. 0d.		£5 6s. 8d.		£6 7s. 9d.	
Cost of all extra diet ordered by Medical Officer for prisoners not in hospital,	£3 3s. 6d.		£4 10s. 8d.		£4 18s. 9d.		£3 18s. 10d.	

2 A

SOUTH DISTRICT.

Wicklow County Gaol.

Hospital.

The hospital building was unoccupied at the time of my visit. It is detached. Prisoners of both sexes are treated in it. The wards for females are above, those for males below.

The sanitary condition of the gaol is satisfactory; and I desire to record my appreciation of the unceasing attention of the Medical Officer in the discharge of his duties in the prison. During the month which proceeded my inspection he had paid twenty-nine visits to the prison.

Books and Accounts.

Net cost of Gaol, including Diet and Salaries.

1872, . £1,661 18s. 7d. | 1873, . £1,783 4s. 1d. | 1874, . £1,770 3s. 9d.

Total cost of Officers, including Clothing, value of Rations, &c.

1872, . £807 15s. 7d. | 1873, . £925 18s. 4d. | 1874, . £836 18s. 4d.

Average cost of each Prisoner per annum.

1872, . £44 16s. 4d. | 1873, . £43 4s. 9d. | 1874, . £41 3s. 4d.

Amounts repaid by the War Department for Military Prisoners.

1872, . £1 6s. 0d. | 1873, . £1 11s. 0d. | 1874, . £2 8s. 0d.

Amounts repaid from the Consolidated Fund for the Maintenance, &c., of Prisoners.

1872, . £172 9s. 11d. | 1873, . £184 8s. 7d. | 1874, . £154 18s. 5d.

Books.

The books and accounts in this prison are most carefully kept by the Governor. He is assisted by the warder in charge of the gate, but the Governor himself checks and examines every item of expenditure.

The journals of the Local Inspector and Governor are very full, and in them are noted all matters which occur in the management of the establishment. Both these gentlemen are very attentive in the discharge of their duties in the prison; and I have much pleasure in repeating the observations made by my colleague in his report for 1874, when bearing testimony to their zeal and efficiency as prison officers. The Medical Officer, likewise, is most attentive to his duties in the prison, and the preceding table of attendance shows the large number of visits he paid to the prison during the year. His journal is well kept. The Chaplains, likewise, have journals, in which they state the duty they perform.

Board of Superintendence.

Sir George Hodson, bart., D.L., J.P.
Charles Tottenham, esq., J.P.
Colonel Cuninghame, D.L., J.P.

Robert F. Ellis, esq., J.P.
Rev. John Drought.
Henry Pomeroy Truell, esq., J.P.
William Magee, esq., J.P.
Julius Casement, esq., J.P.

Wm. Jones Westby, esq., J.P.
Major Grogan, J.P.
Edwd. A. Dennis, esq., J.P.
Francis W. Green, esq., J.P.

Board.

The meetings of the Board are held on the second Monday of each month, when incidentals and the salaries of the subordinate staff are paid. The salaries of the extern officers, contractors, and large amounts are paid by presentment half-yearly at assizes.

My colleague and I have, year after year, pointed out the unnecessary expense incurred in the maintenance of the bridewell at Tinahely, which should be closed.

STATE OF BRIDEWELLS.

	Baltinglass District Bridewell.		Tinahely.	
	M.	F.	M.	F.
No. of Committals in past year,	90	11	11	7
Of whom were Drunkards,	13	–	–	1
No. of Committals in the quarter preceding inspection,	8	–	4	2
Of whom were Drunkards,	1	–	–	–

	Baltinglass District Bridewell.	Tinahely.
Petty Sessions and Transmittals, how often?	Fortnightly at Baltinglass and Dunlavin; monthly at Hacketstown. Transmittals on Mondays.	Fortnightly at Tinahely, Carnew, and Coolkevin.
Committals,	Regular.	Regular.
Registry,	Correctly kept.	Correctly kept.
Repairs and Order,	In good repair and order.	In fair repair, except that one of the doors is unsound, and marks of damp in keeper's apartment.
Security,	Secure; walls high.	Yards very insecure, pipe from roof in both yards.
Accommodation,	Males—two day-rooms, one used as a store, and five cells; females, day-room and two cells, a third used as a store. No sashes to cell windows, which are very small; one day-room for males has no window, except in door; upper day-room for males has no glass in sash.	Day-room and two cells for each sex.
Furniture, Bedding, and Utensils.	Bedding and furniture sufficient; clothes for prisoners are kept in store.	Sufficient; two pair of new blankets lately provided.
Water, how supplied?	Pumps, in order; one in each yard.	The pump was dry at the time of inspection, and water from town insufficient.
Sewerage,	Effective; the privies should be altered to water-closets.	Sufficient.
Cleanliness, Dryness, and Ventilation.	Clean and orderly, but damp; ventilation improved.	Clean, and ventilation sufficient.
Cost of Dietary,	5¼d. for all prisoners.	6¼d. males; 5¼d. females.
Salary of Keeper, and whether he follows any other employment.	Keeper, £50; Matron, £20; Turnkey, £25, with rations, valued at 3s. 6d. per week. None.	£25; wife, £5. Court-keeper, salary, £8.
Date of Inspection,	9th November, 1875.	6th September, 1875.
Remarks,	The Keeper is allowed 6s. per day travelling expenses to Wicklow, the Turnkey 4s., and to Blessington 2s. 6d. No prisoner in charge when I visited. As this is a district bridewell prisoners are sometimes kept in it for long periods, and their private clothes should be fumigated and disinfected. A fumigating box should therefore be provided.	I found seven males in charge; six committed from Shillelagh Union Workhouse for applying for relief, they having been relieved in said workhouse within two days previously, and one having maliciously torn his clothes. The seventh prisoner in charge was committed for stealing a chemise.

JOHN LENTAIGNE, *Inspector-General.*

DUBLIN: Printed by ALEXANDER THOM, 87 & 88, Abbey-street,
Printer to the Queen's Most Excellent Majesty. .
For Her Majesty's Stationery Office.

www.ingramcontent.com/pod-product-compliance
Lightning Source LLC
Chambersburg PA
CBHW030909270326
41929CB00008B/632